PSYCHOLOGICAL ASSESSMENT OF CHILDREN

Best Practices for School and Clinical Settings

SECOND EDITION

Edited by

H. Booney Vance

John Wiley & Sons, Inc.

New York • Chichester • Weinheim • Brisbane • Singapore • Toronto

Library of Congress Cataloging-in-Publication Data:

Psychological assessment of children : best practices for school and
   clinical settings / edited by H. Booney Vance.—2nd ed.
      p.   cm.
    Rev. ed. of: Best practices in assessment for school and clinical
settings / H. Booney Vance, editor, c1993.
    Includes bibliographical references and index.
    ISBN 0-471-19301-1 (cloth : alk. paper)
    1. Handicapped children—Education—United States. 2. Handicapped
children—United States—Psychological testing. 3. Clinical child
psychology. I. Vance, H. Booney, 1941–   . II. Best practices for
school and clinical settings.
    [DNLM: 1. Psychological Tests—in infancy & childhood. 2. Child,
Exceptional—psychology. 3. Psychology, Educational—methods. WS
105.5.E8 P945 1998]
LC4031.B43 1998
371.91'0973—DC21
DNLM/DLC
for Library of Congress
                                            97-11277
                                              CIP

Printed in the United States of America

10 9 8 7 6 5 4 3 2 1

Contributor List ——————————————————

Rose M. Allinder
University of Nebraska-Lincoln
Lincoln, Nebraska

Eva A. Altizer
East Tennessee State University
Johnson City, Tennessee

Abeer M. Awadh
Sabah Hospital
Kuwait City, Kuwait

Larry M. Bolen
East Carolina University
Greenville, North Carolina

Mary M. Chittooran
University of Tennessee-Chattanooga
Chattanooga, Tennessee

MaryAnn Demchak
University of Nevada-Reno
Reno, Nevada

Sandy D. Devlin
Mississippi State University
Mississippi State, Mississippi

Sarah Drinkwater
Federal Way Public Schools
Federal Way, Washington

Ronald C. Eaves
Auburn University
Auburn, Alabama

G. Franklin Elrod
Mississippi State University
Mississippi State, Mississippi

Douglas Fuchs
Vanderbilt University
Nashville, Tennessee

Lynn S. Fuchs
Vanderbilt University
Nashville, Tennessee

Carole G. Fuller
Rogersville Public Schools
Rogersville, Tennessee

Gerald B. Fuller
Walden University
Traverse City, Michigan

Bruce Gordon
Royal University Hospital
Saskatoon, Saskatchewan, Canada

Denise K. Hildebrand
University of Saskatchewan
Saskatoon, Saskatchewan, Canada

LaMont Johnson
University of Nevada-Reno
Reno, Nevada

Cleborne D. Maddux
University of Nevada-Reno
Reno, Nevada

Koressa Kutsick Malcolm
School Psychologist
McDowell, Virginia

Lawrence E. Melamed
Kent State University
Kent, Ohio

Kenneth W. Merrell
The University of Iowa
Iowa City, Iowa

Ted L. Miller
University of Tennessee-Chattanooga
Chattanooga, Tennessee

Margaret R. Rogers
University of Maryland
College Park, Maryland

David A. Sabatino
East Tennessee State University
Johnson City, Tennessee

David Saklofske
University of Saskatchewan
Saskatoon, Saskatchewan, Canada

Dennis G. Tesolowski
Clemson University
Clemson, South Carolina

H. Booney Vance
East Tennessee State University
Johnson City, Tennessee

Jeffrey R. Wozniak
Kent State University
Kent, Ohio

Preface

Assessment plays a major role in clinical and school settings. Whether one is using standardized tests or other assessment procedures, the need to keep current and use state-of-the-art practices is imperative. The measurement of various psychological constructs from intelligence to social skills plays a major role in the assessment of children for various clinical and school programs. There are major changes in this second edition of *Best Practices in Assessment for School and Clinical Settings.* The new title, *Psychological Assessment of Children,* reflects the broad scope of current assessment and its focus on *children,* who pose different assessment challenges than do adults. Clinical assessment of children is more complex and somewhat more difficult than the assessment of adults.

The title of the original volume, *Best Practices for School and Clinical Settings,* has been retained as the subtitle because leading national and international practitioners with substantial real-world assessment experience have set forth the highest caliber assessment techniques for a variety of school settings and clinical populations. Best practices emphasizes the proper interpretation of assessment instruments in the context of the domains they measure, communicates new and updated information, and provides opportunities to learn through case examples.

This thorough revision includes a new structure, organized into topical sections that parallel instruction programs in child assessment, which provides more experienced readers a logical format for quick reference. The 16 chapters are divided into three major parts. The first part, "Assessment Approaches," introduces the assessment process and discusses specific approaches to evaluation. The second part, "Skill and Behavioral Assessment," describes tests that measure specific skills or domains of behavior such as peer relations, perceptual-motor skills, cognitive abilities, and adaptive behavior. The final section, "Assessing Special Populations," focuses on the assessment of the populations that often represent a difficult task for psychologists. This third part presents a comprehensive discussion of infant and preschooler assessment, the assessment of culturally diverse children and children with mental retardation, the evaluation of autistic disorders, and the use of vocational assessment techniques with special learners. The organization of individual chapters includes a historical review, an overview of current theory, practice examples of relevant instruments, trends, and illustrative case examples. Extensive reference lists provide current and classic support for the ideas expressed and rich resources for the reader.

The second edition was written for two reasons. First, there was a need to update the materials presented in the first edition since the field of psychological assessment—in thought and practice—is rapidly changing and growing. Second, the editor wanted to provide an opportunity for distinguished authorities in various areas of assessment to write from their own clinical backgrounds. The chapters retained have been thoroughly updated to include current issues, trends, and professional practices, and to provide the connection between gathering assessment data and integrating it into a report that helps decision making. The new edition also features seven completely new chapters on the following subjects:

- Assessing current psychological status
- Assessing cognitive abilities using the Woodcock-Johnson Psycho-Educational Battery-Revised
- Assessing intelligence using the Wechsler Intelligence Scale for Children-Third Edition
- Assessing social skills and peer relations
- Assessing perceptual-motor skills
- Assessing and diagnosing autistic disorders
- Assessing children with mental retardation

A chief strength of this text remains its balanced coverage of formal and informal assessment with excellent applied case examples. I have chosen to include not only popular assessment procedures but lesser known ones that are distinctive in the field, such as neuropsychological assessment, current psychological status, social skills and peer relations, perceptual-motor skills, assessment of autistic disorders, assessment of culturally diverse children and youth, and vocation assessment.

This book was written with several potential users in mind. It is intended for a graduate-level course in assessment for those whose careers require comprehension of various assessment practices and instruments but can serve as a refresher for the psychologist who needs to update his or her skills. The text is also a reference source for clinicians, educational diagnosticians, clinical child psychologists, and child psychiatrists. A secondary audience may include special-education teachers, counselors, social workers, speech and language specialists, preschool educators, and educational administrators. Merely reading this book will not make one competent in the use of best practices in his or her area of expertise but will make the reader more aware of best practices in using the assessment instruments and procedures described herein.

There were many times when I wondered whether the second edition of this book would ever see the light of day. The constant support, patience, and encouragement of my friends, colleagues, and family, however, made the task more enjoyable. Invaluable critical feedback came from trusted colleagues. I would like to personally thank the contributors for their conscientious and detailed work as well as for their perspectives on the various areas of assessment. Their hard work and valuable time is very much appreciated.

Gerald B. Fuller, colleague and mentor from whom I have learned much, has been a guiding force behind this book. I am grateful for his constant support and friendship. I would like to especially thank a few people who know who they are and have taught me how to live one day at a time. The contributions of Kelly Franklin, acting for John Wiley & Sons, Inc., are acknowledged with gratitude. Candace Morton, the production editor at Huron Valley Graphics who reviewed the chapters, did a stupendous job. Her assistance was invaluable.

Contents

Part I   Assessment Approaches

Part III   Assessing Special Populations

Chapter 1

BEST PRACTICES IN ASSESSMENT OF CHILDREN: ISSUES AND TRENDS

H. BOONEY VANCE AND ABEER M. AWADH

Many advances have been made in the field of assessment since the publication of the first edition of this book. The fundamentals have remained the same. Assessment is still a child/student-oriented process. It still consists of obtaining information about the child's functioning in a typical environment as well as clinical setting that will be used to determine a child's need and eligibility for special services, define the services required, and measure progress. As such, assessment remains an important and ongoing responsibility of the professionals who serve students, children, and their families.

In the early stages of the field's development, the parameters of assessment were neither as restricted nor as defined by federal, state, and local regulations as they have come to be over the past decades. Moreover, the parameters of assessment are now influenced by the theories that have come to govern and define *best practices*.

Best assessment practices mandate that psychologists working in school or clinical settings have a solid understanding of assessment concepts and practices; training in the administration of various psychoeducational instruments; skills in the clinical application of these concepts and practices; the ability to effectively communicate their findings; and the willingness to keep abreast of new instruments, new regulations, and new trends as well as issues involving ethics and the law. Readers of this text are advised to study the standards, guidelines, and laws in order to ensure that he or she is using best practices in the clinical or educational assessment of children and youth.

FUNCTIONS OF ASSESSMENT

Assessment is a process of gathering information used in screening, diagnosing, and determining eligibility, program planning and service delivery, and monitoring progress during treatment or intervention. All these assessment functions pose challenges for psychologists working in applied settings. A number of questions must be asked: (1) Should the client be referred? And if so, what type of referral is called for? (2) What assessment and screening procedures should be used? Multiple domain assessment? Norm-referenced or criterion-referenced screening? And if norm-referenced is to be used, what are the psychometric properties? Is the psychologist qualified to conduct the assessment?

To make a simple analogy, the problems faced by the clinician assessing any client may be likened to the problems faced by the detective attempting to solve a crime. Both have little or no previous knowledge of the case, face gaps in reliable information, and must rely on observations and interviews to uncover other problems or clues, all the while continuing to gather data. Both must observe, form hypotheses, and continually test and revise those hypotheses. Assessment is a continuous and ongoing process.

AREAS OF BEST PRACTICES

What are some areas of best assessment practice? Kamphaus (1993) has suggested three—test standards, ethics, and test selection—and discussed them as they concern the practicing clinician. McLean, Bailey, and Wolery (1996) have described additional areas in which the psychologist should be able to demonstrate best assessment practices. They indicate that the role of families in the assessment process has been limited to providing background information. But those in the assessment field should move toward greater utilization of families as evaluators. Recent research (eg., Bricker & Squires, 1989; Dale, 1991) has demonstrated that families can be reliable judges of their children's behavior, even in areas where their judgment has traditionally been thought unreliable.

Instruments have been developed to strengthen the collaborative relationship possible between families and clinicians. The AEPS Family Report Instrument (Bricker, 1993) and the Parent/Professional Preschool Performance Profile (Block, 1987) encourage evaluation by families and professionals. The Communications and Symbolic Behavior Scale (Wetherly & Prizant, 1993) allows for direct family participation in the assessment process. During the administration of this test, the examiner and parent(s) sit on either side of the child and either or both administer the test, depending on whom the child prefers to interact with.

Sharing the assessment finding at the end of the evaluation is another means of building a collaborative relationship between the clinician and the family. Yet other ways are (1) involving the parents, not at the end but at the beginning of the assessment process, by asking them to develop or complete a family profile; (2) asking parents to complete a developmental assessment and/or give their impressions of the assessment; and (3) sharing assessment information as it is being collected—it is crucial however, that the information be shared in a way that is useful to the families, promotes feelings of self-worth, and facilitates ownership of the decisions by the family. Building collaborative relationships with families and across disciplines can help to determine the assessment contents, activities, and results, and can help to build a relationship of trust and respect between family members and clinicians. Conscienciously followed this practice should lead to the kind of collaborative decision making central to the quality assessment of students and clients. Best practices would dictate that clinicians nurture such relationships.

CULTURAL COMPETENCY

Exemplary assessment requires not only a set of highly technical skills but an awareness of and sensitive response to the diverse characteristics of the people served. Psychologists, social theorists, politicians, lawyers, and administrators have wrestled with such terms as *nonbiased assessment, cultural nonbiased, nondiscriminatory assessment, culturally and linguistically different, pluralistic-multiculture approaches, appropriateness of instrument,* and *disproportionate placement.* Although litigation has not been able to provide an acceptable definition for many of these terms, a number of significant legal actions have influenced assessment practices and have brought such catchwords to the forefront of the field. Such laws as Public Law 99–457 (now titled the Disabilities Education Act, P.L. 102–119 of 1991) and Public Law 99–142, and the Rehabilitation Act, Section 504 have significantly affected the assessment practices of clinicians. A thorough discussion of the public law and court decisions that have influenced assessment is beyond the scope of this chapter; interested readers are advised to see other sources such as Elliott (1987).

Changing demographics (estimates are that by the year 2003, 41% of the nation's children will be Latino or other minority children) have forced psychologists to examine methods and explore avenues that ensure the assessment is neither culturally nor linguistically biased and that services are rendered in ways effective across cultures. Best practices thus mandate knowledge of the ever-changing family, acquisition of culture-specific information, and a commitment to selecting the most appropriate instrument of service-delivery. Cases involving children who are bilingual or non-English speaking will require the presence of an interpreter. Lynch (1992) has offered suggestions and guidelines for working more effectively with interpreters.

NONDISCRIMINATORY ASSESSMENT

Assessment procedures can be biased against individuals on the basis of gender, race, linguistic background, culture, religion, or disability (McLoughlin & Lewis, 1994). Numerous volumes have been written investigating nondiscriminatory assessment practices and test-item biases (Jensen, 1980; Kamphaus, 1993; Reynolds, 1982; Zucherman, 1990). Most have focused on the psychometric approach of test bias (mean-score difference bias; content-, construct-, and predictive-validity bias; and item bias). This section will focus briefly on some issues that are not often emphasized when discussing test-assessment bias.

Determining which instrument in an assessment battery is the most culturally, linguistically, and psychometrically appropriate constitutes a major issue. Valencia (1990) has discussed the difficulty involved in creating equivalent instruments for different cultural and linguistic populations. Valencia and Rankin (1985) conducted a study using the standard version of the McCarthy Scales of Children's Abilities and its Spanish translation, and found item and content bias in both editions (6 of the 16 McCarthy subtests showed some type of bias). As a result they cautioned more than a decade ago that sound research would be needed to develop tests that

Table 1-1. Code of Fair Testing Practices in Education

Developing/Selecting Appropriate Tests

1. Define the purpose for testing in the population to be tested. Then, select a test for that purpose and that population based on a thorough review of the available information.
2. Investigate potential useful sources of information, in addition to test scores, to corroborate the information provided by tests.
3. Become familiar with how and when the test was developed and tried.
4. Read independent evaluations of the test and, if possible, alternative measures. Look for evidence to support the claims of test developers.
5. Select and use only those tests for which the skills needed to administer the test and interpret scores correctly are available.

Interpretation of Test Scores

1. Obtain information about the scale used for reporting scores, the characteristics of any norms or comparison group(s), and the limitation of these scores.
2. Interpret scores taking into account any major differences between the norms or comparison group(s) and the actual test takers. Also take into account any differences in test administration practices or familiarity with specific questions in the test.
3. Avoid using tests for purposes not specifically recommended by the test developer unless evidence is obtained to support the alternate use.
4. Explain how any passing scores were set and gather evidence to support the appropriateness of the scores.
5. Obtain evidence to show the test is meeting its intended purpose(s).

Striving for Fairness

1. Evaluate the procedures used by test developers to avoid potentially insensitive content or language.
2. Review the performance of test takers of different race, gender, and ethnic background when samples of sufficient size are available. Evaluate the extent to which performance differences may have been caused by inappropriate characteristics of the test.
3. When necessary and feasible, use appropriately modified forms of tests or administration procedures for test takers with handicapping conditions. Interpret standard norms with care in the light of the modifications made.

Informing Examinees

1. When a test is optional, provide test takers or their parents or guardians with information to help them judge whether the test should be taken or whether an available alternative should be used.
2. Provide test takers information about coverage of the test, types of question formats, directions, and appropriate test taking strategies. Strive to make such information equally available to all test takers.
3. Provide test takers or their parents or guardians with information describing rights test takers may have to obtain copies of tests and completed answer sheets, retake tests, or have tests rescored or scores cancelled.
4. Tell test takers or their parents/guardians how long scores will be kept on file and indicate to whom and under what circumstances they will or will not be released.
5. Describe the procedures that test takers or their parents or guardians may use to register complaints and have problems resolved.

can be administered without linguistic or cultural bias. Is the instrument available in the child's native language? Are norms appropriate for comparison? Has his or her cultural group been included in the norms or has the instrument merely been translated? If these questions are answered in the negative, nonstandardized measures may be appropriate.

The Code of Fair Testing Practices in Education (1988) addressed the problems of test development and selection (Table 1–1), and the American Psychological Association (1985) has issued formal codes of ethics and standards of competency governing the administration and interpretation of tests. These standards are must reading. But as Kamphaus pointed out in a 1991 article well worth reading no gains have been made in devising specific tests for specific populations. Kamphaus (1991), however, documented many areas of competency needed by clinicians who assess multicultural clients.

AFFECTIVE DIMENSION OF ASSESSMENT

An often omitted or neglected dimension of psychoeducational assessment is the emotional aspect of the clinical setting. How do the psychologist's feelings affect the assessment procedures as the data is gathered, interpreted, and used to make decisions? As certain aspects of a client's behavior are evaluated, do nonverbal as well as verbal prompts come into play, even though clinicians are taught to adhere strictly to the test manual's instructions? Is there a "halo affective" of wanting a child found eligible to receive services or be admitted to certain programs? This area of affective domain must be further researched to more clearly understand and determine how and if emotions affect practices. Do clinicians become so addicted to the WISC-III or Binet test that administering them becomes routine? Professional clinicians working in a school or clinical environment must be aware of and prepared to deal with their own emotions. Perhaps universities that train professionals would be wise to spend as much time teaching an appreciation and understanding of the affective domain of assessment as they spend teaching the administration of tests.

EDUCATIONAL REFORM/MINIMUM COMPETENCY TESTING

What roles, if any, will the psychologist play in the educational reform movement? Assessment and evaluation of all students is a major goal in most educational reform movements. Ysseldyke, Algozzine, and Thurlow (1992) have indicated that in Kentucky all students are measured in terms of basic goals and learning outcomes. Such assessment devices as authentic, performance-based measures, portfolios, and even group-based measures are being used. How has this movement affected the assessment of special needs students? Best practices would mandate that psychologists working in schools become actively involved in designing assessment systems that meet the needs of not only the school but, more importantly, the learner. Psychologists are in a unique position to offer advice, training, and assistance to school counselors, teachers, and administrators involved in designing and administering assessment programs for students in systems where emphasis is placed on evaluating learning outcomes.

THE ASSESSMENT PROCESS

The field of psychological and educational assessment has expanded rapidly during the last 20 years. Numerous new and exciting instruments have been added to the clinician's battery of tests. Often the clinician is left to his or her own judgment when evaluating the psychometric soundness of an instrument. Vance in a 1987 speech to the Arizona Educational Diagnostic Convention addressed the issue of why clinicians use bad tests. Buros in 1961 said, "at present, no matter how poor a test may be, if it is needed, packaged so that it promises to do all sort of things which no test can do, the test will find many gullible buyers" (p. 1781). His observation holds true today. Best assessment practices mandate that clinicians select the instrument that is most firmly grounded in theory and has the best possible psychometric properties. This may be the most important decision in the assessment process.

Assessment practices are often poorly understood. The acquisition of clinical skills may be related to personality (Kamphaus, 1993). Clinical skills require more than the ability to follow the appropriate directions when administering a test. Best practices mandate such skills as rapport building, positive interactions, test interpretation, inference drawing, interviewing, and observation. Sattler (1988) has provided excellent suggestions for the new clinician who may lack familiarity with the instruments or experience working with young children, and Kutsick's chapter in the present volume provides the clinician with both sound and practical advice about best practices in assessing infants. As Matarazzo (1990) pointed out, "the assessment of intelligence, personality type or level of impairment is a highly complex operation that involves extracting diagnostic meaning from an individual's personal history and objectively recorded test scores. Rather than being totally objective assessment involved a subjective component" (p. 1000). That is, assessment is not the summation of scores from a battery of tests. A clinician's effectiveness also depends on his or her ability to listen, and to know and relate to others.

EMERGING TRENDS

Assessment is at a crucial, if not critical, juncture of development. Attacks on assessment procedures, practices, and instruments are almost a daily occurrence. The critics are vocal and are demanding reforms. In fact, it is safe to say that assessment is in a state of flux and that in many educational and clinical settings psychological assessment has fallen into disrepute during the past 20 years. Some educational professionals, and others as well, find the results of tests irrelevant, untimely, and in general unresponsive to the clinical or educational needs of children. This problem has probably developed because psychologists have, in some cases, formed a misguided and self-destructive loyalty to the standard battery of tests (Draw-A-Person, WISC-II, Bender Gestalt, and WRAT-R) and administered them in situations where their use is inappropriate. There are many movements outside the field of assessment that will have direct implications for the field.

REGULAR EDUCATION INITIATIVE

The regular education initiative, the movement to provide services to students with disabilities through a more integrated system of general and special education, continues. A major reconceptualization of assessment will occur as a result of this movement, according to McLoughlin and Lewis (1994), who suggest that "many of the current procedures will become inappropriate and useless" (p. 580). Perhaps the regular education initiative might expand the role of the clinician working in the schools in such areas as authentic assessment, portfolio, curriculum-based, and other informal techniques related to the general education curriculum, accountability, and minimum competency testing. Assessment in the arena (school) will require the clinician and diagnostic team to not only establish the eligibility of and the services needed by a client but a prognosis based on the severity of disability should such services be provided.

ARENA ASSESSMENT

Many public laws relating to assessment procedures require that assessment be a multidisciplinary effort (P.L. 101–476, P.L. 102–119, P.L. 99–457, 99–142). For instance, Parts B and H of 34CFR Sec. 303.17 call for the "involvement of two or more disciplines or professionals in the provision of integrated and coordinated services, including evaluation and assessment." How professionals from two or more disciplines organize themselves and relate to one another is important, for interdisciplinary assessment is difficult. Overlap in function, professional rivalry, and lack of communication are but three of the problems affecting cooperation. Competition, role conflict, and economics will all be forces as each specialty continues to develop its own expertise.

Arena assessment has been defined as the simultaneous evaluation of the child by multiple professionals of different disciplines (Linder, 1993), an approach that allows not only an immediate sharing of data, experience, and expertise regarding certain client behaviors, but reduces the assessment time required by each professional since each has immediate access to the data, skills, and knowledge of the others (Foley, 1990). The rationale for arena assessment is based on the difficulty of separating the physical, cognitive, and sensory domains of childhood development (McLean et al., 1996). This assessment format is both common and popular in the evaluation of young children, since it allows the team of experts to adapt their testing methods to the individual needs of the child and his or her family. In this regard, arena assessment promotes a more detailed understanding of how the child uses his or her emotionality or intellectual functions in response to a certain task in a certain environment, by providing more reliable and perhaps more valid observations. In addition, it allows clinicians to describe learning and behavioral disabilities in much greater detail.

DIAGNOSING THE SEVERITY OF DISABILITY

As provisions governing federal and state funding for the handicapped continue to be revised, teams of experts will have to assess more than the client's eligibility. They will have to determine not only the disability but the severity of the disability as well and design a treatment intervention program based on cost of service. Not every handicapping condition will receive the same amount of money. This trend will become more important as advances in modern medicine save more and more profoundly impaired children who will then come to school. Sabatino, Miller, and Vance (1993) suggested that in the face of divided resources, the more efficient use of clinicians' time, technology, and assessment instruments will be a major concern. A major problem with assessment as practiced by many psychologists who seek to determine eligibility or disability is that it fails to deal with etiological and ecological factors and fails to establish a prognosis (Sabatino et al., 1993). Best practices could mandate that psychologists go beyond administering tests and measure learner characteristics, behavior, rate of learning, and reaction time, and determine what intervention techniques are best suited for a particular handicapping condition.

COMPUTERIZED ADAPTIVE TESTING

Vance (1993) indicated that adaptive testing will become more applicable to a wide range of assessment instruments. Anastasi (1993) pointed out that the "most exciting event with regard to assessment devices is the development of computerized adaptive testing" (p. 40). Adaptive testing enables a clinician to custom-build a test for a client while he or she is taking the test. Adaptive testing procedures will increase the flexibility and facility with which tests can be give by computer-examiner interaction. A major advantage of interactive-adaptive testing is that it uses a decision model that takes into account not only the items and tasks of a test but also the level of errors or accuracy in the examinee's responses (ceiling levels) and where to begin testing (basal levels). Computerized adaptive testing allows for clearer and more accurate test scores by taking into account the statistical properties of the test items as well as the number of correct responses. Special training, however, will be required to make full use of this procedure (Golden et al., 1990).

CHROMOMETRIC TECHNIQUES

In a interview with R.W. Kamphaus (1993), Arthur Jenson suggested that chromometric techniques will propel the study of the information-processing component of mental ability into the twenty-first century. Chromometric techniques are simple to use and provide a very reliable measurement of the individual subject's reaction time, making it possible to measure individual differences in mental ability by means that are virtually independent of acquired intellectual contents and skills. According to Jensen, clinicians will be able to localize strengths and weaknesses in the various components of the information-processing system reflected in chromometric techniques, and by applying chromometry measure processing speed from preschool to old age. The time unit used is a ratio scale, which has the scientific advantage of being an absolute measurement scale.

As Jensen's and numerous other studies attest, assessment, and particularly what comprises best practices, remains an elusive topic. McLean et al. (1996) pointed out that "no one method or instrument is identified as capable of detecting and/or predicting all children in need of intervention or evaluating the effects of intervention regimen" (p. 70).

What held true in the 1980s may still hold true today: As the public and private interest in tests and assessment continues to increase, that interest may be directly related to self-survival as well as to a desire to improve the assessment process. It is eminently clear from this chapter and the following chapters that best practices in assessment—in reality—depends on the clinicians: their professionalism, training, sensitivity to individual differences, and desire to be well informed about the instruments of assessment and how best to use them.

REFERENCES

Anastasi, A. (1993). Personal interviews. In R.W. Kamphaus (Eds.), *Clinical assessment of children's abilities.* Needham Heights, MA: Allyn & Bacon.

Block, J. (1987). *Parent/Professional Preschool Performance Profile.* Syosset, NY: Variety Pre-Schoolers' Workshop.

Bricker, D. (1993). *Assessment, evaluation, and programming system for children: AEPS measurement for birth to three years* (Vol. 1). Baltimore: Paul H. Brookes.

Bricker, D., & Squires, J. (1989). The effectiveness of parental screening of at-risk infants: The infant monitoring questionnaire. *Topics in Early Childhood Special Education, 9,* 67–85.

Buros, O.K. (1961). *Tests in print: A comprehensive bibliography of tests for use in education, psychology, and industry.* Highland Park, NJ: Gryphon Press.

Dale, P. (1991). The validity of a parent report measure of vocabulary and syntax at 24 months. *Journal of Speech and Hearing Research, 34,* 565–571.

Elliott, R. (1987). *Litigating intelligence: IQ tests, special education and social science in the courtroom.* Dover, MA: Alvin House.

Foley, G.B. (1990). Portrait of the arena evaluation: Assessment in the transdisciplinary approach. In E. Gibbs & D. Jeti (Eds.), *Interdisciplinary assessment of infants: A guide for early intervention* (pp. 271–286). Baltimore: Paul H. Brookes.

Golden, C.J., Sawichi, R.F., & Frazen, M.D. (1990). Test construction. In G. Goldstein & H. Hersen (Eds.), *Handbook of psychological assessment* (pp. 21–40). New York: Pergamon Press.

Jensen, A.R. (1980). *Bias in mental testing.* New York: The Free Press.

Kamphaus, R.W. (1991, October). Multicultural expertise. *Child Assessment News,* pp. 1, 8–10.

Kamphaus, R.W. (1993). *Clinical assessment of children's intelligence.* Boston: Allyn & Bacon.

Linder, T.W. (1993). *Transdisciplinary play-based assessment: A functional approach to working with young adults* (Rev. ed.). Baltimore: Paul H. Brookes.

Lynch, E.W. (1992). Developing cross-cultural competence. In E.W. Lynch & M.J. Hanson (Eds.), *Developing cross cultural competence: A guide for working with young children and families.* Baltimore: Johns Hopkins University Press.

Matarazzo, J.D. (1990). *Psychological assessment versus psychological testing: Validation from Binet to the school, clinic, and courtroom.* Washington, DC: American Psychological Association.

McLean, M., Bailey, D.B., & Wolery, M. (1996). *Assessing infants and preschoolers with special needs.* Englewood Cliffs, NJ: Prentice-Hall.

McLoughlin, J.A., & Lewis, R.B. (1994). *Assessing special students.* Englewood Cliffs, NJ: Prentice-Hall.

Reynolds, C.R. (1982). The problem of bias in psychological assessment. In C.R. Reynolds & T.B. Gutkin (Eds.), *The handbook of school psychology.* New York: Wiley.

Sabatino, D., Miller, T., & Vance, H.B. (1993). Defining best diagnostic practices. In H.B. Vance (Ed.), *Best practices in assessment: School and clinical settings* (pp. 1–28). Brandon, VT: Clinical Psychology Publishing Co.; New York: Wiley.

Sattler, J.M. (1988). *Assessment of children* (3rd ed.). San Diego, CA. Sattler Publication.

Valencia, R.R. (1990). Clinical assessment of young children with the McCarthy Scales of Children Abilities. In C.R. Reynolds & R.W. Kamphaus (Eds.), *Handbook of psychological and educational assessment of children: Intelligence and achievement.* New York: Guilford.

Vance, H.B. (1987, April). Why people use bad tests. Keynote Speech. Arizona Chapter of Teachers of Exceptional Children. Flagstaff, AZ.

Vance, H.B. (1993). Future trends in assessment. In H.B. Vance (Ed.), *Best practices in assessment: School and clinical settings* (pp. 525–535). Brandon, VT: Clinical Psychology Publishing Co.; New York: Wiley.

Wetherly, A., & Prizant, B. (1993). *Communication and symbolic behavior scale.* Chicago: Riverside.

Ysseldyke, J.E., Algozzine, B., & Thurlow, M.L. (1992). *Critical issues in special education* (2nd ed.). Boston: Houghton Mifflin.

Zucherman, M. (1990). Some dubious premises in research and theory on racial differences: Scientific, social, and ethical issues. *American Psychologist, 45,* 1297–1303.

Part I

Assessment Approaches

Chapter 2

INFORMAL ASSESSMENT

MARY M. CHITTOORAN AND TED L. MILLER

INTRODUCTION

The accurate assessment of children's functioning continues to be a critical concern to teachers and school psychologists. According to Stiggins (1992), teachers spend as much as one-third to one-half of their professional time on assessment, and surveys of school psychologists indicate that assessment accounts for at least 50% of their professional practice (Stinnett, Havey, & Oehler-Stinnett, 1994; Wilson & Reschly, 1996). Despite its obvious importance, the issue of assessment remains marked by controversy. One reason for this has been the growing realization that traditional norm-referenced assessment, despite early indications to the contrary, has limited utility for teachers and others involved in delivering instruction to children. Criticism of formal assessment has ranged from its lack of relevance to classroom instruction to its limitations with children from culturally diverse groups (Worthen & Spandel, 1991).

Characteristics of Informal Assessment

The continuing debate over formal assessment has resulted in the resurgence of informal assessment, which offers the promise of a richer, more complete understanding of a child's performance. Although there are a number of definitions of informal assessment (e.g., McLoughlin & Lewis, 1994; Sattler, 1988; Witt, Elliott, Kramer, & Gresham, 1994), most include variations of the following: Informal assessment is a structured and systematic problem-solving approach to assessment designed to gather information about a child's strengths and weaknesses in academic, cognitive, and social-behavioral domains that can then be translated into instructional objectives. Unlike norm-referenced assessment, it is not generally quantitative in nature and is not normally used to compare a child's performance against previously established standards. It is generally used in classrooms and often developed by classroom teachers, although that is certainly not always the

We would like to thank our graduate assistants at the University of Tennessee at Chattanooga, Karen L. White and Pamela J. Wing, for their library assistance during the writing of this manuscript.

Correspondence concerning this chapter should be directed to Mary M. Chittooran, Graduate Studies Division, the University of Tennessee-Chattanooga, 615 McCallie Avenue, Chattanooga, TN 37403.

case. Salvia and Ysseldyke (1995) view informal assessment as any assessment that is *not* formal and consider the two approaches to be qualitatively different with regard to their purposes, methods, and outcomes; however, others such as Houtz and Krug (1995) and Stiggins (1994) regard them as complementary, sometimes overlapping approaches that can provide a comprehensive understanding of a child's functioning.

The conceptual basis for informal assessment is not new; in fact, such assessment, with its relatively easy translation into effective instructional practice, is actually a precursor to formal assessment. One can almost imagine a cave father demonstrating hunting skills to his son, monitoring the boy's performance and then modifying instruction to facilitate his son's mastery of the task that would one day be so critical to his survival. According to Witt et al. (1994) and Sattler (1988), there are several assumptions upon which the use of assessment in general and informal assessment in particular must be predicated; a disregard of these could result in faulty interpretations and inappropriate interventions. First, all tests, whether formal or informal, are simply samples of current functioning; one must therefore extrapolate from these samples to an estimate of typical functioning. Second, all assessment results must be interpreted in light of the unique environmental contexts within which a particular child functions; without these connections, results are neither meaningful nor useful. Third, the aim of all informal assessment is to enhance the utility of instructional interventions, whether these are academic or social-behavioral. Finally, all assessment involves a certain degree of error; while this cannot be entirely eliminated, it can certainly be minimized by the competent examiner.

Advantages of Informal Assessment

Informal assessment offers a number of advantages to the school professional. Perhaps most important among these is its direct relevance to instruction, in that such assessment not only helps determine the content of instruction but also suggests methods and activities that might be beneficial. Unlike standardized norm-referenced tests, many of the methods and materials used in informal assessment are easily accessible to teachers and other professionals and are therefore routinely used. Such tests, with their sensitivity to small improvements in instructional outcomes, can be used to document instructional effectiveness to a degree that is not possible with the more broad-based norm-referenced measures. Informal measures can also be readily developed when no adequate formal instrument is available.

Another advantage of informal assessment is its flexibility. It can be used in a number of settings by individuals with varying levels of education. It does not generally require extensive training and is therefore relatively inexpensive. Informal assessment also has a greater degree of specificity than norm-referenced assessment (McLoughlin & Lewis, 1994); while formal measures usually assess a large number of content areas, specific skills within each of those areas are assessed by only a few items. On the other hand, informal assessment can be used to assess a number of specific skills with a large number of items. It is clear that informal assessment can accomplish some important educational functions, particularly the effective monitoring of progress and the measurement of changes in specific learning outcomes.

Informal Assessment for Individuals with Special Needs

One of the main criticisms of formal assessment is its limitation with certain populations. For example, when it comes to children with certain kinds of disabilities, formal measures simply cannot provide the in-depth information that informal measures can. Informal methods such as behavioral observations, dynamic assessments, curriculum-based assessment, and nonverbal tasks have been proposed for use in school psychology with a variety of populations (Rosenfield & Reynolds, 1990).

Informal assessment has been seen as a viable option for preschool bilingual children (Gutierrez-Clellen, Pena, & Quinn, 1995), adults and children with psychiatric or psychological disorders (Leitner, 1995), infants with prenatal cocaine exposure (Edmondson & Smith, 1994), learning-disabled children with psychiatric disorders (Audet & Hummel, 1990), children with attention-deficit/hyperactivity disorder (Fiorello & Burcham, 1996; Landau & Burcham, 1995; Reid, 1995), and those with traumatic brain injury (Farmer & Peterson, 1995). It is clear that the potential uses of informal assessment span all settings and all disabilities.

Disadvantages of Informal Assessment

Despite its many advantages, informal assessment still has a number of detractors, primarily among those professionals who believe that it lacks an established theoretical foundation. Others cite limited evidence of reliability and validity, and warn against the premature acceptance of assessment results obtained in this manner. According to Witt et al. (1994), the relative subjectivity of informal measures may reduce the validity of the results. Further, differences in administration and interpretation across raters suggest that interrater reliability may be a very real concern. To many, the very name *informal assessment* implies an approach that is less serious or important than formal assessment, although its methods are often just as rigorous. Another objection is that many examiners do not have the familiarity with the specific content areas required by such assessment. Finally, there is some concern about the fact that although informal assessment is touted as being the more economical of the two approaches, its hidden costs are not widely apparent. For example, according to McLoughlin and Lewis (1994), informal measures are often not as time or cost efficient as norm-referenced measures in that they require more teacher time, both to develop and to administer. Despite these objections, most authors recognize that informal assessment, when used in conjunction with traditional methods of assessment, can yield valuable information about a child's functioning that may not be available with traditional, norm-referenced tests alone (Sattler, 1988).

Informal Assessment and Alternative Assessment: A Clarification

The recent literature reveals a certain amount of confusion surrounding the use of the terms *informal assessment* and *alternative assessment*. Although they appear to be used interchangeably in the literature, there are subtle differences between the two, particularly with regard to their origins. Whereas informal assessment stands in contrast to the norm-referenced standardized tests used in special education, the term *alternative assessment* arose out of general education in the late eighties in direct opposition to the group-administered, multiple-choice, standardized achievement tests used to assess pupil progress (McLoughlin & Lewis, 1994; Miller & Legg, 1993; Worthen, 1993; Worthen & Leopold, 1992). These tests, like the ones used in special education, were criticized for their failure to be instructionally relevant, their inability to measure higher-order cognitive skills, and the disjointed manner in which they assessed important school skills (McLoughlin & Lewis, 1994; Popham, 1993).

Alternative assessment, then, represented a departure from traditional assessment and a move toward innovative ways to assess children's functioning. Nationwide efforts have been directed at bringing about general education reform and developing complex large-scale assessments and high performance standards for all children. The movement gathered force with the passing of *Goals 2000* in 1994 and is slowly gaining acceptance in related fields like school psychology and special education (Braden, 1996).

The growing interest in informal and alternative forms of assessment is evident in the fact that computer resources for proponents of this approach are now available. In fact, the authors recently discovered a database entitled *Alternative Assessments in Practice* that provides access to hundreds of methods of assessment as well as reviews of selected measures.[†] In an effort to avoid confusion, this chapter will use the term *informal assessment* to refer to approaches that have traditionally been considered informal as well as more recent approaches that are subsumed under the term *alternative assessment*.

The remainder of this chapter will provide an overview of the major approaches to informal assessment as well as a description of how informal assessment may be used in specific academic domains such as reading, mathematics, and language. A discussion of informal assessment with specific populations is included, as is a section on the use of computers in informal assessment. A case study is offered to show how the results of formal and informal assessment can be integrated to provide a comprehensive picture of a child's functioning as well as a foundation upon which to build academic and/or behavioral interventions. Finally, the chapter considers the future of informal assessment and provides directions for further research.

INFORMAL ASSESSMENT APPROACHES

According to McLoughlin and Lewis (1994), informal measures can be differentiated along two dimensions: their level of obtrusiveness and whether they are direct

---

[†]The Internet address for the *Alternative Assessments in Practice Database* is
http://www.cresst96.cse.ucla.edu/database.htm.

or indirect measures of behavior. These dimensions can be used to classify informal assessment into three general groups: direct and unobtrusive measures, such as behavioral observations, task analysis, and ecological analysis; direct and obtrusive measures, such as curriculum-based measurement, classroom inventories, work samples, and criterion-referenced measures; and indirect and obtrusive measures, such as checklists, questionnaires, and interviews (McLoughlin & Lewis, 1994).

Behavioral Observation Strategies

No discussion of informal assessment is complete without the inclusion of behavioral observations. However, because the procedures outlined here are well known, only a brief outline is offered. Guerin and Maier (1983) dichotomize observation into methods that may be considered direct and those that may be considered indirect. Direct measures demand a high level of behavioral specificity, employ observation of the student's activities at the time of occurrence, and result in an immediate and precise record of behavior. Direct observation is generally used to describe prespecified, directly observable behaviors. Indirect observation procedures often have a format which results in information that is a summary of prior experiences. These procedures are generally used to obtain an overview of less specific, perhaps less readily observable behaviors.

Direct Approaches to Observation

There are many variations of direct observation. The simplest form is the *sequence sample* (sometimes referred to as the *anecdotal record*), in which the observer notes instances of specific types of behaviors as they occur. The observer notes all that appears after the behavioral event and, to the extent possible, reconstructs all that occurred prior to the event. A more specific adaptation of this approach has been termed *functional analysis* (Bijou & Peterson, 1970). According to Drew and Hardman (1995), the approach is founded in behavioral analysis and is especially applicable for assessment in early childhood (see Bergan, 1977, for a more specific rationale). Direct observation is employed in the setting in which the identified behavior is of concern (i.e., artificial clinical settings are not used). As Drew and Hardman note, that behavior is usually recorded with respect to inappropriate stimulus control and behavioral deficits or excesses. The result is a record that specifies the precise elements of the intervention program. This approach appears to be exceptionally useful with individuals who have severe disabilities.

In *chronolog recording,* the observer provides a description of all events that are ongoing during a particular time frame. Properly constructed, this report yields a detailed description of events as they occur: *Frequency* or *duration recordings* note the number of occurrences or the length of occurrences of specific predetermined behaviors during some specified time and in some specified location. Finally, in the *trait sample technique,* specific predetermined trait characteristics are recorded, usually by frequency. This is a closed system in which the behaviors have been prespecified, often on the basis of some heuristic model. Techniques such as these have been extensively applied to the analysis of teacher-pupil interaction, and the observer's task is to specify not only the behaviors but the sequence of the behaviors. These approaches are sometimes termed *observational systems* (see Simon & Boyer, 1974). A very sophisticated variation, currently more likely to be used in the laboratory than in the classroom, has been termed the *lag sequential approach* (Sackett, 1979). In this approach, relationships among behaviors—not strictly absolute quantities of behaviors—can be statistically ascertained. An example of the lag sequential approach may be found in Slate and Saudargas (1987).

Each of these approaches to direct observation has specific strengths and weaknesses. The techniques vary in suitability for the specific circumstances in which data are to be collected, ease of use in terms of observer training, and level of attainable reliability and validity. Oosterhof (1996) has recently provided an excellent set of guidelines for improving the generalizability of observations.

One variation of direct observation lies less in specific techniques than in the responsibility of the examinee; that is, the examinee may sometimes be the observer. Such self-observation (Mahoney & Thoreson, 1974; Meichenbaum, 1979; Watson & Tharp, 1989) can be extremely useful in monitoring behaviors such as time-on-task. These procedures have generally gained favor in altering student behavior but are also useful for monitoring behavior prior to some intervention. All of these approaches are techniques of analysis that must be specified for a particular case. The practitioner must become familiar with these techniques and competent at adapting them to the peculiarities of specific settings. Guidelines for the use of these procedures are readily available. And, because observation strategies are often the basis for evaluating the effects of behavioral assessment (Bellack & Hersen, 1988), single-subject research (Tawney & Gast, 1984), and classroom management strategies (Alberto & Troutman, 1995; Kazdin, 1995; Walker & Shea, 1988), practical descriptions can be found in textbooks devoted to these topics.

Indirect Approaches to Observation

Indirect approaches to observation also offer the practitioner many techniques and are equally prominent in practice. All of these procedures are dependent upon the recall and judgment of the observer and can be used to examine developmental history, current life circumstances, and beliefs and attitudes (Guerin & Maier, 1983). Indirect measures have the advantage of being able to evaluate a broad range of behaviors and to investigate topics of interest that may not be readily observable. Typically, such approaches are used to summarize impressions gathered over some lengthy period of time. They are also generally less cumbersome to the observer because they do not require either the direct involvement or the time investment that direct measures do. The following sections describe some frequently used indirect approaches to observation.

Checklists

When checklists are used for the assessment of social-emotional functioning, they generally include a list of behavioral indicators that may be grouped in some way or stated in the form of a question. The respondent marks "Yes" if the behavior is observed and "No" if it is not. Checklists to determine whether academic skills have been mastered are similarly developed and used. The main advantages of checklists are the speed with which they can be completed, the ease of data interpretation, the fact that they can be group administered, and their comprehensiveness. They provide a detailed record of a student's progress and can be readministered several times with impunity. Their main disadavantage is that the respondent has only two choices and is therefore limited to stating that the behavior occurs without being able to describe the frequency, duration, or severity of the response. This results in the loss of some potentially valuable information; for example, a child whose teacher marks "Yes" for "Steals" because the child stole a classmate's pencil on one occasion can hardly be compared to another child who steals whenever the occasion presents itself.

An additional problem with checklists is the difficulty of summarizing a child's performance in some convenient form (Airasian, 1994; Merrell, 1994). It is possible with some checklists to obtain a sum of "Yes" and "No" responses, but a global summary score is not possible. Checklists are also susceptible to inaccuracy, either because of errors in individual judgment or because of errors in the reporting process. Pigford (1989) has recently criticized the use of behavioral checklists for teacher evaluation. Among his more prominent concerns is the reduction in adequacy of information and the misleading outcomes that can arise from a data technique that sacrifices subtleties in the interest of expediency. In the face of such concerns, indirect measures such as checklists have often been considered best utilized when reserved for initial clinical investigations. Some examples of checklists are the Mooney Problem Checklist (Mooney & Gordon, 1992) and the Autism Behavior Checklist (Krug, Arick, & Almond, 1988).

Rating Scales

Rating scales are similar to checklists in that they contain behavioral descriptors of some kind to which the rater is expected to respond. Like checklists, they provide idiographic descriptions of behavior; that is, they are designed to assess an individual's perceptions of another person's behaviors. Rating scales differ from checklists in that the respondent is not limited to the dichotomy of "Yes" and "No" responses but is, instead, able to make finer discriminations between observed behaviors. Merrell (1994) describes rating scales as an "algebraic summation" of discrete observations in that raters are able to weight behaviors differentially according to their frequency or severity. This is contrasted with the "additive" nature of checklists, which are necessarily limited in the kind of information they can provide about a child's behavior.

There are a variety of rating scales and response options. The most frequently used scales include *category ratings,* with the observer selecting a word or phrase that best characterizes a person or event; *forced choice items,* which require the observer to select a response that is not graduated (for example, the rater is forced to indicate "Always" or "Never" and is limited to these choices); and finally, responses that indicate some level of concurrence on a continuum of possibilities (e.g., "Agree," "Somewhat agree," "Disagree").

Rating scales may be completed by one or more respondents and ratings can be used to provide multiple comparisons of a child's behavior. For example, both a parent and a teacher may complete rating scales on a child and these ratings can then be compared both quantitatively, by examining obtained scores, and qualitatively, by studying response patterns or individual comments marked by both raters.

Although rating scales were viewed with some suspicion before the 1970s, vast improvements in rating-scale technology have taken place since 1975 that have allowed such scales to become the most frequently used measurement device for verifying and determining the degree of social maladjustment (Martin, 1988). These changes have also been attributed to a growing understanding that problem behaviors are best understood from a multisource, multisetting, multimethod perspective (Martin, 1988). Many rating scales identify the presence or absence of abnormality and some also indicate the type of abnormality present. For example, the Burks' Behavior Rating Scale (Burks, 1980) provides information about whether a behavior is significant or nonsignificant but does not further describe or quantify the behavior, while the Child Behavior Checklist (Achenbach, 1991), which includes teacher, parent, and youth self-report ratings, provides T scores, information about the presence of problem behaviors and their severity, and classifies behaviors according to type (e.g., social withdrawal or delinquent behaviors) and dimension (externalizing or internalizing).

Martin (1988), Merrell (1994), and Sattler (1988) provide a comprehensive justification for the use of rating scales with children and adolescents. For one thing, they are relatively easy to administer, score, and interpret and, as such, are cost efficient. They are able to identify low-frequency behaviors that may not be noted during direct behavioral observations. They are an objective method of assessment and provide information that is more reliable than that gathered through unstructured interviews and projective techniques. They can be used to describe the behaviors of individuals who are unable to provide information about themselves. Because they essentially provide a summation of behavior, they capitalize on the fact that the respondent bases ratings on a series of observations rather than on an isolated case. They are also useful in that the raters are usually parents or teachers who have primary observation opportunities.

The main disadvantage of rating scales, according to Barkley (1987), is that "such scales, despite their apparent objectivity, are simply quantifications of adult opinions. As a result they are subject to the same sources of unreliability as those opinions" (p. 219). Sources of variance have been attributed to response bias; for example, raters may assume an unusually lenient or critical stance and provide corresponding ratings of a child's behaviors. Further, because of the situational specificity of behavior, raters may not observe behaviors of interest in all settings and so may not note them as occurring. Readers are referred to Martin (1988) for a more complete discussion of error variance. Rating scales are further limited in that the discriminations between levels of behavior may not be fine enough and so may not accurately reflect the severity or frequency of a particular behavior. A number of commercially developed instruments are available, such as Achenbach's (1991) Child Behavior Checklist and McCarney and Leigh's (1990) Behavior Evaluation Scale-2; alternatively, the teacher can develop instruments designed for a particular purpose.

Self-Report Measures

Informal measures that describe an individual's perceptions of his or her own behaviors are known as self-report measures and bear the distinction of being the oldest form of personality tests (Martin, 1988). Although they fell out of favor in the seventies and eighties, there has been a renewed interest in their use with children and adolescents. Self-report measures are useful in that they provide critical information about aspects of functioning that are not directly observable, such as thoughts, perceptions, attitudes, values, and interests. Such information can, of course, be gathered during an interview, but some respondents may feel uncomfortable discussing information of a personal nature during a face-to-face interaction.

The main advantage of self-report measures is that they tap aspects of functioning that may not be accessible through any other means. The primary disadvantage of such measures is that they are subject to several types of response bias that can increase error variance and so reduce the validity of results. Martin (1988) has noted that children and adolescents exhibit a tendency to dissemble or to respond in a defensive manner, particularly if the outcome of the assessment is seen as threatening. Although many of these problems can be circumvented by using a multisource approach to assessment, there is no guarantee that inaccuracies will always be identified; Martin therefore recommends a cautious interpretation of the results of self-report measures. Some examples of self-report measures are the Youth Self-Report Form of the Child Behavior Checklist (Achenbach, 1991) designed to be used by adolescents between the ages of 11 and 18 and the Piers-Harris Children's Self-Concept Scale (Piers & Harris, 1984).

Questionnaires

Questionnaires are frequently utilized in informal assessment and are most useful when students can read and write at an appropriate level. Although most questionnaires in use are teacher developed, there are a few that are commercially available. Essentially, questionnaires consist of a selected number of questions designed to gather information about an individual's functioning in one or more domains. They can be used for the assessment of specific academic skills or to determine a student's attitudes and beliefs. Questionnaires may be of the sentence-completion variety or may require a constructed response to a question or statement. Some questionnaires are open-ended (e.g., Describe your relationship with your mother); others contain questions of the closed variety (e.g., How old are you?); and a third type contains both open and closed questions. In any event, each type of questionnaire yields valuable albeit different kinds of information.

Despite the efficiency that is possible with questionnaires (unlike interviews, they can be group administered, for example), there are at least three potential drawbacks to their use. First, we must make the assumption—not ·always accurate—that students can read and write at a satisfactory level. Second, individuals must be able to comprehend the questions and formulate accurate responses, and this is certainly not always the case. In some cases, questions may be read to the examinee; however, the presence of the reader, and his or her gender, age, and ethnicity may influence the way the individual responds. Third, we must be relatively assured that the student is motivated to answer the questions in a satisfactory manner. Some students may be so disenchanted with the necessity of composition and so anxious to get the task done that their responses are not only abbreviated but inaccurate. Thus, in many cases, to ensure acceptable validity the evaluator should forego questionnaires and conduct interviews instead.

Clinical Interviews

One special approach to indirect observation, the clinical interview, actually contains elements of direct observation in that the interviewer observes the interviewee face-to-face and in so doing has some opportunity to judge the supplied information. The clinical interview is a purposeful, face-to-face interaction between two persons, the interviewer and the interviewee, which is conducted for the primary purpose of gathering information about a referral problem (Sattler, 1988). Interviews are flexible assessment tools because they provide greater scope for data collection than many other methods. In excellent discussions of the interview as a data-gathering tool, Lanyon and Goldstein (1982) and Sattler (1988) discuss four advantages to such an assessment approach. First, the conversational nature of the interview serves to enhance the rapport between interviewer and interviewee; this in turn increases the likelihood that accurate information will be exchanged. Second, the relatively unstructured format of many interviews lends itself to flexible administration, giving the interviewer the prerogative of additional probing and questioning. In addition, interviews allow for the documentation of the "context and chronicity of behaviors" and the clarification of uncertain responses. Third, the interview is a useful tool with individuals who because of intellectual, social, or emotional deficits cannot be assessed through more conventional means. And finally, the interviewer gains information not only about specific issues but about the interviewee's personality and lifestyle that may be critical to problem solution (Sattler, 1988).

Although interviews can yield extremely useful information, their greatest weakness as an assessment technique is, arguably, the limited reliability and validity of the information gathered. However, Martin (1988) and Merrell (1994) have offered suggestions to enhance the reliability of information, including the selection of a quiet setting that is relatively free of distractions, the establishment and maintenance of rapport, the recognition and appropriate use of power, and the modeling of appropriate behaviors such as active listening, empathy, and genuineness. Other disadavantages of the interview are that the results are heavily dependent upon the interviewer's interpersonal skills and the interviewee's willingness to self-disclose, the rapport that exists between them, and in the case of unstructured interviews the relevance or omission of important questions. According to Sattler (1988), these problems may be exacerbated when it comes to cross-cultural or cross-class interviewing. He suggests improving the chances of success by learning about the cultural norms of the group that the interviewee represents, being willing to consider alternate perspectives, and being aware of one's own prejudices.

Another issue that complicates the use of interviews is that an interviewee's responses to questions are a function of the individual's developmental level. Adolescents, for example, may be wary of providing information about sexual matters and recreational activities, or may resent adult interference in private matters. Preschoolers may require extensive rapport-building sessions, may be easily distracted, and may not provide much meaningful information. Children who are intellectually deficient may not be functioning at a level commensurate with chronological age, and this must be considered during interviews. An interviewer who uses "developmentally sensitive" interviewing techniques (Martin, 1988) recognizes interviewee differences in the content and style of responses and structures the interview accordingly; one who does not, runs the risk of gathering little usable information.

Some of the problems inherent in unstructured interviews have led authors to advocate for more structured interviews as a way of increasing both the reliability and validity of information. For example, the Semistructured Clinical Interview has been recommended by McConaughy and Achenbach (1996) as a supplement to behavior-rating scales such as the Child Behavior Checklist (Achenbach, 1991). Structured interviews have been advocated for use in academic evaluation (Gable & Henderson, 1990; Howell & Kaplan, 1980; McLoughlin & Lewis, 1994; Zigmond, Vallecorsa, & Silverman, 1983), and the technique has also been used to measure learning aptitudes, career and vocational goals, adaptive behavior, and social-emotional concerns. Good interviewing practices require considerable training, and the practitioner who is unfamiliar with the approach is encouraged to seek formal training. Excellent descriptions of the essentials of interviewing can be found in Guerin and Maier (1983), Hughes and Baker (1990), McLoughlin and Lewis (1994), and Martin (1988).

Ecological Analysis

In recent years, there has been a growing recognition of the close link between student behavior and environmental influences. This recognition has been attributed to the emerging emphasis on and success of the behavioral orientation in assessment and programming. A variation of this orientation has been termed *ecological analysis*. As noted by Wallace and Larsen (1992), the professional who employs an ecological perspective attempts to view children in relationship to their total environment(s), not merely to discrete and unrelated influences. Much of the rationale for this approach is drawn from ethnological studies and, more recently, from ecological psychology. For some, the theoretical underpinnings and practical assessment procedures associated with ecological assessment are little more than a modified approach to traditional behavioral methods (Baer, 1977). For others, the approach may be seen as a partial departure from the emphasis of assessment and the subsequent conceptualization of treatment strategies (Rogers-Warren & Warren, 1977; Scott, 1980; Willems, 1974).

A number of concepts are relatively unique to the ecological analysis of behavior. For example, Scott (1980) defined the *behavioral setting*, a key concept of ecological analysis, as a collection of time, place, and object properties that demonstrate a standing pattern of behavior. A specific classroom might be identified as a behavioral setting in that it contains object properties unique to it and displays a standing pattern of behavior at some particular time (e.g., arithmetic instruction). The ecologist would suggest that this standing pattern of behavior displays similarity from one occasion to the next and that persons entering this setting would tend to blend in (i.e., adopt behaviors that are characteristic of the setting's major structures). In ecological analysis, observation of these setting characteristics is considered essential if the behavior of an individual is to be properly described, characterized, and understood.

Simeonsson (1986) has identified overlapping components of the behavioral and ecological approaches. Both strategies rely on systematic observation as the primary means of assessment (although observation approaches vary in focus, precision, and methodology). Both approaches may be considered age irrelevant; that is, identical procedures may be used regardless of the child's age or disability. Finally, all data are criterion referenced. Simeonsson notes that "the value of ecological and behavioral approaches is that they provide means whereby the contextual and functional influences of the environment can be assessed" (p. 99). However, the procedures and assumptions of the methods diverge somewhat at this juncture. Simeonsson notes that whereas ecological methods focus on the context of the behavior, behavioral approaches focus on stimulus-behavior relationships. Ecological analysis places great emphasis on nonobtrusive observation, whereas behavioral methods emphasize measurement under conditions of experimental control. Whereas behavioral methods operationalize behavior prior to observation, the ecological approach produces inferences only after all recordings have been completed. Finally, the ecological approach views patterns and sequences of behavior as the primary unit of analysis, while the behavioral approach usually measures frequency or duration of a particular behavior.

Data collection procedures associated with ecological analysis are neither simple nor efficient to use. Data collection generally begins with a long narrative record, often generated by a transcribed tape recording. The intent of the record is to thoroughly describe the events experienced by the child. The record is extensive and comprehensive but is not, at this stage, evaluative. Generally, several records are collected, resulting in many pages of descriptive text. The evaluator then attempts the process of unitization; that is, structural units of naturally occurring behaviors are identified and characterized. These activity units (AUs) are identified by beginning and ending points of behavior sequences and are then categorized. Typical AU titles might be "talks with classmates," "stares out window," "runs from wall to wall," "attempts to attract teacher's attention," and so on. Ultimately, a summary of the AUs is developed, often accompanied by the percentage of time the student engages in them.

Although the methods of ecological analysis are complex and time consuming, the procedure does tend to reveal insights into student behavior that may otherwise be overlooked. The evaluator may discover proportions of time that are devoted to specific behaviors or identify specific environmental antecedents to specific behaviors. These data can help establish areas in which an emphasis on behavioral change should be considered. The data can also be invaluable for the identification of environmental components that support undesirable behaviors. Moreover, the data are unique in that no prestructured elements are specified, and unnoticed or unanticipated elements of behavior can emerge without the transducer or filtering process (Barker, 1965; Schoggen, 1978) imposed by more traditional, structured, obtrusive data-collection procedures. For readers with a particular interest in ecobehavioral analysis, excellent resources are Benner (1992) and Schroeder (1990).

Criterion-Referenced Tests

Among the oldest of the informal measures for the assessment of academic skills, criterion-referenced tests are so familiar that a discussion of them in this section does not seem warranted. Readers who desire a background in these measures are referred to works by Gronlund (1993) and Sattler (1988), which contain comprehensive discussions of the nature, characteristics, and use of criterion-referenced tests.

Curriculum-Based Assessment

Numerous authors (e.g., Evans, Evans, & Mercer, 1986; Salvia & Hughes, 1990; Taylor, 1989) have provided substantial descriptions of the concept of curriculum-based assessment. But, in fact, "Curriculum-based assessment (CBA) is a new term for a teaching practice that is as old as teaching itself: using the material to be learned as the basis for assessing the degree to which it has been learned" (Tucker, 1985, p. 199). More recently, Salvia and Hughes (1990) have stated that CBA must have seven capabilities: curricular match, direct measurement of pupil performance, evaluation of pupil progress on specific objectives as well as more general goals, frequent administration, provision of valid inferences about instructional modification, reliability, and sensitivity to small but important changes in pupil performance. These criteria represent a refinement of the essential characteristics described by Gronlund (1993). The reader is encouraged to investigate the applications that have been devised, especially for exceptional populations (Evans et al., 1986; Fuchs, 1994; Idol, Nevin, & Paolucci-Whitcomb, 1986; Salvia & Hughes, 1990; Tindal & Marston, 1990).

ASSESSMENT DOMAINS

The following sections are intended to provide a synopsis of the procedures most commonly used within specific domains of assessment. Specialized approaches are described where warranted.

Reading

The assessment of reading, as is the case with many academic areas of instruction, commonly involves both formal and informal procedures. Unlike some areas of academic instruction, a significant number of formal measures are available (Salvia & Ysseldyke, 1995), although some of the procedures generally described as formal measures also display characteristics associated with informal techniques. For example, several published oral reading tests are technically inadequate for use as formal measures but may be useful when employed to respond to issues more characteristic of informal assessment (Salvia & Ysseldyke, 1995). Whether particular instruments are best considered formal or informal is problematic for the practitioner. Thus, because of the importance of reading, its multiple conceptualizations as a process (Tindal & Marston, 1990), the number of measurement instruments available, and the sometimes blurred distinction between formal and informal assessment devices, readers with a particular interest in reading assessment are strongly encouraged to begin their study with a thorough examination of the conceptualization of the reading process and the devices fully accepted as formal measurement techniques.

As might be expected, such remarkable controversy makes a discussion of reading assessment difficult and more or less satisfactory depending upon the perspective one holds on the activity termed *reading*. Many but certainly not all discussions of reading assessment emphasize devices designed to assess word attack/word sequence (sometimes simply decoding) and/or reading comprehension (usually divided into subcomponents such as literal and inferential comprehension). Tindal and Marston (1990), among others, do not agree that this traditional view remains an effective construct. These authors cite extensive research to support their contention that reading is best conceptualized as a unitary model "in which the focus is not on identifying separate subskills of the reading process" (p. 143). Obviously, such a dramatically modified approach, if generally accepted, has extensive implications for virtually all current formal and informal assessment procedures. For the present many reviewers continue to discuss reading according to the dichotomy outlined above. Recent years have, however, seen an increasing theoretical interest in and corresponding measurement emphasis directed toward the assessment of comprehension as opposed to decoding. Luftig (1989) has provided an excellent overview of the procedures commonly used in the measurement of reading. A staggering array of procedures (generally considered formal) include reading tests, oral reading tests, and reading comprehension tests. Informal measures include observations, informal reading inventories, error analysis, checklists, and the cloze procedure. McLoughlin and Lewis (1994) expand this list of informal procedures to include diagnostic reading procedures and criterion-referenced tests. Salvia and Hughes (1990) discuss curriculum-based assessment of reading and emphasize the concept of performance measures applied to various aspects of reading assessment. As may be seen, there does not appear to be consensus regarding which procedures can be considered informal measures of reading. Some of the more generally accepted measures are briefly described below.

Criterion-Referenced Tests

The practitioner can certainly construct useful criterion-referenced tests along the lines described by Gronlund (1993) and others. Additionally, a number of published criterion-referenced reading tests are available to the practitioner. Among the more popular of these devices are the Brigance Diagnostic Comprehensive Inventory of Basic Skills (Brigance, 1983) and System FORE (Bagai & Bagai, 1979), both of which contain various assessments of skills in basic reading and reading comprehension. Other systems are described and evaluated for specific technical merit in Luftig (1989), McLoughlin and Lewis (1994), and Salvia and Ysseldyke (1995).

Observations

Specific behavioral observation strategies can follow any of the general approaches described earlier in this chapter. However, many other assessment approaches mentioned in this section contain, as part of the procedure, elements that could easily be termed *observation*. Informal inventories, error-analysis strategies, the cloze procedure, and other methods all include some elements of observation. Observation can also be used to monitor student time-on-task and other variables involved in reading. The teacher can, for example, count the number of occasions when a student leaves his or her seat during a reading lesson, the number of questions asked, or the duration of reading activity. These procedures can be more or less direct and measure more or less specific behaviors. Additionally, in some cases, the teacher may find it useful to utilize self-monitoring by directing the student to observe and record personal behavior.

In practice, observation may be more directed to the analysis of decoding than to the analysis of comprehension, but this is not always the case. When a teacher notes answers to questions that parallel reading assignments, he or she is employing a form of observation. Variations of this approach are fairly abundant. One interesting illustration of the use of observation to assess comprehension can be found in a subtest (Reading/Understanding) of the Kaufman Assessment Battery for Children (K-ABC; Kaufman & Kaufman, 1983). Although the K-ABC is a formal test, the basic approach could be readily adapted to measure specific instructions of importance or possibly to gauge comprehension levels. The subtest requires students to read a passage and then pantomime a statement. For example, the statement might request that the child pretend to mix some paint. The examiner then observes the child's actions to determine whether the directions have been understood. This approach uses observation effectively and in a manner that children seem to enjoy. As may be seen, observation is a useful and integral part of the reading assessment. The evaluator is certain to use observation techniques whether independently or as part of other informal approaches.

Checklists

Observation procedures in reading assessment must be directed (focused upon critical points that are to be measured), and checklists are often utilized for this function. There are several ways checklists can be used for the measurement of reading. First, there are checklists that are focused primarily on decoding skills, usually organized by skills to be learned at particular grade levels. Other checklists focus on comprehension skills. Sometimes a more or less integrated network is offered within a single checklist. Finally, because reading is so fundamental to success in academic activities, there are checklists that examine attitudes toward reading and cognitive development in relationship to reading behaviors. Useful checklists can be found in Evans, Evans, and Mercer (1986), Guerin and Maier (1983), Hammill (1987), and McLoughlin and Lewis (1994).

The practitioner must be careful to examine checklists for their suitability for a particular use. For example, it is very important to use curriculum-skill checklists that correspond to the curriculum taught (curriculum-based assessment) and to use attitudinal indices that are developmentally appropriate.

Informal Reading Inventories

Informal reading inventories (IRIs) are among the most popular informal devices for assessing the reading proficiency of children, adolescents (Olson & Gillis, 1987), and adults (Cheek, Kritsonis, & Lindsey, 1987). Published examples have been provided by Burns and Roe (1993), Ekwall (1986), Silvaroli (1986), and others.

Structurally, virtually all forms of IRIs contain a graded word list and a series of graded word passages. The latter are established for grade-level representation using any of several procedures to estimate reading level (Evans et al., 1986; Fry, 1972). Generally, the word lists are used to quickly establish the grade level of the passages that should be used to initiate the student's oral reading (Duffelmeyer, Robinson, & Squier, 1989). The student then reads passages aloud while the teacher scores oral reading errors using unique symbols to denote specific types of predesignated errors. Subsequent examination for oral reading miscues (i.e., consistent patterns of inappropriate reading responses) is termed *error analysis* (Luftig, 1989). At the end of specific passages, students are asked to answer questions that provide an indication of comprehension. Generally, questions are stated in such a fashion that a number of possible types of comprehension can be assessed. Finally, based upon specific criteria that vary from test to test, the student is profiled for levels at which reading can be conducted independently, is considered useful for instruction (with teacher assistance), or is likely to result in frustration and therefore should not be attempted at this time. In some cases, specific tests may include listening comprehension, a level at which the student cannot read but can profit from others reading aloud. Informal reading inventories are thus used to estimate suitability of reading materials for particular students, describe decoding errors that are made in oral reading, and estimate comprehension by level and type.

Informal reading inventories contain an intrinsic diagnostic face validity and can be useful if outcomes of the devices are not overgeneralized. Despite their popularity, the instruments have significant technical deficiencies and therefore some degree of measurement error. Some authors (e.g., Anderson, 1986; McKenna, 1983) have pointed out technical weaknesses that should be carefully considered, such as small samples of behavior, standardization inadequacies of published examples, and varying estimates of passage difficulty (e.g., variations in the formats of published tests such as the types of errors that are scored and the degree of curriculum parallel that is apparent). As a result, it is impossible to assume that responses on one test necessarily correlate with results from another test, a significant problem if the examiner wishes to equate outcomes (McKenna, 1983). Spache (1981) has also questioned the logic of inferring silent reading capacity from measures of oral reading.

Due to the measurement error frequently associated with published IRIs, the teacher is often well advised to utilize reading materials known to have been (or will be) used by the child. Reading difficulty formulas (for estimating paragraph reading difficulty) can be found in many sources, including Evans et al. (1986). Recommendations for text selection for adolescent students have been offered by Olson and Gillis (1987), while a discussion of considerations in the use of IRIs (and other informal assessment devices) with adults has been provided by Cheek et al. (1987). Any of the oral reading error guidelines available can be used, and an excellent summary of guidelines for evaluating comprehension can be found in Luftig (1989) and Nessel (1987). Although somewhat time-consuming, teachers and other diagnosticians can often benefit from constructing personalized IRIs. Whether commercial or personally developed IRIs, the approach is not difficult to use and the diagnostician should encounter little trouble attaining proficiency in this area.

Cloze Procedure

The cloze procedure was first introduced by Taylor (1953), although the technique seems to have been popularized by Bormuth (1968). This approach is used to determine the suitability of graded reading material for a particular student. Variations exist in the development of the procedure (see Tindal & Marston, 1990, pp. 168–169), but one popular approach advises the teacher to select passages at known grade level. Each passage is approximately 250 words in length. Every fifth word is then blocked out and, in a typed copy of the sample, equal-length lines are inserted in place of the missing words. According to Bormuth (1968), if the student supplies between 44 and 57% of the missing words, the passage is at the student's instructional level. Levels above this indicate that the passage is acceptable for independent reading. There is debate regarding the meaning of these results. Tindal and Marston (1990), for example, presented a summary of studies which suggests that the outcomes of the cloze procedure are only moderately correlated with teacher judgments of grade placement and more traditional measures of reading comprehension. A partial explanation of this discrepancy may reside in two factors. First, the cloze procedure is based upon a quite different view of achievement than most contemporary measures, drawn as it is from Gestalt psychology's concept of closure. Second, regardless of the merits of the general approach, variations in the technique for conducting the cloze procedure are certain to introduce additional variance in the comparisons of scores with performance estimates drawn from other sources. As a result, there is concern for the validity of the procedure; in fact, Tindal and Marston (1990) indicated that there are questions as to exactly what the test does measure. Still, there is a considerable amount of research on the cloze technique and many researchers appear to feel it is a valuable if perhaps eccentric measure of reading comprehension.

Categorizing Errors in Reading (Error Analysis)

Morsink and Gable (1990) have proposed a system for evaluating student reading proficiency based upon systematic analysis of the student's errors. In effect, the process is a logical extension of several procedures and is made up of several steps. Step 1 requires the examiner to initiate a systematic sampling technique in order to identify error patterns. While the student reads orally, the teacher notes errors but does not correct them, a process that Salvia & Hughes (1990) have referred to as *topological analysis*. The process may be conducted with materials of varying difficulty, and both qualitative and quantitative information is acquired. Typically, patterns of decoding errors are noted, but it is quite likely that the examiner will also wish to conduct measures of comprehension, perhaps utilizing miscue analysis (Goodman & Burke, 1972). Step 2 requires retesting to confirm that any original patterns of errors are in fact standing patterns and not simply the result of carelessness or anxiety. Step 3 is a structured interview of the student during which faulty approaches to decoding are verbally conveyed. If the student is unresponsive, the evaluator may ask specific questions based on hypotheses formulated on the basis of the original testing. Step 4 is the construction of a record of findings to provide a basis for initiating instruction and, logically, a baseline by which to evaluate instructional effects.

Performance Measures

Salvia and Hughes (1990) have described a procedure termed *performance measures*. This procedure first assesses the student's ability to pronounce letters and groups of letters in isolation and then the student's pronunciation of words in passages taken from school reading books. The emphasis is on both accuracy and speed. A specific seven-step sequence of performance measures is outlined: "fluency in saying sounds in isolation, fluency in saying nonsense words, fluency in saying phonetically regular words, oral reading accuracy, and rate on passages from text, fluency in saying prefixes and suffixes in isolation, fluency in saying endings, prefixes, and suffixes with nonsense root words, fluency in saying words that can be analyzed structurally" (Salvia & Hughes, 1990, pp. 128–132). This approach appears to be an easily devised technique that can be readily adapted from classroom materials to yield useful informal assessment results.

Retellings, Think Alouds, and Dictated Stories

A number of unique approaches to the assessment of specific aspects of reading are available in the literature; three of these are presented here.

As the name implies, *retellings* of stories are restatements or rewritten versions of original stories. According to Kalmbach (1986), retellings have been used for at least 60 years to assess a variety of topics, the most prevalent of which is comprehension, especially reading comprehension. Although the approach may be more closely associated with the laboratory as a research tool than with the classroom as a diagnostic tool, Kalmbach argues that the device is useful to teachers if "instead of comparing retellings to original stories, teachers analyze the structure of retellings as stories" (Kalmbach, 1986, p. 327). In particular, Kalmbach suggests that teachers can learn about the meaning students get from stories and the problems they face in organizing the various story elements. The author provides considerable detail about the procedure and offers valuable illustrations for the practitioner who conducts this measurement of reading comprehension.

Wade (1990) indicates that even informal assessment devices have received criticism as being too narrow in their emphasis on mastery of serially related discrete skills. The author points out that research in comprehension and metacognition suggests that reading is a very complex process that exceeds a conceptualization of it as simply a collection of discrete skills. *Think alouds* are "verbal self-reports about . . . thinking processes . . . to obtain information about how students attempt to construct meaning from text" (Wade, 1990, p. 442). Hoy and Gregg (1994) have described this general technique as a form of dynamic assessment in which the evaluator is more interested in the interaction of the environment, student, and task than in the learning product. Wade provides an overview of the processes involved in comprehension, a taxonomy of different types of comprehension that might be encountered, and a discussion of instructional approaches as well as an assessment of the strengths and weaknesses of the approach. His article provides sufficient detail for the reader to implement the approach, though additional information can be found in Afflerbach and Johnson (1984) and Myers and Lytle (1986).

Agnew (1982) emphasizes that young children are often not aware of the technical features of reading—that is, the code conventions that make reading possible. In Agnew's view, *dictation* (a part of the whole language approach) provides a means by which the teacher can probe the child's understanding of these conventions. As might be expected, the process begins with the development of a story by a child or a group of children. A seven-step procedure is then initiated. These steps are relatively simple to accomplish and appear to be capable of yielding interesting and valuable information. The reader is referred to Agnew (1982) for the specific details of this process.

Mathematics

Mathematics assessment is generally considered to be more straightforward than is reading assessment (Salvia & Ysseldyke, 1995). In formal testing, this translates into fewer diagnostic tests and more similarity between those tests that are available. Diagnostic tests usually sample content, operations, and applications and, in general, most informal tests measure mathematics achievement in one or more of these areas. As noted by VanDevender and Harris (1987), informal techniques are necessary for pinpointing exactly what the student has learned and precisely what is to be taught.

Luftig (1989) suggests that at least the following approaches can be used in the assessment of mathematics: measures of prerequisite abilities, including intelligence measures and developmental readiness (see Guerin & Maier, 1983, for an excellent discussion of these dimensions); formal assessment devices, including diagnostic tests and other commercially prepared tests; criterion-referenced tests; and, finally, informal procedures. Luftig indicates that the following may be considered informal measures: mathematical inventories (of which at least five are widely available), checklists, interviews, and error analysis. McLoughlin and Lewis (1994) include the concepts of probes and questionnaires. The reader has been introduced to many of these general approaches through previous discussion, particularly in the section on reading assessment.

Mathematics Inventories

Inventories are especially useful in the assessment of mathematics because there is generally more agreement on specific skills to be learned and specific sequences of introduction. Luftig (1989) notes that it is often advisable for the teacher to create the inventory from the particular curriculum because this will be most likely to assure a match between assessment and the skills taught. Guerin and Maier (1983) have provided a useful if somewhat abbreviated skill sequence for practitioners who choose to accept a model rather than create a sequence through curriculum analysis. More detailed skill hierarchies can be found in Bartel (1986), Enright (1983), and Reisman (1978). A very thoughtful and useful content taxonomy was developed by Tindal and Marston (1990) based upon the work of Glennon and Wilson (1972), in which the authors provide an integrated model of assessment that corresponds to the taxonomy, as well as specific guidelines for assessment practice.

Checklists

Checklists used for the informal assessment of mathematics are effective at providing the practitioner with a quick method for evaluating the completion of some specific task by a student or for indicating those skills that are already mastered (i.e., for maintaining a record of student accomplishments). Checklists are technically most accurate and defensible as assessment devices when used in parallel with skill hierarchies as described above. When using checklists, the practitioner should exercise care to be certain that (1) the correct skills in the correct sequence are being investigated, (2) behaviors are sampled more than once, thus minimizing errors in the judgment of student competency, and (3) the skill hierarchy is followed with precision.

Interviews

Ginsburg (1987) has described a flexible interviewing technique that appears to be very useful in the assessment of mathematics. The author notes that the technique "has great potential for instructional assessment" (p. 443) and is "an enormously powerful technique for identifying students' thinking and learning processes" (p. 459). Ginsburg considers flexible interviewing to be a complex process that has four components: establishing rapport, discovering thinking processes and strategies, describing how these processes operate, and ascertaining levels of competence. Guidelines are presented for readers who wish to attempt the approach.

Error Analysis

Described in nearly all discussions of the informal assessment of mathematics, error analysis has long been utilized and in some ways is a counterpart to the oral reading analysis procedures described earlier. There are several variations of error analysis that are used in the assessment of mathematics. One of the most comprehensive discussions currently available is offered by Ashlock (1993), who describes the four categories of errors identified by Roberts (1968): wrong operation, obvious computational error, defective algorithm, and random response. Roberts noted that the largest proportion of errors was the result of defective algorithms except among students in the lowest quartile, in which students made more random responses, a probable indication of near total failure to learn the algorithms. Ashlock (1993) provides some discussion on frequently observed patterns of errors as well as reasoned estimates of why particular error patterns emerge. His book includes guidelines for instructional practices that help prevent the appearance of defective algorithms and other inappropriate learning. However, possibly the most important contribution of this book is its presentation of children's error patterns in a format designed to instruct the reader in detecting algorithmic errors. The text also includes a useful bibliography for the assessment of mathematics.

Questionnaires

These can be used in the assessment of mathematics to address concerns ranging from specific skills the student has or has not attained to attitudes regarding mathematics and mathematics instruction. Because of the difficulties inherent in the use of questionnaires, described elsewhere in this chapter, it is recommended that their use in mathematics assessment be limited and that interviews be substituted.

Thinking Aloud and Building Sentences

VanDevender and Harris (1987) describe two techniques somewhat similar to those described by Kalmbach (1986) and Wade (1990) for reading instruction. *Thinking aloud* simply requires the student to describe the steps being applied in the algorithm to solve the problem. The strategy not only spares the evaluator the deductive process of determining the error from work samples but can also provide insight into the student's cognitive strategies for solving the stated problems.

The authors also describe a process termed *building sentences*. In this process, the student may use wood blocks to illustrate the meaning of problems or may be required to verbalize the steps in the solution of word problems. In either case, the practitioner has the opportunity to investigate the student's thought processes relative to solving the problem.

Written Language

McLoughlin and Lewis (1994) note the complexity of written language and the fact that the development of the skill occurs late in the communication sequence that begins with speech. Further, they note that written language is related to but quite distinct from other forms of communication, especially in that writing is a solitary act that eliminates all immediate possibility for clarification that can emerge from spoken language (e.g., restatements that occur as a result of the facial expressions of a receiving individual). There are certainly many skills involved in the development of written messages. First, the writer must conceptualize a message, whether it be a note of reminder to purchase cat food or the far more complex task of constructing a convincing letter describing the quality of the cat food to the manufacturer. Part of this conceptualization may require research. The writer must then demonstrate several skills that are essential to the final written message. These include knowledge of grammar, punctuation, spelling and possibly vocabulary (though assessment of vocabulary is often conducted in terms of receptive language skills and reading), and production of text (by hand or by keyboard). Considering the complexity of these components, and there are probably others, it is little wonder that written communication is generally considered one of the most advanced human skills.

Although many of the areas described above are assessed, two factors need to be considered. First, many of the components are judged in a very informal manner.

Judgment of the theme or content of written material, whether for creativity or clarity of the message, for example, is generally very subjective. Why is one author's style particularly appealing? Why is a book eloquent to one person and obscene to another? Such complex issues, even with classroom compositions, are often difficult to address. The second factor relates to the fact that much assessment of written composition tends to emphasize the mechanical aspects of writing, such as spelling, grammar, punctuation, and production of script. We will concentrate on a few illustrations in the measurement of written expression and spelling.

The informal assessment of written expression generally consists of adaptations of techniques, previously discussed, which include rating scales and checklists, sample analysis, and observation, including observation of interest in writing. A few features of writing assessment are unique: measures of fluency (often using thought [T] units), sentence analysis by structure and type (Polloway & Smith, 1982), and specialized vocabulary analysis (Cartwright, 1969; Polloway & Smith, 1982) are among these.

A number of approaches are often attempted to facilitate the assessment of spelling. These include work samples (that is, error analysis conducted on work samples) and informal inventories of words, often drawn from classroom texts, to determine the student's ability to spell a selected group of words. The words selected may be based on a specific configuration of structural components (i.e., specific vowel sounds or syllabication patterns). Other methods that might be used are observation strategies, interviewing techniques, the cloze procedure, or teacher-made, criterion-referenced tests. It is apparent that many of the basic techniques used in the assessment of reading and mathematics are similarly useful in the assessment of spelling.

INNOVATIVE APPROACHES TO INFORMAL ASSESSMENT

Authentic Assessment

One of the best-known forms of alternative assessment, authentic assessment, is described by Jones (1994) as representing one of the most influential trends in the contemporary move away from traditional assessment practices. The primary distinction between traditional testing and authentic assessment lies in the way learning is measured. Authentic assessment represents a paradigmatic shift in the way we view assessment and is not so much a group of techniques or strategies as it is a *philosophy.* Assessments are authentic when they have "meaning in themselves, when the learning they measure has value beyond the classroom and is meaningful to the learner. All authentic assessment refers to direct examination of student performance on significant tasks that are relevant to life outside of school" (Worthen, 1993, p. 45). Authentic assessment tasks are analogues, if not identical representations of real-world tasks—that is, activities that might be encountered outside the classroom (Archbald, 1991; Burke, 1994; Kerka, 1995).

According to Lopez (1996), authentic assessment addresses tasks that are "important and authentic, rather than trivial and contrived" (p. 1). For example, having a child use real money to purchase a desired item at a dollar store is an important and authentic task, one that will be needed in the world outside of school; however, having that same child complete 20 math problems that involve getting change from a dollar might be contrived and trivial. Perhaps because of its intuitive appeal, authentic assessment is fast becoming the approach of choice in a variety of educational and non-educational settings; for example, it is being used in vocational education classes, infant and toddler rooms, and university settings. Formats available for authentic assessment all represent alternatives to traditional multiple-choice question formats. Among these are standardized patient, audiovisual context setting, computer-based problem solving, multiple choice with justification, latent image, performance, and portfolio (Jones, 1994).

Authentic Assessment and Instruction

Authentic assessment lends itself very nicely to authentic instruction. For example, an authentic assessment might involve asking a child to write a letter to the school board about an important issue and then correcting the letter for punctuation and capitalization; an inauthentic assessment would require the child to complete a worksheet of sentences that are incorrectly punctuated. The results of authentic assessment suggest instructional activities in a way that is not possible with standardized assessment. In this case, for example, the teacher could go back and give the student help on specific writing skills. An added advantage would be that this kind of instruction obviates the frequent concern that in-class instruction is unrelated to real-world activities.

Advantages and Disadvantages of Authentic Assessment

According to Lopez (1996), authentic assessment acknowledges the existence of multiple intelligences; that is, implicit in this approach is the idea that intelligence can be manifested in a variety of ways. Traditional assessment is not always able to tap into these intelligences; however, authentic assessment has the potential to do so. It is also more likely to accommodate a variety of learning styles. Although some writers (e.g., Lopez, 1996) have cautioned against the careless use of authentic assessment, particularly with culturally diverse students, there is on the whole strong support of such assessment (e.g., Meller & Ohr, 1996).

Authentic assessment requires school professionals to abandon traditional perspectives about evaluation and be willing to embrace a whole new way of thinking about assessment, and this may be difficult for those who are deeply engrained in the old ways (Christenson, 1991). Authentic assessments are time intensive in terms of task preparation and training in administration and implementation. Although they are intended to improve the validity of assessment (Kamphaus, 1991), they lack adequate validity and reliability, at least at this point in their development. They are also fiscally demanding (Bateson, 1994; Elliott, 1992; Gresham, 1991; Popham, 1993). Although Hipps (1993) states that traditional methods of evaluation like validity, reliability, and objectivity are not suitable criteria for the evaluation of authentic assessment, these authors' contention as it is Bateson's (1994) that such criteria *must* be part of the evaluation. Hipps suggests that criteria such as trustworthiness (credibility, transferability, dependability, and confirmability) and authenticity (knowing, action, and fairness) be used to judge authentic assessments; however, there is limited information about these criteria and their use in authentic assessment.

Approaches to authentic assessment can be categorized into the following often-overlapping categories: (1) performance-based tasks and exhibitions, (2) portfolios, and (3) documentation of learning over time or formative evaluation (Hipps, 1993). Performance assessment and portfolio assessment will be discussed in the following sections.

Performance Assessment

Referred to most commonly as *performance assessment,* this approach is also referred to as *performance testing* or *performance-based assessment* (Cancelli & Arena, 1996). The term is also used interchangeably with the term *authentic assessment,* although in fact a performance assessment is simply one approach to authentic assessment. Regardless of the terminology, these approaches are similar in that they entail "observing and judging a pupil's skill in actually carrying out a physical activity (e.g., giving a speech) or producing a product (e.g., building a birdhouse)" (Airasian, 1994, p. 426). The concept of performance assessment is not new; indeed, in some fields assessment has always been authentic and performance based. For example, students taking driver education courses have to actually drive a car before they can pass the course, students in advanced computer programming courses have to write and run their programs, and students in shop classes have to demonstrate that they can use tools to build an object.

The measurement of many aspects of student learning outcomes in special education is not compatible with the traditional purposes of informal testing. That is, tests of knowledge such as those described above measure student skills indirectly. The examiner is left to assume that the appearance of conditions in real-life situations will evoke correct responses. This may be a poor assumption, particularly with exceptional students who may have difficulties not only in remembering but in recognizing the conditions that specify the elicitation of learned behaviors. Accordingly, performance assessment attempts to measure skill outcomes in ecologies that are close to the conditions within which the skill will ultimately be used. Unfortunately, performance assessments are not adequately utilized because they can be much more difficult to prepare and score and also because "our past emphasis on norm-referenced measurement has made indirect measurement acceptable" (Gronlund, 1993, p. 85). The emphasis in special education on specific skill development makes performance assessment a procedure of choice wherever feasible.

A performance assessment can be thought of as an increasingly accurate simulation of a real event. The realism of the simulation can vary from a paper-and-pencil abstraction to completion of the actual activity. The degree of realism is often dictated by expense or safety concerns, and the learner often undergoes a series of evaluations in which successive tests are increasingly reflective of the actual situation. Gronlund (1993) notes that such tests can focus more on the student's knowledge of procedure than on the student's product or a combination of both. Generally, about four levels of realism are required. First, paper-and-pencil tests are designed that place emphasis upon the application of previously learned facts. A second level is often referred to as an identification test, and at this level the student can identify anything from tools to probable sources of malfunctions. The third step is simulated performance (e.g., calculating appropriate change with student customers in a classroom-based store purchase). In the final step, the student actually carries through the specified activity in a totally, or certainly almost totally, realistic manner.

A good illustration of the performance examination sequence occurs in driver education. Usually, students learn conventional information such as the meaning of signs and then specific capabilities of automobile components. This is usually followed by brief, supervised excursions on a closed course. Finally, the student operates the car in real traffic situations. Few teachers would risk omission of the first three steps in which the learning of essential prerequisite skills is ensured, and transfer of these skills can be judged in limited and carefully monitored fashion.

According to Howell and Rueda (1996), performance assessment is based on a constructivist model of learning. Unlike traditional approaches to learning, which focus on the passive acquisition of unconnected pieces of information, this approach emphasizes the meaningfulness of learning. It describes the active construction of a personal knowledge of the world through the making of meaningful connections with previously known information; however, these connections are made through the filter of one's experience. Differences in experience, therefore, lead to unique, individualized conceptions of knowledge. In the constructivist approach to learning, students engage in learning activities that are most likely to help them develop these knowledge bases and assessment focuses on their progress toward that goal. Howell and Rueda consider performance assessment to be the ideal accompaniment to the constructivist model of learning as such assessment encourages self-exploration, documents student progress, and emphasizes continuing improvement.

School professionals are often able to design performance assessments of their own; however, there are commercially available materials. One performance-based assessment described in Hennings and Hughes (1992) that serves as both a testing and a teaching diagnostic tool is Roswell and Chall's Diagnostic Assessments of Reading with Trial Teaching Strategies (DARTTS), which includes short tests that assess strengths and weaknesses in six areas of reading and language, such as word recognition, word analysis, oral reading, silent reading comprehension, spelling, and word meaning. Other work in this area has far-reaching implications; for example, those who are concerned about high-stakes testing are attempting to develop large-scale, performance-based assessments to replace standardized achievement testing in schools. Indeed, the state of Ohio has already experimented with substituting performance assessments for the group-administered Iowa Test of Basic Skills (Cancelli & Arena, 1996), and preliminary reports indicate that this effort has been a success.

Problems with the Use of Performance Assessment

There has been a regrettable tendency on the part of school professionals to jump on the bandwagon of every movement that promises an improvement in services to children. A hasty acceptance of approaches that have not been tested could lead to problems—and this is true for performance assessment (Cancelli & Arena, 1996). One of the main concerns relates to the lack of commonly accepted evaluation standards. Evaluations of performance assessment have typically been so subjective that they have compromised reliability. Some of these concerns are being addressed by the use of multiple raters and objective performance standards known as *scoring rubrics;* however, the issue has not been settled. It is also considerably more difficult and sometimes risky for the teacher to produce the conditions for performance testing, at least at the most complex levels of the test; once again, this limits the utility of the approach. The issue of validity is another important concern; although its proponents argue that performance assessment is valid because it translates directly to real life, there are others who are concerned about the lack of generalizability in that success on a particular task does not guarantee success on other tasks, even those that are closely related. A final concern has to do with the expense involved in performance assessment—in terms of staff, resources, and funding (Baker, O'Neil, & Linn, 1993).

Despite these problems, performance testing should be viewed as an essential form of informal assessment for at least two reasons. First, it is the only way that the instructor can be certain that skills are appropriately transferred to the locations in which they are needed. Second, by close observation of students, the instructor can gain insight into the legitimacy of the trained task. This ensures that the skills that are taught are valuable in actual application.

Portfolio Assessments

Another type of authentic assessment rapidly gaining a foothold in a variety of disparate fields is that of portfolio assessment, defined by Arter and Spandel (1992) as a "purposeful collection of student work that exhibits the student's efforts, progress, and achievements in one or more areas. The collection must include student participation in selecting contents, criteria for selection, evaluation criteria, and evidence of student self-reflection" (p. 37). Like many other informal measures, portfolio assessment is not a new concept; for years artists and photographers have collected their best or most representative work in portfolios and presented it to prospective employers. A folder of a child's best work laid out on a desk during a school open house as evidence of learning is really an example of a basic portfolio.

Characteristics of Portfolio Assessments

Darling-Hammond (1993), Jorgensen (1994), Paulson, Paulson, and Meyer (1991) and Wolf (1989) have offered useful guidelines for developing portfolios that include some of the following suggestions. The portfolio is completed and assembled by the student. It must include goals, a list of contents, and a well-considered rationale for inclusion. Portfolios must also include material that is illustrative of continued growth so, for example, a student might include partially completed works or a series of assignments which show noticeable improvement. Also necessary are evaluation criteria and student or teacher judgments about portfolio items.

Portfolio items may reflect the student's own interests or follow state-prescribed guidelines for evidence of learning. The teacher's role is that of a monitor and facilitator, but it is the student who is active in his or her own learning and the evaluation of that learning. Students are generally provided with models of completed portfolios, and they practice developing components of a portfolio.

Advantages and Disadvantages of Portfolio Assessment

The unique quality of a portfolio is its ability to document not only the products of learning but the process. Where traditional assessment allows for the inclusion of static outcomes that can be quantified, portfolio assessment is dynamic, allowing for the inclusion of materials that reveal learning in progress. The portfolio reveals the student-as-becoming, in the act of creating, problem solving, and self-reflecting. It provides a complete and comprehensive view of student performance, but performance placed within the larger context of learning. Portfolios provide students with the opportunity to demonstrate not just what they know but what they can do. They encourage the use of metacognitive strategies, self-reflection, and high-level cognitive skills; emphasize direct methods of assessment, the product and process of learning, a high degree of realism, and creativity; and demand that students be able to publicly justify their progress (Burke, 1994; Darling-Hammond, 1994; Jones, 1994).

Several authors, including Bateson (1994), have cautioned against the over-enthusiastic acceptance of portfolio assessment. Such an approach is still in the experimental stage and should not be engaged in without training and preparation. Reliability and validity issues remain paramount. The limitation of portfolios when it comes to comparing one student to another has also been of concern. Despite these objections, Paulson, Paulson, and Meyer (1991) describe portfolios as permitting the "intersection of assessment and instruction" in ways that are not possible with standardized tests. The portfolio concept is rapidly becoming one of the most popular ways of assessing student learning at all levels; in fact, even students in university teacher-training programs are being encouraged to develop portfolios that document their growth as student teachers.

INFORMAL ASSESSMENT OF INFANTS AND PRESCHOOLERS

A separate section has been devoted to this issue because children under the age of six pose a unique set of problems for the examiner. The use of standardized tests with this age group has been problematic for reasons that range from the dearth of valid and reliable tests developed for young children to their lack of relevance for instruction. An issue that complicates the assessment of young children is that many of them are not in school. Primary caregivers must be included in the assessment in order to gain a complete understanding of the child's functioning, and home-school collaboration is not always a simple undertaking. A distinct hindrance in working with this population is that very young children cannot control their behaviors to the extent that is required in an assessment situation. Interviews are difficult to conduct because of preschoolers' limited vocabulary and immature conceptual development. They also have difficulty understanding what Martin (1988) refers to as "assessment cues," which include both written and spoken instructions and stimuli. Further, some interview questions require complex information processing abilities that many preschoolers have not attained and a level of sophistication that escapes the very young.

Informal or alternative approaches to assessment are a promising solution for children of this age; in fact, some would say they are the only solution. Also important is the fact that children change so rapidly during these early years that the ongoing, formative evaluation of such approaches can be used to document small changes as they occur. Informal or alternative approaches lend themselves well to planning instructional objectives. For example, developmental checklists of the criterion-referenced type like the Brigance Diagnostic Inventory of Early Development-Revised (Brigance, 1991), the Hawaii Early Learning Profile (HELP; Furuno, O'Reilly, Hosaka, Inatsuka, Zeisloft-Folbey, & Allman, 1990), and the Early Learning Accomplishment Profile (E-LAP; Glover, Perminger, & Sanford, 1988) can be used profitably for this purpose. A child who has not mastered the lower-level skills that form the foundation of more complex skills can be taught those specific skills.

Several other informal approaches have been offered, including arena assessment, transdisciplinary play-based assessment (Linder, 1990), and dynamic assessment, which uses a test-teach-test approach. Behavior checklists and rating scales become critically important at this juncture, and both parents and teachers can provide useful information about the child's functioning at home and at school. Interviews and questionnaires may also be used with parents and teachers of young children. Readers with an interest in this area are referred to the chapter on this topic elsewhere in this volume. There are also comprehensive accounts of approaches to infant and preschool assessment in the works of Bracken (1990), Lowenthal (1992), McLean, Bailey, and Wolery (1996), Meller and Ohr (1996), and Sattler (1988).

COMPUTERS AND INFORMAL ASSESSMENT

The use of the computer for assessment purposes is growing dramatically, due partly to the advent of new and sophisticated technologies. Although the focus of much of this work is in the area of formal assessment, the computer is finding increasing acceptance in informal assessment, particularly as a way to engage in the formative evaluation of student learning. For example, Haapa and Lewis (1992) have described the use of *Write This Way,* a word processing package for students with disabilities that completes an error analysis in capitalization, punctuation, spelling, grammar, and style. *Monitoring Basic Skills Progress* by Fuchs, Hamlett, and Fuchs (1990) is a computerized curriculum-based, data-collection device that allows teachers to assess students' progress in basic academic areas.

Expert systems, which are a relatively new approach to assessment, are computer-based systems that are designed to emulate a human expert's decision-making strategies. They offer considerable promise in the area of informal assessment and, in fact, several expert systems in education and related areas have already been developed. Hofmeister and Lubke (1988) have discussed the *Written Language Consultant,* an expert system that examines writing samples of special-education students and suggests modifications. Balajithy (1989) has described the RD2P (System Reading Difficulties-Diagnosis and Prescription), which guides teachers in the informal assessment of reading difficulties and suggests instructional interventions based on assessment results. Chittooran (1995) developed an expert system, *ADHDEXPERT,* that uses the results of informal assessments such as observations and interviews in conjunction with scores from norm-referenced measures to help teachers identify children who meet preliminary criteria for attention-deficit/hyperactivity disorder (ADHD). As is true with all new approaches to assessment, there is great potential for the misuse of computers in education. Guidelines for the responsible and ethical use of computers in assessment can be found in the American Psychological Association's (1986) *Guidelines for Computer-Based Tests and Interpretations.*

INFORMAL ASSESSMENT WITH LINGUISTICALLY AND CULTURALLY DIVERSE POPULATIONS

The use of norm-referenced assessment with linguistically and culturally diverse populations has engendered so much controversy that school professionals searching for alternatives to traditional assessments with these children have frequently turned to informal assessments (Cancelli & Arena, 1996; Sattler, 1988; Suzuki, Meller, & Ponterotto, 1996). In California, the 1979 case of *Larry P. v. Riles,* which prevented California schools from using norm-referenced assessment to place minority students, is an important case in point.

Various forms of informal and alternative assessments have been proposed for linguistically and culturally diverse populations, including authentic assessment, portfolio assessment, dynamic assessment, observations, rating scales, interviews, questionnaires, examinations of social history, and checklists. The reader is referred to Thomas and Grimes (1995), Sattler (1988) and Suzuki, Meller, and Ponterotto's (1996) *Handbook of Multicultural Assessment* for excellent discussions of informal assessment with these populations.

INFORMAL ASSESSMENT AND INTERVENTION

There are several reasons that justify the inclusion of informal measures as precursors to intervention. Several authors (Linn & Gronlund, 1995; Nitko, 1996; Stiggins, 1994) have clearly outlined the relationship between informal measures and intervention. Linn and Gronlund (1995) assert an interdependence between teaching, learning, and assessment, and Nitko (1996) provides an extensive review of formative evaluation techniques (informal assessment) that are seen as very important in educational interventions. We must note here that virtually all discussions of informal assessment stress the technical adequacy of the measures; that is, assurances must be available with regard to the technical adequacy of the particular devices. That accomplished, there are several reasons to promote the use of informal measures in virtually all interventions. These include the following:

Flexibility. The devices can be developed to meet the unique demands of the learner or the instructional task.

Parallel with curriculum. The devices help ensure that the assessment is aligned with curriculum content.

Adequacy of sample. The devices allow the developer to vary the size of the sample over a specified content domain.

Unobtrusive. The devices can often be so closely integrated with teaching that they do not appear to the student as stand-alone test activities.

Sensitivity. The devices are sensitive to small changes in behavior that are characteristic of complex tasks or of the performance of individuals who struggle with the subject matter.

Mastery. The instruments can be designed to measure levels of mastery; that is, specific criteria can be established and measured.

Replicability. Since most informal instruments are criterion referenced in nature, they can often be repeated, or adaptations of them can be readily devised. This ensures that repeated measures can be obtained during the intervention period.

Ease of interpretation. In general, these instruments are reported in percentages or some other easy-to-explain format. The simplicity of the scores is useful in explaining outcomes to parents and can often be used as an incentive for the learner.

As can be seen, these qualities tend to make informal measures important tools in the intervention process. There remains a need to integrate the findings from both formal and informal devices since the information provided is often complementary and occasionally unique to the type of instrument used. However, the characteristics described above are generally accepted as strengths of informal devices and, as such, clearly establish a place for the instruments in the development and monitoring of most educational interventions. The following case study is designed to show how the results of both formal and informal assessment can be used concomitantly to explain a child's functioning and how this information can be used to suggest relevant and effective interventions.

As can be seen from Case Example 2–1, the results of both formal and informal assessment were used to make a decision about Laurie and to suggest academic and social-behavioral interventions. The "numbers" are still required to document special education eligibility in Laurie's home state, and did, in fact, show that Laurie met state criteria for a Specific Learning Disability in Basic Reading Skills. Results of informal measures indicate that Laurie is also experiencing significant difficulty with reading comprehension and other reading-related skills, although she does not qualify for special services in these areas at this time. Informal measures confirm reports about social-behavioral functioning provided by her parents and teachers; in fact, many of her behaviors do seem to stem from her academic problems.

Case Example 2–1.   "Laurie: The case of the reluctant reader"

PSYCHOEDUCATIONAL EVALUATION
CONFIDENTIAL

NAME: Laurie Jackson   PARENTS: Dennis and Anne Jackson
DATE OF BIRTH: 5-14-88   AGE: 8-0
SCHOOL: Hilltop Elementary   GRADE: 3

REASON FOR REFERRAL

Laurie Jackson was referred to the Child Development Clinic by her adoptive parents following complaints from her teachers about failing grades in reading and increasing problems with self-esteem. Anne Jackson stated that Laurie "just doesn't seem to get it" and expressed some concern that Laurie may have inherited her biological mother's learning problems.

METHODS OF EVALUATION

Acuity Screening

Wechsler Intelligence Scale for Children-Third Edition

Woodcock-Johnson Psycho-Educational Battery-Revised, Tests of Achievement

Child Behavior Checklist

Brigance Diagnostic Inventory of Basic Skills

Informal Reading Inventory

Reading Portfolio

Teacher-made Tests

Work Samples

Clinical Interviews

Direct Observations

Record Review

BACKGROUND INFORMATION

Laurie is an 8-year-old from Glenwood, who was adopted by the Jacksons when she was 1 year old. Dennis Jackson is an emergency medical technician while his wife, Anne, is a graduate student in history. The Jacksons have two sons, Matt, age 15, and Sam, age 13. According to Mrs. Jackson, Laurie's relationship with her parents is not close; she tells her parents that they love the boys more than they do her. Although the Jacksons do not have much information about Laurie's birth parents or the circumstances surrounding her birth, Mrs. Jackson did report that the mother "drank like a fish during the entire pregnancy." Laurie was born 3 weeks premature but weighed 7 pounds at birth. Developmental milestones were attained within normal limits and there were no significant illnesses, hospitalizations, or accidents.

Laurie is in the third grade at Hilltop Elementary and is making Bs and Cs in math, social studies, science, and English. She has received failing grades in reading for two of the last three grading periods. According to Mrs. Jackson, Laurie has always had difficulty with reading, but "it seems to have gotten worse and she just will not try." Laurie

(continued)

Case Example 2–1.   *(Continued)*

comes home every day saying she hates school and that no one likes her. She often has stomachaches, generally in the morning, just before she has to leave for school. Twice in the last week she called her mother at work, begging to come home because she had a headache. Mrs. Jackson indicated that she was taking four graduate courses at the university and just did not "have the time to be running up and down after her."

Mrs. Jackson stated that she spends approximately 3 or 4 hours with Laurie every day, trying to teach her to read, and experiences extreme frustration and helplessness at their lack of progress. She described sitting at the kitchen table with Laurie, both in tears, shouting at her daughter, "You *have* to read! No Jackson ever failed school before!" She stated that she could not "bear the thought that she's that slow, even if she *is* adopted." Laurie's phonetic skills are reported to be relatively poor and she "seems unable to put the sounds together to make words." Her mother also reported that Laurie struggles so much to read the words that she does not focus on what the words mean. She does better when a story is read to her. Mrs. Jackson reported that Matt and Sam make excellent grades. They tease Laurie about her reading difficulty and refer to her as "Sorry Laurie."

Laurie plays soccer with a local recreational team and is said to enjoy the sport. She has a puppy, Maxie, with whom she spends most of her free time. Her mother stated that Laurie did not have chores because "she needs to spend all of her time learning to read."

TEST CONDITIONS AND BEHAVIORS

Laurie presented as a neatly dressed, well-groomed young girl in apparent good health. She wore neither glasses nor hearing aids, exhibited right-hand dominance, and appeared to have adequate posture, gait, and coordination. Testing was completed in a small, well-lit room with minimal distractions, and Laurie was given breaks between tests as needed.

At first, Laurie appeared rather shy and hesitant about leaving her mother; however, she accompanied the examiner when asked if she'd like to see pictures of her children. Laurie was polite and rather reserved; however, she was not unfriendly and she did cooperate with the examiner. She did not initiate any conversation during the session, had difficulty maintaining eye contact, and responded in a soft whispery voice when addressed. Laurie appeared to understand task demands without difficulty and followed directions easily. She worked hard, maintained attention to task, and was not distracted by extraneous stimuli.

Laurie appeared uncertain of her ability to answer correctly and always provided her answers in the form of a question; however, she did not ask directly for examiner feedback. She also exhibited a tendency to say "I don't know" almost immediately on difficult items, and examiner efforts to encourage her proved unsuccessful. On two occasions, she asked the examiner if her mother and brothers were going to see her papers. When reassured, she said, "That's good, because they think I'm dumb anyway." Overall, results are judged to be a valid and reliable estimate of Laurie's current psychoeducational functioning.

EVALUATION RESULTS AND INTERPRETATION

Acuity Screening. Laurie's hearing and vision were assessed using the Puretone Audiometer and the Keystone Telebinocular Vision Screening Test. Results indicate that her hearing and vision are within normal limits and therefore adequate for testing purposes.

Case Example 2–1. *(Continued)*

Wechsler Intelligence Scale for Children-Revised (WISC-III). Descriptions of tests have been omitted because of space limitations. Laurie obtained the following scores on this administration of the WISC-III:

	IQ Scores/Index Scores	*Percentile Rank*
Verbal IQ	99	47
Performance IQ	95	37
Full Scale IQ	97	42
Verbal Comprehension	98	45
Perceptual Organization	90	25
Freedom from Distractibility	106	66
Processing Speed	109	73

Verbal Scale		*Performance Scale*	
Subtest	*Scaled Score*	*Subtest*	*Scaled Score*
Information	10	Picture Completion	10
Similarities	13	Coding	13
Arithmetic	11	Picture Arrangement	9
Vocabulary	10	Block Design	7
Comprehension	5	Object Assembly	7
Digit Span	11	Symbol Search	10

Results indicate that Laurie's general, verbal, and nonverbal intellectual abilities fall in the average range of functioning for chronological age with a 90% probability that the range of scores from 92 to 102 includes her true overall IQ. Results suggest that she is able to process nonverbal, visually presented information as well as she does verbal, auditorily presented information. Laurie's attention and concentration are adequate and she is not overly distractible. Although her ability to process visual information is in the average range, she does significantly better on pencil-and-paper tasks that require her to make quick and accurate discriminations of visually presented information. Laurie exhibits significant difficulty on verbal tasks that require her to apply her intelligence or use common sense to solve practical problems.

Woodcock-Johnson Psycho-Educational Battery-Revised, Tests of Achievement

Subtest	*Standard Score*	*Percentile Rank*
Letter-Word Identification	78	7
Passage Comprehension	84	15
Word Attack	80	9
Calculation	118	89
Applied Problems	105	63

Results indicate significant weaknesses in basic reading skills including sight word recognition and the use of phonetic and structural analysis skills to decode unfamiliar nonsense words. Laurie consistently sounded out the first syllable or two of a word and then apparently guessed at the rest. She exhibited average performance in reading

(continued)

Case Example 2–1.   *(Continued)*

comprehension; however, on this subtest, she used the picture cues accompanying some of the items to figure out the answer, saying, "my mom says the pictures can give me hints." She obtained average to high-average scores on subtests that measured math reasoning and mathematical operations.

Child Behavior Checklist. Forms were completed by both Mrs. Jackson and Laurie's teacher, Ms. Helms. Provided below is a comparative summary of significant scores:

Subscale	T Score	
	Mother	Teacher
Social Withdrawal	62	75
Anxiety/Depression	78	72

Results indicate that both mother and teacher see Laurie as exhibiting anxious or depressive behaviors. Her teacher also seems to think that Laurie is socially withdrawn; however, her mother rated this as less significant. No other problems were reported.

Brigance Diagnostic Inventory of Basic Skills. Laurie was administered selected sections of the Brigance to assess mastery of reading skills and to identify strengths and weaknesses. Her sight word reading level is at the first-grade level; she was able to read 80 out of 250 sight words. She read first-grade words such as *work, children, kitten,* and *daddy;* however, she was unable to read most second-grade words such as *street, again,* and *back.* She mentioned several times that she had never seen the words before and couldn't read words she had not seen. Laurie was able to identify common signs such as *go, stop, out, in, women,* and *danger.* She read a passage aloud at the primer level and was able to answer three out of five detail questions about the passage, also at the primer level. However, when stories were read out loud to her, she was able to answer literal and inferential questions at the third-grade level.

Informal Reading Inventory. Results of the informal reading inventory revealed that Laurie's instructional level is at the first grade and that she is able to read independently at the primer level. She reaches frustration with material at the second-grade level. The kinds of errors she made most often were omissions, particularly of medial and final sounds. She made two errors of substitution but corrected herself immediately. When asked questions about passages she had read, she was able to recall details but was not able to identify the main idea or cause and effect. Laurie's listening comprehension is at the fourth-grade level.

Reading Portfolio. Laurie, like the other children in her class, has a reading portfolio. The teacher described this as experimental and stated that she wanted to see whether it could work with young children before she made it a permanent requirement. The following were included in Laurie's reading portfolio: a table of contents, a form entitled "How My Portfolio Is Organized," which included room to justify inclusion of items, student-teacher conference notes, a reading log that described books read during the year and student reflections on reading progress, a parent portfolio rating form, and a teacher evaluation form.

Case Example 2–1.   *(Continued)*

Ms. Helms stated that Laurie had extreme difficulty deciding what to include in her portfolio, saying, "I don't *have* a best work." Her mother had commented, "I don't believe that this portfolio represents Laurie's actual ability." The teacher evaluation form rated her progress as below average but her effort as superior. Reading logs indicated that three books were completed for the year (the other children averaged nine): "Curious George Goes to the Hospital," "The Berenstain Bears," and "The Very Hungry Caterpillar." Among Laurie's notes on her reading progress were "I'm bad in reading" and "I like picture books not word books."

Teacher-made Tests. Results of written class tests showed grades ranging between 70 and 85 in math, English, science, and social studies. On unit tests in reading, Laurie obtained grades of 81, 74, and 66; her most frequent errors related to understanding what she was reading. Ms. Helms stated that Laurie exhibited significant anxiety before tests and did best when she had unlimited time to complete them.

Work Samples. A review of samples of Laurie's work shows that her progress in math is generally good; in fact, she consistently makes Bs and an occasional A in this subject. In the area of reading, she is able to complete classwork with teacher assistance but has been unable to do any class assignments independently. Two of her assignments were better than the others; on these, Laurie had been allowed to use picture cues to make up a new ending for a story in her reader. Error analysis indicated problems understanding what she reads; she is able to pick out details accurately but has trouble getting the big picture. Laurie's homework is always completed accurately; when asked about this, she says her mother helps and makes sure she gets it right even if they have to stay up all night. Her writing is careful, neat, and precise, and all of her papers are clean and have minimal erasures.

Clinical Interviews. Laurie was interviewed by the examiner and when asked to describe one thing she was good at, could not find anything positive to say about herself. She also made several self-deprecating statements such as "I'm kinda dumb" and "I'm prob'ly never gonna be a good reader." She stated that she was tired of reading and school. She said she might drop out of school and become a famous soccer player like Mia Hamm. Interviews with Ms. Helms, the teacher, revealed that Laurie is a quiet child who is no trouble, tries hard to please, and stays out of everyone's way. With regard to her academics, Ms. Helms stated that Laurie "will do anything to hide the fact that she can't read, although the kids do know, and some of them make fun of her." During round-robin reading, Laurie tries to change places with her classmates without the teacher noticing, so that she will not be called on. When her turn does come, she begins to cough and blow her nose or asks to go to the bathroom. The Jacksons told the examiner they were concerned about Laurie. They said she would often come home crying, saying that she was "the dumbest in the whole class." They also noted that Laurie had sleep disturbances at least five times over the previous 3 weeks. On these occasions, she got up crying and called out, but would not tell anyone what was bothering her.

Direct Observations. Anecdotal recordings of Laurie's behavior were completed on two separate days, first during reading and recess and then during math. During oral reading, she started to sneeze before her name was called. She asked to be excused to

(continued)

Case Example 2–1. *(Continued)*

get a tissue from the office and returned 8 minutes later; by this time, her turn had passed. When the teacher did call on her, she became red but started to read, slowly and hesitantly. She was helped by the teacher with every second or third word, and it was noted that a little girl next to her was whispering the reading passage to her. At recess, Laurie sat on a rock and watched the others play. She did not initiate any activity with her peers and no one came up to her. On the second occasion Laurie was observed, during math; she completed her worksheets without help, switched her sheets with a partner to grade each other's work, and remained quiet and attentive.

SUMMARY AND DIAGNOSTIC IMPRESSIONS

Laurie Jackson is an 8-year-old female who was referred for an assessment because of failing grades in reading and low self-esteem. Results of this evaluation suggest intellectual functioning in the average range. She exhibits average performance in mathematics, but has more difficulty with word problems. She experiences significant difficulty on reading tasks that involve word recognition and decoding. She is able to identify sight words at the first-grade level, but her oral reading is at the primer level and she has poor word attack skills. Her reading comprehension is within the low-average range for chronological age but she relies heavily on picture cues to help her understand what she reads; she does significantly worse on such tasks when there are no cues. When asked about what she has read, Laurie is able to answer literal questions but not inferential ones; however, she is able to answer inferential questions when stories are read to her (her listening comprehension is at or above grade level).

Results of interviews and observations indicate that Laurie is a quiet, reserved child. She has no close friends and does not have close relationships with family members. She does not seem to feel good about either herself or her reading. She exhibits signs of anxiety and unhappiness that appear to be exacerbated by her family and peers' attitudes toward her. She is also described as experiencing severe test anxiety and does better on tests when there is no time limit. She is experiencing physical symptoms such as stomachaches, headaches, and sleep disturbances that may be a result of her difficulties in school.

There is a significant difference between Laurie's intellectual ability and her reading performance that does not seem to be the result of lack of effort, poor teaching, or other factors. Results of this evaluation suggest that Laurie meets State Department of Education criteria for a Specific Learning Disability in Basic Reading Skills and that she qualifies for special services in this area. It is important that Laurie be given the help she needs before she falls further behind and loses interest in school altogether.

RECOMMENDATIONS

The following recommendations are offered to Laurie's family and teachers to help her function at her maximum potential:

General. Schedule an appointment with a physician for a complete medical examination to rule out the possibility of physical reasons for Laurie's stomachaches, headaches, and sleep disturbances. Such complaints, regardless of whether they have a physical or emotional origin, are not normal for a child her age.

Work through the school to get Laurie special services in basic reading skills as soon as possible. Adequate reading skills become increasingly critical at higher grade levels, and it is important that she be given a strong foundation in reading at this time.

Case Example 2–1. *(Continued)*

Laurie would probably benefit most—both academically and socially—from an inclusive or resource room placement. Such a placement would allow her to spend a major part of the school day in a regular education setting where she can be with other children her age, both with and without disabilities.

Parent involvement is desirable; however, in this case, Mrs. Jackson seems to be overinvolved, has unreasonable expectations for Laurie's success, and is letting her frustration show in front of her daughter. It is strongly recommended that she back off a little and be careful about what she and her sons say about Laurie's reading. It is also important that she guard against negative comments about Laurie's biological family.

It is not necessary for an 8-year-old child to spend three or four hours on homework every day, particularly when it is so frustrating for both Laurie and her mother; work with the teacher to make alternative arrangements, schedule brief study periods, and allow Laurie to take breaks and come back to a difficult reading assignment.

Laurie needs someone to talk with about her anxiety and frustration. Counseling is recommended, either through the school or through private sources. Teach her some ways to handle test anxiety, such as relaxation and simple cognitive-behavioral strategies.

Arrange for the family to do fun things together that have nothing to do with academics. Most of Laurie's interactions with her family seem to center around schoolwork, an arena in which she is not experiencing success. Also schedule some private time for the parents to spend alone with Laurie, without her brothers, and use this time for activities she likes. These efforts may help Laurie feel like an important and valued member of the family and may cut down on some of her uncertainty regarding her parents' love for her.

Find alternate ways for Laurie to take exams. Try unlimited-time tests or working for accuracy, not speed. Teach her to go back and check her work after she is done.

Encourage peer involvement; have a friend come over, or take Laurie and another child from the soccer team to a movie.

Make Laurie responsible for some chores—perhaps feeding her puppy, Maxie, or taking him out for a walk. Help her feel like an important, contributing member of the household. Reading should not serve as a substitute for all other activities.

Continue Laurie's involvement in soccer. She is successful in this area and needs to feel as though she is good at something.

Reading. Encourage and reward all of Laurie's attempts at reading. Help her build a personal library, set up a reading corner for her in her room, or join a book exchange or book club. Play reading games or word games. Buy computer software that teaches reading skills to young children. It is important that Laurie view reading as a pleasure, not a chore.

It is suggested that Laurie's parents and brothers read to her as much as possible, even if she does not understand everything that is read; alternatively, have her read to her family members. Reading into a tape recorder can also be beneficial.

Let Laurie become a member of the local library. Don't worry too much about her choice of books; let her pick simple picture books if she wants to, even if they seem too young for her. Enroll her in summer reading programs that do not stress accuracy, but number of books read.

(continued)

Case Example 2–1. *(Continued)*

Get Laurie her own subscription to magazines of interest; National Geographic's *World* is full of appealing pictures with minimal text, while *Sports Illustrated for Kids* and *Soccer, Jr.* have articles about soccer that she would enjoy.

Have Laurie read street signs, billboards, sale notices, and labels on grocery items. Help her see that reading is a valuable skill that she can actually use outside the classroom.

Although Laurie's standardized test scores do not indicate that she has a learning disability in reading comprehension, all other information points to weaknesses in this area. Monitor her performance and get help as needed. She may experience increasing difficulty in this area as she progresses through the grades and as reading material becomes more complex.

Have a peer tutor work with Laurie on basic reading skills. Also, have Laurie tutor a younger child or teach a classmate a skill that the other child has not mastered, perhaps in math. Such involvement will result in academic and social benefits for both children. Cooperative learning activities are also a good way to help children like Laurie.

When attempting to teach reading, work at Laurie's instructional level, which is first grade. Material at this level presents a challenge without being so frustrating that she makes no progress.

Teach Laurie simple strategies for handling unfamiliar words. For example, when she comes across a word she does not know, have her guess at it, using context cues or picture cues. Have her try to sound it out and see whether that helps (children often know or understand words that they may not be able to recognize in print). Have her look the word up in a dictionary; its meaning may give her clues as to what the word is. If necessary, encourage her to ask an adult or friend what the word is. Finally, simply skip the word altogether; it may not be critical to understanding the passage.

Teach Laurie strategies for noting all parts of a word, not just the first part. Help her use simple metacognitive strategies that allow her to think about her learning.

Work on phonetic and structural analysis skills so that she can decode new words independently; however, try to avoid drills. These are unnecessary and boring for most children. There are several published books and software packages that address reading strategies for children with learning disabilities.

Teach Laurie to read for meaning. Ask her questions about stories she has read or ask her to tell you a story she has read.

Do not discourage Laurie from using visual cues to help her understand reading material; she relies on them and they have worked for her in the past. However, because advanced reading material does not always have accompanying pictures, also help her develop some alternate strategies.

Laurie seems to have a good imagination. Use this to help her improve her reading and writing skills. Have her dictate a story to you and write it on a chalkboard or in a special book. Rewrite it and have her read it back to you. Alternatively, teach her to use a word processor to type her story. Use the story to teach her new words and new skills.

Allow Laurie to keep a private journal in which she jots down thoughts, feelings, new words, or exciting experiences. Tell her not to worry about grammar or spelling and assure her that she does not have to share her journal unless she wants to. Reading over her entries will give her additional practice in reading even if the words are inaccurately spelled or the grammar is incorrect. Reading and writing are interrelated skills and children who write a great deal generally seem to be successful readers.

Identified deficits in basic reading skills can be used to develop goals and objectives for Laurie; counseling could also be recommended as a related service. These can be written into her individualized education plan (IEP) and can be systematically addressed throughout the year. Other information gathered about Laurie's functioning may not be part of her IEP but can still be used to plan a comprehensive and individualized program for her, with both teachers and parents working together to help her succeed. Laurie's progress can be monitored with the use of informal assessment techniques, and goals and objectives can be modified accordingly.

CONCLUSION

Informal assessment is gaining increasing importance in school psychology, education, and related areas as school professionals begin to truly understand that traditional norm-referenced assessment has failed to live up to its promise. This will become even more apparent as we move into the twenty-first century and as schools face the responsibility of meeting the assessment and instructional needs of an increasingly diverse group of children. Informal assessment, with its myriad approaches, may offer one solution to this dilemma.

It is expected that informal assessment will become increasingly technical in nature over the next 20 or 30 years. As computer assessments become more commonplace, more technically sophisticated, and less expensive, they will not only be used more often, but will be used in ways not yet conceivable to us with our limited vision.

Assessment and instruction will change dramatically as educational reform efforts sweep the country. According to Braden (1996), the focus on measuring student learning outcomes will mean a corresponding shift from measuring the psychological characteristics of children (e.g., intelligence) to assessing educational performance (e.g., academic achievement). Braden also predicts that assessment of student performance will become more complex as schools vie with each other to find ways to accurately assess functioning. "Multiple choice tests will give way to portfolios, on-demand performance assessments and other authentic methods for measuring student outcomes" (p. 11). According to the National Center on Educational Outcomes (1995), the emphasis on accountability has resulted in large-scale assessment systems and uniform standards being developed in 45 out of 50 states. Success in these ventures could very well change the face of assessment as we know it.

Such changes also demand a need for additional research into what children learn, how they learn, and how we can measure what they learn. These studies must focus on all children; not just "average" children in regular education, but those with disabilities. Further information is needed on the differences between school systems, administrators, and faculty that lead to differential educational outcomes among students. We will truly be making progress when we can use the results of such studies to inform our actions as concerned professionals.

Although this chapter has described many approaches to informal assessment, they are admittedly not the only way to gather useful information about children. In truth, there may be times when informal assessment at its present level of sophistication cannot provide the kind of comparative information about a child that is needed—for example, for eligibility determination. There is a very real danger to the premature and unquestioning acceptance of any approach that has not been validated with the populations with which it will be used. Inaccurate assessments can result in incomplete or erroneous information about a child's strengths and weaknesses, which can lead to corresponding impediments to instructional effectiveness. If we are willing, however, to heed the warnings of authors such as Barnett and Macmann (1992), Braden (1996), and Cizek, (1991), we will be better equipped to select the tools that are most likely to enhance our decision making. In this way, we can discard that which is of no use and retain those methods that work best in our search for accurate assessments of children's functioning.

REFERENCES

Achenbach, T.M. (1991). *The Child Behavior Checklist.* Burlington: University of Vermont, Department of Psychiatry.

Afflerbach, P., & Johnson, P. (1984). Research methodology on the use of verbal reports in reading research. *Journal of Reading Behavior, 16,* 307–322.

Agnew, A.T. (1982). Using children's dictated stories to assess co-subconsciousness. *The Reading Teacher, 35,* 450–454.

Airasian, P.W. (1994). *Classroom assessment* (2nd ed.). New York: McGraw-Hill.

Alberto, R.A., & Troutman, A.C. (1995). *Applied behavior analysis for teachers: Influencing student performance* (4th ed.). Columbus, OH: Macmillan.

American Psychological Association. (1986). *Guidelines for computer-based tests and interpretations.* Washington, DC: Author.

Anderson, B. (1986, April). *A report on IRI scoring and interpretation.* Paper presented at the International Reading Association Convention, Philadelphia, PA.

Archbald, D.A. (1991). Authentic assessment: Principles, practices, and issues. *School Psychology Quarterly, 6*(4), 279–293.

Arter, J.A., & Spandel, V. (1992). Using portfolios of student work in instruction and assessment. *Educational Measurement: Issues and Practices, 11*(1), 36–44.

Ashlock, R.B. (1993). *Error patterns in computation* (6th ed.). Columbus, OH: Merrill.

Audet, L.R., & Hummel, L.J. (1990). A framework for assessment and treatment of language-learning disabled children with psychiatric disorders. *Topics in Language Disorders, 10*(4), 57–74.

Baer, D.M. (1977). A note on the absence of Santa Claus in any known ecosystem. In A. Rogers-Warren & S.F. Warren (Eds.), *Ecological perspectives in behavioral analysis* (pp. 33–36). Baltimore: University Park Press.

Bagai, E., & Bagai, J. (1979). *System FORE handbook.* North Hollywood, CA: Foreworks.

Baker, E.L., O'Neil, H.F., & Linn, R.L. (1993). Policy and validity prospects for performance-based assessment. *American Psychologist, 48,* 1210–1218.

Balajithy, E. (1989). Operation and structure of an artificial intelligence expert consultative system for reading and learning. *Journal of Reading, Writing, & Learning Disabilities International, 4*(3), 201–214.

Barker, R. (1965). Explorations in ecological psychology. *American Psychologist, 20,* 1–14.

Barkley, R.A. (1987). The assessment of attention-deficit hyperactivity disorder. *Behavioral Assessment, 9,* 207–233.

Barnett, D.W., & Macmann, G.M. (1992). Decision reliability and validity: Contributions and limitations of alternative assessment strategies. *Journal of Special Education, 25*(4), 431–452.

Bartel, N.B. (1986). Problems in mathematics achievement. In D.D. Hammill & N.R. Bartel (Eds.), *Teaching children with learning and behavioral problems* (4th ed., pp. 178–223). Boston: Allyn & Bacon.

Bateson, D. (1994). Psychometric and philosophic problems in "authentic" assessment: Performance tasks and portfolios [Special issue on: cognition and assessment]. *Alberta Journal of Educational Research, 40*(2), 233–245.

Bellack, A.S., & Hersen, M.H. (Eds.). (1988). *Behavioral assessment: A practical handbook* (3rd ed.). Elmsford, NY: Pergamon.

Benner, S.M. (1992). *Assessing young children with special needs: An ecological perspective.* White Plains, NY: Longman.

Bergan, J.R. (1977). *Behavioral consultation.* Columbus, OH: Merrill.

Bijou, S.W., & Peterson, R.F. (1970). The psychological assessment of children: A functional analysis. In P. McReynolds (Ed.), *Advances in psychological assessment* (Vol. 2, pp. 63-78). Palo Alto: Science & Behavior.

Bormuth, J.R. (1968). Cloze test readability: Criterion-referenced scores. *Journal of Educational Measurement, 5,* 189–196.

Brachen, B.A. (1990). The psychoeducational assessment of preschool children (2nd ed.). Boston: Allyn & Bacon.

Braden, J.P. (1996). Assessment and educational reform. *Communique, 24*(7), 9–10.

Brigance, A.H. (1983). *Brigance Diagnostic Comprehensive Inventory of Basic Skills.* North Billerica, MA: Curriculum Associates.

Brigance, A.H. (1991). *Brigance Diagnostic Inventory of Early Development-Revised.* North Billerica, MA: Curriculum Associates.

Burke, K. (1994). *The Mindful School: The portfolio connection, K-College.* Palatine, IL: Skylight Publishing. (ERIC Document Reproduction Service No. ED 382 373)

Burks, H.F. (1980). *Burks' Behavior Rating Scales.* Los Angeles, CA: Western Psychological Services.

Burns, P.C., & Roe, B.D. (1993). *Burns/Roe Informal Reading Inventory.* Boston, MA: Houghton Mifflin.

Cancelli, A.A., & Arena, S.T. (1996). Multicultural implications of performance-based assessment. In L.A. Suzuki, P.J. Meller, & J.G. Ponterotto (Eds.), *Handbook of multicultural assessment: Clinical, psychological, and educational applications* (pp. 319–347). San Francisco: Jossey-Bass.

Cartwright, G.P. (1969). Written expression and spelling. In R. Smith (Ed.), *Teacher diagnosis of educational difficulties* (pp. 68–91). Columbus, OH: Merrill.

Cheek, E.H., Kritsonis, D., & Lindsey, J.D. (1987). Informal reading assessment strategies for adult readers. *Lifelong learning: An omnibus of practice and research, 10*(7), 8015.

Chittooran, M.M. (1995). ADHDEXPERT: The development of a prototype expert system for the identification of attention-deficit hyperactivity disorder. (Doctoral dissertation, Mississippi State University, 1991) *Dissertation Abstracts International, 56*(06), 3499B.

Christenson, S.L. (1991). Authentic assessment: Straw man or prescription for progress? *School Psychology Quarterly, 6*(4), 294–299.

Cizek, G.J. (1991, May). Innovation or enervation? Performance assessment in perspective. *Phi Delta Kappan,* 695–699.

Darling-Hammond, L. (1993). *Authentic assessment in practice: A collection of portfolios, performance tasks, exhibitions, and documentation.* Columbia University Teachers College National Center for Restructuring Education, Schools, and Teaching. (ERIC Document Reproduction Service No. ED 377 226)

Darling-Hammond, L. (1994). Setting standards for students: The case for authentic assessment. *Educational Forum, 59*(1), 14–21.

Drew, C.J., & Hardman, M.L. (1995). *Mental retardation: A life style approach* (6th ed.). Columbus, OH: Merrill.

Duffelmeyer, F.A., Robinson, S.S., & Squier, S.E. (1989). Vocabulary questions on informal reading inventories. *The Reading Teacher, 43*(2), 142–148.

Edmondson, R., & Smith, T.M. (1994). Temperament and behavior of infants prenatally exposed to drugs: Clinical implications for the mother-infant dyad. *Infant Mental Health Journal, 15*(4), 368–379.

Ekwall, E.E. (1986). *Ekwall Reading Inventory* (2nd ed.). Boston: Allyn & Bacon.

Elliott, S. (1992, October). Authentic assessment: A case report of system change. *"Communique,"* pp. 1, 4–5.

Enright, B.E. (1983). *ENRIGHT Diagnostic Inventory of Basic Arithmetic Skills.* North Billerica, MA: Curriculum Associates.

Evans, S.S., Evans, W.H., & Mercer, C.D. (1986). *Assessment for instruction.* Boston: Allyn & Bacon.

Farmer, J.E., & Peterson, L. (1995). Pediatric traumatic brain injury: Promoting successful school reentry. *School Psychology Review, 24*(2), 230–243.

Federal Resource Center. (1993). *Task force report: Cultural and linguistic diversity in education.* Washington, DC: Office of Special Education Programs, U.S. Department of Education.

Fiorello, C.A., & Burcham, B. (1996). Educational identification of ADHD: Best practices for school practitioners. *"Communique,"* 24(5), 17–18.

Fry, E. (1972). *Reading instruction for classroom and clinic.* New York: McGraw Hill.

Fuchs, L.S. (1994). General educators' specialized adaptation for students with learning disabilities. *Exceptional Children, 61*(5), 440–459.

Fuchs, L.S., Hamlett, C., & Fuchs, D.S. (1990). Monitoring basic skills progress [Computer program]. Austin, TX: PRO-ED.

Furuno, S., O'Reilly, K.A., Hosaka, C.M., Inatsuka, T.T., Zeisloft-Folbey, B., & Allman, T. (1990). *Hawaii Early Learning Profile.* Palo Alto, CA: VORT.

Gable R.A., & Henderson, J.M. (Eds.). (1990). *Assessing students with special needs: A sourcebook for analyzing and correcting errors in academics.* New York: Longman.

Ginsburg, H.P. (1987). Assessment techniques: Tests, interviews and analytic teaching. In D.D. Hammill (Ed.), *Assessing the abilities and instructional needs of students* (pp. 441–462). Austin, TX: PRO-ED.

Glennon, V.J., & Wilson, J.W. (1972). Diagnostic-prescriptive teaching. In *National Council for Teachers of Mathematics: The slow learner in mathematics: The 35th Yearbook.* Reston, VA: NCTM.

Glover, M.E., Preminger, J.L., & Sanford, A.R. (1988). *Early Learning Accomplishment Profile.* Winston-Salem, NC: Kaplan.

Goodman, Y.M., & Burke, C.L. (1972). *Reading Miscue Inventory: Manual of procedure for diagnosis and evaluation.* New York: Macmillan.

Gresham, F.M. (1991). Alternative psychometrics for authentic assessment? *School Psychology Quarterly, 6*(4), 305–309.

Gronlund, N.E. (1993). *How to make achievement tests and assessments* (5th ed.). Englewood Cliffs, NJ: Prentice-Hall.

Guerin, G.R., & Maier, A.S. (1983). *Informal assessment in education.* Palo Alto: Mayfield.

Gutierrez-Clellen, V.F., Pena, E., and Quinn, R. (1995). Accommodating cultural differences in narrative style: A multicultural perspective. *Topics in Language Disorders, 15*(4), 54–67.

Haapa, B.L., & Lewis, R.B. (1992). Designing word processing software for specific populations: Individuals with hearing impairments and those with learning disabilities. *Closing the Gap, 10*(6), 12, 15.

Hammill, D.D. (Ed.). (1987). *Assessing the abilities and instructional needs of students.* Austin, TX: PRO-ED.

Henk, W.A. (1993). New directions in reading assessment. *Reading and Writing Quarterly: Overcoming learning difficulties, 9*(10), 103–120.

Hennings, S.S., & Hughes, K.E. (1992, April). *Building a performance-based assessment system to diagnose strengths and weaknesses in reading achievement.* Paper presented at the Annual Meeting of the American Educational Research Association, San Franciso, CA. (EDRS Document Reproduction Service No. ED 346 160)

Hipps, J.A. (1993, April). *Trustworthiness and authenticity: Alternative ways to judge authentic assessments.* Paper presented at the Annual Meeting of the American Educational Research Association, Atlanta, GA. (ERIC Document Reproduction Service No. ED 376 195)

Hofmeister, A.M., & Lubke, M.M. (1988). Expert systems: Implications for the diagnosis and treatment of learning disabilities. *Learning Disability Quarterly, 11*(3), 287–291.

Houtz, J.C., & Krug, D.A. (1995). Assessment of creativity: Resolving a mid-life crisis. [Special Issue: Toward an educational psychology of creativity: II]. *Educational Psychology Review, 7*(3), 269–300.

Howell, K.W., & Kaplan, J.J. (1980). *Diagnosing basic skills: A handbook for deciding what to teach.* Columbus, OH: Merrill.

Howell, K.W., & Rueda, R. (1996). Achievement testing with culturally and linguistically diverse students. In L.A. Suzuki, P.J. Meller, & J.G. Ponterotto (Eds.), *Handbook of multicultural assessment: Clinical, psychological, and educational applications* (pp. 253–290). San Francisco, CA: Jossey-Bass Publishers.

Hoy, C., & Gregg, N. (1994). *Assessment: The special educator's role.* Pacific Grove, CA: Brooks/Cole.

Hughes, J.N., & Baker, D.B. (1990). *The clinical child interview.* New York: Guilford Press.

Idol, L., Nevin, A., & Paolucci-Whitcomb, P. (1986). *Models of curriculum-based assessment.* Rockville, MD: Aspen.

Jitendra, A.K., & Rohena-Diaz, E. (1996). Language assessment of students who are culturally diverse: Why a discrete approach is not the answer. *School Psychology Review, 25*(1), 40–56.

Jones, R.W. (1994). *Performance and alternative assessment techniques: Meeting the challenge of alternative evaluation strategies.* Paper presented at the International Conference on Educational Evaluation and Assessment, 2nd Pretoria, Republic of South Africa. (ERIC Document Reproduction Service No. ED 380 483)

Jorgensen, M. (1994, April). *Alternative assessment from the perspective of six different school systems: An experience in consensus building.* Paper presented at the annual meeting of the American Educational Research Association, New Orleans, LA. (ERIC Document Reproduction Service No. ED 372 089)

Kalmbach, J.R. (1986). Getting at the point of retellings. *Journal of Reading, 29,* 326–333.

Kamphaus, R.W. (1991). Authentic assessment and content validity. *School Psychology Quarterly, 6*(4), 300–304.

Kaufman, A.S., & Kaufman, N.L. (1983). *Kaufman Assessment Battery for Children, Interpretive Manual.* Circle Pines, MN: American Guidance Service.

Kazdin, A.E. (1995). *Behavior modification in applied settings* (Rev. ed.). Homewood, IL: Dorsey.

Kerka, S. (1995). *Techniques for authentic assessment* [Practice application brief]. Washington, DC: Office of Educational Research and Improvement. (ERIC Document Reproduction Service No. ED 381 688)

Krug, D.A., Arick, J.R., & Almond, P.J. (1988). *Autism Behavior Checklist.* Portland, OR: ASIEP Education Company.

Landau, S., & Burcham, B. (1995). Best practices in the assessment of children with attention disorders. In A. Thomas & J. Grimes (Eds.), *Best practices in school psychology-III* (pp. 817–829). Bethesda, MD: National Association of School Psychologists.

Lanyon, R.I., & Goldstein, L.D. (1982). *Personality assessment* (2nd ed.). New York: Wiley.

Leitner, L.M. (1995). Dispositional assessment techniques in experiential personal construct psychotherapy. *Journal of Constructivist Psychology, 8*(1), 53–74.

Linder, T.W. (1990). *Transdisciplinary play-based assessment: A functional approach to working with young children.* Baltimore, MD: Paul H. Brookes.

Linn, R.L., & Gronlund, N.E. (1995). *Measurement and assessment in teaching* (7th ed.). Englewood Cliffs, NJ: Prentice-Hall.

Lopez, R. (1996). Authentic assessment: What it does and what it doesn't do. *Tennessee School Psychologist, 12*(1), 7–8.

Lowenthal, B.N. (1992). Assessment of young children with disabilities in the mainstream. *Early Child Development and Care, 79,* 39–45.

Loyola, J.L., & Loyola, J. (1996, March). *Practical guidelines for the psychoeducational assessment of monolingual and bilingual/bicultural Hispanic and Hispanic-American students.* Workshop presented at the 28th Annual Convention of the National Association of School Psychologists, Atlanta, GA.

Luftig, R.L. (1989). *Assessment of learners with special needs.* Boston: Allyn & Bacon.

Mahoney, M.J., & Thoreson, C.E. (1974). *Self-control: Power to the person.* Monterey, CA: Brooks.

Martin, R.P. (1988). *Assessment of personality and behavior problems: Infancy through adolescence.* New York: Guilford.

McCarney, S.B., & Leigh, J.E. (1990). *The Behavior Evaluation Scale* (2nd ed.). Columbia, MO: Hawthorne Educational Services.

McConaughy, S.H., & Achenbach, T.M. (1996). Contributions of a child interview to multimethod assessment of children with EBD and LD. *School Psychology Review, 25*(1), 24–39.

McKenna, M.C. (1983). Informal reading inventories: A review of issues. *The Reading Teacher, 37,* 670–678.

McLean, M., Bailey, Jr., D.B., & Wolery, M. (1996). *Assessing infants and preschoolers with special needs* (2nd ed.). Englewood Cliffs, NJ: Prentice-Hall.

McLoughlin, J.A., & Lewis, R.B. (1994). *Assessing special students* (4th ed.). Englewood Cliffs, NJ: Prentice-Hall.

Meichenbaum, D. (1979). *Cognitive behavior modification: An integrative approach.* New York: Plenum.

Meller, P.J., & Ohr, P.S. (1996). The assessment of culturally diverse infants and preschool children. In Suzuki, L.A., Meller, P.J., & Ponterotto, J.G. (Eds.), *Handbook of multicultural assessment: Clinical, psychological and educational applications* (pp. 509–559). San Francisco: Jossey-Bass.

Merrell, K.W. (1994). *Assessment of behavioral, social, & emotional problems: Direct and objective methods for use with children and adolescents.* New York: Longman.

Miller, M.D., & Legg, S.M. (1993). Alternative assessment in a high-stakes environment. *Educational Measurement Issues and Practice, 12*(2), 9–15.

Mooney, R.L., & Gordon, L.V. (1992). *The Mooney Problem Checklist.* San Antonio, TX: The Psychological Corporation.

Morsink, C.V., & Gable, R.A. (1990). Errors in reading. In R.A. Gable & J.M. Hendrickson (Eds.), *Assessing students with special needs: A sourcebook for analyzing and correcting errors in academics* (pp. 46–62). New York: Longman.

Myers, J., & Lytle, S. (1986). Assessment of the learning process. *Exceptional Children, 53,* 138–144.

National Center on Educational Outcomes (1995). *State special education outcomes.* Minneapolis, MN: Author.

Nessel, D. (1987). Reading comprehension: Asking the right questions. *Phi Delta Kappan, 68,* 442–445.

Nitko, A.J. (1996). *Educational assessment of students* (2nd ed.). Englewood Cliffs, NJ: Prentice-Hall.

Olson, M.W., & Gillis, M.K. (1987). Text type and text structure: An analysis of three secondary informal reading inventories. *Reading Horizons, 28*(1), 70–80.

Oosterhof, A. (1996). *Developing and using classroom assessments.* Englewood Cliffs, NJ: Prentice-Hall.

Paulson, F.L., Paulson, P.R., & Meyer, C.A. (1991). What makes a portfolio a portfolio? *Educational Leadership, 49*(5), 60–63.

Piers, E.V., & Harris, D.B. (1984). *The Piers-Harris Children's Self-Concept Scale.* Los Angeles, CA: Western Psychological Services.

Pigford, A.B. (1989). Evaluation by checklist: Debating the effectiveness. *NASSP Bulletin, 73*(520), 81–84.

Polloway, E.A., & Smith, J.E., (1982). *Teaching language skills to exceptional learners.* Denver, CO: Love.

Popham W.J. (1993). Educational testing in America: What's right, what's wrong? A criterion-referenced perspective. *Educational Measurement Issues and Practice, 12*(1), 11–14.

Reid, R. (1995). Assessment of ADHD with culturally different groups: The use of behavioral rating scales. *School Psychology Review, 24*(4), 537–560.

Reisman, F.K. (1978). *A guide to the diagnostic teaching of arithmetic* (2nd ed.). Columbus, OH: Merrill.

Roberts, G.H. (1968). The failure strategies of third-grade arithmetic pupils. *The Arithmetic Teacher, 15,* 442–446.

Rogers-Warren, A., & Warren, S.F. (Eds.). (1977). Ecological perspectives in behavioral analysis. Baltimore: University Park Press.

Rosenfield, S., & Reynolds, M.C. (1990). Mainstreaming school psychology: A proposal to develop and evaluate alternative assessment methods and intervention strategies. *School Psychology Quarterly, 5*(1), 55–65.

Sackett, G. (1979). The lag sequential analysis of contingency and cyclicity in behavioral interaction research. In J. Osofsky (Ed.), *Handbook of infant development* (pp. 623–634). New York: Wiley.

Salvia, J., & Hughes, C. (1990). *Curriculum-based assessment: Testing what is taught.* New York: Macmillan.

Salvia, J., & Ysseldyke, J.E. (1995). *Assessment* (6th ed.). Boston: Houghton Mifflin.

Sattler, J.M. (1988). *Assessment of children* (3rd ed.). San Diego, CA: Jerome M. Sattler.

Schoggen, P. (1978). Ecological psychology and mental retardation. In G.P. Sackett (Ed.), *Observing behavior: Theory and application in mental retardation* (Vol. 1, pp. 108–142). Baltimore: University Park Press.

Schroeder, S.R. (Ed.). (1990). *Ecobehavioral analysis and developmental disabilities: The twenty-first century.* New York: Springer-Verlag.

Scott, M. (1980). Ecological theory and methods for research in special education. *Journal of Special Education, 14,* 279–294.

Silvaroli, N.J. (1986). *Classroom reading inventory* (5th ed.). Dubuque, IA: Brown.

Simeonsson, R.J. (1986). *Psychological and developmental assessment of special children.* Boston: Allyn & Bacon.

Simon, A., & Boyer, E.G. (Eds.). (1974). *Mirrors for behavior: An anthology of observation instruments.* Wyncott, PA: Communication Materials Center.

Slate, J.R., & Saudargas, R.A. (1987). Classroom behaviors of LD, seriously emotionally disturbed, and average children: A sequential analysis. *Learning Disabilities Quarterly, 10,* 125–134.

Spache, G. (1981). *Diagnosing and correcting reading disabilities.* Boston: Allyn & Bacon.

Stiggins, R.J. (1992). High quality classroom assessment: What does it really mean? *Educational Measurement: Issues and Practice, 11*(2), 35–39.

Stiggins, R.J. (1994). *Classroom assessment for teaching and learning.* New York: Merrill.

Stinnett, T.A., Havey, J.M., & Oehler-Stinnett, J. (1994). Current test usage by practicing school psychologists: A national survey. *Journal of Psychoeducational Assessment, 12*(4), 331-350.

Suzuki, L.A., & Meller, P.J., and Ponterotto, J.G. (Eds.). (1996). *Handbook of multicultural assessment: Clinical, psychological and educational applications.* San Francisco: Jossey-Bass.

Tawney, J.W., & Gast, D.L. (1984). *Single subject research in special education.* Columbus, OH: Merrill.

Taylor, W.L. (1953). Cloze procedure: A new tool for measuring readability. *Journalism Quarterly, 30,* 414–438.

Taylor, L. (1989). *Assessment of exceptional students: Eductional and psychological procedures* (2nd ed.). Englewood Cliffs, NJ: Prentice-Hall.

Thomas, A., and Grimes, J. (Eds.). (1995). *Best practices in school psychology-III.* Bethesda, MD: National Association of School Psychologists.

Tindal, G.A., & Marston, D.B. (1990). *Classroom-based assessment: Evaluating instructional outcomes.* Columbus, OH: Merrill.

Tucker, J.A. (Ed.). (1985). Curriculum-based assessment. *Exceptional Children, 52,* 199–298.

VanDevender, E.M., & Harris, M.J. (1987). Why students make math errors. *Academic Therapy, 23*(1), 79–85.

Wade, S.E. (1990). Using think alouds to assess comprehension. *The Reading Teacher, 43,* 442–451.

Walker, J.E., & Shea, T.M. (1988). *Behavior management: A practical approach for educators* (4th ed.). Columbus, OH: Merrill.

Wallace, G., & Larsen, S.C. (1992). *Educational assessment of learning problems: Testing for teaching* (2nd ed.). Boston: Allyn & Bacon.

Watson, D.L., & Tharp, R.G. (1989). *Self-directed behavior: Self-modification for personal adjustment* (5th ed.). Pacific Grove, CA: Brooks.

Willems, E.P. (1974). Behavioral technology and behavioral ecology. *Journal of Applied Behavioral Analysis, 7,* 151–165.

Wilson, M.S., & Reschly, D.J. (1996). Assessment in school psychology training and practice. *School Psychology Review, 25*(1), 9–23.

Witt, J.C., Elliott, S.N., Kramer, J.J., & Gresham, F.M. (1994). *Assessment of children: Fundamental methods and practices.* Madison, WI: Brown & Benchmark.

Wolf, D.P. (1989). Portfolio assessment: Sampling student work. *Educational Leadership, 46*(7), 35–39.

Worthen, B.R. (1993). Critical issues that will determine the future of alternative assessment. *Phi Delta Kappan, 74,* 444–454.

Worthen B.R., & Leopold, G.D. (1992). Impediments to implementing alternative assessment: Some emerging issues. *New Directions for Education Reform 1*(2), 1–20.

Worthen B.R., & Spandel, V. (1991). Putting the standardized test debate in perspective. *Educational Leadership, 48*(5), 65–69.

Zigmond, N., Vallecorsa, A., & Silverman, R. (1983). *Assessment for instructional planning in special education.* Englewood Cliffs, NJ: Prentice-Hall.

Chapter 3

NEUROPSYCHOLOGICAL ASSESSMENT

LAWRENCE E. MELAMED AND JEFFREY R. WOZNIAK

INTRODUCTION

A Unique History

Neuropsychological assessment is perhaps a unique assessment area in psychology. Its deepest roots are not in psychometric or psychological theory but rather in nineteenth-century behavioral neurology. When Broca or Jackson or Lichtheim, to name a few of the so-called immortals, argued about the nature of the cognitive deficit experienced by a particular patient, their arguments were usually buttressed by acute clinical observations denoting the circumstances under which they occurred. Often these clinically derived observations of behavior led to models of cognitive processes that are remarkably similar to those found in current work in cognitive psychology or, more accurately, cognitive neuropsychology.

In the century or so since this golden age of behavioral neurology it might be expected that psychometric roots, a kind of archaeological evidence that psychologists are present, be evident now in neuropsychological assessment. Although a few recent instruments (e.g., the Wechsler Memory Scale-Revised, 1987) demonstrate a major concern with psychometric properties, most widely employed instruments have been developed without an apparent primary interest in these matters. Aside from tests appropriated from other domains—for example, the Wechsler Adult Intelligence Scale-Revised (WAIS-R)—most neuropsychological assessment instruments appear to still have their source in clinical acumen (e.g., the Benton Revised Visual Retention Test, 1974) or in conceptualizations of functional neuroanatomy that have evolved over the past several decades, such as the contributions of Goldstein (1944), Halstead (1947), and Luria (1980). The value of these instruments was considered until recently to be in their success at denoting brain damage or in localizing sites of injury rather than in conceptualizing functional consequences as in the early work in behavioral neurology. There has been a resurgence of interest in the latter issue in the past decade or so in clinical neuropsychology as remediation and rehabilitation planning have become core elements of the assessment task. Recently, there has been some movement in incorporating constructs from experimental psychology and cognitive science into neuropsychological test design in a more fundamental way than had been done previously. Important examples of such instruments are the California Verbal Learning Test (Delis, Kramer, Kaplan, &

Ober, 1987), the Recognition Memory Test (Warrington, 1984), and the Learning Efficiency Test-II (LET-II; Webster, 1992).

Distinguishing Characteristics

The most distinguishing feature of neuropsychological testing compared to other means of psychological assessment is probably its thoroughness. Instruments are employed that examine highly integrative cognitive functions, such as those found in intelligence tests, as well as those that are focused on more limited cognitive operations, such as visual, auditory, and tactual perception, linguistic functions, and memory. Additionally, most assessment batteries in neuropsychology have extensive components dealing with attentional processes and motor functions. Specific suggestions on instruments for evaluation in these various areas will be presented later. It is obvious from the breadth of this testing that strategies for integrating assessment data and making inferences about the nature of neuropsychological deficits is of primary concern.

A second distinguishing feature of neuropsychological assessment is its increasingly closer ties to fundamental research in experimental psychology and other life and behavioral sciences. The influence of basic science is extensive. As indicated earlier, models from cognitive science are being used in the design of neuropsychological instruments. There are continuing advances in the development of cognitive rehabilitation procedures that are based on models of normative functioning. These models, in turn, often have their origin in cognitive neuropsychology research, which involves the study of cognitive functioning in individuals with brain lesions. As McCarthy and Warrington (1990) note, "The functional analysis of patients with selective deficits provides a very clear window through which one can observe the organization and procedures of normal cognition. No account of 'how the brain works' would even approach completeness without this level of analysis" (p. 1).

It can be argued that one of the most important components of one's work in clinical neuropsychology is staying abreast of work in cognitive psychology and cognitive neuropsychology, which helps to provide not only a general understanding of what clinically derived tests measure but often reasonable hypotheses for conceptualizing cognitive deficits and possible remediation strategies. Notable in this regard is the work of Posner (1989) on selective attention and Baddeley (1986) on working memory.

A final distinguishing feature of neuropsychological assessment is the "neuro" component. This aspect of the assessment requires that very direct ties to the medical community and its knowledge base exist. It is necessary to develop a working knowledge of a wide range of neuropathologies and their treatment. An excellent introduction to this material can be found in Lezak (1995). Certainly, one must be reasonably informed about current diagnostic procedures such as the EEG, CT scan, and MRI. It is axiomatic that familiarity with neuroanatomy is required along with an understanding of the physical effects of various types of brain damage. Probably no neuropsychologist feels terribly secure in his or her medically related information and must therefore continually upgrade that information. An additional influence of the "neuro" orientation is the help it provides in conceptualizing the nature of the deficits the individual is experiencing. At times, it is much easier to conceptualize deficits as, for example, left hemispheric or frontal than it is to place them within a functional framework. When working with a nonacquired disorder such as a learning disability, an analysis that takes cognizance of functional neuroanatomy can be very helpful even when its speculative nature precludes giving it any more status than a working hypothesis (e.g., Bakker's [1994] conceptualization of L- and P-type dyslexia). It is the manner in which neuropsychological hypotheses integrate seemingly disparate data that gives them their force.

Applications of Neuropsychological Assessment

Neuropsychological assessment is being employed in an ever-increasing set of circumstances. Traditionally, it has been employed in two major areas, the first being the need to characterize the cognitive consequences of head injury, stroke, and diseases that affect neural tissue in order to facilitate rehabilitation planning and decisions on employment and living arrangements. This is probably still the fastest growing area of clinical neuropsychology given the growth of rehabilitation medicine and the aging of the population. The second traditional application has been in answering the question of "organicity" posed generally by psychiatrists. This question is presented in a wider variety of situations today. Examples would be (1) discriminating between dementia and pseudo-dementia or depression, (2) attempting to classify schizophrenia as Type I or Type II where the latter involves negative symptoms such as flattened affect and may be related to structural changes in the brain, and (3) offering information about the neuropsychological profile of an individual who has known organic deficits coexisting with a major emotional disorder and therefore presents many complicated diagnostic and social service questions.

There are two newer areas of neuropsychological assessment today that show considerable growth. One is in the area of forensic application where neuropsychologists are called upon to offer assistance in myriad ways. Common questions have to do with evaluating the cognitive complaints that clients report after motor-vehicle or industrial accidents or in medical malpractice suits. Very complicated issues in criminal cases can arise, such as the effect of a brain injury, after the commission of a crime, on an individual's behavior during a trial or probationary evaluation.

The other area in which application of neuropsychological assessment strategies has become more widespread is in the evaluation of learning disabilities and attention-deficit/hyperactivity disorder (ADHD). Child neuropsychology has been a particularly active area of research and it includes considerable work on learning disabilities. This research has primarily focused on two issues. One has been the prediction of academic achievement using neuropsychological variables. Several longitudinal studies have demonstrated the efficacy of early assessment in predicting the level of success several years hence (Fletcher & Satz, 1980; Melamed & Rugle, 1989; Rourke & Orr, 1977). This research argues for the application of neuropsychological assessment strategies in the kindergarten screening process. The other issue is that of subtype analysis. This has been an exceedingly active area in which several strategies have been employed to determine whether reliable subtypes of children with learning disabilities can be discerned from the assessment data. These strategies have included clinical evaluations of profiles (e.g., Mattis, French, & Rapin, 1975) as well as a wide variety of statistical procedures such as cluster analysis (e.g., Watson, Goldgar, & Ryschon, 1983). Hynd, Connor, and Nieves (1988) present a very thorough review of this literature. Although this literature does indicate that more than two subtypes of learning-disabled children can be reliably discriminated, Hynd et al. point out that the tests used to create these subtypes are generally not useful in furthering an understanding of the nature of the deficits that define the subtypes. This understanding would be very important for remediation. For a highly critical analysis of the application of neuropsychological assessment to learning disabilities the reader is referred to the at times cogent, at times very overdrawn comments of Reschly and Gresham (1989).

As evaluating learning disabilities, both in adults and children, is increasingly common in neuropsychological assessment and will be a focus of the examples presented later in this chapter, it seems useful to indicate the situations in which such an assessment would be advisable, given the time commitment and expense of these procedure. First of all, a neuropsychological assessment would be warranted in almost all situations in which the child or adult has a history of head injury, even if relatively mild. This would also be true for a history of stroke, seizure disorder, and various systemic and genetic disorders. Additionally, even if the individual's history is negative for the above factors, the presence of an appreciable number of soft signs such as very delayed language development and severe motor immaturity would warrant the neuropsychological approach. An additional indication, not often considered, is the failure of academic intervention for reasons that are not evident. This circumstance can be masking an inadequate conceptualization of the disorder. Obvious examples are the continued application of language experience or phonics programs in reading after years of little or no progress by the student. A neuropsychological approach furthermore can often alleviate the stress for the child or family that can build up from the reality or perception of being offered only incomplete or poorly focused information about the correlates of the learning disorder.

A tremendous amount of interest has also recently been generated concerning the potential contributions of neuropsychology to the study of behavior disorders including ADHD and conduct disorder (CD). A number of studies have demonstrated that children with ADHD and/or CD show higher rates of neuropsychological deficits (especially verbal and executive deficits) than their peers (Moffitt & Silva, 1988). Children with ADHD and/or CD also show much higher rates of learning disabilities. A number of neuropathological models have been proposed for these disorders, the most well developed of which are based on frontal-lobe pathology. A good deal of evidence seems to support frontal-lobe deficits in children with ADHD (Barkley, Grodzinsky, & DuPaul, 1992; Shue & Douglas, 1992). Frontal-lobe pathology is often associated with attentional problems, a dysexecutive syndrome, a disinhibited syndrome, or a combination of these difficulties (Mega & Cummings, 1994). All of these underlying syndromes are thought to contribute to ADHD and, perhaps, to CD as well. Particularly important are executive function deficits. Executive functions are those involved in the planning and organizing of activity to reach goals. They also include those processes involved in the initiation and regulation of this behavior and in its adjustment to changing circumstances. Tests sensitive to frontal-lobe functioning are typically used in investigating these functions. Therefore, verbal and visual fluency, learning and problem solving, motor programming, and selective attention measures are often employed in investigating these functions.

Neuropsychological assessment can provide important diagnostic information to be used in conjunction with interview and observational data in identifying these disorders and in differentiating among them. Welsh (1994) provides a particularly strong case for the use of neuropsychological assessment in ADHD and also discusses a comprehensive executive function battery for this purpose. Despite the strength of the models and the evidence, Barkley's (1991) caution about the limited "ecological validity" of many neuropsychological tests used in ADHD research is worth noting. It should be noted that in addition to aiding in differential diagnosis among these disorders, neuropsychological assessment may be helpful in reducing the heterogeneity within the diagnostic groups. For example, a number of recent studies have demonstrated the ability of neuropsychological measures to discriminate ADD with hyperactivity from ADD without hyperactivity (Goodyear & Hynd, 1992). Similarly, neuropsychological assessment should be helpful in employing the new *Diagnostic and Statistical Manual of Mental Disorders* (*DSM-IV*) classification scheme for ADHD, which includes an *inattentive* type, a *hyperactive* type, and a *combined* type (American Psychiatric Association, 1994). At present, the rationale for utilizing attentional and executive measures in diagnosing ADHD is fairly sound, but assessment strategies will surely become more sophisticated in the coming years. One likely trend will be to incorporate our understanding of developmental neuropsychology and more carefully tailor our choice of assessment techniques to the client's age and/or developmental status. This type of refinement will be particularly relevant to the assessment of ADHD and CD as frontal-lobe development has been shown to proceed in stages throughout childhood, leveling off only in early adolescence (Welsh, Pennington, & Groisser, 1991).

BRAIN–BEHAVIOR RELATIONSHIPS

Probably nothing is more self-evident in the practice of neuropsychological assessment than the need for familiarity with functional neuroanatomy, that is, brain-behavior relationships. The starting point in developing this knowledge is to become acquainted with brain anatomy. At a beginning level this means becoming familiar with the major landmarks—gyri and fissures—of the cerebral cortex and the denoting of lobes. Figure 3–1 is a simplified lateral view of the left cerebral cortex. Besides denoting the four lobes, the sulci used in defining their boundaries are given. Subsequent study would require becoming familiar with the wide range of landmarks such as the angular gyrus in alexia that have become relevant to understanding various disorders. Of course, study would not be limited to struc-

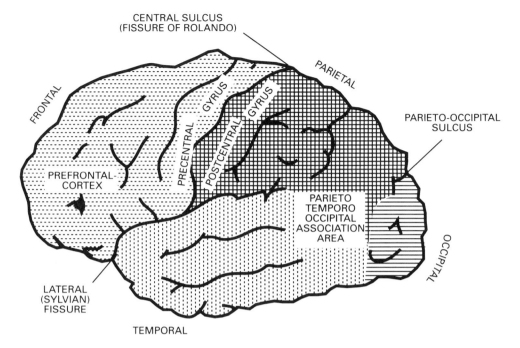

Figure 3–1. Lobes and important landmarks of the cerebral cortex

Note: From *Neuropsychological Assessment,* by M. Lezak. Copyright © 1983 by Oxford University Press. Reprinted with permission.

tures evident on the lateral views of the cortex but would extend to those observed from bottom (ventral) or central (medial) views. Additionally, knowing the location and expected size and shape of the fluid-filled cavities of the brain, the ventricles, is important for understanding the effects of many disease processes and injuries on the brain. Becoming familiar with all these elements of neuroanatomy is best met by an investment in a brain atlas such as the photographic one compiled by DeArmond, Fusco, and Dewey (1989). Further, it could even be argued today that becoming familiar with CT scans and MRI studies of the brain should be an aspect of one's preparation for neuropsychological practice. A helpful book for this purpose is that of Bigler, Yeo, and Turkheimer (1989). Once all this neuroanatomical material is familiar, the next step is to connect it to the existing lore on functional significance. Typically, this knowledge base relating function to cortical location uses partitions based on hemisphere and/or lobe. Compendia of this lore can be found in Lezak (1995) and Kolb and Whishaw (1995).

Another very important aspect of cortical anatomy is the distribution of the major arteries. Figure 3–2 is a medial view of this distribution. In understanding the cognitive consequences of an ischemic event such as a stroke, one has to consider the area irrigated by the blood vessel whose flow is decreased or interrupted. An excellent discussion of these cerebrovascular disorders can be found in Funkenstein (1988).

Although specifying cortical site by lobe and/or prominent landmark may appear to be rather exacting localization, it is in actuality not fine grained enough for many purposes. In neuroscience in general and in many neuropsychological applications,

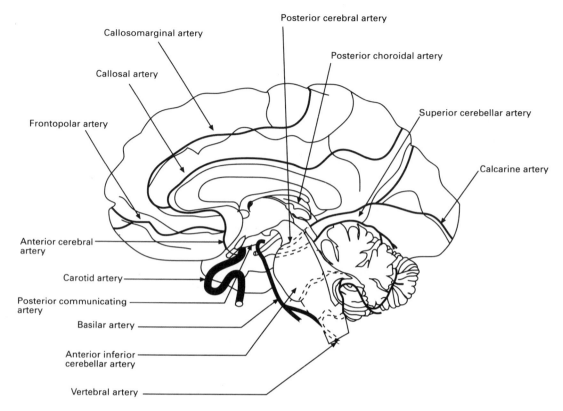

Figure 3–2. A medial view of the cortical arteries

Note: From *Structure of the Human Brain: A Photographic Atlas,* by S.J. DeArmond, M.M. Fusco, & M.M. Dewey (1989). Copyright © 1989 by Oxford University Press. Reprinted with permission.

anatomical localization within the neocortex is specified by Brodmann numbers, a system established over 80 years ago. In Figure 3–3, these numbers are presented for both a lateral and a medial view of the cortex. In this scheme, neighboring areas with discernibly different cell types are given different numbers. It can be seen that each lobe is divided into many different areas by this method. The frontal lobe is remarkable in its apparent diversity. Interestingly, there are sizable areas that overlap traditionally designated lobes, such as Area 39, which appears to border on the parietal, occipital, and temporal lobes.

One very prominent approach to understanding the functional significance of this extraordinary diversity of cortical areas is the model proposed by the great Russian pioneer in neuropsychology, Luria (1980). Luria proposes three functional units underlying cortical activity. The first, the *unit for regulating tone and waking and mental states,* involves the arousal level and is dependent upon subcortical and brain-stem mechanisms and is therefore not within the focus of our concern here. The second unit, that for *receiving, analyzing, and storing information,* involves the posterior neocortex, beyond the central sulcus. This can be thought of as the sensory cortex and is involved in processing visual, auditory, and somesthetic information. The third functional unit is that located anterior to the central sulcus and is described as the motor unit. More formally, it is the *unit for programming, regula-*

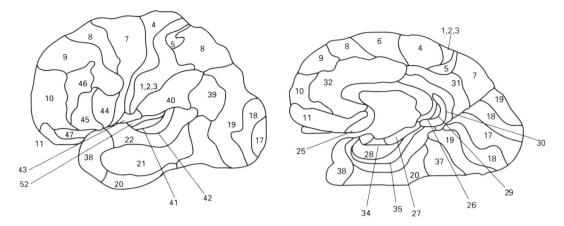

Figure 3–3. Brodmann cortical map

Note: From *Fundamental Neuroanatomy,* by W.J.H. Nauta & M. Feirtig. Copyright © 1986 by W.H. Freeman and Company. Reprinted with permission.

tion, and verification of activity. For Luria, this final unit serves to organize conscious activity. It deals with the development of intentions and the planning and programming of activity and its verification.

In addition to the designation of these functional units, Luria proposed that there is a hierarchical structure that is characteristic of all regions of the cortex. For the posterior or sensory system, *primary* cortex contains cells that are for the most part modality specific and respond to the elementary features of stimulation. Examples in terms of Brodmann numbers would be Area 17 for vision and Area 41 for audition. *Secondary* zones receive projections from the primary ones. Luria sees these as less modality specific and more integrative, producing the organization evident in perceptual experiences. For vision, the secondary areas include 18 and 19, while Areas 22 and 42 are examples for audition. At the pinnacle of the hierarchical structure for the sensory cortex, according to Luria, are the *tertiary* zones. These are areas in which the great majority of neurons are multimodal and process general features such as spatial arrangement. Most importantly, these tertiary regions serve to translate the visual experience into a symbolic one for higher-order cognitive functioning. Large areas of the posterior cortex are tertiary in function. These include Area 7 and portions of 22, 37, 39, and 40. Many of these areas are at the boundary of the parietal, temporal, and occipital lobes—the P-T-O junction. It should be apparent that Luria's system leads to an understanding of the qualitative differences in deficits that occur when, for example, Area 17 is damaged compared to Area 37—the difference between the occurrence of a blind spot in the visual field and an inability to recognize faces.

For the anterior or motor cortex, the primary area is Brodmann Area 4, a motor command area for fine movements. The secondary is Area 6, the premotor area in which motor programs are generated that are executed by the primary cortex. The anterior tertiary zone includes Areas 9, 10, and 11 as well as others. The prefrontal cortex is decisive, according to Luria, in the formation of intentions and programs for behavior as well as in the regulation and verification of this behavior.

Luria's formulation of functional neuroanatomy is widely respected and employed but is not without critics. A particularly cogent analysis is presented in Kolb and Whishaw (1995).

ASSESSMENT FUNDAMENTALS

In this section, an introduction to the various strategies for creating a neuropsychological battery and for conducting the assessment will be presented. In particular, Kaplan's (1989) very stimulating suggestions on how an assessment might be conducted to facilitate an evaluation of a patient's compensatory strategies will be covered. Additionally, normative batteries for comprehensive adult and child evaluations will be described along with examples of the contents of specialized or briefer batteries that may be employed for assessment of dementia, learning disability, and so forth.

Assessment Strategies

In general, there seem to be three denotable approaches to neuropsychological assessment. The first is termed *fixed* by Kaplan (1989) and *actuarial* by Lezak (1984). In this approach, there is a relatively systematic use of the same set of tests from individual to individual. Interpretation of the test results depends upon there being a body of knowledge relating specific test profiles and pathognomonic signs to various organic or functional criteria. There are two widely employed examples of this approach to neuropsychological assessment, the Halstead-Reitan Battery (Reitan & Wolfson, 1985) and the Luria-Nebraska Neuropsychological Battery (Golden, 1981). These are very different instruments: The first is based on experimental investigations into frontal-lobe function by Halstead (1947) and the latter on an attempt to make over a masterfully conducted examination from behavioral neurology (cf. Christensen, 1975) into an instrument with scales denoted (e.g., memory), quantitative measurement, and, potentially, specifiable patterns and pathognomonic signs for various diagnostic purposes. Although space limitations do not allow an overview of the Halstead-Reitan instrument, some of the tests are often incorporated into the flexible batteries emphasized in this chapter and will be introduced later. The Luria-Nebraska instrument has been the source of much contention in the neuropsychological assessment literature and is generally given a negative evaluation by those not in the camp. The problems enumerated concern methodological issues, validity concerns, and statistical and psychometric problems (Lezak, 1995; Spiers, 1982; Stambrook, 1983).

Several criticisms of the fixed battery approach have been raised. The major problem probably has been that the tests employed are often extremely difficult to interpret in terms of the cognitive skills being evaluated. Partly it is an issue of the measure tapping into many functions, that is, of being overdetermined. Without additional measures exploring more fundamental skills, it is very difficult to interpret the test results. Further difficulty of interpretation comes about because of weak construct validity. When measures of language or memory or perception are present, they are often only tenuously related to the level of theoretical development in cognitive science or tap into a very limited portion of the component processes that need to be evaluated. Both the Halstead-Reitan and the Luria-Nebraska are very weak in their assessment of memory, perceptual functions, and language processes. The practical difficulty of using instruments with weak construct validity and hard-to-interpret procedures is that test results do not readily lead to the formulation of remediation or rehabilitation strategies. At this point, one might question the value of the fixed battery approach in general. It is necessary to point out that this approach retains considerable usefulness when questions of organicity are dominant. The overdetermination of test procedures or, more positively, their dependence on integration of functions, makes them very sensitive to brain damage. Recently, two extended Halstead-Reitan batteries have been developed that retain the fixed battery approach and address the limitations in content. These are the Halstead-Russell Neuropsychological Evaluation System (Russell & Starkey, 1993) and Heaton, Grant, and Mathews' (1991) Comprehensive Norms for an Expanded Halstead-Reitan Battery.

Perhaps the polar opposite of the fixed battery approach is what Kaplan (1989) terms the *clinical investigative* approach. This is best exemplified by the work of Luria (1980) in its original form. Luria was very critical of psychometric tests because of the inability to clinically, that is, qualitatively, evaluate performance on them. His attack was to focus on how a problem was solved rather than on determining the number of correct answers. Although a wide range of tests would be employed, from those investigating sensory functions to those focusing on more complex integrative functions, the strategy of assessment was paramount. Luria was most concerned with the *structural dynamics* of a response. Tasks were continuously modified, made harder or different, so as to converge on the most adequate interpretation of the functional deficit and its physiological basis. The limitation of the strong clinical approach represented by Luria's work is in its aversion to quantification and the resulting difficulty in then documenting procedures so that others can duplicate them. Christensen's (1975) attempt to do this with Luria's work is clearly commendable. A related approach that is becoming very influential is the process orientation of Edith Kaplan (1989). This approach also focuses on the strategies that the patient employs in solving tasks. In using this approach, some common instruments such as the WAIS-R (Kaplan, Fein, Morris, & Delis, 1991) are administered and scored in novel ways, at times with new or extended components. Unlike Luria's approach, qualitative aspects of performance are quantified and norms are produced. Procedures can be standardized so that others can reproduce them. It is likely that these innovations of Kaplan's will become a common aspect of neuropsychological assessment over the next decade. The power of this approach becomes apparent when evaluating patients with cerebral vascular accidents (CVA) or other localized lesions for cognitive rehabilitation.

The third strategy in neuropsychological assessment is the individualized approach, perhaps best formulated by Lezak (1984), in which the assessment is "tailored to the patient's problems, limitations, and situations." This procedure uses standardized instruments but considers the individual's social and medical history, their mental status, and the purpose of the assessment (e.g., rehabilitation planning, differential diagnosis, etc.). Although there may be considerable overlap in the testing battery established for assessing the results of, say, a closed-head injury, and that established for investigating an apparent learning disability in an adult, there will be differences in the range and depth of testing in the various areas. Lezak (1984) describes the conceptual structure of the individualized approach to be *deficit measurement.* Deficits are considered with reference to both normative information and the patient's history. Thus, an average WAIS-R Similarities score may appear to indicate a deficit for an individual who graduated from a prestigious university. When a pattern of impairment is established from the deficit analysis, according to Lezak the examiner uses his or her knowledge of brain function and disease, along with information about the patient's background and present situation, to produce an interpretation that allows for diagnostic inferences, predictions, management, and rehabilitation strategies.

The strategy favored by the present authors is the individualized approach of Lezak (1984). The application of this strategy will be demonstrated in a later section of this chapter. There is a modest difference in emphasis between the strategy presented in this chapter and the manner in which Lezak introduces this approach. The difference is found in the direct acknowledgment of the role of hypothesis testing in the current presentation. This multifaceted role includes tailoring and adjusting the final assessment battery as well as interpreting the pattern of deficits. As an example, when establishing a test battery for a person who has experienced a closed-head injury as a result of a motor-vehicle accident, there are certain expectations that guide the choice of evaluative instruments so that measures of executive functions and attentional processes usually dominate. On the other hand, it may appear likely to the investigator that problem-solving deficits are only modest in this individual, that, for example, compromised language skills or memory deficits are more primary in understanding this individual's functional deficits. These hypotheses would have to be followed up both by using appropriate language and memory test instruments and by adjusting the manner in which executive functions are examined to see whether performance improves when memory or language skills are less essential to task performance.

The Problem of Norms

Psychologists are very familiar with tests that have an advanced level of norming such as the Wechsler tests or achievement batteries such as the Woodcock-Johnson-Revised or personality instruments such as the Minnesota Multiphasic Personality Inventory-2 (MMPI-2). When getting started in neuropsychological assessment, the generally poor quality of norms comes as a shock. Eventually, one is simply pleased to find norms on a sample of at least modest size that has some characteristics of the people one is assessing. Very few exceptions exist, the Wechsler Memory Scale-Revised comes to mind. Even there, the sample size at any age range is only 50. Newer instruments do often have norms—the California Verbal Learning Test and the Boston Naming Test—but samples are small, and very little in the way of sophisticated examinations of reliability and measurement error are conducted. The reasons for this situation are likely complex. One factor is the long history with clinical investigative methods in this field. It should be noted that psychometric procedures have made few inroads into behavioral neurology. Second, it is very expensive and time consuming to norm tests, and most investigators do not have the resources to conduct extensive norming research. Perhaps most important is the fact (or realization) that an investigator is primarily looking for obvious impairment. Lezak (1984) uses a standard deviation of 2 from expectancy criterion in defining a significant deficit. In clinical practice, deficits are often so discrepant from expectancy that percentile ranks are far below the first percentile and standard scores are obviously distorted, being 4 or more standard deviations below the norming sample. Finely graded performance distinctions are less important under such circumstances.

Practitioners in neuropsychology find it necessary to develop files of norms from published articles and books. Three journals often publish norms that have been created in various clinical settings. These are *Archives of Clinical Neuropsychology, The Clinical Neuropsychologist,* and *Developmental Neuropsychology.* Lezak's (1995) assessment text, an article by Bornstein (1985), and recent books by Spreen and Strauss (1991) and Heaton, Grant, and Mathews (1991) are other good sources.

A Comprehensive Adult Battery

The purpose of this section is to present the contents of a comprehensive adult neuropsychological test battery assuming that an individualized or flexible battery approach is being employed. Useful instruments for the different assessment areas will also be introduced. The number of tests or procedures employed in any one area would depend upon the purpose of the assessment, the individual circumstances of the client, and the effort required to arrive at an acceptable characterization of the nature of the deficit the client is experiencing. The purpose of the assessment can often include such items as rehabilitation planning or a vocational evaluation. *Individual circumstances* refers to the nature of the injury or illness as well as the person's premorbid medical and social history. An individual may have suffered a stroke but, in addition, have a history of long-term alcohol abuse. Diffuse brain damage such as in closed-head injuries and certain dementias demand elaborate assessment.

The several areas of investigation in a comprehensive neuropsychological assessment are listed in Table 3–1. References are given for the less-familiar instruments. The sequence in which they are presented here is not meaningful, although it is probably customary to begin with the intellectual (cognitive ability) measures because of their breadth and because certain subtests of the Wechsler instruments lend themselves to an elaboration by the process approach (Kaplan, 1989) or some related procedure. Only a portion of the tests listed in each area here would be given in any assessment, no matter how comprehensive. In practice, most assessments are comprehensive with respect to breadth of areas to explore. How elaborate testing will be in any one area, as indicated earlier, will depend upon the degree to which it is necessary to finely characterize an individual's cognitive profile in order to bring closure to the hypothesis testing the investigator has been engaged in.

Table 3–1. Areas of investigation in neuropsychological assessment

Cognitive Ability
  WAIS-R
  Raven's Progressive Matrices
  Shipley Institute of Living Scale
Attention/Concentration
  Knox's Cube Test (Stone & Wright, 1980)
  Trail Making A,B (Reitan & Wolfson, 1985)
  Wechsler Memory Scale-Revised, Mental Control subtest
  Stroop Test (Trenerry et al., 1989)
  Visual Search and Attention Test (Trenerry et al., 1990)
  Paced Auditory Serial Addition Test (Lezak, 1995)
Language Functions
  Multilingual Aphasia Examination (Benton & Hamsher, 1983)
  Boston Naming Test (Kaplan et al., 1983)
  Boston Diagnostic Aphasia Examination (Goodglass & Kaplan, 1983)
  Revised Token Test (McNeil & Prescott, 1978)
  Peabody Picture Vocabulary Test
Visual Perceptual/Visual Motor
  Rey-Osterreith Complex Figure Test (Lezak, 1995)
  Hooper Visual Organization Test
  Facial Recognition (Benton et al., 1983)
  Judgment of Line Orientation (Benton et al., 1983)
  Visual Form Discrimination (Benton et al., 1983)
Executive Functions
  Wisconsin Card Sorting Test
  Category Test (Reitan & Wolfson, 1985)
  Porteus Maze Test
  WISC-R/WISC-III Mazes
  Tower of Hanoi/London
  Tinker Toy Test (Lezak, 1995)
  Verbal Fluency (oral and written)
  Visual Fluency
Memory: General Batteries
  Wechsler Memory Scale-Revised
  Memory Assessment Scales (Williams, 1991)
Memory: Restricted
  California Verbal Learning Test (Delis et al., 1987)
  Recognition Memory Test (Warrington, 1984)
  Rey Auditory Verbal Learning Test (Lezak, 1995)
  Benton Visual Retention Test (Sivan, 1992)
  Learning Efficiency Test-II (LET-II, Webster, 1992)
  Selective Reminding Test (Buschke, 1974)
Motor Skills
  Grooved Pegboard Test
  Finger Oscillation
  Lateral Dominance Examination
  Pin Test
Academic Skills
  Wide Range Achievement Test (WRAT-3)
  Gray Oral Reading Test (GORT-3)

A Comprehensive Children's Battery

In creating a neuropsychological battery for children, a number of issues are of relevance. Very desirable is that the instruments used be sensitive to developmental changes in cognitive function. The domain of functions assessed by a neuropsychological instrument should reflect the findings of more basic research on cognitive development. Very few instruments, whether developed originally in neuropsychology or for other purposes, such as in the fields of speech pathology or educational testing, meet this requirement today. Perhaps it is best to think of this requirement as a goal for future test development. A related and more manageable concern is the availability of norms. Norms are probably more important in child assessment than in adult work, particularly since the purpose for assessment can be the evaluation of learning disabilities or attentional difficulties, which can vary widely in degree and expression. Additionally, these are problems for which there is no identified cortical lesion and, therefore, there is very little likelihood of predictable and extremely severe deficits occurring that have obvious clinical significance.

It is also necessary to consider that the purpose of a neuropsychological assessment with children almost always involves remediation, which in turn means educational programming. Cognitive rehabilitation—for example, for unilateral neglect—may also be required and may employ procedures that differ little from those used with adults. Because of this need for remediation, coordinated planning with the schools is a must. School personnel such as the school psychologist are likely to be reading the assessment report, and it must therefore be seen as relevant by them and as sensitive to their requirements for treating the child. Here, treatment means more than placement recommendations. It also includes suggestions for instruction and social guidance.

Two minor points should be noted here. First, the assessment battery will have to have within it widely accepted, quality measures of academically pertinent skills. One cannot simply use the Wide Range Achievement Test (WRAT-3) and expect to be able to come up with many educationally relevant recommendations for classroom instruction. Second, in conducting the neuropsychological assessment, a series of relatively brief sessions, especially for younger children, is most appropriate. It is not unusual to have the assessment take place all on one day with a few breaks interspersed, especially in hospital settings. It would seem that much more accurate data could be obtained by having several sessions scheduled during the time of day when the child is best able to perform intellectual tasks. This is especially important for observing executive functions and academic skills.

In presenting the elements of the comprehensive child's battery in Table 3–2, it is assumed that an individualized approach to assessment is being employed. It will be noted that the component areas of the child's battery are basically the same as in the adult battery. Wider choices exist in the child's battery in cognitive ability, language, and visual perceptual assessment. Somewhat more restricted choices are evident for the attention/concentration and memory areas. Executive function, memory, and motor measures are very similar in the two batteries. In the latter areas and selectively in others, the same test is often used as with adults because of the existence of child norms. At times, the child's test is a simplified or reduced

Table 3–2. Comprehensive Neuropsychological Battery for Children

Cognitive Ability
   WISC-R / WISC-III / WAIS-R
   Raven's Colored Progressive Matrices
   Raven's Standard Matrices
Attention/Concentration
   Knox's Cube Test
   Trail Making A,B
   Seashore Rhythm Test (Reitan & Wolfson, 1985)
   WISC-R / WISC-III Freedom from Distractibility Quotient
   Continuous Performance Test (many versions available)
   Token Test for Children (response pattern)
Language Functions
   TOLD-I:2 / TOLD-P:2 / TOAL-3
   TOWL / TOWL-2 / TOWL-3
   Fullerton Language Test for Adolescents
   Token Test for Children
   Comprehensive Receptive and Expressive Vocabulary Test (CREVT)
   Test of Word Finding (TWF, TAWF)
   CELF
   Expressive/Receptive One Word Picture Vocabulary Tests
   Wepman Auditory Series
   Multilingual Aphasia Examination (Schum et al., 1989)
   McCarthy Scales (selected verbal subtests)
Visual Perceptual/Visual Motor
   Bender Gestalt
   Developmental Test of Visual Motor Integration (VMI)
   Motor-Free Visual Perception Test
   Test of Visual Motor Integration (TVMI)
   Kent Visual Perceptual Test
   Jordan Left-Right Reversal Test
   Test of Visual Perceptual Skills
   Bieger Test of Visual Discrimination (Bieger, 1982)
   McCarthy Scales (selected perceptual subtests)
Executive Functions
   Category Test / Intermediate Booklet Category Test
   Children's Category Test
   Wisconsin Card Sorting Test
   Porteus Mazes
   WISC-R / WISC-III Mazes
   Tower of Hanoi / London
   Verbal Fluency Measures (oral and written)
   Stroop Test
Memory
   Wechsler Memory Scale-Revised (older adolescents)
   Wepman Visual Series
   McCarthy Scales (selected memory subtests)
   Learning Efficiency Test-II

Table 3–2. *(Continued)*

Children's Auditory Verbal Learning Test
Selective Reminding Test (Clodfelter et al., 1987)
Wide Range Assessment of Memory and Learning (WRAML)
Test of Memory and Learning (TOMAL)
Motor Skills
Finger Oscillation
Grooved Pegboard
Lateral Dominance Examination
Tactual Perceptual
Elements of Halstead-Reitan Sensory Perceptual Exam
Academic Achievement
Various standardized instruments including diagnostic reading, math, and written
    expression tests.

version of the adult test, that is, the category test. It will be noted in the listings below that some common educational and psychological tests are suggested. The use of such tests is a common practice in child neuropsychological assessment. Telzrow (1989) argues that this approach allows the clinician to select tasks more appropriate to the functioning level and response limitations of the child. She further notes that the use of common instruments allows for a description of the neuropsychological assets of the child in a way that is understandable to school personnel. It also avoids an emphasis on descriptions of brain impairment, which is certainly appropriate in LD cases and even, perhaps, in those where the child has an acquired disorder but where referral issues primarily concern remediation. Of course, at least passable norms exist for such instruments. This is not the case for many traditional instruments in child neuropsychology, such as for those derived from the Halstead-Reitan Battery. Two helpful sets of norms for such instruments are those of Knights and Norwood (1980) and Spreen and Gaddes (1969). The compendium of norms put together by Spreen and Strauss (1991) is very useful in the breadth of tests covered. However, most of the samples covered are very limited in size and other characteristics. Those norms provided for children in such widely used and important tests as Facial Recognition are very limited. The problem of norms for common neuropsychological instruments is most acute for adolescents where less norming has been conducted than for younger children. Perhaps the best practice is to continually check the research literature for norming studies and periodically evaluate the new, better-normed instruments for children that are continually arriving on the market, and make modifications of one's battery where clinical (qualitative) usefulness of the information provided is not compromised.

INTERPRETIVE STRATEGIES

Once the assessment is completed, the data must be evaluated for meaningfulness or interpretability, summarized, and integrated. The result of this process is the formation of a hypothesis or set of hypotheses consistent with the assessment findings and the current neuropsychological literature on brain-behavior relationships in general. The emphasis in one's conclusions today is more likely to be on functional interpretations of the assessment data and their significance in rehabilitation planning than on neurologically oriented specifications of the disorder. In this section, two separable tasks are denoted in the summarizing process. The first is the actual analysis of the test results. The second concerns the strategies for synthesizing these findings.

Analyzing Test Results

In analyzing test results, the most common procedure, which cuts across all assessment strategy approaches, is a level of performance or deficit analysis technique. Here, an individual's performance is compared to norms or cut-off scores. When norms are poorly constructed and/or when evaluating child data, this procedure can lead to the observation of more pathology than is justified given the variability and unreliability of the comparison data. Further, the discrepancies from expectation based solely on norms does not take into account an individual's unique background. For instance, deficits of less than a standard deviation from the mean on some measure—for example, a problem-solving task—can be highly informative when it is likely that premorbid functioning was at a superior level, say, when the patient is a physicist. In general, the background factors to be considered would be the person's native language, handedness, occupation, and premorbid cognitive ability (Orsini, Van Gorp, & Boone, 1988). Related to deficit analysis is the use of pathognomonic signs such as hemispatial neglect or moderate to severe anomia. These markers for brain damage are important to note even in the flexible battery approach to assessment where one's interest is less likely to be on confirming or identifying lesions and more on describing cognitive functions. Intervention planning, the primary goal of this approach, often makes such deficits the initial target of rehabilitation efforts.

Two other common procedures employed in summarizing test results are pattern analysis and the evaluation of lateralizing signs. In the latter case, such factors as asymmetrical deficits in motor speed and tactual perception are used to infer a generalized hemispheric weakness or locus of deficit. The variables employed are generally not at a pathognomonic level. Pattern analysis has been most widely developed in child neuropsychological assessment for learning disabilities. This subtype analysis has generated a very large literature with considerable consistency in findings (Hynd, Connor, & Nieves, 1988). Practical application with respect to remediation has been limited but there are some promising starts (Lyon, Moats, & Flynn, 1988). It is not surprising that this type of analysis has evolved in the learning disability area. In this area, the diagnostic focus can only be a pattern of functional strengths and weaknesses. All brain-behavior interpretations are secondary and often problematic. The major handicap in employing subtype analysis is the variability within subtype profiles. Hynd et al. (1988) make the further point that the variables used in constructing the profiles frequently show weak correlations, at best, with academic skill deficits.

Synthesizing and Interpreting Test Information

As has already been noted, the flexible battery approach is recommended here for most assessment purposes. Most typically, one identifies a pattern of *intraindividual variability* in performance (Telzrow, 1989) and a list of pathognomonic signs from analyzing the test results. It is then necessary to attempt to characterize any evident neuropsychological impairment *and* develop recommendations for intervention. How does one integrate assessment data to produce this interpretation or characterization? The process involved requires the use of medical information and knowledge concerning premorbid functioning, education, work history, and cultural-linguistic background. Even information on test-taking behavior is essential to consider; fatigue, impulsive responding, and potential feigning of deficit all have to be considered. The actual synthesizing of the data follows one of two tracks—separately or simultaneously. The first is the investigation of hypotheses derived from knowledge of brain and behavior relationships from clinical research or from that conducted in cognitive neuropsychology. The cognitive deficits are seen as a pattern related to parameters of brain damage. In this way they are explained. Their severity and mode of expression are still a unique element and require their own elaboration for purposes of remediation.

The second technique for synthesizing neuropsychological assessment data follows what has been termed the *strong inference method* by Fennell and Bauer (1989) because of its association with the model of inductive inference created by Platt (1964). This approach is especially appropriate and efficient when attempting to characterize the functional deficits of the individual. Basically, one creates a series of related hypotheses to explain the result of an assessment task such as poor copying in a visual-constructional task. These hypotheses have to be such that data from another task will support some hypotheses and disconfirm others; for example, in examining a child it may be noted that he or she does well on nonmotoric tests of visual perception, thus ruling out a visual-sensory or visual-perceptual explanation for the constructional deficits on the drawing test. One continues the process of considering hypotheses until only one or perhaps more realistically a small set remains viable, that is, not disconfirmed. In the present example, one would need to consider test data on motor skills independent of visual guidance and on frontal-lobe type tasks that examine planning and organizing skills to track down the deficit appearing on the drawing task. A more formal presentation of this approach for perceptual testing is found in Melamed and Melamed (1985).

REMEDIATION AND REHABILITATION

The results of both procedures for integrating data and characterizing a person's neuropsychological profile, as outlined above, would be used in creating a program of cognitive rehabilitation or, in the case of an LD child, academic remediation. Recovery from brain damage is ordinarily described as involving two processes (Rothi & Horner, 1983). The first is a physiological event in which pathways regain function and active inhibition of cortical areas is lessened or terminated. The second process is termed *substitution* by Rothi and Horner and results from a *reorganization* of the functional system underlying the skill, in Luria's (1980) terms, by adding new subroutines and dropping impaired aspects. One can also include the use of assistive devices in this mode of recovery. Cognitive rehabilitation for acquired brain damage generally focuses on both the use of these assistive devices and the fostering of the development of new functional systems. At times, particularly in the early stages of recovery, an attempt to stimulate certain functions such as sustained attention may be attempted. On the other hand, for disorders such as learning disabilities and attentional deficits, which are not approached as acquired deficits in most circumstances, the use of assistive devices and compensatory strategies dominates in neuropsychologically based interventions. For instance, Hartlage and Telzrow (1983) suggest both matching treatment to learner aptitudes following the lead of Chronbach and Snow (1977) and employing assistive devices. Here, aptitudes are the neuropsychological strengths from the child's assessment profile. A very interesting approach to educational remediation is offered by Hynd (1986), who uses a compensatory strategy that combines the use of the child's strengths with an interpretation of the process of reading based on models developed from research in neurolinguistics and cognitive neuropsychology. Thus a visual-spatial whole word approach to vocabulary building such as the Edmark Reading Program would be recommended for a phonological dyslexic, that is, a child who can read familiar words well, especially nouns, but has difficulty with phoneme-to-grapheme correspondence rules.

Case Example 3–1.   Cognitive rehabilitation—Child with CVA

This case has all the elements that make an assessment very difficult. The case concerns a 7-year-old boy (W. E.), who suffered a right hemispheric infarct following cardiac surgery at age 4. A recent CT scan indicated that such structures as the middle frontal gyrus, right lentiform nucleus, and external capsule were involved. The child has left hemiplegia and reoccurring partial complex seizures although their severity has decreased. He is considered very hyperactive by his family and a physician. The remainder of W. E.'s medical history is unremarkable. As this child's lesion occurred early in life, there is no really useful premorbid school or testing history with which to compare current findings. W. E. was brought for assessment because he was making little progress in his first-grade work and the school was considering having him repeat first grade. His mother was concerned that W. E. required specialized educational intervention that was tailored to his unique cognitive and behavioral profile and would not benefit by simply repeating first grade.

The most prominent aspect of W. E.'s behavior during assessment was his constant motion. He demonstrated significant difficulty in both engaging and sustaining his attention. He could be echolalic, repeating words voiced by the examiner and then perseverate on them. It was possible to get valid data by using a reward system for time-on-task and by gaining W. E.'s attention through the examiner randomly modulating his voice and changing his seating pattern.

Case Example 3–1. *(Continued)*

A Full Scale WISC-R IQ of 78 was obtained with Verbal and Performance IQs of 75 and 85, respectively. Scatter was from 3 (Information, Block Design) to 10 (Picture Arrangement, Object Assembly). Since this test was given by the school psychologist, no information was available about W. E.'s strategies on some of these tasks. His performance on the Raven's test was somewhat higher (Standard Score or IQ = 80) than might be expected by his 3 in Block Design, indicating that the motor requirements of the latter task likely interfered with his performance. W. E.'s academic achievement, as measured by the WRAT-R, was very limited. He knew only his uppercase letters. He was unable to read any word and could not make reasonable guesses. He did not demonstrate any decoding strategies. With respect to arithmetic, he did not consistently respond correctly to the + and − symbols. He could do single-digit addition problems orally that he could not do in written form, as long as the sum remained below 7.

With respect to visual perceptual skills, W. E. performed very poorly whether a motor response was required (comparing DTVMI and Bender drawings with performance on the Motor-Free Test of Visual Perception). He appeared to have great difficulty with visual analysis, finding it very difficult to discriminate individual form features. Using subtests from the McCarthy battery and spatial memory tests such as the one by Wepman demonstrated spatial confusion, poor immediate visual memory, and severe visual-motor deficits. His performance level was typically at about the 5-year-old level except for more complex reasoning tasks where he was typically at about a 6-year-old level of performance. Several strategies for assessing unilateral spatial neglect were used and failed to demonstrate its occurrence.

A wide range of language tests were employed with W. E. given his poor performance on the WISC-R Verbal scale and the fact that there is a rather large research literature on the linguistic consequences of unilateral right hemisphere lesions in childhood. Most of the instruments employed were standard ones, such as the McCarthy verbal subtests, the TOLD-P, Token Test, and the EOWPVT and ROWPVT. Additionally, measures of fluency and phonemic discrimination were employed. W. E. showed a pattern of results that was consistent with the research literature: adequate grammatical skills and articulation, reduced confrontational naming, some dysfluency, and occasional stuttering. Overall, receptive language skills were superior to expressive ones. W. E. was marginally better dealing with semantic aspects than syntactic features.

The final area of testing concerned tactual perceptual skills and motor behavior. Instruments employed were primarily from the Reitan Battery for Young Children. W. E. could only employ his right hand and was able to demonstrate good fine-motor skills on a pegboard task, adequate ballistic speed, good tactual form perception, and normative spatial localization.

In the case of W. E., the major source of hypotheses about his deficits came from knowledge about his illness and the research literature on the cognitive consequences of such lesions. Additionally, testing was very thorough in the perceptual and language areas in order to aid in the development of a strategy for educational intervention at his beginning reading level. Because of W. E.'s attentional deficits, the overall testing was limited in scope, with memory evaluation being most affected. In the final report to the school, W. E.'s neuropsychological profile was presented in considerable detail

(continued)

Case Example 3–1. *(Continued)*

with the deficits indicated above presented very clearly along with somewhat of an explanation of how they relate to his illness. It was argued in this report that W. E. would need an individualized educational plan that is tailored to his complex neuropsychological profile and a classroom environment that could minimize his attentional drift and allow for the involved and adaptable programming required to help him. Instructional recommendations included suggestions for increasing his verbal fluency and clarifying his perception of other children's feelings. With respect to reading, the suggestion was made to use a multisensory approach given the limitations he shows in visual perception and phonemic discrimination. His adequate tactual perceptual skills should benefit him in this approach. Given his severe visual-constructional deficits, it was suggested that he begin on computer work very soon, particularly if writing instruction remains frustrating and offers little success. The strategy suggested for arithmetic was based on a substitution strategy in which he verbalizes arithmetic operations as he performs them.

Case Example 3–2.   Academic remediation—Adolescent with ADHD

As an example of using neuropsychological assessment techniques for the analysis of an ADHD condition, the case of a 15-year-old Caucasian female will be discussed here. The presenting problem was very typical of referrals for this condition. L. Y. was considered a very bright child by her parents and, indeed, had a record of strong academic performance in the elementary grades. During middle school, her performance became somewhat more variable but was still in the upper B range overall. For her high-school career, she transferred to a very competitive parochial school and found it very difficult to maintain her previous performance level. Her first three semesters produced grades that were in the C range or below and she was receiving much individual attention from teachers in many areas, including foreign language and algebra. She was not able to keep up with homework assignments and special projects. She had fallen weeks behind in some courses and had no coherent strategy for gaining ground. In discussing her academic difficulties, L. Y. noted that she had particular difficulty in written work, including essay-type exams where she had problems finding appropriate words and in working quickly enough. She also reported difficulty keeping up with most teachers in her attempts at note taking. With respect to attentional difficulties, L. Y. reports that she has always had difficulty concentrating in class but that this problem is more acute in high school because of the challenging curriculum. Her mother reports that L. Y. will occasionally "zone out," that is, not listen when she gets bored. To counter this behavior, her mother will ask L. Y. to repeat things to make sure she is attending. Interestingly, in the area of executive functions, L. Y. is described as flexible, sufficiently organized, and able to accommodate changing circumstances. As is not uncommon in these referrals, L. Y.'s general affect at this time indicated the likelihood of depression. It should be pointed out that L. Y. was performing at a higher level than many similar clients seen in the previous few years where the modal client has been an adolescent male with high-average or superior WISC-III

Case Example 3–2. *(Continued)*

performance and low grades. Almost always, there is the same pattern of good early school performance with dramatic changes around the middle-school years or a little earlier. As is typically the case in these individuals, L. Y. had an unremarkable medical history. Her mother indicated that there were no pregnancy or delivery problems and that her daughter's early medical history was uneventful. There was no history of otitis media, head injury, or seizure disorder. Developmental milestones were met at a normal pace or sooner.

Before indicating the results of L. Y.'s assessment, it is necessary to discuss the differences that exist between an assessment used to support a *DSM-IV* diagnosis of ADHD and that used to characterize an impairment of attentional mechanisms from a neuropsychological point of view. The *DSM-IV* criteria refer to symptoms of inattention and/or hyperactivity-impulsivity as reflected in everyday behavior. Thus inattention refers to such behaviors as making careless mistakes, not listening when spoken to, and being reluctant to engage in tasks that take sustained effort. Hyperactivity and impulsivity require even less reference to inference about behaviors such as leaving one's seat in the classroom or blurting out answers before questions have been completed. There is a hint, for want of a better word, of a connection with a model of attentional processes in the criteria for inattention, that is, difficulty *sustaining* attention. In neuropsychology, the focus is less on observational data and questionnaires referring to observation and more on determining the individual's ability to demonstrate normative attentional skills as these are understood in cognitive neuroscience (Grodzinsky & Diamond, 1992; Loge, Staton, & Beatty, 1990; Posner & Peterson, 1990). The focus is on mechanisms for controlling, directing, and sustaining attention and those for underlying executive functions. The cortical areas involved are primarily the parietal and frontal lobes. Tests are employed which are thought to measure skills that are associated with these constructs. Typically measures of sustained, selective, alternating, and perhaps divided attention are employed (cf. Lezak, 1995). Additionally, assessment of executive functions, such as the ability to plan, organize, and effectively carry out one's goal-directed activities, are examined using a wide range of frontal-lobe measures. These include tests of motor planning, verbal fluency, conceptual reasoning, and mental flexibility.

Test results confirmed that L. Y. had above-average cognitive ability although the accompanying WISC-III profile was exceptional, with a Verbal IQ of 101 and a Performance IQ of 125. There was even a greater discrepancy when the Verbal Comprehension factor score (104) and Perceptual Organization factor score (130) were compared. L. Y.'s performance was only in the average range on subtests thought to be most directly related to attentional and executive processes (Freedom from Distractibility factor score = 96; Coding score = 9; Mazes score = 11). On measures of academic skills, L. Y. demonstrated abilities in mathematics superior to those in reading and written expression. In all these areas, her performance had characteristics that were consistent with attentional difficulties. In mathematics, her score was not in the superior range only because of a number of careless, uncorrected mistakes. None of the errors were conceptual. She read exceptionally fast on the GORT-3 with average accuracy and comprehension. She claimed she would do even worse in comprehension if she read more slowly. It was clear that she depended strongly on context cues in

(continued)

Case Example 3–2. *(Continued)*

gaining comprehension. Her written language performance (TOWL) was her poorest, in the low-average range. She did adequately on such measures as vocabulary and handwriting but was very inattentive to visual information and organizational demands in her spontaneous writing sample. The same thing was true on a more structured subtest where allegiance to style conventions was required.

On measures of sustained (Trail Making Part A, Knox's Cube Test), selective (Stroop Test), and alternating attention (Trail Making Part B), L. Y. performed, at best, in the below-average range. In contrast, she did quite well on executive function tasks such as the Wisconsin Card Sorting Test. Her only below-average score was on a verbal fluency task. On measures of visual perceptual, somesthetic perception, and motor skills, she did very well. On the other hand, L. Y.'s performance on language measures was mixed, with mild difficulties apparent in confrontational naming, repetition, and fluency. Memory scores were above average to superior in all domains. L. Y. performed quite well on verbal-learning procedures that were effortful and required active strategizing. It should be noted that personality testing indicated a moderate elevation in both depression and anxiety. Her cognitive difficulties did not appear to derive from the emotional difficulties for a number of reasons, including their chronicity, the particular profile with its emphasis on linguistic deficits, and her ability to strategize effectively and perform well on effortful tasks.

The impression from this assessment was that L. Y. is an individual of superior nonverbal cognitive ability along with average verbal processing skills. Her academic skills were seen as moderately below expectancy, particularly in the areas of basic reading skills and written expression—more so if her Performance IQ is considered a more appropriate as an ability measure. Her school performance appeared to be negatively impacted by two factors: (1) an uneven development of linguistic processes that includes a difficulty in organizing and sequencing elements in both oral and written production and (2) an ADHD condition (*DSM-IV:* 314.00, Predominantly Inattentive Type). She demonstrated consistent deficits on all attention measures. It was very difficult to concentrate for long periods of time, to shift set between tasks or components of tasks, and for her to ignore irrelevant information and maintain her focus on the task at hand. To a much lesser extent, she also demonstrated executive function deficits such as in her ability to organize her verbal output. Within our clinical practice, the *DSM-IV* diagnosis of Predominantly Inattentive Type is that assigned to most adolescent and adult clients. However, the typical profile more likely involves executive function deficits rather than the attentional difficulties demonstrated by L. Y.

The specific recommendations for L. Y. reflected the nature of her ADHD condition along with the emotional distress she demonstrated. She was referred to a pediatric psychiatrist for possible pharmacological intervention. She was also provided with a number of strategies for sustaining her vigilance in the classroom. Examples include monitoring class activity with a time sheet and employing subvocal, self-initiated prompts. Recommendations for homework included the use of distributed sessions and monitoring. L. Y. was also provided a description of study strategies that would aid her retrieval of material on exams. Finally, recommendations also included strategies for compensating for her difficulties in written expression. The argument was made that L. Y. was experiencing the consequences of a specific learning difficulty in this area, so suggested accommodations and intervention strategies were recommended for the school.

CONCLUSION

Neuropsychological assessment is a field that has deep roots in both the clinical science of behavioral neurology and experimental cognitive science. It is a field that requires an interest in both neuroscience and behavior. In this chapter it has been demonstrated how a continuous process of development has been taking place in clinical neuropsychology in which constructs from these two fields have been combined to produce effective strategies for assessing and interpreting the effects of brain damage or anomalous development on behavior. What is most promising is the accelerated rate at which new assessment instruments have been created that reflect the constructs being developed in the cognitive science area. Perhaps equally important has been the progress in the development of assessment strategies, such as the process approach, and the clarification of the advantages of the use of a flexible assessment battery, as the focus of clinical neuropsychological practice has shifted to intervention. It is in this last area where progress has not been altogether satisfactory. Progress in the development of cognitive rehabilitation strategies and research on their effectiveness has not kept pace with advances in assessment. Given the close association desired today between assessment and treatment, this relative neglect of rehabilitation is likely to lessen in the near future.

REFERENCES

American Psychiatric Association. (1994). *Diagnostic and Statistical Manual-IV.* Washington DC: Author.

Baddeley, A.D. (1986). *Working memory.* Oxford: Clarendon.

Bakker, D.J. (1994). Dyslexia and the ecological brain. *Journal of Clinical & Experimental Neuropsychology, 16,* 734–743.

Barkley, R.A. (1991). The ecological validity of laboratory and analogue assessment methods of ADHD symptoms. *Journal of Abnormal Child Psychology, 19,* 149–178.

Barkley, R.A., Godzinsky, G.M., & DuPaul, G.J. (1992). Frontal lobe functioning in Attention Deficit disorder with and without hyperactivity: A review and research report. *Journal of Abnormal Child Psychology, 20,* 163–188.

Benton, A.L. (1974). *The Revised Visual Retention Test.* New York: Psychological Corporation.

Benton, A.L., & Hamsher, K. deS. (1983). *Multilingual Aphasia Examination.* Iowa City: AJA Associates.

Benton, A.L., Hamsher, K. deS., Varney, N.R., & Spreen, O. (1983). *Contributions to neuropsychological assessment: A clinical manual.* New York: Oxford.

Bieger, E. (1982). *Bieger Test of Visual Discrimination.* Chicago: Stoelting.

Bigler, E.D., Yeo, R.A., & Turkheimer, E. (1989). *Neuropsychological function and brain imaging.* New York: Plenum Press.

Bornstein, R.A. (1985). Normative data on selected neuropsychological measures from a nonclinical sample. *Journal of Clinical Psychology, 41,* 651–659.

Buschke, H., & Fuld, P.A. (1974). Evaluating storage, retention, and retrieval in disordered memory and learning. *Neurology, 24,* 1019–1025.

Christensen, A. (1975). *Luria's neuropsychological investigation: Text.* New York: Spectrum.

Chronbach, L.J., & Snow, R.E. (1977). *Aptitudes and instructional methods.* New York: Irvington.

Clodfelter, C.J., Dickson, A.L., Wilkes, C.N., & Johnson, R.B. (1987). Alternate forms of selective reminding for children. *The Clinical Neuropsychologist, 1,* 243–249.

DeArmond, S.J., Fusco, M.M., & Dewey, M.M. (1989). *Structure of the human brain: A photographic atlas* (3rd ed.). New York: Oxford University Press.

Delis, D.C., Kramer, J.H., Kaplan, E., & Ober, B.A. (1987). *California Verbal Learning Test.* New York: Harcourt Brace Jovanovich.

Fennell, E.B., & Bauer, R.M. (1989). Models of inference in evaluating brain-behavior relationships in children. In C.R. Reynolds & E. Fletcher-Janzen (Eds.), *Handbook of clinical child neuropsychology* (pp. 167–177). New York: Plenum Press.

Fletcher, J.M., & Satz, P. (1980). Developmental changes in the neuropsychological correlates of reading achievement: A six-year longitudinal follow-up. *Journal of Clinical Neuropsychology, 2,* 23–37.

Funkenstein, H.H. (1988). Cerebrovascular disorders. In M.S. Albert & M.B. Moss (Eds.), *Geriatric neuropsychology* (pp.179–207). New York: Guilford Press.

Golden, C.J. (1981). A standardized version of Luria's neuropsychological tests. In S. Filskow & T.J. Boll (Eds.), *Handbook of clinical neuropsychology* (pp. 608–642). New York: Wiley.

Goldstein, K. (1944). The mental changes due to frontal lobe damage. *Journal of Psychology, 17,* 187–208.

Goodglass, H., & Kaplan, E. (1983). *The assessment of aphasia and related disorders* (2nd ed.). Philadelphia: Lea & Febiger.

Goodyear, P., & Hynd, G.W. (1992). Attention-Deficit Disorder with (ADD/H) and without (ADD/WO) Hyperactivity: Behavioral and Neuropsychological Differentiation. *Journal of Clinical Child Psychology, 21,* 273–305.

Grodzinsky, G.M., & Diamond, R. (1992). Frontal lobe functioning in boys with attention-deficit hyperactivity disorder. *Developmental Neuropsychology, 8,* 427–445.

Halstead, W.C. (1947). *Brain and intelligence: A quantitative study of the frontal lobe.* Chicago: University of Chicago Press.

Hartlage, L.C., & Telzrow, C.F. (1983). The neuropsychological bases of educational intervention. *Journal of Learning Disabilities, 16,* 521–528.

Heaton, R.K, Grant, I., & Mathews, C.G. (1991). *Comprehensive norms for an expanded Halstead-Reitan battery.* Odessa, FL: Psychological Assessment Resources.

Hynd, C.R. (1986). Educational intervention in children with developmental learning disorders. In J.E. Obrzut & G.W. Hynd (Eds.), *Child neuropsychology: Clinical practice* (pp. 265–297). New York: Academic Press.

Hynd, G.W., Connor, R.T., & Nieves, N. (1988). Learning disability subtypes: Perspectives and methodological issues in clinical assessment. In M.G. Tramontana & S.R. Hooper (Eds.), *Assessment issues in child neuropsychology* (pp. 281–312). New York: Plenum Press.

Kaplan, E. (1989). A process approach to neuropsychological assessment. In T. Boll & B.K. Bryant (Eds.), *Clinical neuropsychology and brain function: Research, measurement, and practice* (pp. 129–167). Washington, DC: American Psychological Association.

Kaplan, E., Fein, D., Morris, R., & Delis, D.C. (1991). *The Wechsler Adult Intelligence Scale-Revised as a Neuropsychological Instrument.* San Antonio, TX: The Psychological Corporation.

Kaplan, E., Goodglass, H., & Weintraub, S. (1983). *Boston Naming Test.* Philadelphia: Lea & Febiger.

Knights, R.M., & Norwood, J.A. (1980). *Revised smooth normative data on the neuropsychological test battery for children.* Ottawa: Knights Psychological Consultants.

Kolb, B., & Whishaw, I.Q. (1995). *Fundamentals of human neuropsychology* (4th ed.). New York: W.H. Freeman & Co.

Lezak, M.D. (1984). An individualized approach to neuropsychological assessment. In P.E. Logue & J.M. Schear (Eds.), *Clinical neuropsychology: A multidisciplinary approach* (pp. 29–49). Springfield: Charles C. Thomas.

Lezak, M.D. (1995). *Neuropsychological assessment* (3rd ed.). New York: Oxford University Press.

Loge, D.V., Staton, R.D., & Beatty, W.W. (1990). Performance of children with ADHD on tests sensitive to frontal lobe dysfunction. *Journal of the American Academy of Child and Adolescent Psychiatry, 29,* 540–545.

Luria, A.R. (1980). *Higher cortical function in man* (2nd ed.). New York: Basic Books.

Lyon, G.R., Moats, L., & Flynn, J.M. (1988). From assessment to treatment: Linkage to interventions with children. In M.G. Tramontana & S.R. Hooper (Eds.), *Assessment issues in child neuropsychology* (pp. 113–144). New York: Plenum Press.

Mattis, S., French, J. H., & Rapin, I. (1975). Dyslexia in children and young adults: Three independent neuropsychological syndromes. *Developmental Medicine and Child Neurology, 17,* 150–163.

McCarthy, R.A., & Warrington, E.K. (1990). *Cognitive neuropsychology: A clinical introduction.* New York: Academic Press.

McNeil, M.R., & Prescott, T.E. (1978). *Revised Token Test.* Baltimore: University Park Press.

Mega, M.S., & Cummings, J.L. (1994). Frontal-subcortical circuits and neuropsychiatric disorders. *The Journal of Neuropsychiatry and Clinical Neurosciences, 6,* 358–370.

Melamed, L.E., & Melamed, E.C. (1985). Neuropsychology of perception. In L.C. Hartlage & C.F. Telzrow (Eds.), *The neuropsychology of individual differences* (pp. 61–91). New York: Plenum Press.

Melamed, L.E., & Rugle, L. (1989). Neuropsychological correlates of school achievement in young children: Longitudinal findings with a construct valid perceptual processing instrument. *Journal of Clinical and Experimental Neuropsychology, 11,* 745–762.

Moffitt, T.E., & Silva, P. A. (1988). Self-reported delinquency, neuropsychological deficit, and history of attention deficit disorder. *Journal of Abnormal Child Psychology, 16,* 553–569.

Orsini, D.L., Van Gorp, W.G., & Boone, K.B. (1988). *The neuropsychology casebook.* New York: Springer-Verlag.

Platt, J.R. (1964). Strong inference. *Science, 146,* 347–353.

Posner, M.I. (1989). Structure and functions of selective attention. In T. Boll & B.K. Bryant (Eds.), *Clinical neuropsychology and brain function: Research, measurement, and practice* (pp. 173–202). Washington DC: American Psychological Association.

Posner, M.I., & Peterson, S.E. (1990). The attention system of the human brain. *Annual Review of Neuroscience, 13,* 25–42.

Reitan, R.M., & Wolfson, D. (1985). *The Halstead-Reitan Neuropsychological Test Battery: Theory and clinical interpretation.* Tucson, Az: Neuropsychology Press.

Reschly, D.J., & Gresham, F.M. (1989). Current neuropsychological diagnosis of learning problems: A leap of faith. In C.R. Reynolds & E. Fletcher-Janzen (Eds.), *Handbook of clinical child neuropsychology* (pp. 503–519). New York: Plenum Press.

Rothi, L.J., & Horner, J. (1983). Restitution and substitution: Two theories of recovery with application to neurobehavioral treatment. *Journal of Clinical Neuropsychology, 5,* 73–81.

Rourke, B.P., & Orr, R.L. (1977). Prediction of the reading and spelling performance of normal and retarded readers: Four-year follow-up. *Journal of Abnormal Child Psychology, 5,* 9–20.

Russell, E.W., & Starkey, R.I. (1993). *Halstead Russell Neuropsychological Evaluation System.* Los Angeles: Western Psychological Services.

Schum, R.L., Sivan, A.B., & Benton, A.R. (1989). Multilingual Aphasia Examination: Norms for children. *The Clinical Neuropsychologist, 3,* 375–383.

Shue, K.L., & Douglas V.I. (1992). Attention deficit hyperactivity disorder and the frontal lobe syndrome. *Brain and Cognition, 20,* 104–124.

Sivan, A.B. (1992). *Benton Visual Retention Test* (5th edition). San Antonio, TX: The Psychological Corporation.

Spiers, P.A. (1982). The Luria-Nebraska Neuropsychology Battery revisited: A theory in practice or just practicing? *Journal of Consulting and Clinical Psychology, 50,* 301–306.

Spreen, O., & Gaddes, W. (1969). Developmental norms for fifteen neuropsychological tests for ages 6 to 15. *Cortex, 5,* 171–191.

Spreen, O., & Strauss, E. (1991). *A compendium of neuropsychological tests: Administration, norms, and commentary.* New York: Oxford University Press.

Stambrook, M. (1983). The Luria-Nebraska Neuropsychological Battery: A promise that *may* be partly fulfilled. *Journal of Clinical Neuropsychology, 5,* 247–269.

Stone, M.H., & Wright, B.D. (1980). *Knox's Cube Test.* Chicago: Stoelting.

Telzrow, C.F. (1989). Neuropsychological applications of common educational and psychological tests. In C.R. Reynolds & E. Fletcher-Janzen (Eds.), *Handbook of clinical child neuropsychology* (pp. 227–246). New York: Plenum Press.

Trenerry, M.R., Crosson, B., DeBoe, J., & Leber, W.R. (1989). *The Stroop Neuropsychological Screening Test.* Odessa, FL: Psychological Assessment Resources.

Trenerry, M.R., Crosson, B., DeBoe, J., & Leber, W.R. (1990). *Visual Search and Attention Test.* Odessa, FL: Psychological Assessment Resources.

Warrington, E.K. (1984). *Recognition Memory Test.* Windsor: Nelson.

Watson, B.U., Goldgar, D.E., & Ryschon, K.L. (1983). Subtypes of reading disability. *Journal of Clinical Neuropsychology, 5,* 377–399.

Webster, R.E. (1992). *Learning Efficiency Test-II.* Novato, CA: Academic Therapy Publications.

Wechsler, D.A. (1987). *Wechsler Memory Scale-Revised.* New York: Harcourt Brace Jovanovich.

Welsh, M.C. (1994). Executive function and the assessment of attention deficit hyperactivity disorder. In N.C. Jordon & J. Goldsmith (Eds.), *Learning disabilities: New directions for assessment and intervention* (pp. 21–42). Boston: Allyn & Bacon.

Welsh, M.C., Pennington, B.F., & Groisser, D.B. (1991). A normative-developmental study of executive function: A window on prefrontal function in children. *Developmental Neuropsychology, 7,* 131–149.

Williams, J.M. (1991). *Memory Assessment Scales.* Odessa, FL: Psychological Assessment Resources.

Chapter 4

COMPUTER-ASSISTED ASSESSMENT

CLEBORNE D. MADDUX AND LAMONT JOHNSON

The 1980s was a decade of rapid growth in the implementation of computer technology in education and related endeavors such as psychology and counseling. One of the most rapidly growing uses of computing continues to be in the area of assessment. A clear trend toward automating assessment procedures was emerging in the mid-to-late 1980s. For example, Meier and Geiger (1986) suggested that "human services professionals are witnessing an unprecedented growth in the automation of instruments for psychological and career assessment" (p. 29). Green (1988) asserted that "small, versatile computers are changing the way tests are given, and changing the kinds of tests being given" (p. 223). Madsen (1986) predicted that during the next decade, computer-assisted testing would increase tenfold; Johnson (1979) went even further and predicted that by the next century, *all* testing would be done by computer.

There are probably several reasons for the rapid growth during the 1980s and 1990s in use of computers in assessment. Increasing caseloads of human services personnel in the face of budget cuts in social programs (another trend of the 1980s) undoubtedly played a role. Walker and Myrick (1985) alluded to this factor when they wrote, "This new technology seems to have the potential to revolutionize the testing responsibilities of school psychologists, particularly those with heavy testing loads" (p. 51). Then, too, it was not until the eighties that powerful but inexpensive microcomputers first became widely available (Eberly & Cech, 1986).

Whatever the reasons for increased interest in incorporating computers into the assessment process, the growth trend is now well established. Jacob and Brantley (1987) surveyed 268 school psychologists and reported that 72% used computers in their assessment work. Further, of those who did not use computers at the time of the survey, many reported that they planned to use them in the future (33% planned to use them for data storage, 30% for test scoring, and 30% for report writing). By 1993, it became evident that earlier predictions were clearly on target. Mead and Drasgow (1993), after a thorough review, concluded that

> Clinical instruments, personality scales, job attitude surveys, and cognitive tests are among the many types of psychological assessment instruments that have been converted to computerized administration. Such computerized assessments are easy to administer; usually require fewer proctors and less proctor training; provide faster results; are less prone to errors; and, in some cases, allow fewer opportunities for

cheating. Moreover, as personal computers become less expensive, the costs associated with computerized assessment continue to decrease. Clearly, computerized assessments of psychological variables are already popular and seem to be growing in usage. (p. 449)

Another indication of the growing interest in the use of computers in assessment is the recent appearance of a number of new journals, including *Computers in Human Behavior, Computers in Human Services, Computers in Psychiatry/Psychology,* and *Computers in the Schools* (Kramer, 1988). In addition, the American Psychological Association's Committee on Professional Standards, in conjunction with the Committee on Psychological Tests and Assessment, has published *Standards for Computer-Based Tests and Interpretations* (APA, 1986).

HISTORY AND DEVELOPMENT

Neither computerized assessment procedures, in general, nor automated testing, in particular, is new. One of the earliest proponents of automated testing was Sidney Pressey (1926, 1927). Pressey noted that objective tests, used widely in the military during World War I, were becoming commonplace in schools. Pressey feared that teachers would soon be overwhelmed by bookkeeping and other routine tasks related to administering and scoring these tests. To solve this problem, he developed an experimental testing machine to administer multiple-choice items to students.

Pressey's device presented a question followed by several alternative answers. In the earliest version of the device, both question and answer appeared in a slot on the machine. Later versions had questions and alternatives on a printed page (Travers, 1967). Pressey also experimented with the machine's potential for instruction. Although many educators and psychologists were interested in Pressey's device, it was never widely implemented.

B.F. Skinner (1954, 1958) was responsible for the next cycle of interest in what came to be termed *teaching machines.* Skinner's machine differed from Pressey's in several respects, including the ability to handle essay-type questions:

Material is printed in 30 radial frames on a 12-inch disk. The student inserts the disk and closes the machine. He cannot proceed until the machine has been locked, and, once he has begun, the machine cannot be unlocked. All but a corner of one frame is visible through a window. The student writes his response on a paper strip exposed through a second opening. By lifting a lever on the front of the machine, he moves what he has written under a transparent cover and uncovers the correct response in the remaining corner of the frame. If the two responses correspond, he moves the lever horizontally. This movement punches a hole in the paper opposite his response, recording the fact that he called it correct, and alters the machine so that the frame will not appear again when the student works around the disk a second time. Whether the response was correct or not, a second frame appears when the lever is returned to its starting position. The student proceeds in this way until he has responded to all frames. He then works around the disk a second time, but only those frames appear to which he has not correctly responded. When the disk revolves without stopping, the assignment is finished. (Skinner, 1958, p. 974)

Many others became interested in teaching machines. However, once again, the machines never really caught on, although a number of different designs were successfully built and tested.

Although teaching machines were never widely implemented, the principles employed by Skinner and others (especially task analysis and reinforcement) were later applied to printed materials such as books and workbooks. The use of such materials came to be termed *programmed instruction*. The programmed instruction movement gained a considerable following, peaked during the early 1960s, and declined rapidly thereafter. Readers who are interested in the history of this movement are referred to excellent analyses by Criswell (1989), Gayeski (1989), Osguthorpe and Zhou (1989), and Skinner himself (1986).

At about the same time that programmed instruction gained its brief popularity, there were a number of experimental educational computing projects that incorporated assessment components. The Programmed Logic for Automatic Teaching Operations Project (PLATO) and the Stanford Project were the most well known as well as the most ambitious of these ventures.

The PLATO project was developed at the University of Illinois. This system, which may have been the largest computer-assisted instructional and testing system ever developed (Burke, 1982), began as a student workstation connected to a large, mainframe computer and evolved into a highly interactive network through which entire courses could be offered to many learners, each using the special PLATO terminal. Over a thousand separate PLATO programs were developed, and the system was installed on mainframe computers housed on a number of university campuses.

The Stanford Project was headed by Patrick Suppes and Richard Atkinson and was aimed at improving instruction in math and reading. This computer project was to involve three levels: drill and practice, tutorials, and questioning routines. The first two of these levels were successfully implemented, but the questioning routines were never perfected.

Projects such as PLATO and the Stanford Project were widely discussed and extensively written about but never widely used. One of the problems with such systems was their expense. Microcomputers did not exist, and these systems required use of a mainframe computer. Mainframes were immensely expensive; experienced frequent, costly breakdowns; required a large operational staff; and allowed few users at any one time. Therefore, rental of time on these machines was costly. The special workstations and the telephone lines required were other expenses that most public school systems were unable or unwilling to accept. There were other problems as well, including the fact that most teachers were unfamiliar with the technology involved and did not know how to make good use of such systems. Then, too, at about this time federal support for educational research and development began to decline, making funding even more difficult.

Thus, although education and psychology experienced a number of periods marked by interest in a variety of computerized assessment applications, it was not until recently that such applications became widely—and inexpensively—available. With wide availability, however, has come a variety of real and potential advantages and disadvantages. This chapter will discuss both and will provide some guidelines for educators and others who are contemplating the use of computerized assessment procedures. No attempt will be made to review specific software. Not only would a comprehensive review be far beyond the scope of a single chapter, but changes are occurring so rapidly that such a review would be out of date before it was published. Instead, this chapter will concentrate on providing guidelines to help assessment professionals choose among the software currently available as well as among software that will become available in the future.

SOME GENERAL PROBLEMS IN COMPUTING AND IN ASSESSMENT

Before beginning a discussion of the use of computers in assessment, it may be helpful to discuss general problems in each of these areas that may have important implications for those who would combine the two activities.

Some General Considerations Related to Computing

Few would argue that computers have enjoyed wide acceptance, approval, and implementation in business, the military, and many other walks of life. There are many reasons for this near-universal acceptance, and space will not permit a comprehensive discussion. What is most relevant to the present discussion, however, is a lesson from cultural anthropology. Anthropologists have long realized that successful technological change is always linked to the values a society endorses (Kneller, 1965). Americans associate computers with a variety of powerful values about work, including belief in the importance of speed, accuracy, precision, and the removal of human error from work activities (Maddux, Johnson, & Willis, in press).

Because computers are perceived as promoting these goals, they were widely accepted first by the military and business subcultures, and they were then sanctioned for use in schools by those who control school policy. (In this country, school boards are the most common controllers, and these boards are usually dominated by successful businessmen [Boocock, 1980]).

The point is that since Americans associate computers with these respected values, they have a tendency to believe that computerizing an activity automatically improves it in some important way. Weizenbaum (1976) has addressed this phenomenon:

> It is important to understand very clearly that strengthening a particular technique—putting muscles on it—contributes nothing to its validity. For example, there are computer programs that carry out with great precision all the calculations required to cast the horoscope of an individual whose time and place of birth are known. Because the computer does all the tedious symbol manipulations, they can be done much more quickly and in much more detail than is normally possible for a human astrologer. But

such an improvement in the technique of horoscope casting is irrelevant to the validity of astrological forecasting. If astrology is nonsense, then computerized astrology is just as surely nonsense. (pp. 34–35)

Thus, there is a tendency to believe that whenever techniques are computerized, progress has been made. Actually, computerizing often (but not always) stream-lines or otherwise improves the way an idea is put into action. Improving the way an idea is operationalized, however, does not necessarily improve the idea itself. Com-puters may simply make it easier, faster, or more convenient to continue carrying out a bad idea. For example, if the analysis of discrepancies between verbal and achievement IQ scores does not contribute to accuracy in diagnosis or remediation, speeding up that analysis or improving the accuracy of the calculations by employ-ing computers does not address the real problem.

The illusion of progress is dangerous because it may cause us to neglect thinking about and evaluating the concepts that underlie our actions and cause us to focus exclusively on putting muscles on existing techniques. Thus, while computers may or may not help us be innovative in our approach to technique, they have a tendency to make us more conservative and less likely to consider and adopt new ideas.

Another contributor to this phenomenon is the fact that computerizing requires considerable time, effort, and expense. Therefore, once this process is viewed as completed and computers are in place, there is often great reluctance to make even minor adjustments. It is not unusual for consultants to be told to make recommenda-tions concerning changes in any and every aspect of an organization's functioning with the exception of some aspect that has been recently computerized. Administra-tors and workers alike often feel that too much time, effort, and expense went into a recent computer implementation to consider any changes for at least several years.

These problems are related to a larger phenomenon we have called the *Everest Syndrome* (Maddux, 1984). This syndrome is characterized by the belief that com-puters should be implemented simply because they are there. Those who indulge in this syndrome do so because they have neglected to ask what tasks ought to be submitted to computer solutions, and assume that computers should be used to do whatever they *can* be made to do. Eberly and Cech (1986) refer to this problem: "Computer technology has been almost uncritically integrated into the counseling process" (p. 24). This chapter will attempt to *make* the case that while many assessment tasks can be turned over to computers, some clearly should not be computerized.

Some General Considerations Related to Assessment

There are a number of reasons why caution should be exercised in integrating computers and assessment. Standardized testing is currently misunderstood by the public and by many educators, parents, and other consumers of assessment results. Many people incorrectly assume that test scores are as highly accurate as are measurements of the physical world. As most assessment professionals realize, however, the state of the art in psychological assessment is in its infancy. (This can be appreciated in light of the fact that individual psychology is only about 100 years old.) Then, too, psychologists, unlike physicists, do not make direct measurements of independently existing variables but are instead forced to measure behavior they believe is related to some hypothetical construct.

Why has this mistaken idea concerning the precision of test scores come to be accepted? There are undoubtedly many reasons, including the following:

1. In the Western world, many people suffer from what Papert (1980) has termed *mathophobia,* or an unreasonable fear of mathematics. Because many people feel intimidated by numbers, and because scientists and others have developed highly accurate numerical descriptors for the physical world, some people assume that any psychological trait that has been quantified enjoys the same accuracy and precision as that reflected in the measurement of heat, weight, and distance.

2. The media contributes to an unrealistic valuing of the results of standardized testing. Television programs and movies often employ plots that imply that the state of the art in psychological testing is far more advanced than it really is.

3. Many people are aware of the great emphasis placed upon precision in standardization, administration, and scoring of formal tests. Such people erroneously assume that the results obtained from such techniques are as precise as the procedures used to produce them.

4. Assessment professionals have sometimes encouraged the overvaluing of tests. We have frequently failed to emphasize the tentative nature of test scores. We have, in fact, reinforced public misunderstanding by referring to IQ scores as if they were attributes analogous to eye color, by reporting observed scores rather than confidence intervals, and by otherwise overtly or covertly supporting the notion of the infallibility of testing.

Since testing is already highly overvalued, we should engage in careful thought before deciding to convert highly visible assessment procedures to computer implementation. Bringing computers into the process is almost sure to contribute further to the overvaluing of testing, since many people already associate precision, power, accuracy, and prestige to any activity carried out in whole or in part by computer.

COMPUTERS IN ASSESSMENT

There are a number of assessment-related tasks that are sometimes carried out partially or completely by computers. These include (1) administration of standardized tests, (2) scoring of test items, (3) arithmetic manipulation or transformation of test or subtest scores, (4) interpretation of test results, (5) production of test or assessment reports, and (6) storage of test scores or other assessment data.

Computer Administration of Standardized Tests

Professionals cite a number of reasons for wanting computer implementations of assessment instruments:

1. *Computer administration can save time.* Even a casual reading of the literature reveals that this is the most commonly cited advantage for using the computer to administer tests (e.g., Halpern, 1986; Madsen, 1986; Moe & Johnson, 1988; Olsen, Maynes, Slawson, & Ho, 1989; Ronau & Battista, 1988; Sampson, 1986; Schuerholz, 1984–1985; Sternberg, 1986; Turner, 1987; Walker & Myrick, 1985; Wise & Plake, 1989).

2. *Assessment personnel will be freed from routine data gathering* and will, consequently, be able to devote more time to more professional services to clients (Sampson, 1986).

3. *Test takers will gain a greater sense of control,* leading to more active, and less passive participation in the educational or counseling activity (Eberly & Cech, 1986).

4. *Precisely standardized administration procedures will be guaranteed.* Computers, can, for example, administer items at precisely timed intervals. Then, too, computers are patient and nonjudgmental. These factors could eliminate problems due to examiner bias (Eberly & Cech, 1986; Eller, Kaufman, & McLean, 1986; Schuerholz, 1984–1985).

5. *Examinees will have more flexibility* in when and where they take the test. This advantage will become more apparent as computer technology expands beyond our present concept of what a computer is and what it can do. Consider, for example, George Gilder's (1994) view of tomorrow's computer: "The new system will be the telecomputer, or 'teleputer,' a personal computer adapted for video processing and connected by fiber-optic threads to other teleputers all around the world. Using a two-way system of signals like telephones do, rather than broadcasting one-way like TV, the teleputer will surpass the television in video communication just as the telephone surpassed the telegraph in verbal communication" (p. 45). An example of how new technology can provide more flexibility in assessment with regard to time and place has been demonstrated by Baer, Brown-Beasley, Sorce, and Henriques (1993). These researchers demonstrated that certain screening scales commonly used by psychiatrists to indicate the need for intervention could be administered just as effectively by a hybrid computer-telephone system that utilizes digitized human voice as by the more traditional paper and pencil system or a telephone system where a clinician was actually present at the time of administration. Access for handicapped individuals whose condition precludes traditional test formats (Becker & Schur, 1986; Schuerholz, 1984–1985) is another area where such increased flexibility will be valuable.

6. *Most examinees have a good attitude* toward computerized testing and will be motivated to try their hardest (Ronau & Battista, 1988; Schuerholz, 1984–1985; Watkins & Kush, 1988). One of the conclusions drawn from a research study by Flowers, Boorman, and Schwartz (1993) was that counseling clients "often prefer computer-administered tests to paper-and-pencil ones" (p. 13).

7. *Examinees may receive their scores immediately* after taking the test. This can be a great advantage where admission to programs is dependent on the rapid reporting of test scores. Traditionally, tests were often scored by a test company or agency that sent the results through the mail, often causing anxious moments for the applicant. The Graduate Record Examination (GRE) can now be taken by computer, with test scores available upon completion of the exam.

8. *Computers will permit the development of new kinds of tests* (Turner, 1987; Wise & Plake, 1989), that gather nontraditional data (such as response latency) as well as those employing animation or other nontraditional presentation or response modes. Bridgeman and Rock (1993) conducted research on developing new types of test items that take advantage of the computer's ability to manipulate data. Their research was specifically aimed at developing items for the GRE General Test. They concluded that their new items could "more closely simulate the kind of evaluation of alternative hypotheses that is a common feature of graduate education" (p. 326). To accomplish this, these researchers capitalized on the computer's ability to present a series of branching questions.

Currently, two general types of computerized testing are in use: *computer-based* (CB) and *computerized-adaptive* (CA) tests. Wise and Plake (1989) provide an excellent analysis of research findings related to each type. Computer-based testing refers to the use of the computer to administer a conventional test, which has often merely been transferred from paper and pencil to computer screen. Computerized-adaptive testing, on the other hand, refers to tests in which choice of the next item to be administered is made by reference to the examinees's performance on earlier items. Most computerized testing is presently available only in CB format (Turner, 1987).

It may appear that there would be few if any problems involved in converting objective format tests from paper and pencil to computerized administration mode. Indeed, the actual programming to accomplish this conversion is relatively simple. However, there are many problems, including the following:

1. *As a general rule, the computer version of a test cannot be assumed to be equivalent to the original, paper-and-pencil version.* Indeed, Watkins and Kush (1988) suggest that "translating conventional tests to a computer format simply duplicates the weaknesses of conventional testing methods while confounding them with new sources of error (e.g., keyboard unfamiliarity)" (p. 87). This is unfortunate, indeed, since lack of equivalence means that the computer version of the test must be restandardized and renormed, a costly and time-consuming process. Moe and Johnson (1988) administered both a paper-and-pencil and a computer version of a standardized aptitude test to 315 students in grades 8 to 12, then surveyed them about their experiences. Although the students were positive about the computer experience, more than half reported experiencing problems: 63% said their eyes got tired during the test, 39% indicated that the screen was too bright, and 27.6% said there was glare on the screen. Furthermore, in the computer testing, girls were more likely to report nervousness than were boys, and girls reported having a wider variety of problems than did boys, even though there was no difference by gender in the amount of previous computer experience.

We strongly advise test users to look carefully at the computer version of any test to ensure that it has been carefully standardized. There is evidence, however, that when careful comparisons are made between paper-and-pencil and computer versions of certain types of tests, their equivalency is remarkably close. Mead and Drasgow (1993), after conducting a meta-analysis of the paper-and-pencil versus the computer version of the GRE, concluded that "the verbal and quantitative abilities measured by the computerized version of the GRE are the same verbal and quantitative abilities assessed by the paper-and-pencil GRE" (p. 457). There is also growing evidence that the benefits of computerized versions of certain types of tests justify the time and expense required to develop a good computer version where reliability and validity checks are made. Kobak, Reynolds, and Greist (1993) developed a computerized version of the Hamilton Anxiety Scale that correlated at an extremely high level ($r = .92$) with its traditional clinical version. Tucker and Gillespie (1993) found high correlations ($r = .84$ to $r = .86$) between a computer version of the Meyers-Briggs Type Indicator and the traditional paper-and-pencil version of the instrument.

2. *Many kinds of tests do not lend themselves to computer implementation,* due to the nature of required communication with the examinees or the crude state of the art of the technology (Schuerholz, 1984–1985). Many reading tests require the subject to read a passage orally and then respond to oral questions. Speech synthesis problems such as lack of sophistication and standardization also mitigate against immediate implementation.

3. *Inadequate hardware and software can diminish the effectiveness of computerized testing.* There are several ways the hardware and software arrangements being used in a testing situation can interfere with test effectiveness. In some cases, the testing software is poorly designed and will not permit the examinees to review previous questions and answers, skip items, or return to earlier items to change answers (Ronau & Battista, 1988). Although research results are somewhat contradictory, there is evidence that scores on tests that do not permit skipping, review, or revision of previous answers will be lower than scores on otherwise equivalent paper-and-pencil versions that do (Wise & Plake, 1989). Some computer tests employ flawed programs or poor error-trapping procedures that result in program crashes during testing (Walker & Myrick, 1985). Consumers should carefully check the software to be sure that the programming is accurate (correct order of items, proper spelling, accurate calculation of raw scores, etc.).

Lack of standardization of computers and peripherals can compromise the reliability of a computerized test, as demonstrated by Madsen (1986). There is great variance in screen size, color, and resolution; keyboards; display fonts; furniture; and room lighting. Effects of such variables are unknown and are probably test specific. Therefore, resolution of this problem will require separate norming and standardization of computer implementations. Sarvela and Noonan (1988) discuss these and a number of psychometric problems in computer assessment.

Another hardware and software consideration for effective computer-administered testing is that computerized testing will require extensive equipment maintenance and staff training (Jacob & Brantley, 1987; Madsen, 1986; Meier & Geiger, 1986). Without adequate planning for proper hardware and software maintenance, the effectiveness of employing computerized versions of tests will be compromised.

It is obvious that as technology improves and as access to state-of-the-art technology for assessment purposes becomes more standard and more universally available, some of the problems to which we have alluded will be alleviated.

4. *There is evidence that computerized tests are completed faster* than paper-and-pencil versions (Wise & Plake, 1989). Therefore, the computerized versions of timed tests will require different, probably shorter, time limits.

5. *Computerized testing could dehumanize the assessment process* (Eller et al., 1986; Madsen, 1986; Sampson, 1986). One danger is that professionals will begin to rely excessively on computerized testing and approach the assessment process in a mechanical fashion. Subjects should be observed while using the computer, and professionals must be sensitive to subjects' general emotional state as well as attitudes toward computers. As Eberly and Cech (1986) point out, the computer should not be used to avoid subjective evaluation by the assessment professional.

There are no problems with the use of computers to administer tests as long as the professionals are aware of the problems referred to and make every effort to deal with them. Given these problems, however, it should be remembered that most of the advantages listed are conjectural and have not been empirically established (Eberly & Cech, 1986). Given the experimental nature of this computer application, great caution in its implementation is advised.

Scoring of Test Items

Computerized scoring of objective items has been used successfully for years. Problems in the future, however, can be envisioned in this area, however, as complicated scanning devices become more sophisticated. Such devices may eventually be employed to score short-answer or even essay formats. The objection to computerized scoring is that it usurps expert judgment in determing correctness of responses, for most test manuals give considerable leeway to experienced examiners in judging correctness, and human examiners become expert at sensing when a child is too tired or inattentive to continue, or when to probe a response (Maddux, Johnson, & Willis, in press).

Arithmetic Manipulation or Transformation of Scores

Of all the possible uses for computers in assessment, this is the most appropriate one. Procedures such as calculating a subject's chronological age; adding the number of correct items; calculating z scores or other standard scores; transferring raw scores to grade-equivalent or age-equivalent scores through use of extensive tables; and plotting scores on a graph are tedious, boring, time-consuming, and error-prone tasks for humans. Computers, on the other hand, are ideally suited to perform such complicated, mechanical, rote activities.

The only concern about this computer implementation is related to accuracy of the program controlling these manipulations. A number of programs contain errors that would lead users to inaccurate conclusions about performance. This is compounded by the fact that many assessment professionals have a tendency to blindly accept as accurate results obtained from a computer program. Purchasers should therefore validate software accuracy by comparing computer results to hand calculations known to be accurate (Maddux et al., in press).

Interpretation of Test Results

This is one of the fastest growing applications of computers in the assessment process. In 1984, Krug located over 190 computer programs intended for test interpretation, and many more are now available. Kramer suggested in 1988 that there were more than a dozen commercial programs for interpreting the WISC-III alone. Such programs continue to proliferate.

Of all computer applications in assessment, interpretation is the most questionable. Interpretation of test results calls for a form of subjectivity often called *clinical judgment* or *professional expertise*. One reason that computers cannot be invested with good clinical judgment is that development of this skill in people is a mysterious, little understood process. It seems to emerge from a synthesis of wide and varied experience, intelligence, common sense, factual knowledge, intuition, and a mixture of human affective qualities such as compassion, empathy, and wisdom. Computers are ill suited to make diagnostic and other decisions about human beings because they lack both human intelligence and the human affective qualities. Furthermore, computers cannot be invested with human intelligence or affective qualities since human experiences are required in their formation. Weizenbaum (1976) refers to the dilemma faced by those who would invest computers with intelligence:

> I have argued that the individual human being, like any other organism, is defined by the problems he confronts. The human is unique by virtue of the fact that he must necessarily confront problems that arise from his unique biological and emotional needs. . . . No other organism, and certainly no computer, can be made to confront genuine human problems in human terms. And, since the domain of human intelligence is, except for a small set of formal problems, determined by man's humanity, every other intelligence, however great, must necessarily be alien to the human domain. (p. 223)

The formal problems to which Weizenbaum refers are the rare ones that *do* yield to computer solutions and are referred to by Dreyfus and Dreyfus (1988) as *structured problems*. Structured problems are those for which there are sequential, step-by-step, convergent solutions. These solutions yield to IF-THEN strategies, a paradigm developed for computers. Examples include warehouse inventory control, mathematical processes, delivery truck routing, optimal weight distribution of objects in cargo holds of airplanes, and other such problems. Dreyfus and Dreyfus (1988) say of structured problems, "Here the goal and what information is relevant are clear, the effects of decisions are known, and verifiable solutions can be reasoned out" (p. 20).

Unfortunately, nearly all important human problems are unstructured and do not yield to IF-THEN logic or to straightforward, sequential thinking of any kind. Examples of unstructured problems in everyday life include riding a bicycle, identifying a faint odor, and recognizing a human face. Such problems are characterized by "a potentially unlimited number of possibly relevant facts and features, and the ways those elements interrelate and determine other events is unclear" (Dreyfus & Dreyfus, 1988, p. 20). It is precisely such problems that are the stuff of nursing, counseling, and of assessment itself.

Computer programs have been developed that are attempts to invest computers with human expertise. Such programs are known as *expert systems* and are part of a larger effort known as *artificial intelligence.* So far, such intelligence is artificial indeed, and Dreyfus and Dreyfus (1988) suggest that efforts to apply artificial intelligence to unstructured problems is one of the great commercial failures of this century. Many companies dedicated to developing expert system software have either gone out of business or changed their focus. Dreyfus and Dreyfus (1988) maintain that although there has been limited success in creating expert systems for structured problems, no one has even come close to writing a program that can emulate the kind of complex human expertise necessary for the solution of the vast majority of important (and unstructured) human problems.

Yet this is precisely what would be required if the plethora of interpretation programs on the market were to do their jobs as well as a human expert. Kramer (1988) conducted an analysis of interpretation programs and concluded that:

> They often make general statements about the client that would apply to almost every human being (a phenomenon referred to as the "Barnum effect"); and they often suggest specific remedial strategies that go far beyond published data on the efficacy of the original test. (p. 147)

Perhaps because of the above shortcomings, Jacob and Brantley (1987), in their survey of 268 school psychologists, found that 33% reported problems with such programs and 57% anticipated future problems.

Not only do commercial programs exist to interpret individual tests, but there is a rapidly growing number of programs designed to accept test scores and other data about a student and to then produce the student's legally mandated individual education plan (IEP). The IEP contains a diagnosis as to whether the student qualifies for special education, the handicapping condition he or she is suffering from, and even long-term and short-term instructional goals.

The requirement for an IEP to be written for every special-education student is one of the great educational experiments of our time. The intent of the law that requires it (P.L. 94–142) was that the IEP be written by an interdisciplinary team of experts during a problem-solving meeting that included the child's parents and, when appropriate, the child.

The potential for abuse through the use of expert systems for the writing of IEPs can be seen in the following endorsement of computer IEP programs by Guilbeau (1984): "In the old days—a couple of years ago—it took educators . . . as much as an hour to develop and prepare IEPs. . . . Today, IEP development . . . requires only five to 15 minutes for each student" (p. 43). Is there any doubt at all that an IEP program used in this fashion violates the letter and spirit of the law, which calls for the careful consideration of evidence, professional debate among experts, consultation with parents, and the reaching of eventual consensus concerning the best course of action?

The suggestion that IEPs be written in 5 to 15 minutes per student calls to mind a similar proposal concerning psychotherapy and Joseph Weizenbaum's (1976) ELIZA program. ELIZA was a simple program designed to demonstrate that a computer could be made to respond to natural language comments entered by a user. There was no pretense made that ELIZA actually comprehended what was entered by the user or that its responses were anything but mindlessly rote in nature. About ELIZA, Weizenbaum wrote:

> ELIZA was a program consisting mainly of general methods for analyzing sentences and sentence fragments, locating so-called key words in texts, assembling sentences from fragments, and so on. It had, in other words, no built-in contextual framework or universe of discourse. This was supplied to it by a "script." In a sense ELIZA was an actress who commanded a set of techniques but who had nothing of her own to say. . . . The first extensive script I prepared for ELIZA was one that enabled it to parody the responses of a nondirective psychotherapist in an initial psychiatric interview. I chose this script because it enabled me to temporarily sidestep the problem of giving the program a data base of real-world knowledge. (pp. 188–189)

Weizenbaum was shocked and horrified to learn that a psychoanalyst who learned of his work actually made the suggestion that ELIZA might be profitably used to automate psychiatry, and that such programs would soon be able to handle several hundred patients per hour. Of this suggestion, he wrote, "What must a psychiatrist who makes such a suggestion think he is doing while treating a patient, that he can view the simplest mechanical parody of a single interviewing technique as having captured anything of the essence of a human encounter?" (p. 6). The same might be asked of Guilbeau concerning his 5-minute IEP meetings.

The psychotherapy suggestion referred to should not be viewed as an antiquated remnant of an unenlightened past. In 1986 Eberly and Cech suggested that computerized counseling programs could be helpful and that "interpersonal interaction as such may not be necessary for positive personal changes" (p. 19). In light of such suggestions, Weizenbaum's question seems as relevant now as it did in 1976.

The use of most interpretation programs is inappropriate at this time, as they encourage the use of assessment instruments by personnel who are not fully competent in their use, and they apply a simplistic paradigm (IF-THEN) to the solution of complex human assessment problems. Weizenbaum came to a similar conclusion about the application of computers to any unstructured human problem: "What emerges as the most elementary insight is that, since we do not now have any ways of making computers wise, we ought not now to give computers tasks that demand wisdom" (p. 227). Caution in the use of interpretation programs is therefore recommended, for their disadvantages generally outweigh their advantages, and they have great potential for abuse. When computer interpretation programs such as those used with the Minnesota Multiphasic Personality Inventory (MMPI) are used, the resulting computer interpretation is probably no worse than other cookbook approaches to interpreting such tests. The question is, Should any cookbook approaches be used?

Production of Test or Assessment Reports

There are few problems with computer assistance in the production of reports as long as such reports do not usurp professional judgment by involving computer *interpretation*. Word processors, for example, are valuable and appropriate aids to the production of reports. Word-processing templates (blank forms stored on diskette) can be produced using school district or other human service agency forms. Users then fill in the blanks on their computers and print as many copies as they need.

Storage of Test Scores or Other Assessment Data

The concern with computer storage of assessment information is related to problems of ensuring privacy and confidentiality. With respect to these issues, the principal rule should be that the assessment professional is responsible for ensuring that the individual has the right to approve or disapprove the gathering of information and the right to control access to that data (Meier & Geiger, 1986). Johnson (1979) provides a chilling, Orwellian suggestion that serves as an illustration of the potential for abuse in this regard: That physiological monitoring equipment be teamed with automated testing to check the truthfulness of a testee's responses.

Jacob and Brantley (1987) have also expressed concern about these issues. When they surveyed 268 school psychologists, they found that 3% indicated they had experienced problems of unauthorized access to records and 6% suggested that schools they were associated with had failed to notify parents of the existence of computerized pupil records. More telling, perhaps, 35% and 40% indicated they expected future problems in these two areas, respectively. Other, related problems were "failure to maintain adequate back-up copies of computer records to assure that pupil information is not lost in the event of equipment problems" and "use of computerized records for employee accountability studies without the knowledge and consent of personnel involved" (p. 73).

These problems are indicative of unaddressed philosophical issues, especially those related to ethics. There are other, more practical concerns, however. It is not recommended that assessment data or other personal data be placed on hard-disk drives or file servers. Hard-disk drives are usually accessible to anyone who uses the computer, and file servers are often accessible to all members of the computer network. Although security systems are available for use with these devices, they are often cumbersome, and none are foolproof. Such data should be saved on floppy diskettes that are duplicated, and both copies should be kept under lock and key. Of course, a record should be kept of all those allowed access to this data. If data *is* kept on hard-disk drives or file servers, code numbers should be substituted for names, the key to the code numbers should be kept secure in a separate location, and at least one floppy disk or hard copy should be made.

Another problem is created by public attitudes about data displayed on computer monitors. Many people seem to view such data as public information. Although such individuals would probably never pick up and read the contents of a file folder located on another professional's desk, they may have no qualms about reading data displayed on another's computer screen. Hopefully, this attitude will change as computers become more common and we begin to extend the courtesy of privacy to computer displays. Until then, computer users should develop the habit of switching off their computer monitors when colleagues or others approach or when the computer is left unattended. Turning off the monitor will have no effect on any programs that are running, and the monitor can be switched back on and work resumed at any time.

The enormous growth and development of networked computers on both small and large scales in the past few years will obviously stimulate the development of more sophisticated ways to store and protect information. Large institutions are increasingly being faced with issues of privacy—how to make sensitive information readily available to those who need it and still protect it from unauthorized access. Institutions and agencies that use computerized testing will need to adopt such security methods and procedures as they are developed.

CONCLUSION

Although computers hold considerable promise for enhancing the assessment process, they also contain the potential for abuse. This chapter has argued that computers are appropriately used to perform rote tasks and data storage and that they are inappropriately used when they usurp expert judgment, and has attempted to make this point with reference to assessment. Dreyfus and Dreyfus (1988) do a good job of summing up this position with respect to the business world: "It turns out, then, that at every level of business from the factory floor to the board room, wherever skills are involved, formal models fail to capture human expertise" (p. 189).

What then, is the solution? Should we rebel mindlessly against computers in general? There are modern-day Luddites, both inside and outside the human services professions who are engaging in such a rebellion. The *Whole Earth Review* published a "computer as poison" special issue (Dreyfus & Dreyfus, 1988). In the early 1980s, the beginning of a backlash against educational computing could be detected. Such a backlash, however, has not succeeded. The computer is here to stay. Indeed, it is destined to proliferate enormously. It is such a powerful tool that pressure for implementation has become an irresistible force. The question is not whether to involve computers in assessment but how to do so intelligently. As we work toward that end, we would do well to heed Dreyfus and Dreyfus (1988):

> What we do now will determine what sort of society and what sort of human beings we are to become. We can make such a decision wisely only if we have some understanding of what sort of human beings we already are. If we think of ourselves only as repositories of factual knowledge and of information processing procedures, then we understand ourselves as someday to be surpassed by bigger and faster machines run-

ning bigger and more sophisticated programs. . . . But fortunately, there are other possibilities. We can use computers to track the vast array of facts and law-governed relationships of our modern technological world, yet continue to nurture the human expertise that inference engines cannot share by encouraging learners to pass from rule following to experience-based intuition. If we do so, our experts will be empowered by their computer aids to make better use of their wisdom in grappling with the still unresolved problems of technological society. The chips are down, the choice is being made right now. (205–206)

Case Example 4–1.   A hypothetical example of best practices in computer-assisted assessment

---

George Smith, a computer-using school psychologist, has just received a referral on Sue Jones, a fourth-grade student. George has met with two of Sue's teachers, talked to Sue's parents, and observed Sue in the classroom. Sue was referred because both her parents and teachers are concerned that she is not keeping up in her schoolwork. Sue seems bright enough, but is not completing assignments and is scoring poorly on tests. Since among parents and teachers opinion is mixed as to the cause and remedy for Sue's problem, George has decided to conduct a thorough assessment, including a battery of tests that he believes will provide important information.

In cases like this, George usually administers three standardized tests: an extensive norm-referenced achievement test, a criterion-referenced achievement test, and a general intelligence test. The information he gathers from these three tests along with other information he has gleaned is then analyzed and condensed into a report that forms the basis for the IEP.

The first test administered is a criterion-referenced achievement test. The administration of such a test used to be very cumbersome since it required the test administrator to weave through a massive amount of test items and keep track of a large number of facts in order to focus in on those portions of the test that are best suited to the level of the subject. George now uses a computer to make this a much smoother and more efficient experience. While the actual test items are administered in the traditional manner, the computer keeps track of Sue's performance and helps George focus on those sections of the test that will provide the most fruitful information. Consequently, George is now more free to observe and make clinical notes about such things as Sue's problem-solving strategies.

The second test is a computer-administered intelligence test. This test has been normed for computer administration, and George is familiar enough with the test that he has confidence in the results it yields. He feels the reliability of the test is enhanced by the increased objectivity of the computer administration. While Sue is taking the test, George is able to carefully observe and take notes about how she interacts with the test items. The computer scores as well as administers this test.

The final test is a norm-referenced achievement test. This test is administered one-on-one with George again making careful notes while scoring the test. The computer comes into play only after the testing session is completed. Instead of having to do all the clerical work by hand, a process that was very time consuming and error prone, George is able to use a computer-scoring program that he has complete confidence in.

Case Example 4–1.   *(Continued)*

This program manipulates the scores quickly and accurately. The computer program also prints out various types of profiles and score comparisons depending on the options George chooses.

The most difficult part of George's job is to pull all the information he has collected together in an organized manner that will begin to form a picture of why Sue is falling behind in her schoolwork. George uses the computer in two ways at this point. First, he enters into specialized software pertinent information that he has gathered through interviews, clinical notes, observations, and testing. This software is designed to assist in organizing the information so it can be efficiently analyzed and woven into a final report. Next, George uses a special expert-system program that helps him consider a wide variety of options in making sense of the information he has gathered. George harbors no illusions that the computer can make decisions about Sue or arrive at useful conclusions about the cause and treatment of her problem. What his expert system program can do is expand the range of options to be considered beyond what he might consider on his own. The program does this by comparing a summary of the information gathered on Sue with similar cases and allows George to review what other school psychologists have concluded and recommended. George realizes that this information is only suggestive in nature and cannot supplant his own clinical expertise. He does find, however, that sometimes his attention is focused on aspects of the case that he would not have thought of and that need to be explored as options. This program allows George to do something that is akin to consulting with his colleagues and discussing Sue's case—a luxury that is not otherwise possible.

Once George has gathered information, organized it, and analyzed it, he is ready to put it all together in a well-organized report that will form the basis for an IEP that will be prepared by an IEP committee. At this stage, the computer becomes an essential tool for George. Using a format template with his word processor, he can select items of information he has stored elsewhere for inclusion in the report. He can add, delete, and modify the contents of the report until he is thoroughly satisfied that it is the best summarization he can provide. A final polish can be placed on the report by running it through a word processor and a grammar checker. George has learned to use his computer as a clerical aid and has found that the quality of his reports is superior to those he submitted before the computer was available.

Finally George saves his report in a database of cases in a manner that he feels is secure. This database serves as both a storage facility and a diagnostic aid for George. Besides being able to store many cases in a very small space, he can retrieve designated cases quickly and efficiently. Beyond these obvious advantages, however, George can use the database in a more powerful way. Since the information is organized into records and categories, a wide variety of searches and sorts can be performed on the entire database. George can, for example, call up all children he has tested who have a similar intelligence test pattern as Sue's or he can review all the cases where the child has been diagnosed as learning disabled.

In this example, we have spoken in generalities and have not used specific tests or computer-program names. This was done by design. Our intent in this example is to illustrate the ideal uses of a computer in assessment. Our example is based on what we think constitutes the wise use of the computer in assessment and is possible by carefully planning and selecting the appropriate hardware, software, and procedures.

REFERENCES

American Psychological Association Committee on Professional Standards and Committee on Psychological Tests and Assessment. (1986). *Guidelines for computer-based tests and interpretations.* Washington, DC: Author.

Baer, L., Brown-Beasley, M.W., Sorce, J., & Henriques, A.I. (1993). Computer-assisted telephone administration of a structured interview for obsessive-compulsive disorder. *American Journal of Psychiatry, 105*(11), 1737–1738.

Becker, H., & Schur, S. (1986). Advantages of using microcomputer-based assessment with moderately and severely handicapped individuals. *Journal of Special Education Technology, 8*(2), 53–57.

Boocock, S.S. (1980). *Sociology of education: An introduction* (2nd ed.). Boston: Houghton Mifflin.

Bridgeman, B., & Rock, D.A. (1993). Relationships among multiple choice and open-ended analytical questions. *Journal of Educational Measurement, 30*(4), 313–329.

Burke, R.L. (1982). *CAI sourcebook.* Englewood Cliffs, NJ: Prentice-Hall.

Criswell, E.L. (1989). *The design of computer-based instruction.* New York: Macmillan.

Dreyfus, H.L., & Dreyfus, S.E. (1988). *Mind over machine: The power of human intuition and expertise in the era of the computer.* New York: The Free Press.

Eberly, C.G., & Cech, E.J. (1986, April). Integrating computer-assisted testing and assessment into the counseling process. *Measurement and Evaluation in Counseling and Development,* 18–28. Eller, B.F., Kaufman, A.S., & McLean, J.E. (1986). Computer-based assessment of cognitive abilities: Current status/future directions. *Journal of Educational Technology Systems, 15*(2), 137–147.

Flowers, J.V., Boorman, C.D., and Schwartz, B. (1993). Impact of computerized rapid assessment instruments on counseling and client outcome. *Computers in Human Services, 10*(2), 9–15.

Gayeski, D. (1989). Why information technologies fail. *Educational Technology, 29*(9), 9–17.

Gilder, G. (1994). *Life after television.* New York: W.W. Norton.

Green, B.F. (1988). Critical problems in computer-based psychological measurement. *Applied Measurement in Education, 1*(3), 223–231.

Guilbeau, J.J. (1984). Micros for the special ed administrator: PROFILE: A Louisiana district's network of special educators. *Electronic Learning, 3*(5), 43.

Halpern, M. (1986, Winter). Evolving trends in testing. *Education Libraries, 11,* 12–15.

Jacob, S., & Brantley, J.C. (1987). Ethical-legal problems with computer use and suggestions for best practices: A national survey. *School Psychology Review, 16*(1), 69–77.

Johnson, J. (1979). Technology. In T. Williams & J. Johnson (Eds.), *Mental health in the 21st century* (pp. 7–9). Lexington, MA: D.C. Heath.

Kneller, G.F. (1965). *Educational anthropology: An introduction.* New York: Wiley.

Kobak, K.A., Reynolds, W.M., & Greist, J.H. (1993). Development and validation of a computer-administered version of the Hamilton Anxiety Scale. *Psychological Assessment, 5*(4), 487–492.

Kramer, J.J. (1988). Computer-based test interpretation in psychoeducational assessment: An initial appraisal. *Journal of School Psychology, 26,* 143–153.

Krug, S.E. (1984). *Psychware.* Kansas City, MO: Test Corporation of America.

Maddux, C.D. (1984). Breaking the Everest syndrome in educational computing: An interview with Gregory Jackson and Judah L. Schwartz. *Computers in the Schools, 1*(2), 37–48.

Maddux, C.D., Johnson, L., & Willis, J. (in press). *Educational computing: Learning with tomorrow's technologies.* Boston: Allyn & Bacon.

Madsen, D.H. (1986, April). Computer-assisted testing and assessment in counseling: Computer applications for test administration and scoring. *Measurement and Evaluation in Counseling and Development*, 6–14.

Mead, A.D., & Drasgow, F. (1993). Equivalence of computerized and paper-and-pencil cognitive ability tests: A meta-analyisis. *Psychological Bulletin, 114*(3), 449–458.

Meier, S.T., & Geiger, S.M. (1986, April). Implications of computer-assisted testing and assessment for professional practice and training. *Measurement and Evaluation in Counseling and Development*, 29–37.

Moe, K.C., & Johnson, M.F. (1988). Participants' reactions to computerized testing. *Journal of Educational Computing Research, 4*(1), 79–86.

Olsen, J.B., Maynes, D.D., Slawson, D., & Ho, K. (1989). Comparisons of paper-administered, computer-administered, and computerized adaptive achievement tests. *Journal of Educational Computing Research, 5*(3), 311–326.

Osguthorpe, R.T., & Zhou, L. (1989). Instructional science: What is it and where did it come from? *Educational Technology, 29*(6), 7–17.

Papert, S. (1980). *Mindstorms: Children, computers, and powerful ideas.* New York: Basic Books.

Pressey, S.L. (1926). A simple apparatus which gives tests and scores—and teaches. *School and Society, 23,* 373–376.

Pressey, S.L. (1927). A machine for automatic teaching of drill material. *School and Society, 25,* 549–552.

Ronau, R.N., & Battista, M.T. (1988, Spring). Microcomputer versus paper-and-pencil testing of student errors in ratio and proportion. *Journal of Computers in Mathematics and Science Testing, 7,* 33–38.

Sampson, J.P. (1986). Computer technology and counseling psychology: Regression toward the machine? *The Counseling Psychologist, 14*(4), 567–583.

Sarvela, P.D., & Noonan, J.V. (1988). Testing and computer-based instruction: Psychometric considerations. *Educational Technology, 28*(5), 17–20.

Schuerholz, L.J. (1984–1985). The use of technology and media in the assessment of exceptional children. *Diagnostique, 10,* 197–208.

Skinner, B.F. (1954). The science of learning and the art of teaching. *Harvard Educational Review, 24,* 86–97.

Skinner, B.F. (1958). Teaching machines. *Science, 128,* 969–977.

Skinner, B.F. (1986). Programmed instruction revisited. *Phi Delta Kappan, 68*(2), 103–110.

Sternberg, R.J. (1986, Fall). The future of intelligence testing. *Educational Measurement: Issues and Practice,* 19–22.

Travers, R.M. (1967). *Essentials of learning* (2nd ed.). New York: Macmillan.

Tucker, I.F., & Gillespie, B.V. (1993). Correlations among three measures of personality type. *Perceptual and Motor Skills, 77*(2), 650.

Turner, G.A. (1987). Computers in testing and assessment: Contemporary issues. *International Journal of Instructional Media, 14*(3), 187–197.

Walker, N.W., & Myrick, C.C. (1985). Ethical considerations in the use of computers in psychological testing and assessment. *Journal of School Psychology, 23,* 51–57.

Watkins, M.W., & Kush, J.C. (1988). Assessment of academic skills of learning disabled students with classroom microcomputers. *School Psychology Review, 17*(1), 81–88.

Weizenbaum, J. (1976). *Computer power and human reason.* New York: W.H. Freeman.

Wise, S.L., & Plake, B.S. (1989, Fall). Research on the effects of administering tests via computers. *Educational Measurement: Issues and Practice, 8,* 5–10.

Chapter 5

CURRICULUM-BASED MEASUREMENT

ROSE M. ALLINDER, LYNN S. FUCHS, AND DOUGLAS FUCHS

Curriculum-based measurement (CBM; Deno, 1985) is an established process for monitoring student progress in academic areas (Deno & Fuchs, 1987; Shinn, 1989). Consisting of prescribed procedures conducted in a standardized format, CBM offers school psychologists, special-education teachers, and administrators a technically strong assessment system.

Curriculum-based measurement has been used for a variety of purposes, including program evaluation (Tindal, 1992); screening, referral, and identification for special-education services (Shinn, 1989) and reintegration of students with disabilities into general-education classes (Fuchs, Fuchs, & Fernstrom, 1992; Shinn, Habedank, Rodden-Nord, & Knutson, 1993). It was developed specifically as a method of assisting teachers to improve student academic performance (Deno, 1992). Used in this manner, CBM shifts the focus of assessment from the student to the interaction between student and instruction (Tindal & Marston, 1990).

The emphasis of CBM on improving student achievement distinguishes it from the more common form of school assessment: norm-referenced testing (NRT). The emphasis of NRT on evaluating an individual student's discrepancy from same-age peers limits its utility for evaluating student progress across time and the effectiveness of instructional plans for individual students. NRTs lack sensitivity to growth over time (Marston, Fuchs, & Deno, 1986), are questionably matched to the curriculum (Jenkins & Pany, 1978; Shapiro & Derr, 1987), and consist of only one or two forms, thus limiting the frequency with which they can be administered and making it impossible to measure change in student performance over time (Carver, 1974).

In contrast, CBM offers a reliable, valid method of monitoring student progress. Relying on graphic representation of student progress over the school year, CBM provides a process by which teachers can compare a student's actual to expected progress and thus evaluate the impact of their instructional plans for that student. Rooted in applied-behavior analysis, CBM (Deno, 1992) provides the teacher and school psychologist a single-subject research tool for conducting educational interventions (Casey, Deno, Marston, & Skiba, 1988). A teacher designs an instructional plan, collects ongoing data, and evaluates the effects of the instruction.

Although CBM is a variation of curriculum-based assessment (CBA), CBM's unique characteristics distinguish it from other forms of CBA (Shinn, Rosenfield, &

Knutson, 1989). All forms of CBA are marked by repeated assessments, the linking of assessment and instruction, and the use of material from local curricula (Tucker, 1987). CBM, however, offers practitioners the following advantages: a focus on long-term goals rather than short-term objectives, standardized administration and scoring of assessments, and validated technical adequacy. Data are the result of direct measurement of student proficiency in reading, mathematics, spelling, and written expression (Shinn et al., 1993), and represent a general outcome measure of student proficiency in an academic area (Deno, 1992; Fuchs & Deno, 1991).

During the development of CBM, four properties that distinguish it from NRT and other forms of CBA were emphasized (Deno, 1992, 1985): (1) technical adequacy, which includes both reliability and validity; (2) ease of administration, which facilitates use; (3) repeated and frequent measurement, which enhances its ability to document growth over time; and (4) low cost in terms of time and money. All CBM methods are based on these four properties, which will be discussed in the following sections.

Curriculum-based measurement consists of standardized administration and scoring procedures (Shinn, 1989) in which the school psychologist or special- or general-education teacher presents the student(s) with short, timed tests called *probes*. With most criterion-referenced tests or other types of CBA, tests are developed and administered without regard for consistency across time or students, and with limited or no concern for reliability or validity. In contrast, CBM is a set of prescribed procedures with demonstrated reliability and validity and detailed directions for administration and scoring (Shinn, 1989). This allows the school psychologist or special education teacher to follow rather than create measurement procedures that result in accurate and meaningful scores consistent across academic areas and across students (Fuchs, Fuchs, & Hamlett, 1990).

OVERVIEW OF CBM PROCEDURES

This section reviews the basic administration and scoring procedures of the Reading, Spelling, Written Expression, and Math probes. For further information on administration and scoring as well as materials development, the reader is referred to Shinn (1989). For further information regarding CBM software, the reader is referred to Fuchs, Hamlett, and Fuchs (1990). A brief discussion of graphing and decision-making procedures follows (Case Example 5–1 summarizes the section).

Reading test administration. The student is given a passage of approximately 300 words to read, which is selected randomly from his or her end-of-year, goal-level curriculum material. Procedures to be followed are outlined here (Deno & Fuchs, 1987; Shinn, 1989):

1. Create or obtain two copies of each passage. The examiner's copy will be numbered along the right-hand border with a cumulative count of number of words. The student's copy will be unnumbered. Place this copy in front of the student.

2. Say to the student: "When I say 'start,' begin reading aloud at the top of this page. Try to read each word. If you wait for a word too long, I'll tell you the word. You can skip words you don't know how to read. At the end of 1 minute, I'll say 'stop.' " (Give the student 3 seconds before supplying a word.)

3. As you say "Start," trigger the stopwatch.

4. As the student reads, follow along on your copy. Circle all incorrectly read words (omissions, substitutions, mispronunciations, reversals). Incorrect words the student self-corrects within 3 seconds are not counted as errors.

5. After 1 minute, say "Stop," place a slash after the last word read, and turn off the stopwatch.

6. Count the number of words correct and the number of errors. (The examiner copy lists the number of words per line.)

7. Record the number of correct words on an equal-interval graph labeled "Number of Words Read Aloud from Text Passage."

8. Repeat Steps 1 through 7 at least twice weekly.

Spelling test administration. Words randomly chosen from the goal-level material are dictated to students, who write them on numbered lists. The following procedures outline specific steps to be taken (Deno & Fuchs, 1987; Shinn, 1989):

1. Give the student a pencil and piece of paper numbered 1–20.

2. Say to the student: "I am going to read some words to you. I want you to write the words on the sheet I just gave you. I'll give you 10 seconds to spell each word. When I say the next word, try to write it even if you haven't finished the last one."

3. Say, "Let's begin," as you trigger the stopwatch.

4. Dictate each word in order. If the word is a homonym, use a short sentence incorporating the appropriate use of the word.

5. Present each word upon the student's completion of the previous word. After 10 seconds, present the next word even if the student has not completed the previous word.

6. Dictate words for 2 minutes. If the student is near the completion of a word and the time is up, allow the student to finish that word. Do not present any new words in the last 3 seconds of the test.

7. Count the number of correct letter sequences (pairs of letters in the correct sequence). (See Tindal and Marston [1990] for scoring letter sequences.)

8. Record the number of correct letter sequences on an equal-interval graph labeled "Number of Letter Sequences Correct."

9. Repeat Steps 1 through 8 at least twice weekly.

Written Expression test administration. In written expression, the student writes in response to a story starter. The basic quantitative scoring procedure is number of words written. (See Tindal & Marston [1990] for additional quantitative scoring and qualitative scoring procedures.) The following procedures are followed in administering the written expression probes (Deno & Fuchs, 1987; Shinn, 1989):

1. Give the student a pencil and lined paper.
2. Say to the student: "I want you to write a story. I am going to read a sentence to you first, and then I want you to write a short story about what happens. You will have 1 minute to think about the story you want to write and then 3 minutes to write it. When I say 'begin,' start writing."
3. Time the student as he or she writes for 3 minutes and then tell the student to stop writing.
4. Count the total number of words, including words spelled incorrectly. Count all personal nouns and names. Do not count numbers.
5. Record the total number of words written on an equal-interval graph labeled "Number of Words Written."
6. Repeat Steps 1 through 5 at least twice weekly.

Math test administration. In math, the student responds to probes containing math problems. These probes may be single-problem probes (i.e., all addition facts), mixed-problem probes (i.e., addition, subtraction, multiplication, etc.), or application probes (i.e., time, money, measurement, etc.). The scoring procedure is the number of correct digits written (i.e., correct numerals in correct place value). (See Tindal & Marston [1990] for scoring procedures.) The following procedures are followed in administering the math probes (Shinn, 1989):

1. Give the student a pencil and math probe.
2. For single-problem probes, say to the student: "All of the problems are addition (or subtraction or multiplication or division) facts."
   For mixed-problem probes, say to the student: "There are several types of problems on the sheet. Some are addition, some are subtraction, some are multiplication, some are division. Look at each problem carefully before you answer it."
   For application probes, say to the student: "There are several types of problems on the sheet. Some are time, some are money, some are measurement. Look at each problem carefully before you answer it."
   To all students, say: "When I say 'start,' begin answering the problems. Do the best work you can."
3. Say "Start," and trigger the stopwatch.
4. At the end of the allotted time period, say "Stop" and turn off the stopwatch.
5. Count the number of digits (i.e., correct numerals) in the correct place value.
6. Record the total number of digits on an equal-interval graph labeled "Number of Correct Digits."
7. Repeat Steps 1 through 6 at least twice weekly.

Graphing and decision making. Evidence from numerous research studies indicates that administering CBM probes alone does not significantly affect student academic progress (Allinder, in press; Fuchs, 1988; Wesson, Skiba, Sevcik, King, & Deno, 1984). Thoughtful and instrumental use of the data collected through CBM is necessary to bring about higher academic gains. Two specific uses of CBM data are discussed below.

Teachers must set a specific, end-of-year goal for a student in the academic area of interest (e.g., "When given a passage randomly chosen from the fifth-grade level of the Barkley Reading Series, Tommy will read aloud 85 words correctly in 1 minute with no more than 2 errors"; "When given a list of 20 words randomly chosen from Grade 3 Columbus Spelling Curriculum, Jane will write 105 letter sequences correctly in 3 minutes"). The degree to which this specific, end-of-year goal is ambitious appears to be related to the amount of progress a student makes (Allinder, in press; Fuchs, Fuchs, & Hamlett, 1989a).

Once the end-of-year goal is determined, practitioners are guided to examine student progress toward this goal using a set of decision rules on a biweekly basis. To examine student progress, first a line is drawn on the graph, which connects the student's proficiency at the beginning of the year to the end-of-year goal. This is the *goal line* that indicates the rate of progress the student must approximate if he or she is to meet the end-of-year goal. Next, eight scores are added to the graph, and a trend line is drawn through them. Comparison of student progress toward the end-of-year goal is based on the comparison of the goal line (expected progress) with the student's trend line (actual progress). This results in one of three decisions. If student progress is greater than expected, the end-of-year goal should be increased. If progress is less than expected, an instructional change should be made. If actual progress approximates the expected progress, the goal and the instructional plan should be maintained. Continual application of this set of decision-making rules results in greater gains (Fuchs, 1988).

Case Example 5–1. Using curriculum-based measurement

Ms. Fernandez is a school psychologist in an elementary school. She has worked extensively with Ms. Green, a fifth-grade general-education teacher, and Mr. Campbell, the special-education resource-consultant, with regard to a student named Taylor. Taylor has been verified as having a learning disability in the areas of reading and written expression. Taylor receives instruction in Ms. Green's class in all content areas, with Mr. Campbell providing consultant services. This appears to be effective in reading: Mr. Campbell provides extensive prereading activities to a small group of students, including Taylor, prior to reading assignments in content area textbooks, and then Taylor successfully completes his assignments in these texts. In written expression, particularly spelling, however, neither Ms. Green nor Mr. Campbell is satisfied with Taylor's performance. Ms. Green has reported that Taylor's writing would meet minimal qualitative measures she considers important, such as organization of ideas, variety of vocabulary, and cohesion. However, both teachers are concerned about

Case Example 5–1.   *(Continued)*

Taylor's spelling. At the beginning of the year, when given the weekly 25-word spelling test in fifth-grade material, Taylor's score was never above 25%. Ms. Green and Mr. Campbell tried two different approaches to spelling instruction within the whole class that did not prove effective in increasing Taylor's spelling achievement. After consulting with Ms. Fernandez, Mr. Campbell began providing spelling instruction in a small group setting. To monitor the effectiveness of this, Ms. Fernandez suggested that Mr. Campbell use CBM.

To teach Mr. Campbell and Ms. Green how to use CBM, Ms. Fernandez decided to use a computerized approach (see Fuchs, Hamlett, & Fuchs, 1990 for further information). Ms. Fernandez suggested this approach because previous research has demonstrated that (1) students can learn to complete CBM probes independently at computers; (2) use of computers decreases the amount of time teachers must spend in administering the probes (Fuchs, Hamlett, Fuchs, Stecker, & Ferguson, 1988); (3) computers can provide immediate feedback before and after each CBM probe, which can be important because the effect of seeing the most recent score plotted immediately on a graph is positive for students (Glor-Scheib & Zigmond, 1993); and (4) the software provides skills analysis, which assists teachers in modifying instruction (Fuchs, Fuchs, Hamlett, & Allinder, 1991; Fuchs, Fuchs, Hamlett, & Stecker, 1990).

Mr. Campbell had Taylor practice keyboarding skills at the computer for 2 weeks to help ensure that Taylor's scores on the CBM probes would not be affected by typing ability. Ms. Fernandez choose an end-of-year goal for Taylor. With input from the two teachers, it was decided that Taylor's end-of-year goal in spelling would be to be proficient in fourth-grade spelling. Next, Ms. Fernandez entered all the spelling words from the fourth-grade level of the schools' spelling curriculum into the computer program. From this, she generated twenty-five 20-word probes; each probe contained words that were selected randomly from all the fourth-grade words. Therefore, every probe was of equal difficulty and each represented the end-of-year goal.

Mr. Campbell taught Taylor how to use the CBM software in two 15-minute sessions. He also made sure that Taylor understood the graph presented immediately before and after each spelling probe. This graph showed Taylor his past growth in spelling as well as highlighting the most recent score after the probe. To take the spelling probes, Mr. Campbell read aloud a list of 20 words at 15-second intervals for 3 minutes. Taylor typed each word within the time period. After the 3 minutes were up, the computer scored each word according to letter sequences (LS), or pairs of letters in the correct sequence. On a separate screen, Taylor saw the total number of correct letter sequences earned that day. Next, a graph was displayed with the most recent score highlighted.

After Taylor had taken five spelling probes, Mr. Campbell, Ms. Fernandez, and Ms. Green examined Taylor's initial spelling performance on the CBM probes. The median score Taylor earned in fourth-grade spelling for this time period was 45 correct letter sequences. Ms. Fernandez explained that they would be monitoring letter sequences rather than whole words because this was a more sensitive measure of change over time.

"Now," explained Ms. Fernandez, "we need to decide on a specific end-of-year goal for Taylor in spelling. We had decided we wanted Taylor to be proficient at fourth-

(continued)

Case Example 5–1.   *(Continued)*

grade spelling, but exactly how many letter sequences do we expect Taylor to write by the end of the school year?"

Mr. Campbell turned to Ms. Fernandez and said, "How do you know what is an appropriate goal for a student like Taylor in spelling?"

"Well," explained Ms. Fernandez, "we could base it on what the typical student does at the end of the school year in fourth-grade spelling. Or we could use what previous research indicates is good growth in spelling for students with learning disabilities. In this case, we might expect Taylor to make average gains in spelling equal to 1.5 letter sequences per week. If we go with this approach, we would set Taylor's end-of-year goal at 81. There are 24 weeks until the end of the school year; 1.5 digits per week would be 36 additional digits. Add this to Taylor's median baseline score of 45, and you get 81 correct letter sequences."

"Sounds good to me," said Mr. Campbell. "Now what do we do?"

Ms. Fernandez responded, "We are going to add this goal to Taylor's graph. A vertical line at this date will indicate when we set the end-of-year goal. You also see a diagonal line connecting the present level of performance (45) with the end-of-year goal of 81 (see Figure 5–1). This is the goal line. It's what we expect Taylor's progress in spelling to look like. If Taylor's progress follows this goal line, reaching the goal will be easy. If Taylor's actual progress turns out to be greater than we expected, we will raise the end-of-year goal. This is important because the research all indicates that when teachers set ambitious goals, their students achieve more. On the other hand, if Taylor's performance is less than expected, we will have to make some modification in the instructional plan to increase the likeliness of Taylor reaching the goal. For now,

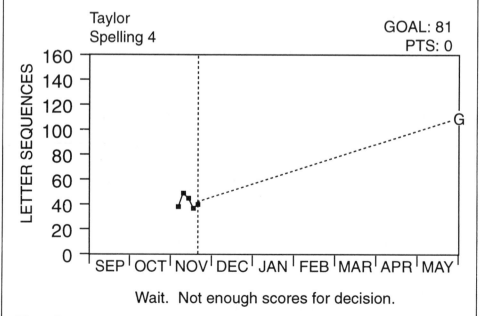

Figure 5–1.   Taylor's graph after Ms. Fernandez set the initial end-of-year goal

Case Example 5–1.   *(Continued)*

continue with the instructional plan you are currently using with Taylor. Also, continue having Taylor take two spelling probes per week. When there are eight scores after the last vertical line, we will make some decisions."

"What kind of decisions?" asked Ms. Green.

"After eight scores have been added to the graph, we will have enough information to look for overall trends in Taylor's performance in spelling and the effectiveness of the instructional plan. It's important that there are eight scores before we decide whether the instructional plan is working. Any one score shouldn't overinfluence us. Taking two probes a week means that eight scores would be gathered in one month's time, a good amount of time to allow an instructional plan to work."

Both teachers agreed to this arrangement. Mr. Campbell continued to implement the instructional plan written for Taylor, which involved having him complete the *I Can Spell* computer program independently. Mr. Campbell allotted 40 minutes per week for this spelling instruction.

After 4 weeks, Ms. Fernandez scheduled a meeting with Mr. Campbell and Ms. Green.

"I wanted to meet with you today to examine Taylor's progress in spelling. When we met last time, we agreed that you, Mr. Campbell, would continue providing spelling instruction for Taylor and that he would take two spelling probes a week. How has this assessment plan worked?"

"It's been fine. At first I tended to forget to have Taylor take the spelling probes twice a week. However, your recommendation to list this within my plan book as a reminder to myself really helped."

"Good. Let's examine Taylor's graph now. We will use the teacher disk of this CBM software. We simply boot it up, select Taylor's name, and look at the graph. As you remember, the dotted diagonal line is the goal line—the amount of progress we expect Taylor to make to reach the end-of-year goal. Each score represents Taylor's overall performance on fourth-grade material, *not* the score earned on a weekly list of words from the spelling curriculum. The scores appear to be somewhat 'bouncy,' but that's not unexpected. Through Taylor's actual scores is a dotted diagonal line. This is the trend line. As you can see, Taylor's actual progress, as indicated by the trend line, is greater than the expected progress. Therefore, we should raise the goal. We will indicate this on the graph with another vertical line" (See Figure 5–2).

"Wonderful," said Ms. Green. "Tell me, though, how is Taylor responding to the spelling probes? I've been concerned about him having to type a word in 15 seconds or less. Does this make Taylor nervous?"

"No," replied Mr. Campbell, "Taylor doesn't seem the least bit bothered by the time component. I explained that while we want the word to be spelled correctly, it's also important to spell it in a reasonable amount of time. To tell you the truth, Taylor almost always finishes a word before the 15 seconds are up."

"Well," interjected Ms. Fernandez, "it looks like the instructional plan you are using seems to be working. Let's continue to have Taylor take two CBM spelling probes a week."

(continued)

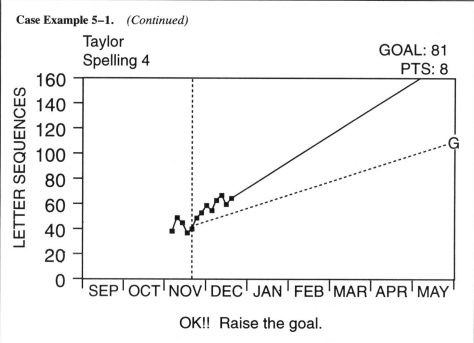

OK!! Raise the goal.

Figure 5–2. Taylor's graph with eight additional scores plotted

The team met again 4 weeks later. Again, Ms. Fernandez led Mr. Campbell through, using the teacher disk and examining Taylor's graph.

"As you see, Taylor's rate of progress appears to be flattening out. At this rate of progress, it is doubtful that the end-of-year goal will be met" (see Figure 5–3).

"I see," said Mr. Campbell. "What happens now?"

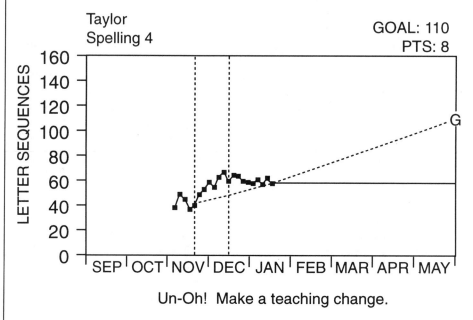

Un-Oh! Make a teaching change.

Figure 5–3. Taylor's graph after the goal was raised to 110 and eight additional scores plotted

Case Example 5–1.   *(Continued)*

"First, let's indicate on the graph with a vertical line that an instructional change is being made on this date. To make an instructional change, let's review the current instructional plan. One advantage that CBM software offers is skills analysis, which can analyze Taylor's performance on the most recent 50 words of the CBM spelling probes. First, we see the numbers and percentages of words that were spelled correctly, nearly correct, not-nearly correct, or completely wrong. In addition, we can see the types of phonetic errors made. The software prioritizes these errors and lets us know which are the most common" (see Figure 5–4).

"I see," said Mr. Campbell. "It looks like Taylor makes most errors in final *e* words, final vowels, and words with double consonants."

Ms. Green added, "How interesting. These are exactly the types of errors I've noticed Taylor making in the papers he turns in."

NAME: Taylor   Spelling 4

Corrects (100% LS)	15 word(s)
Near Misses (60–99% LS)	17 word(s)
Moderate Misses (20–59% LS)	10 word(s)
Far Misses (0–19% LS)	8 word(s)

Type	Correct	Possible	Pct	Type	Correct	Possible	Pct
Sing cons	40	43	93	Final vowel	4	8	50
Blend	11	15	73	Double	2	9	22
FLSZ	1	2	50	c/s	0	1	0
Single vowel	27	35	77	c/ck	1	3	33
Digraph	3	3	100	-le	1	2	50
Vowel + N	11	13	84	ch/tch	2	3	66
Dual cons	16	25	64	-dge	0	1	0
Final e	0	3	0	Vowel team	5	12	41
igh/ign	0	0	100	Suffix	3	4	75
ild/old	0	0	100	tion/sion	0	0	100
a+l+con	0	0	100	ance/ence	0	0	100
Vowel + R	10	15	66	sure/ture	0	1	0

KEY ERRORS

Final e		Final vowel		Double	
meantime	– MEANTIM	taste	– tast	suggest	– sugest
rare	– rar	arrange	– ARRAN	pattern	– patern
cube	– cub	hero	– hearow	odd	– od
		lunlucky	– unluke	mistress	– mistre
				committee	– comity
				giggle	– gelle

Figure 5–4.   Skills analysis for first instructional change

(continued)

Case Example 5–1.   *(Continued)*

"Well," said Mr. Campbell, "it looks like that's what I should be focusing my instruction on. I think that is the instructional change I should make. I really liked that computer program Taylor was using, but I think I'll put that on hold for a while. In addition to changing the skill I think I should change my teaching strategy. To teach these phonetic rules, I'll use teacher presentation, modeling, guided practice, and *then* independent practice."

"Good," said Ms. Fernandez. "Let's document these changes and continue probing."

After four weeks, Ms. Fernandez met with Mr. Campbell and Ms. Green. Mr. Campbell was very excited: "I went ahead and printed out Taylor's graph and skills analysis for our meeting today. The graph shows definite improvement overall in spelling, suggesting we again raise the end-of-year goal" (see Figure 5–5).

"This is great," said Ms. Fernandez. "A month ago you decided to change the spelling skill focused on as well as your teaching strategy. It looks like this worked."

"Yes, I have to agree," said Mr. Campbell. "The skills analysis shows that Taylor made no mistakes with final-vowel words or with double-consonant words. Using the presentation and modeling approach before having Taylor do guided or independent practice appears to have been the best approach."

"I agree," said Ms. Fernandez. "Now it's time to raise the goal, insert a new vertical line into Taylor's graph, and continue with instruction."

Mr. Campbell responded, "True. I would also like to make another instructional change. While I like the teaching strategies I've been using with Taylor, the skill should be new. According to the skills analysis, the most common problem is with digraphs and vowels + *n* words. That's what we will tackle next" (see Figure 5–6).

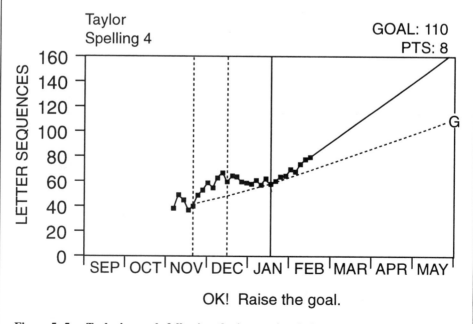

OK! Raise the goal.

Figure 5–5.   Taylor's graph following the instructional change

Case Example 5–1.   *(Continued)*

NAME: Taylor			Spelling 4			

Corrects (100% LS)   15 word(s)
Near Misses (60–99% LS)   17 word(s)
Moderate Misses (20–59% LS)   15 word(s)
Far Misses (0–19% LS)   3 word(s)

Type	Correct	Possible	Pct	Type	Correct	Possible	Pct
Sing cons	40	49	81	Final vowel	0	2	0
Blend	15	16	93	Double	1	5	20
FLSZ	0	1	0	c/s	2	7	28
Single vowel	27	38	69	c/ck	3	3	100
Digraph	4	7	57	-le	1	2	50
Vowel + N	4	10	40	ch/tch	0	1	0
Dual cons	10	20	50	-dge	0	0	100
Final e	3	8	37	Vowel team	8	17	47
igh/ign	0	0	100	Suffix	0	2	0
ild/old	0	0	100	tion/sion	0	1	0
a+l+con	0	1	0	ance/ence	0	1	0
Vowel + R	5	9	55	sure/ture	0	0	100

KEY ERRORS

Digraph		Vowel + N		Dual cons	
parachute	– pishust	frank	– frunk	student	– studen
wheat	– wars	grunt	– grut	mumble	– munble
ashore	– oust	carton	– carter	grunt	– grut
		entrance	– intranc	gulp	– gulm
		inland	– inli	earnest	– east
		loosen	– loster	inland	– inli

Figure 5–6.   Second skills analysis

RELIABILITY AND VALIDITY

The reliability and validity of CBM are a distinct advantage to school psychologists. Developed through multiple studies across several years, results generally support CBM as a technically strong assessment system. The sections below briefly review, separately, the reliability and validity of CBM measures in reading, spelling, written expression, and math.

Reliability

Reading

Prevailing forms of reading assessment in CBM include reading from a passage, list, cloze, or maze for a fixed, brief period of time. Of these types, reading words aloud for 1 minute and replacing blanks in maze passages for 2.5 minutes are used most frequently. For oral reading, the tester marks errors while students read aloud from a passage. Errors are considered to be omissions, substitutions, deletions, and hesitations of more than 3 seconds; self-corrections and insertions are not considered errors. Interjudge reliability for this form of CBM has been reported between 96% and 99% with children reading aloud to adults (Deno, Marston, Mirkin, Lowry, Sindelar, & Jenkins, 1982); 98.8% for narrative and 97.5% for expository material when adults in an adult literacy program read aloud (Bean & Lane, 1990); and between 94.8% and 100% when children's scoring was compared with adults' scoring (Bentz, Shinn, & Gleason, 1990). Test-retest reliability has been reported as ranging from 93 to 96% (Fuchs, Deno, & Marston, 1983).

Spelling

For CBM in the area of spelling, lists of 20 words randomly chosen to represent an end-of-year spelling goal are dictated to students, who have no more than 10 seconds to write each word, with a maximum of 2.5 minutes across lists (Shinn, 1989). Performance, then, is scored as the number of words written correctly and the number of correct letter sequences, or pairs of letters, written in correct sequence.

Marston (1989) summarized reliability studies of CBM spelling by both words correct and letter sequences correct. Test-retest reliabilities at 2, 5, 10, and 20 weeks were, respectively, .94, .85, .87, and .91 for words correct and .93, .83, .92, and .86, for letter sequences correct. Parallel-form reliabilities ranged from .82 to .96 for words correct and .82 and .97 for letter sequences correct. Parallel-form/test-retest reliabilities ranged from .80 to .85 for words correct and .87 to .84 for letter sequences correct. Interjudge reliabilities were .99 and .91 for words correct and letter sequences correct.

Written Expression

In written expression CBM, students typically are given a story starter (i.e., *It was a dark and stormy night when I suddenly heard a loud . . .*), with the directions to think for 1 minute about what they will write. Next, students are given 3 minutes to write in response to the story starter. Resulting stories can be scored in a quantitative or qualitative fashion. Reliabilities of both quantitative and qualitative measures have been reported. First, we present the quantitative measures.

Marston (1989) summarized earlier reliability studies of CBM written expression for three frequent scores: total words written, words correctly spelled, and correct letter sequences written in a 1-minute writing sample. Test-retest reliabilities for total words ranged from .42 (10 weeks) to .91 (1 day); for words correctly spelled from .46 (10 weeks) to .81 (1 day); and for correct letter sequences from .51 (10 weeks) to .92 (1 day). Split-half reliability was reported as .99, .96, and .98 for total words, correct words, and correct letter sequences, respectively. Parallel-form reliability for total words ranged from .58 (10 forms, 1 week apart) to .95 (two forms, same day); for correct words from .59 (parallel forms, 1 week apart) to .95 (two forms, same day); for correct letter sequences from .64 (parallel forms, 1 week apart) to .96 (two forms, same day). Interjudge reliabilities ranged from .98 to .99 for the three metrics.

In more recent studies, interjudge reliability of common quantitative CBM written expression measures have been reported as .99 for number of words written in a 3-minute sample; a range of .97 to .98 for number of words spelled correctly; a range of .87 to .98 for number of correct word sequences; and .95 for number of legible words (Parker, Tindal, & Hasbrouck, 1991; Tindal & Parker, 1991). Split-half reliability for CBM written expression has been reported as .77 for number of words written in a 3-minute sample; .78 for number of correctly spelled words; .81 for number of legible words; and .75 for number of correct word sequences (Parker, Tindal, & Hasbrouck, 1991; Tindal & Parker, 1991). Test-retest reliability for these quantitative measures of CBM Written Expression include .82 for total words written in a 3-minute sample; .75 for number of correctly spelled words; .83 for number of legible words; and .65 for number of correct word sequences (Parker et al., 1991; Tindal & Parker, 1991).

Qualitative measures of CBM written expression generally have not produced reliabilities of the magnitude of those reported for quantitative measures. Interjudge reliability for story idea, organization and cohesion, and writing conventions have been reported as .79, .73, and .75, respectively (Tindal & Parker, 1991).

Math

In CBM math assessments, students are given math problems to answer under timed conditions. Math probes may be single-problem probes containing only one type of computation problem, mixed-problem probes containing several types of computation problems, or application probes containing several types of application problems, such as place value, money, measurement, and time.

In a summary of CBM math computation reliability studies (Marston, 1989), five types of reliability were reported. Internal consistency was reported as .93 for mixed probes; test-retest ranged from .78 for division-only probes to .93 for mixed probes; parallel-form reliability ranged from .48 to .72; and interscorer reliability ranged from .93 to .98 on mixed probes.

Validity

Reading

Content validity of CBM reading measures is assumed to be sufficient, given that probes may be developed from local curricular materials. Several studies have demonstrated that CBM reading procedures have strong discriminant validity to differentiate among students at different grade levels and with varying abilities (Shinn et al., 1989). Construct validity for CBM reading procedures has been partially provided in a study by Fuchs, Fuchs, and Maxwell (1988), which compared question-answering tests, recall procedures, oral passage reading measures, and cloze technique with two global, standardized measures of reading: the Word Study Skills (WS) and Reading Comprehension (RC) subtests of the Stanford Achievement Test (SAT). Results indicated that the correlation between the oral passage reading test and the SAT RC subtest was .92. This was significantly higher than the correlation between the oral passage reading test and the SAT WS subtest (.81).

The preponderance of CBM validity studies in the area of reading addresses criterion validity. CBM is an assessment system that does not measure specific skills but generalized outcomes or proficiency (Fuchs & Deno, 1991; Jenkins & Jewell, 1993). To index overall proficiency, the most commonly used measure is number of words read aloud correctly from a passage in 1 minute. The validity of this approach to reading assessment is sometimes challenged (Potter & Wamre, 1990). Much research has investigated the validity of the 1-minute oral reading method of assessing reading.

In an early study of the validity of CBM reading measures, correlations were reported among three simple measures of reading aloud (words in isolation, words in context, and oral reading of a passage) and standardized norm-referenced measures of reading achievement (Deno, Mirkin, & Chiang, 1982). Correlations between 1-minute oral reading and the Reading Comprehension subtest of the Standard Diagnostic Reading Test (SDRT; Karlsen, Madden, & Gardner, 1975) and the Word Identification and Word Comprehension subtests of the Woodcock Reading Mastery Test (Woodcock, 1973) ranged from .73 to .91. When these three CBM measures were correlated with the Peabody Individual Achievement Test (Dunn & Markwardt, 1970) and the Reading Comprehension subtest of the SDRT results again were supportive of the CBM measures. Oral reading correlations with the standardized measures were .78 and .80 for Literal and Inferential Comprehension, respectively, and .67 and .71 for cloze measures. The higher correlations between oral reading and the standardized measures give support to oral reading as a more valid measure of reading comprehension (Deno et al., 1982).

Further evidence of the concurrent validity of CBM oral passage reading has been made available. Jenkins and Jewell (1993) compared this measure of reading with two global, norm-referenced reading tests: the Gates-MacGinitie Reading Test (MacGinitie, Kamons, Kowalski, MacGinitie, & McKay, 1978) and the Metropolitan Achievement Test (MAT; Prescott, Balow, Hogan, & Farr, 1984). Results indicated the correlations between CBM oral passage reading and the Gates-MacGinitie and the MAT were .88 and .80, respectively. Bain and Garlock (1992) reported correlations between CBM oral passage reading and the total Reading Scores from the Comprehensive Test of Basic Skills (CTBS/McGraw-Hill, 1983) ranging from .54 to .79. Wilson, Schendel, and Ulman (1992) reported correlations between CBM oral passage reading and the Illinois Test of Basic Skills ranging from .39 (Vocabulary subtest) to .52 (Word Analysis subtest).

Development of software to facilitate CBM implementation (Fuchs, Hamlett, & Fuchs, 1990) has made the use of CBM in maze reading passages more common; therefore, information about the validity of this CBM reading measure is important to consider. Jenkins and Jewell (1992) reported that the mean correlation between CBM maze and Gates-MacGinitie reading test was .85; between CBM maze and MAT, .80. The correlation between CBM maze and oral passage reading ranged between .81 and .89 (Jenkins & Jewell, 1992). Espin, Deno, Maruyama, and Cohen (1989) reported the correlation between oral reading and number of filled-in maze blanks as .85. Similarly, Fuchs and Fuchs (1992) reported the correlation between these two informal reading measures as .83; furthermore, in this study, the correlation between maze and the Reading Comprehension subtest of the SAT was .77.

Written Expression

As in reading, content validity of CBM written expression measures is supported through the direct measurement of the skill addressed. Several studies assessing the criterion validity of quantitative CBM written expression measures have been conducted and report the following correlations: (1) for total words written, from .41 with the Test of Written Language subtests to .84 with the Developmental Scoring Sentence; (2) for words correctly spelled, from .45 to .92 with the Test of Written Language; and (3) for correct letter sequence, .57 with the Test of Written Language subtests to .86 with the Developmental Scoring Sentence (see Marston, 1989). These findings were corroborated with results of more recent validation studies (Parker et al., 1991), which report that the range of correlations between CBM written expression and subtests of the Test of Written Language was between −.09 (for total words written and handwriting) and .74 (for percentage of correctly spelled words and spelling).

The validity of CBM written expression measures has been examined with regard to qualitative aspects also. Results indicate that the range of correlations between teachers' holistic ratings and number of total words written was .26 to .61; number of correctly spelled words, .47 to .61; percentage of correctly spelled words, .27 to .76; number of legible words, .34 to .65; percentage of legible words, .53 to .72; and number of correct word sequences, .60 to .71 (Parker et al., 1991).

Spelling

Criterion validity studies in the area of spelling have been summarized by Marston (1989) and include the Test of Written Spelling (TOWS), Peabody Individual Achievement Test (PIAT), and the Stanford Achievement Test, Spelling subtest (SAT-S) as criterion measures. Correlations between the CBM spelling words correct measure and these criterion measures range from .83 with the SAT-S to .95 with the TOWS. Correlations between the CBM correct letter sequences measure and the criterion measures ranged from .80 with the SAT-S to .90 with the PIAT.

Math

In the area of math, early research on the validity of CBM math measures resulted in generally lower correlations than in other areas. Correlations ranged for math computation probes and various criterion measures between .27 for district criterion-referenced tests with first- and second-grade students to .67 for district criterion-referenced tests with fifth- and sixth-grade students (Marston, 1989). In a more recent analysis of CBM math validity, Fuchs, Hamlett, and Fuchs (1990) reported that the criterion validity of CBM math procedures conducted via computer software programs and the Math Computation Test-Revised (MCT-R; Fuchs, Fuchs, Hamlett, & Stecker, 1991) was from .66 to .91 with problems correct and .77 to .87 with digits correct. Correlations also were reported between this computerized version of CBM math and the Concepts of Number (NC) and Math Computation (MC) subtests of the Stanford Achievement Test. Results were .49 to .88 for NC and .55 to .93 for MC. Explanation for these stronger correlations may be related to the differences in CBM measures. In earlier studies the majority of CBM probes consisted of single-problem types; the computerized CBM math probes consisted of mixed probes that contained addition, subtraction, multiplication, and division of whole numbers, fractions, and decimals.

In an examination of the validity of CBM application probes, correlations ranged between .64 and .81 for the CBM application probes and the Comprehensive Test of Basic Skills; correlations between the CBM application measures and computation measures ranged from .63 to .81 (Fuchs, Fuchs, Hamlett, Thompson, Roberts, Kubek, & Stecker, 1994).

TREATMENT VALIDITY

In addition to the research demonstrating technical aspects of CBM, a substantial body of research provides evidence of CBM efficacy relative to student achievement and student metacognition.

Student Achievement

Several studies have provided evidence that teacher use of CBM procedures can positively affect student achievement in reading. Fuchs, Deno, and Mirkin (1984) found that when teachers of students with mild disabilities used CBM procedures in reading, they saw significantly greater gains than did teachers in a control group, both on a passage-reading test and a standardized norm-referenced test. Similarly, Jones and Krouse (1988) reported that student teachers who implemented CBM oral reading progress monitoring and decision making saw significantly greater growth than that of a control group with respect to both a passage-reading test and the Reading Comprehension subtest of the California Achievement Test. Fuchs, Fuchs, and Hamlett (1989) demonstrated that students whose teachers monitored reading progress and who responded to lack of student progress by modifying instruction made significantly greater gains on the Reading Comprehension subtest of the SAT. In this study, the effect size associated with this CBM group and a control group was .72. An effect size of .36 was reported between a CBM group that only monitored student progress but did not use progress monitoring data to adjust instructional plans. Similar results support the need for complete and instrumental use of CBM procedures to affect student growth in reading (Wesson et al., 1984).

Reading is not the only area in which research has demonstrated that teacher implementation of CBM affects student achievement. In spelling, Fuchs, Fuchs, and Hamlett (1989b) reported significantly greater gains for students whose teachers implemented CBM using a computerized system that required they assess student graphed data and formulate decisions (Fuchs, Fuchs, & Hamlett, 1989c).

Student Metacognition

When teachers use CBM to monitor student progress, students appear to respond positively. Students whose teachers implement CBM appear to have greater and more accurate awareness of goals in reading (Fuchs, Deno, & Mirkin, 1984) and in spelling (Fuchs, Butterworth, & Fuchs, 1989). Learners who are provided graphic feedback within CBM are reported to be more motivated (Bean & Lane, 1989); have less variability in scores (Fuchs, Fuchs, Hamlett, & Whinnery, 1991); and have increased self-perceptions of competence in reading (Glor-Scheib & Zigmond, 1993).

ADDRESSING LIMITATIONS WITH INNOVATING EXTENSIONS TO CBM

While the technical adequacy of CBM has been established and the efficacy of teacher use of CBM to enhance student achievement has been demonstrated, some limitations exist. Mehrens and Clarizio (1993) pinpoint the chief limitation: "In short, although CBM has the potential for telling us *when* to modify instruction, it does not link assessment with instruction by telling us, a priori, *what* to teach or *how* best to teach" (p. 252). Lack of sufficient progress toward the end-of-year goals tells the teacher to modify the existing instructional plan, but the graphed data are restricted in helping the teacher decide what to change instructionally. To address this limitation, two avenues have been explored: skills analyses and expert systems, and combining CBM with portfolio assessment.

Skills Analyses and Expert Systems

Skills analyses and expert systems have been investigated as components of the software version of CBM—Monitoring Basic Skills Progress (MBSP; Fuchs, Hamlett, & Fuchs, 1990). This software enables students to take CBM probes independently at Apple computers; it assists teachers in implementing CBM by graphing student scores and applying decisions regarding adequacy of end-of-year goal and sufficiency of student progress toward that goal. In addition, MBSP provides teachers with a skills analysis that is qualitative rather than quantitative in nature. In math, the degree of mastery of each subskill the student attempted is depicted for the teacher to use in making instructional changes. Thus, as guided by the skills analysis, the teacher might begin teaching a new math subskill, teach a prerequisite skill, or provide maintenance practice on another skill. In spelling, the skills analysis portion of MBSP informs the teacher of the types of phonetic spelling errors the student made and identifies key errors for instruction.

The treatment validity of incorporating skills analysis and expert systems into CBM monitoring procedures is well established. Experimental studies comparing treatment and control groups have demonstrated significant effects associated with the use of skills analysis and expert systems in reading (Fuchs, Fuchs, Hamlett, & Ferguson, 1992), spelling (Fuchs, Fuchs, Hamlett, & Allinder, 1991), and math (Fuchs, Fuchs, Hamlett, & Stecker, 1991). Furthermore, the addition of these components is associated with differences in teacher instructional planning and delivery: Teachers who used skills analyses and expert systems employed a more diverse set of teaching strategies, targeted a wider range and more specific components of instruction to reteach, and attempted to increase student motivation (Fuchs, Fuchs, & Hamlett, 1994).

Given that CBM data must be reliable and valid so that decisions regarding *when* to make instructional changes are technically adequate, information from the skills analysis portions of MBSP regarding *how* to modify instruction should be reliable and valid also. Evidence suggests this is so. In math, reliability of problem-type-by-problem-type agreement at different mastery levels at 1-week intervals was .83; in spelling, reliability of .87 was reported for different error types at 1-week intervals. The validity of the skills analysis was assessed by correlating the skill-by-skill analysis with the median score graphed for the same time period. In math, the correlation was .73 (.87 for students with disabilities); in spelling, the correlation was .87 (Fuchs, Fuchs, Hamlett, & Allinder, 1989).

Combining CBM and Portfolio Assessment

A second approach to remediating the limitation denoted by Mehrens and Clarizio (1993) regarding the lack of information CBM provides for knowing *what* or *how* to change instruction focuses on the combination of CBM and portfolio assessment in reading and written expression. The more common CBM assessments in reading (oral passage reading) and written expression (total words written, total thought-units written, total word sequences, etc.) are quantitative in nature, while the qualitative analysis is conspicuous by its absence. In combining CBM measures with portfolio assessment, both aspects may be addressed (Wesson & King, 1992). In writing, the teacher would conduct CBM measures by setting a long-range goal with the student, having the student complete two written expression probes under timed conditions, and graphing the student's progress toward that goal. The teacher would incorporate the portfolio component by developing an instructional plan with the student and generating and collecting writing samples from daily instructional lessons. Jointly, teacher and student would analyze graphed progress toward the long-term goal, and if changes in the instructional plan were warranted by lack of progress toward that goal, teacher and student would together analyze the collected writing samples and modify the instructional plan.

In reading, the combination of CBM and portfolio assessment may rely on the inclusion of miscue analyses of student oral passage reading. While many types of miscue analyses are available (e.g., Goodman & Burke, 1972; Pflaum, 1980), most have little or no support (Leu, 1982; Wixson, 1979). Parker, Hasbrouck, and Tindal (1992), however, combined a variation of Pflaum (1980) with traditional CBM oral passage reading measures. In this procedure, teachers analyzed student errors in reading as (1) corrected or uncorrected and (2) severe, minimal, or no meaning change. Adding information such as this to the quantitative number of words read correctly may provide teachers with insight into *what* or *how* to change their reading instruction if the student is not making sufficient progress toward his or her end-of-year reading goal.

PROGRAM RECOMMENDATIONS

This section addresses recommendations for using CBM with specific regard to the importance of the fidelity of treatment implementation and classwide applications. When CBM is used to monitor and enhance student achievement by evaluating and modifying instructional plans, it appears important that all components of CBM are implemented with high fidelity. Previous research has indicated that poor quality of implementation lessens the positive effect on student progress (Allinder, in press; Fuchs, 1988; Wesson et al., 1984). Practitioners appear to be able to perform some aspects of CBM with greater ease than other aspects. Specifically, practitioners have students complete probes frequently, set ambitious goals, and increase goals with good fidelity; however, they are less apt to make instructional decisions in a timely fashion or to modify instructional programs when student progress is less than sufficient (Allinder & BeckBest, 1995; Allinder & Oats, 1997). While the first set of components is important for enhancing student progress, the latter components may be more critical.

CBM was developed to be used (and has primarily been) with students on an individualized basis (Deno, 1992). While this practice is laudatory and meets both the spirit and letter of Public Law 94–142, it may not be the method of first choice in every situation. Students with disabilities are increasingly receiving larger amounts of instruction in the general classroom (Graden, Zins, & Curtis, 1989). Within the general classroom, individual monitoring of student progress may not be feasible or desirable for a variety of reasons: Prohibitive amounts of time are required to monitor students individually; large amounts of student data generated by individual student monitoring may make interpretation difficult for general education teachers; and if student data indicate the need for instructional modifications, general education teachers rarely are prepared to implement these changes (Fuchs, Fuchs, & Hamlett, 1994). To meet the challenges associated with monitoring student performance within the general education classroom, specific classwide CBM procedures have been developed (e.g., Fuchs, Fuchs, Phillips, Hamlett, & Karnes, in press).

Using computer applications, students complete CBM assessments in reading or in math. Information from the assessments is stored, analyzed, and presented to the classroom teacher twice monthly. Teacher feedback includes individual student graphs, a class graph, a class skills profile, recommendations for instructional groupings and instructional delivery, and peer tutoring pairs (Fuchs, Fuchs, Hamlett, Phillips, & Bentz, 1994; Phillips, Hamlett, Fuchs, & Fuchs, 1993). Results from these investigations indicate that the combination of CBM and instructional recommendations effected significantly greater growth among students, including students with learning disabilities.

CONCLUSION

CBM is a technically reliable set of procedures whose use for progress monitoring in basic academic skills has been demonstrated to have strong treatment validity. As illustrated in the case study, school psychologists may use CBM as a means of documenting and evaluating the effectiveness of suggested instructional interventions as implemented by special education and general education teachers. Because of (1) the simplicity of the procedures, (2) the development of computer-assisted CBM programs for individuals and groups of students, which provides additional information in the form of skills analysis and group profiles, and (3) the research demonstrating strong reliability and validity of all procedures, school psychologists can confidently include CBM in their repertoire of assessment techniques.

As education continues to struggle to understand and refine assessment practices, strategic analysis of the *why* of assessment must remain as important as the *how* of assessment. School psychologists, teachers, and administrators are well advised to delineate the purposes of assessing children and then to match this purpose carefully and thoughtfully to the appropriate assessment procedures. Although norm-referenced tests will undoubtedly continue to fulfill certain purposes, they will not meet the requirements of progress monitoring and intervention evaluation. As school psychologists and teachers seek to design and implement instruction for students with special needs, individual-referenced tests such as CBM will continue to best fulfill the purpose of determining the success of these plans.

REFERENCES

Allinder, R.M. (1996). When some is not better than none: Effects of differential implementation on curriculum-based measurement. *Exceptional Children, 62,* 525–536.

Allinder, R.M., & BeckBest, M. (1995). Differential effects of two approaches to supporting teachers' use of curriculum-based measurement. *School Psychology Review, 24*(2), 285–296.

Allinder, R.M., & Oats, R. (1997). Effects of acceptability on teachers' implementation of curriculum-based measurement and student achievement in mathematics computation. *Remedial and Special Education, 18,* 113–120.

Bain, S.K., & Garlock, J.W. (1992). Cross-validation of criterion-related validity for CBM reading passages. *Diagnostique, 17,* 202–208.

Bean, R.M., & Lane, S. (1990). Implementing curriculum-based measures of reading in an adult literacy program. *Remedial and Special Education, 11* (5), 39–46.

Bentz, J., Shinn, M.R., & Gleason, M.M. (1990). Training general education pupils to monitor reading using curriculum-based measurement procedures. *School Psychology Review, 19,* 23–32.

Carver, R.P. (1974). Two dimensions of tests: Psychometric and edumetric. *American Psychologist, 29,* 512–518.

Casey, A., Deno, S., Marston, D., & Skiba, R. (1988). Experimental teaching: Changing beliefs about effective instructional practices. *Teaching Education and Special Education, 11*(3), 123–131.

CTB/McGraw-Hill (1983). *Comprehensive Test of Basic Skills, Forms U & V.* Monterery, CA: Author.

Deno, S.L. (1985). Curriculum-based measurement: The emerging alternative. *Exceptional Children, 52,* 219–232.

Deno, S.L. (1992). The nature and development of curriculum-based measurement. *Preventing School Failure, 36,* 5–10.

Deno, S.L., & Fuchs, L.S. (1987). Developing curriculum-based measurement systems for data-based special education problem solving. *Focus on Exceptional Children, 19*(8), 1–16.

Deno, S.L., Marston, D., Mirkin, P.K., Lowry, L., Sindelar, P., & Jenkins, J.R. (1982). *The use of standard tasks to measure achievement in reading, spelling, and written expression: A normative and developmental study* (Research Report No. 87). Minneapolis, MN: University of Minnesota, Institute for Research on Learning Disabilities.

Deno, S.L., Mirkin, P.K., & Chiang, B. (1982). Identifying valid measures of reading. *Exceptional Children, 49*, 36–47.

Dunn, L.M., & Markwardt, F.C. (1970). *Peabody individual achievement test.* Circle Pines, MN: American Guidance Service.

Espin, C., Deno, S.L., Maruyama, G., & Cohen, C. (1989). *The Basic Academic Skills Samples (BASS): An instrument for the screening and identification of children at risk for failure in regular education classrooms.* Paper presented at the annual meeting of the American Educational Research Association.

Fuchs, D., Fuchs, L.S., & Fernstrom, P. (1992). Case-by-case reintegration of students with learning disabilities. *The Elementary School Journal, 92*, 261–281.

Fuchs, L.S. (1988). Effects of computer-managed instruction on teachers' implementation of systematic monitoring programs and student achievement. *Journal of Educational Research, 81*, 294–304.

Fuchs, L.S., Butterworth, J.R., & Fuchs, D. (1989). Effects of ongoing curriculum-based measurement on student awareness of goals and progress. *Education and Treatment of Children, 12*(1), 63–72.

Fuchs, L.S., & Deno, S.L. (1991). Paradigmatic distinctions between instructionally relevant measurement models. *Exceptional Children, 57*, 488–500.

Fuchs, L.S., Deno, S.L., & Marston, D. (1983). Improving the reliability of curriculum-based measures of academic skills for psychoeducational decision making. *Diagnostique, 8*, 135–149.

Fuchs, L.S., Deno, S.L., & Mirkin, P.K. (1984). The effects of frequent curriculum-based measurement and evaluation on pedagogy, student achievement, and student awareness of learning. *American Educational Research Journal, 21*, 449–460.

Fuchs, L.S., & Fuchs, D. (1992). Identifying a measure for monitoring student reading process. *School Psychology Review, 21*(1), 45–58.

Fuchs, L.S., Fuchs, D., & Hamlett, C.L. (1989a). Effects of instrumental use of curriculum-based measurement to enhance instructional programs. *Remedial and Special Education, 10*(2), 43–52.

Fuchs, L.S., Fuchs, D., & Hamlett, C.L. (1989b). Computers and curriculum-based measurement: Effects of teacher feedback systems. *School Psychology Review, 18*(1), 112–125.

Fuchs, L.S., Fuchs, D., & Hamlett, C.L. (1989c). Effects of alternative goal structures within curriculum-based measurement. *Exceptional Children, 55*, 429–438.

Fuchs, L.S., Fuchs, D., & Hamlett, C.L. (1990). Curriculum-based measurement: A standardized, long-term goal approach to monitoring student progress. *Academic Therapy, 25*, 615–632.

Fuchs, L.S., Fuchs, D., & Hamlett, C.L. (1994). Strengthening the connection between assessment and instructional planning with expert systems. *Exceptional Children, 61*, 138–146.

Fuchs, L.S., Fuchs, D., Hamlett, C.L., & Allinder, R.M. (1989). The reliability and validity of skills analysis in curriculum-based measurement. *Diagnostique, 14*, 203–221.

Fuchs, L.S., Fuchs, D., Hamlett, C.L., & Allinder, R.M. (1991). The contribution of skills analysis to curriculum-based measurement in spelling. *Exceptional Children, 57*, 443–452.

Fuchs, L.S., Fuchs, D., Hamlett, C.L., & Ferguson, C. (1992). Effects of expert system consultation within curriculum-based measurement using a reading maze task. *Exceptional Children, 58,* 436–450.

Fuchs, L.S., Fuchs, D., Hamlett, C.L., Phillips, N.B., & Bentz, J. (1994). Classwide curriculum-based measurement: Helping general educators meet the challenge of student diversity. *Exceptional Children, 60,* 518–537.

Fuchs, L.S., Fuchs, D., Hamlett, C.L., & Stecker, P.M. (1990). The role of skills analysis in curriculum-based measurement in math. *School Psychology Review, 19,* 6–22.

Fuchs, L.S., Fuchs, D., Hamlett, C.L., & Stecker, P.M. (1991). Effects of curriculum-based measurement and consultation on teacher planning and student achievement. *American Educational Research Journal, 28,* 617–624.

Fuchs, L.S., Fuchs, D., Hamlett, C.L., Thompson, A., Roberts, P.H., Kubek, P., & Stecker, P.M. (1994). Technical features of a mathematics concepts and applications curriculum-based measurement system. *Diagnostique, 19,* 23–49.

Fuchs, L.S., Fuchs, D., Hamlett, C.L., & Whinnery, K. (1991). Effects of goal line feedback on level, slope, and stability of performance within curriculum-based measurement. *Learning Disabilities: Research & Practice, 6,* 66–74.

Fuchs, L.S., Fuchs, D., & Maxwell, L. (1988). The validity of informal reading comprehension measures. *Remedial and Special Education, 9*(2), 20–28.

Fuchs, L.S., Fuchs, D., Phillips, N.B., Hamlett, C.L., & Karnes, C. (in press). Acquisition and transfer effects of classwide peer-assisted learning strategies in mathematics for students with varying learning histories. *School Psychology Review.*

Fuchs, L.S., Hamlett, C.L., & Fuchs, D. (1990). *Monitoring Basic Skills Progress* [computer programs]. Austin, TX: PRO-ED.

Fuchs, L.S., Hamlett, C.L., Fuchs, D., Stecker, P.M., & Ferguson, C. (1988). Conducting curriculum-based measurement with computerized data collection: Effects on efficiency and teacher satisfaction. *Journal of Special Education Technology, 9,* 73–86.

Glor-Scheib, S., & Zigmond, N. (1993). Exploring the potential motivational properties of curriculum-based measurement in reading among middle school students with learning disabilities. *Learning Disabilities, 4,* 35–43.

Goodman, Y.M., & Burke, C.L. (1972). *Reading miscue inventory.* New York: Macmillan.

Graden, J.L., Zins, J.E., & Curtis, M.J. (1989). *Alternative educational delivery systems: Enhancing instructional options for all students.* Washington, DC: National Association of School Psychologists.

Jenkins, J.R., & Jewell, M. (1993). Examining the validity of two measures for formative teaching: Reading aloud and maze. *Exceptional Children, 59,* 421–432.

Jenkins, J.R., & Pany, D. (1978). Standardized achievement tests: How useful for special education students? *Exceptional Children, 44,* 448–453.

Jones, E.D., & Krouse, J.P. (1988). The effectiveness of data-based instruction by student teachers in classrooms for pupils with mild learning handicaps. *Teacher Education and Special Education, 11(1),* 9–19.

Karlsen, B., Madden, R., & Gardner, E.F. (1975). *Stanford diagnostic reading test* (Green Level Form B). New York: Harcourt Brace Jovanovich.

Leu, K.J. (1982). Oral reading error analysis: A critical review of research and application. *Reading Research Quarterly, 17,* 420–437.

MacGinitie, W.H., Kamons, J., Kowalski, R.L., MacGinitie, R.K., & McKay, T. (1978). *Gates-MacGinitie Reading Tests* (2nd ed.). Chicago: Riverside.

Marston, D.B. (1989). A curriculum-based measurement approach to assessing academic performance: What it is and why do it. In M.R. Shinn (Ed.), *Curriculum-based measurement: Assessing special children* (pp. 18–78). New York: Guilford Press.

Marston, D., Fuchs, L.S., & Deno, S.L. (1986). Measuring pupil progress: A comparison of standardized achievement tests and curriculum-related measures. *Diagnostique, 11,* 77–90.

Mehrens, W.A., & Clarizio, H.F. (1993). Curriculum-based measurement: Conceptual and psychometric considerations. *Psychology in the Schools, 30,* 241–254.

Parker, R., Hasbrouck, J.E., & Tindal, G. (1992). Greater validity for oral reading fluency: Can miscues help? *The Journal of Special Education, 25,* 492–503.

Parker, R.I., Tindal, G., & Hasbrouck, J. (1991). Progress monitoring with objective measures of writing performance for students with mild disabilities. *Exceptional Children, 58,* 61–73.

Pflaum, S.W. (1980). Diagnosis of oral reading. *The Reading Teacher, 33,* 278–284.

Phillips, N.B., Hamlett, C.L., Fuchs, L.S., & Fuchs, D. (1993). Combining classwide curriculum-based measurement and peer tutoring to help general educators provide adaptive education. *Learning Disabilities: Research & Practice, 8,* 148–156.

Potter, M.L., & Wamre, H.M. (1990). Curriculum-based measurement and developmental reading models: Opportunities for cross-validation. *Exceptional Children, 57,* 16–25.

Prescott, G.A., Balow, I.H., Hogan, T.P., & Farr, R.C. (1984). *Metropolitan Achievement Tests (MAT-6).* San Antonio, TX: The Psychological Corporation.

Shapiro, E.S., & Derr, T.F. (1987). An examination of the overlap between reading curricula and standardized tests. *The Journal of Special Education, 21,* 59–67.

Shinn, M.R. (1989). Case study of Ann H: From referral to annual review. In M.R. Shinn (Ed.), *Curriculum-based measurement: Assessing special children* (pp. 79–89). New York: Guilford Press.

Shinn, M.R., Habedank, L., Rodden-Nord, K., & Knutson, N. (1993). Using CBM to identify potential candidates for reintegration into general education. *The Journal of Special Education, 27,* 202.

Shinn, M.R., Rosenfield, S., & Knutson, N. (1989). Curriculum-based assessment: A comparison of models. *School Psychology Review, 18,* 299–316.

Tindal, G. (1992). Evaluating instructional programs using curriculum-based measurement. *Preventing School Failure, 36,* 39–42.

Tindal, G.A., & Marston, D.B. (1990). *Classroom-based assessment: Evaluating instructional outcomes.* Columbus, OH: Merrill.

Tindal, G., & Parker, R. (1991). Identifying measures for evaluating written expression. *Learning Disabilities: Research & Practice, 6,* 211–218.

Tucker, J.A. (1987). Curriculum-based assessment is not a fad. *The Collaborative Educator, 1* (4), 4, 10.

Wesson, C.L., & King, R.P. (1992). The role of curriculum-based measurement in portfolio assessment. *Diagnostique, 18*(1), 27–37.

Wesson, C.L., Skiba, R., Sevcik, B., King, R.P., & Deno, S. (1984). The effects of technically adequate instructional data on achievement. *Remedial and Special Education, 5*(5), 17–22.

Wilson, M.S., Schendel, J.M., & Ulman, J.E. (1992). Curriculum-based measures, teachers' ratings, and group achievement scores: Alternative screening measures. *Journal of School Psychology, 30,* 59–76.

Wixson, K.L. (1979). Miscue analysis: A critical review. *Journal of Reading Behavior, 11,* 165–175.

Woodock, R.W. (1973). *Woodcock reading mastery tests* (Form A). Circle Pines, MN: American Guidance Service.

Part II

Skill and Behavioral Assessment

Chapter 6

ASSESSING CURRENT PSYCHOLOGICAL STATUS

DAVID A. SABATINO, CAROLE G. FULLER, AND EVA A. ALTIZER

This chapter reviews selected diagnostic procedures, including the mental status examination (MSE), used in describing personality development in children with emotional disturbance. The evaluation process with children has a long history of being overly dependent upon test data without use of the MSE. Test data including self-report questionnaires and observational data reported from those in role relationships with the child (i.e., teacher, day or evening care provider) are not substitutes for MSE but are collaborative aspects of the clinical decision-making process. Personality assessment requires the examiner to obtain descriptive historic and current developmental, social-personal, medical-health, educational, and psychological data. Mental status examinations require obtaining intake data while simultaneously observing and obtaining client responses to gross- and fine-motor development (including gait and balance), sensory function, samples of motor speech and language, expression of affect, mood, adaptive behaviors, communications of thoughts and feeling awareness, social-personal interactions, and unusual, unique, or predominate behaviors.

Most psychological reports on adults contain descriptions of the client's current mental status. In sharp contrast, few school or child clinical psychological reports include mental status examinations. The MSE is the diagnostic process of interacting with the child in an attempt to understand the responses, reactions, beliefs, and motivations that underlie his or her observable behavior. Simply observing and reporting behaviors does not constitute a mental process examination but turns a psychological examination into a social work report.

This chapter will explore a systematic means of observing and interacting with clients during the clinical interview to obtain the data necessary for determining current psychological status. As well as examining several selected behavioral rating devices, the chapter looks at two newer and more comprehensive child and adolescent self-rating personality tests: the Minnesota Multiphasic Personality Inventory-Adolescent (MMPI-A; Butcher, Williams, Graham, Archer, Tellegen, Ben-Porath, & Kaemmer, 1992) and the Behavioral Assessment System for Children (BASC; Reynolds & Kamphaus, 1992). A brief section will discuss some of the older projective diagnostic procedures—not a complete review, since most of these techniques have existed for years and have a substantial literature base. Then, too, while many of the older procedures such as the Kinetic Family Drawings (Burns & Kaufman, 1972) have been updated and are useful in a dynamic sense, the central focus of this chapter is on the mental status examination itself, which occurs at the end of the chapter.

Unfortunately, many psychological reports label children as *seriously emotionally disturbed* on the basis of two diagnostic procedures, such as a human-figure drawing and a behavioral checklist. A child's psychological status cannot be ascertained by his or her drawing of a human figure or from someone's behavioral observations. Some practitioners insist on using test data to state overdrawn conclusions derived from other subjective means. In many of these cases the so-called diagnosis of seriously emotionally disturbed was made by the teacher at the time of the referral. The psychologist only legitimized it. These reports rarely convey even a brief description of the child's current prevailing mood or his or her feelings, awareness, or responsiveness to that mood—factors central to a mental status examination.

PROJECTIVE TECHNIQUES OF PERSONALITY ASSESSMENT

Projective techniques are based on the psychoanalytic defense mechanism of projection. Freud (1949) thought projection allowed the client to attribute his or her own weaknesses or unacceptable desires to other people, thus decreasing the anxiety the client felt. Projective procedures (Gefland, Jenson, & Drew, 1988) assume that children are driven by psychological forces blocked from consciousness. The child reveals these unconscious conflicts through ambiguous projective test stimuli.

The use of projectives came to the forefront during World War II when clinical psychology was responding to the crisis demands of the military. Bellak (1992) attributed the decrease in usage of projectives after this period to three factors. The first factor was the growing dependence on medication. The second was the decreasing emphasis in long-term psychotherapy on growth in community mental health. The third factor was the increase in behaviorism and decrease in dynamic psychology. Still another factor contributing to the decline in popularity of projective personality instruments was the perception that projective methods failed to meet psychometric standards.

In a now classic book, Meehl (1954) described the actuarial versus the clinical approach to prediction. Meehl's work demonstrated that the actuarial approach relied more on objectivity and less on situational circumstances. Psychological assessment instruments of any type are expected to adhere to five psychometric standards, which are set forth by the American Psychological Association (1985): (1) *validity,* which refers to the "appropriateness, meaningfulness, and usefulness of the specific inferences made from test scores" (APA, 1985); (2) *reliability,* or test stability, which is the consistency of scores from the same test over various administrations; (3) *test development,* which assumes that tests are developed on sound scientific research; (4) *scaling, norming, score comparability, and equating,* subtest and score comparability, which assists interpretation; and (5) *technical manuals and user guides,* which detail the appropriate use, administration, scoring, and interpretation of the instrument.

Projective instruments generally display validity (1) and have a test publication (5); however, the subjective nature of scoring generates low reliability, making interpretation difficult. Different clinicians using the same scoring systems derive scores which may vary greatly as demonstrated by Exner (1986), who studied the use of the Rorschach.

Despite the shortcomings in psychometric properties and the emergence of objective personality instruments, projective tests are still among those most frequently administered. In a survey of 36 clinics by Piotrowski, Sherry, and Keller (1985), the most frequently administered projective tests were the Rorschach and Thematic Apperception Test (TAT). However, the Minnesota Multiphasic Personality Inventory (MMPI; Hathaway & McKinley, 1943) is also reported as being the most frequently administered personality assessment instrument (Lubin, Larsen, Matarazzo, & Seever, 1985).

An example of a modernized projective technique is the children's form of the Picture-Frustration Test (Rosenzweig, 1981), which is used to ascertain children's thought content when dealing with frustrating circumstances. This tool consists of 24 cartoon-like pictures that show normal, everyday frustrating events. The pictures contain balloons in which the children write captions about what they think the child in the picture is thinking in response to these frustrating events. From these caption words, 11 response types are generated. The captions are then used to determine the type of aggression portrayed (obstacle dominance, ego defense and need persistence) portrayed and the direction of the aggression (extra-aggression, intra-aggression, and im-aggression). Test theory and initial research indicated the test could classify changes in children's aggression by type and direction. More recent research by Graybill (1990) suggested that the 11 response types are more stable indicators of frustration than type or direction of aggression.

SELF-REPORT, BEHAVIORAL OBSERVATIONAL PROCEDURES, AND CLINICAL INTERVIEW

This section clarifies the differences among the data sources commonly used in the diagnostic process. Frequently, various diagnostic procedures are used to provide the examiner with similar information from different sources and informants.

Self-Report Instruments

Self-report or questionnaire instruments are usually lengthy, containing in the case of the MMPI-A, 478 individual test items. Often the responses are forced choice, requiring a "True" or "False" answer. Most of these tests recommend that the child read the item, but an option exists for the questions to be read. Understanding item meaning is critical.

The strength of the self-report personality test is the objectivity it provides. Self-report instruments often contain validity scales as well as descriptive scales, all of which are frequently profiled into various personality traits. The applicability of each item has been determined according to its ability to correctly differentiate between clinical and normal populations.

The objective self-report questionnaire approach to personality assessment is the most common personality diagnostic procedure for three very good reasons: (1) A number of these approaches have validity indices (as do both the MMPI-A and the BASC); (2) the better objective personality tests have expanding databases containing current research; and (3) unlike apperceptive and other subjective personality approaches, the examiner's bias and perceptions are held to a minimum. Butcher, Graham, and Ben-Porath (1995) wrote, "The questionnaire method is one of the most versatile and user-friendly approaches to personality assessment in contemporary psychology" (p. 320). The significance of self-report measures is the ability to provide information from several sources (differing observational vantage points), using the same or different observers, including the person taking the test. The more objective self-report systems provide substantial information on the validity and consistency the observer has for his or her own thinking and feeling processes. The MMPI-A and BASC are two current self-report instruments investigated next.

The Minnesota Multiphasic Personality Inventory has a rich history in clinical and research applications. The MMPI was first published by the University of Minnesota Press and has become the most frequently used objective test of personality (Lubin et al., 1985). The original MMPI consisted of 550 items to which the respondent answered "True" or "False." During construction of the test, prospective items were administered to control groups and criterion groups that contained previously classified clinical patients. Those items that showed a statistically significant differentiation between the various clinical populations were retained. The MMPI was constructed with 10 clinical scales and 3 validity scales designed to detect response sets and attitudinal factors.

The original version of the MMPI was used to assess psychopathology in adolescents for many years (Graham, 1987). Adolescents tended to have elevated K (fake good) scores on the MMPI. Since the MMPI was normed on adults (Archer, 1987), it did not appear to be sensitive to the number of false-positive adolescent personality profiles (Chase, Chaffin, & Morrison, 1975).

The MMPI-A was designed to assess characteristics of personality in adolescent populations using the theoretical orientation of the original MMPI. The MMPI-A maintains the 10 clinical scales of the original MMPI and the MMPI-2 (listed with their code number): Hypochondriasis (1), Depression (2), Conversion Hysteria (3), Psychopathic Deviance (4), Masculinity/Femininity (5), Paranoia (6), Psychasthenia (7), Schizophrenia (8), Hypomania (9), and Social Introversion (0). The MMPI-A also retains the Infrequency (F), Lie (L), and Defensiveness (K) validity scales. Four new validity scales were also added, Variable Response Inconsistency (VRIN), True Response Inconsistency (TRIN), Infrequency 1 ($F1$), and Infrequency 2 ($F2$). High scores on the VRIN scale suggest a random, or variable, response pattern. The TRIN scale is designed to detect individuals who respond to items in a predominantly "True" or "False" pattern. The three F scales (F, $F1$, $F2$) contain items related to odd thoughts, sensations, and experiences, as well as antisocial attitudes and behaviors.

The MMPI-A added 15 content scales geared directly to the adolescent population. They include scales such as Adolescent-Anxiety (A-anx), Adolescent-Family Problems (A-fam), and Adolescent-School Problems (A-sch). In addition there are six supplemental scales that complete the MMPI-A profile: MacAndrew Alcoholism-Revised (MAC-R), Alcohol/Drug Acknowledgment (ACK), Alcohol/ Drug Proneness (PRO), Immaturity (IMM), Anxiety (A), and Repression (R). The MAC-R scale contains 49 items that are expected to correlate with an increased likelihood of alcohol or drug abuse, self-indulgence, and impulsivity; of a conduct disorder diagnosis; and of violation of social norms. The ACK scale contains 13 items that indicate the level of acknowledgment of and attitudes toward drug or alcohol use. The PRO scale, composed of 36 items, indicates an increased tendency for drug and alcohol problems. Factors considered in the PRO scale include family and peer characteristics, antisocial behaviors or beliefs, and academic interests and behaviors. The IMM scale contains 43 items that measure psychological maturation based on Loevinger's concept of ego development. The Anxiety scale correlates with individuals who are tense, anxious, fearful, maladjusted, guilty, and self-critical (Archer, 1992). High scores on the R scale indicate individuals who show little feeling and are overcontrolled, inhibited, constricted, and pessimistic (Archer, 1992).

Adding the highest two clinical scales together produces a code type, coded on the number corresponding to the 10 clinical scales. Three Attention-Seeking two-point code types, defined by the two clinical scales with the highest elevations, are unique to adolescents in the MMPI/MMPI-A literature. The 1/3 and 3/1 code type contains the clinical scales of Hypochondriasis and Hysteria as the two high clinical scales. Adolescents with this code type are frequently seen as insecure, manipulative, lacking in interpersonal or social skills, noncompetitive in academic and social environments, and failing to obtain peer and adult recognition through socially approved mechanisms (Archer, 1992).

The 2/8 and 8/2 code types, clinical scales of Depression and Schizophrenia, are associated with low self-esteem and an impaired self-concept, being emotionally volatile, and having difficulty in monitoring emotional expressions (Archer, 1992). A third code type common in troubled adolescents is the 6/8-8/6, clinical scales of Paranoia and Schizophrenia. This code type generally indicates the presence of severe psychopathology. Adolescents exhibiting this code type are perceived as hostile, with inappropriate and unpredictable outbursts of aggression (Archer, 1992).

Archer and Gordon (1994) determined the stability of 70 MMPI items that were modified for inclusion in the MMPI-A. They found that the modified items did not produce changes in correlations with the original items. Archer, Belevich, and Elkins (1994) examined the item and the scale level of the MMPI-A using factor analysis. Sixteen hundred and twenty junior- and senior high-school students from eight states served as subjects. An item matrix was constructed producing 14 factors upon oblique rotation. Three hundred and eighty-nine of the 478 MMPI-A items accounted for 81% of the variance with eigenvalues of 1, with no item in the loading having a value less than plus or minus .25. In addition to the item rotations, scale rotations were obtained with an eigenvalue of 1 accounting for 93.5% of the scale variance. Eight factors resulted from that factor analysis and were named (1) General Maladjustment, (2) Immaturity, (3) Disinhibition/Excitatory Potential, (4) Social Comfort, (5) Health Concerns, (6) Naivete, (7) Familial Alienation, and (8) Psychoticism. The authors concluded that the MMPI-A factors were consistent with those obtained in prior studies on the MMPI. Unique factors were Developmental Symptomatology on the item level and Immaturity on the scale level. These factors were felt to be specific to adolescent development. It was concluded based on these data that the MMPI-A has the capacity to assess the characteristic features unique to adolescence.

The Behavior Assessment System for Children (BASC; Reynolds & Kamphaus, 1992) is a system or group of specific instruments designed for children and adolescents ages 4 to 18. The different components available include a Structured Observation System, Structured Developmental History, Teacher Rating Form (ages 4 to 18), Parent Rating Form (ages 4 to 18), and Self-Report Form (ages 8 to 18). While few personality measures differentiate between children and adolescents, the BASC offers preschool (ages 4 to 5), child (ages 6 to 11), and adolescent (ages 12 to 18) forms. Each age-sensitive form provides the opportunity to obtain parental and teacher ratings. A self-rating form exists for children, ages 8 to 11, and adolescents, ages 12 to 18. Each behavior is rated on a 4-point scale from "Never" to "Almost Always." The self-rating forms provide a validity index containing F (faking bad), L (faking good), and V (validity or random responding) scales. The parent and teacher rating scales provide an F index only.

The BASC SRP-A is a 186-item True/False survey that possesses three validity indices: F, L, and V. The BASC F index resembles the MMPI-A Infrequency scale, detecting those who may attempt to "fake bad." High F scores may be indicative of difficulty reading the items or inability to follow directions. The L index is responsive to subjects trying to "fake good" and is indicative of good reading ability and following directions. High scores may indicate "psychological naivete" and an inability to achieve insight into one's thoughts and feelings. The V index is composed of nonsense items to detect individuals who may not be reading the items or are uncooperative. Also included are 16 critical items that should be considered when several are responded to as "True."

The BASC is composed of Clinical and Adaptive scales that factor into three composites (clinical, school, and personal). Clinical scales include Anxiety, Atypicality, Depression, and Somatization. Adaptive scales include Interpersonal Relations, Relations with Parents, and Self-Esteem. Scales comprising the Emotional Symptoms index are referred to as the SAD triad—Social Stress, Anxiety, and Depression.

The behavioral dimensions rated on the teacher and parent rating forms are aggression, hyperactivity, conduct problems, anxiety, depression, somatization, attention problems, learning problems, atypicality, withdrawal, adaptability, leadership, social skills, and study skills. Preschoolers are not rated on conduct problems, learning problems, leadership, or study skills. Adolescents are not rated on leadership. The scales are grouped according to the following clinical composites: internalizing problems (anxiety, depression, and somatization), externalizing problems (hyperactivity, aggression, and conduct problems), school problems (attention problems and learning problems), adaptive skills (adaptability, social skills, leadership, and study skills), and other problems (atypicality and withdrawal). A special scale on the parent form (consisting of previously rated dimensions) is the behavioral symptoms index, which consists of aggression, hyperactivity, anxiety, depression, and atypicality.

The self-rating forms provide four composites and one index. The four composites are clinical maladjustment (anxiety, atypicality, locus of control, social stress, and somatization), school maladjustment (attitudes toward school, attitudes toward teachers, and sensation seeking), other problems (depression and sense of inadequacy), and personal adjustment (relations with parents, interpersonal relations, self-esteem, and self-reliance). There is an emotional symptoms index that provides a global measure of serious emotional disturbance. It includes the behavioral dimensions of anxiety, social stress, interpersonal relations, self-esteem, and sense of inadequacy. The differences between the child and adolescent self-report scales are that the child form does not include the somatization and sensation seeking scales.

The test authors reported reliability from internal consistency on the teacher form as .82 to .90, as .74 to .80 for the parent form, and as .80 to .82 for the self-report form. Internal consistencies are higher for composite scores across the age range. Test-retest reliability for the composite teacher form is .81 to .96. The test-retest reliability for the parent form is .85 for the preschool, .88 for the child, and .70 for the adolescent form. Test-retest reliability for the self-reports ranges from .64 to .85 for the individual behavioral scales and .78 to 86 for the composites. Interrater reliability between teachers on the composite scores were .47 to .76 for the preschool form and .69 to .89 for ages 6 through 11.

Validity in the form of agreement between the BASC and MMPI is .52 to .60. Norms are provided for students with both emotional and behavior disorders. This is an attempt to provide norms for special-education students with educational classifications based on operational definitions that are consistent with the federal definition (Flanagan, 1995).

Fuller and Sabatino (1994) compared the MMPI-A and BASC on an at-risk population of 50 adolescents, ages 14 through 18, from four alternative schools. Seventy-four percent were male; 82%, caucasian. Thirty-six percent reported they had committed repeated school violations. The MMPI-A validity scales generated mean T scores of 64 on F and 65 on $F1$ (a T score of 65 is the criterion cutoff). All three validity indices on the BASC were well within the normal range.

Several significant relationships existed between MMPI-A and BASC corresponding scales. The BASC Anxiety scale correlated significantly ($r > .70$) with the MMPI-A A-Anxiety Content scale ($r = .77$), Anxiety Supplemental scale ($r = .71$), and Schizophrenia scale ($r = .72$). Four BASC scales correlated highly ($r > .70$) with the Psychasthenia and Schizophrenia scales of the MMPI-A. These include Atypicality, Locus of Control, Somatization, and Sense of Inadequacy. Atypicality also had a strong positive relationship with Paranoia and the Content scale A-Bizarre Mentation.

Significant correlations ($r > .70$) were also obtained between the number of critical items (designated by the authors to warrant further examination) endorsed on the BASC and MMPI-A scales. These scales included Paranoia ($r = .72$), Psychasthenia ($r = .76$), Schizophrenia ($r = .78$), and A-Depression ($r = .70$).

Another group of scales that should have had corresponding content included MMPI-A Hypochondriasis and A-Health Concerns and BASC Somatization. Hypochondriasis and A-Health Concerns had an extremely high positive correlation ($r = .96$). Correlations between the MMPI-A A-Health Concerns and A-Hypochondriasis and BASC Somatization correlated modestly at .61 and .64, respectively.

A group of corresponding named scales across the two tests showed only minimal correlations. BASC Depression and A-Depression had the highest correlations ($r = .60$). Depression and A-Depression from the MMPI-A correlated at .43. The Depression scales from both tests correlated only at the .23 level.

The BASC Atypicality scale related in a strong positive manner with MMPI-A Paranoia ($r = .75$), MMPI-A Schizophrenia ($r = .75$), MMPI-A Psychasthenia ($r = .74$), and MMPI-A A-Bizarre Mentations ($r = .72$). The BASC Atypicality scale was designed to evaluate thought patterns, behaviors and/or perceptions that are often symptomatic of severe psychopathology, including schizoid response patterns. MMPI-A Paranoia, MMPI-A Psychasthenia, and MMPI-A Schizophrenia correlated highly with the BASC Clinical Maladjustment Composite (.76, .83, and .83, respectively).

The school-based scales of the two personality tests loaded factorially but did not generate a significant correlational relationship. The MMPI-A A-School Problems scale produced modest correlations with the BASC Attitude to School ($r = .61$), BASC Attitude to Teachers ($r = .56$), and BASC School Maladjustment Composite ($r = .62$).

The validity scales of both tests produced no significant relationships. The MMPI-A $F1$ and $F2$ correlated highly with the MMPI-A F scale because both scales contribute to the MMPI-A F scale.

Principal-component factor analysis isolated six factors with 72% cumulative variance and eigenvalues greater than 1 using a varimax orthogonal rotation (Kaiser, 1958). Factorial loadings were described by including the variable that loaded the highest and coming down .30. No variable below .36 was considered to constitute a factor within a principal component. The six factors were Defensiveness/Hopelessness, Attention-Seeking, Antisocial Disorders, Conduct Disorders, Interpersonal Problems, and Family Relationship Problems.

Each of these two tests appears to have specific strengths. Correlations were of low-to-moderate value on scales with the same name across the two tests, the Anxiety scales being the exception. The MMPI-A does yield a more specific profile and more data for deriving a multi-axial *DSM-IV* diagnosis. The BASC, however, provides the three perspectives (self, parent, and teacher) and removes some of the bias associated with self-report measures. The BASC is also easily understood and completed by parents and teachers, yielding information from the school setting that is often relevant to presenting problems.

The MMPI-A is stronger in identifying alcohol and/or drug problems, conduct disorders, legal involvement, and violations of social norms (Archer, 1992). Mac-

Andrew Alcoholism-Revised loaded into the Defensiveness/Hopelessness factor. The other supplemental scales dealing with substance use/abuse (ACK, PRO, and IMM) loaded into the Conduct Disorders factor.

The single most remarkable result was that no BASC scale mean score for the at-risk subject population reached the level of either at-risk consideration or clinical significance. In contrast, the mean profile on the MMPI-A produced a 4/9-9/4 two-point code type. Individuals exhibiting this code type are described as impulsive, frequently acting out, and having a disregard for social norms (Archer, 1992). These adolescents are also externalizers, sensation seekers, easily frustrated, and often diagnosed with conduct disorders.

Published in 1992, both the MMPI-A and BASC are relatively new to the field and consequently have not yet generated much research. Both instruments were developed utilizing the empirical criterion keying method of test construction. Items were selected based upon their ability to discriminate among clinical and "normal" groups. Both tests also use scoring that transforms raw scores to T scores with a mean of 50 and a standard deviation of 10. The MMPI-A resulted from the MMPI-2 Restandardization Project, which updated the original MMPI. This gives the MMPI-A the ability to share in the well-established credibility of the MMPI and MMPI-2.

The BASC offers a number of composite scales that place greater emphasis on school adjustment. The MMPI-A and BASC scale names are useful to teachers and other professionals in the schools. The BASC parent and teacher forms are easy to read, and the items are not confusing. The self-rating forms are also concise and easily read by most students. On both these tests the examiner must first determine whether the child has the reading comprehension and vocabulary levels needed to read the items and understand key words with ease.

Finally there is the issue of age limitations. The MMPI-A was designed for adolescents ages 14 to 18. The BASC may be used on children and adolescents ages 4 to 18. Two different instruments that can serve a range of purposes and thus greatly aid the clinician are now available.

Behavior Rating Scales

Behavioral rating scales require someone in a role relationship with the child to observe selected behaviors and record the frequency and, in some cases, the intensity. Behavioral rating scales are usually quick and easy to use as they place few requirements on the observer. Because rating scales contain only a few items, test stability (test-retest reliability) may be limited. The resulting scores from behavioral rating scales will show frequencies of behavioral occurrences in selected environments by selected respondents. The resulting range of reported behaviors may be restricted for this reason.

Clarizio and Higgins (1989) surveyed 83 school psychologists to determine common assessment practices. School psychologists most commonly used the following battery to assess severely emotionally disturbed (SED) children: the Wechsler Intelligence Scale for Children-Revised (1969–1974), Wide Range Achievement Test (Jastak, Wilkinson & Jastak, 1984), Bender Visual Motor Gestalt Test (1946),

Incomplete Sentence Test, a behavioral rating scale, classroom observation, and informal interviews (96% interviewed the teacher and child, 91% interviewed the parents). Clarizio and Higgins (1989) reported that the most common behavioral checklists were the Behavior Rating Profile (34%; Brown & Hammil, 1978, 1983), Conners' (1969) Teachers Rating Scale (32%), Devereux Elementary Behavior Scale (23%; Spivack & Swift, 1966–1967), Behavioral Problem Checklist (21%; Quay & Peterson, 1975, 1987), Walker (1970) Problem Behavior Checklist and Behavior Evaluation Scale (16%; McCarney, Leigh, & Cornbleet, 1983), Achenbach's (1991) Child Behavior Checklist (12%), and Miller's (1977–1981) School Behavior Checklist (5%).

Similarly Hutton, Dubes, and Muir (1992) also reviewed the most frequently used behavioral lists by school psychologists. These researchers surveyed 1,000 randomly selected members of the National Association of School Psychologists. The results indicated the following usage: the Devereux Child Behavioral Rating Scales (Spivack & Spotts, 1966) and Devereux Adolescent Behavioral Rating Scales (Spivack, Spotts, & Haimes, 1967; both used 67% of the time), Devereux Elementary School Behavior Rating Scale II (44%; Swift, 1982), Burks' (1968, 1969) Behavior Rating Scale (10%), Hahnermann Elementary School Behavior Rating Scale (9%; Spivack & Swift, 1975), Walker (1970) Behavior Problem Checklist (8%), Behavior Rating Profile (7%; Brown & Hammil, 1978, 1983), and Behavior Evaluation Scale (4%; McCarney et al., 1983).

It would appear that the dependence of the field on behavioral rating scales has grown through the years. Only intelligence and achievement tests outrank these rating scales in popularity. How psychometrically reliable and valid are most of these commonly used behavior rating scales? Naglieri and Flanagan (1993) examined 14 of the more commonly used behavioral rating scales and found that only 3 possessed acceptable reliability and validity drawn from representative samples to provide user confidence. Hutton et al. (1992) candidly noted, "It is alarming that some instruments with less than favorable psychometrically sound characteristics continue to be used, these practices, . . . constitute a lack of professional responsibility" (p. 283).

Naglieri, Bardos, and LeBuffe (1995) tout the use of the Devereux Behavior Rating Scale-School Form (DBRS-SF; Naglieri, LeBuffe, & Pfeiffer, 1993), a 40-item scale for ages 5 to 18. This rating scale has four subscales: Interpersonal Relations, Inappropriate Behaviors/Feelings, Depression, and Physical Symptoms/Fears. Without providing any evidence on stability or interrater reliability for the specific population of children previously classified as "seriously emotionally disturbed" (an undifferentiated mass of poorly classified children by diagnostic standards), they reported that this particular behavioral rating scale identified 76.7% and 74.3% of two age-level samples correctly. These findings suggest that the DBRS-SF correctly identifies 75% of the presorted samples of children. What about the other 25%? This research does not make a case for the use of a specific behavioral rating scale (two of the researchers are authors of the DBRS-SF). It does make the case that behavior ratings by teachers may be considered one aspect, with many other forms of data, in the decision-making process regarding children's psychopathology. It is important that readers understand that these authors recommend behavioral rating scales that will classify children using a volatile label (seriously emotionally disturbed) without deriving a mental status diagnosis.

Achenbach, McConaughy, and Howell (1987) wisely advise that the observations of parents, teachers, and other informants must be considered important. Discrepancies among different sources of information may be useful in diagnosis and treatment (Kendall, Kortlander, Chansky, & Brady, 1992). Even so, few guidelines exist to clarify how to integrate and process multiple informant information in the diagnostic process (Piacentini et al., 1992). Different behavioral terms on behavioral rating scales may have different meanings to informants. While inservice training of the informants enhances communications in the use of behavioral rating scales, only the diagnostician will be aware of the informant's relationship with the client and possible bias.

The following are some examples of recently published behavioral checklists. The New Devereux Adolescent Behavior Rating Scales (DAB; Ben-Porath, Williams, & Uchiyama, 1989) was designed to be administered to adolescents in residential treatment settings by clinical personnel. This rating scale has four subscales: Acting Out Behavior (AOB), Heterosexual Interests (HI), Neurotic Dependent Behavior (NDB), and Withdrawn/Timid Behavior (WTB). The DAB has an internal consistency range of .80 to .95.

The Child Behavior Checklist (CBC; Achenbach, 1991a) is a 138-item checklist to be completed by parents. The checklist has 118 items that measure behavior problems and 20 items that measure social competence. The CBC contains the following scales: Withdrawn, Somatic Complaints, Anxious/Depressed, Social Problems, Thought Problems, Attention Problems, Delinquent Behavior, and Aggressive Behavior. The CBC-Teacher Report Form (TRF) consists of 118 items to be completed by the teacher. There is also a CBC Youth Self-Report (Achenbach, 1991b) version that contains 119 items to be answered by 11- to 18-year-olds. The CBC's teacher and parent forms were designed to identify psychopathology in 4- to 18-year-olds, not to define subtle or mild behavior difficulties that would not be considered as abnormal in psychopathological terms. These can be used in identifying children who have more severe behavior/social problems.

McConaughy, Mattison, and Peterson (1994) conducted research using the CBC parent and teacher forms to differentiate between severely emotionally disturbed (SED) and learning disabled (LD) students. The results indicated that the SED children were rated higher than the LD children on all of the TRF scales and all but one (somatic complaints) of the CBC scales. When SED children were rated by the teachers, the most important behavioral predictor was aggressive behavior. Other scale predictors for the SED children were higher rates of attention problems, delinquent behavior, social problems, thought problems, and withdrawal.

The Adjustment Scales for Children and Adolescents (ASCA; McDermott, Marston, & Stott, 1993) is a 123-item (indicator) checklist to be used with children ages 5 to 17. Different versions exist for males and females. Ninety-seven problem behavior items and 26 positive behavior indicators are assessed in 29 specific situations. The 97 problem items assess the following syndromes: Attention-Deficit/Hyperactive, Provocative Solitary Aggressive, Impulsive Solitary Aggressive, Oppositional Defiant, Diffident, and Avoidant. These syndromes had internal consis-

fficients ranging between .75 and .86. The syndromes also produced
nal consistency and considerable interobserver and test-retest reliabil-
's verity and severity of pathology should be determined by examining
viors in many different environments.

ely used example of a behavioral rating scale is the Personality Inventory for
en (PIC; Wirt, Lachar, Klinedinst, & Seat, 1984), a 280-item true/false checklist to be rated by parents, teachers, or clinicians. This version contains the following
scales: Lie, Frequency, Defensiveness, Adjustment (used for screening), Achievement, Intellectual Screening, Development, Somatic Concern, Depression, Family
Relations, Delinquency, Withdrawal, Anxiety, Psychosis, Hyperactivity, Social
Skills, and a general screening scale. The Lie, Frequency, and Defensiveness scales
are validity scales. This inventory is used to assess children ages 3 to 16 for cognitive-
scholastic functioning and emotional or conduct problems. Kline, Lachar, and
Boersma (1993) conducted research using the PIC to differentiate between children
in regular classrooms and special-education classes who are learning disabled,
emotionally/behaviorally disabled, or mentally impaired. The children's mothers
served as the informants. The PIC differentiated correctly between the regular class
and special-education children at a rate of 90%. This percentage dropped to 50 in
differentiating students with learning disabilities from students with emotional/
behavioral problems.

Clinical Interview

The clinical interview is more flexible and less objective than either the self-report
or behavioral checklist. A principal difference between the clinical interview and
self-report questionnaire or symptom checklist is often described as *progressive
flexibility*. Flexibility is obtained when clinicians are able to follow information
leads and veer into areas not normally included on a behavioral inventory or
checklist. Self-report systems attempt to objectively quantify the child's responses.
The previously developed questions are usually ones that differentiated clinical
from normal populations. A behavioral checklist or rating scale asks the rater to
determine the presence or absence of a specific behavior, often to some degree
(i.e., Is the child hyperactive/hypoactive, or does he display inappropriate [as the
form is usually specified] behaviors?) Behavioral rating scales are often used to
determine the frequency of a behavior; rarely are the scales used to determine the
intensity of a behavior. These devices are not designed to ascertain children's
thoughts, feelings, or moods, only their behavioral responses.

Which one is more important: the more open clinical interview, or the more
objective, structured questionnaire, and/or the behavioral rating scale? Although
this question has been argued for years, the departure taken in this chapter is that
the three procedures should be used together. The clinical interview in the hands of
an experienced and well-trained clinician is both powerful and efficient in following
up on questions raised (clinical hypothesis construction) by personality and behavioral rating devices. The interview process is not simply an open-ended conversation; it should become a systematic search for answers to clinical hypotheses. The
clinical interview is a balance of systematic information gathering and additional

exploratory follow-up into areas as they arise. The price of not being systematic is terminating the interview without plausible diagnostic constructs leading to diagnosis. Every experienced psychologist has returned to examine test and interview data after the client has left only to see gaping holes where vital information was missing.

Barnett and Macmann (1992) placed clinical diagnosis into a decision tree analysis to encourage the systematic clinical interview. They argued that "relatively little knowledge may be gained through the analysis of individual scales and assessment techniques without placing them within" a consistently systematic decision-making context based on a holistic view of people (p. 431). They offered three concerns about being overly dependent upon observational rating scales. (1) Different rating scales (methods of measurement) produce different results even for the same specified behavioral trait being observed. (2) Diagnostic profiles containing individual symptoms and syndromes are too restrictive to provide for specific treatment interventions. (3) Behavior rating scales frequently fail to specify the severity of the behavior, this providing little or no prognostic value.

The reason for obtaining broad-based systematic data is that it maximizes the development of clinical hypotheses. Self-report questionnaires and behavioral reporting devices, when used without the clinical interview, limit symptom exploration and may result in premature diagnostic conclusions. The development of clinical hypotheses is addressed by Kazdin (1995) in what he called *forced reductions* in the range of symptoms, prematurely ruling out diagnostic factors that could be important.

One such factor is the possibility of co-morbidity. Co-morbidity is the presence of at least two distinct and separate disabilities (pathologies) within the same person. Although they may have a common origin or etiology, all the pathologies are classified as disparate. Reber (1992) reported that most mental disorders can coexist. The prevalence of co-morbidity in children is much greater than previously reported (Bregman, 1991).

Bird et al. (1988) reported high rates (as high as 50%) of co-morbidity among conduct disorders and attention-deficit/hyperactivity disorders (ADHD), depression and anxiety, and autism and mental retardation, to name just a few. This data suggests that effective treatment considerations are contingent upon appropriate diagnostic procedures capable of identifying more than one mental disorder or other condition in combination. Behavioral rating scales cannot make that determination, only clinicians can. Test data is helpful, but consolidation and interpretation of data from all sources is absolute in the clinical decision-making process.

DETERMINING PSYCHOLOGICAL STATUS

The client history and mental status examination (MSE) provide the data for the development and implementation of treatment plans. These activities bring the psychologist, child, family, and other caregivers into close communication and relationship. The psychologist must be empathetic, interested, and uncritical. Ridicule, sarcasm, and fault finding do not enhance trust and confidence, without which there can be no relationship. Intake interviews containing history and the MSE as a diagnostic procedure are discussed in the following sections. Developing and implementing treatment plans is beyond the scope of this diagnostic chapter.

History

Intake information from parents, siblings, extended family, and caregivers can be helpful in seeing the child's problem from several viewpoints. This important two-way communication process permits the clinician to assuage some of the family's and immediate care providers' concerns and enlist their cooperation. And while taking the history, impressions of child behavior and child and family interactions are obtained. Histories are filled with the judgments of others, which means the informant's perceptions and bias must be considered and understood. It is not unusual for families to relate the history as they want it to be told, not as it is. Certainly, when confronting the defense mechanism of denial, this observation is true. Denial, as a faulty psychological structure, protects the family from the threat imposed by fact; therefore, the examiner must be alert to denial and aware that the information is filtered. Denial inhibits the family from receiving and giving factual information. Parents in denial may prove to be of limited help in the diagnostic process. In the presence of denial, the clinician is advised to stop the information exchange and begin working the parents carefully through denial.

Many families search for what they want to hear and fix blame where it least affects them. Guilt can lead some parents to clinic shopping and, frequently, to disharmony in family relationships. Other parents become trapped in their own guilt and are willing to shoulder all the responsibility to the point of depression.

If the examiner sees the child's difficulties resulting from the manner in which she interacts with the important figures in her life, then the external reality is somewhat less important than the child's perceptions of what reality exists in her world. A child's ability to define and test reality is critical to the developmental task of describing self. Reality is often distorted when children feel they are controlled by others, that their wants and feelings and being are not important. The impression children often have is that adult examiners (authority figures) side with parents in an adult-against-children configuration.

Reason for Referral

With adults the initial history starts with the direct question, "Why are you here?" or "What seems to be the problem?" Children may find these question threatening, so the initial approach with them should be much more open-ended and less direct. Even with late preschool and school-age children it is important to establish what they perceive. Children should be asked, "What do your teachers and your parents say (think) about you?" followed by "What would make things better at home (or in school) now?" Avoid using the word "why." If the child knew why things were not going well, he or she might well change them. A response to the "why" question usually results in further rationalization as to why the problem exists.

As the interview proceeds a continuing question to be raised is "What do you want?" It is open-ended, and the examiner can ask it against different relationships, environments, and tasks. As the responses are elicited, they should be written down only and not responded to at this time. The examiner will review them later to see whether the person is still interested in a specific wish and will add another question, "What are you willing to do about it?"

The examiner should interfere as little as possible with the child's language flow, eliciting and not inhibiting self-talk. With preschool children, puppets, dolls, playhouses, and talking pictures are useful in eliciting self-talk. Self-talk will provide the examiner with more insight into internal feelings than any other diagnostic procedure. The examiner is interested in when the problem began, how it began, any factors that seem significantly related to the onset, the course of the present presenting symptoms, what has been attempted to modify them, and, if so, with what success.

Early childhood memories are particularly susceptible to distortion. The child's memory of such events is critical in determining *retrospective falsification,* in which the child changes the reporting of past events or is selective in remembering them. The child may reinterpret events or even make up stories to serve a particular psychological need. Younger children will pay more attention to detail than older ones.

The child's perceptions of how well he or she is accepted in the family or classroom are very important. Was the child's birth planned? Did (and does) he or she feel wanted? Changes in interactions among family members should be examined at different periods of the child's life. If specific events were traumatic, it is not only the event itself that is important but also the reaction of the child and others.

Histories are rarely well-ordered chronologies of events. More often they are filled with repetition, digression, and occasional rambling. Children both like and dislike to talk about themselves. The effort is to place the focus on them, often by highlighting events in their lives. The examiner will usually go from the general to the specific, noting not only what the child says but what he or she tells with movement and body language. Especially important to note are the child's responses to various family members and the attitudes and emotions expressed toward them.

Family History

A description of the child's family of origin, nuclear family, and extended family should include specific information on the role relationship members play with one another. Family histories may reveal any pattern of significant medical, neurological, and mental disorders across and within generations. The family as a whole is considered through its biographical data, in age, occupation, composition, social status, and cultural, religious, and ethnic background. The aim is to formulate a clear picture of the family members in interaction with one another.

If the mother serves as the informant, pregnancy and birth information should be obtained. What was the child like at birth? What was his or her temperament? At what age were important developmental milestones achieved? What was the child's general style of behavior and speech? How did the child get along with playmates? What was the child's attitude toward the family? Were there any markedly outstanding developmental disturbances, such as speech or language changes, tics, bedwetting, phobias, or night terrors?

Important events at various stages in life are covered in detail. Are there signs of abuse, neglect, or rejection? Was there maternal deprivation of any kind? What was the father's role in the childrearing? How frequent were baby-sitters, child-care providers, and preschool programs provided and what was the child's relationship to these people and environments?

Have there been any significant relationship changes in the family structure such as divorce, remarriage, or blended families, and what is the child's reaction to these factors. Is the child living with the parent of choice, and how does he or she feel about the other parent and manifest those feelings? Are there any unusual sexual behaviors?

Care should be taken to find the extended family members who have the best relationship with the child and obtain their opinions as well. This may be a baby-sitter or grandparent.

School Histories

A complete school and social history will provide an awareness of the range of social learning experiences, interpersonal interactions, expectations for success, and feelings of threat, rejection, and peer recognition. School history includes grade level achieved, actual academic performance levels, difference between actual and expected academic performance levels, actual grades earned, social interactions, friends, overall adjustment to school, relationships with teachers, favorite subjects, and extracurricular interests. What predominant behaviors has the child displayed toward teachers and peers? What did the child think of pre-school and early school experiences? What feelings and responses were there to school and leaving home? Does the child have homework and feel responsible for it?

Medical History

The child's medical history should be examined for any accidents or illnesses that required hospitalization, surgery, or long-term use of medications. The emotional facts surrounding any illness or accident and the attitudes toward the illness of significant people in the child's life should be ascertained.

Important are any symptoms that may indicate neurological disease or head injury. Does the child experience dizziness, muscle weakness, trouble with vision, fainting spells, staring spells, or muscle twitching? If the child reports headaches, are they unilateral, bilateral, steady, throbbing, or associated with scotomata? A history of grand-mal or petit-mal seizures should be investigated, especially if confusion, incontinence, or explosive behaviors are reported. How does the child sleep and eat? Depression is associated with frequent awakening, whereas anxiety is associated with difficulty in falling asleep. New stress or acute stress frequently curtails appetite, while prolonged low-grade stress may frequently send the child to the refrigerator for comfort.

Mental Status Examination

The purpose of the MSE is to define the presenting problem in terms of mental disorders or other clinical pathology, detailing the severity. The MSE focuses on bringing information from the child's observable behaviors into agreement (or understanding the disagreement) with information obtained from the history and formal diagnostic procedures. The psychologist begins this process by observing motor movement, hand and finger coordination, gaze or gaze aversion, motor speech and language usage, need for communications and personal interaction, and general orientation and awareness of self and others. Does the child have age-appropriate orientation to time, place, persons, and situation (environmental event)?

Symptoms of mental disorders can be seen in a child's general appearance, attitude toward the examiner and others, and overall level of comfort with various people in the clinical and school environments. Initial observations include:

1. Physical health, physical size, shape, posture, and gait.
2. Hearing, vision, and motor speech.
3. Dress, grooming, and facial expressions. (Do they match the child's emotions?)
4. Social comfort, personal comfort, freedom from threat. (Is the child defensive, hostile, or guarded?)
5. Is the expression of emotionality age appropriate? Is the child cooperative, interested in the activities available, or verbally or physically aggressive? Is there evidence of recurrent dreams or fantasies, gender identification issues, conscience or values development, punishment, social relationships (close friendships) or social popularity, group or gang activities, social rule violation, or pattern of poor decision making?
6. Are there unusual presenting behaviors (i.e., hyperactivity, inattentiveness, lack of impulse control, tics and uncontrollable muscular movements, mood swings, and stereotyped movements, rigidity of muscle movement, or repetitive behaviors and speech)?
7. Is there a series of changes or recent changes in personality, interests, mood, attitudes toward others, level of tenseness, irritability, patterns of aggression, passivity, anxiety, antisocial behavior, or in interactions with siblings and playmates?

The next six factors are considered important in observing and reporting the MSE: (1) Mood and Emotional Reaction, (2) Speech and Language, (3) Thought Content, (4) Sensorium, (5) Judgment, and (6) Insight.

Mood and Emotional Reaction. Mood refers to prevailing feelings. Moods or feelings may be described in terms of their intensity, duration, and fluctuations. Work, play, and sleep can all influence mood changes. Likewise, hallucinatory experiences may produce certain moods. Anxiety, anger, ecstasy, general warmth, affection, and boredom represent a range of moods. Is the child's expression of moods consistent with how he or she describes feelings, circumstances, and conditions? As the child moves across subject areas are mood fluctuations congruent; if not, are they guarded or is the relative level of awareness absent?

In both a dynamic and behavioral sense, are there reinforcers or conditions that create or prolong specific behaviors, feelings, or thoughts? Are there particular emotional or physical problems: nightmares, phobias, masturbation, bedwetting, running away, delinquency, smoking, drug or alcohol use, anorexia, bulimia, weight problems, feeling of inferiority, or psychosexual preoccupation?

Speech and Language. Is the rate, rhythm, fluency, and inflection of speech age appropriate? Do the speech patterns flow in a fairly smooth manner or are there hesitations, stuttering, blocking, or an abrupt cessation of speech? Is the volume reasonable, or does it seem too loud or too soft? Are there word-finding problems, confusion in monitoring what he or she is saying, or confusion in the language structures (supra-segmentals). Is the child able to monitor what is being said? Is he or she able to disregard ambient background noise? Does the child communicate thoughts through connected sensible language?

Thought Content. Thought content is the rate of verbalized thoughts to assess whether there is a paucity or seeming abundance of ideas. Is there a flight of ideas; does the child jump from one idea to another seemingly without pause? Is speech guarded? Is speech limited to answering questions? The examiner notes the presence of associative processing. Are the answers to questions relevant or irrelevant? If they are not relevant are they circumstantial, reflecting a tendency to avoid central issues? Are they tangential; do they split off in a direction not warranted by the questions? Is there evidence of neologisms, made-up words condensed to express feelings and ideas that are incomprehensible? Are there other incomprehensible or incoherent answers?

The examiner is also interested in the general content of the child's thoughts. Ideas of reference are beliefs that one's actions and thoughts are controlled by others. Somatic delusions are beliefs that something is wrong with the body. Fears and phobias suggesting the presence of irrational anxieties should also be looked for.

Sensorium. The sensorium includes a number of capabilities, consciousness, orientation, memory, and intellectual tasks. The level of consciousness is the ability to attend to and concentrate on directed stimuli. Reduced awareness of the environment varies from confusion to stupor to coma.

Orientation is usually assessed with respect to time, place, and person. Greater significance is given to difficulties concerning person than to difficulties of time or place, and more significance is given to place than to time. Orientation to place is obtained by asking the child to describe the present location, where he or she just came from, and where he or she is going; orientation for person, by ascertaining whether the child is aware of or recognizes persons around her. Time is tested by asking the child the date (year, month, day of the week) and his or her birthday.

Typically, memory is divided into recent and remote. Recent memory deteriorates first in organic mental impairment. Remote memory can be examined by asking about important events that occurred in their lives. Recent memory is frequently assessed by asking the child to name three items early in the interview and then to recall them later. Immediate retention is frequently tested by memory of sentences (verbal) or digits (dichotic). Loss of memory may be classified as retrograde (loss of memory before the event) or anterograde (loss of memory after the event).

A number of intellectual tasks can be presented to estimate the child's general fund of knowledge and intellectual functioning, including reading, writing, and arithmetic. What is the child's cognitive and motor development? When did he or she learn to read and perform other intellectual and motor skills? Is there evidence of minimal cerebral dysfunctions, learning disabilities, or any measured cognitive dysfunctions? If so, how does the child manage and what effects do these dysfunctions have?

Judgment. Does the child show impaired judgment? What would happen if the child was in the street and a car was coming? What would the child do in response to seeing a house on fire? Can the patient discriminate critical differences that require judgment at age-appropriate levels?

Insight. The examiner should determine whether the child has any insight into his or her problem. What are the circumstances that brought the child to the examiner? Does the child feel that treatment is necessary? Are the child's problems blamed on others, or is there an awareness that some of the problems stem from his or her own particular emotional thoughts or feelings?

Case Example 6–1. Determining psychological status—School dropout

The client was 16 years and 3 months old, a white male who dropped out of school during the 11th grade. He lived with his mother and stepfather. His biological father had died the year before. He was referred by the public defenders office to determine his current psychological status in response to two questions: (1) his predicted response to rehabilitation as a juvenile and (2) the type and amount of rehabilitation needed to achieve long-term stability. He was charged with maternal homicide.

FAMILY HISTORY

According to records from a local mental-health center, his early intellectual and physical development were within normal limits, with no evidence of serious accidents or illnesses. The stability of his home environment strongly suggests that early and continued social learning occurred in a highly dysfunctional family with verbal abuse and emotional neglect. The mother was a product of sexual, physical, and emotional abuse and neglect. The client's mother and her siblings received repeated psychiatric treatment, including hospitalization, for chronic depression and anxiety. She married an older man as a teenager to escape her home. The client's father provided the client with the only source of stability in the family until the time of his death. His stepfather and his mother were in rehabilitation for substance dependency and alcoholism. The abusive parental figures justified their own abuse as children by creating an abusive home environment for this client. The stepfather was physically abusive to the client's mother and frequently left the home for extended periods of time.

EDUCATIONAL HISTORY

School records indicated that the client passed the hearing and vision screening tests when last administered. Family instability caused him to change schools frequently in

(continued)

Case Example 6–1.   *(Continued)*

the elementary grades. Between 1983 and 1989, he was in four schools. He received As and Bs and had excellent attendance except for a 34-day absence in fourth grade because of a move. No conduct or behavioral problems were ever reported in elementary school.

In the seventh grade he began to produce mostly Cs and some Ds. His school attendance was still very good. He liked most subjects, and standardized achievement tests indicated that he generally performed at the 70th percentile. No conduct or behavioral problems were reported in junior high school. His grades were actually better in the ninth grade and then began to slide downward in the tenth grade. He was absent 7 days in the tenth grade.

He now sees school as a support system and wishes he had remained in school. His behavioral pattern in school had consistently been one of social withdrawal. After dropping out he isolated himself in his room, escaping through television and video games.

INTERVIEW

The client was seen by the examiner on two consecutive days at a children's detention center. He had been in that environment since his arrest. He appeared for the examination in good spirits and was casually dressed in a loose-fitting shirt and slacks. He is physically large to the point of obesity, weighing 255 pounds on a 5'5" frame. He has dark hair, blue eyes, and clear skin. He has a fair but ruddy complexion, with heightened coloration in his cheeks. He maintained good eye contact and was very willing to relate to the examiner. He demonstrated good thought orientation through intact language usage, with no threat to mental or emotional integrity (devoid of hallucinations, voices, or distortions in reality). He discussed the antecedents and incident reluctantly but vividly.

MOOD

He demonstrated appropriate emotional responses in relating the events. He could describe mood using only two gross emotional descriptors, "up" or "down." Finer emotional distinctions were seemingly impossible for him to make. His recent mood was described as so "down" that he could not go out of the house or meet people. The more he withdrew, the greater the internal pressures to escape and the more unreal his world became.

He ran away from home frequently. Upon being returned, the poor relationship between his mother and him grew more intense. She used the running away and petty thefts (taking a few dollars from her purse) as a reason to place him on juvenile probation, which he interpreted as another example of her rejection. Systematic parental support structures promoting love and acceptance were not present, fostering severe limitations in reality testing mechanisms, delays and denial in emotional development, and underlying anger caused by inconsistencies in human attachment.

CURRENT PSYCHOLOGICAL STATUS

He withdraws from emotional threat by disassociating himself from his feelings of emotional hurt and rejection. He describes his father's death as "sad." His best prompted description of his feelings at the time of the incident was "bad." He is aware of his mother's death and his role only because of what he was told by the police. He has been dependent upon the psychological defense mechanisms of denial and rational-

Case Example 6–1.   *(Continued)*

ization as a protection from the pain of maternal rejection and parental conflict. He repeatedly remarked that he was happier now (in the detention center) than he had been in his life. His level of emotional awareness (awareness of his own emotions) is critically below age level.

SENSORIUM

His sensorium is filled with poor judgment and lacks personal insight. He is intelligent and can see and feel things around him except for those feelings associated with interactions between his mother and himself. There are few things that he is definitive about and he is incapable of making personal decisions based on values. His thoughts seem to be easily influenced, and his level of self-directed decision making is very limited. His values (moral development) are at a very early preadolescent level.

His orientation to persons, place, time, and past events is undistorted (*X*4). His immediate and remote memories appear to be age appropriate. He appears to relate in a positive manner, and uses feeling-expressive language such as "I *love* (not loved) my mother."

THOUGHT AND LANGUAGE

His speech was clear and his language fully functional with no evidence of any bizarre thought disorder. He is now fully aware of his behaviors. However, while he is able to express his thoughts using language associated with emotional expression and human feelings, there is a vagueness and uncertainty about the meaning of his emotional responses. His therapist had described this disassociation of appropriate emotional feeling. Restoration of feeling awareness had become her major treatment goal. The disassociation is heard in his speech, which usually is normal in intonation, inflection, and the supra-segmental structures. When he talks about himself, he has hesitancies and patterns of intonation associated with mumbling, which he apparently used at times to avoid responding.

DIAGNOSTIC FINDINGS

Results from the Bender Visual Motor Gestalt Test indicate no scoreable errors. On the academic achievement tests he showed at or above grade-level performance.

WRAT-R	*Raw Score*	*Standard Score*	*Grade Level*
Word Recognition	50	113	Post High School
Spelling	40	101	High School
Arithmetic	49	122	Post High School
Kaufman Test of Educational Achievement			
Reading Comprehension	49	115	above 12.9

The academic achievement test scores indicate that he could be academically competitive and successful in school. Results describing his cognitive function on the intellectual subtests administered (Wechsler Intelligence Scale for Children-III) suggest above-average verbal ability and superior performance ability. There is a clinically significant difference between the two (Verbal and Performance) scales.

(continued)

Case Example 6–1.   *(Continued)*

Verbal 109.6–118.9	115	84	*High Average*	111.1–117.4
Performance 130.0–141.8	139	99.53	*Very Superior*	132.0–139.8
Full Scale 123.6–132.0	129	97	*Superior*	125.0–130.7

Results of subtest scores and factor analysis suggest visual-motor and nonverbal learning strengths at a superior level of intelligence. Relative weaknesses occur in making comparisons between sound and word units carrying limited information. His ability to comprehend and use vocabulary meaningfully is in the above-average range of intelligence. These findings are in sharp contrast to those produced by the local mental-health agency that placed him in the borderline intellectual range.

The Kinetic Family Drawing produced mature drawings of three adults with full social features. He identified the slightly heavier adult as himself. The two figures of similar height with sexual and weight distinctions were identified as his aunt and uncle. Tubbie, the dog, was also identified in the drawings. He is concerned about Tubbie's care. He believes Tubbie is being fed by his aunt and uncle. He describes them as loving and caring, and seems delighted that they have visited him. When asked about his own sister, he noted that she was angry with him for killing his mother. Results on the self-rating (ages 12 to 18) Behavioral Assessment System for Children produced the following *T* scores.

Scale	*T Score*
Attitude to School	37
Attitude to Teachers	53
Sensation Seeking	38
School Maladjustment Composite	41
Atypicality	46
Locus of Control	59
Somatization	45
Social Stress	55
Anxiety	47
Clinical Maladjustment Composite	50
Depression	46
Sense of Inadequacy	41
Relations with Parents	18*
Interpersonal Relations	49
Self-Esteem	26*
Self-Reliance	59
Personal Adjustment Composite	34
Emotional Index	53
Validity Index	*F* Index 2 Acceptable Range
	L Index 0 Acceptable Range

*T scores below 30

Case Example 6–1.   *(Continued)*

The findings on this scale did not produce any clinically significant *T* scores (above 70). High *T* scores were obtained for Locus of Control and Self-Esteem. These scores indicate that his decision-making behavior is based on external factors. His self-esteem and self-reliance have not developed and are not on the same level of independence from parents achieved by most 16-year-olds. He feels trapped into a dependent but destructive relationship with his parents. He is more depressed than the rating scale indicated and has a pervasive dissatisfaction with himself. The overall interpretation of these findings is that the absence of self-reliance reduces his ability to test reality and sustain a psychological balance in a painful environment.

One of the strengths of the Behavior Assessment System for Children is that it can also be used as a behavioral observation device in other environments. The counselor at the detention center completed a BASC on the client. The report indicates:

Scale	*T Score*
Hyperactivity	40
Aggression	46
Conduct Problems	44
Externalizing Problems Composite	42
Anxiety	37
Depression	42
Somatization	43
Internalizing Problems Composite	38
Attention Problems	39
Learning Problems	39
School Problems Composite	38
Atypicality	42
Withdrawal	57*
Behavioral Symptoms Index	37
Social Skills	48
Leadership	48
Study Skills	57
Adaptive Skills Composite	51
F-Index 0 Acceptable	

*T scores of 60 or above are at-risk

The BASC indicates that his counselor at the juvenile detention center thinks he will respond in an expected manner, with a tendency for social withdrawal. This normal sample of behavior—in contrast to what he has displayed—can be explained only by the fact that he will act from reason when provided the opportunity to do so.

Results of the MMPI-A failed to produce any clinical significance. The Validity Indices (*F*1, *F*2, *F, L, K,* VRIN and TRIN) were all within acceptable limits. The scales were as follows:

(continued)

Case Example 6–1.   *(Continued)*

Validity Index	T Score
Variable Response Inconsistency (VRIN)	54
True Response Inconsistency (TRIN)	54
Infrequency 1 (*F*1)	46
Infrequency 2 (*F*2)	40
Infrequency (*F*)	43
Lie (*L*)	55
Defensiveness (*K*)	59

Scales	T Score
Hypochondriasis (*Hs*)	37
Depression (*D*)	55
Conversion Hysteria (*Hy*)	46
Psychopathic Deviate (*Pd*)	55
Masculinity-Femininity (*Mf*)	49
Paranoia (*Pa*)	44
Psychasthenia (*Pt*)	38
Schizophrenia (*Sc*)	43
Hypomania (*Ma*)	39
Social Inversion (*Si*)	49

The profile does not place him into the at-risk group (above 60) on any clinical scale dimensions. The slightly elevated (not at-risk) Depression scale might suggest feelings of hopelessness and dissatisfaction with his life, observed in his obesity and inability to achieve his adolescent need for independence (from adults) and peer recognition. The elevated (but not at-risk) Psychopathic-Deviate scale might suggest his overall inability to describe his feelings at an age level appropriateness, with an unresolved but stilted need for love and acceptance in the presence of rejection and anger. He is beginning to experience awareness of feelings and behaviors that he has not understood, such as compulsive stealing, lying, and temper outbursts with his mother. These behaviors now trouble him greatly.

DIAGNOSTIC IMPRESSIONS

He has above-average intelligence, demonstrating academic achievement at and above grade level. He is physically obese with no other medical or health problems reported. His social-personal development evidences limited decision-making ability based on poorly defined value development. His personality development has been influenced by parental neglect, rejection, and emotional abuse. He is filled with self-doubts driven by hopelessness as a result of parental rejection and demeaning emotional abuse. He was a victim with no place to escape the pain and humiliation that threatened his emotional being. The threat to his personal-social development is observed in the bipolar disorder (depression) and fluctuating mood changes reported clinically since 1991.

His child-rearing experiences forced maternal dependency. He fought this depen-

Case Example 6–1. *(Continued)*

dency by seeking comfort in compulsive eating, social isolation, and avoiding peer and adult confrontation. He has literally spent his life avoiding conflict and yet he thinks and reacts defensively. He is socially and emotionally an early preadolescent in terms of his understanding of feelings, inhibited by disassociative emotional awareness. He says he loves his mother, but he loves the ideal of what his mother could have been. He loves something he never experienced.

CONCLUSION

In the reported actual case study the objective projective tests opened avenues of inquiry but did not result in solutions. The MSE provides the specific usable information in response to the hypotheses raised. Without the MSE the diagnosis could not have been arrived at. It is interesting that he was never referred for school psychological examination and that his school counselors did not follow up when he left school. The communication between mental-health personnel and the schools did not exist.

Describing mental disorders that constitute the broad category emotional disturbance requires integrating test, interview, and observational data into a systematic structure called the mental status examination. In this chapter we have attempted to discuss the mechanics of the MSE, specifying the observational and intake data needed to judge current interpersonal interactions with selected people in specified environments on specified tasks. Decisions regarding emotional development are derived from observing and questioning the client, family, and caregiver on a number of issues. Among these issues are impulse control, arousal/attention, self-control, predominant moods, frequency and duration of moods, trust for self and others, feeling awareness, organization of thought, preoccupying thought or behaviors, psychotic features, and other dynamic factors (forces, pressures, needs, and type and amount of behavioral response to them).

The entire MSE process rests on knowledge of the various symptoms and conditions that comprise each discrete mental disorder. Knowledge of the *Diagnostic and Statistical Manual of Mental Disorders-IV* (*DSM-IV;* 1994) is extremely helpful. Diagnosis should be guided by the multiaxial classification scheme consisting of five axes. Axis I includes all the disorders and conditions listed in *DSM-IV,* except for personality disorders and specific developmental disorders, which are included in Axis II. Axis III includes physical (health) disorders and conditions. Axis IV relates to the severity of psychosocial stressors and Axis V, the current Global Assessment of Functioning (GAF), addresses overall severity. The following is an example of the *DSM-IV* classification that the case-study client might receive.

Axis I V61.20 Parent-Child (severe emotional neglect and abuse)
Axis II 300.60 Depersonalization Disorder
      301.6 Dependent Personality Disorder
      301.82 Avoidant Personality Disorder

Axis III Obesity (secondary to compulsive eating)

Axis IV Severity of Psychosocial Stressors-Extreme V

Axis V Current GAF = 30 (serious impairment in judgment)

Past GAF = unknown

Diagnosis of mental disorders is more than nosological pigeon-holing. From the diagnosis the clinician can form a longitudinal picture of the patient's life—the past condition—and a cross-sectional view—the current condition. Together with the diagnosis, the MSE enables the clinician to establish prognosis. These factors permit development of a treatment plan.

The early history of special education services may have contributed to current confusion in the diagnosis of emotional disturbances (mental disorders) in school-age children. Many of the early disability groups were classified to receive services on the basis of sensory and physical disability. Later, high-incidence disability groups were added to the service receiving programs on the basis of intellectual, adaptive, and cognitive dysfunctions. Clinicians learned to use test scores to consistently classify children needing special education.

Not all disabling conditions are tangible. Many are relative to cognitive dysfunctions in information processing behaviors such as learning disabilities; others are products of attentional or impulse control factors, and still others to inter- and intrapersonal adjustment factors. This group of relative disabilities has been difficult to categorize with precision. For example, ADHD is defined by the presence of six symptoms from a list of nine that describe inattentiveness or hyperactivity and impulsivity. If six of nine symptoms from both the hyperactive-impulsive and inattentive symptom lists are present, the combination of the two conditions coexist. The definition for ADHD in the *DSM-IV* requires clinical observations that use the language "often fails," "often has difficulty," and "often does not . . ." (pp. 83–85). ADHD requires that a subjective clinical decision be made. It is not concretely defined by a test score or other measure of sensory or motor performance having a relative nature.

When first defined by Kirk (1962), ADHD required the measured presence of cognitive dysfunction (deficits in basic psychological processes). There was never any precision in the definition, and children were inconsistently classified. To control for the number of children labeled as having a learning disability, a statistical procedure (or control to prevent abuse of clinical practice) was imposed as a discrepancy between academic achievement and global cognitive function. In this government-dispensed formula to make the diagnosis consistent, a discrepancy of one standard deviation was to exist between any measured academic achievement subject area and an IQ score. The practice is fraught with statistical and clinical issues. The relative nature of this disability begged definition and ended up defined as academic underachievement for financial and regulatory control. It would appear that the conclusion drawn by regulating agencies was that practitioners could not be trusted to make important clinical judgments. The truth that learning disabilities were relative to the method of measurement was apparently incomprehensible.

If the relative cognitive aspect of children with learning disabilities cannot be measured easily, then socially relative mental disorders would be more resistive. Bower's (1982) observation that "emotion is nonrational, nonlinear, and so far has been pretty elusive to being pinned down by precise prose" (pp. 55–56) certainly appears accurate. Coleman (1995) notes that "there are certainly no tests or battery of tests that can answer the question satisfactorily" (p. 451).

In opposition to tests alone, this chapter offers the clinician a very old and trusted procedure, the MSE. Our argument is that this time-tested process will clarify the ambiguity in children's mental disorders. No one said *DSM-IV* did justice to children, but diagnosis is much better than differentiating through classification in the development of treatment plans. Our position is that serious emotional disturbance must be defined against the child's current psychological status. Can the socially relative and unstable emotional responses in children be made concrete? In operational terminology, diagnosis must begin by revisiting Jessor and Jessor's (1977) dominant theory. This theory views multiple behaviors as serving similar emotional needs for children. It is essential that diagnostic practices with emotionally disturbed children identify those needs.

REFERENCES

Achenbach, T.M. (1991a). *Manual for the Child Behavior Checklist/4–18 and 1991 profile.* Burlington: University of Vermont, Department of Psychiatry.

Achenbach, T.M. (1991b). *Manual for the Youth Self-Report Form and 1991 profile.* Burlington: University of Vermont, Department of Psychiatry.

Achenbach, T.M., McConaughy, S.H., & Howell, C.T. (1987). Child/Adolescent behavioral and emotional problems: Implications of cross-informant correlations for situational specificity. *Psychological Bulletin, 101,* 213–232.

American Psychiatric Association. (1987). *Diagnostic and statistical manual of mental disorders—Third edition revised (DSM-III-R).* Washington, DC: Author.

American Psychiatric Association. (1994). *Diagnostic and statistical manual of mental disorders—Fourth edition (DSM-IV).* Washington, DC: Author.

American Psychological Association. (1985). *Standards for educational and psychological testing.* Washington, DC: APA.

Archer, R.P. (1987). *Using the MMPI with adolescents.* Hillsdale, NJ: Erlbaum.

Archer, R.P. (1992). *MMPI-A: Assessing adolescent psychopathology.* Hillsdale, NJ: Erlbaum.

Archer, R.P., Belevich, J.K.S., & Elkins, D.E. (1994). Item-level and scale-level factor structures of the MMPI-A. *Journal of Personality Assessment, 62,* 332–345.

Archer, R.P., & Gordon, R. (1994). Psychometric stability of MMPI-A item modifications. *Journal of Personality Assessment, 62,* 416–426.

Barnett, D.W., & Macmann, G.M. (1992). Decision reliability and validity: Contributions and limitations of alternative assessment strategies. *The Journal of Special Education, 25,* 431–452.

Bellak, L. (1992). Projective techniques in the computer age. *Journal of Personality Assessment, 58,* 445–453.

Bender, L. (1946). *Instructions for the use of the Visual Motor Gestalt Test.* New York: American Orthopsychiatric Association.

Ben-Porath, Y.S., Williams, C.L, & Uchiyama, C. (1989). New scales for the Devereux Adolescent Behavior Rating Scale. *Psychological Assessment: A Journal of Consulting and Clinical Psychology, 1,* 58–60.

Bird, H.R., Canino, G., Rubio-Stipec, M., Gould, M.S., Ribera, J., Sesman, M., Woodbury, M., Huertas-Goldman, S., Pagan, A., Sanchez-Lacey, A., & Moscoso, M. (1988). Estimates of the prevalence of childhood maladjustment in a community survey of Puerto Rico: The use of combined measures. *Archives of General Psychiatry, 45,* 1120–1126.

Bower, E. (1982). Defining emotional disturbance: Public policy and research. *Psychology in the Schools, 19,* 55–60.

Bregman, J. (1991). Current developments in the understanding of mental retardation. Part II: Psychopathology. *Journal of the American Academy of Child and Adolescent Psychiatry, 30,* 861–872.

Brown, L.L., & Hammil, D.D. (1978, 1983). *Behavior Rating Profile: An ecological approach.* Austin, TX: PRO-ED.

Burkes, H.F. (1968–1969). *Burkes Behavior Rating Scales.* In-print status uncertain. Huntington Beach, CA: Arden Press.

Burns, R., & Kaufman, S. (1972). *Kinetic Family Drawings (K-F-D): An introduction to understanding children through kinetic drawings.* New York: Brunner/Mazel.

Butcher, J.N., Graham, J.R. & Ben-Porath, Y.S. (1995). Methodological problems and issues in MMPI, MMPI-2, and MMPI-A research. *Psychological Assessment, 7,* 320–329.

Butcher, J., Williams, C., Graham, J., Archer, R., Tellegen, A., Ben-Porath, Y., & Kaemmer, B. (1992). *Minnesota Multiphasic Personality Inventory—Adolescent: Manual for administration, scoring, and interpretation.* Minneapolis: University of Minnesota Press.

Chase, T.V., Chaffin, S., & Morrison, S.D. (1975). False positive adolescent's MMPI profiles. *Adolescence, 10,* 507–519.

Clarizio, H.F., & Higgins, M.M. (1989). Assessment of severe emotional impairment practices and problems. *Psychology in the Schools, 26,* 154–162.

Coleman, M. (1995). Turning the Corner. In B.L. Brooks and D.A. Sabatino (Eds.), *Personal perspectives on emotional disturbance/behavioral disorders* (pp. 50–71). Austin, TX: PRO-ED.

Conners, C.K. (1969). A Teacher Rating Scale for use in drug studies with children. *American Journal of Psychiatry, 126,* 884–888.

Exner, J.E., Jr. (1986). *The Rorschach: A comprehensive system* (Vol. 1, 2nd ed.). New York: Wiley.

Flanagan, R. (1995). A review of the Behavior Assessment System for Children (BASC): Assessment consistent with the requirements of the Individuals with Disabilities Education Act (IDEA). *Journal of School Psychology, 33,* 177–186.

Freud, S. (1949). *An outline of psychoanalysis.* New York: Norton.

Fuller, C., & Sabatino, D. (1994). Factorial structures of the MMPI-A and BASC with at-risk adolescents. Manuscript in preparation. Johnson City, TN: East Tennessee State University.

Gefland, D., Jenson, W., & Drew, C. (1988). *Understanding child behavior disorders: An introduction to child psychopathology.* Fort Worth, TX: Holt, Rinehart and Winston.

Graham, J. (1987). *The MMPI—A practical guide.* New York: Oxford University Press.

Graybill, D. (1990). Developmental changes in the response types versus aggression categories on the Rosenzweig Picture-Frustration Study, Children's Form. *Journal of Personality Assessment, 55,* 603–609.

Hathaway, S.R., & McKinley, J. (1943). *Minnesota Multiphasic Personality Inventory.* Minneapolis: University of Minnesota Press.

Hutton, J.B., Dubes, R., & Muir, S. (1992). Assessment practices of school psychologists: Ten years later. *School Psychology Review, 21,* 271–284.

Jastak, S., Wilkinson, G.S., & Jastak J. (1984). *Wide Range Achievement Test.* Wilmington, DE: Jastak Associates.

Jessor, R., & Jessor, S. (1977). *Problem behavior and psychological development: A longitudinal study of youth.* San Diego, CA: Academic Press.

Kaiser, H. (1958). The varimax criterion for analytic rotation in factor analysis. *Psychometrika. 23,* 187–200.

Kazdin, A.E. (1995). Scope of child and adolescent psychotherapy research: Limited sampling of dysfunctions, treatments, and client characteristics. *Journal of Clinical Child Psychology, 24,* 125–140.

Kendall, P.C., Kortlander, E., Chansky, T.E., & Brady, E.U. (1992). Comorbidity of anxiety and depression in youth: Treatment implications. *Journal of Consulting and Clinical Psychology, 60,* 869–880.

Kirk, S.A. (1962). *Educating exceptional children.* Boston: Houghton Mifflin.

Kline, R.B., Lachar, D., & Boersma, D.C. (1993). Identification of special education needs with the Personality Inventory for Children (PIC): A hierarchical classification model. *Psychological Assessment, 5,* 307–316.

Lubin, B., Larsen, R., Matarazzo, J.D., & Seever, M. (1985). Psychological test usage patterns in five professional settings. *American Psychologist, 40,* 857–861.

McCarney, S.B., Leigh, J.E., & Cornbleet, J.A. (1983). *The Behavior Evaluation Scale.* Columbia, MO: Educational Services.

McConaughy, S.H., Mattison, R.E., & Peterson, R.F. (1994). Behavioral/emotional problems of children with serious emotional disturbances and learning disabilities. *School Psychology Review, 23(1),* 81–98.

McDermott, P.A., Marston, N.C., & Stott, D.H. (1993). *Adjustment Scales for Children and Adolescents.* Philadelphia, PA: Edumetric and Clinical Science.

Meehl, P. (1954). *Clinical versus statistical prediction: A theoretical analysis and a review of the evidence.* Minneapolis: University of Minnesota Press.

Miller, L.C. (1977–1981). *School Behavior Checklist.* Los Angeles: Western Psychological Services.

Naglieri, J.A., Bardos, A.N., & LeBuffe, P.A. (1995). Discriminant validity of the Devereux Behavior Rating Scale-School Form for students with serious emotional disturbance. *School Psychology Review, 24,* 104–111.

Naglieri, J.A., & Flanagan, D.P. (1993). Psychometric characteristics of commonly used behavior rating scales. *Comprehensive Mental Health, 2,* 225–239.

Naglieri, J.A., LeBuffe, P.A., & Pfeiffer, S.I. (1993). *Devereux Behavior Rating Scale-School Form.* San Antonio, TX: The Psychological Corporation.

Piacentini, J.C., Cohen, P., & Cohen, J. (1992). Combining discrepant diagnostic information from multiple sources: Are complex algorithms better than simple ones? *Journal of Abnormal Child Psychology, 20,* 51–63.

Piotrowski, C., Sherry, D., & Keller, J. (1985). Psychodiagnostic test usage: A survey of the Society of Personality Assessment. *Journal of Personality Assessment. 49,* 115–119.

Quay, H.C., & Peterson, D.R. (1975). *Manual for the Behavior Problem Checklist.* Unpublished manuscript.

Quay, H.C., & Peterson, D.R. (1987). *Manual for the Revised Behavior Problem Checklist.* Available from H.C. Quay, Box 248074, University of Miami, Coral Gables, FL 33124.

Reber, M. (1992). Dual diagnosis-psychiatric disorders and mental retardation. In M.L. Batshaw & Y.M. Perret (Eds.), *Children with disabilities—A medical primer* (p. 421–440). Baltimore: Paul H. Brookes.

Reynolds, C.R., & Kamphaus, R.W. (1992). *Behavior Assessment System for Children— Manual.* Circle Pines, MN: American Guidance Service.

Rosenzweig, S. (1981). *Children's form supplement to the basic manual of the Rosenzweig Picture-Frustration Study.* St. Louis: Rana House.

Spivack, G., & Spotts, J. (1966). *Devereux Child Behavioral Rating Scale.* Devon, PA: Devereux Foundation.

Spivack, G., Spotts, J., & Haimes, P.E. (1967). *Devereux Adolescent Behavior Rating Scale.* Devon, PA: Devereux Foundation.

Spivack, G., & Swift, M. (1966–1967). *Devereux Elementary School Behavior Rating Scale.* Devon, PA: Devereux Foundation.

Spivack, G., & Swift, M. (1975). *Hahnermann Elementary School Behavior Rating Scale.* Philadelphia, PA: Department of Mental Health Sciences at Hahnermann Medical College and Hospital.

Swift, M. (1982). *Devereux Elementary School Behavior Rating Scale II Manual.* Devon, PA: Devereux Foundation.

Walker, H.M. (1970). *Walker Problem Behavior Identification Checklist (WPBIC) Manual.* Los Angeles: Western Psychological Services.

Wechsler, D. (1969–1974). *Manual for the Wechsler Intelligence Scale for Children-Revised.* New York: The Psychological Corporation.

Wirt, R.D., Lachar, D. Klinedinst, J.K., & Seat, P.D. (1984). *Multidimensional description of child personality: A manual for the Personality Inventory for Children.* Los Angeles: Western Psychological Services.

Chapter 7

ASSESSING COGNITIVE ABILITIES USING THE WOODCOCK-JOHNSON

LARRY M. BOLEN

CRYSTALLIZED AND FLUID INTELLIGENCE

There has been a progression in intelligence testing from early theories of a general or global intelligence to multiple-factor theories of intelligence. Early two-factor theories proposed one overall intellectual entity represented by numerous subsets of activities or specific skills. Multifactor theories, in contrast, suggested an intelligence model composed of various abilities including memory, number concepts, reasoning, visual/spatial processing and speed, and verbal meaning (McGrew & Flanagan, 1996). Moreover, the multifactor theorists do not necessarily agree that there is an overall or general (*g*) intelligence factor.

In 1941, Raymond B. Cattell hypothesized two types of intelligence—fluid intelligence (*Gf*) and crystallized intelligence (*Gc*). Cattell's theoretical approach was significantly influenced by the work of both Charles Spearman, L.L. Thurstone, and E.L. Thorndike. Cattell worked as a research associate with Charles Spearman in the 1930s. In his book *The Abilities of Man* Spearman (1927) hypothesized a two-factor hierarchical structure in the understanding of intelligence. He theorized that general intelligence (*g*) represented the overlying mental ability necessary for all intelligent behavior. An individual's performance, then, was attributed to a combination of *g* and a factor specific to the task. The second factor (*s*) represented a variety of specific cognitive abilities that one may or may not have. Included were the so-called special abilities such as musical aptitude, mechanical skill, and unique talents. In 1909 E.L. Thorndike, in direct opposition to Spearman, tested the hypothesis of *g* on a set of measures similar to those Spearman had used in his original 1904 study and concluded that instead of *g* that intelligence was a complex set of bonds between thought and content. L.L. Thurstone (1938), also in opposition to Spearman's theory of only one intellectual entity, proposed a factor analytic model of intelligence hypothesizing nine primary mental abilities (PMA) believed to represent

Grateful appreciation is expressed to my Graduate Research Assistant, Kathy Launey, for her excellent editing skills. Her years of experience as a special-education classroom teacher proved most beneficial, especially with regard to her penetrating questions and comments regarding interpretation of certain aspects of the WJ-R COG ability clusters and their relevance to remedial recommendations for students experiencing learning and behavior problems.

actual characteristics of the person. Later, these primary mental abilities were re-duced to six (Space, Perceptual Speed, Number, Verbal Meaning, Memory, and Inductive Reasoning). Cattell's model somewhat reconciles the two theories of Spearman and Thurstone (Cattell, 1963). Fluid intelligence (*Gf*) is similar to Spear-man's *g* or general intelligence for problem solving and also includes concepts of Thurstone's primary mental abilities (inductive reasoning, for example). Cattell (1979) states that *Gf* is more related to physiological factors, influenced by genetic factors, and predominates in childhood before declining after adolescence and is not easily influenced by schooling. Sattler (1992) describes fluid intelligence as "essen-tially nonverbal, relatively culture-free mental efficiency" (p. 86). Crystallized intelli-gence (*Gc*), on the other hand, is similar to Spearman's specific abilities and includes aspects of Thurstone's PMA (number facility, verbal meaning and understanding, and word fluency, for example). *Gc* is related to education and special training and experience, predominates in adulthood, and is influenced by environmental factors. Sattler (1992) describes crystallized intelligence as "acquired skills and knowledge that are strongly dependent for their development on exposure to culture" (p. 86).

MULTIPLE INTELLIGENCE MODELS

The two-factor *Gf-Gc* theory has been gradually expanded since Cattell's 1940 introduction of the fluid-crystallized model. Horn, a former student of Cattell's, identified additional factors after 1965 and completed further refinements in *Gf-Gc* theory by 1985 (Horn, 1986a, 1986b). Ten abilities, including two sensory detectors, were described along with the possibility of a broad language factor separate from *Gc*. Second-order factors were identified, many of which closely resemble those first identified by Thurstone and Thurstone (1941). Horn's 1991 model lists nine broad *Gf-Gc* abilities. Seven factors comprise the basis for the cognitive scales of the WJ-R Tests of Cognitive Ability (Woodcock & Johnson, 1989). The eighth factor, Quantitative Ability (*Gq*), is placed on the WJ-R Tests of Achievement (Woodcock & Johnson, 1989), while measurement of the ninth factor, Correct Decision Speed (*Gd*), "has been difficult" (McGrew, 1994, p. 34) and was not included in the development of the WJ-R tests.

Horn (1991), like Cattell (1941), did not think that there is an underlying *g* factor. He maintained that the nine *Gf-Gc* abilities identified represent the basic building blocks of intelligent behavior and saw no need (or particular use) for a higher-order general intelligence factor. Woodcock (1990) noted that one of the more important aspects of *Gf-Gc* theory is the concept of broad versus narrow abilities. The narrower abilities, established through factor analytic research, are often referred to as "primary mental abilities" or "first-order factors." Each of these primary mental abilities could be measured using a variety of different tasks. Crystallized intelligence, for example, could be measured by tests of vocabulary, general information, knowledge of science, and so forth, each measuring a differ-ent, narrow aspect of the broad ability.

Prior to the introduction of the revised WJ-R Tests of Cognitive Ability in 1989, a number of theoretical models of multiple intelligences had been proposed or

---

Stratum III—General Intelligence (*g*)

Stratum II—Eight Broad Abilities

    Fluid Intelligence

    Crystallized Intelligence

    General Memory & Learning

    Broad Visual Perception

    Broad Auditory Perception

    Broad Retrieval Ability

    Broad Cognitive Speediness

    Processing Speed

Stratum I—Narrow Cognitive Abilities

        (Carroll lists 69 specific abilities)

Figure 7–1. Carroll's Three-Stratum theory

expanded. Guilford's (1959, 1967) Structure of Intellect model was one of the earlier models following Cattell's (1941) work. The serious practitioner should also become familiar with Gardner's (1983) theory of multiple intelligences, Sternberg's (1985) triarchic theory, and Vernon's (1979) hierarchical model.

A review and factor analysis of the extant literature on intelligence was completed by Carroll in the early 1990s. Based on his meta-analysis, Carroll (1989, 1993) proposes a Three-Stratum theory, which is remarkably similar to Horn's identified broad abilities with the exclusion of a quantitative ability. Moreover, Carroll's model also includes Spearman's *g*. Figure 7–1 presents an overview of Carroll's model of the major domains of human intelligence. Determination of the model is the result of reviews and reanalysis of over 460 different sets of data spanning 50 years of published research on intelligence by Carroll (1993). This text is an essential reference for anyone following multiple models of intellectual functioning.

THE WJ-R TESTS OF COGNITIVE ABILITY

Not to be confused with the 1977 Woodcock-Johnson Psycho-Educational Battery, the 1989 revision is a substantial improvement based on the Horn-Cattell model of intellectual processing (Horn, 1976, 1985, 1988; Horn & Cattell, 1966). In fact, Cummings (1992) noted that the revised WJ cognitive scales reflect the advice of a group of consultants—Carroll, Haywood, Horn, and McGrew.

The WJ-R Tests of Cognitive Ability (WJ-R COG) is composed of 21 tests. It is not, however, designed to be administered in its entirety. Rather, selective scales are used depending on the referral questions and assessment need. The WJ-R COG is divided into standard and extended batteries. The Standard Battery is composed of seven tests, each representing one of the Horn-Cattell abilities. Administration of the first seven tests results in a Standard Cognitive Ability (IQ score) factor score representing the individual's overall intellectual ability. An Early Development scale, which is intended for use with preschoolers (2 to 6 years of age), is composed of five of the standard subtests. The next seven tests comprise the Supplemental Battery, with each test also representing one of the Horn-Cattell abilities. Woodcock (1990) cautions that no single test can be interpreted as representative of a

Table 7–1. Cognitive factors and tests of the WJ-R COG

Cognitive Cluster/Broad Ability	Test (Narrow Ability)
Long-Term Retrieval (*Glr*): Ability to encode, store, and retrieve information for later use	1. Memory for Names 8. Visual-Auditory Learning 15. Delayed Recall/Memory for Names 16. Delayed Recall/Visual Auditory Learning
Short-Term Memory (*Gsm*): Ability to attend and store semantically meaningful information in immediate auditory memory and orally recall it correctly	2. Memory for Sentences 9. Memory for Words 17. Numbers Reversed
Processing Speed (*Gs*): Fine-motor speed under timed limits on	3. Visual Matching 10. Cross Out
Auditory Processing (*Ga*): Perception and understanding of rhythms and patterns and language development	4. Incomplete Words 11. Sound Blending 18. Sound Patterns
Visual Processing (*Gv*): Identification of visual patterns and spatial relations	5. Visual Closure 12. Picture Recognition 19. Spatial Relations
Comprehension-Knowledge (*Gc*): The ability to understand and apply procedural reasoning skills; related to depth of knowledge and experience.	6. Picture Vocabulary 13. Oral Vocabulary 20. Listening Comprehension 21. Verbal Analogies
Fluid Reasoning (*Gf*): Ability to reason abstractly, draw inferences, and understand implications	7. Analysis-Synthesis 14. Concept Formation 19. Spatial Relations
Quantitative Reasoning (*Gq*): The ability to think, reason, and solve numerical problems.	24. Calculations[a] 25. Applied Problems[a]

[a] Subtests from the WJ-R Test of Achievement

Stratum III

General intelligence (*g*) represented by the WJ-R Broad Cognitive Ability index factor score (BCA), which is analogous to a composite Full Scale IQ score.

Stratum II

Broad abilities represented by the seven cognitive clusters on the WJ-R COG and the quantitative cluster on the WJ-R Tests of Achievement (*Gf, Gc, Ga, Gv, Glr, Gsm, Gs,* and *Gq*).

Stratum I

29 Narrow abilities represented by the 21 subtests comprising the WJ-R COG and 8 tests comprising the WJ-R Tests of Achievement.

Figure 7–2. WJ-R *Gf-Gc* representational model of intelligence

broad (Stratum II) ability. Only the cognitive clusters (i.e., broad ability), which are composed of a minimum of two subtests representing specific measures of narrow abilities, can be interpreted at the Stratum II level. The Extended Battery, composed of the standard and supplemental tests, provides an Extended Broad Cognitive Ability (IQ) factor score and factor scores for seven of the nine Horn-Cattell *Gf-Gc* cognitive factors. These seven cognitive processing factors (and the Quantitative factor from the WJ-R Tests of Achievement), along with the specific/narrow abilities measures, are described in Table 7–1 (Hicks & Bolen, 1996) adapted from Woodcock (1990).

A careful review of the cognitive clusters reveals the basis of the WJ-R tests of cognitive abilities in terms of multiple intelligence representation. The WJ-R, compared to Carroll's (1993) Three-Stratum theory, would follow the model outlined in Figure 7–2.

Standardization

The normative sample included 6,359 individuals, ranging from 2 years through 90 years of age, from over 100 geographically diverse U.S. communities. There is a slight oversampling of racial/ethnic minorities; otherwise, the 1980 U.S. Bureau of the Census distribution of demographic characteristics was well matched. Stratification variables included gender, geographic region, community size, and race (White, Black, Native American, African Pacific, Hispanic, and Other). All normative data were obtained between 1986 and 1988. For children below age 5, the early developmental scale is based on a sample of 705 cases; the sample for kindergarten through 12th grade included 3,245 cases. Handicapped students, who were mainstreamed at least part-time, were also included. The 916 students from higher education institutions included in the sample produced "distinct college/university norms" (Woodcock, 1990, p. 231). The WJ-R standardization utilized a unique procedure to control for family socioeconomic status (SES) variables (Kamphaus, 1993). Communities were selected during standardization based on SES, as determined by adult educational attainment, type and status of occupation, and household income. For the adult population, direct measures of SES were determined on the basis of educational attainment and occupation.

Reliability

The WJ-R Technical Manual (McGrew, Werder, & Woodcock, 1991) provides specific reliability information for each test on the WJ-R COG. Total test reliability for the Standard Broad Cognitive Ability index (based on the first seven tests) is reported as .94. This is a median internal consistency coefficient, corrected by the Spearman-Brown formula (Woodcock & Mather, 1989). For the preschool sample, the Broad Cognitive Ability index internal consistency coefficient was reported as .96 for ages 2 and 4. The median reliability for the Extended Scale (based on the first 14 tests) exceeded .95 for all sample groups.

Individual reliabilities for the 14 tests comprising the Standard and Supplemental Cognitive Battery ranged from the mid-.70s to mid-.90s, with the majority falling in the .80s. The Visual Closure subtest reliabilities, for ages 6 through 39, are somewhat lower (.60), while reliabilities for Visual Matching are in the .70s. Although these reliabilities compare favorably to other individual measures of cognitive ability, McGrew (1994) appropriately cautions that "the lack of consistent reliability at or above the .90 level for each individual test argues against the use of a single WJRCA-R [WJ-R COG] cognitive cluster as the sole basis for an important educational decision [e.g., special class placement]" (p. 85).

For the seven cognitive processing factors, internal consistency coefficients are quite high. These median reliability coefficients ranged from .816 for Visual Processing to .946 for Fluid Reasoning (McGrew, 1994, p. 85). Test-retest (stability) coefficients for the Processing Speed factor were calculated by Mosier's (1943) procedure since they are timed tests. Median test-retest reliability coefficients ranged from .60 to .90 for the individually timed tests and .81 to .96 for the Processing Speed factor.

Validity

Content, concurrent, predictive, and construct validity are discussed in the technical manual (Woodcock & Mather, 1989; Woodcock, 1990). Limited validity information is presented for either content or predictive validation; detailed validity information is presented for concurrent and factorial validation.

Content Validity

Content validity was established by having experts select test items and then subjecting those items to item validity studies and retaining only those meeting specific psychometric properties. However, criteria used to select the original items and the qualifications of these experts was not revealed. As Cummings (1992) notes, "whether individuals who would bring alternative racial/ethnic perspectives to the scrutiny of [these] items is not stated" (p. 1114). One method of assessing adequate content involves examining test items for adequate "floor" and "ceiling" effects within each test. Floor effects occur when a test does not have enough easy items for discriminative measurement at the lower developmental levels (the child misses all of the items). Ceiling effects occur when a test does not have enough difficult items for discriminative measurement at the upper developmental levels (the children all receive perfect scores). For the WJ-R COG, floor and ceiling effects appear satisfactory (Hicks & Bolen, 1996). Thus, item discrimination among abilities does not appear to be a problem. Adequacy of item representation within specific developmental ranges, however, is suspect. For example, analysis of the Memory for Sentences test shows poor item representation for the 1st through 12th grade levels as there are only 10 items included for this developmental range. In contrast, there are 39 items to differentiate the preschool and kindergarten range (ages 2 to 6 years, 3 months). Similar concerns are noted for the Visual Closure, Incomplete Words, Memory for Words, and Sound Blending tests. Lack of sufficient items within specific age and grade ranges on some scales distorts score interpretation. Relative Mastery Index (RMIs) and the *W* score, as well as stability of the standard based score are affected. These issues are discussed further in the section on administration and scoring of the WJ-R.

Concurrent Validity

Concurrent validity was investigated across different age levels (ages 3, 9, and 17) using common intellectual measures—the Kaufman Assessment Battery for Children (K-ABC; Kaufman, 1983), the McCarthy (McCarthy, 1972), the Stanford-Binet Intelligence Scale-Fourth Edition (SB-IV; Thorndike, Hagen, & Sattler, 1986), the WAIS-R (Wechsler, 1981), and the WISC-R (Wechsler, 1974). The concurrent validity coefficients for the sixty-four 3-year-olds ranged from .463 to .69 depending on the specific instrument used. The WJ-R COG Early Developmental scale correlated .69 with the K-ABC Mental Processing composite; .62 with the McCarthy GCI, and .69 with the SB-IV (Kamphaus, 1993). Concurrent validity coefficients were considered much lower than expected by Kamphaus, since the WJ-R COG is a "multisubtest measure of intelligence" (p. 299). At the 9-year-old level, concurrent validity coefficients for the Standard Battery (based on the first 7 tests of the COG) Broad Cognitive Ability were .46, .53, and .52 with the K-ABC, SB-IV, and WISC-R, respectively. When the Extended Battery Broad Cognitive Ability scale is used (based on the first 14 tests of the COG), validity coefficients increase substantially, from the mid-.60s to low .70s (Cummings, 1992). McGrew (1994) also details concurrent correlations with tests such as the McCarthy Scales, K-ABC, WISC-R, WAIS-R, and SB-IV.

One of the more obvious omissions in the concurrent validity discussion is the absence of mean score comparisons across tests. Standard score mean comparisons are essential in establishing concurrent validation. Moderate to strong correlations by themselves are insufficient to indicate concurrent measurement. Beginning students should carefully consider that the correlation shows only the agreement between the two tests being compared in terms of the individual's relative rank or position on that test. That is, if the concurrent validity between two tests was extremely high, this would indicate that an individual who scored the highest of the group on test one would tend to also score the highest on the second test. But there is nothing that suggests the two scores are equivalent qualitatively. The highest obtained IQ score could easily be 55 on the first test and 120 on the second. The rank order or position remains unchanged, but the two tests clearly do not measure ability in the same manner. Thus, for concurrent validation it is also necessary to know the group means for each test as well as the variance. There should be no statistically significant difference in group performance on the two instruments being compared if concurrent validation is to be established. (See also Anastasi, 1988, Chapter 7, for a discussion of slope and intercept bias in measurement.)

As Cummings (1992) notes, "Information on the comparison of mean scores for the WJ-R with the original 1977 version of the Woodcock-Johnson and with other anchor measures of cognitive ability and measures of achievement would have provided a context for interpretation of any differences noted when comparing old scores to the WJ-R scores in the situation of a 3-year re-evaluation" (p. 1115). Thus, to date, there is only limited data supporting the concurrent validity of the WJ-R COG. In the next 3 years, a considerable amount of data should be available for review in the research literature as independent studies are completed.

Construct and Factorial Validity

Woodcock (1990) provides extensive information regarding the factor analytic studies of the WJ-R COG. Three data sets from the norming sample were analyzed: a sample of 2,261 subjects administered the 16 tests representing the primary measures of the eight clusters; a sample of 3,063 subjects administered 27 tests (21 COG tests and 6 ACHV tests); and a follow-up sample of 1,425 subjects also administered the 27 tests in which the data were analyzed by two independently conducted confirmatory factor analyses and by an oblique rotation factor analysis. Additionally, McGrew (1994) and McGrew et al. (1991) provide a comprehensive discussion of the factorial-based construct validity of the WJ-R COG along with further details of three specific samples, including third-grade students ($N = 89$), a group of 9-year-olds ($N = 70$), and a group of 17-year-olds ($N = 53$).

Confirmatory and exploratory factor analyses across grade and age levels were performed to determine the fit of the WJ-R COG to the Horn-Cattell *Gf-Gc* model. McGrew et al. (1991) report the results of a confirmatory factor analysis of the 14 cognitive tests that make up the seven processing factors for six different age groups in the WJ-R COG standardization sample. The goodness-of-fit and adjusted goodness-of-fit statistics were above .90 and .80, respectively; and the root-mean-square residual value was below .10. This suggests a good fit between the hypothesized structure and the WJ-R COG cognitive factors. Additional confirmatory and joint factor analysis studies using a variety of other aptitude tests are reported in McGrew (1994, Chapters 4 and 8) and by Bickley, Keith, and Wolfle (1995).

Independent review of Woodcock's factor analyses of the WJ-R COG was completed by Reschly (1990), Kaufman (1990), and Ysseldyke (1990). These researchers conclude that the WJ-R COG is psychometrically robust with strong factor analytic support for the construct validity of the test battery (Hicks & Bolen, 1996).

Administration, Scoring, and Interpretation of the WJ-R COG

The WJ-R COG should be administered and interpreted only by trained school, clinical, or educational psychologists. Ease of administration is simplified by the easel format presentation of each test. Directions, sample and/or teaching items, and basal and ceiling rules are clearly presented on both the test easel and test record forms. Several subtests do require the use of a tape recorder (not provided), and the beginning examiner requires some practice in including these tests without disrupting pace and attention. For the Auditory Processing and Short-Term Memory tests, the tape recorder helps ensure uniformity and continuity in administration. The examiner manuals are comprehensively written and present a number of examples and descriptive activities to introduce the novice examiner to proper administration and scoring practices. Various checklists of learning activities are introduced along with sample protocols, detailed case examples, and scoring exercises. A tape pronunciation guide for the phonics coding is also provided. One feature especially evident is the objective nature in the scoring of individual test items. Error variance, often associated with the WISC-III in the scoring of Comprehension, Similarities, and Vocabulary items, is minimized in the WJ-R COG.

For the preschool child, there is an obvious lack of manipulative items when compared to the Wechsler Preschool and Primary Scale, the K-ABC, or the McCarthy scales. Woodcock and Mather (1989) stress that the WJ-R COG can be easily modified to accommodate ESL (English as a second language) students, the hearing impaired, the visually impaired, individuals with traumatic brain injury, and the physically handicapped.

For each of the 21 tests scores and seven cognitive processing factors, a variety of derived scores are provided. Grade and age equivalents are obtained directly from the test record form. Once raw scores are obtained, the practitioner is well advised to utilize the *Report Writer for the WJ-R* (Schrank & Woodcock, 1995), as hand scoring is extremely laborious and subject to computational error. The computer-generated scoring printout provides developmental level bands and instructional ranges plotted on an age/grade scale, allowing determination of easy and difficult levels of performance. The Relative Mastery Index (RMI) shows the examinee's percentage of success on tasks performed with 90% accuracy, by either age or grade reference group comparison. Percentile rank scores are also provided to show a student's relative standing. A standard score index (based on a mean of 100 and a standard deviation of 15) is printed for each test as well as for each of the seven cognitive processing factors. The WJ-R COG (1989) continues to provide the *W* scale measurement. The *W* scale is based on the Rasch Log Ability Scale and is used to provide a basis for making interpretive and comparative analyses of the student's performance in relation to the difficulty level of the items. A *W* score of 500, for example, represents average level performance comparable to that of the average fifth-grade student. Utilization of these types of scores is much more beneficial than the traditional clinical-based procedure of using standard scores for diagnosis (e.g.,

Table 7–2.   Classification based on standard scores for the WJ-R COG

Standard Score Range	Descriptive Classification
131 and above	Very Superior
121–130	Superior
111–120	High Average
90–110	Average
80–89	Low Average
70–79	Low
Below 69	Very Low

< 70 is often equated with retardation) as they describe and compare performance to a norm. For example, the WJ-R also provides extended age- and grade-equivalent scores at the lower end of the distribution, using a superscript to represent the percentile rank of the child compared to that age level. An age equivalent reported as AE 2.0[15] would mean that the child obtained a score at the 15th percentile rank for 2-year-olds.

Qualitative interpretation of standard scores, based on a mean of 100 and a standard deviation of 15, follows the descriptive classification as provided in Table 7–2.

Administration of the WJ-R COG individual subtests involves a straightforward procedure, enhancing uniformity of presentation and inquiry as well as determining basal and ceiling levels. Clear basal and ceiling rules, starting points, and scoring criteria are presented on the test record form and/or on the easel.

A description of each WJ-R COG subtest, and administration and scoring comments, is presented next:

1. *Memory for Names:* a task requiring learning of names of a number of space creatures. The test measures the narrow ability involved in learning visual-auditory associations between novel stimuli. Scoring is very objective in that the examinee points to the space creature. The task provides an opportunity for clinical observation, as the learning/association process is directly observed by the examiner and incorrect responses are corrected immediately by the examiner (who shows the correct response until item 64). Items are scored as 1 or 0.

2. *Memory for Sentences:* an auditory task requiring the examinee to repeat exactly the phrase or sentence presented on the tape player. In the unusual cases of hearing impairment, the examiner may read the items; otherwise, the tape player ensures uniformity in presentation (voice inflection, pace, pronunciation, etc.). Scoring examples are provided directly on the examiner's easel. Items are scored as 2, 1, or 0.

3. *Visual Matching:* a visual-motor task requiring the examinee to visually identify two numerals that are alike in a row of six numbers. The task increases in difficulty from single digits to triple digits and has a 3-minute time limit. Bonus points are awarded for rapid completion. Scoring is objective, and the

examiner has an opportunity to observe task vigilance (sustained attending) as well as distractibility and/or off-task tendencies. Items are scored as 1 or 0.

4. *Incomplete Words:* a task requiring auditory closure (phonics coding). One (or more) phoneme of a word is omitted during oral presentation via the tape player. Sounds omitted may be the beginning, middle, or ending sounds of the word. The examinee states the complete word aloud to the examiner. Scoring is objective in that acceptable responses are clearly printed on the examiner's easel; items are scored as 1 or 0.

5. *Visual Closure:* a task requiring oral identification of incomplete pictures/drawings of objects. The examinee is required to provide the correct name of the object; thus, language and verbal concept formation may be involved in task success. Scoring is objective as acceptable responses are clearly provided on the examiner's easel. Items are scored as 1 or 0.

6. *Picture Vocabulary:* a task requiring the naming of both familiar and unfamiliar pictured objects. Scoring is objective and items are scored as 1 or 0.

7. *Analysis-Synthesis:* a unique measure of deductive reasoning. The task requires the examinee to analyze a puzzle composed of colored squares. This appears to be a rather powerful task in that (1) the examinee is provided several practice/training examples during various portions of the test; (2) the task increases in difficulty through a step-by-step learning gradient; (3) a key is provided on each page for the examinee's use, which reduces reliance on rote memory and helps ensure that the task is a power measure; (4) ample time for problem solving is allowed; and (5) feedback is provided by the examiner for incorrect responses until the very last section of the test. The upper-level items have a 1-minute time limit (earlier items are not timed). The examinee cannot complete this task if he or she is color-blind, and a simple screening measure for color identification is provided prior to administration. Scoring is objective and items are scored as either 1 or 0.

8. *Visual-Auditory Learning:* a measure of visual-auditory association using a rebus approach. Reading passages increase in complexity as the examinee is taught new symbols throughout the test. Scoring is objective as the examinee "reads" the rebuses aloud. Incorrect responses to a rebus are immediately corrected by the examiner. Each incorrect response is counted; thus, the higher the raw score, the poorer the performance. Combined with the Memory for Names test, this test contributes to the Long-Term Memory cluster (*Glm*).

9. *Memory for Words:* a serial auditory memory task requiring the examinee to recall, in correct sequence, a list of words presented via the tape player. Each word sequence is grouped into three units with a ceiling designated whenever a unit of three word groups of the same length is missed. The sequences of words in the first group begin with three and increase to seven. Scoring is objective with each word group scored as 1 or 0. Test 9 is combined with Test 2 to form the Short-Term Memory cluster (*Glm*).

10. *Cross Out:* a fine-motor task requiring visual discrimination. The examinee must locate and mark 5 drawings in a row of 20 that match the first item in

the row. Speed and accuracy is required as the test has a 3-minute time limit. Bonus points are awarded for rapid task completion, even if errors are made. A nice feature of this task is that it provides a way of adjusting the raw score if the examiner makes a timing error (i.e. exceeds the 3-minute time limt). Scoring is objective, and each row is scored as 1 or 0. Combined with Test 3, these measures represent the Processing Speed cognitive cluster (*Gs*).

11. *Sound Blending:* an auditory task requiring phonics coding. Various parts of words (syllables or phonemes) are presented, and the examinee attempts to integrate the sounds into a whole word form. Use of the tape player helps ensure consistency in presentation and oral pronunciation of the word parts. The task requires a shift in auditory perception by the examinee midway through as items switch (without warning or instruction) from a blending of the word syllables to phonetic spelling of the phonemes within each word. Scoring is objective with acceptable responses clearly presented on the easel. Items are scored as 1 or 0. This test combines with Test 4 to form the Auditory Processing cluster (*Ga*).

12. *Picture Recognition:* a visual memory task requiring the examinee to recognize one or more previously pictured items from a group of similar images. Scoring is objective, and items are scored as either 1 or 0. This task combines with Test 5 to form the Visual Processing cluster (*Gv*).

13. *Oral Vocabulary:* a test measuring the examinee's knowledge of word meanings. The test is divided into two parts: synonyms and antonyms. Scoring is objective, and each pair of items is scored as 1 or 0. The total score is the sum of both parts. This test combines with Test 6 to form the measure of crystallized intelligence (*Gc*).

14. *Concept Formation:* a unique reasoning test measuring the ability of the examinee to deduce relations. Geometric figures are utilized and presented in such a manner as to encompass one or more of four primary concepts: size (large/small), shape (round/square), quantity (single/double), and color (red/yellow). The examinee must determine the rule for any particular combination of the geometric figures. Additionally, class inclusion is involved as the examinee must often stipulate two or more rules and/or components (e.g., round and two; small and square). Scoring is objective as the examinee must orally state the rule utilizing the four concepts. The test appears to be a powerful measure in that (1) prior experience is not likely a feature of successful performance (although as one graduate student observed knowledge of set theory could be an advantage); (2) practice/training test items are presented periodically throughout the test as new concepts are introduced; and (3) corrective feedback is presented by the examiner until the very last section of the test. Item scoring is either 1 or 0. This test combines with Test 7 to form the fluid intelligence cognitive cluster (*Gf*).

15. *Delayed Recall, Memory for Names:* based on a 1 to 8 day delay, this test is used to measure the ability of the examinee to recall the space creatures presented in Test 1, Memory for Names. A random order display is presented. The examinee is not informed that subsequent testing will occur. Test

15 is then combined with Tests 1 and 8 to form a stronger long-term memory cognitive cluster (*Glm*).

16. *Delayed Recall, Visual-Auditory Learning:* also based on a 1 to 8 day delay, this test is used to measure delayed recall of the rebus items previously learned in Test 8. The examinee is shown each rebus symbol and asked to state its name. The examinee is not informed that subsequent testing will occur. Test 16 is then combined with Tests 1 and 8 to form a stronger long-term memory cognitive cluster (*Glm*).

17. *Numbers Reversed:* a memory test requiring the examinee to repeat a series of random numbers backward (items are presented from the audio tape). Item difficulty increases as more numbers are added to the series. Woodcock considers this task more of a perceptual reorganization task than a memory task *per se,* as numbers repeated forward would represent. Thus, Test 17 represents a mix of short-term memory, attention, and possible fluid intelligence.

18. *Sound Patterns:* a unique test measuring the ability to discriminate pairs of complex sound patterns as the same or different. A voice synthesizer is used, and no meaningful language component is involved. An audio tape is required. The test is thought to represent a measure of both auditory processing (*Ga*) and fluid intelligence (*Gf*).

19. *Spatial Relations:* a task requiring the examinee to select from a visual list the component parts needed to complete a whole shape. This visual-processing task involves visual discrimination, matching, and reasoning as the items become increasingly more complex and abstract. Thus, the test is thought to represent a mix of visual processing (*Gv*) and fluid intelligence (*Gf*).

20. *Listening Comprehension:* a task requiring the examinee to listen to a short tape-recorded passage in which a single word is missing. This oral cloze procedure is thought to require a reasoning component as well as vocabulary and comprehension knowledge. Thus, both verbal comprehension (*Gc*) and fluid reasoning (*Gf*) may be represented.

21. *Verbal Analogies:* a test measuring the ability to finish a phrase with the appropriate word to represent the analogy. Verbal relationships become more complex although the required vocabulary remains fairly easy. Both fluid intelligence (*Cf*) and crystallized intelligence (*Gc*) are hypothesized to be involved in successful completion of the task.

Broad Cognitive Ability Standard Scale, Early Development Scale,
and Extended Scale

The Broad Cognitive Ability (BCA) Standard Scale is an equally weighted combination of the first seven tests in the WJ-R COG representing a broad-based measure of general intellectual ability. No cluster (Broad Abilities) scores are obtained, however, when only the Standard Scale is administered. For children at the preschool level, or for individuals at any age who are functioning at very low levels, the Early Developmental Scale, composed of five equally weighted tests (Memory for Names, Memory for Sentences, Incomplete Words, Visual Closure, and Picture Vocabulary), is administered. Again, no Broad Abilities are obtained. When the first 14 tests are administered (Standard Scale Tests 1–7 and Supplemental Battery Tests 8–14), a BCA Extended Scale score based on an equally weighted combination of the first 14 cognitive tests is obtained. In addition, the seven Broad Ability clusters are produced, and cluster interpretation, along with intrascale analysis of profile strengths and weaknesses, is now considered appropriate. Additional tests in the Supplemental Battery (Tests 15–21), along with tests from the WJ-R ACHV, may be used to provide additional information (scholastic aptitude estimates and oral language measures, for example).

The Cognitive Clusters and Interpretation of the BCA Standard Score

Interpretation of the individual subtest is specifically de-emphasized. In fact, Woodcock (1993) strongly cautions the examiner *not* to attempt individual test interpretation or individual test profile analysis. Cluster interpretation, however, provides a "higher validity because more than one component of a broad ability comprises the score that serves as the basis for interpretation" (p. 21). Extended interpretive strategies are presented by McGrew (1994, Chapter 6) and Hessler (1993, Chapter 5).

When analyzing standard scores for the ability clusters, the examiner will quickly ascertain that the factor cluster standard score is not an average of the two standard scores obtained on each cluster. For example, a child obtained a standard score of 125 on the Visual Matching subtest and 123 on the Cross Out subtest, which results in a standard score of 127 on the Processing Speed factor (composed of these two subtests). This is because the probability of performing well on both tests of the factor is less than the probability of performing well on only one of the two tests. Conversely, when the examinee performs poorly on both subtests of a factor, the factor score will be lower than the average of the two test scores. Again, the probability of performing poorly on both tests of the factor is less than the probability of performing poorly on only one of the two tests. Moreover, when interpreting the BCA (Ext. Scale), which is based on a mean of 100 and standard deviation of 15, it also becomes apparent that the BCA index score is not an average of the seven cognitive factor scores. This can cause considerable difficulty, initially, for the examiner in interpreting of the score profile and overall ability index.

Woodcock (1990) states that the BCA (Std. and Ext. Scales) is not based on an arithmetic average of the seven factor scores. This might imply that each factor, then, is uniquely weighted based on its variance contribution in the measurement of intelligence. This is not, apparently, the case even though Woodcock (1990) states, "All cognitive batteries provide a broad measure of intellectual ability based on average subtest performance" (p. 250). He also reports that for the WJ-R Broad Cognitive Ability index, there are two measures for each of the seven factors, and "the two measures for each factor contribute approximately 14% each toward the total score" (p. 251). The scaling of the BCA, however, does not result in an average of the seven-factor standard scores as the BCA composite. For example, if a child obtains the seven-factor standard scores of *Glm* 57, *Gsm* 60, *Gs* 47, *Ga* 30, *Gv* 52, *Gc* 28, and *Gf* 49, the BCA (Ext. Scale) standard score is actually 20, which is considerably lower than 46, the average of the seven factors. Again, this is because the probability of performing poorly on all seven factors is less than the probability of performing poorly on only one or two of the seven factors. In the

Table 7–3. Comparison of average standard scores on the WISC-III and WJ-R COG to the composite: The average of the parts does not equal the total

WISC-III Subtest	Scale Score	Standard Score $(M = 10\ SD = 3)$	WJ-R COG	$(M = 100\ SD = 15)$
Information	4	70	Glr	77
Similarities	4	70	Gsm	77
Arithmetic	4	70	Gs	71
Vocabulary	4	70	Ga	76
Comprehension	4	70	Gv	70
Picture Completion	4	70	Gc	76
Picture Arrangement	4	70	Gf	75
Block Design	4	70		
Object Assembly	4	70		
Coding	4	70		
Average Standard Score	70		Average	74.57
Full Scale Standard Score	59		BCA	61
Difference	−11			−13.57

same manner of interpretation, if an examinee performs poorly on all seven factors, prediction of school failure globally would be best represented by the BCA (Ext. Scale) rather than any one factor or the average of all seven factors. This aspect of the WJ-R COG does present some difficulties, however, which are discussed in the case examples.

This phenomenon is also present on other tests of intelligence (e.g., the WISC-III), but due to differences in intercorrelations among subtests and factors (the amount of uniqueness in measurement by each test or factor), the discrepancy between standard scores on any one test and its composite on the WJ-R COG may range from only a few to as much as 15 to 20 points. McGrew (1994) provides a striking example using the WISC-R, which is taken from Chapter 8 of his text *Clinical Interpretation of the Woodcock-Johnson Tests of Cognitive Ability-Revised.* McGrew's WISC-III example is compared to a simulated test performance on the WJ-R COG of a youngster 11 years old. These comparisons are presented in Table 7–3.

The magnitude of the discrepancy will be larger on the WJ-R COG BCA than on other intelligence batteries because the *Gf-Gc* factors on the COG better represent measures of unique abilities (lower intercorrelations among factors = more unique measure of separate cognitive abilities). As McGrew (1994) noted, the only time the full scale IQ could equal the *average* of the individual tests is when all individual tests are perfectly correlated. By default, then, one and only one ability could be represented on that intelligence test measure, which defeats the very purpose of having a battery of individual tests to measure different abilities.

Recommended Interpretive Model for the WJ-R

Woodcock (1990) recommends the following approach in factor-score interpretation:

1. The clinician, teacher, or counselor must be knowledgeable about the factorial composition of each test in the battery; not just about the names but about the behavior being sampled.

2. Information is needed from at least two "clean" measures of a cognitive factor before generalizing about a subject's ability in that area.

3. A mixed factor cannot be interpreted to represent a unique ability. For example, the WJ-R Spatial Relations subtests, composed of *Gv* and *Gf* measures, cannot be interpreted as a measure of visual reasoning.

4. The clinician should be prepared to "cross" batteries to obtain a set of measures required for a particular assessment.

In addition, four levels of interpretation of the WJ-R COG, following earlier schemas developed by Kaufman (1979, 1990) are suggested. This process involves Level 1, Qualitative Information; Level 2, Level of Development; Level 3, Indices of Proficiency; and Level 4, Indices of Relative Standing in a group. Guidelines for interpreting the WJ-R COG would incorporate each of the following steps:

1. Interpret the Broad Cognitive Ability Index (Std. or Ext. Scale) and corresponding percentile rank, using Woodcock's (1990) classification system, as the best representation of the subject's overall ability *g*. The BCA (Ext.) index is a global estimate of the child's level of cognitive ability based on the first 14 WJ-R cognitive subtests and is also reported in age and grade equivalencies and RMIs. The BCA (Std.) Index is also a global measure of the child's cognitive ability but is based on the first seven subtests. It is used primarily for reevaluation purposes, as well as for screening, and *Gf-Gc* factor clusters are not obtained.

2. Only when the Extended Scale is administered can the examiner analyze and compare the intracognitive factors and interpret the profile of seven cognitive factors. Next, the examiner develops hypotheses regarding intracognitive discrepancies, especially in conjunction with the reason for referral and prior information about the subject's schooling, background, and language. If the examiner identifies a specific need to investigate further, long-term retrieval, for example, then subtests 15 and 16 could be administered and combined with subtests 1 and 8 for a more robust assessment of that particular ability. Likewise, language proficiency and other specific clusters could be the focus.

3. Compare each of the seven cognitive clusters, using RMIs, to establish a cognitive profile of strengths and weaknesses. Table 7–4 (see Case Example 7–1), adapted from Hessler (1993), relates levels of proficiency based on RMI comparisons. Utilization of this method is outlined in one of the case studies presented at the end of the chapter. An alternative procedure is to compare standard score discrepancies provided on the WJ-R Report Writer (Schrank & Woodcock, 1995) analysis printout, adopting a criteria of at least 1.5 standard deviation units for significance. When using intracognitive discrepancy scores to identify strengths and weaknesses between factor clusters, an un-

Table 7–4.   Levels of proficiency as determined by analysis of RMIs

RMI	W Difference	Proficiency Level	Difficulty Gradient Related to Academics
100/90	+34 and above	Very Advanced	Extremely Easy
98/90 to 99/90	+14 to +26	Advanced	Very Easy
82/90 to 95/90	−6 to +6	Average	Manageable
34/90 to 67/90	−26 to −14	Limited	Difficult
5/90 to 18/90	−46 to −34	Very Limited	Extremely Difficult
0/90 to 2/90	−54 and below	Negligible	Impossible

Source: Adapted from Hessler (1993, p. 34).

usual occurrence is defined as a difference that occurs less than 13% of the time (McGrew, 1994). The 1.5 standard deviation of difference identifies approximately 13% of the population as having either a positive or negative intracognitive discrepancy in each cognitive area. This procedure, automated on the WJ-R Report Writer, provides an analysis of relative processing strengths and weaknesses, and should lead to the development of specific hypotheses regarding educational needs and/or remedial recommendations.

4. Carefully examine each of the (two) test clusters comprising a broad cognitive ability. Do the two test scores correspond reasonably well or do they differ significantly? If the two differ by 33 *W* score points or more, interpretation of the cognitive cluster may be unreliable. These comparisons must be cautiously examined due to errors associated with multiple comparison. Nonetheless, it is valuable to understand the consistency or inconsistency of a student's performance within each factor. For example, the Processing Speed factor is composed of Tests 3 and 10, and both are completed within a 3-minute time limit. If a child scores 105 on Test 3 and 80 on Test 10, what can reliably be concluded about processing speed? This divergence within a broad ability factor does not give us confidence that we have a dependable measure of the child's processing speed. Clinical observation during the evaluation, however, may have simply noted that the child was now fatigued after having worked assiduously on the nine previous tests. The clinician should remain very cautious, however, in interpreting individual subtest performance without compelling data from other sources.

5. Examine each cognitive processing factor in terms of actual versus expected performance levels. Compare the aptitude cluster in relation to the expected level of performance and identify areas reflecting discrepant cognitive processing.

6. Determine aptitude/achievement discrepancies. A special section describing three types of psychoeducational discrepancies—the disparity between certain intellectual abilities and achievement—as well as identification of learning disabilities is presented on pages 31 to 36.

7. Examine intrasubtest patterns in terms of item gradients. Does the subject miss easier level items while successfully completing more difficult items

above his or her age or grade level? There is a qualitative difference between a child who completes the first ten items of a test ($RS = 10$) before reaching ceiling and one who misses every other item or so until reaching ceiling at item 25 ($RS = 10$). This could possibly indicate attentional, memory, motivational, or other cognitive deficiencies requiring additional analysis. Are there any tests in which performance is extremely low or represented by a raw score of zero? A specific processing disorder may be implicated or, perhaps, a test with a lower basal level (< 2.0 years) may be needed, such as the Bayley Scales of Infant Development.

8. Examine the subject's responses for qualitative features involving the ability to conceptualize, verbal expressiveness, motivation (tendency to give up, task persistence), ability to self-monitor, impulsivity, anxiety, and so forth. Did the child generally understand directions? Was the child able to attend? Were learning strategies apparent?

9. Determine the clinical significance of any specific responses that may suggest pathology. This level of analysis focuses on specific item failures and the nature of the actual response the child provides. The quality of the verbal responses as well as nonverbal behavior should be evaluated.

Scholastic Aptitude Clusters

Four scholastic aptitude clusters are obtained when Tests 1 through 14 are administered. These are Reading Aptitude, Mathematics Aptitude, Written Language Aptitude, and Knowledge Aptitude. The aptitude measures are designed specifically to provide information about the examinee's expected achievement. Aptitude clusters are based on an equally weighted combination of four (various) tests and, according to Woodcock (1991), provide a psychologically meaningful determination of the presence or severity of an aptitude/achievement discrepancy:

Reading Aptitude: Consisting of Test 2 (Memory for Sentences), Test 3 (Visual Matching), Test 11 (Sound Blending), and Test 13 (Oral Vocabulary), this aptitude cluster provides an expected score to be used for comparison to the actual score an examinee obtains on tests of reading achievement.

Mathematics Aptitude: Consisting of Test 3 (Visual Matching), Test 7 (Analysis-Synthesis), Test 13 (Oral Vocabulary), and Test 14 (Concept Formation), this aptitude cluster provides an expected score to be used for comparison to the actual score an examinee obtains on tests of mathematics achievement.

Written Language Aptitude: Consisting of Test 3 (Visual Matching), Test 8 (Visual-Auditory Learning), Test 11 (Sound Blending), and Test 14 (Concept Formation), this aptitude cluster provides an expected score to be used for comparison to the actual score an examinee obtains on tests of written language.

Knowledge Aptitude: Consisting of Test 2 (Memory for Sentences), Test 5 (Visual Closure), Test 11 (Sound Blending), and Test 14 (Concept Formation), this aptitude cluster provides an expected score to be used for comparison to the actual score an examinee obtains on tests of knowledge in the content areas.

Two additional clusters that may be obtained include Oral Language and Oral Language Aptitude. The Oral Language cluster consists of Test 2 (Memory for Sentences), Test 6 (Picture Vocabulary), Test 13 (Oral Vocabulary), Test 20 (Listening Comprehension), and Test 21 (Verbal Analogies). This cluster is thought to represent a broad measure of oral language ability. The Oral Language Aptitude cluster consists of Test 12 (Picture Recognition), Test 14 (Concept Formation), Test 17 (Numbers Reversed), and Test 18 (Sound Patterns). As an aptitude cluster, it provides the expected score for comparison to the examinee's actual scores obtained on the Oral Language cluster.

Educational Uses of the WJ-R

Woodcock (1990, 1993) reports that the information provided by the WJ-R is especially appropriate for determining three basic types of psychoeducational discrepancies:

1. Aptitude/achievement discrepancies
2. Intracognitive discrepancies
3. Intraachievement discrepancies

A Type 1 (aptitude/achievement) discrepancy shows the difference between one's expected academic performance and actual academic performance. One's expected level is determined by an estimate of the individual's broad cognitive ability. Unlike the IQ/achievement discrepancy model adopted by many states in the identification of learning disabilities, an individual's achievement would be compared to the aptitude cluster, not the global IQ score. The comparison is unidirectional; only discrepancies in which achievement is lower than the predicted performance are of concern.

A Type 2 (intracognitive) discrepancy examines cluster differences for processing disorders or specific cognitive deficits such as delayed language or visual processing. Comparison is bidirectional as there is equal interest in any cognitive cluster. Some individuals, at certain times in their education, may not demonstrate an achievement discrepancy (due to compensation, special training, curricular demands, learning strategy applications, particular tests used, etc.); but the processing disorder continues to show itself via this type of analysis, evidenced by disparate processing abilities. This type of analysis also helps provide insights into curriculum needs and program planning for the individual.

A Type 3 (intraachievement) discrepancy shows achievement deficits such as reading comprehension or deficient math skills. The comparison is also bidirectional and the type of information obtained is useful for specific instructional planning.

Educational Misuses of the WJ-R

1. Do not interpret a low score on an individual subtest such as Memory for Names as indicating poor overall long-term memory.

2. Do not use the WJ-R Broad Cognitive Index score in isolation to classify the individual as mentally retarded.

3. Do not interpret any specific performance on any of the seven cognitive clusters as a direct indicator of attention deficit disorder.

4. Do not interpret a low score on any specific cognitive cluster as indicating brain damage or neurological impairment.

5. Do not interpret the Broad Cognitive Index as an indicator of innate intellectual capacity.

6. Do not report factor scores when physical limitations invalidate test administration. For example, for the hearing impaired, the Auditory Processing factor may be invalidated; for children suffering from cerebral palsy, the Processing Speed factor may be invalidated.

Expanded *Gf-Gc* Test Clusters

McGrew (1994) reports that the 21 individual tests comprising the WJ-R COG can be expanded into broader test groupings, some of which support specific *Gf-Gc* clusters while others add new information. Expanded test clusters and the corresponding individual tests were identified by McGrew as follows:

1. *Expanded Long-Term Retrieval (Glr)*: Visual-Auditory Learning, Memory for Names, Picture Recognition, Visual Closure, Delayed Recall-VAL, and Delayed Recall-MN.

2. *Expanded Short-Term Memory (Gsm)*: Memory for Sentences, Memory for Words, Numbers Reversed, and Listening Comprehension.

3. *Expanded Processing Speed (Gs):* Visual Matching, Cross out, and Numbers Reversed.

4. *Expanded Comprehension-Knowledge (Gc)*: Picture Vocabulary, Oral Vocabulary, Memory for Sentences, Visual Closure, Incomplete Words, Verbal Analogies, and Listening Comprehension.

5. *Expanded Fluid Reasoning (Gf)*: Concept Formation, Analysis-Synthesis, Oral Vocabulary, Spatial Relations, Verbal Analogies, Listening Comprehension, Numbers Reversed, and Sound Patterns.

6. *Auditory Sequential Processing Memory:* Memory for Sentences, Memory for Words, Incomplete Words, Sound Blending, Numbers Reversed, and Sound Patterns.

7. *Visual Perceptual Fluency:* Cross Out, Visual Matching, Visual Closure, Picture Recognition, and Spatial Relations.

8. *Auditory Attention/Listening:* Incomplete Words, Sound Blending, Sound Patterns, and Listening Comprehension.

9. *New Learning Efficiency:* Memory for Names, Visual-Auditory Learning, Analysis-Synthesis, and Concept Formation.

10. *Broad Synthesis Ability:* Incomplete Words, Sound Blending, Visual Closure, and Spatial Relations.

11. *Word Finding/Verbal Retrieval:* Picture Vocabulary, Oral Vocabulary, Incomplete Words, Sound Blending, and Visual Closure.

12. *Nonverbal Ability (nonspeeded):* Visual Closure, Picture Recognition, Concept Formation, Analysis-Synthesis, Memory for Names, Delayed Recall-MN, Delayed Recall-VAL, and Spatial Relations.

Although these expanded groupings are based on empirical analyses that suggest shared abilities among the test groupings, the robustness of any one cluster would not necessarily match any one of the seven established *Gf-Gc* cognitive clusters previously identified. Nonetheless, these groupings may provide helpful insight into intracognitive discrepancy analysis for specific cases and the utility of these test groupings—as well as others not yet developed—can be determined only through future research and test application.

Cross-Battery Assessment

One of the potentially rich benefits of the WJ-R COG, then, may well be the examiner's leeway to examine new clusters as previously outlined (procedures for deriving new clusters are described in the WJ-R *Examiner's Manual* [Woodcock & Johnson, 1989]). Depending on the referral question, various combinations of tests may be used for special diagnostic and/or research purposes. In addition, it is not a requirement that new clusters be drawn only from the WJ-R. McGrew and Flanagan (1996) recently proposed "a cross-battery approach to assessing and interpreting cognitive abilities" (personal communication) during a 2-day seminar at the 1996 National Association of School Psychiatrists convention in Atlanta, Georgia. Acknowledging that not all subtests are created equally, a rationale for inclusion of selected tests from various test batteries was presented to represent "stronger or purer measures of their respective broad *Gf-Gc* constructs" (p. 3). Implications for cross-battery assessment are highly intriguing, and the next decade should see considerable research into this idea. McGrew and Flanagan (1996) maintain that cross-battery assessment will (1) result in more thorough assessment of an individual's broad *Gf-Gc* abilities, (2) increase the validity of the interpretations that can be derived, (3) improve communication between and among professionals, (4) improve understanding of the relationship between cognitive abilities and a variety of achievement tests, and (5) may increase identification of important aptitude-treatment interactions (ATIs).

Intelligence testing appears to have entered a new frontier, based on multiple intelligence theory. Tests such as the WJ-R COG, the Kaufman Adult Intelligence Test (KAIT; 1993), and the Differential Ability Scale (DAS; Elliott, 1990), among others, are now available. The history of intelligence testing, particularly in using tests to only measure *g* (how well individuals express their intelligence verbally or nonverbally), is likely past.

Case Example 7–1.   WJ-R COG analysis and interpretation—Kathy

Kathy, a 13 years, 1 month, 7th grade student, is currently identified as educable mentally handicapped (EMH) and placed in the EMH resource special-education class. Kathy was referred for the triennial evaluation of her special-education eligibility. She had been receiving special-education services for 15 hours per week (60% of the day) since the first grade. Results from previous tests administered when Kathy was in fifth grade showed all academic skills between the K.1 and 1.2 grade level. Her WISC-III VIQ was 48; PIQ, 47; and FSIQ, 44. Additionally, it was well documented that Kathy's level of acculturation, based on her rural environment and parents' extremely low socioeconomic status, was very weak.

REFERRAL QUESTION

What is Kathy's overall level of intellectual functioning? Does she exhibit a specific cognitive profile of strengths and weaknesses? What are her levels of achievement? What are appropriate educational recommendations?

Because of cultural and environmental concerns and their effect on test performance, the WJ-R was selected as the instrument of choice. Certain test clusters (e.g., *Gc*) may not provide a valid measure of Kathy's ability, as the Comprehension-Knowledge factor is known to reflect learning in the context of a particular culture (Hessler, 1993); but the WJ-R COG provides other factors less influenced by culture and environmental learning that can be directly compared.

TEST RESULTS

Kathy obtained a BCA (Ext.) score of 45 (below the first percentile) on the WJ-R COG. Analysis of her seven-factor scores, however, reveals erratic performance and a profile of cognitive strengths and weaknesses. Of the three factors most highly affected by culture, Kathy obtained the following standard scores and RMIs. (RMIs are used to determine the student's level of proficiency in any one factor cluster.) Kathy's Levels of Proficiency are based on Table 7–4.

Using the RMIs and referring back to Table 7–4, Kathy's test profile, based on her WJ-R COG test performance, would be summarized for the factors most affected by culture:

Broad Ability	Standard Score	RMI	Proficiency
Comprehension-Knowledge	28	0/90	negligible proficiency
Auditory Processing	30	2/90	negligible proficiency
Short-Term Memory	60	3/90	negligible proficiency

Results of the factors less affected by acculturation would be listed as follows:

Long-Term Retrieval	57	29/90	very limited proficiency
Processing Speed	47	8/90	negligible proficiency
Visual Processing	52	29/90	very limited proficiency
Fluid Reasoning	69	32/90	limited proficiency

Kathy's performance was fairly consistent and overall much better on the factors less affected by acculturation. Cognitive strengths relative to her overall abilities are shown in Long-Term Retrieval, Visual Processing, and Fluid Reasoning. These intra-

Case Example 7–1. *(Continued)*

cogntive discrepancies are also found to be statistically significant when reviewing the *Report Writer for the WJ-R* computer-scoring results. Not surprisingly, Kathy's age-equivalent level of cognitive functioning was below 6 years.

A cognitive proficiency comparison, using RMIs, between Auditory and Visual Processing suggests that Kathy may have significantly greater ability to visually analyze information than to encode and process auditory information.

29 (*Gv*)   very limited to limited Visual Processing
 2 (*Ga*)   negligible Auditory Processing

A cognitive proficiency comparison between long-term retrieval and short-term memory suggests that Kathy's ability to recall information once it has been learned may be greater than her short-term rote-memory ability.

29 (*Glr*)   very limited to limited long-term retrieval
 3 (*Gsm*)   negligible Short-Term Memory

A cognitive proficiency comparison between Comprehension-Knowledge and Fluid Reasoning indicates a significant difference in ability and suggests that Kathy has experienced considerable difficulty in acquiring new information from her environment; she has much better ability, however, in problem solving independently.

 0 (*Gc*)   negligible Comprehension-Knowledge
32 (*Gf*)   limited Fluid Reasoning ability

Kathy's achievement results also support the need for extensive individualized and structured assistance. Her standard scores and RMIs on the three broad achievement composites are as follows:

	Standard Score	RMI
Broad Reading	33	0/90
Broad Math	17	0/90
Broad Written Language	34	1/90

Achievement composites are slightly lower than the overall BCA (Ext.) index. Kathy demonstrates some cognitive strengths (*Glr, Gv,* and *Gf*) relative to the BCA (5/90), but all achievement areas except writing samples were at RMIs of 0/90 or 1/90. Thus, Kathy appears to *not* be achieving at a level commensurate with her abilities, and RMIs on three of the cognitive factors suggest that she may have considerably more potential (in terms of academic mastery) than she currently demonstrates on the achievement tests (since *Gf* is significantly higher than *Gc*). Kathy's low *Gc* may reflect the poor quality of her environment and, if this is indeed the case, intensive one-on-one remedial emphasis in the basic skills of reading, math, and writing appears warranted. Remedial instruction should utilize a whole word approach (since *Gv* is significantly higher than *Ga*) rather than a phonics approach. Learning practices utilizing drill, repetition, and practice are also strongly indicated for mastery of basic academics, as *Gsm* is very weak and *Glr* is relatively strong.

Case Example 7–2.   WJ-R COG analysis and interpretation—Shannon

Referred to determine eligibility for academically gifted program placement, Shannon is almost 10 years old and is in the fourth grade at a parochial school. Her achievement levels have already been established at the 95th percentile rank or higher in all areas. The psychoeducational report format follows a general standard used by the school system in reporting results to parents and teachers.

PSYCHOEDUCATIONAL REPORT
CONFIDENTIAL

NAME: Shannon   DATE OF TEST: March 11, 1996
AGE: 9 years, 11 months   DATE OF BIRTH: March 14, 1986
PARENTS: Ted & Lynne   GRADE: 4
102 Blue Banks Drive   SCHOOL: St. Gabriel's Catholic School
Anywhere, USA 10001

TEST ADMINISTERED
   Woodcock-Johnson Tests of Cognitive Abilities-Revised

REASON FOR REFERRAL
   Shannon was referred for intellectual evaluation to determine her current level of functioning and to establish her cognitive profile of strengths and weaknesses. Assessment of achievement levels, completed at school, show all her percentiles fall at or above the 95th percentile ranks. Eligibility for academically gifted services, based on current North Carolina Department of Instructional Services guidelines, requires that Shannon obtain a BCA (Ext.) ability index at or above the 91st percentile rank.

TEST RESULTS

Woodcock-Johnson Tests of Cognitive Ability-Revised. The WJ-R cognitive battery is designed to provide an aptitude profile that includes a measure of broad intellectual ability and indications of strengths and weaknesses in specific areas of cognitive processing. The extended scale was administered, and scores for the subtests as well as Shannon's BCA IQ score (Ext.) are given below (a standard score of 100 is average, corresponding to a 50th percentile rank).

	Standard Score	*Percentile*
Broad Cognitive Ability	121	92

   The BCA (Std.) score represents a global measure of individual aptitude (IQ). Shannon's score of 121 falls at the 92nd percentile rank: that is, 92% of the students obtain IQ scores lower than hers; 8% earn scores that are higher. This score places Shannon in the superior range of cognitive ability. She demonstrated an erratic cognitive profile, however, which indicates that each processing factor should be examined independently.

Case Example 7–2. *(Continued)*

Seven Cognitive Factors. Administration of the extended battery of the WJ-R Tests of Cognitive Ability provides two measures for each of seven cognitive factors. A brief description of each factor and Shannon's standard scores and percentiles are presented next:

Factor	Standard Score	Percentile
Long-Term Retrieval (Effectiveness in storing information & retrieving it over time)	110	74
Short-Term Memory (Processing information and utilizing it over a short period of time)	122	93
Processing Speed (Performing fine-motor cognitive tasks quickly)	130	98
Auditory Processing (Phonetic coding of auditory patterns)	88	22
Visual Processing (Understanding & processing visual patterns)	130	98
Comprehension-Knowledge (Factual knowledge & effective application)	109	73
Fluid Reasoning (Conceptual reasoning ability)	119	89

Intracognitive Discrepancies. Shannon demonstrated cognitive strengths in Fluid Reasoning, Visual Processing, Processing Speed, and Short-Term Memory. A distinct weakness (low-average) was observed in Auditory Processing. The remaining two cognitive processing areas were high-average.

Shannon demonstrated excellent task persistence as well as vigilance. She is able to process information visually and motorically at superior levels. Conceptual Reasoning ability (*Gf*) was also superior along with Short-Term Memory (*Gsm*, rote retrieval of semantically meaningful material). Although high-average, Comprehension-Knowledge (*Gc*, factual knowledge) and Long-Term Memory Processing (*Glr*) are considered relative weaknesses for Shannon. She demonstrated one specific weakness in Phonetic Coding (*Ga*). She had considerable difficulty processing phonetic information that involved sound-symbol correspondence. Overall, the ability to apply phonics was a weakness. This lowered processing area affects and diminishes her total BCA by approximately 10 points.

Based on State Department of Education guidelines, her overall BCA percentile rank was at a level (at or above the 95th percentile) that would qualify Shannon for academically gifted (AG) eligibility. It was a pleasure working with Shannon. She showed herself to be a young person with superior cognitive abilities overall and excellent motivation. (Signature and credentials of the examiner ends the report.)

Case Example 7–3. WJ-R COG analysis and interpretation—Stephen

A middle-school student was referred for reevaluation of his Learning Disability placement. He is 12 years old and in the 7th grade, and he continues to struggle daily in his academics. Resource services were recommended 3 years earlier but he has been mainstreamed in all classes.

The evaluation is to establish whether the student continues to qualify for Learning Disability services, to identify specific areas of need, to determine achievement levels, and to look for various processing deficits.

In North Carolina, learning disability eligibility is determined either by a 15-point aptitude-achievement discrepancy in one of the basic achievement areas of reading, math, or written language, or (alternatively) by identifying and documenting a cognitive processing disorder. The alternative LD model not only involves identification of a cognitive processing disorder but also requires establishing a history of learning difficulty, documented work samples, teacher recommendation, and parent input as well as current test findings. The report is written using standard score interpretations across factors in relation to the BCA and achievement results. RMIs, though more informative than the standard score alone, are not utilized. Thus, the report may resemble more of a Wechsler scale interpretive format than the previous case studies presented in terms of determining eligibility for learning disability services via the aptitude/achievement discrepancy model.

PSYCHOLOGICAL TEST RESULTS
CONFIDENTIAL: TO BE VIEWED BY
AUTHORIZED PERSONS ONLY

NAME: Stephen C. DATE OF TESTS: 9–24–96
SCHOOL: South Middle School DATE OF BIRTH: 6–19–84
GRADE: 7 CHRONOLOGICAL AGE: 12–3
PARENTS: Tom & Shirley C.
Rt. 1, Box 199
Anywhere, USA 27858

PROCEDURES

Woodcock-Johnson Tests of Cognitive Ability-Revised (WJ-R COG)

Woodcock-Johnson Tests of Achievement-Revised (WJ-R ACH)

Bender Visual Motor Gestalt Test (Bender Gestalt)

Learning Efficiency Test-2nd Edition (LET-II)

Parent Interview and Record Review

REASON FOR REFERRAL AND BACKGROUND INFORMATION

Stephen was referred for psychological reevaluation in order to update his previous learning disability testing from 1993. He initially qualified as a learning-disabled student in math and written language in 1990 while a first-grade student attending Elmhurst Elementary. Stephen is currently attending South Middle School and is a B/C student. A review of Stephen's previous assessments reveals his 1993 WISC-R FSIQ was 97; VIQ, 101; and PIQ, 93. Average visual-motor integration was reported. WJ-R

Case Example 7–3. *(Continued)*

achievement score levels were average in reading (94) and math (98) but low-average in written language (85). He exhibited a 12-point aptitude/achievement discrepancy at this time in written language. Specific difficulty was observed in spelling and written language skills. His 1990 WISC-R FSIQ was 101; VIQ, 103; and PIQ, 100. WJPB achievement scores were 95 in reading, 69 in math, and 83 in written language.

His mother reports that Stephen continues to demonstrate basic language-skill deficits. He has required continuing assistance in the form of tutors. Stephen has maintained very acceptable grades in school and works diligently to do so. Stephen is currently a 7th-grade, middle-school student who has college ambitions.

Stephen is the only child of Tom and Shirley C. His mother is 34 years old, completed postgraduate study, and is employed by Aviation Consultants as a Certified FAA inspector. His father is 38, completed junior college, and is self-employed as a farmer. Maternal and paternal relatives in the immediate families have reported experiencing academic difficulties.

Developmentally, Stephen was the product of a full-term pregnancy and weighed 6 pounds and 2 ounces at birth. His mother experienced significant weight gain and toxemia during a pregnancy complicated by high blood pressure. There were no difficulties during the birth, however. Sleeping and activity schedules were reported as normal during the first year. Stephen did experience feeding difficulties. He was colicky and allergic to milk.

Stephen's medical history reveals the possibility of one seizure related to a high fever suffered during a case of the flu. He was hospitalized. Additionally, head injuries occurred while he was jumping on the bed at 4 years of age and 2 years later he suffered a three-wheeler accident. Subsequent head X rays were reported as normal. Stephen did undergo surgery on his finger as the result of an accident in 1994. Visual and hearing screening, completed in 1994 and 1996, were reported as within normal limits. Stephen is currently on no medications.

Development history reveals average childhood milestones. Stephen sat alone at 5 ½ months, crawled at 6 months, and walked alone at 9 months. Toilet training was within normal limits and Stephen established right-hand dominance. Language development was reported within average ranges, though speech was thought to be too low and soft. Some concern was expressed regarding Stephen's expressive vocabulary. Fine- and gross-motor control was thought to be well developed. Stephen is considered well coordinated.

Behaviorally, Stephen is perceived as somewhat shy and a worrier. He does not appear to particularly enjoy new experiences and does not like speaking in front of groups. He does not exhibit a temper or show anger very often. He can work independently and delay gratification. He has a number of acquaintances and two or three close friends.

Educationally, Stephen attended preschool and has never repeated a grade. Letter and number reversals were observed at that time. Stephen completed the Test of Cognitive Skills in 1992 and 1995. He earned a CSI IQ of 102 and 95, respectively. He has benefited from after-school tutoring throughout school. Due to poor performance on the mandatory End-of-Grade (EOG) testing, Stephen has been required by his school system to attend summer school for the past 2 years or be retained if he elected not to do so.

(continued)

Case Example 7–3.   *(Continued)*

BEHAVIORAL OBSERVATIONS

Stephen appeared to be of slender build and average weight compared to same-aged peers. He was dressed typically in jeans, golf shirt, and tennis shoes. Stephen was alert and maintained steady eye contact when conversing with the examiner. He appeared slightly anxious at first, but easily settled down, demonstrating excellent attention and concentration during the one-on-one session. Speech was low in volume and tone, though easily understood in the quiet setting.

Rapport was easily established, and Stephen was cooperative and persistent throughout the examination. Occasionally he wondered aloud how he was performing on various items and maintained a high level of motivation throughout. He self-monitored his progress, accepted failure on high-level, difficult items, and preferred accuracy over speed of responding. Based on these behaviors, Stephen's tests results are thought to represent a reliable assessment of his current level of functioning.

Stephen indicated that he especially enjoyed golf (with quite a low handicap) and looked forward to playing at the high-school level. Indeed, he had placed first in a southeastern regional golf tournament for juniors the month before.

TEST RESULTS AND INTERPRETATIONS

Woodcock-Johnson Tests of Cognitive Ability-Revised. The WJ-R cognitive battery is designed to provide an aptitude profile that includes not only a measure of broad intellectual ability but also an indication of strengths and weaknesses in specific areas of cognitive processing. The extended scale of fourteen subtests was administered, and Stephen's scores for the test clusters as well as the BCA (Ext.) score are printed below (a standard score of 100 is average, corresponding to a 50th percentile rank).

WJ-R Cognitive Battery	*Standard Score*	*Percentile*
Broad Cognitive Ability	94	34

The BCA Standard score is considered a global measure of individual aptitude that is comparable to the Wechsler Full Scale IQ score. Stephen's score falls in the average range compared to same-aged peers.

Seven Cognitive Factors: Administration of the WJ-R Cognitive Battery subtests provides two measures each for seven cognitive factors. The factors, a brief description of each, and Stephen's standard scores and percentile ranks are listed next:

WJ-R Cognitive Factor	*Standard Score*	*Percentile*
Long-Term Retrieval	89	23
(Ability to store and retrieve symbol names over a period of time)		
Short-Term Memory	94	35
(Ability to recall and use information within a short period of time)		
Processing Speed	88	21
(Performing fine-motor cognitive tasks quickly)		

Case Example 7–3.   *(Continued)*

Auditory Processing (Ability to analyze and interpret sounds in words)	98	44
Visual Processing (Perceiving and thinking with visual patterns)	118	89
Comprehension-Knowledge (Range of knowledge and its effective application)	98	45
Fluid Reasoning (Ability to develop concepts and organize and classify ideas)	93	31

Intracognitive Discrepancies: Intracognitive discrepancies provide indications of a student's specific strengths and weaknesses relative to his own test performance. Stephen displayed strength in Visual Processing (*Gv*), which involves the ability to understand and reason using visual patterns. The remaining six cognitive processing abilities were evenly developed. There were no relative cognitive processing strengths or weaknesses in relation to his BCA IQ score of 94.

Woodcock-Johnson Tests of Achievement-Revised. The WJ-R ACH was administered to estimate Stephen's achievement level. Stephen obtained the following standard scores based on age.

WJ-R Subtest	*Standard Score*	*Percentile*
Word Identification	88	33
Passage Comprehension	83	13
Math Calculations	88	33
Applied Problems	84	28
Dictation	75	5
Writing Samples	72	3

WJ-R Composites	*Standard Score*	*Percentile*	*Discrepancy*
Broad Reading	82	12	−12
Broad Math	84	14	−10
Written Language	70	2	−24

Stephen is currently achieving significantly below his estimated ability in reading, math, and writing. His written language skills are especially weak when compared to his measured aptitude based on the WJ-R Tests of Cognitive Abilities. Overall, Stephen appears to be functioning more than three grade levels below his current grade placement in terms of basic academic skill mastery. Spelling, along with written expression, continues to be a weakness. Stephen attempts to spell phonetically, and his errors often closely approximate the stimulus word. Homophones are particularly difficult for him (e.g., sole/soul; knight/night; feat/feet). Stephen also read unfamiliar words phonetically. In spelling, medial vowels were again sources of error (e.g., poise/pose) as was omission of consonants (e.g., sparse/spare), and he had some difficulty with syllabication.

(continued)

Case Example 7–3.   *(Continued)*

Math reasoning skills were lower (low-average) than expected. Stephen had particular difficulty with place value for both whole numbers and decimals (units, tenths, hundredths, etc.) and in expressing a decimal fraction as a common fraction. In terms of actual math computation skills, Stephen was able to complete a number of the higher-level items (solving for one unknown, perimeter). Errors often occurred on lower-level items (single-digit multiplication, adding common fractions with like/ different denominators, and multiplying a unit fraction by a whole number).

Reading comprehension was also low-average. Analysis of Stephen's errors suggests difficulty in isolating the main point and providing tangential details instead. Following directions and oral expression in responding were average.

Written-language skills were borderline and well below his expected level of performance. Although Stephen is quite able to verbally describe or produce thoughts coherently, he has a very difficult time writing these thoughts. He generated very good ideas but his organization was weak. Vocabulary usage was below his grade level, as Stephen had a tendency to use simple word forms. Thus, expressive vocabulary appears somewhat weak. This affects sentence structure; although constructed correctly, his sentences would either be too choppy or run on with two or more different ideas expressed. Stephen did not appear to experience any difficulty with capitalization or punctuation.

Bender Visual Motor Gestalt Test. The Bender Gestalt was administered to determine visual motor skills. According to the Koppitz scoring criteria, Stephen made two errors (angularity). At his age, no errors are expected on the Bender Gestalt (when scored by the Koppitz system), and his performance yields a standard score of 94 when compared to the highest, 11-year, 11-month age-normative group. Qualitative analysis of his performance indicates that problems may be due to motor output, which corresponds to his Processing Speed performance on the WJ-R Tests of Cognitive Ability.

Learning Efficiency Test-2nd Edition. The LET-II was administered to assess Stephen's information processing efficiency and effectiveness. He received a standard score of 115 on the Visual Processing scale (high-average) and a standard score of 86 on the Auditory Processing scale (low-average).

On the visual memory subtests, Stephen appeared to have no difficulty with concentration. He did show a tendency to merge new information with information previously presented when the information must be remembered sequentially. A visual sequential memory deficit was identified for short-term memory processing, though Stephen showed no deficit in terms of initial encoding.

On the auditory subtests, Stephen also seemed to merge new information with previously presented information when order was a criteria. His initial auditory processing was average (ordered or unordered), but short-term retention was deficient for ordered information. Retrieval for unordered information was high average. Individual string-length scores follow (10 is average):

	Visual Ordered	*Visual Unordered*
Immediate Recall	15	14
Short-Term Recall	1	13
Long-Term Recall	1	13

Case Example 7–3.   *(Continued)*

	Auditory Ordered	*Auditory Unordered*
Immediate Recall	10	11
Short-Term Recall	1	13
Long-Term Recall	2	11

SUMMARY

Stephen is a Caucasian male, 12 years, 3 months old, who is currently functioning in the average range of intellectual ability based on the WJ-R COG. Achievement scores based on the WJ-R ACH fall in the low-average range in reading and mathematics and the borderline range in writing. The Bender Gestalt indicates that Stephen's visual motor development is slightly behind that of his peers, and his problems appear related to motor output difficulties. The LET-II estimates that Stephen's visual memory and auditory memory for unordered processing falls in the high-average range. Sequential memory processes for initial input is superior for visual processing and average for auditory processing. Retention of ordered information, whether visually or audibly processed, however, is deficient and appears affected by proactive interference.

Diagnostic Impressions

Developmental Writing Disorder

Information Processing Disorder: Auditory and Visual Sequential Memory

Based on SDPI "Discrepancy Guidelines for Eligibility for Learning Disability Services," Stephen is eligible for special-education services in written language administered through the Learning Disability program.

Recommendations. Based on SDPI criteria, Stephen qualifies for LD services in written language. Compared to measured aptitude, he has discrepancies of 24 points in this area, as well as demonstrated sequential processing difficulties as measured by the LET-II. In order to compete with peers academically and perform to his ability, Stephen may benefit from modifications in testing and class instruction.

In terms of learning strategies, Stephen would appear to require considerable exposure to cognitive processing strategies, especially recoding and chunking strategies. He appears to attempt to remember everything by relying on rote-memory processing (which is excellent for unordered material). Information to be remembered in order, however, is not retained once processed. Thus, chunking and recoding strategies should be particularly useful.

Stephen continues to display specific math weaknesses in understanding decimals, place values, and fractions. A basic tutorial review could augment the transition to high school mathematics. Additionally, periodic tutoring in his math courses may be helpful.

Writing continues to be affected by basic language-skill deficits. Spelling is particularly weak, primarily due to an inability to apply phonics correctly, especially in medial vowel sounds. Use of a word processor and spelling program is recommended. This may also make it easier for him to organize and edit his writing assignments. Stephen would need to master typing skills first. A whole-word approach to spelling is suggested using the Fernald or VAKT (visual-auditory-kinesthetic-tactile) methods.

(continued)

Case Example 7–3.   *(Continued)*

Verbal rehearsal is also a technique that should be helpful for Stephen. He should read aloud his assignments, chapters, and test questions. Comprehension would be expected to improve by this method. Stephen should also be taught with a combination of visual and auditory input. He easily remembers what he sees (not necessarily in the right order), and if a learning strategy is introduced, he should improve in retrieval of ordered information. Various learning strategies, especially those using mnemonics, need to be utilized for sequentially ordered information.

Studying techniques should follow the PQ4R method. This sequential, step-by-step method must be rehearsed numerous times before Stephen could be expected to follow through on his own. A copy of the method is attached.

It was a pleasure working with Stephen. If I can be of further assistance, please do not hesitate to call.

REFERENCES

Anastasi, A. (1988). *Psychological testing* (6th ed.). New York: MacMillan.

Bickley, P.G., Keith, T.A., & Wolfle, L.M. (1995). The three-stratum theory of cognitive abilities: test of the structure of intelligence across the life span. *Intelligence, 10,* 309–328.

Carroll, J.B. (1989). Factor analysis since Spearman: Where do we stand? What do we know? In R. Kanfer, P.L. Acherman, & R. Cudek (Eds.), *Abilities, motivation and methodology* (pp. 43–67). Hillsdale, NJ: Erlbaum.

Carroll, J.B. (1993). *Human cognitive abilities: A survey of factor-analytic studies.* New York: Cambridge University Press.

Cattell, R.B. (1940). A culture-fair intelligence test. *Journal of Educational Psychology, 31,* 161–170.

Cattell, R.B. (1941). Some theoretical issues in adult intelligence testing. *Psychological Bulletin, 38,* 592.

Cattell, R.B. (1963). Theory for fluid and crystallized intelligence: A critical experiment. *Journal of Educational Psychology, 54,* 1–22.

Cattell, R.B. (1979). Are culture fair intelligence tests possible and necessary? *Journal of Research and Development in Education, 12,* 3–13.

Cattell, R.B., & Horn, J.L. (1978). A check on the theory of fluid and crystallized intelligence with description of new subtest designs. *Journal of Educational Measurement, 15,* 139–164.

Cummings, J.A. (1992). Review of the Woodcock-Johnson Tests of Mental Ability, Revised. In J.J. Kramer & J.C. Conoley (Eds.), *The Eleventh Mental Measurements Yearbook.* Lincoln: The Buros Institute of Mental Measurement, University of Nebraska.

Elliott, C.D. (1990). *Differential ability scales: Introductory and technical handbook.* San Antonio, TX: The Psychological Corporation.

Gardner, H. (1983). *Frames of mind: The theory of multiple intelligences.* New York: Basic Books.

Guilford, J.P. (1959). The three faces of intellect. *American Psychologist, 14,* 469–479.

Guilford, J.P. (1967). *The nature of human intelligence.* New York: McGraw-Hill.

Hessler, G.L. (1993). *Use and interpretation of the Woodcock-Johnson Psycho-Educational Battery-Revised.* Chicago: Riverside.

Hicks, P., & Bolen, L.M. (1996). Review of the Woodcock-Johnson Psycho-Educational Battery-Revised. *Journal of School Psychology, 34,* 93–102.

Horn, J.L. (1976). Human abilities: A review of research and theory in the early 1970s. *Annual Review of Psychology, 27,* 437–485.

Horn, J.L. (1979). The rise and fall of human abilities. *Journal of Research and Development in Education, 12,* 59–78.

Horn, J.L. (1985). Remodeling old models of intelligence. In B.B. Wolman (Ed.), *Handbook of intelligence: Theories, measurements, and applications.* (pp. 267–300). New York: Wiley.

Horn, J.L. (1986a). Intellectual ability concepts. In R.J.L. Sternberg (Ed.), *Advances in the psychology of human intelligence* (Vol. 3, pp. 35–37). Hillsdale, NJ: Erlbaum.

Horn, J.L. (1986b). Some thoughts about intelligence. In R.J. Sternberg & D.K. Detterman (Eds.), *What is intelligence? Contemporary viewpoints on its nature and definition* (pp. 91–96). Norwood, NJ: Ablex.

Horn, J.L. (1988). Thinking about human abilities. In J.R. Nesselroade (Ed.), *Handbook of multivariate psychology* (pp. 645–685). New York: Academic Press.

Horn, J.L. (1991). Measurement of intellectual capabilities: A review of theory. In K.S. McGrew, J.K. Werder, & R.W. Woodcock, *WJ-R technical manual,* Chicago: Riverside.

Horn, J.L., & Cattell, R.B. (1966). Refinement and test of the theory of fluid and crystallized intelligence. *Journal of Educational Psychology, 57,* 253–270.

Kamphaus, R.W. (1993). *Clinical assessment of children's intelligence.* Needham Heights, MA: Allyn & Bacon.

Kaufman, A.S. (1979). *Intelligent testing with the WISC-R.* New York: Wiley-Interscience.

Kaufman, A.S. & Kaufman, N.L. (1993). *The Kaufman Adolescent and Adult Intelligence Test.* Circle Pines, MN: American Guidance Service.

Kaufman, A.S. & Kaufman, N.L. (1983). *Administration and scoring manual for the Kaufman Assessment Battery for Children.* Circle Pines, MN: American Guidance Service.

Kaufman, A.S. (1990). *Assessing adolescent and adult intelligence.* Needham Heights, MA: Allyn & Bacon.

Mather, N. (1991). *An instructional guide to the Woodcock-Johnson Psycho-Educational Battery-Revised.* Brandon, VT: Clinical Psychology Publishing; New York: Wiley.

Mather, N. (1993). Critical issues in the diagnosis of learning disabilities addressed by the Woodcock-Johnson Psycho-Educational Battery-Revised. *Journal of Psychoeducational Assessment, Monograph Series: WJ-R Monograph,* 103–122.

McCarthy, (1972) *McCarthy Scales of Children's Abilities.* New York: The Psychological Corporation.

McGhee, R. (1993). Fluid and crystallized intelligence: Confirmatory factor analysis of the Differential Abilities Scale, Detroit Test of Learning Aptitude-3, and Woodcock-Johnson Psycho-Educational Battery-Revised. *Journal of Psychoeducational Assessment,* WJ-R Monograph, 20–38.

McGrew, K.S. (1994). *Clinical interpretation of the Woodcock-Johnson Test of Cognitive Ability-Revised.* Needham Heights, MA: Allyn & Bacon.

McGrew, K.S., & Flanagan, D.P. (1996). A cross-battery approach to intelligence test interpretation. Workshop presented at the National Association of School Psychologists, Atlanta, GA.

McGrew, K.S., & Murphy, S. (1995). Uniqueness and general factor characteristics of the Woodcock-Johnson Tests of Cognitive Ability-Revised. *Journal of School Psychology, 33,* 235–245.

McGrew, K.S., Werder, J.K., & Woodcock, R.W. (1991). *WJ-R technical manual.* Chicago: Riverside.

Mosier, C.I. (1943). On the reliability of a weighted composite. *Psychometrika, 8,* 161–168.

Reschly, D.J. (1990). Found: Our intelligences: What do they mean? *Journal of Psychoeducational Assessment, 8,* 259–267.

Sattler, J.M. (1992). *Assessment of children* (3rd ed.). San Diego, CA: Jerome M. Sattler.

Schrank, F.A., & Woodcock, R.J. (1995). *Report writer for the WJ-R* (version 1.0). Chicago: Riverside.

Spearman, C.E. (1904). "General Intelligence," objectively determined and measured. *American Journal of Psychiatry, 15,* 201–293.

Spearman, C.E. (1927). *The abilities of man: Their nature and measurement.* New York: Macmillan.

Sternberg, R.J. (1985). *Beyond IQ: A triarchic theory of intelligence.* London: Cambridge University Press.

Thorndike, R.L., Hagen, E.P., & Sattler, J.M. (1986). *Technical manual for the Stanford-Binet Intelligence Scale: Fourth Edition.* Chicago: Riverside.

Thurstone, L.L. (1938). *Primary mental abilities.* Chicago: University of Chicago Press.

Thurstone, L.L., & Thurstone, T.G. (1941). Factorial studies of intelligence. *Psychometric Monographs, 2.*

Vernon, P.E. (1979). *Intelligence: Heredity and environment.* San Francisco: Freeman.

Wechsler, D. (1974). *Wechsler Intelligence Scale for Children-Revised.* San Antonio, TX: The Psychological Corporation.

Wechsler, D. (1981). *Wechsler Adult Intelligence Scale, Revised.* San Antonio, TX: The Psychological Corporation.

Wechsler, D. (1991). *Wechsler Intelligence Scale for Children-Third Edition.* San Antonio, TX: The Psychological Corporation.

Woodcock, R.W. (1990). Theoretical foundations of the WJ-R measures of cognitive ability. *Journal of Psychoeducational Assessment, 8,* 231–258.

Woodcock, R.W. (1993). An information processing view of *Gf-Gc* theory. *Journal of Psychoeducational Assessment, Monograph Series: WJ-R Monograph,* 80–102.

Woodcock, R.W., & Johnson, M.B. (1977). *Woodcock-Johnson Psycho-Educational Battery.* Chicago: Riverside.

Woodcock, R.W., & Johnson, M.B. (1989). *Woodcock-Johnson Psycho-Educational Battery-Revised.* Chicago: Riverside.

Woodcock, R.W., & Mather, N. (1989). *Woodcock-Johnson Tests of Cognitive Ability—Standard and Supplemental Batteries: Examiner's Manual.* In R.W. Woodcock and M.B. Johnson (Eds.), *Woodcock-Johnson Psycho-Educational Battery-Revised.* Chicago: Riverside.

Ysseldyke, J.E. (1990). Goodness of fit of the Woodcock-Johnson Psycho-Educational Battery-Revised to the Horn-Cattell *Gf-Gc* theory. *Journal of Psychoeducational Assessment, 8,* 268–275.

Chapter 8

ASSESSING INTELLIGENCE USING THE WISC-III

LARRY M. BOLEN

HISTORY AND DEVELOPMENT

Psychological tests are used for such varied purposes as identifying and analyzing individual differences in personality traits, vocational preferences, mechanical aptitudes, educational achievement, and for measuring general intellectual ability. The most common use of psychological tests since the introduction of the Stanford-Binet, however, has been the assessment of individual intellectual functioning.

Individually administered psychological tests of general intelligence have a documented history of use in the United States that begins prior to World War II (Aiken, 1987). Attempts to differentiate individual mental abilities were recorded by Jean Esquirol (1772–1840) and Edouard Seguin (1812–1880). These two Frenchmen also distinguished among levels of mental deficiency that later influenced Binet and Simon's three-level classification system of moron, imbecile, and idiot (Freeman, 1962). The roots of formal psychological assessment can be traced back to ancient China (2000 B.C.), where oral examinations were common in determining eligibility for government employment (Aiken, 1987).

The Binet-Simon Scales

From 1916 until the late 1950s, the most frequently administered individual intelligence test was the Stanford-Binet. Lewis Terman adapted and revised the Binet-Simon intelligence scale and published the Stanford Revision and Extension of the Binet-Simon Intelligence Scale in 1916 (Aiken, 1987). The number of items was increased from 54 to 90. Terman's intent was to have a test that could not only identify mentally retarded individuals (Binet and Simon's goal) but also differenti-

I wish to thank those who contributed to this work in one way or another. Appreciation is expressed to Dr. Booney Vance for his invitation to write about the WISC-III. Writing this chapter forced me to synthesize my previous 20 years experience with the Wechsler scales into an integrated presentation. Thanks is expressed to Dr. Charles C. Mitchell for his time in reviewing the manuscript and thoughtful consideration when I raised various questions or concerns in test administration, analyses and interpretation schemes, factor structures, or training issues. Lastly, I would like to compliment Page Jerzak for her quality editing and ability to find my split infinitives.

ate among degrees of intellectual ability in a normal population and predict scholastic performance.

The Binet-Simon scale, like the Stanford-Binet revision, was not initially developed for use with adults. Additionally, the Binet scales were primarily verbal in orientation and age based, using mental age and IQ.

The Wechsler Scales

The development of the Wechsler Adult Intelligence Scale in 1939 met the need for a scale measuring adolescents and adults, and introduced several new components in the measurement and understanding of intellectual functioning (Freeman, 1962). First, nonverbal or performance scales were included that involved the ability to reason using visual images. That is, perceptual and spatial organization and reasoning of situations and problems (rather than words and numerals) were assessed. Second, the verbal and nonverbal item content was arranged in ascending order of difficulty within each subtest. For example, vocabulary began with the easiest item and progressively became more difficult. Interestingly, the vocabulary subtest on the 1937 Wechsler scale was considered a supplemental or alternate subtest (Wechsler, 1939). The reason for this was that Wechsler, chief psychologist at Bellevue Psychiatric Hospital in New York City, needed to assess mentally disordered patients. Here, the initial test development was accomplished in the hospital clinic (hence, the name of the adult scale is the Wechsler-Bellevue test) with patients who were often nonverbal or psychotic. Third, substituting the deviation IQ for Binet's mental age scale was a major contribution in the quantification and measurement of individual differences (Wechsler, 1946, 1949). The reader may recall the ratio IQ index of MA/CA × 100 as a concept introduced by William Stern (1914) and subsequently utilized on the Stanford-Binet. Fourth, and perhaps the most important aspect of Wechsler's contribution to intelligence measurement, was the introduction of tasks in which examinees could express their intelligence in a nonverbal manner. Performance-based subtests became a necessary condition for future item/test development. The general-factor theory, or Spearman's g factor (1927), was the accepted basis for understanding the nature of intelligence in intelligence testing. Thus, while both the Verbal IQ (VIQ) and the Performance IQ (PIQ) measure contributed to an overall or Full Scale IQ index (FSIQ), representing an individual's general intellectual ability (g), the Wechsler scales now provided both verbal and performance measures of intellectual functioning. The Wechsler scales represented a shift from a g or unitary measure to verbal and performance subsets representing two distinct ways in which an individual could express intelligence (McGrew, 1996, personal communication). Although Binet clearly understood that intelligence was not unitary (Matarazzo, 1972), this distinction was apparently lost during subsequent revision, interpretation, and use of the Binet IQ score in the United States between 1916 and 1939.

David Wechsler

David Wechsler's personal history is reported in detail by Matarazzo (1972) and is selectively summarized here.

David Wechsler was born in Lespedi, Romania, on January 12, 1896, the youngest of seven children (four girls and three boys). His parents immigrated to New York City in 1902. He earned a B.A. degree in 1916 from the College of the City of New York and an M.A. degree from Columbia University in 1917. After induction into the U.S. Army, Wechsler was assigned to the psychology unit at Fort Logan, Texas, where he assessed recruits with the Stanford-Binet, the Yerkes Point Scale, and the Army Individual Performance Scales. This early introduction into the measurement of intelligence set the stage for his theoretical conceptualization of intelligence, and he was influenced by his brief work with both Pearson and Spearman at the University of London in 1919. Matarazzo (1972) reports that in his later years Wechsler "reluctantly abandoned Spearman's unique (bifactor) theory" (p. 74), viewing intelligence instead as an interaction of abilities and eventually defining intelligence as the aggregate or global capacity of the individual to act purposefully, to think rationally, and to deal effectively with the environment (Wechsler, 1958).

Wechsler Intelligence Scale For Children

First published in 1949, the WISC was developed as a downward extension of the Wechsler Adult Intelligence Scale. The WISC was designed to assess the intellectual functioning of children ranging in age from 5 years through 15 years, 11 months. A number of criticisms surrounded the WISC, one being that it was merely a simplification of the Wechsler-Bellevue Scale with two adult-oriented items (Aiken, 1987). In 1974, the test was revised, and the WISC-R gained in acceptance and use. This form was normed for children ranging in age from 6 years to 16 years, 11 months. The age change reflected the earlier (1967) publication of the Wechsler Preschool and Primary Scale of Intelligence (WPPSI) for children ranging in age from 4 to 6 years, 7 months, and 15 days. Thus, the age range of the WPPSI and WISC-R overlap from 6 years to 6 years, 7 months, 15 days, while the age range of the WISC-R and WAIS overlap from 16 years to 16 years, 11 months.

Although the WISC-R is less adult oriented than the WISC, more than two-thirds of the items are the same. Gender and race bias, however, was more carefully examined, and various subtests were lengthened to improve reliability. Like the WISC, the WISC-R was composed of 12 subtests—6 each for both the Verbal and Performance scales. Two of the 12 subtests were optional—Digit Span on the Verbal scale and Mazes on the Performance scale. Direct subtest substitution was not appropriate except when Mazes was substituted for Coding. Subtest substitution was allowable when a subtest was incorrectly administered or when a child's handicapping condition prohibited administration of a particular subtest.

IQ scores are calculated from the administration of 10 subtests, 5 verbal and 5 performance. It was recommended, however, that all 12 subtests be administered if time permitted. The WISC-R was standardized on 200 children at each of 11 age ranges (n = 2,200); but unlike the WISC, which was composed of an all-white sample, children were proportionally selected on the stratification variables of age, sex, race, geographic region, occupation of head of household, and urban-rural residence from the 1970 U.S census data.

Reanchoring and Revision: The WISC-III

Published in 1991, the WISC-III was a substantial revision of the WISC-R. Based on the 1988 U.S. census data, the procedures for norming closely followed the WISC-R standardization as well as sound principles of test construction. Each item was analyzed for bias in terms of gender, race/ethnicity, and age (Cohen, Swerdlik, & Smith, 1992). Final norming was based on 2,200 children (200 at each of 11 age levels divided equally by gender). Additional testing was conducted with Hispanic and Black children for item bias analyses as well as test-retest reliability. Furthermore, additional testing for same-subject performance on the WPPSI-R and WISC-III (200 children 6 years of age), WISC-R and WISC-III (200 children across the age range), and WAIS-R and WISC-III (200 children 16 years of age) was completed. Cohen et al. (1992) estimated that 4,500 children around the country were tested (when including the item trial testing, reliability studies, and final norming sampling).

Aesthetics Become More Important

Aesthetic improvement of several subtests was also accomplished. The addition of color to artwork on the Picture Arrangement, Picture Completion, and Object Assembly subtests is a vast improvement over the WISC-R. Enlarged print for Coding and Mazes considerably aids performance, and left-handed subjects are no longer penalized, since the Coding key was moved to the top of the page. Further, the recommended order of subtest administration was changed with the intention of gradually introducing the child to the testing process in a less threatening manner.

More substantial changes included lengthening the Coding subtest, adding items at both ends of the Arithmetic subtest, and providing additional examples or trial items for Block Design, Similarities, and Comprehension. A new subtest, Symbol Search, was added, a supplemental performance subtest expected to provide a measure of cognitive processing speed along with the Coding subtest.

Extending the WISC-III to Measure Four Factors

In addition to the Verbal, Performance, and Full Scale IQ scores, the WISC-III was designed to provide four factor-based index scores: (1) Verbal Comprehension (composed of Information, Similarities, Vocabulary, and Comprehension); (2) Perceptual Organization (composed of Picture Completion, Picture Arrangement, Block Design, and Object Assembly); (3) Freedom from Distractibility (composed of Arithmetic and Digit Span); and (4) Processing Speed (composed of Coding and Symbol Search). Although factor analytic studies generally supported a small third factor on the WISC-R, Sattler (1992) cautioned against its use on the WISC-III because the factor appeared highly unstable across the age ranges. As later detailed in the section on psychometric properties, two of the four intended factors were not well supported and may cause the user to make faulty assumptions (Little, 1991).

IQ AND INDEX SCORES

Quantitative interpretation of the Verbal, Performance, and Full Scale IQ scores and the four factor-based index scores are based on a mean of 100 and a standard deviation of 15 points. At any age, a deviation IQ score of 100 defines average performance on each scale, corresponding to the 50th percentile rank for that particular age group. In terms of the normal distribution, it is expected that 68% of the population within each age range will obtain IQ scores ranging from 85 to 115 ($\pm$ 1 *SD*). The VIQ and PIQ scales have a predetermined range of 46 to 155 while the FSIQ scale ranges from 40 to 160. The four factor-based index scores each range from 50 to 150.

Qualitative interpretation of WISC-III IQs follow a classification system provided by Wechsler (1991, Table 2.8, p. 32) and, with slight modification, is presented next for review (see Table 8–1).

Of special interest in Wechsler's classification system is the division between Average and Superior and the two additional categories between Intellectually Deficient and Average. This system does not follow the normal distribution statistical model so rigorously taught in statistics classes. The statistical model would simply use the standard deviations as classification markers, so that Average IQ is between 85 and 115, Above Average is between 115 and 130, and Below Average is less than 85. Wechsler's classification allows for much more practical use and for appreciation of differences in intellectual performance. Note the use of the term "Intellectually Deficient" rather than "mentally retarded." Test users should realize that an IQ score by itself is not sufficient evidence for determining retardation. This follows the standards recommended by the American Association on Mental Deficiency (AAMD; Grossman, 1983) and the federal guidelines set forth in Public Law 94–142. Several classification systems have been developed and may be of interest (see Kamphaus, 1993; Kaufman, 1994).

Scaling and Subtest Ranges

WISC-III subtest scores are set to a predetermined mean of 10 and standard deviation of 3. Subtest scales have a range of 1 to 19 across the age groups with the following exceptions:

Table 8–1. Qualitative descriptions of WISC-III Full Scale IQ Scores

IQ Range	Classification	WISC-III Sample Percentage Distribution
130 and above	Very Superior	2.1
120–129	Superior	8.3
110–119	High Average	16.1
90–109	Average	50.3
80–89	Low Average	14.8
70–79	Borderline	6.5
69 and below	Intellectually Deficient	1.9

Mazes: range 1 to 18 beginning with age group 12

Picture Completion: range 1 to 18 beginning with age group 14, then 1 to 17 beginning with age group 16

Information: range 1 to 18 beginning with age group 15, then 1 to 17 beginning with age group 16

Arithmetic: range 1 to 18 beginning with age group 16

Comprehension, Block Design, Object Assembly, and *Symbol Search:* range 1 to 18 beginning with age group 16

Common Misuse of WISC-III Scale Scores

Unfortunately, experienced clinicians and regular users of psychoeducational test reports (school-based committees, placement or advisory teams, etc.) often ignore the relationship of WISC subtest scores to IQ classification level. Table 8–2 illustrates this relationship, following Wechsler's classification system.

The interesting feature about this classification system is that it directly involves qualitative interpretation of the individual subtest scale scores. According to

Table 8–2.   WISC-III scaled scores and corresponding classification system

Score	SD unit	IQ Equivalent	Classification
19	+3	145	
18	+2⅔		
17	+2⅓		
16	+2	130	Very Superior
15	+1⅔	125	
14	+1⅓	120	Superior
13	++1	115	
12	+⅔	110	High Average
11	+⅓	105	
10	+0	100	
9	−⅓	95	
8	−⅓	90	Average
7	−1	85	
6	−1⅓	80	Low Average
5	−1⅔	75	
4	−2	70	Borderline
3	−2⅓	65	Intellectually
2	−2⅔	60	Deficient
1	−3	55	

Wechsler's system, a scale score of 5 on the Information subtest, for example, suggests (upper) borderline versus below average or intellectually deficient performance. This performance level is often referred to as the "slow learner" range to distinguish it from the concept of a retarded learner. A mentally retarded child, with the exception of normal deviations due to measurement error, would be expected to exhibit a subtest scale score profile ranging from 1 to 4. When children obtain a WISC-III profile with scale scores uniformly above 4, less than two standard deviations below the mean, the idea of mental retardation is summarily dismissed. The utility of the classification, however, often does not match available educational programs. The *slow learner* is often classified as educable mentally handicapped (EMH) regardless—as one teacher related, so the child could "get the help that he [or she] needs." Not only is it unfair to classify children on this basis, but continuing to do so simply removes the school system from educational accountability. Too often children are made to fit into existing programs rather than the programs and curriculums modified to meet the learner's needs. A review of case law and litigation since 1967 regarding the use and abuse of IQ tests for classification of mental retardation and placement in special (i.e., restricted) services aptly supports these concerns (e.g., *Hobson v. Hansen*, 1967; *Diana v. State Board of Education*, 1970; *Larry P. v. Riles*, 1974; *PASE*, 1980).

SUBTESTS: DESCRIPTIONS, CHANGES FROM THE WISC-R, AND INTERPRETIVE IMPLICATIONS

Table 8–3 (from Wechsler, 1991, p. 5) lists the subtests under their respective groupings (Verbal or Performance); the number preceding each subtest denotes its position in the standard order of administration. Note that Verbal and Performance subtests are administered in alternating order with the intention of maintaining the child's attention during testing.

Table 8–3.   The WISC-III subtests grouped according to scale and administration order

Verbal	Performance
2. Information	1. Picture Completion
4. Similarities	3. Coding
6. Arithmetic	5. Picture Arrangement
8. Vocabulary	7. Block Design
10. Comprehension	9. Object Assembly
[a]12. Digit Span	[b]11. Symbol Search
	[a]13. Mazes

[a]Supplementary subtest.
[b]Supplementary subtest that can substitute only for Coding.
Source: D. Wechsler, *Manual for the Wechsler Intelligence Scale for Children-Third Edition*, 1991, p. 5. San Antonio, TX: The Psychological Corporation.

Verbal Subtests

Information

Consisting of 30 general information questions (21 unchanged, 7 new, and 2 significantly altered). The scale items are arranged in order of difficulty and have one essential correct answer. Responses are scored 0 (incorrect) or 1 (correct). Since the content reflects learned material—at home or in school—the test is thought to reflect a strong measure of crystallized (*Gc*) ability (Horn, 1991; Woodcock, 1990; Kaufman, 1994; McGrew, 1996).

Numerous authors have reported that the Information subtest measures basic factual knowledge, which, therefore, requires intact long-term memory processing. It is also hypothesized that the child's performance is affected by familial and cultural backgrounds (including language proficiency) as well as by achievement motivation or anxiety features (Kaufman, 1994; Kamphaus, 1993; Sattler, 1988, 1992). Research has suggested that the Information subtest is one of the more difficult subtests for exceptional groups (Cooper, 1995).

Similarities

Now, a total of 19 items rather than 17 (11 unchanged, 2 modified, and 6 new items). This scale measures a range of relational and conceptual reasoning. A sample item was added to allow the child initial exposure to this type of test item. Items are scored 0 (incorrect and representing a misunderstanding), 1 (demonstrating concrete understanding or its function), or 2 (showing abstract reasoning or categorical thinking). Additional sample responses to facilitate scoring are also provided that should substantially improve scorer reliability.

Researchers such as Kaufman (1979) and Sattler (1992) have reported that item performance may be influenced by subject interest and outside reading, while others hypothesize that low scores reflect "a rigidly concrete mode of thinking or sometimes private or distorted conceptual thinking" (Aiken, 1987, p. 153). Interestingly, vocabulary knowledge (or lack of) does not play a significant role in terms of poor performance, according to Wechsler (1958). The essential feature of whether the child understands the notion of "sameness" more closely resembles the Piagetian concept of cognitive development. Glasser and Zimmerman (1967) reported on the WISC that Similarities measured the qualitative aspects of hierarchical relationships, which is an abstract function (*Gf*) rather than a concrete process (*Gc*). Kaufman (1994) classified Similarities as representing both crystallized intelligence (*Gc*) and fluid (*Gf*) intelligence (p. 51). Woodcock (1990) and McGrew and Flanagan (1996), however, consider it as only a strong measure of crystallized intelligence.

Arithmetic

Composed of 24 arithmetic problems, 14 unchanged and 10 new items (extending the floor and ceiling limits). Arithmetic is presented orally, though the last 6 items are read aloud by the child. The examiner may supply unknown words or read the item if it becomes apparent that the child cannot read the problem. The child may not, however, use any external aids such as pencil and paper or a calculator (though many children finger count). This is a timed subtest measuring elementary knowledge of basic arithmetic, while higher level items may require one- or two-step reasoning processes. Bonus points are awarded for quick and accurate solutions to items 19 to 24. Wechsler (1958) noted that success on Arithmetic was a sign of mental alertness that he thought correlated highly with global intelligence. Further, he thought that children who are unable to perform satisfactorily on this subtest are very likely to experience difficulty in their other school subjects.

Test performance is thought to be influenced by anxiety factors; thus, low performance is often described as reflecting poor attention or concentration, distractibility, or poor school learning (Kaufman, 1979b, 1990; Sattler, 1992; Kamphaus, 1993). Arithmetic is one of only three subtests to load on a third factor, identified as *Freedom from Distractibility* by Kaufman (1979), in analyzing the WISC-R. The factor appears unstable, however, on the WISC-III, and Sattler (1992) recommends a moratorium on interpreting the third factor for the present time. According to the crystallized-fluid (*Gc-Gf*) model of intelligence (Horn, 1991), the Arithmetic subtest represents a fluid measure overall, and also falls on the Short-Term Acquisition and Retrieval factor along with Digit Span (Horn, 1991; Kaufman, 1994). McGrew (1996), however, now considers Arithmetic a strong measure of quantitative ability rather than fluid (*Gf*) intelligence.

Cooper (1995) notes that the Arithmetic subtest utilizes a variety of different functions at different points within the scale items, ranging from basic one-to-one correspondence in counting, to attending to a sequential auditory presentation, to holding the information in short-term auditory memory, to abstracting the nature of the problem, to utilizing one's own long-term memory for math rules and operations, to applying those rules to the data in short-term memory, and to finally providing a solution. Also, at the highest levels, Arithmetic items require reading a series of items aloud before engaging in problem-solving cognitive actions.

Vocabulary

An expressive vocabulary measure, this scale is now comprised of 30 items rather than the 32 found on the WISC-R (19 unchanged), in which the child must produce a verbal definition of a word meaning. Scoring is weighted with 0 (incorrect response), 1 (concrete or partial understanding demonstrated), and 2 (showing complete and accurate understanding of the word). Wechsler (1958) maintained that vocabulary reflects level of education and basic fund of verbal information, and serves as an index of general intelligence.

High scores are hypothesized to reflect good integration into the mainstream culture and schooling (Glasser & Zimmerman, 1967; Aiken, 1987; Kaufman, 1990b), while low scores may reflect limited cultural opportunities, poor school learning, or limited outside reading (Kaufman, 1979, 1994; Sattler, 1992; Kamphaus, 1993). Vocabulary continues to be the single best Verbal subtest measure in predicting scholastic performance and is often used as an overall representation of crystallized (*Gc*) ability (Horn, 1991; McGrew & Flanagan, 1996). The Vocabulary subtest also continues to be one of the more difficult for the mentally retarded population (Kaufman & Van Hagen, 1977; Clarizio & Bernard, 1981; Kaufman, 1990b).

Comprehension

Composed of 18 questions presented orally by the examiner, 12 unchanged and 6 new items (5 outdated items eliminated and a new item added). The scale requires detailed verbal response to demonstrate an understanding of a variety of social situations and problems. Scored 0, 1, or 2, eight of the items require two responses that the child is prompted to provide. Additional sample responses to facilitate scoring were developed.

This subtest was described by Wechsler (1958) as a test of common sense, but as Kaufman (1994) noted his reason for including the subtest was its rich clinical basis in understanding individual pathology. Comprehension is often described as a measure of social judgment, or knowledge of social conventions, and may be influenced by cultural opportunities at home and type of upbringing (Kaufman, 1979; Sattler, 1992). Numerous researchers agree with Wechsler that the Comprehension subtest often reveals significant clinical findings about a child's personality (Glasser & Zimmerman, 1967; Sattler, 1992; Kamphaus, 1993; Cooper, 1995), especially as related to social conformity and one's moral conscience. Conduct-disordered children, for example, may provide highly socially deviant responses (Kamphaus, 1993). Following the crystallized-fluid (Gc-Gf) categorization of intelligence, Comprehension is a strong measure of crystallized (Gc) intelligence along with Information, Vocabulary, and Similarities (Woodcock, 1990; Horn, 1991; Kaufman, 1994; McGrew & Flanagan, 1996). The child who is linguistically deficient could experience severe difficulty on this test; studies on mentally retarded individuals, however, "have found that the Comprehension subtest is of variable difficulty for this population" (Cooper, 1995, p. 218).

Digit Span

The 7 digits forward and 7 digits backward items from the WISC-R remain unchanged. A two-digit item was added as a downward extension of the subtest. Although it has long been noted that most children perform better on digits forward than digits backward, cumulative frequency data is provided for the first time in the WISC-III manual (Wechsler, 1991, Table B.6). Kamphaus (1993) recommended caution in the interpretation of Digit Span as a strength or weakness without corroboration from other measures or considerable experience in testing. Digit Span is a supplementary Verbal subtest that may be substituted in cases where a subtest is invalidated or cannot be administered due to the examinee's handicapping condition.

Included as part of the Freedom from Distractibility Index, poor performance on Digit Span was hypothesized to reflect anxiety, impulsivity, inattention, or distractibility on the WISC-R (Sattler, 1988; Kaufman, 1979; Glasser & Zimmerman, 1967). Digit Span, on the WISC-III, may no longer be interpreted in this manner, as discussed in the validity section of this chapter. Additionally, children with auditory discrimination problems or low achievement motivation, or those simply fatigued or bored, may perform poorly (Kamphaus, 1993). Sattler (1992) suggested that Digit Span forward is a measure of sequential processing and short-term memory, while Digit Span backward involves both planning ability and sequential processing. Based on the crystallized-fluid (Gc-Gf) model, Digit Span falls on the Short-Term Acquisition and Retrieval factor (Woodcock, 1990; Horn, 1991; Kaufman, 1994; McGrew & Flanagan, 1996).

Performance Subtests

Picture Completion

Thirty items, 15 unchanged, measuring visual alertness to detail, comprise the first subtest of the WISC-III administered to the child. Picture Completion is relatively nonthreatening and colorful and includes a sample item to help the child become familiar with the task, which is to indicate, either verbally or by pointing, what part is missing in a picture. This subtest is now administered, before Information, which was the first subtest administered in both the WISC and WISC-R. It was thought that Picture Completion was one of the least threatening subtests (i.e., perceived by the child as school related like the Information subtest) and would facilitate rapport building. Research suggested that Picture Completion is one of the easier subtests on the WISC-R, especially for handicapped groups (Clarizio & Bernard, 1981; Hale & Landino, 1981).

Performance is affected by poor attention and concentration (Glasser & Zimmerman, 1967) as well as anxiety (Aiken, 1987). Kaufman (1979, 1990b) suggested that Picture Completion reflects holistic or right-brain processing and also noted, in 1994, that children's performance may reflect cognitive style (field dependence-field independence) as well as the ability to work under time constraints. Horn (1991) and Kaufman (1994) report that Picture Completion is one of three subtests falling on the Broad Visualization (*Gv*) factor. McGrew and Flanagan (1996) also place it on the *Gv* factor but consider it a rather weak, secondary factor.

Coding

A symbol-encoding measure requiring visual discrimination and fine-motor speed and accuracy in copying. The two levels of the subtest, Coding A and Coding B, were retained from the WISC-R, as was the 120-second time limit. The number of items was increased from 45 to 59 on Coding A and from 93 to 119 on Coding B. Bonus points are earned for quick and accurate performance. All symbols and rows were slightly enlarged, and the red pencil is no longer required as on the WISC and WISC-R. Not mentioned in the WISC-III manual is its economic savings, since Coding is now included as a perforated sheet in the Test Record Form rather than as a separate booklet, which necessitated additional expense for the WISC-R. Unfortunately, as pointed out by Kamphaus (1993), the instructions have been lengthened and interfere with administration pace and continuity.

Performance is subject to influence by anxiety, distractibility, and the effects of time pressure (Kaufman, 1979; 1990b). Poor performance may reflect motor skill output deficits, visual discrimination problems, fatigue, or low motivation (Sattler, 1992; Kamphaus, 1993). Based on Horn's (1985) crystallized-fluid model of intelligence, Coding was the only WISC subtest to fall on the Processing Speed factor. Kaufman (1994) reported that Symbol Search should also fall on the Processing Speed factor. Wechsler (1958) felt that Coding simply required an association among certain symbols with other symbols, "and the speed and accuracy with which [the task is completed] serves as a measure of his [or her] intellectual ability" (p. 81).

Picture Arrangement

Fourteen sets of cards (7 original and/or slightly modified and a redrawn sample item) are designed to measure sequential reasoning (ordering), contributing to the overall measurement of perceptual organization abilities. Wechsler (1958) described Picture Arrangement as "a series of pictures, that when placed in the right sequence, tell a little story" (p. 74). He believed that this subtest measured the ability to comprehend and size up a total situation, and he referred to this ability as "social intelligence" (p. 75). Factor analytic studies show this subtest secondarily loaded on the Verbal Comprehension factor (Kaufman, 1990b; Sattler, 1992), and it was the weakest of the four Performance tests that make up the Perceptual Organization factor index. Research on the WISC-R (Cooper, 1994) suggests that the Picture Arrangement subtest is somewhat variable in difficulty, though it is generally one of the easier subtests for handicapped children.

Low scores have been hypothesized as indicative of problems in nonverbal planning (Aiken, 1987; Blatt & Allison, 1968), and are subject to the influence of creativity, cultural opportunities at home, exposure to comic strips, and working under time pressure (Kaufman, 1990b; Kamphaus, 1993). Initially, according to the crystallized-fluid model of intelligence, Picture Arrangement was reported as reflecting fluid intelligence (Horn, 1985; Kaufman, 1994). It has since been classified as loading on both *Gc* and *Gf* factors (Horn, 1991; Kaufman, 1994) or as a very weak Visual Processing (*Gv*) ability (McGrew & Flanagan, 1996).

Block Design

A test measuring spatial reasoning ability consisting of 12 geometric and abstract designs. The test remains unchanged except for the addition of one easier level, two-block design and the substitution of a more difficult, nine-block design for a relatively easy nine-block item. Wechsler (1958) reported that this subtest was originally developed by Kochs (1923), who felt it represented a comprehensive measure of nonverbal intelligence.

Poor performance was hypothesized to reflect perceptual problems and poor spatial conceptualization (Aiken, 1987). Block Design continues to be the best of the Performance subtests for measuring general intellectual ability. Block Design has long been regarded as a spatial reasoning task. This feature suggested that Block Design represents (1) right-brain (holistic) processing (Kaufman, 1979b; 1990); (2) a measure of fluid (nonverbal) ability (Horn, 1985) as well as falling on the Broad Visualization (*Gv*) factor (Kaufman, 1994; McGrew & Flanagan, 1996); and (3) overall perceptual organizational ability (Sattler, 1992).

Object Assembly

A perceptual organization measure, it consists of five items (four original and one new item) and the sample item from the WISC-R. The five puzzles are timed, and bonus points are earned for quick, accurate performance. Although Wechsler did not originally think this subtest should be included on the WAIS, its placement on the original WISC was thought to serve as a source of clinical value because it often revealed the child's mode (holistic/analytic) of perception, his or her degree of trial-and-error problem-solving methodology, and the child's task persistence and/or reaction to failure (Cooper, 1995).

Poor performance was hypothesized to reflect unfamiliarity with puzzles (Kaufman, 1994), anxiety, or deficient visual-perceptual development (Kaufman, 1990b). Kamphaus (1993) theorized specific behavioral aspects to investigate, which include visual discrimination, achievement motivation, and impulsivity. According to the crystallized-fluid model of intelligence, Object Assembly reflects fluid intelligence (Horn, 1986; Kaufman, 1990) and also contributes to Broad Visualization (*Gv*) and Processing Speed (*Gs*) (Horn, 1991; Kaufman, 1994). McGrew and Flanagan (1996) consider it a strong measure of *Gv* and not subtantially contributing to the other *Gf-Gc* abilities.

Mazes

Provided on a separate record form, the WISC-III retains all of the mazes from the WISC-R and adds one additional difficult maze, for a total of 10. This is a timed subtest, and bonus points are earned for quick, accurate performance. Mazes is a supplementary Performance subtest and may be used as a substitute in those cases where one of the standard subtests was invalidated. Additionally, Mazes may be substituted if an examinee's handicapping condition prohibits administration of one of the other standard subtests. If Mazes is administered in *addition* to the five standard Performance subtests, it is not included in the calculation of the PIQ score.

According to Cooper (1995), Wechsler did not discuss the Mazes subtest when writing about the individual subtests developed originally for the WAIS. Sattler (1992) reported that the Mazes subtest measures the child's planning and perceptual organizational abilities. Kaufman (1979) stated that the Mazes subtest on the WISC-R may reflect a number of hypothesized functions to be considered, including integrated brain functioning, planning ability, nonverbal reasoning, visual-motor coordination, the ability to respond when uncertain, past experience in solving mazes, and working under time pressure. Mazes' unique feature, however, involves measurement of the child's ability to follow a visual pattern and to use foresight. Interestingly, Mazes was excluded from the crystallized-fluid model of intelligence (Horn, 1991; Kaufman, 1990b, 1994). Cooper (1995) reported that "there has been very little research focused specifically on the Mazes subtest" (p. 241); it could be one of the subtests that handicapped or exceptional children perform more adequately on than other WISC tasks.

Poor performance was hypothesized to reflect anxiety, visual and/or motor integration problems, or impulsiveness (Kaufman, 1990b; Kamphaus, 1993). Sattler (1992) suggested that performance is related to adequate visual-motor control combined with motoric speed and accuracy.

Symbol Search

A new supplementary subtest, it has two levels, A and B, included on the separate record form with Mazes. This is a visual discrimination task, with a time limit of 120 seconds, in which the child indicates whether a target symbol appears in a search group. The test was designed to be used as a substitution *only* for the Coding subtest in determining the examinee's IQ scores.

The initial purpose in adding Symbol Search was to develop a measure that would complement the Freedom from Distractibility factor identified on the WISC-R. That is, it was intended to provide additional information in the measurement of attentional and memory features. Factor analytic procedures, however, suggested that Symbol Search may actually represent a fourth factor, labeled *Processing Speed*, along with the Coding subtest. As later discussed in the construct validity section, further research is necessary before assuming direct interpretation of this fourth factor. Sattler (1992) reported that the speed and accuracy with which the child performs this type of task provides a measure of overall ability. He thought that the task required visual discrimination and visual perceptual scanning. It is currently assumed (Kaufman, 1994) that Symbol Search may fall on the Processing Speed factor in the crystallized-fluid model of intelligence proposed by Horn (1985, 1991), although research is just now emerging on this topic. Cooper (1995) summarized the available literature and concluded that children with language or learning disabilities perform more poorly on Symbol Search than do nonimpaired children, while research on ADHD children was inconsistent.

Although research on this subtest is somewhat limited, Kamphaus (1993) listed a number of cognitive hypotheses that may explain poor performance. These include poor motor coordination, poor visual discrimination, poor short-term memory, or inability to follow instructions. Deficient performance may indicate problems in visual analysis, deficits in concentration or impulse control, or motivational problems (Cooper, 1995).

PSYCHOMETRIC PROPERTIES

The interpretive value of any test is defined quantitatively by its psychometric characteristics. Indeed, a test's reliability and validity determine whether interpretation should even be attempted, whether the test represents its hypothesized construct, and the extent a measure of current behavior can be used as an indicator of future performance.

For intellectual assessment and subsequent score interpretation, the essential elements include reliability (internal consistency, test-retest, and scorer reliability for certain subtests) and validity (content, predictive, concurrent, and construct). Foremost, the intelligence test must have a sound underlying theoretical base. The WISC-III is now presented as a four-factor model: Verbal Comprehension, Perceptual Organization, Freedom from Distractibility, and Processing Speed (Wechsler, 1991). Each subtest, as well as each of the Factor Index scales, should, then, meet minimum psychometric requirements if interpretive explanations, diagnoses, or classifications are made based on administration of the test. Psychometric properties of the WISC-III are presented next.

Reliability

Internal Consistency

For the WISC-III, as well as previous versions, the internal reliability (internal consistency) coefficients for the Full Scale, Verbal, and Performance IQ scales are outstanding. The average Full Scale IQ internal consistency coefficient is .96; for the Verbal IQ, .95; and for the Performance IQ, .91. These values suggest confidence in the estimates of global, verbal, and performance functioning on the WISC-III.

Since fewer subtests contribute to reliability measurement, the reliability for the Factor Index scales diminishes, as expected, from very adequate to adequate/fair. The average reliability coefficients (all ages) for the Verbal Comprehension factor Index is .94; for the Perceptual Organization Index, .90; for the Freedom from Distractibility Index, .87; and for the Processing Speed Index, .85 (Wechsler, 1991, p. 166, Table 5.1). Anastasi (1988) suggested that for individually administered tests of mental functioning, average reliability coefficients of .90 or higher are expected for global measurements. Thus, these factor index reliabilities may be considered psychometrically adequate.

For the WISC-III individual subtests, an erratic and age-related pattern of reliabilities are observed, ranging from .65 (poor) to .90 (adequate). Since subtests vary with regard to the number of items contained in each, it would be expected that lower reliabilities are associated with subtests containing the fewest items and samples of behavior. Generally, this holds true. Additionally, one would usually expect lower reliabilities at the younger ages due to instability of the trait or aptitude measured as well as expected developmental changes over time. Interestingly, this pattern was observed on the WISC-III Verbal scale, but the opposite pattern was found on several Performance subtests where lower reliabilities were consistently obtained for the higher age groups compared to the younger age groups.

For all ages on the Verbal scale, the Comprehension (.72 to .85) and Arithmetic (.71 to .81) subtests have the lowest reliabilities. This is not surprising for Comprehension, because of the measurement error due to scorer reliability difficulties (Slate & Chick, 1989; Slate & Saddler, 1990). Even though the manual now provides additional scoring examples, the nature of the 2, 1, and 0 scoring and the inconsistency of the examiner in appropriately querying for additional explanations contribute to the lowered reliability. The lowered reliability for Arithmetic, however, is somewhat surprising. First, Arithmetic is composed of 24 items, while Comprehension has only 18. Since it is based on a larger item sample, Arithmetic should have better internal consistency. Secondly, Arithmetic responses are scored as either correct or incorrect (with bonus points for quick and accurate responses). These two facets should ensure better reliability, but that is not the case. What could possibly explain the lowered reliability? Perhaps it results from a difference in application of the administration rules for establishing a ceiling on the two subtests. Both subtests establish a ceiling when three consecutive items are missed. On Comprehension, however, the examiner is required to ask for additional responses on 8 of the 18 items, whereas on Arithmetic, the examinee either solves the problem correctly or misses it altogether. Moreover, Arithmetic is a timed subtest (while

Comprehension is considered a power subtest) and this time factor may also contribute to measurement variability. Overall, the individual subtest reliabilities for the Comprehension and Arithmetic subtests are inadequate for specific profile pattern analysis and interpretation.

As has been the case since the WISC, the Vocabulary subtest continues to exhibit the highest average internal consistency of all Verbal subtests. For all ages, Vocabulary ranged from .79 to .91 with an average reliability of .87. The Vocabulary subtest was less reliable for the younger age groups (age 6, 7, and 9), with the remaining age groups at .88 or higher. Interestingly, the Digit Span subtest had the second highest average reliability across the 6-to-16-year age span, ranging from .79 to .89.

Internal consistency reliabilities for the Coding and Symbol Search subtests were not obtained for all age groups. Rather, interpolation of internal reliabilities for age groups 8, 9, 12, and 13 and extrapolation for age group 16 is provided. For all ages on the Performance scale, Mazes has the lowest average reliability (.70). Here, the younger the child, the more reliable his or her performance on Mazes (.80 for the 6-year-old age group versus .61 for the 17-year-old age group). As noted earlier, some of the Performance subtests (Mazes, Picture Arrangement, and Picture Completion) had much better reliabilities at the younger age groups compared to the older. Block Design, as was the case since the introduction of the first WISC, continues to be the most reliable performance subtest (.77 to .92), with an average reliability coefficient of .87 across the 6-to-16-year age span. Overall, the individual reliabilities for the Picture Completion, Picture Arrangement, Object Assembly, Mazes, and Symbol Search subtests are too low to support individual subtest analysis and interpretation. Coding is too low at the younger ages (ages 6 through 14), but may be adequately reliable at the 15-year-old age.

Test-Retest Reliability

When examining the test-retest reliabilities, Kamphaus (1993) noted that the "estimates of reliability drop precipitously" compared to internal consistency estimates (p. 129). Analysis of Table 5.5 (Wechsler, 1991, p. 172) reveals adequate test-retest reliabilities for Verbal and Performance IQ scales (.94 and .87, respectively), while the Full Scale IQ average reliability across the age span was .94. Factor index reliabilities were also lower, with Freedom from Distractibility .82 and Processing Speed .84. Moreover, some of the individual subtest reliabilities show sharp decreases: Digit Span, .73; Picture Arrangement, .64; Object Assembly, .66; and Mazes, .57. These test-retest reliabilities reflect considerable instability in measurement. Caution is advised, since test-retest reliabilities are provided for only three age groupings (6 to 7, 10 to 11, and 14 to 15) rather than across all age groups.

Based on the available (or lack of) evidence, it must be concluded that profile analysis, diagnostic labeling (e.g., brain damaged), and interpretation of individual subtest score scatter cannot be supported (McDermott, Fantuzzo, & Glutting, 1990). Only the most experienced clinician may attempt profile or diagnostic analyses and interpretation when accompanied by additional and compelling data. The examiner is well advised to draw hypotheses concerning the examinee's areas of strengths and weaknesses that are supported by additional sources of behavioral information or other test data. In fact, Sattler (1988) stated that:

unfortunately, research studies have not provided any firm basis for making diagnostic classification decisions from profile analysis. Using profile analysis with the WISC-R, WPPSI, and WAIS-R is problematic because the subtests are not as reliable as the Deviation IQs and do not measure unique processes (p. 166).

So it is with the WISC-III.

Standard Error of Measurement and Confidence Intervals

Wechsler (1991) provided a secondary index of reliability of the WISC-III by establishing the standard error of measurement for the IQ scales, factor index scores, and subtest scores. The standard error of measurement estimates the amount of error in a student's observed test scores and is inversely related to the reliability coefficient; that is, the larger the standard error of measurement, the smaller the reliability. The smaller the standard error of measurement, the more confidence in the accuracy of the estimated IQ as an indicator of the student's true score. Since the IQ and factor index scores are based on a mean of 100 and standard deviation of 15, and the WISC-III subtest scores on a mean scale of 10 and standard deviation of 3, direct comparison of standard error of measurement is not appropriate. Confidence intervals must be established to determine the accuracy of each IQ or scale score.

Confidence intervals for each IQ and index score as well as the individual subtest scores were reported in the WISC-III manual norms tables (Wechsler, 1991, pp. 251–257). Intervals were determined using both the alpha .05 and .01 levels. The average standard error of measurement for the FSIQ is 3.20. Thus, the FSIQ has the smallest confidence interval compared to the other IQ or factor index scores, making it the most accurate of the predictors of intellectual functioning. The Verbal IQ scale with a standard error of measurement of 3.53 remains close to the FSIQ standard error of measurement, while the Performance IQ scale balloons up to 4.54 (the Performance subtests were the least reliable overall, therefore displaying more measurement error). Factor index standard error of measurements were 3.78 (Verbal Comprehension); 4.68 (Perceptual Organization); 5.43 (Freedom from Distractibility); and 5.83 (Processing Speed). From a practical point of view, what this means is that a student who obtains an estimated Processing Speed Index score of 80 would have a Confidence Interval between 68 and 91 at the alpha .05 level. This can also be expressed as 80 ± 11.43. The confidence interval spans the below-average- to average-range classification, however, and places the examiner in a dilemma regarding interpretation, since the student's true score could fall on one side or the other of the estimated factor index score of 80. When interpreting IQ scales, a good rule of thumb is to use appropriate tables and age-based confidence intervals reported in the WISC-III manual.

For the WISC-III subtests, the average standard error of measurements on the Verbal subtests range from 1.08 (Vocabulary) to 1.45 (Comprehension). For the Performance subtests, the average standard error of measurements range from 1.11 (Block Design) to 1.67 (Object Assembly). Although these standard error of measurements look small, application to their respective subtests reflects the lack of overall reliability among the subtest measures. For example, a 9-year-old stu-

Table 8-4.   WISC-III tests in order of appearance on a 9-year-old student's test record form

Subtest	Scaled Score	Confidence Interval
Picture Completion	7	4.37–9.63
Information	8	5.43–10.57
Coding	9	6.34–11.76
Similarities	6	3.37–9.63
Picture Arrangement	8	4.88–11.12
Arithmetic	6	2.82–8.18
Block Design	8	5.73–10.27
Vocabulary	5	2.51–7.49
Object Assembly	7	4.06–9.94
Comprehension	7	4.00–10.00
Symbol Search	10	6.88–13.12
Digit Span	9	6.51–11.49
Mazes	9	5.57–12.43

dent who obtained a VIQ of 80, PIQ of 86, and FSIQ of 81 would have WISC-III standard scale scores outlined in Table 8–4. The corresponding standard error of measurements (see Wechsler, 1991, p. 168, Table 5.2, for standard error of measurements by age group) range from a low of ± 1.16 (Block Design) to a high of ± 1.75 points (Mazes) across the subtests. Now, individual subtest interpretation becomes problematic.

Interpretation of any single subtest leaves one in doubt regarding the estimated true score, since the confidence intervals are so large. Does the child's score of 7 on Picture Completion indicate functioning in the low-average range? His or her true score falls between 4.37 and 9.63. Likewise, Comprehension's confidence interval ranges from 4 to 10. Thus, the child's score spans the lower borderline to average range. Therefore, individual score estimates are highly variable (68% confidence that the child's true score falls in the range of 4 to 10), as considerable measurement error is represented. The examiner should follow a data-based analysis process whereby additional information is utilized prior to interpreting any one subtest score as clinically useful.

Subtest Specificity

The issue of intelligent test interpretation, generally, and individual subtest interpretation, specifically, has been expanded by Kaufman (1979, 1994) and is now requisite curriculum training for school psychologists. Models of interpretive systems are presented in a later section, although subtest specificity requires a special note at this point. Subtest specificity is the opposite of subtest variance, that is, how much each individual subtest contributes to the FSIQ, which represents global ability or g. Kaufman (1994) notes that a subtest has reliable variance that is shared with other subtests (and g) and also has a portion of its reliable variance that is unique only to itself. Whether the unique variance should be interpreted is the question. Kaufman suggests that if a given subtest's unique variance is at least 25% or more of the total

Table 8–5.   Subtest specificities for the WISC-III

Ample Specificity	Adequate Specificity
Digit Span (.63/.15)	Symbol Search (.34/.26)
Coding (.49/.23)	Arithmetic (.30/.22)
Picture Arrangement (.48/.24)	Comprehension (.30/.23)
Picture Completion (.39/.23)	Information (.25/.16)
Block Design (.34/.13)	Vocabulary (.24/.13)
	Similarities (.23/.19)

Note: Object Assembly is the only subtest with inadequate subtest specificity (.26/.31).

variance while also exceeding the error variance, then it *could* be reasonable to interpret that subtest's unique contribution to the test battery. However, whether one *should* make specific inferences about subtests depends on other factors.

Kamphaus and Platt (1992) calculated the subtest specificities for each of the WISC-III subtests using the squared multiple correlations (r^2) as the estimate of the common (shared) variance for each subtest. To determine the unique variance of the subtest, the common variance is then subtracted from the reliability coefficient for that subtest. Error variance is easily calculated since $1 - r_{tt}$ represents error. Thus, unique and error variance can be readily compared.

Based on Kamphaus and Platt's (1992) calculations, subtests were identified as having *ample, adequate,* or *inadequate* specificity (Kamphaus, 1993). These results are shown in Table 8–5. The values in parentheses indicate the subtest specificity (reliable unique variance), followed by its error variance.

Trait Stability between the WISC-III and WISC-R IQs

Although the WISC-III and WISC-R IQ scores exhibit high correlations, mean score differences (averaging more than 5 points) have been reported. Whenever an intelligence test is revised, practitioners are particularly concerned with performance differences between not only the revised and original test but the revised and other established tests. The WISC-III generated over 25 published or presented studies between 1991 and 1994 comparing various groups of children's performances on the WISC-III with the WISC-R. When tests are compared in this manner, trait stability of the measurement over time is obtained and this provides information about the comparability or equivalence of the two instruments. Weiss (1995) summarized 22 studies comparing WISC-III and WISC-R IQ scores for a variety of children's groups including learning disabled, gifted, epileptic, severely language impaired, Tourette's Syndrome, and mentally retarded (p. 5).

For the Verbal IQ, the weighted average difference between the WISC-R and WISC-III was −4.57 points, with the WISC-III scores lower. For the Performance IQ, the weighted average difference was −5.73 across all studies, with WISC-III PIQ scores lower. For the FSIQ, the weighted average difference was −5.69, again with WISC-III scores lower. Weiss (1995) maintained that these findings are consistent with the expected rate of change of approximately one-third IQ point per year over time. There are multiple explanations for changes in IQ between generations as well as fundamental changes within norm groups. A discussion of these factors is presented by Kaufman (1994) in *Intelligent Testing with the WISC-III* (pp. 37–39).

For the practitioner, retesting or reevaluation of a child previously tested with the WISC-R should produce lower IQ scores on the WISC-III by an average of 5.5 points, although for individual cases the difference could be much greater, depending on the type of referral. The clinician should become well versed in providing accurate explanations for why the child's IQ score is lower, especially if the child no longer qualifies for special services such as gifted education. Weiss (1995) compared children's heights today to those of children 20 years ago: On average, children today are taller than their same-age peers 20 years ago. Likewise, on average, children today are smarter when compared to their peers 20 years earlier. To earn an average score on today's newly normed test, children must perform better than their same-age peers performed decades ago.

Test-Retest Practice Effects

The final type of reliability issue involves retesting with the same instrument and obtaining differences in the IQ scores. The differences in IQ scores between the two testings is often attributed to practice effects.

Wechsler (1991) provided data for children who were tested with the WISC-III an average of 23 days apart. As expected, the Verbal IQ did not significantly change with retesting; it was no more than 2 or 3 points higher. Practice effects on the Performance IQ, however, can substantially increase scores between the first and the second testing. Practice effects of 12 to 13 points were found for age groups 6 to 7, 10 to 11, and 14 to 15. Analysis of Tables 5.3, 5.4, and 5.5 in the WISC-III manual (Wechsler, 1991) reveal that the Coding and Picture Arrangement subtests substantially contributed to the PIQ increase for all three of the age groups analyzed, while Picture Completion had an additional effect for the 14 to 15 group. Symbol Search appeared to exhibit a substantial increase for these three age groups as well, but since it is a supplementary test, it is not used in the IQ estimation.

The implications for the practitioner are obvious. A child should not be retested with the same instrument for at least one calendar year. (Case Examples 8–1 and 8–2 illustrate this point.)

Conflicting Test Information

The clinician might observe that when retesting with a different instrument test results often do not coincide with previous results, even when comparing IQ scores, academic achievement in specific content areas, visual-motor functioning, or behavior. This is especially troublesome when two or more tests are designed to measure the same thing. A crucial question is how much difference between tests that measure the same skill or aptitude is necessary to be considered a significant difference? Sattler (1982) suggested as a general rule that a difference equal to or greater than 1 standard deviation between the two test scores is a significant difference. This suggestion works particularly well when the tests have high reliabilities and, therefore, small SEMs. Moreover, there are several reasons why highly reliable tests that measure the same general abilities may produce highly discrepant results. Bracken's (1988) article on "Ten Psychometric Reasons Why Similar Tests Produce Dissimilar

---

Case Example 8–1.   Test-retest practice effect—A slow learner

---

A child who is a slow learner and is currently failing his or her grade is referred and tested with the WISC-III. The child obtained the following scores on the WISC-III: VIQ, 75; PIQ, 78; and FSIQ, 75. Does the child qualify for special (exceptional) services? (The Board of Education policy requires, among other data, IQ scores of 75 or lower for special services.) A tough call, and supporting data could be just as borderline and inconclusive. Given that the decision is to wait a month and retest, what is expected to happen on the retest? The VIQ will be an average of *at least* 2 or 3 points higher (now 77 to 78) and the PIQ will be an average of 12 to 13 points higher (80 to 83), which subsequently changes the FSIQ to 81 or 82. These new scores suggest that the first testing was unreliable when, in fact, practice effects of this magnitude are expected on the second testing. Additionally, for the statistically minded reader, regression effects toward the test mean would also be expected to raise the IQ score slightly with the second testing.

Case Example 8–2.   Test-retest practice effect—A gifted child

---

A child is referred for the gifted program. In this example, the Board of Education's policy requires a minimum FSIQ score of 121 for eligibility. The child obtained a FSIQ score of 118 on the first testing. Retesting will almost certainly qualify the child, as practice effects may cancel regression effects toward the mean and increase the child's FSIQ. Yet the first testing is the reliable estimate of ability, since known practice effects explain the IQ increase on the second testing. This situation, like Case Example 8–1, presents special problems for the clinician unless the second testing in both cases is accomplished with a different instrument approved for the measurement of intellectual functioning.

Results" is strongly recommended for anyone who may attempt to interpret test scores, explain variation in test scores, or explain why a child's performance on one test significantly differs from his or her performance on another, similar test. Bracken thoroughly discussed the ten problematic variables of floor effects, ceiling effects, item gradients, norm table differences, inappropriate use of grade or age equivalents, reliability differences, skill differences across tests, content differences, differences in publication dates, and norming sample representativeness. Consulting standard assessment texts for a review of human-related reasons for score differences (e.g., motivation, fatigue, practice effects, cultural/economic factors, primary language, etc.) is also recommended.

Validity

Perhaps the most disappointing feature of the WISC-III is the limited validity evidence actually presented in the manual. Salvia and Ysseldyke (1995) reviewed the WISC-III and reported that "most of the information presented in the WISC-III manual in support of the validity of the test consists of information on the validity of the WISC-R. The two measures are not the same" (p. 352).

Conversely, the Psychological Corporation (Wechsler, 1991) maintained that because of the similarities between the WISC-R and the WISC-III, the accumulated validity evidence for the WISC-R should be considered in determining the validity of the WISC-III. According to the standards for educational and psychological testing developed jointly by the American Educational Research Association, American Psychological Association, and Council on Measurement in Education (1985), it is the responsibility of the test developer to provide adequate evidence for the instrument's validity. The following review may shed some light on whether this has been accomplished.

Predictive Validity

Perhaps the most important issue in intellectual assessment concerns evidence for predictive validity of any test. Limited evidence for the predictive validity of the WISC-III was presented in the manual. Two studies were reported. In the first study, the WISC-III was compared to the WISC-R, which had been administered to 23 gifted children 5 to 20 months earlier (age and IQ not reported). All IQs were lower on the WISC-III: −4.9 for FSIQ, −5.8 for VIQ, and −1.1 for PIQ. In the second study, the WISC-III was again compared with the WISC-R, which had been administered this time to 28 retarded children 14 to 37 months earlier (age and IQ not reported). All IQs were lower on the WISC-III: −8.9 for FSIQ, −8.9 for VIQ, and −6.8 for PIQ. These two validity studies (on small samples of exceptional children) do not appear to provide substantive empirical data regarding the predictive validity of the WISC-III. The test developer appeared to rely on numerous references to the WISC-R and accumulated studies of the WISC-R over the last 15 years.

Since the original WISC was a downward extension of the Wechsler-Bellevue Scale, and was not based on any particular developmental theory of intelligence (Aiken, 1987), the consistent lack of predictive validation along with only moderate construct validation raised grave concerns (Salvia & Ysseldyke, 1995). Keith and Witta (1994) maintained that "little more is known about the constructs or structure underlying the WISC-III than was known about the WISC-R" (p. 27). Evidence for convergent (described as internal validity in the manual) and discriminant validity, however, was presented in the manual. Verbal subtests interrelate more highly with each other than they do with performance subtests; likewise, the performance subtests interrelate more highly with each other than with the verbal subtests.

Construct Validity

Much of the validation effort for the WISC-III centered on factor analytic methods and studies of the standardization sample. Sattler (1992) stated that "the test adequately measures two factors that correspond to the Verbal and Performance scales of the tests . . . [and] the test provides a fair measure of general intelligence" (p. 1043). Forty-three percent of the variance on the test was attributable to g.

Both exploratory and confirmatory factor analyses were conducted for the total sample ($N = 2,200$) and for four age-group subsamples: ages 6 to 7 ($n = 400$), ages 8

Table 8–6.   Factor loadings for the WISC-III and WISC-R on the identified factors

		WISC-III	WISC-R
Verbal Comprehension	Information	(.72)	(.63)
	Similarities	(.72)	(.64)
	Vocabulary	(.79)	(.72)
	Comprehension	(.65)	(.64)
	[Arithmetic	(.41)]	(.37)
Perceptual Organization	Picture Completion	(.53)	(.57)
	Picture Arrangement	(.37)	(.41)
	Block Design	(.70)	(.66)
	Object Assembly	(.69)	(.65)
	[Mazes	(.36)	(.47)]
Freedom from Distractibility	Arithmetic	(.73)	(.58)
	Digit Span	(.34)	(.56)
	Coding		(.42)
Processing Speed	Coding	(.79)	N/A
	Symbol Search	(.56)	N/A

Note. Data summarized from the WISC-R (Wechsler, 1974) and WISC-III (Wechsler, 1991) manuals. San Antonio, TX: The Psychological Corporation.

to 10 ($n = 600$), ages 11 to 13 ($n = 600$), and ages 14 to 16 ($n = 600$). Wechsler (1991) concluded that the results of the numerous factor analyses strongly suggest a four-factor solution for the WISC-III. The first two factors, Verbal Comprehension (VC) and Perceptual Organization (PO), were identical to the WISC-R factors. The third factor, Freedom from Distractibility (FFD) slightly differed from the WISC-R third factor. A new, fourth factor—Processing Speed (PS)—was identified due to the addition of the new test, Symbol Search. The identified factors were compared to those originally identified on the WISC-R and are presented in Table 8–6 for careful study.

Analysis of Table 8–6 shows substantial agreement between the two tests for the Verbal Comprehension and Perceptual Organization factors. Although Arithmetic is not included in the Verbal Comprehension factor, it has a marginal loading. For the Perceptual Organization factor, Picture Arrangement loads poorly. It does not associate itself with any factor, rather contributing a portion of its variance to Verbal Comprehension, Perceptual Organization, and Processing Speed. Factor three, Freedom from Distractibility, is composed of only two subtests on the WISC-III; on the WISC-R, Coding made up the third subtest of the triad, loading .42. Factor three appears very weak, as Digit Span loads only a mediocre .34. The addition of Symbol Search was intended to strengthen the third factor. Instead, a completely new factor, Processing Speed, emerged. Initial data suggest that the fourth factor, although weak, is more meaningful than the controversial third factor. Keith and Witta (Keith, in press) noted that the subsequent formation of a fourth factor with Coding, confuses rather than clarifies the nature of the constructs measured by the WISC-III.

A hierarchical and cross-age confirmatory factor analysis of the WISC-III standardization data was completed by Keith and Witta (in press). Two basic research questions were examined: Does the WISC-III measure the same constructs or ability across its 11-year age span, and What abilities are measured by the WISC-III? The results provided mixed support for the construct validity of the WISC-III, which was found to be "remarkably consistent" (p. 25) in its measurement across the 11 age levels and to consistently reflect a four-factor theoretical structure. Freedom from Distractibility was not supported as a third factor. Based on the hierarchical analysis, the third factor was thought to represent a measure of quantitative reasoning and, interestingly, was regarded as one of the best measures of general intelligence (*g*). The fourth factor was tentatively supported as a Processing Speed factor.

What do these data mean for the clinician?

1. The WISC-III, when not included with other intelligence test measures, represents a two-factor measurement: Verbal and Performance IQ scales may be interpreted independently.

2. There are specific subtests that do not load satisfactorily on any factor (and may not be interpretable). These include Picture Arrangement, Mazes, and Digit Span. Kamphaus (1993) referred to these types of tests as mavericks or outliers, especially Picture Arrangement.

3. The third factor is not likely a distractibility factor nor does it appear to contribute sufficient variance to be examined independently. One of its subtests, Arithmetic, also loads secondarily on the Verbal Comprehension factor.

4. The fourth factor appears more meaningful than the third factor, but additional studies for predictive validation are needed before the clinician can routinely interpret this factor.

5. Digit Span continues to be placed on the Verbal scale, yet it consistently has not contributed significantly to the measurement variance of the Verbal scale, whether examining the WISC-III or WISC-R. Thus, it is not an ideal test to use as a substitute for any of the verbal tests. Picture Completion loads substantially higher (.38) on the Verbal Comprehension factor than Digit Span (.26).

6. Coding has a very poor loading on the Perceptual Organization factor (.13), suggesting that it does not contribute significant variance to the computation of the PIQ. Yet it is integral to the computation of the PIQ. Thus, Coding may not be interpreted independently, and the clinician should exercise considerable caution in profile analysis of this measure. Symbol Search, a supplementary subtest, actually loads higher on Perceptual Organization (.35) than Coding and, according to Kaufman (1994), would be a more appropriate substitute on the Performance scale for IQ calculation.

7. Inexperienced clinicians should utilize only the first two factors in the analysis and interpretation of intellectual functioning until validation of the third and fourth factors occurs. Detailed review of the research by Sattler (1992), Roid, Prifitera and Weiss (1993), and Kamphaus, Benson, Hutchinson, and Platt (1994) suggests that there will be continuing debate over the number of factors and under what circumstances they are appropriate for the WISC-III.

Concurrent Validity

Evidence for concurrent validation, at first glance, appears adequate. A number of correlations between the WISC-III and the WISC-R as well as between the WISC-III and other tests of intelligence were reported. These correlations are generally strong (.85 to .92). Sattler (1992) stated, however, that "the concurrent validity studies of the WISC-III with the WISC-R, WAIS-R, and WPPSI-R do not allow us to determine with precision how the WISC-III IQs compare with those on the other Wechsler tests" (p. 1040).

The explanation for exercising caution results from a confounding effect identified in the concurrent validity studies. That is, the WISC-III was administered in counterbalanced order with the other Wechsler scales, producing scores on the test's second administration confounded by practice effects. Sattler (1992) noted that in order to know whether scores on two tests actually differ, independent test administration is needed. Another caution was offered by Anastasi (1988), who noted that concurrent validity does not ensure that the test actually measures what it purports to measure.

The *Journal of Psychoeducational Assessment* published a special monograph edition in 1993 on research examining the construct- and criterion-related validity of the WISC-III (see Shaw, Swerdlik, & Laurent, 1993; Edwards & Edwards, 1993; Sternberg, 1993). Various exceptional groups were analyzed, including language-disordered children (Phelps, Leguori, Nisewaner, & Parker, 1993); normal, learning-disabled, and ADHD children (Prifitera & Dersh, 1993; Roid et al., 1993; Schwean, Saklofske, Yackulic, & Quinn, 1993), and emotionally disturbed students (Teeter & Smith, 1993). Selected studies are summarized next. It should be noted, however, that in each study the initial standardization version, which differed from the final published version, of the WISC-III was administered. Thus, the authors advise caution in the interpretation and application of the findings.

Doll and Boren (1993) examined the performance of severely language-impaired students on the WISC-III. Seventeen of the 25 severely language-impaired students had been administered the WISC-R as part of their original placement, which allowed for a comparison of differences in their performance. Doll and Boren expected to find a decline in WISC-III IQ scores relative to those of the WISC-R, stable VIQ levels, and larger Verbal-Performance IQ differences on the WISC-III than on the WISC-R. These expectations were not confirmed. In fact, the decline in VIQ on the WISC-III was "more than twice as large as in other non-language disabled samples" (p. 84). Additionally, severely language-impaired students exhibited more variability on the WISC-III than on the WISC-R Performance subtests.

In another study, 26 children with developmental dyslexia were identified by use of the WISC-R and were tested 1 to 5 years later with the standardization version of the WISC-III (Newby, Recht, Cladwell, & Schafer, 1993). VIQ and FSIA significantly declined by 4.9 and 4.8 points, respectively, from the WISC-R to the WISC-III, while PIQ showed a smaller and nonsignificant decline of 3.4 points. The authors noted that this pattern of VIQ and PIQ change is the opposite of what would be expected from a short-term, counterbalanced comparison for the two WISC forms.

Using at-risk and special-education students, Hishinuma and Yamakawa (1993) examined the construct- and criterion-related validity of the WISC-III. Forty-two of the 78 subjects previously had been administered the WISC-R, with FSIQs that ranged from 76 to 142. IQs were lower for the WISC-III in comparision to the WISC-R: 4.6 points lower for both the FSIQ and VIQ, and 4.0 points lower on the

PIQ. They reported correlations of .88 between the WISC-R and WISC-III FSIQs, .91 betweeen VIQs, but only .74 between PIQs. Hishinuma and Yamakawa (1993) concluded that the overall pattern of results was supportive of the construct- and criterion-related validity of the WISC-III. They also noted, however, that the addition of Symbol Search increased "the interpretive complexity [and] further research is needed to explicate the applicability of the based measures" (p. 103).

Since 1993, more than 25 comparison studies of the performance of cognitively disabled children on the WISC-R and WISC-III have been published (Bolen, Aichinger, Hall, & Webster, 1995; Slate & Saarnio, 1995). Although the expected decrement in composite IQ scales is well established, the nature of the intercorrelations among WISC-III and WISC-R subtests with exceptional students suggest the need for caution in assuming the WISC-III is simply a replacement of the WISC-R.

MULTITUDE (THEORETICAL) PATHS OF WISC-III INTERPRETATION

One of the more difficult if not confusing tasks of the beginning examiner is learning how to interpret the WISC-III meaningfully. Since the introduction of the original WISC, numerous models or categorizations have been developed over the years. One of the earlier models of intelligence, Guilford's Structure of Intellect Model (SOI; Guilford, 1967), was adapted by Meeker (1969) for use with the WISC as well as the Stanford-Binet. Various templates were developed for scoring each of the SOI factors. Kaufman (1994) provided an outline of SOI classifications of WISC-III subtests based on Guilford's cognitive operations (Cognition, Memory, Evaluation, and Convergent Production) and three content dimensions (Semantic, Figural, and Symbolic). These groupings are presented in Table 8–7. Note that some subtests include more than one type of operation and/or content.

Bannatyne (1974) published a recategorization of the WISC-R that he thought was of particular use in diagnosing dyslexic children. Although these categorizations are produced by the current WISC-III report writer, the reader is cautioned to consider that the original work has not been updated. Thus, Symbol Search is missing and Picture Arrangement failed to meet minimum criteria for inclusion on any of the four categories. Nonetheless, as Kaufman (1994) noted, the Bannatyne approach has been one of the more popular (based on the number of studies reported in the literature) and may retain utilitarian value for use in general descriptions of cognitive functioning (i.e., showing a child's Verbal Conceptualization ability as a strength or

Table 8–7. SOI classifications of WISC-III subtests

Operations	Semantic	Figural	Symbolic
Cognition	S, V, A	PC, BD, OA	
Memory	I		A, DS
Evaluation	C, PA	PC, BD, OA, Cod. B, Cod. A, Symbol S	
Convergent	PA	Cod. A, Symbol S	Cod. B

Table 8–8. Summary of Bannatyne's recategorization system

Verbal Conceptualization Ability	*Spatial Ability*
Similarities	Picture Completion
Vocabulary	Block Design
Comprehension	Object Assembly
Acquired Knowledge	*Sequencing Ability*
Information	Arithmetic
Arithmetic	Digit Span
Vocabulary	Coding

weakness, or better developed Spatial Ability than Acquired Knowledge, etc.). Bannatyne's (1974) recategorization system is presented in Table 8–8.

INTERPRETIVE SCHEMES FOR THE WISC-III

Kaufman (1979) was one of the first to advocate a systematic interpretive approach to the WISC-R that has been expanded and generally applied to intelligence test interpretation. This "successive level approach" to test interpretation is highly useful in integrating WISC data. The original six steps are briefly outlined.

1. Interpret the Full Scale IQ.
2. Interpret the Verbal and Performance IQs: Analyze Verbal-Performance discrepancies; if not interpretable, then analyze VC and PO factors; if appropriate, analyze remaining factor scores.
3. Analyze subtest variability within scales.
4. Examine intrasubtest variability.
5. Examine intersubtest variability.
6. Complete a qualitative analysis.

Kaufman (1994, Chapter 3) expanded the interpretive model for the WISC-III. The interested reader should carefully study these methods and exceptions to the rules.

Kamphaus (1993, pp. 159–168) proposed an integrative method of test interpretation following nine principles. This procedure utilizes not only the WISC-III scores but the examiner's observations, intuitions, and clinical sense. The principles are:

1. Collect and integrate data from numerous sources.
2. Corroborate conclusions with multiple data sources.
3. Support conclusions with research.
4. Individualize interpretation.
5. Emphasize reliable and valid conclusions.
6. De-emphasize subtest profile analysis.

Table 8–9.   Grouping of WISC-III verbal subtests based on verbal input and vocal output by categories of duration and verbal expression

	Long Duration Stimuli	Brief Duration Stimuli
Much Expression	Comprehension	Similarities Vocabulary
Little Expression	Information Arithmetic	Digit Span

7. Minimize calculations.
8. Utilize an iterative process.
9. Emphasize a priori interpretation.

The Information Processing Model: WISC-III Interpretation

The Kaufman (1979, 1994) and Kamphaus (1993) approaches are not mutually exclusive, and practitioners would do well to integrate these procedures for WISC-III interpretation. Another emerging area of interest in the interpretation of the WISC-III requires further development. This involves interpretation of the WISC-III from an Information Processing model. Kaufman (1994) presented an initial overview from an information-processing point of reference by examining WISC-III subtests from an Input-Integration-Storage-Output model. He divided the Verbal and Performance subtests into basic types of tasks. The stimuli for the Verbal subtests were divided into two categories based on the duration of the stimuli and the degree of verbal expressiveness required. Verbal subtests are classified as outlined in Table 8–9.

The stimuli for the Performance subtests were divided into two categories, based on the meaningfulness of the stimuli (degree of abstractness) and the type of response required (visual organization or visual-motor integration). Performance subtests are classified in Table 8–10.

Kaufman noted some exceptions. For example, Symbol Search could be included in the Visual Organization category for some children, since scoring is not determined on the basis of neatness or fine-motor coordination.

All of the interpretive models reviewed provide the clinician with a method of formulating hypotheses to explain WISC-III performance. Empirical studies utilizing information processing approaches in the interpretation of the WISC-III have not yet been designed. Nevertheless, intuitive examination and analysis of each WISC-III subtest following the Input-Integration-Storage-Output model suggested by Kaufman (1994) may assist the clinician in formulating clinically rich hypotheses regarding the child's cognitive functioning.

Table 8–10.   Grouping of WISC-III performance subtests based on visual input and motor output by categories of meaningfulness and type of response

	Meaningful Stimuli	Abstract Stimuli
Visual Organization	Picture Completion Picture Arrangement	
Visual-Motor *Coordination*	Object Assembly	Block Design, Coding and Symbol Search

Guidelines for Interpreting the WISC-III

This chapter has surveyed several interpretive schemes useful in developing hypotheses regarding the child's abilities as represented by his or her WISC-III performance. The most appropriate interpretive system for the beginning clinician involves eight basic steps, summarized from the works of Kaufman (1979, 1994), Sattler (1993), and Kamphaus (1993).

1. Interpret the Full Scale IQ (and its corresponding percentile rank) using Wechsler's classification system as the best representation of the child's overall ability. If there is a VIQ-PIQ difference of more than 20 points, do not interpret the FSIQ; each scale must be interpreted independently (see Step 2 below). If there is no significant VIQ-PIQ difference, evaluate the implication of the FSIQ in terms of prediction of academic success.

2. Compare and interpret the Verbal and Performance IQ scales (and corresponding percentile ranks). Determine the percent of the standardization sample that obtained a difference equal to or greater than the child's VIQ-PIQ difference. Determine whether the child has significantly better developed verbal or nonverbal abilities. Develop hypotheses regarding the VIQ and PIQ scores, discrepancies (if any), and implications, especially in conjunction with the reason for referral and prior information about the child's schooling, background, and language.

3. Compare each Verbal subtest score to the mean Verbal scale score. Differences of 3 or more points are considered meaningful from a statistical perspective. Determine relative strengths and weaknesses within the Verbal scale by identifying differences of 3 or more points.

4. Compare each Performance subtest to the mean Performance scale score. Differences of 4 or more points are considered meaningful from a statistical perspective. Determine relative strengths and weaknesses within the Performance scale by identifying differences of 4 or more points.

5. Compare the Verbal Comprehension and Perceptual Organization factor indexes to the VIQ and PIQ to determine whether factor scores provide additional meaningfulness in understanding the child's intellectual performance.

6. Examine the Processing Speed factor index to determine its relevance in terms of a processing strength or weakness.

7. Examine intrasubtest patterns for each subtest. Compare verbal to performance patterns in terms of item gradients. Does the child often miss easier level verbal items while later correctly completing more difficult items? Does the child display expected basal and ceiling levels for his or her age? Are there one or two subtests in which performance is extremely low or represented by a raw score of one or zero (no correct item on the scale)?

8. Examine the child's responses for qualitative features involving ability to conceptualize, verbal expressiveness, motivation (tendency to quickly give up or state "I don't know"), task persistence and/or perseveration, reaction to failure, ability to self-monitor, impulsive response style, and anxiety. Determine the clinical significance of any specific responses that may suggest

pathology—for example, responding to a Comprehension item such as "What should you do if you find an ATM card lying on the ground and the PIN number is written on the back?" with the answer "you are supposed to turn it in [laughs] to the bank but I would get all the money [out of the ATM] first."

The beginning clinician should not

1. Use subtest scores to describe specific cognitive functions (e.g., Rhonda's low score on Digit Span indicates the presence of an attention-deficit disorder).
2. Use the IQ score to classify the child as mentally retarded (e.g., Rhonda's FSIQ of 72 shows that she is mentally retarded).
3. Interpret the Freedom from Distractibility factor index score as an indicator of ADHD.
4. Generate high-level inferences regarding subtest patterns (e.g., Rhonda's low Block Design score suggests brain damage—or right-hemisphere dysfunction, for the neurologically inclined).
5. Interpret the WISC-III as indicating future potential; it is not a measure of how motivated the child is or a determinant of actual (innate) intellectual capacity.
6. Report IQ scores when mitigating circumstances invalidate test results. Rather, carefully explain why test results are not valid without reporting invalid scores.
7. Rely on computer-generated psychological interpretation of WISC-III scales or psychoeducational reports. It is the psychologist's ethical obligation to provide test interpretation and analysis as well as appropriate recommendations.

The Use of Computerized Test Software

The last decade has witnessed an explosive growth of computer-based software scoring and interpretive programs. Various professional organizations, including the American Educational Research Association, National Council on Measurement in Education, APA, and NASP, have provided standards for educational and psychological testing. NASP's *Principles for Professional Ethics* (1986) and the updated NASP *Code of Conduct Manual* (1994), together with the APA's *Ethical Principles of Psychologists* (1989), *Standards for Educational and Psychological Testing (1985),* and *Guidelines for Computer-Based Tests and Interpretations* (1986), clearly point out the psychologist's responsibility for individual test interpretation rather than relying on computer-generated test interpretive reports.

An acceptable use of computer software, however, involves raw-score conversions and cross-scale comparisons. One of the early articles dealing with computerized scoring suggested that microcomputers handle the mundane clerical tasks of converting raw scores to standard scores much more accurately and quickly than can the clinician (Jacob & Brantley, 1987). Moreover, the software may identify errors during data entry, calculate chronological age correctly, and report a variety of standard scores useful to the clinician in formulating hypotheses to help understand the nature of the child's performance.

Thus, the distinction is between software that provides computerized interpretation (and report generation) and computerized assistance in scoring (and standard score generation). The ethical clinician (and student trainee) will refrain from using computer-generated interpretive reports. Schrank (1994) pointed out that substitution of the computer-generated score profile in lieu of the individually written interpretive report is specifically addressed (and not approved) by the Test User Training Work Group of the Joint Committee on Testing Practices (1993).

Future computer application is likely to involve the use of real-time computer intelligence testing, referred to as Computerized Adaptive Testing (CAT). Here, on-line test administration may soon replace individual intelligence assessment as it is currently practiced.

Case Example 8–3. Analysis and interpretation—Academically gifted

The following report was completed at the request of a boy's parents for a school-recommended referral to the academically gifted (AG) program for their son. Subsequent group testing at school resulted in an IQ score of 106 (average) and the son's failure to qualify for AG enrichment services. For the individual assessment, only the Full Scale IQ was of paramount importance to the parents and school officials, since the child had to obtain a FSIQ of at least 121 to qualify for enrichment.

CONFIDENTIAL
PSYCHOLOGICAL TEST REPORT

NAME: John   SCHOOL: Primary
PARENT: Larry & Nancy   GRADE: 3
ADDRESS: 127 Middle Class Lane   DATE OF BIRTH: 10/22/86
Anywhere, USA 00001   CHRONOLOGICAL AGE: 9 years, 5
                                           months
EXAMINER: Janet R. Adams, M.A.   DATE OF TEST: 3/22/96
Licensed Psychological Associate

TEST ADMINISTERED
   Wechsler Intelligence Scale for Children-Third Edition

REASON FOR REFERRAL
   John was referred for intellectual evaluation by his parents. Test results are to be used as part of the process for determining eligibility for admission into the Academically Gifted program.
   According to the mother, John's academic record reveals above-average performance. Course grades on a yearly average were consistently in the high As. Results from in-school group IQ testing, however, did not correspond to John's superior performance in class.

BEHAVIORAL OBSERVATIONS
   John presented as a pleasant and alert youngster who initially seemed to display very mild test anxiety. He exhibited a strong desire to perform his best and often asked

(continued)

Case Example 8–3. *(Continued)*

if he was correct in his responses. John was able to self-monitor the accuracy of his performance, rolling his eyes or exclaiming "where did that come from?" when items exceeded his ability level. He was highly motivated and persistent. He exhibited a methodical approach to problem solving and always rechecked his work. Language skills and vocabulary were excellent for his age and grade level.

John displayed well-developed interpersonal social skills for his age. He seemed somewhat precocious as well as showing a high level of achievement motivation. He did not demonstrate any obvious physical or sensory handicaps. Concentration and attention were good, and no signs of an underlying learning problem, ADHD, or other processing disorder were observed.

TEST RESULTS: WECHSLER INTELLIGENCE SCALE FOR CHILDREN-III

	Standard Score	*Percentile*
Verbal IQ	113	81
Performance IQ	111	77
Full Scale IQ	113	81

John's Full Scale IQ score on the WISC-III places his overall performance within the high-average range of intellectual functioning, at the 81st percentile in comparison with other children his age. Profile analysis of John's IQ scores suggests verbal and performance abilities are not significantly discrepant, with a majority of the students in the standardization sample exhibiting a difference of at least 3 points.

The Verbal IQ scale was high-average. John demonstrated evenly developed verbal abilities and no relative weaknesses. His lowest score was on the Digit Span test (and was not utilized in calculating the VIQ scale), which is primarily a measure of short-term auditory memory. On this subtest, John's score was average.

The Performance IQ was also high-average. Qualitative analysis, however, shows that performance abilities were in fact slightly less well developed than verbal abilities. John exhibited a significant strength on the Coding subtest, which requires fine-motor speed in copying. Also, he showed a strength on the Object Assembly subtest, which requires visual processing ability. The remaining three Performance subtest scores were average and consistently lower than the Verbal scale subtest scores.

Following the factor index model approach for WISC-III interpretation clarifies John's intellectual strengths and weaknesses. John obtained a Verbal Comprehension Factor score of 113 (81st percentile) and a Perceptual Organization Factor score of 105 (63rd percentile). The 8-point difference was not statistically significant, although a clear trend of slightly higher Verbal Comprehension compared to Perceptual Organization ability was apparent. A superior strength was observed on the Processing Speed factor, as shown by John's factor index score of 119 (90th percentile).

An explanation of each WISC-III subtest is now provided (a scaled score of 10 is the mean; scores from 7 to 13 define the average range).

Scaled Score	*Verbal Subtests*
12	*Information*—Measures knowledge of basic facts, requires long-term memory.

Case Example 8–3.   *(Continued)*

13	*Similarities*—Measures verbal concept formation, relational and categorical reasoning.
12	*Arithmetic*—Measures numerical reasoning, requires good attending skills.
13	*Vocabulary*—Measures word knowledge.
11	*Comprehension*—Measures judgment and reasoning in a variety of social situations.
9	*Digit Span*—Measures short-term auditory memory requiring attention & concentration skills.

Scaled Score	*Performance Subtests*
9	*Picture Completion*—Measures visual alertness to details.
15	*Coding*—Measures speed and accuracy of visual and fine-motor coordination skills.
10	*Picture Arrangement*—Measures the ability to apply logical reasoning sequentially.
10	*Block Design*—Measures visual processing, requires visual analysis and synthesis.
14	*Object Assembly*—Measures visual processing, requires perceptual organization.
12	*Symbol Search*—Measures visual processing, requires speed and visual discrimination.

CONCLUSIONS

John exhibited high-average ability in global intellectual functioning. His WISC-III FSIQ score fell at the 81st percentile. Factor profile analysis of his performance indicated that Verbal Comprehension abilities are high-average; Perceptual Organization abilities are average; and Processing Speed is superior.

The verbal profile was evenly developed and high-average. Nonverbal aptitudes were unevenly developed with two strengths: fine-motor speed and accuracy and visual processing. John displayed a high level of achievement motivation. With his skills and abilities, he appears quite able to perform satisfactorily in an academic setting.

ACADEMICALLY GIFTED ELIGIBILITY

Based on current Department of Public Instruction guidelines, John did not meet eligibility requirements for AG services. His WISC-III score pattern, however, did suggest above-average ability. Continued encouragement for academic mastery is strongly recommended and End Of Grade (EOG) test results should be carefully reviewed at the end of fourth grade to determine whether his overall score levels have reached the minimum criteria for AG eligibility. John should be encouraged to continue developing academic, social, and leadership roles by considering group/club involvement and school organization membership. In addition, continuing to provide John with challenging and advanced curriculum is recommended.

It was a pleasure working with John. Please call if I can be of further service.

Case Example 8–4.   WISC-III analysis and interpretation—Learning disabled

This child's teacher observed problems in mastering basic writing skills and suggested to the mother that a psychological evaluation was needed. Concerns were also expressed about letter and numeral reversals. The child was subsequently scheduled to have a comprehensive evaluation through the Scottish Rites Dyslexia Foundation, and results of the intelligence test were to be forwarded to that agency.

PSYCHOLOGICAL EVALUATION
CONFIDENTIAL

NAME: Mark   TESTING DATE: 11/18/96
AGE: 6 years, 10 months   DATE OF BIRTH: 12/30/90
SCHOOL: Primary   EXAMINER: R.J. Rose
GRADE: 1   School Psychology
                                Graduate Student

PSYCHOLOGICAL TEST BATTERY

  Wechsler Intelligence Scale for Children-III

  Bender Visual Motor Gestalt Integration

  Record Review

REASON FOR REFERRAL

  Mark was referred for evaluation to determine global intellectual functioning. He is currently enrolled in first grade. Individual testing results are to be forwarded to the Director of the Scottish Rites Dyslexia Foundation for follow-up dyslexic evaluation and written language remedial therapeutic services.

RELEVANT BACKGROUND INFORMATION

  Mark is currently residing with his father, mother, and twin brother. His mother indicated her interest in finding out his abilities in order to determine what needs to be accomplished to improve his school performance. Mark has not yet mastered basic readiness skills in reading, math, and writing for first-grade success. He "becomes confused" when copying or printing letters, according to his teacher.

BEHAVIORAL OBSERVATIONS

  Mark appeared to be of average height and weight for his age. At the time of the evaluation, Mark had a raspy cough. His mother indicated that he had a slight cold but that he was not running a fever or showing excess fatigue. He was, however, very fidgety throughout the testing session. Also, Mark constantly mumbled to himself that he had to do his best or "make it perfect." He seemed slightly uncomfortable and anxious as he tended to play with his hair and slide up and down in his seat. Both eye contact and spontaneous, friendly conversation were maintained, however, throughout the evaluation. Mark appeared observant and able to self-monitor his progress. On the Vocabulary section, for example, Mark commented—as the items became more difficult—that it was "too hard; the word is too big for my little mouth."

  After testing was completed, Mark talked openly about the current television show

Case Example 8–4. *(Continued)*

"Power Rangers." He described all the characters in detail and their specific abilities. Many of the words on the show are complex; however, Mark had no problem in saying or explaining to what they referred. He offered to bring all his action figures from the show and their weapons the next time he came to the office. It is the examiner's opinion that Mark's performance during the testing situation was a reliable reflection of his current ability. It was a pleasure to work with this young boy.

TEST RESULTS AND INTERPRETATIONS

Wechsler Intelligence Scale for Children (WISC-III). Mark obtained a Full Scale IQ score of 102 on the WISC-III, which placed him at the 55th percentile. He obtained a Verbal IQ of 108, placing him at the 70th percentile. This score represents his ability to express verbally and to understand verbal information. On the Performance section of the test, he obtained a Performance IQ of 95 (37th percentile). This score reflects his ability to perform spatial and perceptual tasks. No significant discrepancy between Verbal and Performance scores was present, which indicates equal development in his Perceptual Organization and Verbal Comprehension abilities.

The subtest scores on the WISC-III were as follows:

Verbal		Performance	
Subtest Scores	Scaled Scores	Subtest	Scaled
Information	12	Picture Completion	14
Similarities	11	Coding	7
Arithmetic	7	Picture Arrangement	7
Vocabulary	16	Block Design	7
Comprehension	11	Object Assembly	11
Digit Span	13	Symbol Search	6

On the Verbal portion of the WISC-III, Mark's subtest scores fell primarily in the average range with the exception of Vocabulary, which was superior. Mark demonstrated significant strengths in his expressive fluency and word knowledge. Mark demonstrated a relative weakness in his numerical reasoning ability. However, his performance in this area is average when compared to other children of the same age. High-average ability was demonstrated in his overall Verbal Comprehension.

On the Performance portion of the WISC-III, Mark's subtest scores fell in the average range with the exception of Picture Completion, which was above-average, and Symbol Search, which was low-average. Perceptual Organization abilities were unevenly developed.

Processing Speed was a weakness as shown by his factor index score of 83 (13th percentile). Mark had considerable difficulty with fine-motor execution and control. He often lost his place and had to work laboriously on both the Coding and Symbol Search tasks.

Bender Visual Motor Gestalt Test. Mark was also administered the Bender to assess his visual-motor integration, fine-motor coordination, and spatial perception. He com-

(continued)

Case Example 8–4.   *(Continued)*

pleted the test in 7 minutes and 55 seconds. Mark made 10 errors on the test and obtained a standard score of 88 based on the Koppitz Developmental Scoring System. His errors involved distortion of shapes (misshapen figures, dots converted to circles, angles drawn as curves and vice versa), perseveration (continuing a shape instead of stopping), and integration (problems in integrating figures together). Qualitative analysis suggested that Mark is experiencing some delay in visual-motor integration development. As writing demands increase in both complexity and length over time, this may become problematic for school success. Additionally, Mark exhibited an inappropriate pencil grasp, holding the pencil in a tight fist grip while copying.

SUMMARY AND RECOMMENDATIONS

Mark is a white male, 6 years and 10 months old, who has been referred by his mother for evaluation to determine his global intellectual abilities. He was friendly and determined to do his best. His verbal and perceptual abilities were measured equally within the average range. Difficulty on tasks measuring visual and motor integration was noted, which was consistent with the referral question of possible dyslexia and directionality confusion. Follow-up diagnostic and remedial services are to be provided through the Scottish Rites Dyslexia Foundation.

Case Example 8–5.   Analysis and interpretation—Academically delayed

This child was a private referral. Parent concerns specifically centered on school readiness, the possibility and need for retention, and general developmental issues.

PSYCHOLOGICAL EVALUATION
CONFIDENTIAL

NAME: J. Alan   DATE OF TEST: 6/28/96
AGE: 6 years, 4 months   DATE OF BIRTH: 1/30/90
SCHOOL: Smith Elementary   GRADE: Kindergarten
PARENTS: John & Alissa
900 J Executive Lane
Golden Pond, MA 20103

REASON FOR REFERRAL

Alan was referred for a psychoeducational evaluation because of parent concerns regarding readiness for first grade. Placement issues were of particular importance, as Alan's identical twin brother, Randy, experienced severe delays in attaining basic readiness skills during kindergarten.

PROCEDURES AND TESTS ADMINISTERED

Wechsler Intelligence Scale for Children-III
Woodcock-Johnson Tests of Achievement-Revised

Case Example 8–5. *(Continued)*

Bender Visual Motor Gestalt Test for Young Children

Achenbach Child Behavior Checklist: Parent Edition

Jordan Left-Right Reversals Test

Goodenough Draw-A-Person Test

Parent Interview

Vineland Adaptive Behavior Scales: Expanded Edition

BACKGROUND INFORMATION

Alan lives with both parents, his identical twin brother, Randy, and his older sister, Ginna, who is 9 years old and in the fourth grade. His father is a college graduate and is self-employed as a federal wildlife officer. His mother is also a college graduate and operates her own travel agency.

The parents have been concerned about the twins' school placement for several months. Alan was described as generally faster in grasping concepts, with significantly better language development skills than Randy. Alan has shown significant improvement since the beginning of school, knowing all of his letters and most letter sounds. He does still confuse some of his numbers.

Based on referral information, Alan gets along equally well with his parents and with his brother and sister. He is able to play by himself as well as with other children. He is described as a happy child, friendly and outgoing, and affectionate. Alan likes school. There does appear to be sibling rivalry with Randy, as any temper outburst by Alan generally results from a confrontation with his brother. They do like to tease and imitate each other, prompting the parents to place them in separate kindergarten classes.

Alan, like Randy, enjoys swimming, bike riding, and tee-ball. He also enjoys singing and building and making things, as well as playing with Ninja Turtles. He has several friends with whom he spends a limited amount of time playing. Also like Randy, Alan participates in seasonal sports, such as tee-ball, soccer, and basketball. Chores around the home include putting away his toys, putting away his dishes, taking his own bath, and getting ready for bed.

SCHOOL READINESS SCREENING

School readiness testing was completed in September of 1995, when Alan completed the Early Prevention of School Failure testing. Seven areas were measured. Both Alan's and Randy's performance levels are summarized below for review:

Area	*Rating*	
	(Randy)	(Alan)
Receptive Language:	Moderate Need	Moderate
Expressive Language:	Moderate Need	Average
Auditory:	Considerable Need	Moderate
Visual Memory:	Moderate Need	Moderate
Visual Discrimination:	Average	Moderate
Fine Motor:	Average	Moderate
Gross Motor:	Average	Average

(continued)

Case Example 8–5.   *(Continued)*

Screening results suggested mild delays in Alan's receptive language and auditory based processing levels compared to the other children entering kindergarten. Alan's area ratings were higher than Randy's on two, the same on three, and lower on two. The major difference appeared to be in Alan's somewhat better readiness level in the Expressive Language and Auditory Processing areas when the twins began kindergarten. End-of-year testing results just received by the parents revealed considerable improvement by both children on this screening test, with Alan scoring slightly higher than Randy overall.

Alan's kindergarten performance was reported as satisfactory by his teacher, Ms. Donna Johnson. Alan was assigned to first grade, but his parents were concerned about the twins' readiness as well as the effects of retention and promotion, especially if one twin is retained and the other is not. The parents' concerns were about developmental maturity and ability to handle first-grade academics successfully.

DEVELOPMENTAL HISTORY

Pregnancy history revealed a 7-month term, with Alan born first and weighing 4 pounds and 9 ounces. It was not a difficult delivery according to the mother, though she had been hospitalized and placed on various medications 2 weeks prior to delivery because of the possibility of a premature delivery. Immediately after birth, however, the twins encountered difficulties with breathing (anoxia) and feeding. They remained in the hospital for 6 weeks.

MEDICAL HISTORY AND EARLY DEVELOPMENTAL MILESTONES

There were no major illnesses or injuries noted except for chronic ear infections during the early years. Both Alan and Randy had tubes inserted at 18 months of age. Developmental milestones were reported within late-normal limits in sitting (8 months), crawling (10 months), and walking alone (15 months). Bowel and bladder control were achieved by 36 months. Alan established right-hand dominance earlier than Randy. Beginning words were noted by 20 months. Alan did not show the articulation problems (with *l, th,* and *r* sounds), experienced by Randy, or word finding and retrieval problems. Fine- and gross-motor skills were described as adequately developed: Alan can catch a ball fairly well; he can ride a bike and roller-blade without difficulty.

CHILD BEHAVIOR CHECKLIST RATINGS

Alan was rated by his mother on the Child Behavior Checklist. His ratings were compared to the ratings of other 6-year-old children on nine clinical scales. Alan's ratings were well within the normal range on all nine scales. An average but slightly elevated rating was noted on the Aggressive scale. That is, in behavior (and behavior frequency) characterized by arguing, stubbornness, teasing, and being loud, Alan's mother perceived some immaturity.

BEHAVIORAL OBSERVATIONS

Alan presented as serious and somewhat concerned about having to be tested. He did not really want to separate from his mother but did so, with reluctance in his demeanor. He was able to relate in a socially appropriate manner. Alan has very light

Case Example 8–5. *(Continued)*

brown hair and was neatly groomed and dressed. He wore a large ring on his right-hand middle finger and explained he had found it at the pool. He showed good task focus and seemed to relax and become more comfortable as the testing progressed. Alan would usually scrunch up his face after a question or task was presented, perhaps in concentration. He was concerned about performing well and occasionally glanced at what the examiner was writing. Alan worked in a slow and methodical manner, using a rather analytical approach. He seemed to have difficulty elaborating on verbal responses when queried, generally just repeating what he had previously stated.

Alan exhibited an appropriate pencil grasp, using a three-finger position. He showed little sense of organization and sequence, often writing over previous work. Sometimes Alan started in the middle of the page and other times at the bottom, and often worked right-to-left only to proceed left-to-right the next time. He was unsure of his date of birth, although he knew his age.

TEST RESULTS

On the Wechsler Intelligence Scale for Children-III, Alan obtained the following scores:

Verbal IQ	100	Average
Performance IQ	85	Low-Average
Full Scale IQ	91	Average

His resulting Full Scale IQ percentile rank was 27. This means that 73% of children Alan's age scored above him. There was a significant 15-point difference between his Verbal and Performance IQ scores, suggesting that his overall cognitive abilities are unevenly developed. The FSIQ provided an assessment of general intelligence and scholastic aptitude, but the 15-point discrepancy suggested that it may not accurately represent Alan's abilities. An examination of each scale is necessary to more accurately understand his cognitive abilities, strengths, and weaknesses.

Alan obtained the following subtest scale scores on the Wechsler Intelligence Scale for Children-Revised.

Verbal Scale	*Score*	*Performance Scale*	*Score*
Information	8	Picture Completion	6
Similarities	11	Picture Arrangement	9
Arithmetic	11	Block Design	10
Vocabulary	10	Object Assembly	6
Comprehension	10	Coding	8
Digit Span	(8)	Symbol Search	7

Note: A scaled score of 10 is average; scores from 7 to 13 define the average range.

Alan's Verbal Comprehension scores are average (50th percentile), with no relative weaknesses noted. His performance suggested evenly developed verbal aptitudes. His Verbal IQ, which fell at the 50th percentile, provided an indication of verbal aptitudes,

(continued)

Case Example 8–5. *(Continued)*

which include the ability to reason with words, to learn verbal materials, and to process verbal information.

His Perceptual Reasoning abilities were significantly lower, at the 16th percentile rank, with no relative strengths. Perceptual Reasoning abilities were consistently lower than Verbal Reasoning abilities. The PIQ contributed an understanding of Alan's perceptual organization, which involves the ability to employ visual images in thinking and the ability to process visual material efficiently.

Analysis of the Processing Speed factor of the WISC-III revealed a standard factor index score of 88 (21st percentile). This factor measures visual discrimination and requires visual-perceptual scanning and speed. Concentration and task persistence as well as speed and accuracy in fine-motor execution are the components necessary for successful task completion.

Results from Alan's individual achievement testing are listed below.

Woodcock-Johnson Tests of Achievement-Revised

Subtests	*Standard Score*	*Discrepancy*	*Grade Equivalent*
Letter-Word Identification	82	−9	12
Passage Comprehension	97	6	42
Calculation	73	−18	4
Applied Problems	90	−1	26
Dictation	93	2	32
Writing Samples	87	−4	20
Broad Reading	89	−2	24
Broad Math	70	−21	2
Broad Written Language	89	−2	23

Alan's achievement scores were generally at the expected range of performance based on his WISC-III estimated ability levels except for mathematics. Analysis of his subtest performance is presented next.

Letter-Word Identification: Alan relied on rote memory skills for letter identification. He would not attempt to read out or sound out any of the two- or three-letter words presented. Letter identification was immediate and he made only one error, identifying the letter *S* as *C*. His letter-word identification skills were measured at the middle grade level (K.5), the same level as Randy's.

Passage Comprehension: Alan was able to understand unknown words from pictorial context. His reading comprehension was slightly erratic, though, as he missed three items below his age level while successfully completing one item above his grade level. He relied on his reasoning skills to supply missing words, since he was unable to read any of the words in the sentences. His grade level equivalence was 1.1.

Dictation: Alan earned an average score on the Dictation test. He had no difficulty writing uppercase and lowercase letters. He attempted to write the spelling words using phonics but generally produced the ending sound of the word (the last sound he

Case Example 8–5.   *(Continued)*

heard when repeating the word to himself). Simple punctuation was not understood, as he carefully placed the period in front of the sentence. His work was at the K.7 grade level.

Calculation: Alan demonstrated basic computational skills at the K.5 grade level, writing orally presented numerals. He reversed each numeral when writing, however. He showed confusion about the operational sign (plus, +) and apparently wrote down numbers randomly as answers to the items (e.g., 2 + 2 =). When asked to add by using his fingers, holding two up on one hand, for example, and one on the other, he usually responded with the combination the two numbers made when placed side-by-side (for example 12). Thus, his present performance was borderline and apparently affected by his constant reversals.

Applied Problems: Alan's performance was much higher than his actual computational skills, showing average development in his numerical reasoning skills. Conceptually, Alan was able to add and subtract amounts when a pictorial representation of objects was presented. He was not able to tell time consistently. His numeral reasoning processes were at the K.8 grade level.

Writing Samples: Alan's grade equivalent of K.8 suggested low-average skill development in written language. His fine-motor control for letter formation was weak. He was able to successfully write his name, the last letter in the word *cat*, and the first letter in the word *apple*. Alan would orally say the correct word and also orally identify some of the letters that he could hear in the words. He attempted to sequence these and write them on paper, but had little success.

   In sum, Alan's achievement levels were at his measured ability level, with particularly weak math skills. His levels are generally end-of-kindergarten to early-first-grade equivalent—except for math, which was K.2. Alan's achievement skills in reading and written language were approximately one-to-three months behind his expected grade level.

Bender Gestalt Test. The Bender Gestalt Test (Bender 1938) was completed to assess visual-motor integration functioning. Alan obtained a standard score within the average range for his age based on the Koppitz scoring criteria. He made seven errors involving angularity and integration difficulties. Organizational and sequencing difficulties were observed, as Alan worked from the bottom of the page and then from the top, and he overlapped a number of the items. When asked to write his name, he wrote over several of the items just completed. Thus, his work was somewhat confusing and messy in appearance. He completed the task within a normal amount of time.

Jordan Left-Right Reversals Test. Results of the Jordan Left-Right Reversals Test revealed below-average performance for his age. Alan made nine errors on the letter section and six errors on the numeral section. He identified the letters *E, D, L, W, J,* and *Q* as reversed (they were not) and the letters *S, R,* and *Z* as not reversed (they were). On the numerals, Alan identified *7, 2, 9, 3,* and *6* as reversed (they were not) while identifying a reversed *7* as correct. Children his age, on average, make eight errors on these two parts, so Alan made more than the expected number. In 2 months,

(continued)

Case Example 8–5. *(Continued)*

Alan would be expected to make five errors, suggesting that his visual-spatial (or directional) confusion in letter and numeral shapes could cause him difficulty in learning to read, in mastering numbers, and in copying and writing as he enters first grade.

Goodenough Draw-A-Person Test. Analysis of Alan's Goodenough Draw-A-Person Test was made to estimate his social maturity. He produced an integrated figure and spontaneously added family members. Heavy line pressure was noted. His social maturity level, as scored by the Goodenough-Harris criteria, fell at the 5½ year level consistent with ability measures.

Vineland Adaptive Behavior Scales-Expanded Edition. The Vineland Adaptive Behavior Scales-Expanded Edition (with Alan's mother as informant) was completed as part of the assessment process in determining his social and developmental maturity levels. Alan's score levels were compared to those of other children his age; his rankings are presented next (a score of 100 is average).

Adaptive Domain	Standard Score	Age Equivalent
Communication	70	4.11
Receptive		4.08
Expressive		5.03
Written		5.00
Daily Living	75	4.11
Personal		5.01
Domestic		3.06
Community		5.03
Socialization	86	5.01
Interpersonal		7.00
Play and Leisure		3.06
Coping skills		5.06
Adaptive Behavior Composite	71	4.00

Analysis of the Adaptive ratings suggested that Alan's adaptive behavior levels were rated lower than his cognitive level. He scored generally within the borderline range on the Adaptive scales, while cognitive levels were within the average range. He showed a pattern of adaptive behavior strengths and weakness across the domains.

Communication skills fell within the borderline range. Receptive, Expressive, and Written Communication skills were rated as evenly developed and at the beginning kindergarten level.

Interpersonal skills (socialization) were Alan's highest rankings of all adaptive areas. These levels suggested an ability to socialize effectively in terms of cooperative interaction, functioning within a group, and effective social communication. Play and Leisure skills were one of his lowest areas. Examination of the ratings here suggested that Alan's behavioral interactions with his brother, as previously mentioned in terms of maturity, are a concern.

His lowest area fell in the Daily Living Skills domain, which measured independent functioning. Alan's weak area (as well as Randy's) was within the domestic section. This area deals with the self-help skills of cleaning up after himself, putting things

Case Example 8–5.   *(Continued)*

away, and fixing snacks on his own, as well as assisting before, during, or after a meal in various ways and attempting to make his own bed. Alan's ratings suggested an emerging five-year-old level of independent functioning in this area. Safety needs such as looking both ways before crossing a street were also listed as a concern.

Gross-motor and fine-motor skills fell within the average range compared to children six years of age. Alan had almost no problem with catching a ball, riding his bike, cutting with scissors, or using pencil and paper, according to his mother.

CONCLUSIONS

Test results placed Alan's level of intellectual functioning within the average range. His resulting percentile rank was 27, with Verbal Comprehension abilities significantly better developed than Perceptual Reasoning abilities. Processing Speed was low-average and at levels similar to Perceptual Organization abilities. Achievement scores were at levels expected (except for math) based on Alan's estimated ability. Visual-motor integration was age-appropriate, though some difficulty in spatial organization was suggested. Social maturity levels appeared to be slightly lower than his mental age.

Alan showed overt concerns about his progress and abilities. He seemed to take rather seriously the nature of the testing. Adaptive ratings placed Alan's overall level of adaptive functioning within the borderline range, 1 year below his actual chronological age. These ratings suggested that Alan's adaptive levels were not sufficient to meet independently the required social and adaptive demands of first grade. In contrast, intellectual assessment suggested that Alan was only 3 months below first-grade cognitive readiness.

RECOMMENDATIONS

Retention in kindergarten remained a most difficult issue, since Alan's test results did not clearly differentiate the lack of first-grade readiness. He appeared to be functioning one to three months behind in his basic Language and Written Expression skills. Math skills, however, were almost one year behind. Directionality development, in terms of letter and numeral reversals, was below age expectancy. This weakness appeared to significantly delay Alan's writing, copying, and math skill development. Adaptive behavior skills were erratic, suggesting some delay in his overall maturation. Having an identical twin brother (who experienced considerably more difficulty than Alan) complicated matters both in terms of their self-concept development and interpersonal relationship throughout the school years.

Based on discussions during Randy's parent conference and on the case analysis, the recommendation is that both children enroll in first grade at Smith Elementary School and be independently grouped in their reading and math classes. The issue of first-grade retention may present itself later, but with close monitoring the matter may well be determined before the end of first grade. Tutorial assistance for specific skill development (fine-motor control and visual-spatial organization for written work, phonics application, and math/number concept) is recommended.

Alan will need additional support structure and assistance in terms of tutorial help, extra study sessions, organizational assistance, and rehearsal with feedback. This type of assistance should be provided during the summer, in preparation for first grade. Utilization of the summers for remedial and preparatory training—by participating in

(continued)

Case Example 8–5.   *(Continued)*

the university reading clinic, taking extended educational trips, and joining a beginning reader library program is recommended.

If Alan and Randy enter first grade, it is essential that their instruction begin at their level of readiness, with appropriate educational assistance, or they may be overwhelmed in school. The parents should discuss the children's groupings with the principal, counselor, and first-grade teacher and request frequent updates on their progress.

In terms of Alan's deficit in understanding math (addition), the following steps may help address this problem. After presenting a math problem such as 2 + 3:

1. An adult completes the problem while talking aloud, counting on fingers, or marking lines.
2. Alan performs the same task under the verbal directions of the adult's instruction.
3. Alan performs the task while instructing himself.
4. Alan performs the task while instructing himself silently.
5. Problems of similar difficulty and type are presented, and all errors are demonstrated and re-explained.

Learning strategies and instruction for Alan and Randy should ensure that active cognitive and language processing is occurring. This may include teacher use of

1. Imagery in descriptions and vivid contrasts.
2. Analysis of key words.
3. Facilitating retrieval by chunking information, using mnemonics, and categorizing presented material (chunking = Al-an; Ran-dy, to-get-her).
4. Having Alan verbally repeat directions to ensure comprehension and accuracy.

It is recommended that special LD tutoring be implemented to emphasize directionality for letter and numeral recognition. Fine-motor-control training is also suggested. A multimodality approach that includes a combination of phonics training and whole word (context) instruction is required. Specifically, letters must be mastered in terms of recognition and production from memory first; then letters which represent the single sounds of familiar speech are presented and immediately synthesized into words that carry meaning. Introduce prefix and suffix letter groupings simultaneously through hearing, seeing, and feeling to enhance integration and memory (retrieval). The goal is to develop automatic memory, building in reinforcement and moving as fast as possible but as slow as necessary to master the basic elements.

CONCLUSION

As the case studies demonstrated, the type of format followed may vary. The use of side headings can often facilitate understanding and clarity. Moreover, interpretation of the WISC-III in and of itself may not be particularly revealing—or valid— beyond the global IQ estimate. The consummate clinician will certainly utilize a variety of sources of data, including social history, the referral question, previous test results, behavior and/or teacher descriptions of academic weaknesses, and other information.

The WISC-III provides a global estimate of ability that correlates to a degree with academic success. When used in isolation, its diagnostic utility is severely limited. With the contemporary advances in our understanding and measurement of intelligence, the WISC-III may become secondary to newer and more refined assessment instruments. For different points of view compare Kaufman's (1993) "King WISC the third assumes the throne" and Sternberg's (1993) "Rocky's back again: A review of the WISC-III"; Vance's (1993) *Best Practices in Assessment for School and Clinical Settings* and Post and Mitchell's (1993) "The WISC-III: A reality check."

The work of Carroll (1993a, 1993b), Horn (1979, 1985, 1986a, 1986b, 1991, 1994), Sternberg (1985), Gardner (1983), McGrew (1994), McGrew and Flanagan (1996), and Woodcock (1990, 1993) on multiple intelligences demonstrates that clinicians now have the capability to understand and measure multiple constructs of intelligence in a far more sophisticated manner than represented by any one intelligence test alone. McGrew and Flanagan (1996) called for a "cross battery approach to intelligence test interpretation" that would facilitate a better and more thorough assessment of an individual's abilities, provide a greater understanding of the relation between cognitive ability and a variety of achievement criteria, and enhance our understanding of aptitude-treatment interactions (ATIs).

Multifactored assessments should be the standard throughout the nineties and into the next century. It is the clinician's obligation to develop the appropriate skills necessary in the measurement of cognitive abilities and to become well versed in multifactored assessment and multiple intelligence models. Further research will demonstrate the contribution of the WISC-III in the understanding and measurement of human cognitive abilities.

REFERENCES

Aiken, L.R. (1987). *Assessment of intellectual functioning.* Needham Heights, MA: Allyn & Bacon.

American Educational Research Association, American Psychological Association, & National Council on Measurement in Education. (1985). *Standards for educational and psychological testing.* Washington, DC: American Association of Mental Retardation.

American Psychological Association (1985). *Standards for educational and psychological testing.* Washington, DC: APA.

American Psychological Association (1986). *Guidelines for computer-based tests and interpretations.* Washington, DC: Author.

American Psychological Association (1989). *Ethical principles of psychologists.* Washington, DC: APA.

Anastasi, A. (1988). *Psychological testing* (6th ed.). New York: Macmillan.

Bannatyne, A. (1974). Diagnosis: A note on recategorization of the WISC scaled scores. *Journal of Learning Disabilities, 7,* 272–273.

Bender, L. (1938). A visual motor test and its clinical use. American Orthopsychiatric Association. New York: Research Monograph, 3.

Blatt, S.J., & Allison, J. (1968). The intelligence test in personality assessment. In A.I. Rabin (Ed.), *Projective techniques in personality assessment* (pp. 421–460). New York: Springer.

Bolen, L.M., Aichinger, K.S., Hall, C.W., & Webster, R.E. (1995). A comparison of the performance of cognitively disabled children on the WISC-R and WISC-III. *Journal of Clinical Psychology, 51,* 89–94.

Bracken, B.A. (1988). Ten psychometric reasons why similar tests produce dissimilar results. *Journal of School Psychology, 26,* 155–166.

Bracken, B.A. (1993). Editor's comments. *Journal of Psychoeducational Assessment, Monograph Series, Advances in Psychoeducational Assessment, Wechsler Intelligence Scale for Children: Third Edition, 4–5.*

Carroll, J.B. (1993a). *Human cognitive abilities: A survey of factor-analytic studies.* Cambridge, England: Cambridge University Press.

Carroll, J.B. (1993b). What abilities are measured by the WISC-III? *Journal of Psychoeducational Assessment, Monograph Series, Advances in Psychoeducational Assessment, Wechsler Intelligence Scale for Children, Third Edition, 134–143.*

Clarizio, H., & Bernard, R. (1981). Recategorized WISC-R scores of learning disabled children and differential diagnosis. *Psychology in the Schools, 18,* 5–12.

Cohen, R.J., Swerdlik, M.E., & Smith, D.K. (1992). *Psychological testing and assessment.* Mountain View, CA.: Mayfield Publishing.

Cooper, S. (1995). *The Clinical use and interpretation of the Wechsler Intelligence Scale for Children, Third Edition.* Springfield, IL: Charles C. Thomas Publisher.

Doll, B., & Boren, R. (1993). Performance of severely language-impaired students on the WISC-III, language scales, and academic achievement measures. *Journal of Psychoeducational Assessment, Monograph Series, Advances in Psychoeducational Assessment, Wechsler Intelligence Scale for Children, Third Edition, 77–86.*

Edwards, R., & Edwards, J.L. (1993). The WISC-II: A practitioner perspective. *Journal of Psychoeducational Assessment, Monograph Series, Advances in Psychoeducational Assessment, Wechsler Intelligence Scale for Children: Third Edition, 144–150.*

Freeman, F.S. (1962). *Theory and practice of psychological testing* (3rd ed.). New York: Holt, Rinehart & Winston.

Gardner, H. (1983). *Frames of mind: the theory of multiple intelligences.* New York: Basic Books.

Glasser, A.J., & Zimmerman, I.L. (1967). *Clinical interpretation of the Weschler Intelligence Scale for Children.* New York: Grune & Stratton.

Graf, M.H., & Hinton, R.N. (1994). A three year comparison study of WISC-R and WISC-III IQ scores for a sample of special education students. *Educational and Psychological Measurement, 54,* 128–133.

Grossman, H.J. (Ed). (1983). *Classification in mental retardation.* Washington, DC: American Association on Mental Deficiency.

Guilford, J.P. (1967). *The nature of intelligence.* New York: McGraw-Hill.

Guilford, J.P. (1959). The three faces of intellect. *American Psychologist, 14,* 469–479.

Hale, R.A., & Landino, S.A. (1981). Utility of WISC-R subtest analysis in discriminating among groups of conduct problem, withdrawn, mixed, and nonproblem boys. *Journal of Consulting and Clinical Psychology, 49,* 91–95.

Hishinuma, E.S., & Yamakawa, R. (1993). Construct and criterion-related validity of the WISC-III for exceptional students and those who are "at-risk." *Journal of Psycho-*

educational Assessment, Monograph Series, Advances in Psychoeducational Assessment, Wechsler Intelligence Scale for Children: Third Edition, 94–104.

Horn, J.L. (1979). The rise and fall of human abilities. *Journal of Research and Development in Education, 12*, 59–78.

Horn, J.L. (1985). Remodeling old models of intelligence. In B.B. Wolman (Ed.), *Handbook of intelligence: Theories, measurements, and applications* (pp. 267–300). New York: Wiley.

Horn, J.L. (1986a). Intellectual ability concepts. In R.J.L. Sternberg (Ed.), *Advances in the psychology of human intelligence* (Vol. 3, pp. 35–37). Hillsdale, NJ: Lawrence Erlbaum.

Horn, J.L. (1986b). Some thoughts about intelligence. In R.J. Sternberg & D.K. Detterman (Eds.), *What is intelligence? Contemporary viewpoints on its nature and definition* (pp. 91–96). Norwood, NJ: Ablex.

Horn, J.L. (1991). Measurement of intellectual capabilities: A review of theory. In K.S. McGrew, J.K. Werder, & R.W. Woodcock (Eds.), *Woodcock-Johnson technical manual: A reference on theory and current research* (pp. 197–246). Allen, TX: DLM Teaching Resources.

Horn, J.L. (1994). Theory of fluid and crystallized intelligence. In R.J. Sternberg (Ed. in chief), *Encyclopedia of human intelligence* (pp. 443–451). New York: Macmillan.

Jacob, S., & Brantley, J.C. (1987). Ethical-legal problems with computer use and suggestions for best practices: A national survey. *School Psychology Review, 16*, 69–77.

Kamphaus, R. (1993). *Clinical assessment of children's abilities.* Needham Heights, MA: Allyn & Bacon.

Kamphaus, R.W., Benson, J., Hutchinson, S., & Platt, L.O. (1994). Identification of factor models for the WISC-III. *Educational and Psychological Measurement, 54*, 174–186.

Kamphaus, R.W., & Platt, L.O. (1992). Subtest specificities for the WISC-III. *Psychological Reports, 70*, 899–902.

Kaufman, A.S. (1979). *Intelligent testing with the WISC-R.* New York: Wiley.

Kaufman, A.S. (1990a). *Assessing adolescent and adult intelligence.* Needham Heights, MA: Allyn & Bacon.

Kaufman, A.S. (1990b). Intelligence testing in the schools. In C.R. Reynolds & T.B. Gutkins (Eds.), *The handbook of school psychology: Second edition* (pp. 289–327). New York: Wiley.

Kaufman, A.S. (1993). King WISC the third assumes the throne. *Journal of School Psychology, 31*, 345–354.

Kaufman. A.S. (1994). *Intelligent testing with the WISC-III.* New York: John Wiley & Sons.

Kaufman, A.S., & Van Hagan, J. (1977). Investigation of the WISC-R for use with retarded children: Correlation with the 1972 Stanford-Binet and comparison of WISC and WISC-R profiles. *Psychology in the Schools, 14*, 10–14.

Keith, T.Z., & Witta, E.L. (in press). Hierarchical and cross-age confirmatory factor analysis of the WISC-III: What does it measure. *School Psychology Quarterly.*

Kochs, S.C. (1923). *Intelligence measurement: A psychological and statistical study based upon the Block-Design Test.* New York: Macmillan.

Little, S.G. (1991, October). Is the WISC-III factor structure valid? [letter to the editor]. *Communiqué*, p. 24.

Matarazzo, J.D. (1972). *Wechsler's measurement and appraisal of adult intelligence* (5th ed.). New York: Oxford University Press.

McDermott, P.A., Fantuzzo, J.W., & Glutting, J.J. (1990). Just say no to subtest analysis: A critique on Wechsler theory and practice. *Journal of Psychoeducational Assessment, 8*, 290–302.

McGrew, K.S. (1994). Clinical interpretation of the Woodcock-Johnson Tests of Cognitive Ability-Revised. Needham Heights, MA: Allyn & Bacon.

McGrew, K.S., & Flanagan, D.P. (1996, March). A cross-battery approach to intelligence test interpretation. A symposium presented at the Annual National Association of School Psychology, Atlanta, GA.

Meeker, M.N. (1969). *The structure of intellect.* Columbus, OH: Merrill.

National Association of School Psychologists. (1986). Principles for professional ethics. Silver Springs, MD: NASP.

National Association of School Psychologists. (1994). *Code of conduct manual.* Silver Springs, MD: NASP.

Newby, R.F., Recht, D.R., Cladwell, J., & Shaefer, J. (1993). Comparison of WISC-III and WISC-R IQ changes over a 2-year time span in a sample of children with dyslexia. [WISC-III Monograph]. *Journal of Psychoeducational Assessment.*

Phelps, L., Leguori, S., Nisewaner, K., & Parker, M. (1993). Practical interpretations of the WISC-III with language-disordered children. *Journal of Psychoeducational Assessment, Monograph Series, Advances in Psychoeducational Assessment, Wechsler Intelligence Scale for Children: Third Edition, 71–76.*

Post, K.R., & Mitchell, H.R. (1993). The WISC-III: A reality check. *Journal of School Psychology, 31,* 541–545.

Prifitera, A., & Dersh, J. (1993). Base rates of WISC-II diagnostic subtest patterns among normal, learning-disabled, and ADHD samples. *Journal of Psychoeducational Assessment, Monograph Series, Advances in Psychoeducational Assessment, Wechsler Intelligence Scale for Children: Third Edition, 43–55.*

Roid, G.H., Prifitera, A., & Weiss, L.G. (1993). Replication of the WISC-III factor structure in an independent sample. *Journal of Psychoeducational Assessment, Monograph Series, Advances in Psychoeducational Assessment, Wechsler Intelligence Scale for Children: Third Edition, 6–21.*

Salvia, J., & Ysseldyke, J.E. (1995). *Assessment* (6th ed.) Boston: Houghton Mifflin.

Sattler, J.M. (1982). Assessment of children's intelligence and special abilities (2nd ed.). Boston: Allyn & Bacon.

Sattler, J.M. (1988). *Assessment of children* (3rd ed., Rev. reprint). San Diego: Jerome M. Sattler.

Sattler, J.M. (1992). *Assessment of children: WISC-III and WPPSI-R supplement.* San Diego: Jerome M. Sattler.

Schwean, V.L., Saklofske, D.H., Yackulic, R.A., & Quinn, D. (1993). WISC-III performance of ADHD children. *Journal of Psychoeducational Assessment, Monograph Series, Advances in Psychoeducational Assessment, Wechsler Intelligence Scale for Children: Third Edition, 56–70.*

Shaw, S.R., Swerdlik, M.E., & Laurent, J. (1993). Review of the WISC-III. *Journal of Psychoeducational Assessment, Monograph Series, Advances in Psychoeducational Assessment, Wechsler Intelligence Scale for Children: Third Edition, 151–160.*

Slate, J.R., & Chick, D. (1989). WISC-R examiner errors: Cause for concern. *Psychology in the Schools, 26,* 78–83.

Slate, J.R., & Saarnio, D.A. (1995). Differences between WISC-III and WISC-R IQs: A preliminary investigation. *Journal of Psychoeducational Assessment, 13,* 340–346.

Slate, J.R., & Saddler, C.D. (1990, October). Improved but not perfect. NASP *Communiqué,* p. 20.

Spearman, C. (1927). *The abilities of man.* New York: MacMillan.

Stern, W. (1914). *The psychological methods for testing intelligence.* Baltimore, MD: Warwick & York.

Sternberg, R.J. (1985). *Beyond IQ: A triarchic theory of human intelligence.* London: Cambridge University Press.

Sternberg, R.J. (1993). Rocky's back again: A review of the WISC-III. *Journal of Psychoeducational Assessment, Monograph Series, Advances in Psychoeducational Assessment, Wechsler Intelligence Scale for Children: Third Edition,* 161–164.

Teeter, P.A., & Smith, P.L. (1993). WISC-III and WJ-R predictive and discriminant validity for students with severe emotional disturbance. *Journal of Psychoeducational Assessment, Monograph Series, Advances in Psychoeducational Assessment, Wechsler Intelligence Scale for Children: Third Edition,* 114–124.

Test User Training Work Group of the Joint Committee on Testing Practices (1993). *Responsible test use: Case studies for assessing human behavior.* Washington, DC: APA.

Vance, H.B. (1993). Future trends in assessment. In H.B. Vance (Ed.), *Best practices in assessment for school and clinical settings.* Brandon: Clinical Psychology Publishing Co./ New York: Wiley.

Wechsler, D. (1939). *The measurement of adult intelligence.* Baltimore: Williams & Wilkins.

Wechsler, D. (1946). *The Wechsler-Bellevue Intelligence Scale, Form II.* New York: The Psychological Corporation.

Wechsler, D. (1949). *Manual for the Wechsler Intelligence Scale for Children.* New York: The Psychological Corporation.

Wechsler, D. (1958). *The measurement and appraisal of adult intelligence* (4th ed.). Baltimore: Williams & Wilkins.

Wechsler, D. (1974). *Manual for the Wechsler Intelligence Scale for Children-Revised.* San Antonio, TX: The Psychological Corporation.

Wechsler, D. (1991). *Manual for the Wechsler Intelligence Scale for Children-Third Edition.* San Antonio, TX: The Psychological Corporation.

Weiss, L.G. (1995). *Assessment Focus, 1.* San Antonio, TX: The Psychological Corporation.

Woodcock, R.W. (1990). Theoretical foundations of the WJ-R measures of cognitive ability. *Journal of Psychoeducational Assessment, 8,* 231–258.

Woodcock, R.W. (1993). An information processing view of Gf-Gc theory. [WJ-R Monograph]. *Journal of Psychoeducational Assessment,* 80–102.

Chapter 9 ———————————————————————

ASSESSING SOCIAL SKILLS AND PEER RELATIONS

KENNETH W. MERRELL

In recent years, assessment and treatment of social skills has become an increasingly important endeavor within the fields of school psychology, clinical child psychology, and special education. This chapter provides an overview of some important issues and methods in assessing social skills and peer relations of children and youth. First, the components of social competence are discussed. Next, the importance of social skills and peer relations during the developmental period is addressed. Assessment of social skills and peer relations using behavior rating scales and sociometric procedures is then covered. A case study is presented to illustrate the practical and clinical aspects of social behavior assessment. The chapter ends with a discussion of best practice in assessing social skills and peer relations, including designing and conducting assessments and linking assessment data to interventions.

THE COMPONENTS OF SOCIAL COMPETENCE

Social competence is a complex, multidimensional construct that consists of a variety of behavioral and cognitive variables, as well as different aspects of emotional adjustment, that are useful and necessary in developing adequate social relations and obtaining desirable social outcomes. Gresham (1986) conceptualized the domain of social competence as comprising the following three subdomains: *adaptive behavior, social skills,* and *peer acceptance* (*peer relations*). Each of these three areas is discussed as follows.

Adaptive Behavior

A widely accepted definition of adaptive behavior is that it is "the effectiveness or degree with which the individual meets the standards of personal independence and social responsibility" (Grossman, 1983, p. 1). Adaptive behavior is assumed to be a developmental construct in that expectations for independent and responsible behavior vary based upon age (Reschly, 1990). It is also important to consider that adaptive behaviors must be viewed within cultural and environmental contexts in that expectations and demands for independence and responsibility vary based upon an individual's specific culture or subculture (Reschly, 1990). The assessment of adaptive behavior is a critical aspect in the classification of developmental delays and mental retardation. The most recent definition of mental retardation by the American Association on Mental Retardation (AAMR) includes the construct of adaptive behavior or adaptive functioning as a critical component of assessment and classification (AAMR, 1992).

Social Skills

Social skills have been given cognitive, behavioral, ecological, and social validity definitions (Merrell, Merz, Johnson, & Ring, 1992). For purposes of this chapter, a good working definition of social skills is that they are specific behaviors that when initiated lead to desirable social outcomes. Gresham and Elliott (1984) consider this definition to be from a social validity perspective, because the practical social outcomes of social behaviors are emphasized. From a behavioral standpoint, initiation of social skills increases the probability of reinforcement and decreases the probability of punishment or extinction based upon one's socially related behavior (Gresham & Reschly, 1987a). For children and youth, examples of classes of behavior representing social skills include academic and task-related competence, cooperation with peers, reinforcement of peer behavior, and social initiation behaviors.

Peer Acceptance

Although peer acceptance (which is referred to hereafter by a more generic label, *peer relations*) has been considered to be the third overall component or domain of social competence, it is often thought of as a *result or product* of one's social skills. This view of peer relations is reasonable in that one's social reputation and quality of social relations are in great measure a result of how effectively one interacts socially with peers (Landau & Milich, 1990; Oden & Asher, 1977). Positive peer relations are associated with peer acceptance, while negative peer relations are linked with peer rejection.

Because the assessment of adaptive behavior is addressed elsewhere in this book, and because such assessment is often for different purposes and may require different qualitative approaches than the assessment of social skills and peer relations, it will not be covered in this chapter. In addition to rating scale and sociometric assessment, children's social skills and peer relations can also be evaluated using such methods as direct behavioral observation, interviews, and analogue/role-play situations. However, developing an adequate understanding of these other three techniques would require a substantial and separate treatment of each, which is beyond the scope of this chapter. Therefore, the treatment of the subject of assessing social skills and peer relations will be limited to behavior rating scale and sociometric methods.

SOCIAL SKILLS AND PEER RELATIONS IN CHILDHOOD

A growing body of literature in the fields of child development, education, and psychology collectively points to the conclusion that the development of adequate social skills and peer relationships during childhood has important and far-reaching ramifications. It has been established that development of appropriate social skills is an important foundation for adequate peer relationships (Asher & Taylor, 1981). There is also evidence that childhood social skills and consequent peer relationships have a significant impact on academic success (Walker & Hops, 1976) during the school years. In reviewing the literature on peer relations, Hartup (1983) demonstrated that it is well established that the ability to relate effectively to others provides an essential contribution to the progress and development of the child.

Given that adequate social skills and peer relations are an important foundation for various types of success in life, it stands to reason that inadequate development in these areas is related to a variety of negative outcomes. A classic and frequently cited study by Cowen et al. (1973) involving an 11- to 13-year follow-up study of third-grade students provided convincing evidence that early peer relationship problems are strong predictors of mental health problems later in life. These researchers found that "peer judgment (using a negative peer nomination procedure) was, by far, the most sensitive predictor of later psychiatric difficulty" (p. 438). Other frequently cited studies have suggested that inadequate social skills and poor peer relations during childhood may lead to a variety of other problems later in life, such as juvenile delinquency, school drop-out, termination from employment, conduct-related discharge from military service, chronic unemployment and underemployment, and psychiatric hospitalizations (Loeber, 1985; Parker & Asher, 1987; Roff, 1963; Roff & Sells, 1968; Roff, Sells, & Golden, 1972).

As the literature on the social, emotional, and behavioral characteristics of children with disabilities continues to grow, it has become increasingly clear that these children are at significantly heightened risk for developing social skills deficits and experiencing peer relationship problems. Students identified as learning disabled have been found to experience high rates of social rejection by other children (Bryan, 1974; Cartledge, Frew, & Zacharias, 1985; Sater & French, 1989), be rated by teachers as having poor interpersonal behavior (Gresham & Reschly, 1987b), and exhibit maladaptive social behaviors in instructional settings (Epstein, Cullinan, & Lloyd, 1986; McKinney & Feagans, 1984; McKinney, McClure, & Feagans, 1982). Students identified as mentally retarded have been found to exhibit deficits in adaptive-social competencies (Gresham & Reschly, 1987b), experience high rates of peer rejection (Gresham, 1982), and receive inadequate amounts of social support (Park, Tappe, Carmeto, & Gaylord-Ross, 1990). Likewise, students identified as having behavior disorders have been found to be readily discriminated from nonhandicapped students by their maladaptive social-emotional behaviors (Merrell et al., 1992; Stumme, Gresham, & Scott, 1982; Vaughn, 1987) and experience significant rates of social rejection by other children (Hollinger, 1987). Therefore, clinicians who work with disabled and other at-risk children should be especially aware of the social problems these children face and keep up-to-date on appropriate methods of assessment.

ASSESSMENT WITH BEHAVIOR RATING SCALES

Behavior Rating Scales: An Overview

Behavior rating scales utilize summative paper-and-pencil judgments about a child by an informant who knows him or her well, most often a teacher or parent. These judgments are made using a standardized rating format, which yields scores that allow comparison between the subject and a normative group. Most rating scales now use an *algebraic* rating format, where the rater selects a number or other value that best represents the student's performance on the particular characteristic. For example, an algebraic response format for the item "Is physically aggressive" might have the rater select the value 0 if the statement is not true, 1 if the statement is sometimes true, and 2 if the statement is frequently true. Then, after completing the rating scale, the numerical value of the ratings would be added and compared in different configurations to those of a norm group. This type of format is more sophisticated and sensitive to behavioral change or intensity than a checklist format, which is *additive* in nature, in that the rater simply circles or checks items that seem to be true for the subject and then adds the number checked. Rating scales have gained wide popularity in educational and clinical settings, particularly for behavioral assessment (Merrell, 1994a).

Rating scales have become widely used because they offer several advantages as an assessment method. Although direct behavioral observation is a potentially excellent method for assessing social competence, rating scales are less expensive in terms of professional time and training required and are capable of providing data on low frequency but important behaviors that might not be seen in a limited number of direct observation sessions (Merrell, 1994a; Sattler, 1988). When compared to other assessment methods such as projective techniques and interviews, rating scales provide more objective and reliable data (Martin, Hooper, & Snow, 1986). Rating scales can be used to assess subjects who cannot readily provide information about themselves or be easily observed (e.g., very young children, or adolescents in lock-up units in hospitals or juvenile detention centers). Rating scales also capitalize on observations from the student's normal environment (school and home) and the observations of expert informants (teachers and parents).

Notwithstanding the popularity and advantages of rating scales, there are certain problems associated with their use that need to be considered in order to use them effectively. Two types of problems with rating scales have been discussed by Martin et al. (1986). The first type of problem is referred to as *bias of response,* meaning that the way that informants complete rating scales may create additional error in the resulting scores. Three types of response bias are particularly problematic, including *halo effects* (e.g., a teacher rating a student as having good behavioral characteristics because that student does well on academic work); *leniency or severity* (the tendency of some raters to be overly generous or overly critical in their ratings of all subjects); and *central tendency effects* (the tendency of raters to select midrange rating points and avoid extreme ratings such as "never" or "frequently"). The second type of problem is that rating scale scores are subject to four different kinds of *variance,* including *source variance* (the way that ratings vary between different raters); *setting variance* (the way that ratings might differ across different classroom settings, or between school and home); *temporal variance* (the way that behavior ratings change over time based on changes in the rater or the subject); and *instrument variance* (different results obtained by using different rating scales). The recommended way of dealing with these two types of problems in rating scales is to use a multisource, multisetting, multiinstrument assessment design, which reduces the chance for bias and error by obtaining ratings of the subject from different informants, in different settings, and using different types of rating scales (Martin, 1988; Merrell, 1994a).

A Review of Five Social Skills Rating Scales

Until the mid-1980s, there was a dearth of nationally standardized behavior rating scales for assessing social skills and peer relations. Most rating scales developed prior to this time were designed for the express purpose of assessing behavior problems, and there was a much smaller body of research on children's social competence. However, during the past several years there has been a significant increase in interest and research in children's social competence, and one of the results of this increase has been the development of several psychometrically sound standardized assessment instruments. This section of the chapter provides an overview of five behavior rating scales or systems useful for assessing social competence and peer relations of children and adolescents: the Child Behavior Checklist, the Preschool and Kindergarten Behavior Scales, the School Social Behavior Scales, the Social Skills Rating System, and the Walker-McConnell Scales of Social Competence and School Adjustment. These five instruments do not represent all that is currently available in this area, but they were selected for inclusion in this chapter because they all are norm referenced using nationwide standardization groups, psychometrically acceptable, designed to be specifically useful for assessment of social skills and peer relations, and commercially published and thus widely available. A brief overview of each of these instruments, in alphabetical order, follows.

The Child Behavior Checklist

The Child Behavior Checklist (CBC; Achenbach, 1991a, 1991b) system developed by Achenbach and his colleagues has been considered to be perhaps the most sophisticated problem behavior rating scale system currently available (Martin, 1988). The system includes a parent checklist, a teacher checklist, a self-report form for older children and adolescents, and a direct behavioral observation form. Although the rating scales in this system are best known and best used as instruments for the assessment of child psychopathology, the version for use by parents and parent surrogates, the Child Behavior Checklist, also includes a social competence scale that is useful in social skills assessment in conjunction with problem behavior assessment. The rating scale version for teachers, the Teacher's Report Form (TRF) (Achenbach, 1991b), includes a series of nonbehavior problem items conceptually similar to the Social Competence scale of the CBC, which is referred to as the Adaptive Functioning scale. However, the items on this scale of the TRF are almost entirely related to academic achievement and adjustment and are thus not designed to be a complete measure of social skills or peer relations; therefore, only the Social

Competence scale of the CBC will be overviewed in this chapter. Since the Behavior Problem scales of the CBC are reviewed elsewhere in this book, they will not be covered in this chapter.

The CBC was designed as a rating scale for parents of children and adolescents ages 4 to 18. The Social Competence scale of the CBC is located on the first and second pages of the rating form, just after the demographic information section and before the Behavior Problem scales. The Social Competence scales include 20 items in seven sections wherein the child is rated on participation in various activities such as sports, hobbies, organizations, jobs, and chores, and is rated as to the quality and quantity of relationships with siblings and peers. For children ages 6 and older, the parent also provides a rating of their performance on academic tasks and their behavioral adjustment in school.

Unlike the Behavior Problem scales of the CBC, the Social Competence items do not utilize a common standard rating format for each item—the rating format for each section differs somewhat depending on the nature of the rating task. For example, in Section I, the parent lists up to three sports the child most likes to participate in and in Section II lists up to three hobbies, activities, or games other than sports that the child most likes. The parent then provides an estimate of how much time the child spends at each activity compared to other children (ranging from "less than average" to "more than average") and an estimate of how well the child is able to perform each activity in comparison to same-age peers (ranging from "below average" to "above average"). In Section III the parent lists up to three organizations or clubs the child belongs to and in Section IV lists up to three jobs or chores the child routinely does and then compares the child's participation and effectiveness in these areas to that of same-age peers, ranging from "below average" to "above average." Section V asks the parent to list how many close friends the child has (with rating points ranging from none to 4 or more) and then estimate how well the child gets along with peers and parents, as well as play and work independently. The remaining two sections of the Social Competence scale (VI and VI) ask the parent to rate the child's performance in different academic subjects (ranging from "failing" to "above average") and then respond with a "Yes" or "No" answer to questions related to specific academic issues and problems.

Items on the CBC Social Competence scales are scored using the scoring system outlined in the CBC manual. The directions must be followed carefully, as procedures for scoring items in each of the seven sections vary somewhat. Raw scores are then calculated for three designated areas (Activities, Social, and School) as well as a Social Competence Total. After these area and total raw scores have been calculated, they are converted to normalized T scores ($M = 50$, $SD = 10$), based on the CBC normative samples at different age levels. Higher scores reflect more positive social competence attributes, while lower scores reflect poorer social competence.

The CBC was restandardized in 1991 using a large, nationwide sample. Extensive information on the technical aspects of the CBC standardization is provided in the scale manual, and the psychometric properties of the Social Competence scales are adequate to excellent. Test-retest reliability coefficients by gender and age at 1-week intervals range from .68 to .98 for the three area scores and from .76 to .92 for the total score. The mean r based on gender and age level breakdowns for stability coefficients at 6- and 18-month intervals is .47 to .76. Interrater reliability coefficients for interparent agreement on the combined age and gender samples range from .44 to .81 for the area scores and is reported at .59 for the total score.

The Social Competence scales of the CBC differ from the other scales reviewed in this section of the chapter in that they consist of fewer rating items (20) and provide a different format for rating, but they should still be considered a useful screening tool for assessing social competence. The main limitation of using this part of the CBC for assessing social skills and peer relations is that the number and scope of items is limited, and it thus does not represent the broader domain of social competence in as much detail as some other instruments. However, this instrument has the advantage of being linked to the Behavior Problem scales of the CBC, which are highly regarded for their sophistication in assessing child psychopathology. Thus, the CBC is useful as a screening device for social competence, particularly when the referral issues include the existence of severe behavior problems.

Preschool and Kindergarten Behavior Scales

The Preschool and Kindergarten Behavior Scales (PKBS; Merrell, 1994b) is a 76-item behavior rating scale designed to measure both social skills and problem behaviors in the early childhood/preschool population (ages 3 to 6). This instrument may be completed by parents, teachers, daycare providers, or others who frequently observe a given child's behavior. It was developed with a national normative sample of 2,855 children from 16 different states representing each of the 4 U.S. geographical regions, and that approximated the general U.S. population in terms of gender, ethnicity, and socioeconomic status. For example, 51% of the standardization sample was male and 49% female; 80% of the sample was Caucasian and 20% members of racial or ethnic minority groups (12.1, African American; 5.2, Hispanic; 1.5, Asian or Pacific Islander; .01, American Indian; and 1.2, "other"). Based on parent occupation, general similarity was found in occupational categories of the normative population when compared with the most recent occupational breakdown statistics from the U.S. Bureau of the Census. Rather than being a downward extension of a rating scale designed for use with older children or adolescents, the PKBS and its items were designed specifically with the unique social-emotional aspects of the early childhood/preschool developmental period in mind, employing systematic item development and content validation procedures.

The PKBS items consist of two separate scales, each designed to measure a different domain—a 34-item Social Skills scale (shown in Figure 9–1), and a 42-item Problem Behavior scale. Each of these two scales includes an empirically derived subscale structure. The Social Skills scale includes the following subscales: Social Cooperation (12 items describing cooperative and self-restraint behaviors); Social Interaction (11 items reflecting social initiation behaviors); and Social Independence (11 items reflective of behaviors that are important in gaining independence within the peer group). The Problem Behavior scale includes two broad-band subscales, Internalizing Problems and Externalizing Problems. Consistent with the theoretical and empirical breakdown of the internalizing/externalizing problem dichotomy (see Cicchetti & Toth, 1991), the latter broad-band scale includes 27 items describing undercontrolled behavioral problems such as overactivity, aggression, coercion, and antisocial behaviors, while the former broad-band scale includes 15 items describing

P K B S

Scale A
Social Skills

	Never	Rarely	Sometimes	Often	Scoring Key		
1. Works or plays independently	0	1	2	3			
2. Is cooperative	0	1	2	3			
3. Smiles and laughs with other children	0	1	2	3			
4. Plays with several different children	0	1	2	3			
5. Tries to understand another child's behavior ("Why are you crying?")	0	1	2	3			
6. Is accepted and liked by other children	0	1	2	3			
7. Follows instructions from adults	0	1	2	3			
8. Attempts new tasks before asking for help	0	1	2	3			
9. Makes friends easily	0	1	2	3			
10. Shows self-control	0	1	2	3			
11. Is invited by other children to play	0	1	2	3			
12. Uses free time in an acceptable way	0	1	2	3			
13. Is able to separate from parent without extreme distress	0	1	2	3			
14. Participates in family or classroom discussions	0	1	2	3			
15. Asks for help from adults when needed	0	1	2	3			
16. Sits and listens when stories are being read	0	1	2	3			
17. Stands up for other children's rights ("That's his!")	0	1	2	3			
18. Adapts well to different environments	0	1	2	3			
19. Has skills or abilities that are admired by peers	0	1	2	3			
20. Comforts other children who are upset	0	1	2	3			
21. Invites other children to play	0	1	2	3			
22. Cleans up his/her messes when asked	0	1	2	3			
23. Follows rules	0	1	2	3			
24. Seeks comfort from an adult when hurt	0	1	2	3			
25. Shares toys and other belongings	0	1	2	3			
26. Stands up for his/her rights	0	1	2	3			
27. Apologizes for accidental behavior that may upset others	0	1	2	3			
28. Gives in or compromises with peers when appropriate	0	1	2	3			
29. Accepts decisions made by adults	0	1	2	3			
30. Takes turns with toys and other objects	0	1	2	3			
31. Is confident in social situations	0	1	2	3			
32. Responds appropriately when corrected	0	1	2	3			
33. Is sensitive to adult problems ("Are you sad?")	0	1	2	3			
34. Shows affection for other children	0	1	2	3			
				Totals	A1	A2	A3

Figure 9–1.   Social skills items of the Preschool and Kindergarten Behavior Scales from Page 2 of the PKBS Rating Form (Merrell, 1993a)

overcontrolled behavioral/emotional problems such as social withdrawal, anxiety, somatic complaints, and behaviors consistent with depressive symptomatology. The Externalizing Problems broad-band scale includes three narrow-band scales (Self-Centered/Explosive, Attention Problems/Overactive, and Antisocial/Aggressive), while the Internalizing Problems broad-band scale includes two narrow-band scales (Social Withdrawal and Anxiety/Somatic Problems). Research findings presented in the PKBS test manual provide evidence for adequate to excellent psychometric properties. Internal consistency reliability estimates for the Social Skills and Problem Behavior total scores are .96 and .97, respectively. Test-retest reliability estimates at 3-month intervals were respectively found to be .69 and .78. Child ratings by pre-school teachers and teacher aides for the respective total scores have been shown to correlate at .48 and .59. Validity of the PKBS has thus far been demonstrated through a number of different psychometric procedures detailed in the manual. Content validity has been demonstrated through documentation of the item development procedures and through showing moderate to high correlations between individual items and total scores. Construct validity has been demonstrated through analysis of intrascale relationships, factor analytic findings with structural equation modeling, documentation of sensitivity to gender differences, and differences between develop-mentally delayed and "normal" children. Convergent and discriminant construct validity has been demonstrated through examining relationships with four other established preschool behavior-rating scales (Merrell, 1995). Social skills items of the PKBS are presented in Figure 9–1.

School Social Behavior Scales

The School Social Behavior Scales (SSBS; Merrell, 1993a) is a social behavior rating scale for use by teachers and other school personnel in assessing both social competence and antisocial problem behaviors of students in grades K through 12. It includes two separate scales with a total of 65 items that describe both positive and negative social behaviors that commonly occur in educational settings. Items are rated using a 5-point scale ranging from "never" (1) to "frequently" (5). Each of the two scales of the SSBS yields a total score using a raw to standard score conversion with a mean of 100 and standard deviation of 15. The two scales each have three subscales, with scores reported as four different Social Functioning Levels, includ-ing High Functioning, Average, Moderate Problem, and Significant Problem.

Scale A, Social Competence, includes 32 items that describe adaptive, prosocial behavioral competencies as they commonly occur in educational settings. Subscale A1 (Interpersonal Skills) includes 14 items measuring social skills that are impor-tant in establishing positive relationships with and gaining social acceptance from peers (e.g., "Offers help to other students when needed," and "Interacts with a wide variety of peers"). Subscale A2 (Self-Management Skills) includes 10 items measuring social skills relating to self-restraint, cooperation, and compliance with the demands of school rules and expectations (e.g., "Responds appropriately when corrected by teacher," and "Shows self-restraint"). Subscale A3 (Academic Skills) consists of eight items relating to competent performance and engagement on aca-demic tasks (e.g., "Completes individual seatwork without being prompted," and "Completes assigned activities on time"). The items from the SSBS Social Compe-tence scale are presented in Figure 9–2.

Scale A
Social Competence

	Never	Sometimes		Frequently	Scoring Key
1. Cooperates with other students in a variety of situations	1	2	3	4	5
2. Appropriately transitions between classroom activities	1	2	3	4	5
3. Completes individual seatwork without being prompted	1	2	3	4	5
4. Offers help to other students when needed	1	2	3	4	5
5. Effectively participates in group discussions and activities	1	2	3	4	5
6. Understands other students' problems and needs	1	2	3	4	5
7. Remains calm when problems arise	1	2	3	4	5
8. Listens to and carries out directions from teacher	1	2	3	4	5
9. Invites other students to participate in activities	1	2	3	4	5
10. Asks for clarification of instructions in an appropriate manner	1	2	3	4	5
11. Has skills or abilities that are admired by peers	1	2	3	4	5
12. Is accepting of other students	1	2	3	4	5
13. Accomplishes assignments and other tasks independently	1	2	3	4	5
14. Completes assigned activities on time	1	2	3	4	5
15. Will compromise with peers when appropriate	1	2	3	4	5
16. Follows classroom rules	1	2	3	4	5
17. Behaves appropriately in a variety of school settings	1	2	3	4	5
18. Appropriately asks for assistance as needed	1	2	3	4	5
19. Interacts with a wide variety of peers	1	2	3	4	5
20. Produces work of acceptable quality for his/her ability level	1	2	3	4	5
21. Is skillful at initiating or joining conversations with peers	1	2	3	4	5
22. Is sensitive to feelings of other students	1	2	3	4	5
23. Responds appropriately when corrected by teacher	1	2	3	4	5
24. Controls temper when angry	1	2	3	4	5
25. Appropriately enters ongoing activities with peers	1	2	3	4	5
26. Has good leadership skills	1	2	3	4	5
27. Adjusts to different behavioral expectations across school settings	1	2	3	4	5
28. Compliments others' attributes or accomplishments	1	2	3	4	5
29. Is appropriately assertive when he/she needs to be	1	2	3	4	5
30. Is sought out by peers to join activities	1	2	3	4	5
31. Shows self-restraint	1	2	3	4	5
32. Is "looked up to" or respected by peers	1	2	3	4	5
				Totals	
					A1	A2	A3

Figure 9–2.   Social competence items of the School Social Behavior Scales from Page 2 of the SSBS Rating Form (Merrell, 1993a)

Scale B, Antisocial Behavior, includes 33 negatively worded items describing problematic behaviors that are either other-directed in nature or are likely to lead to negative social consequences such as peer rejection or strained relationships with the teacher. Subscale B1 (Hostile-Irritable) consists of 14 items that describe behaviors considered to be self-centered, annoying, and likely to lead to peer rejection (e.g., "Will not share with other students" and "Argues and quarrels with other students"). Subscale B2, (Antisocial-Aggressive), consists of 10 behavioral descriptors relating to overt violation of school rules and intimidation or harm to others (e.g., "Gets into fights" and "Takes things that are not his/hers"). Subscale B3 (Disruptive-Demanding) includes 9 items that reflect behaviors likely to disrupt ongoing school activities and place excessive and inappropriate demands on others (e.g., "Is overly demanding of teacher's attention" and "Is difficult to control").

A number of studies and procedures are reported in the SSBS manual and elsewhere concerning the psychometric properties and validity of the instrument. The scales were standardized on a group of 1,858 students (kindergarten through grade 12) from the United States, with each of the four U.S. geographical regions represented in the standardization process. The percentage of students with disabilities in various classification categories in the standardization group very closely approximates the national percentages of these figures. Various reliability procedures reported in the SSBS manual indicate the scales have good to excellent stability and consistency. Internal consistency and split-half reliability coefficients range from .91 to .98. Test-retest reliability at 3-week intervals is reported at .76 to .83 for the Social Competence scores and .60 to .73 for the Antisocial Behavior scores. Interrater reliability between resource room teachers and paraprofessional aides ranges from .72 to .83 for the Social Competence scores and .53 to .71 for the Antisocial Behavior scores.

Validity of the scales has been demonstrated in several ways. Moderate to high correlations between the SSBS and five other behavior rating scales (including the Child Behavior Checklist, 39-item version of the Conners Teacher Rating Scale, Teacher's Report Form, Waksman Social Skills Rating Scale, and the adolescent version of the Walker-McConnell Scale of Social Competence and School Adjustment) indicates that the scale has good convergent construct validity. Other findings indicate that the scales can adequately discriminate between gifted and typical students (Merrell & Gill, 1994), special-education and regular-education students (Merrell, 1993b), and behavior disordered and other special-education students (Merrell, Sanders, and Popinga, 1993). The factor structure of the two scales is strong, with all items having a factor loading into their respective subscale of .50 or greater and no items being duplicated across subscales.

The SSBS appears to be useful as a school-based rating scale that provides norm-referenced data on both positive social skills and antisocial problem behavior. It has satisfactory to good psychometric properties, is easy to use, and the items and structure are highly relevant to the types of behavioral issues encountered by school-based professionals. It should be noted that the Antisocial Behavior scale is designed specifically to measure behavior problems that are directly social in nature or that would have an immediate impact on strained relations with peers and teachers. The scale was not designed to measure overcontrolled or internalizing behavior problems such as those associated with depression and anxiety, nor was it designed to measure behavior problems associated with attention deficit/hyperactivity disorder. If these types of problem behavior are a significant issue on an assessment case, the assessment should be bolstered by the addition of an appropriate measure designed specifically for these behaviors.

The Social Skills Rating System

The Social Skills Rating System (SSRS) (Gresham & Elliott, 1990) is a multicomponent social skills rating system that focuses on behaviors that affect parent-child relations, teacher-student relations, and peer acceptance. The system includes separate rating scales for teachers and parents as well as a self-report form for students. Each component of the system can be used alone or in conjunction with the other forms. Separate instruments and norms are provided for each of three developmental groups, which include preschool level (ages 3 to 5), elementary level (grades K to 6), and secondary level (grades 7 to 12). Since a detailed description and review of each of the several SSRS forms is beyond the scope of this chapter, an overview of only the elementary level teacher rating form will be provided herein. Because there are considerable conceptual similarities between the different forms and age-level versions in the system, this description will provide the reader with an understanding that generalizes in many ways to the different forms within the system.

The elementary level teacher rating form of the SSRS consists of 57 items divided over three scales, Social Skills, Problem Behaviors, and Academic Competence. For Social Skills and Problem Behaviors, teachers respond to items using a 3-point response format based on how often a given behavior occurs (0 = never, 1 = sometimes, and 2 = very often). On the Social Skills items, teachers are also asked to rate how important a skill is (on a 3-point scale) to success in the classroom. The importance rating is not used to calculate ratings for each scale but is used for planning interventions. On the Academic Competence scale, teachers rate students as compared to other students on a 5-point scale. Scale raw scores are converted to standard scores ($M = 100$, $SD = 15$) and percentile ranks. Subscale raw scores are converted to estimates of functional ability called Behavior Levels.

The Social Skills scale consists of 30 items that rate social skills in the areas of teacher and peer relations. This scale contains three subscales: Cooperation, Assertion, and Self-Control. The Cooperation subscale identifies compliance behaviors that are important for success in classrooms (e.g., "Finishes class assignments on time" and "Uses time appropriately while waiting for help"). The Assertion subscale includes initiating behaviors that involve making and maintaining friendships and responding to actions of others (e.g., "Invites others to join in activities" and "Appropriately questions rules that may be unfair"). The Self-Control subscale includes responses that occur in conflict situations like turn-taking and peer criticism (e.g., "Cooperates with peers without prompting" and "Responds appropriately to teasing by peers").

The Problem Behaviors scale consists of 18 items reflecting behaviors that might interfere with social skills performance. The items are divided into three subscales: Externalizing Problems, Internalizing Problems, and Hyperactivity. The Externalizing Problems subscale items reflect inappropriate behaviors that indicate verbal and physical aggression toward others and a lack of temper control (e.g., "Threatens or bullies others" and "Has temper tantrums"). The subscale Internalizing Problems includes behaviors that indicate anxiety, sadness, and poor self-esteem (e.g., "Shows anxiety about being with a group of children" and "Likes to be alone"). The Hyperactivity subscale includes activities that involve excessive movement and impulsive actions (e.g., "Disturbs ongoing activities" and "Acts impulsively").

The third scale, Academic Competence, includes nine items that reflect academic functioning, such as performance in specific academic areas, motivation level, general cognitive functioning, and parental support (e.g., "In terms of grade-level expectations, this child's skills in reading are:_____" and "The child's overall motivation to succeed academically is:_____"). Behavior is rated on a 5-point scale that corresponds to percentages, ranging from lowest 10% (1) to highest 10% (5).

The SSRS was standardized on a national sample of more than 4,000 children representing all four U.S. geographical regions. The demographic information is difficult to interpret because the manual does not provide a clear normative breakdown based on the different test forms. However, given the overall large number of subjects rated in the SSRS national standardization, it should most likely be assumed that the norms for each rating form in the system were developed using a sufficient number of cases.

The scale manual states that overall psychometric properties obtained during scale development ranged from adequate to excellent. For the teacher scale, reliability was measured using internal consistency (i.e., alpha coefficients ranged from .74 to .95), interrater, and test-retest (i.e., .75 to .93 correlations across the three scales) procedures. Criterion-related and construct validity were established by finding significant correlations between the SSRS and other rating scales. Subscale dimensions were determined through factor analyses of each scale. Items that met a criterion of a .30 or greater factor loading were considered to load on a given factor.

The SSRS has the distinct strength of consisting of an integrated system of instruments for use by teachers, parents, and students. The manual is extremely well written, and the rating instruments have been designed to be easily usable and understandable. The sections of the instruments that measure social skills are very comprehensive and useful. The sections measuring problem behaviors and academic competence are quite brief and should be considered as short screening sections to be used in conjunction with a social skills assessment.

Walker-McConnell Scales of Social Competence and School Adjustment

The Walker-McConnell Scales of Social Competence and School Adjustment (SSCSA; Walker & McConnell, 1995a, 1995b) are social skills rating scales for teachers and other school-based professionals. Two versions of the scale are available, an elementary version for use with students in grades K to 6 and an adolescent version for use with students in grades 7 to 12. The elementary version contains 43 positively worded items that reflect adaptive social-behavioral competencies within the school environment. The items are rated using a 5-point scale ranging from "never occurs" (1) to "frequently occurs" (5). The scale yields standard scores on three subscales ($M = 10$, $SD = 3$) as well as a total score ($M = 100$, $SD = 15$), which is a composite of the three subscales. Subscale 1 (Teacher-Preferred Social Behavior) includes 16 items that measure peer-related social behaviors highly valued by teachers that reflect their concerns for empathy, sensitivity, self-restraint, and cooperative, socially mature peer relationships (e.g., "Is considerate of the feelings of others" and "Is sensitive to the needs of others"). Subscale 2 (Peer-Preferred Social Behavior) includes 17 items that measure peer-related social behaviors highly valued by other children that reflect peer values involving social relationships, dynamics, and skills in free-play settings (e.g., "Spends recess and free time interacting with peers" and "Invites peers to play or share activities"). Subscale 3 (School Adjustment Behavior) includes 10 items reflecting social-behavior competencies that are especially important in academic instructional settings, such as having good work and study habits, following academic instructions, and behaving in ways conducive to classroom management (e.g., "Attends to assigned tasks" and "Displays independent study skills").

The adolescent version of the scale is very similar to the elementary version in that it was designed as an upward extension of this scale. The adolescent version includes the 43 items from the elementary version (with 9 of the scale items having been revised to better reflect adolescent behavioral content) plus an additional 10 items designed to measure *self-related* social adjustment based on content from an adolescent social skills training curriculum (Walker, Todis, Holmes, & Horton, 1988). The factor structure of the adolescent version includes the same three factors found on the elementary version plus a fourth subscale (the Empathy subscale) containing six items. This fourth factor includes items designed to measure sensitivity and awareness in peer relationships (e.g., "Listens while others are speaking" and "Is considerate of the feelings of others"). The adolescent version of the scale uses the same rating format and scoring system as the elementary version, and the four subscale scores are summed into a total score.

Extensive information on the standardization data and psychometric properties of the two versions of the SSCSA are reported in the scale manual. The scales were standardized on groups of approximately 2,000 students representing all four U.S. geographical regions. Studies undertaken during the development of the scales that are cited in the scale manual indicate adequate to excellent psychometric properties.

Reliability of the scales was established using test-retest (e.g., .88 to .92 correlations over a 3-week period with 323 subjects), internal consistency (e.g., alpha coefficients ranging from .95 to .97), and interrater (e.g., a .53 correlation between teacher and aide ratings on the total score in a day treatment facility) procedures. Validity of the scales was assessed using a variety of procedures. Discriminant validity was established in studies that found the SSCSA to differentiate among groups of students who would be expected to differ behaviorally (behavior disordered and normal, antisocial and normal, behaviorally at-risk and normal, and those with and without learning problems). Criterion-related validity was demonstrated by finding significant correlations between the SSCSA and a number of criterion variables, including other rating scales, sociometric ratings, academic achievement measures, and a systematic behavioral screening procedure. Construct validity of the scales was demonstrated by, among other procedures, finding strong correlations between evaluative comments of subjects by their peers and teacher ratings on the scales and by finding low social skills ratings to be strongly associated with the emergence of antisocial behavior in a longitudinal study of elementary-age boys. A number of other psychometric validation studies are reported in the test manual that substantiate the reliability and validity of the scales. Subsequent investigations have found the SSCSA to correlate highly with other behavioral rating scales (Merrell, 1989) and to accurately discriminate groups of students referred for learning problems from average students (Merrell et al., 1992; Merrell & Shinn, 1990). The six-item Empathy subscale from the adolescent version of the SSCSA has been found to discriminate between a group of antisocial subjects with a record of arrests and an at-risk control group (Walker, Steiber, & Eisert, 1991). The factor structure of the SSCSA scales has been shown to be very strong.

Both versions of the SSCSA are brief, easy to use, and contain items that are highly relevant for assessing social skills in educational settings. The research base behind the scales is truly exemplary, particularly when considering that the scales have only recently been published. Since neither version of the SSCSA was designed to measure problem behaviors, these instruments should be supplemented with an appropriate problem behavior assessment if the referral issues warrant such an assessment.

ASSESSMENT WITH SOCIOMETRIC PROCEDURES

The essence of sociometric assessment procedures is obtaining information from within a peer group (usually in a classroom setting) concerning the social dynamics in that group. The key feature in these procedures is that assessment data on various aspects of social status of persons within the peer group *is obtained directly from its members* rather than through teacher ratings or observations by an impartial outside evaluator. These procedures allow the evaluator to tap directly into the ongoing social dynamics of a group, which is an obvious advantage as there tend to be many things that go on within a classroom environment that students are more aware of than the teacher is (Worthen, Borg, & White, 1993). Sociometric procedures have a long history of use in psychology and education and allow for assessment of such varied qualities as level of popularity, acceptance or rejection status, and attribution of specific positive and negative characteristics such as leadership ability, athletic or academic prowess, aggressiveness, and social awkwardness.

Early researchers in the use of sociometrics tended to view social status in a fairly unidimensional manner (Landau & Milich, 1990). However, more recent efforts in this area have led investigators to conclude that the construct of social status is both complex and multidimensional. For example, Coie, Dodge, and Cappotelli (1982) used peer preference questions in a sociometric technique with a large number ($n = 537$) of elementary and middle-school children, and analyzed the obtained data to develop five different social status groups: popular, rejected, average, neglected, and controversial. An analysis of characteristics of the students indicated that while there was some overlap between categories, each had some distinct features. Popular children were those who were rated by peers as being cooperative, having leadership ability, and engaging in very little disruptive behavior. Rejected children were rated as frequently fighting, being disruptive, and not being cooperative or having leadership traits. Neglected children were those who were largely ignored by other children and were seen as being socially unresponsive. The fourth nonaverage group, controversial children, tended to exhibit features of both the popular and rejected group, being considered disruptive and starting fights but also perceived as being assertive leaders. This conceptualization of social status ratings into five groups, which has been backed up by subsequent research, shows how complex social dynamics within peer groups can be and suggests that sociometric procedures can indeed provide complex and useful social assessment data.

Unlike many other assessment methods, including behavior rating scales, sociometric procedures are usually not norm referenced or commercially published. Instead, they tend to consist of different variations of a few relatively simple methods originally developed for use by researchers, but which are fully capable of being translated into school or clinical practice. The technical and psychometric aspects of these procedures have been researched in several studies and have generally shown favorable evidence of technical soundness. Temporal stability of sociometric assessments has been shown to be relatively high at both short- and long-term stability periods (Hartup, 1983; Roff et al., 1972). Landau and Milich (1990) reviewed several studies of interrater correspondence in sociometric procedures and noted that moderate to high levels of correspondence between raters has generally been found. However, there is one interesting and peculiar finding in this regard—a gender difference on social convergence in ratings wherein both boys and girls tend to ascribe more positive attributes to members of their own sex and more negative attributes to members of the opposite sex. Validity of sociometric assessment procedures has been established in several studies (such as the previously reviewed studies by Cowen et al., 1973, and Roff et al., 1972) wherein social status ratings were predictive of various types of social adjustment and maladjustment later in life. In sum, while sociometric assessment procedures tend not to be standardized or commercially published like most other tests used by psychologists, they have nonetheless been demonstrated to have generally favorable technical properties, and should be viewed as a potentially useful method of assessing peer relations and social status.

Four Sociometric Procedures

It is difficult to divide sociometric procedures into distinct categories because they tend to be nonstandardized and to have considerable overlap. However, there are certain similarities and differences between different methods that make a general categorization possible. This section provides an overview of four general types of sociometric procedures: peer nomination procedures, picture sociometric techniques, guess who measures, and the class play. In some cases these categories involve general descriptions common to many methods within the category. In other cases, the categorical description is rather unique to a specific procedure that has been developed.

Peer Nomination Procedures

The oldest and most widely used sociometric approach, which is the basis for most other types of sociometric measures as well, is the nomination method, originally introduced by Moreno (1934). The basis of the peer nomination technique is that students are asked to nominate or name classmates that they prefer according to specific positive criteria. This approach typically involves naming three classmates the students would most like to study with, play with during free time, work with on a class project, or participate with in some other positive way. For children with sufficient reading and writing ability, peer nomination procedures can be administered either by an item-by-peer matrix or a questionnaire on which they fill in names of classmates on blank lines following questions.

The item-by-peer matrix lists the names of all children in the class across the top of the page and the social interaction items vertically on the left side of the page. The students are instructed to put an *x* under the name(s) of the students to whom they think the item applies (e.g., "Which three students would you most like to have as your best friends?"). Use of a questionnaire format accomplishes essentially the same thing (e.g., "Write the names of three students in your class that you would most like to have as your best friends" followed by three numbered blank lines).

Scoring of peer nominations is typically done by totalling the number of nominations each child receives. Worthen et al. (1993) suggest that the results of positive peer nomination procedures can be classified and interpreted according to a frequently used set of criteria. *Stars* are individuals who are frequently chosen. *Isolates* are individuals who are never chosen in the process. *Neglectees* are those who receive only a few nominations. The results can also be plotted on a *sociogram* showing the patterns of choice for each student, which not only helps in identifying frequently and never-nominated students but is useful in showing cliques and small groups. A *mutual choice* occurs when an individual is chosen by the same student he or she selected. A *cross-sex choice* occurs when a boy chooses a girl or a girl chooses a boy. A *clique* is identified by finding a small group of students who choose each other and make few or no choices outside of that group. *Cleavage* is said to occur when two or more groups within the class or social unit are identified who never choose someone from the other group(s). Using these scoring and classification criteria, one can easily see how a procedure as deceptively simple as the peer nomination method can yield information that is both striking and complex. An example of a sociogram, using the results of a positive peer nomination procedure with a group of elementary-age girls, is presented in Figure 9–3.

Although the peer nomination technique has historically most often involved the use of positive items indicative of high social status, many practitioners and researchers have used variations of this method by employing negative nominations, using items that are created to identify students who are socially rejected by peers (e.g., "Who would you least like to play with" or "Who would you never want to be friends with"). The use of negative peer nomination procedures has proved to be controversial, with ethical questions being raised about the potential for negative effects. Although there is research indicating that sociometric assessment has no

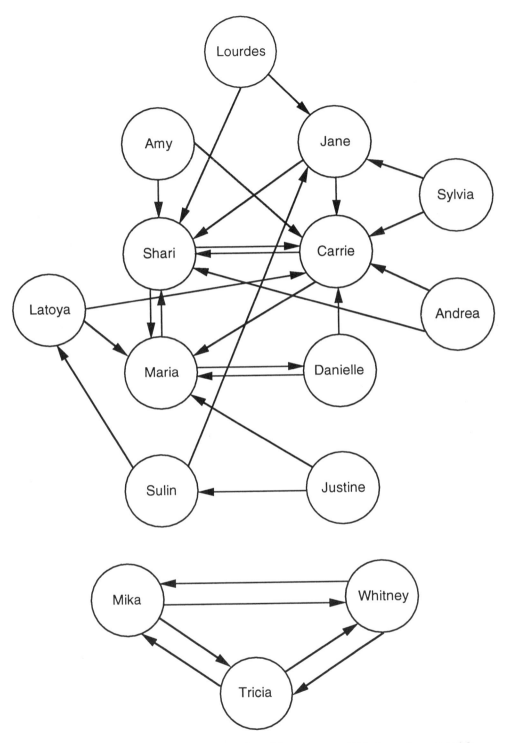

Figure 9–3. An example of a sociogram plotted for a group of 15 elementary-age girls who were asked to select the 2 girls in their classroom with whom they would most like to be friends

consequence on peer interactions (Hayvren & Hymel, 1984), many educators and parents disapprove of the use of these procedures when negative nominations are involved.

Picture Sociometric Techniques

Picture sociometric techniques involve individually presenting each child in a classroom an arbitrary assortment of photographs of each child in the class and then asking the child to answer a series of questions by pointing to or selecting a photograph of a peer. This method is an adaptation of other peer nomination methods that is useful for work with preliterate subjects. Landau and Milich (1990) state that it is the preferred method for preschool through second-grade subjects. Examples of questions that have been used with this technique include "Who do you like to play with the most?" "Who is your best friend?" and "Who is the best student in your class?" As with most other sociometric techniques, specific questions can be developed based on the clinical or research questions, and these questions can be produced to indicate either social acceptance or social rejection.

The original picture sociometric technique and minor variations of it are scored by totalling the number of times each child was nominated by classmates, based on questions indicating positive social status. Using this scoring scheme, rejected or neglected children would have significantly lower scores than accepted children with higher social status. Of course, variations in scoring procedure would be needed if there were any significant deviations in administration method from the original study by McCandless and Marshall (1957). For example, questions that reflect both positive (e.g., "Who do you most like to do schoolwork with?") and negative (e.g., "Who are you afraid to be around on the playground?") social status could be mixed, and the scoring system could be divided into positive and negative status categories.

The use of picture sociometrics was first reported by McCandless and Marshall (1957), and has subsequently been used in a number of other published studies. The psychometric properties of picture sociometric techniques have been shown to be quite good, with relatively high interrater reliability, very high short-term, test-retest reliability, and adequate long-term, test-retest reliability (see Landau & Milich, 1990). Validity of the picture sociometric method has been demonstrated by producing significant discriminations between groups of aggressive, aggressive-withdrawn, and normal boys (Milich & Landau, 1984). Interestingly, this technique has been shown to produce more effective discriminations of social status than information provided by teachers.

Guess Who Measures

The "guess who" technique is a sociometric approach wherein brief descriptions are provided to students and they write down the names of a few other students (usually three or fewer) they think best fit the descriptions. For example, the students might be asked to respond to descriptions such as "Guess who is often in trouble," "Guess who does the best job on schoolwork," "Guess who no one knows very well," or "Guess who is often angry at other children." The descriptions can be provided either verbally or in written format. The content of the items can be made up by the teacher, clinician, or researcher based on specific characteristics they are interested in identifying. The type of measure is scored by making simple frequency counts of each question/description. More elaborate scoring methods are also possible, such as grouping descriptions into categories of similar content (e.g., antisocial behaviors, helping characteristics, peer popularity, etc.) and obtaining frequency counts within each broader category.

An example of a "guess who" measure that has been used with a large number of students and has been carefully investigated is the Revised PRIME Guess Who Measure, which was developed for use in Project PRIME, a large-scale investigation of mildly handicapped students who had been integrated in regular education classrooms for part of their instructional day (Kauffman, Semmell, & Agard, 1974). The original instrument consisted of 29 questions/descriptions and was administered to over 13,000 students in grades 3 to 5. Factor analytic procedures conducted on the instrument divided the items into four major factors, which were labeled "disruptive," "bright," "dull," and "well behaved." A revised scale including 20 items (the 5 items contributing the most to each factor) was developed by Veldman and Sheffield (1979), who reported reliability coefficients ranging from .56 to .77 for each factor score and developed a satisfactory concurrent validity procedure for the instrument by correlating the instrument items with teacher ratings along similar dimensions.

In sum, the "guess who" technique is flexible, easy-to-administer and score, has been used in a large number of studies and projects, and has been found to have satisfactory technical properties. Clinicians and investigators desiring an adaptable, easy-to-administer sociometric measure may find "guess who" techniques to be a useful choice in assessment instrumentation.

The Class Play

The Class Play procedure was first utilized and described by Bower (1969) and has been further revised by Masten, Morrison, and Pelligrini (1985). It is a frequently used sociometric technique that has been employed in several large-scale investigations, including the classic 11-to-13 year follow-up study of elementary-age children by Cowen and his colleagues (1973). The basis of this procedure is that children are asked to assign their peers to various roles (usually both positive and negative roles) in an imaginary play. The original Class Play described by Bower (1969) included both positive (e.g., "someone who will wait their turn") and negative (e.g., "someone who is too bossy") roles, but consisted of a scoring procedure wherein only a single score (negative peer reputation) was derived, which was done by calculating the number of negative roles given to a child and dividing that by the total number of roles given to the child. Large percentages are supposed to indicate a high degree of peer rejection, while low percentages are meant to indicate that the child has higher social status. As is the case with most sociometric approaches, the specification of roles in the Class Play procedure (as well as the method of scoring) can be manipulated by the clinician or researcher to suit their goals. It should be noted that the scoring system advocated by Bower (1969) has been criticized as being on empirically shaky ground (Landau & Milich, 1990).

The use of the Class Play procedure in sociometric assessment is attractive for two reasons other than the measurement capabilities it may have. One advantage is that children (particularly younger children) appear to enjoy participating in make-believe plays and casting their peers into the various roles. The second is that teachers and administrators seem to view this type of procedure more positively than some other sociometric methods and so it is more likely to be supported and approved than some other approaches. Masten et al. (1985) suggest that because of the diversity of roles needed in a play, this procedure will reduce any probability of disapproving labels on children with high negative scores by other children in the rating/casting process.

Some Final Comments on Sociometric Procedures

The sociometric assessment approaches overviewed in this chapter, as well as other types of sociometric measures, have a great deal of appeal to clinicians and researchers and have a long history of use in psychology and education. However, these approaches are not without controversy. Many sociometric methods involve negative ranking or nomination procedures, or having children single out peers based on negative characteristics. Largely because of the use of these negative nomination procedures, parents (and some teachers and administrators) are often hesitant (or outright angry) at the possibility of their children participating in sociometric assessments for fear of their child or other children being singled out by peers and further ostracized because of it. Although there is little empirical evidence to completely warrant this assertion and some evidence to the contrary (Hayvren & Hymel, 1984), there seems to be a common concern that children will compare their responses after the assessment to find out which children were singled out for negative nominations, and this process will end up in increased isolation or social exile for the children who were commonly perceived in negative terms. The author is personally familiar with two separate research projects that had to undergo major methodological modifications when some parents and educators threatened to "shut the study down" because of outrage over the use of negative peer ranking or nomination procedures. Whether such concerns are founded or not, clinicians and researchers desiring to utilize sociometric approaches would do well to carefully pick the most appropriate method for their purposes, communicate closely and carefully with their constituent groups, and educate those involved on the purposes and procedures involved. In the meantime, additional research on any potential peer effects of sociometric measurement involving negative ranking or nomination should be conducted.

CONCLUSION

This chapter concludes with a discussion of best practices in the assessment of social skills and peer relations and an outline of suggested steps to consider in improving the quality and utility of assessments. Two areas of discussion are included. First, best practice issues relating to improving the technical quality and integrity of the assessment process are examined. Then, best practice issues

Case Example 9–1.   Assessing social behaviors—A behavior-disordered student

To illustrate how some of the assessment procedures discussed in this chapter may be utilized in school or clinical practice, a case study report is presented. This case study is based on an actual client who was referred to the author's clinical consulting practice. In order to protect the confidentiality of the case, the client's name and some identifying details have been changed. Only some of the assessment data obtained are actually reported in this case study. The actual assessment involved comprehensive intellectual, academic, and social-behavioral evaluation, much of which is tangential to an illustration of the assessment techniques discussed in this chapter.

NAME: Kayla S.
AGE: 13 years, 2 months
GRADE: 7

REASON FOR REFERRAL

Kayla S., a 13-year-old female student, was referred for this assessment as part of her three-year special-education reevaluation. Kayla is currently placed in the seventh grade at a middle school in an urban area in Utah, where she receives special-education services as behavior disordered under state and federal law. In making the request for this assessment, personnel from the school district specifically requested opinions on the following questions: Should Kayla continue to receive special-education services under her current eligibility category? and what types of intervention programming are most warranted at the present time?

BACKGROUND INFORMATION

Information pertinent to Kayla's academic and behavioral background was obtained through a review of her special-education file, and through interviews with her parents and her special-education teacher. Kayla has a long history of special-education placement for behavioral and learning problems. Reports from as early as her kindergarten year indicate the presence of significant social-emotional behavior problems, including consistent reports of noncompliance, outbursts and tantrums, refusal of requests from school personnel, and strained peer relations. Kayla's parents placed her in a psychiatric hospital for 2 weeks when she was 7 years old, after her noncompliant behavior and other social-emotional problems had escalated to the point where they were extremely difficult to control. Previous assessment and programming data also indicate that Kayla's intellectual ability is in the borderline range (with her most recent full scale IQ score being 76) and that she has academic learning problems in most areas, with mathematics being the most difficult academic task for her. She currently is placed in a self-contained special-education classroom 4 hours per day, and participates in a regular-education classroom (reading and written language block) for 2 hours per day, where she is accompanied and assisted by a special-education classroom aide.

Kayla's ethnic/cultural background is Caucasian, and English is the only language spoken in her home. She lives with both of her parents and her younger brother. Mr. and Mrs. S. have been closely involved in Kayla's education and are reported to be

(continued)

Case Example 9–1.   *(Continued)*

supportive of the school program as well as advocates for Kayla's educational needs. Her younger brother is currently 10 years old and is not reported to have any significant behavioral or academic problems at school. Kayla's parents report that she and her brother get along fairly well, though she frequently instigates fights with him.

ASSESSMENT PROCEDURES

The following assessment procedures were conducted for this assessment:

Direct behavioral observation in the special-education classroom

Child Behavior Checklist (completed by parents and two teachers)

School Social Behavior Scales (completed by special-education teacher)

Peer Nomination Sociometric Procedures in both classrooms

Diagnostic Interview with Kayla

ASSESSMENT RESULTS AND INTERPRETATION

Kayla was observed in her special-education classroom for a 30-minute period. The observation took place during the presentation of a unit on personal health. The observation consisted of an interval recording procedure designed to identify significant social and academic interactions in 20-minute intervals, and included social comparison information on the average behavior data of two other students who were alternately observed during the period. None of Kayla's social or emotional behaviors appeared especially problematic or differed from the comparison students during the observation period. However, Kayla's number of requests for help and clarification from the teacher and classroom assistant were twice as high as anyone else's in the classroom, she appeared to lack independent work skills, and constantly required interaction from adults in the classroom.

The Child Behavior Checklist (CBC) was completed jointly by Kayla's parents. On the Behavior Problems scales, significant elevations were present on the Internalizing ($T = 79$), Externalizing ($T = 78$) and Total ($T = 87$) broad-band scores. Behavior problems were rated as significant across all narrow-band domains, with no isolated problem patterns. On the Social Competence scales of the CBC, Kayla's scores were in the normal range in the Activities area ($T = 40$), but in the problem range in the Social ($T = 25$) and School ($T = 18$) areas. An inspection of the items in these areas revealed that she was rated as having peer relationship problems, having no close friends, and being below average in all academic areas. Kayla's social competence total score ($T = 25$) is also well below the normal score range.

The Teacher Report Form (TRF) of the CBC was completed on Kayla by both her regular and special-education teachers. The rating form completed by her regular-education teacher did not indicate any narrow or broad-band behavioral problem scores in the clinical range (sum $T = 64$) but several items were endorsed indicating peer relationship problems (e.g., "gets teased a lot" and "is not liked by other children"). It should be noted that Kayla is in this teacher's classroom only 2 hours per day and is accompanied by a special-education aide, which likely helps reduce the occurrence of social-behavioral problems. The TRF completed by her special-education

(continued)

Case Example 9–1.   *(Continued)*

teacher indicated a more severe pattern of problems. Both of the broad-band *T* scores (Internalizing = 68, Externalizing = 71) and the Sum *T* score (76) were at or close to the clinical range, and significant elevations were found on five of the narrow-band scores. An inspection of the pattern and endorsed items on the narrow-band scales was indicative of a pattern of problems involving oppositional-defiance, poor peer relationships, social immaturity, and inattentiveness during academic tasks.

Scores from the School Social Behavior Scales, which were completed by her special-education teacher, indicated an overall pattern of significant social skills deficits, accompanied by moderate elevations in antisocial behaviors. On the Social Competence scale, all three subscale scores (Interpersonal Skills, Self-Management Skills, and Academic Skills) were rated at the "significant problem" level, and the Social Competence Total score of 66 (which is at the first percentile or lower) showed a significant pattern of generalized social skills deficits. All three of Kayla's Antisocial Behavior subscale scores (Hostile-Irritable, Antisocial-Aggressive, and Demanding-Disruptive) were rated at the "moderate problem" level and her Antisocial Behavior Total score of 112 (78th percentile) indicated moderate levels of problem behavior excesses.

Sociometric assessment data were obtained earlier in the school year in both of Kayla's classrooms through the use of a peer nomination technique that included items describing both positive and negative social status. Scoring of these procedures was done by obtaining separate sums of positive and negative status items for each student. In terms of positive nominations, Kayla was not nominated by any students in the regular classroom and by only one student in the special-education classroom. On the negative items, Kayla received more nominations than any other student in her regular classroom (specifically, on the items "Who would you not want to be best friends with?" and "Who has problems with schoolwork?"). In the special-education classroom, Kayla's scores on positive items were within the average range for that class but her negative nomination scores were among the highest in the class, particularly on the item "Who is always in trouble with the teacher?" These patterns from the sociometric assessment are indicative of low social status and show a moderate to significant degree of social rejection by peers.

During the diagnostic interview with Kayla, several areas of questioning relevant to social skills and peer relations were pursued. Although she is rated by both teachers and students as having peer relationship problems, Kayla seems to have only a minor amount of insight about this. She stated that she gets along with most other students "just fine" and said that she has "lots of" friends, though she had difficulty naming them. She did admit that when other students tease her she sometimes calls them "dirty names," which usually results in an escalation of the situation. Kayla stated that she liked both of her teachers and her special-education classroom aide but acknowledged that when she gets tired or is in a bad mood she likes to "tell them what I think about them" and becomes uncooperative. The general impression of the interviewer was that Kayla wants to have more friends and to be teased less by other students, but does not seem to recognize either how to go about accomplishing this or the extent to which her negative behaviors affect her relationships with others.

(continued)

Case Example 9–1.   *(Continued)*

SUMMARY AND RECOMMENDATIONS

Kayla S., who has a long history of receiving special-education services as behavior disordered, was referred for a 3-year eligibility reevaluation. This case study involves only the social-emotional behavior aspects of the assessment. A moderate to significant pattern of behavior problems, social skills deficits, and social isolation and rejection was found through the results of the assessment process. It is the opinion of the examiner that Kayla should continue to qualify for special-education services under her current classification due to a longstanding pattern of inappropriate social-emotional behaviors coupled with significant social skills deficits and peer relationship problems.

Although Kayla's current educational placements and IEP goals appear to be appropriate and their continuation is warranted, some additional intervention recommendations are offered, based on the social assessment data, in order to better remediate some of the following concerns.

1. Kayla's intervention goals could be modified to include a plan for increasing her ability to work independently on academic tasks, without constant interaction from teachers. To successfully implement this plan, Kayla will likely need specific training in monitoring her own behavior, developing independent cognitive thinking strategies, and learning a series of steps to follow when she is having difficulties.

2. Kayla could benefit from additional intervention training in the area of self-management skills specifically aimed at helping her learn alternatives to tantrums and oppositional behavior. To successfully implement a goal in this area, Kayla would likely need to work on developing and practicing a list of appropriate alternatives to these negative behaviors, and her progress in this area should be reinforced through an appropriate reward system.

3. Kayla is in need of some specifically designed social skills training. The particular skills she appears to need the most training, modeling, and practice in are friendship making, developing appropriate alternatives to antisocial statements to peers, and increasing her awareness of and sensitivity to other persons.

---

appertaining to the process of linking social-behavioral assessment with interventions are overviewed.

Assessment Procedures

The first set of issues and recommendations discussed for suggested best practices relates to the overall quality of the assessment process. Through the incorporation of careful planning and the implementation of certain procedures, the technical quality and overall utility and success of the assessment process can be greatly enhanced. Four specific suggestions in this area are offered as follows.

Use Rating Scales and Sociometrics Routinely for Early Screening

Effective screening practices involve being able to systematically pick out students who are in the early stages of developing social-behavioral problems with a high degree of accuracy. The identified students are then evaluated more carefully to determine whether their social-behavioral problems warrant special program eligibility and intervention services. The purpose of screening for social-behavioral problems is usually for *secondary intervention,* which is the prevention of the existing problem from becoming worse (Kauffman, 1989). Screening for early intervention is one of the best uses of social skills rating scales and sociometric approaches, as they can potentially cover a wide variety of important behaviors or characteristics and usually take very little time to administer and score. For screening purposes, using rating scales, a criterion of one to one and one half standard deviations is recommended for social skills deficits and problem behavior excesses. While sociometric techniques are generally not standardized to the same extent as rating scales extent, they can be used in screening by including in the screening pool students who show moderate or greater levels of social rejection or social neglect. This practice will narrow the screening pool down to a small to moderate percentage of the overall student population, and this selected group can then be evaluated more comprehensively.

Use the "Aggregation Principle"

When using behavior rating scales for purposes other than routine screening, obtaining aggregated rating scale data is suggested in order to reduce bias of response and variance problems in the assessment. In practice, using aggregated measures means to obtain rating evaluations from different raters in different settings and to use more than one type of rating scale to accomplish this (Martin, Hooper, & Snow, 1986).

Use Multimethod Assessment Procedures

When using rating scales or sociometrics for purposes such as assessment for program eligibility or intervention planning, they should be used in conjunction with other assessment methods. In addition to using behavior rating scales, the use of direct behavioral observation, objective self-report data, and problem-identification interviews with teachers and parents is recommended for a comprehensive, multimethod assessment. A social skills or peer relations assessment using this method is not only technically strengthened but may provide a better basis for forming intervention hypotheses, as some methods of assessment may yield information on social-behavioral problems that other methods do not.

Work Closely with Constituent Groups When Using Sociometric Assessment Methods

This chapter has already alluded to the controversy surrounding the use of certain sociometric techniques (particularly those using negative nomination procedures) and the hesitancy or resistance often encountered from parents or other professionals when attempting to obtain this type of data. One way of avoiding misunderstandings and heated discussions about the assessment process is to work very closely with constituent groups every step of the way. These constituent groups would typically include parents of the children to be assessed and the teachers, specialists, and school administrators involved. Through the process of education and open and frank communication, resistance may be minimized and the outlook for a successful assessment process may be enhanced.

Linking Assessment to Intervention

While the process of assessing social skills and peer relations has many potential purposes, one of the most important of these is using the data to develop appropriate social-behavioral intervention plans. Unfortunately, there is evidence that in many cases where assessment data is obtained on students with special needs, the focus of the assessment process is misdirected to the point where little intervention benefit to the student is derived from it (Fuchs & Fuchs, 1986; Howell, 1986). With this problem in mind, the following four suggestions are offered for using assessment data from rating scales and sociometric approaches within an intervention framework.

Recommended Treatments Should Be Matched to Problems

One of the problems often seen in social-behavioral assessment reports is the tendency for examiners to make generic recommendations such as "this student would benefit from social skills training." Such a broad and vague recommendation does very little to tie assessment data to an effective intervention. One of the major characteristics of effective practices for working with students who have emotional or behavioral problems is that treatments should be closely matched to problems (Peacock Hill Working Group, 1991). When social skills and peer relationship data suggest that a student has deficits in these areas, the suggested approach is to identify the specific problem areas (e.g., interacting appropriately with peers, accepting criticism, showing self-restraint) and then make recommendations for social skills training or other interventions that specifically address the key problems.

Develop IEP Goals by Modifying Rating Scale Items

One of the advantages of using rating scale assessments is that they provide student performance data on a number of standardized items that reflect specific behaviors important to successful social adjustment. By carefully analyzing subtest score patterns and individual items where social-behavioral problems seem to be especially severe, individual items can be selected and reworded in developing IEP or other intervention plan goal statements. For example, if a student had very low scores on the Interpersonal Skills subscale of the School Social Behavior Scales, and a careful content examination revealed that items 4 and 19 were rated as especially problematic, these items could be reworded into general goal statements such as "Steven will increase his level of providing help to other students when it is appropriately needed" and "Steven will increase his number of interactions with classmates in the classroom and on the playground."

Continuously Assess Progress During Intervention

It has been demonstrated that continuous assessment and monitoring of student progress following the initial assessment and intervention is very important in successful implementation of behavioral and academic interventions (Howell & Morehead, 1987; Kerr & Nelson, 1989). Progress toward behavioral goals developed from social skills and peer relations assessment data could be easily assessed on a weekly or semiweekly schedule using appropriate rating scales or nonintrusive and simple sociometric approaches. Additionally, there are other simple ways of assessing progress daily, such as using student performance records.

Follow-up Intervention with Further Assessment

Additional assessment following the intervention can also be a useful process. The main reason for follow-up assessment is to determine how well the intervention effects have been maintained over time (e.g., after 3 months) and how well the behavioral changes have generalized to other settings (e.g., the home setting and other classrooms). In actual practice, a follow-up assessment might involve having teacher(s) and parent(s) complete social competence rating scales on a student or conducting sociometric assessments after a specified time period has elapsed following the student's participation in a social skills training program. The data obtained from this follow-up assessment can be used to determine whether or not follow-up interventions seem appropriate and may be useful in developing future intervention programs if it is determined that social-behavioral gains are not being maintained over time or generalized across specific settings.

REFERENCES

Achenbach, T.M. (1991a). *Manual for the Child Behavior Checklist and 1991 profile.* Burlington: University of Vermont, Department of Psychiatry.

Achenbach, T.M. (1991b). *Manual for the Teacher's Report Form and 1991 Profile.* Burlington: University of Vermont, Department of Psychiatry.

American Association on Mental Retardation (1992). *Mental retardation: Definition, classification, and systems of support* (9th ed.). Washington, DC: Author.

Asher, S.R., & Taylor, A.R. (1981). The social outcomes of mainstreaming: Sociometric assessment and beyond. *Exceptional Children Quarterly, 1,* 13–30.

Bower, E. (1969). *Early identification of emotionally handicapped children in school* (2nd ed.). Springfield, IL: Charles C. Thomas.

Bryan, T. (1974). Peer popularity of learning disabled children. *Journal of Learning Disabilities, 7,* 261–268.

Cartledge, G., Frew, T., & Zacharias, J. (1985). Social skills needs of mainstreamed students: Peer and teacher perceptions. *Learning Disability Quarterly, 8,* 132–140.

Cicchetti, D.A., & Toth, S.L. (1991). A developmental perspective on internalizing and externalizing disorders. In D. Cicchetti & S.L. Toth (Eds.), Internalizing and externalizing expressions of dysfunction (pp. 1–19). Hillsdale, N.J.: Erlbaum.

Coie, J.D., Dodge, K.A., & Cappotelli, H. (1982). Dimensions and types of social status: A cross-age perspective. *Developmental Psychology, 18,* 557–570.

Cowen, E.L., Pederson, A., Babigan, H., Izzo, L.D., & Trost, M.A. (1983). Long-term follow-up of early detected vulnerable children. *Journal of Consulting and Clinical Psychology, 41,* 438–446.

Epstein, M.H., Cullinan, D., & Lloyd, J.W. (1986). Behavior problem patterns among the learning disabled, III: Replication across age and sex. *Learning Disability Quarterly, 9,* 43–54.

Fuchs, L.S., & Fuchs, D. (1986). Linking assessment to instructional intervention: An overview. *School Psychology Review, 15,* 318–323.

Gresham, F.M. (1982). Misguided mainstreaming: The case for social skills training with handicapped students. *Exceptional Children, 48,* 422–433.

Gresham, F.M. (1986). Conceptual issues in the assessment of social competence in children. In P. Strain, M. Guralnick, & H. Walker (Eds.), *Children's social behavior: Development, assessment, and modification* (pp. 143–179). New York: Academic Press.

Gresham, F.M., & Elliott, S.N. (1990). *The social skills rating system.* Circle Pines, MN: American Guidance.

Gresham, F.M., & Elliott, S.N. (1984). Assessment and classification of children's social skills: A review of methods and issues. *School Psychology Review, 13,* 292–301.

Gresham, F.M., & Reschly, D.J. (1987a). Dimensions of social competence: Method factors in the assessment of adaptive behavior, social skills, and peer acceptance. *Journal of School Psychology, 25,* 367–381.

Gresham, F.M., & Reschly, D.J. (1987b). Issues in the conceptualization, classification, and assessment of social skills in the mildly handicapped. In T. Kratochwill (Ed.), *Advances in school psychology* (pp. 203–264). Hillsdale, NJ: Erlbaum.

Grossman, H.J. (Ed.). (1983). *Classification in mental retardation.* Washington DC: American Association on Mental Deficiency.

Hartup, W.W. (1983). Peer relations. In E.M. Hetherington (Ed.), *Handbook of child psychology: (Vol. 4). Socialization, personality, and social development* (pp. 103–198). New York: Wiley.

Hayvren, M., & Hymel, S. (1984). Ethical issues in sociometric testing: Impact of sociometric measures on interaction behavior. *Developmental Psychology, 20,* 844–849.

Hollinger, J.D. (1987). Social skills for behaviorally disordered children as preparation for mainstreaming: Theory, practice, and new directions. *Remedial and Special Education, 11,* 139–149.

Howell, K.W. (1986). Direct assessment of academic performance. *School Psychology Review, 15,* 324–335.

Howell, K.W., & Morehead, M.K. (1987). *Curriculum-based evaluation for special and remediation education.* Columbus, OH: Merrill.

Kauffman, J.M., Semmell, M.I., & Agard, J.A. (1974). PRIME: An overview. *Education and Training for the Mentally Retarded, 9,* 107–112.

Kauffman, J.M. (1989). *Characteristics of behavior disorders of children and youth* (4th ed.). Columbus, OH: Merrill.

Kerr, M.M., & Nelson, C.M. (1989). *Strategies for managing behavior problems in the classroom* (2nd ed.). Columbus, OH: Merrill.

Landau, S., & Milich, R. (1990). Assessment of children's social status and peer relations. In A.M. LaGreca (Ed.), *Through the eyes of the child* (pp. 259–291). Boston: Allyn & Bacon.

Loeber, R. (1985). Patterns of development of antisocial child behavior. *Annals of child development, 2,* 77–116.

Martin, R.P. (1988). *Assessment of personality and behavior problems.* New York: Guilford Press.

Martin, R.P., Hooper, S., & Snow, J.H. (1986). Behavior rating scale approaches to personality assessment in children and adolescents. In H.M. Knoff (Ed.), *The assessment of child and adolescent personality* (pp. 309–351). New York: Guilford Press.

Masten, A.S., Morrison, P., & Pelligrini, D.S. (1985). A revised class play method of peer assessment. *Developmental Psychology, 21*, 523–533.

McCandless, B., & Marshall, H. (1957). A picture sociometric technique for preschool children and its relation to teacher judgments of friendship. *Child Development, 28*, 139–148.

McKinney, J.D., & Feagans, L. (1984). Academic and behavioral characteristics of learning disabled children and average achievers: Longitudinal studies. *Learning Disability Quarterly, 7*, 251–264.

McKinney, J.D., McClure, S., & Feagans, L. (1982). Classroom behavior of learning disabled children. *Learning Disability Quarterly, 5*, 45–52.

Merrell, K.W. (1989). Concurrent relationships between two behavioral rating scales for teachers: An examination of self-control, social competence, and school behavioral adjustment. *Psychology in the Schools, 26*, 267–271.

Merrell, K.W. (1993a). *School Social Behavior Scales.* Brandon, VT: Clinical Psychology Publishing. Austin, TX: PRO-ED.

Merrell, K.W. (1993b). Using behavior rating scales to assess social skills and antisocial behavior in school settings: Development of the school social behavior scales. *School Psychology Review, 22*, 115–133.

Merrell, K.W. (1994a). *Assessment of behavioral, social, and emotional problems: Direct and objective methods for use with children and adolescents.* White Plains, NY: Longman.

Merrell, K.W. (1994b). *Preschool and Kindergarten Behavior Scales.* Brandon, VT: Clinical Psychology Publishing/Austin, TX: PRO-ED.

Merrell, K.W. (1995). Relationships among early childhood behavior rating scales: Convergent and discriminant construct validity of the Preschool and Kindergarten Behavior Scales. *Early Education and Development, 6*, 253–264.

Merrell, K.W., & Gill, S.J. (1994). Using teacher ratings of social behavior to differentiate gifted from non-gifted students. *Roeper Review, 16*(4), 286–289.

Merrell, K.W., Merz, J.N., Johnson, E.R., & Ring, E.N. (1992). Social competence of mildly handicapped and low-achieving students: A comparative study. *School Psychology Review, 21*, 49–58.

Merrell, K.W., Sanders, D.E., & Popinga, M. (1993). Teacher ratings of social behavior as a predictor of special education status: Discriminant validity of the School Social Behavior Scales. *Journal of Psychoeducational Assessment, 11*, 220–231.

Merrell, K.W., & Shinn, M.R. (1990). Critical variables in the learning disabilities identification process. *School Psychology Review, 19*, 74–82.

Milich, R., & Landau, S. (1984). A comparison of the social status and social behavior of aggressive and aggressive/withdrawn boys. *Journal of Abnormal Child Psychology, 12*, 277–288.

Moreno, J.L. (1934). *Who shall survive?* Washington, DC: Nervous and Mental Disease Publishing.

Oden, S.L., & Asher, S.R. (1977). Coaching children in social skills for friendship making. *Child Development, 48*, 496–506.

Park, H.S., Tappe, P., Carmeto, R., & Gaylord-Ross, R. (1990). Social support and quality of life for learning disabled and mildly retarded youth in transition. In R. Gaylord-Ross, S. Siegel, H.S. Park, S. Sacks, & L. Goetz (Eds.), *Readings in ecosocial development* (pp. 293–328). San Francisco: Department of Special Education, San Francisco State University.

Parker, J.G., & Asher, S.R. (1987). Peer relations and later personal development: Are low-accepted children "at-risk"? *Psychological Bulletin, 102,* 357–389.

Peacock Hill Working Group (1991). Problems and promises in special education and related services for children and youth with emotional or behavioral disorders. *Behavioral Disorders, 16,* 299–313.

Reschly, D.J. (1990). Best practices in adaptive behavior. In A. Thomas & J. Grimes (Eds.), *Best practices in school psychology—II* (pp. 29–42). Washington, DC: National Association of School Psychologists.

Roff, M. (1963). Childhood social interactions and young adult psychosis. *Journal of Clinical Psychology, 19,* 152–157.

Roff, M., & Sells, S.B. (1968). Juvenile delinquency in relation to peer acceptance-rejection and sociometric status. *Psychology in the Schools, 5,* 3–18.

Roff, M., Sells, S.B., & Golden, M. (1972). *Social adjustment and personality development in children.* Minneapolis: University of Minnesota Press.

Sater, G.M., & French, D.C. (1989). A comparison of the social competencies of learning disabled and low-achieving elementary age children. *The Journal of Special Education, 23,* 29–42.

Sattler, J.M. (1988). *Assessment of children* (3rd ed.). San Diego: Jerome M. Sattler.

Stumme, V.S., Gresham, F.M., & Scott, N.A. (1982). Validity of social behavior assessment in discriminating emotionally disabled and nonhandicapped students. *Journal of Behavioral Assessment, 4,* 327–341.

Vaughn, S. (1987). TLC—Teaching, learning, and caring: Teaching interpersonal problem-solving skills to behaviorally disordered adolescents. *The Pointer, 31,* 25–30.

Veldman, D.J., & Sheffield, J.R. (1979). The scaling of sociometric nominations. *Educational and Psychological Measurement, 39,* 99–106.

Walker, H.M., & Hops, H. (1976). Increasing academic achievement by reinforcing direct academic performance and/or facilitating nonacademic responses. *Journal of Educational Psychology, 68,* 218–225.

Walker, H.M., & McConnell, S.R. (1995a). *Walker-McConnell Scale of Social Competence and School Adjustment: Elementary Version.* San Diego, CA: Singular Publishing Group.

Walker, H.M., & McConnell, S.R. (1995b). *Walker-McConnell Scale of Social Competence and School Adjustment: Adolescent Version.* San Diego, CA: Singular Publishing Group.

Walker, H.M., Steiber, S., & Eisert, D. (1991). Teacher ratings of adolescent social skills: Psychometric characteristics and factorial replicability. *School Psychology Review, 20,* 301–314.

Walker, H.M., Todis, B., Holmes, D., & Horton, G. (1988). *The Walker social skills curriculum: The ACCESS program (adolescent curriculum for communication and effective social skills).* Austin, TX: PRO-ED.

Worthen, B.R., Borg, W.R., & White, K.R. (1993). *Measurement and evaluation in the schools: A practical guide.* White Plains, NY: Longman.

Chapter 10

ASSESSING PERCEPTUAL-MOTOR SKILLS

GERALD B. FULLER, ABEER M. AWADH, AND H. BOONEY VANCE

HISTORY AND DEVELOPMENT

Perceptual-motor (PM) assessment is deeply rooted in the theoretical and conceptual literature of Gestalt psychology. In the early 1900s Max Wertheimer published a paper based on the work of Koffka and Kohler and himself on perceptual phenomena. Gestalt psychology focuses on the perceptual reactions of the human organism and in doing so formulates certain principles of perception (the relationship of figure to ground). According to Gestalt psychology there are four principles of perception. (1) *Inhomogeneity* or the relationship of figure and ground to perception. In order for a figure to be seen, the ground must be inhomogeneous to the figure (a black figure cannot be seen against a black background). (2) *Interaction of figure and ground:* Koffka (1935) demonstrated that variations of the ground influence one's perception of the figure (see also Goldstein, 1934). In a later study Goldstein and Schaerer (1941), using the Kohs Block Design Test, found that a figure positioned vertically appeared stronger than one positioned horizontally. (3) *The laws of grouping or closure:* These imply that each figure has its own properties and when certain conditions (proximity, similarity, common fate) obtain between the parts a cohesive figure is perceived. The greater the degree of those three conditions, the more stable is the perceived object. (4) *Wertheimer's Law of Pragnanz.* This principle means that there is a tendency to get a decisive structuralization of the perceived object with true orientation.

According to Fuller (1982), these four principles of perception permit stable figures, and the cohesiveness and stability of figures are lessened by converse applications of the same principles. In accordance with these four principles, there is a continuum ranging from cohesiveness and stability to ambiguity and instability for perceived figures (Fuller, 1982). In perceptual-motor assessment the whole is greater than the sum of the parts, so a perceived stimulus (diamond, square, triangle, or letter of the alphabet) has greater meaning for an individual than its component parts. These principles led Wertheimer in 1923 to publish nine geometric designs illustrating the principles of Gestalt psychology. In 1938, Loretta Bender, a physician, used the nine designs as a visual-motor test with adult clinical populations and as a developmental test with children (Sattler, 1988). The Bender

Visual Motor Gestalt Test (Bender, 1938) has become one of the most popular and widely used tests included in a comprehensive psychoeducational assessment battery.

Relationship of Attention to Perception

The correct copying of Gestalt designs involves and requires many different expressive and receptive functions. Such factors as maturational level, medical condition, organization skill, attention-deficit problems, limited intellectual ability, carelessness, interest level, and fine-motor skills all influence the outcome of a given Gestalt. Koppitz (1975) and Palmer (1983) provide excellent reviews of the variables that may affect perceptual-motor functions and interfere with the drawings required by such tests.

Is there a relationship between perception and attention? Wyne and O'Connors' (1979) findings indicate that perception is the active process of selective attention to certain sensory input and the interpretation of that information as a function of stored information and concepts, and higher-order cognitive development. What constitutes cognition or how it can be separated from perception remain unanswered questions. *Selective attention* (ADD) is another confusing term, even though many teachers use it. According to Witt, Elliott, Gresham, and Kramer (1988), selective attention, or the capacity to select and attend to a task, becomes very relevant in the assessment of perceptual-motor abilities. Sattler (1988) also suggests that attention plays a significant role in copying designs. In fact, Fredrick, Fuller, and Hawkins (1969) and Fredrick and Fuller (1973) demonstrated that visual-motor problems can stem from dysfunction in the integrative (memory) or motor (executive) process. In the assessment of perceptive-motor skills it is critical to assess performance by testing the limits when a subject's Gestalt design is different from the one presented. Testing the limits can help determine whether the subject's failure to reproduce the drawing is due to visual, integration, or executional problems. Sattler (1988) and Fuller (1982) provide excellent recommendations for the testing of limits.

Perceptual-Motor Impairment and Academic Achievement/Learning

Perceptual-motor tests were originally designed to be used in adult populations, especially the clinical population of brain-injured adults. Goldstein (1939) pioneered the work of assessing brain-injured adults. In the 1930s, Werner and Strauss studied brain-injured adults at the Wayne County Training School in Detroit, Michigan (Bender, 1992). These two pioneers in the field of visual-motor assessment were able to develop a list of behavioral traits that differentiated the brain injured from the non-brain injured. Werner and Strauss later became interested in differentiating brain-injured from non-brain-injured children. Central to Werner's hypothesis about learning problems in children were perceptual disorders. Within the last 25 years interest in assessing children's learning problems via perceptual-motor tests has increased beyond all expectation. Why is this so? Hallahan and Cruickshank (1973) provide an excellent history surrounding the development and use of perceptual-motor tests to diagnose learning problems in children. A brief synopsis is provided. Most of the early leaders in the field of children's learning problems worked with, were associated with, or were influenced by the work of Werner and Strauss.

During the period Werner and Strauss worked at Wayne County Training Center, Cruickshank, Kirk, and Kephart were associated with the center, as was Ray Barsh. While Kephart was at Purdue, Gerald Gitman worked with him. According to Hallahan and Cruickshank (1973) and Mann (1971), Frostig was influenced by the findings of Werner and Strauss. Each of these professionals made a unique and lasting contribution to perceptual-motor assessment as related to the learning problems of children. The contributions of Kirk, who in 1963 coined the term *learning disabled,* are still far reaching and problematic. For a comprehensive review of reported research using the Bender Gestalt with school-age children, the interested reader is referred to an excellent article by Buckley (1978), which reviews the work completed between 1966 and 1977.

THE BENDER GESTALT

The Bender Gestalt (Bender, 1938) has been the most widely used and most popular visual-motor test (Fuller & Vance, 1993). According to Witt et al. (1988), the Bender Gestalt is by far the most frequently used test of perceptual-motor functioning and "because of its simplicity and ease of administration, it is also one of the most frequently misused tests" (p. 293).

The Bender Gestalt was developed as an aid to differentiate brain-damaged from non-brain-damaged adults. The Bender Gestalt consists of nine geometric figures developed by Wertheimer in 1923. The designs are drawn in black on a 4-by-6 inch white card. The Bender Gestalt is administered individually and is untimed; a subject is asked to draw all nine designs on a sheet of 8 1/2-by-11-inch white paper. Many clinicians begin a testing session with the Bender Gestalt to develop rapport. The average time it takes a child to complete the nine drawings is 5 minutes (Sattler 1988). Variations such as tachistoscopic and memory-phase procedures can be used in administering the Bender Gestalt. The Bender Gestalt also can be given to groups of individuals. Koppitz's (1975) study indicated that reliable results can be obtained whether the Bender Gestalt is individually or group administered. According to Salvia and Ysseldyke (1995), the Bender Gestalt "measures a child's skills in copying geometric designs" (p. 559).

Scoring

Bender Gestalt (1988) provided criteria for scoring the nine designs. Koppitz (1964), however, developed a scoring criteria based on her experiences in a child guidance clinic. The Koppitz Developmental Bender Scoring System (Koppitz 1964, 1975) is the most commonly used system in today's school settings. For those interested in a synthesis of Bender Gestalt research between 1963 and 1973,

Koppitz's second volume of *The Bender Gestalt Test for Young Children* provides an excellent review of the literature. This chapter discusses only the Koppitz Scoring System.

This system consists of a developmental and an emotional indicator scoring system. The developmental scoring system consists of 30 scoring items; each item is scored 0 or 1, depending upon whether an error occurs. There are four types of errors: distortions of shape, rotation, integration difficulties, and perseveration. The number of errors scored for each of the nine drawings is summed to yield the total error score. The total number of errors a child makes is then compared to the norms for the child's age. The higher the raw score, the poorer the performance. The error score is then converted into a percentile ranking used in interpretation. Percentile scores can be used for children ages 5 years to 11 years, 11 months. Sattler (1988) provides a standard score ($M = 100$, $SD = 15$) that is suitable for ages 5 years through 8 years. There are 12 emotional indicators suggested by Koppitz, which are used to evaluate the emotional stability of the child via visual-motor performance; the emotional indicator scoring system, however, is infrequently used in the school setting. Koppitz (1985) provided examples for scoring individual items and presented a new set of normative tables based on the 1974 renorming of the Bender Gestalt. Taylor, Kauffman, and Partenio's (1984) results suggested that the score yielded by the Bender Gestalt should not be considered a developmental score for ages 5 to 11. Taylor et al. (1984) asked whether the developmental scoring system for the Bender Gestalt *was* developmental and concluded "that examiners should be aware of the limited developmental aspects of the test, particularly after age 8. Similarly, the use of standard score tables based on adjusted means should be avoided" (p. 428).

Norms

The 1975 normative sample consisted of 975 elementary children ranging in age from 5 to 11 years. Racial balance and geographic representation were not obtained nor was the sample stratified according to socioeconomic status. The sample size for half-interval age groups are unevenly distributed. It should be noted that the standard deviations after age 8 years, 6 months are about equal to the mean for the 1974 norms. Various reviews of the 1975 norms have been presented elsewhere (Salvia & Ysseldyke, 1995; Sattler, 1988; Witt et al., 1988).

Reliability and Validity

The 1975 manual (Koppitz, 1975) reports two types of reliability findings. Twenty-three studies involving interrater reliability (means score = .89) were reported. These studies suggest that the raters agreed in the total number of errors they scored on the test, which is probably due to the objective scoring criteria. Nine test-retest studies were reported in the manual, over half conducted with kindergarten children. The mean reliability was .71. Koppitz (1975) said that "certainly no diagnosis or major decision should ever be made on the basis of a single scoring point, nor for that matter on the basis of a youngster's total Developmental Bender Test score" (p. 29). Little evidence supporting the construct validity of the Bender Gestalt exists. Fifty-four criterion-related validity studies (Koppitz, 1973), mostly correlating Bender Gestalt with measures of school achievement, are reported in the manual. According to the findings of various studies reported in the manual, the Bender Gestalt is not a useful predictor of academic achievement and accounts for only 5% of the variance in academic success. This finding is further documented by Vance, Fuller and Lester (1986) and by Fuller and Vance (1993). Similar findings hold true for the Bender Gestalt as a measure of intelligence, emotional difficulties, or school readiness. Perhaps Koppitz (1975) said it best when he said, "Because the Bender Gestalt is so deceptively simple, it is probably one of the most overrated, most misunderstood, and most maligned tests currently used" (p. 2). Buckley (1978) further pointed out, "We have no conclusive body of proof that the instrument can be used to predict school achievement, neurological impairment, or emotional problems at a statistically acceptable level, on an individual basis" (p. 336). The same holds true even today.

THE MINNESOTA-PERCEPTO-DIAGNOSTIC TEST-REVISED

History of Development

Preliminary construction of the Minnesota-Percepto-Diagnostic Test (MPDT) was begun in 1962 and development was reported in the professional journals (Fuller, 1962; Fuller, 1963). The MPDT (Fuller and Laird, 1963) was first standardized in 1963 as a research instrument designed to assess and differentiate visual-motor performance in various clinical and educational groups of children and adults. The MPDT consisted of six of Wertheimer's Gestalt designs, which the subject copied. The reproduced designs were scored for degrees of rotation. There was, however, some question about what constituted true rotation. Hutt and Briskin (1960) indicated that rotation in the execution of a Gestalt design is a departure from normalcy. Koppitz (1958) and Fuller and Laird (1963) have documented that rotations are produced by preschool normal children but disappear by the time children are 8 years old. Hutt and Briskin (1960) pointed out three reasons for rotations: The design card may be rotated in reference to the paper, the reproduction of the figure may be rotated in reference to the design card, and the reproduction of the figure may be rotated even when the design card and paper are in direct alignment. Only the last case is considered true rotation. Another troublesome question had to be answered by Fuller in the 1962 construction of the MPDT: How many degrees are necessary before a rotation indicates pathology? Some studies reported that a 15° rotation is significant (Clawson, 1959); others, a 90° rotation (Halpan, 1955). There is no agreement on how many degrees a figure must be rotated before the rotation becomes significant. The ultimate objective was to design a test that eliminated the lack of consistency in scoring for rotation. This became one of Fuller's primary goals.

Fuller and his co-workers undertook a series of investigations to determine whether certain designs are more subject to rotation than others, and whether age and IQ account for rotation as measured by the MPDT. For a comprehensive review of these studies, the interested reader is referred to Fuller (1962, 1963b, 1969, 1982) as well as Fuller and Laird (1963b). In the 1969 version of the MPDT, Fuller revised the norms to control for age and IQ in the scoring system. Norms and tables were developed that would be statistically free of the effect of age and intellectual ability on a subject's execution of the six designs. Individual tables were developed for ages 5 to 14, and subjects over 15 were combined into one group since there was a lack of significant performance differences among them (Fuller, 1969). Two scoring variables were added to rotation, separation, and distortion of figures.

The 1982 Revision of the MPDT

Rationale

The Minnesota-Percepto-Diagnostic Test-Revised (MPDT-R) is a clinical and educational instrument that not only has a firm theoretical base but is also supported by an increasing body of research literature. It is designed to assess visual perception and visual-motor abilities in children and adults. Like the MPDT, it consists of six Gestalt designs the subject copies. The reproduced designs are scored for degrees of rotation, separation, and distortion. The scores have been adjusted for both IQ and age. The MPDT-R provides a rapid and objective source of evidence for differential diagnosis that can be used in conjunction with other information about a client. It provides scores that (1) classify learning disabilities as visual, auditory, or mixed; (2) divide behavioral problems of children into normal, emotionally disturbed, schizophrenic, and organic groups; and (3) distinguish between adults who are normal or brain damaged or who have personality disturbances. The test is geared for practitioners in the fields of school psychology, clinical psychology, learning disabilities, special education, counseling, reading, psychiatry, and/or medical psychology who routinely or occasionally administer a visual-motor instrument. The last MPDT manual was published in 1969, hence the object of the MPDT-R manual was to update the available information and to provide the practitioner with a better organized manual that incorporated current interpretation and research findings. An important feature of the new manual is a five-step diagnostic process that helps lead the examiner to a diagnostic decision.

This version of the MPDT includes a review of the research literature since 1969. An attempt was made to summarize, evaluate, and integrate these published studies into the new manual including judgments concerning the clinical and research status of this testing instrument.

Normative Sample

The MPDT-R norms consisted of 4,000 children and adolescents ages 5 through 20 years. There were 950 Black children included in the sample. The standardization population was from Michigan, Illinois, Georgia, Indiana, New York, Minnesota, Iowa, and Texas. Gender was equal throughout the age levels. Of the original sample of 4,000, 480 had IQs of less than 87. Comparisons between boys and girls were made for each group for both IQ and MPDT-R scores, and no significant gender difference was found. Norm tables provide means, standard deviations, and correlations for the MPDT-R and IQ scores.

The major (1982) revision of the MPDT brought changes in norms, administration, scoring systems, and new tables converting MPDT rotation scores to standard scores ($x = 50$, $SD = 10$). The 1982 manual was organized into three sections: administration and scoring, interpretation and case illustrations, and norm development and test construction. A chapter on clinical interpretation was expanded to help the examiner fully utilize all of the information available from the MPDT-R.

Diagnostic Utility

Numerous studies since the early seventies have investigated the diagnostic validity of the MPDT-R. Ample evidence exists (Fuller, 1982) documenting the use of the MPDT-R with various groups of subjects. Fuller indicated that the reliability of the MPDT-R for different diagnostic groups was high enough to give clinicians confidence that a subject upon retesting would remain in the same diagnostic category. Vance, Lester, and Thatcher (1983) investigated the MPDT-R interscore reliability among novice and professionally trained psychologists. Results indicated that for three of the four MPDT-R scores there was a significant positive correlation between expert and novice scoring criteria. Hence the clinician may have confidence that the MPDT-R can be scored reliably by technicians without postgraduate degrees provided the examiner has received the requisite training in administering and scoring the test (a minimum of five 1-hour training sessions).

Diagnosing Brain Damage

The use of the MPDT-R in providing information for different diagnoses of brain damage has been amply documented (Fuller, 1969, 1982; Fuller & Goh, 1981; Fuller & Laird, 1963). Wallbrown and Fuller (1984) describe a five-step procedure; case studies show how the MPDT-R is used in differential diagnosis of brain damage and other syndromes such as emotional disturbance, reading disability, and childhood schizophrenia. The authors caution against using the MPDT-R alone for differential diagnosis but state that the five-step procedure for the clinical use of the MPDT-R provides a structured, sequential method for generating, testing, and refining a hypothesis based on comprehensive neuropsychological assessment batteries.

The efficacy of the MPDT-R in assessing brain damage in adolescents was compared to that of the Bender Gestalt. Forty-one adolescents were administered, in counterbalanced order, the Bender Gestalt and MPDT-R. The MPDT-R diagnosis was found to have a significant correlation with frequency of correct diagnosis, while the Bender Gestalt demonstrated low correlation with frequency of correct diagnosis. The MPDT-R identified 78% of all subjects; the Bender Gestalt identified 60%. The results can be interpreted as evidence that the MPDT-R provides a more sensitive and accurate measure for identifying brain damage (34 subjects) and non-brain damaged (17 subjects) than the Hutt-scored Bender Gestalt.

Fuller and Doan (1992) compared the performance on the MPDT-R of 60 adult patients with focal cerebrovascular accidents (CVA; 30 with left-cerebral hemisphere lesions, 30 with right-cerebral lesions) to 30 normal adults. This study indicated that the MPDT-R is capable of differentiating brain-damaged groups from non-brain damaged groups. The results showed that the MPDT-R differentiated patients with Alzheimers from CVA patients, but did not differentiate between the two CVA groups. However, in an earlier study by Fuller and Levine (1987), the MPDT-R did significantly differentiate between the two CVA groups. These conflicting results could be due to the heterogeneity of the groups in the two studies. The findings from these studies support the inclusion of the MPDT-R in psychological and neuropsychological test batteries for identification and differentiation of brain-damaged subjects.

Diagnosing Emotional Disturbance

Distinguishing and providing a differentiated diagnosis that will identify emotionally disturbed students from nonemotionally disturbed students continues to be a major difficulty for psychologists. As early as 1966, Buros suggested that the MPDT shows its best discriminatory powers in identifying subjects with brain damage and those with emotional disturbances. The MPDT has always shown good discriminatory power in differential diagnosis when used as part of a comprehensive psychological assessment battery (Fuller & Carroll, 1989; Fuller, 1992).

Unique Features

The MPDT-R consists of six Gestalt designs that the subject copies on a clean sheet of paper. The client is not allowed to turn over the paper or cards. There is no time limit, and erasures and changes are permitted. Only one side of the paper can be used. A protractor that comes with the test is used to measure the degree of rotation. Specific, detailed instructions (which are easily followed) are presented in the manual. In addition, the manual provides guidelines for special scoring problems and a five-step diagnostic process (Fuller, 1982). A diagnostic summary sheet is provided for children and adults. After a MPDT-R protocol is scored, the examiner is able to convert the raw score into a standard score with a mean of 50 and a standard deviation of 10. The conversion tables are easily read, and are separated into two groups (children and adults). An important advantage of the MPDT-R is that it is controlled for age and IQ. For example, if a 12-year-old girl with an IQ of 110 obtained an MPDT-R rotation score of 22, she would receive a T score of 50, which is exactly at the mean of her age and IQ; if a 12-year-old boy received a MPDT-R rotation score of 94, he would receive a T score of 50 for his raw score of 94, and an IQ of 60, which is appropriate for his age and IQ. It is clearly very important to control for age and IQ when administering visual-motor instruments such as the Bender Gestalt and MPDT-R.

When administering any visual-perceptual-motor assessment test it is always advisable to investigate whether the problems lie in output (motor or expressive) or input (perceptual or receptive), as suggested by Sattler (1988). Sattler (1982) provides a set of guidelines helpful in assisting the clinician to determine whether inadequate visual-motor performance is a receptive or expressive difficulty.

Mayes and Vance (1992) investigated the performance of 38 learning-disabled and 16 emotionally impaired children on the WISC-R, WRAT-R, and MPDT-R. The findings suggested that discriminant functional analysis can be useful in the differential diagnosis process. Based on the discriminant scores, 76% of the subjects were correctly identified as Emotionally Disabled (ED) and 81% as Learning Disabled (LD). This finding supported the earlier work of Fuller and Goh (1981) and Vance, Fuller, and Ellis (1983), which found that the MPDT-R can be useful in differentiating learning-disabled children from emotionally impaired children.

Two groups of psychiatric adolescent patients (19 schizophrenics, 22 nonschizophrenics) on an acute inpatient ward were compared for their performance on the MPDT-R. Results supported the efficacy of the test in differentiating between the two groups. A two-factor analysis of variance and analysis of covariance was used to analyze the data. The findings provided evidence that the MPDT-R should be included in a diagnostic battery when one is attempting to differentiate between schizophrenic and nonschizophrenic groups. The MPDT-R correctly identified 79% of those having a personality problem. A major implication of the study supported the cutoff scores established in the revised manual, which makes the test more accurate in diagnosing emotional problems (Fuller, 1992). These findings further support the sensitivity of the MPDT-R in detecting emotional problems in children and adults.

Snow, Hartlage, Hynd, and Grant (1983) compared the relationship of the Luria-Nebraska Neuropsychological Battery for Children-Revised and the MPDT-R for a group of learning-disabled students. No significant correlations were found between the two instruments. The authors suggested that the MPDT-R might be measuring a skill or skills that are relatively independent of any of those assessed by the Luria-Nebraska. Another factor that might have accounted for the finding is that the MPDT-R scores are corrected for age and IQ, whereas the LNNB-Children's Revision T scores do not account for IQ level. Snow et al. (1983) indicated that the MPDT-R provides information concerning dimensions of perceptual organization that are not measured by the LNNB. This makes the findings from the MPDT-R testing less subject to misinterpretation by examiners with relatively little neuropsychological sophistication (Fuller & Levine, 1987).

Articulation Disorders

An interesting finding emerged in an investigation conducted by Carroll, Fuller, and Lindley (1989) to assess differences between children with diagnosed functional disorders and a control group on the variable of visual-motor ability. A group of 34 elementary children with articulation problems were matched with a control group of 34 for sex, age, and grade. Both groups were administered the Goldman-Fristoe Test of Articulation and the MPDT-R. The children in the articulation-disordered group performed significantly more poorly on a measure of visual-motor ability than matched controls did. What was interesting was that when these children were compared as a group, it became evident that as articulation proficiency decreases so does visual-motor functioning. A significant correlation was found between the MPDT-R rotation T scores and articulation errors. As the sounds in word subtests increased and as visual-motor performance deteriorated, articulation errors increased. The implication from this study is that educators should entertain the possibility that the child who severely misarticulates sounds when reading instruction is begun (often in kindergarten or the first grade) may not be developmentally ready to handle the heavy visual-perceptual demands of the task. Perhaps visual-motor assessment should be included in speech and language evaluations.

Ethnic Factors

Fuller and Friedrich (1979) evaluated the performance of 60 Black and 60 White children on achievement and the MPDT. Results from the study indicated that race was not a significant variable in the relationship between achievement levels and MPDT performance.

A study conducted by Fuller, Thomas, and Vance (1987) compared the performance of three different ethnic groups on the MPDT-R and found no significant differences among African American, Hispanic, and Caucasian children in the rotation score. There were significant differences for the configuration scores (Separation of Circle-Diamond [SpCD], Distortion of Circle-Diamond [DCD], and Distortion of Dots [DD]). The African Americans performed significantly less well on the Distortion of Circle-Diamond and Distortion of Dots than did the Caucasians. The Hispanics scored significantly less well than the Caucasians on the SpCD.

A study by Fuller and Friedrich (1979) found no significant differences on the rotation score for African-American high achievers, White high achievers, African-American low achievers, and White low achievers. However, on the DCD configuration score African-American low achievers had significantly more errors than did African-American high achievers, White low achievers, or White high achievers. In both of these studies the MPDT-R rotation score was not different for racial groups. The configuration scores were affected by the child's race. African Americans and Hispanics produced more errors than did Caucasian children. The configuration scores are more dependent on basic motor and kinesthetic expressive variables than on visual receptive ones. This suggests that there is some difference between African Americans and Caucasian and Hispanic children that may reside in their practice of the fine-motor skills needed in using a pencil to copy certain geometric figures, often part of the early home and academic experiences of children. These results provide some empirically based evidence for some racial differences on certain MPDT-R scores. The practitioner must be aware of this when interpreting a child's performance on the MPDT-R.

Fuller and Vance (1995) compared the performance on the MPDT-R of three Native American groups (40 Navajo, 40 Papago, and 40 Hopi) and 40 Caucasian children. One-way analysis of variance and an analysis of covariance (age covaried) were computed along with a Scheffé test. The results indicated significant differences among the four groups on the MPDT-R rotation score and on two of the three configuration scores. When age was controlled for, significant differences were obtained on the MPDT-R scores. The Caucasian children performed significantly better than did the Papago and Hopi children on rotation. They also had significantly less SpCD than the Navajo and significantly less DCD than the Hopi children. Many of the Native American children obtained MPDT-R scores above the range for normal perception. The authors caution the clinician to be careful in determining whether the differences in scores on cross-cultural validity studies are truly a clinical sign or a culturally different reaction or interpretation in visual-motor perception. The findings from the studies referred to provide empirically based evidence that the MPDT-R is sensitive in detecting difference in visual-motor skills of minority children.

COMPARISON OF MPDT-R AND OTHER VISUAL-MOTOR TESTS

Perhaps the most popular visual-motor assessment test is the Bender Gestalt (Bender, 1938). In fact, Kitay (1972) suggested that the Bender Gestalt "be included in every diagnostic exam of adults and children from age 5 because of its unique contribution to the evaluation of perceptual motor functioning, neurological impairment, expressive styles, and maladjustment" (p. 162). In a comprehensive review of the Bender Gestalt over 11 years (from 1965 to 1977), Buckley (1978) concluded that "we have no conclusive body of proof that the instrument can be used to predict school achievement, or emotional problems at a statistically acceptable level on an individual basis" (p. 334). The Bender Gestalt and MPDT-R, however, continue to be popular assessment instruments with psychologists.

Although these two instruments have purported to measure similar visual-motor abilities over the years, limited research comparing the two tests has been conducted. In an early study by Bauman and St. John (1971), the relationship of the Bender Gestalt, MPDT, and Frostig was investigated. Results showed significant correlations between the MPDT and Bender Gestalt, and the MPDT and Frostig Full Scale score. They concluded, however, that because of the low correlation among the instruments they should not be considered interchangeable.

Wallbrown, Wallbrown, and Engin (1977) evaluated the relative effectiveness of the MPDT and Bender Gestalt in identifying achievement-related errors in visual-motor perception of third-grade children. The sample consisted of 153 children (78 boys and 75 girls). The criterion measures were the Reading Vocabulary, Reading Comprehension, Mathematical Computation, Mathematical Concepts and Problems subtests of the California Achievement Test (CAT). Very low (ranging from $-.18$ to $-.27$) but statistically significant correlations were found for the Bender Gestalt and all areas of achievement. The MPDT, however, was found to be a much more sensitive measure of achievement than the Bender Gestalt. The MPDT SpCD error showed a strong significant negative correlation with three of the four achievement criteria (Reading Vocabulary, $r = -.20$; Reading Comprehension, $r = -.18$; Mathematics Computation, $r = -.24$). Significant correlations also were found for the MPDT raw score on rotation (Reading Vocabulary, $r = -.31$; Reading Comprehension, $r = -.24$; and Mathematics Computation, $r = -.26$). Critical ratios were computed to see whether the MPDT SpCD correlations were significantly higher than those of the Bender Gestalt, and they were found to have a significantly stronger relationship with achievement.

Engin, Walkenshaw, Carlton, and Calabria (1976) compared the MPDT and Bender Gestalt on four criteria of CAT academic achievement: Mathematical Comprehension, Mathematical Concepts, Reading Comprehension, and Reading Vocabulary. Both tests were administered to 84 second-graders (41 boys and 43 girls). The children's mean IQ was 114. Once again, the MPDT predicted achievement significantly better than the Bender Gestalt. The most significant correlations were found to be the SpCD (Mathematical Computation, $r = -.52$; Reading Vocabulary, $r = -.51$; and Reading Comprehension, $r = -.47$).

Fuller and Wallbrown (1983) studied the relationship between the Bender Gestalt (Koppitz scoring method) and the MPDT-R for first-grade children on the CAT using the following subtests: Reading Vocabulary, Reading Comprehension, Total Reading, Arithmetic Comprehension and Computation, Total Arithmetic, Language Usage and Grammar, Total Language, Spelling, and Total Battery. Both tests demonstrated significant correlations ($-.26$ to $-.52$) with Reading Vocabulary and Comprehension, Total Reading, Arithmetic Comprehension and Computation, Arithmetic Total, Language Total, Spelling, and Total Battery. Comparisons to determine whether the correlations between the two tests were significant were carried out with t tests for correlated rs. The MPDT-R DCD correlated higher and more significantly than the Bender Gestalt at the .05 level on Reading Vocabulary, Total Reading, and Arithmetic Comprehension. Using the .01 level, the MPDT-R DCD was significantly higher than the Bender Gestalt on Reading Comprehension and Total Battery. These studies indicate that the MPDT-R would be the choice over the Bender Gestalt when predicting achievement in elementary-school children.

Walters (1976) classified third-grade children into one of four conceptual tempo groups (reflective, impulsive, fast-accurate, slow-inaccurate) on the basis of Kagan's Matching Familiar Figures Test. Subjects were then compared on the MPDT IQ, Comprehension, and Vocabulary (from Gates-MacGinitie Reading Test). The MPDT correlated significantly with accuracy (total errors), indicating that as the MPDT rotation score increased, more errors were made. The MPDT also correlated significantly with Reading Comprehension. Tests of significance indicated that accurates, both fast and slow, did significantly better than inaccurates on the MPDT test.

Fuller and Wallbrown (1983) found that several scores on the MPDT-R (Distortion of Dots, Separation of Circle-Diamond) showed a significantly higher correlation with the CAT on Reading Vocabulary, Total Reading, and Arithmetic Computation than the Bender Gestalt. Vance, Fuller, and Lester (1986) compared the performance of 33 children and youth on Bender Gestalt, MPDT-R, WRAT-R, and WISC-R using multiple regression, and a principal component factor analysis with varimax rotation was used in the data analysis. A pattern of pervasive positive correlations was found between the MPDT-R Bender Gestalt distortion of the circle-diamond figure. Lower magnitude but positive correlations indicated that the two instruments measure the ability to copy various Gestalt designs but do so quite differently, and by no means are the two instruments interchangeable. Multiple regression analysis was used with the Bender Gestalt and MPDT-R as predictors, and the WISC-R, FSIQ, and WRAT-R subtest scores as the dependent variable. The results indicated that the SpCD score of the MPDT-R was clearly the best predictor for academic achievement in spelling and math as measured by the WRAT-R, whereas the Total rotation score of the MPDT-R was the best predictor of the WISC-R Full Scale IQ. The results support the claim that the MPDT-R should be the perceptual-motor assessment instrument of choice for predicting the future academic achievement of school-age children and youth.

Vance (1981) provided an excellent discussion of intellectual factors and reading-disabled children. This study documented the efficacy of the MPDT-R over the Bender Gestalt in predicting achievement scores as well as in identifying potential reading-disabled students. A comparison of the MPDT-R and Bender Gestalt in predicting achievement was conducted by Fuller and Vance (1993). The sample consisted of 84 students in the first, third, and fifth grades. The results indicated that the MPDT-R correlated significantly with CAT subtests that measure early reading ability at the first-grade level (Pre-reading, Visual Discrimination, and Sound Match). The MPDT-R DCD score was also correlated with reading subtests at the fifth-grade level (Reading Vocabulary and Reading Comprehension). This finding may suggest that the MPDT-R is a useful instrument for screening reading in the upper-elementary as well as lower-elementary grades.

Intelligence test scores also appeared to be an important factor in predicting achievement on several subtests. However, when IQ was partialed out of correlations in which it was a factor, the SpCD still correlated significantly with achievement at the first-grade level, the MPDT-R raw score correlated significantly with Spelling at the third-grade level, and the Bender Gestalt correlated significantly with Reading Comprehension at the fifth-grade level.

It was also evident that the MPDT-R DCD score correlated significantly with CAT subtests at each grade level. It may be that the MPDT-R and DCD scores in particular would be most helpful if used as a part of a psychoeducational battery at the second-grade level. In this way, a school psychologist could estimate relevant achievement areas (reading, math) with the MPDT-R as well as gain information about a student's perceptual-motor functioning.

Results of this study indicate that the MPDT-R is a better predictor of achievement than is the Bender Gestalt. This seems particularly to be the case at the first- and fifth-grade levels. However, at each grade level the MPDT-R scores correlated with more achievement subtests than did the Bender Gestalt. Therefore, it appears that the MPDT-R is a more appropriate measure of visual-motor perception and a more accurate predictor of achievement in several areas.

ILLUSTRATION OF SELECTED MPDT-R PROTOCOLS

The MPDT-R is merely a set of cards—until the examiner does something with them. Therefore, protocols will be presented to provide the reader with some idea of the interpretive processes involved in formulating tentative hypotheses about the performance of individuals. It should be noted that presenting results of a single test can at best give only an incomplete picture of the subject. All of the subjects were administered an entire battery of tests, but the intent here is simply to illustrate some types of information that might be gained from the MPDT-R.

Since the five-step diagnostic process was used in some of these cases, it will be reviewed here. First, determine the rotation T score (children) or raw score (adult) and check the cutoff scores for different diagnostic groups on the summary sheets. Second, use the actuarial method that is based on the number of separations and distortions as outlined in the MPDT-R manual. Third, use a combination of the first two steps to further verify the diagnosis. Fourth, test the limits to see whether the error is perceived and whether it can be corrected. Fifth, use one of the discriminant analysis (D^2) formulas (as presented on page 22 of the manual).

Case Example 10–1. Mental retardation associated with brain damage

---

John was referred for evaluation because of pronounced behavioral problems and temper tantrums throughout most of his life. He was 17 years old at the time of evaluation. The history reported that the boy had meningitis at 3, encephalitis at 5, and viral meningitis at 9 years of age. He lost his speech at 4 years, 6 months, but slowly regained it.

On examination, John was noted to be an obese boy with effeminate characteristics. He wore glasses but had no apparent physical handicaps. His speech was slow and hesitant, with some stuttering, but understandable. John had previously received a number of IQ scores ranging from 43 to 70, with better performance on nonverbal tests such as the Peabody Picture Vocabulary Test-Revised, where the IQ of 70 was obtained. He was able to read at about the fourth-grade level.

John's actual scores for degrees of rotation were as follows:

Card 1 25°   Card 4 21°
Card 2 2°   Card 5 25°
Card 3 25 ° Card 6 35°

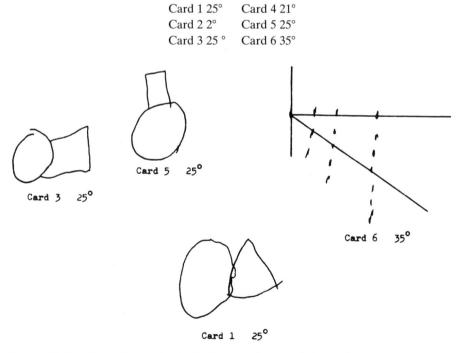

Figure 10–1.   Case of mental retardation associated with brain damage

Case Example 10–1. *(Continued)*

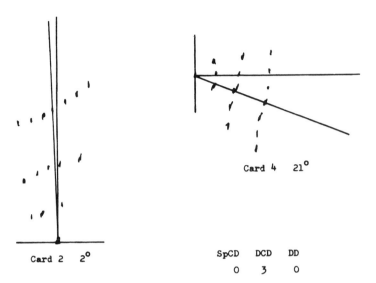

Card 4   21°

Card 2   2°

SpCD	DCD	DD
0	3	0

Figure 10–1. *(continued)*

John obtained raw scores of 25, 2, 25, 21, 25, and 25, and a total raw score of 123. It should be noted that Card 6 was assigned 25 since the actual score was higher than this. Taking his IQ score of 70 with an age of 17, his converted T score would be 30 (use Table 1m in the MPDT-R manual), thus placing him in the brain-damaged range of perception. This is Step 1.

The second step in the diagnosis gave the following results:

SpCD	DCD	DD
0	3	0

Using the guidelines for distortions and separations on page 17 in the manual, these scores further support the diagnosis of brain damage. Since he demonstrated both rotations and distortions (Step 3) of figures, this further suggests right hemispheric damage of a static nature. See Figure 10–1 for illustrations of his MPDT-R test.

When testing the limits (Step 4), John was able to perceive that an error was made but was unable to correct it on a second attempt. In applying Step 5, Formula b was used, since his IQ was below 80.

$$D^2 = -82.8563 + 2.9929 \text{ SpCD} + 4.0129 \text{ DCD} + 7.2558 \text{ DD} + 1.0250 \text{ IQ} + .8864 \text{ MPDTS} + 2.9712 \text{ age.}$$

His actual test scores (SpCD = 0, DCD = 3, DD = 0, IQ = 70, MPDTS = 30) and his age of 17 are substituted in the formula as follows:

$$D^2 = -82.8563 + 2.9929(0) + 4.0129(3) + 7.2558(0) + 1.0250(70) + .8864(30) + 2.9712(17) = 77.66$$

This score of 77.66 is above the cutoff score of 75.48 and once again places him in the brain-damaged group.

Case Example 10–2.   Auditory deficit (primary) reading disability

Richard, age 9, was referred because of poor academic achievement, especially in reading (2 years behind). He showed little motivation and frequently did not attend school. His family situation was described as being very undesirable. On first impression, the psychodynamics could have been explained in terms of emotional disturbance.

Previous findings showed him to be above average, with an IQ of 110. The teacher's report indicated that he demanded a great deal of attention, was very good with his hands, and could not do much writing, reading, or arithmetic. He built models well and often. Richard is not a very verbal child. Richard was given special remedial help concomitant with psychotherapy. After 3 months he did not show improvement and was starting to miss his appointments. At this point, he was referred for evaluation of his academic learning problems, which had been attributed to an emotional disturbance. He was administered a number of tests, including the MPDT-R. On the MPDT-R he received the following actual scores:

Card 1 3°   Card 4 5°
Card 2 6°   Card 5 7°
Card 3 5°   Card 6 4°

This gave him the raw scores of 3, 6, 5, 5, 7, and 4, and a total raw score of 30. By entering Table 1e with his 102 IQ and age of 9, his converted T score was 55. This score placed Richard in the normal range of visual-motor perception. He obtained a Verbal Scale IQ of 90, Performance Scale IQ of 114, and a Full Scale IQ of 102.

The second step in the evaluation elicited the following scores:

SpCD   DCD   DD
  0   1   0

These scores placed him in the non-brain damaged range of perception. Hence, Steps 1 and 2 of the diagnostic procedure suggest that his visual-motor abilities are intact and point to reading problems caused by an auditory deficit (primary) problem. See Figure 10–2 for illustration of his MPDT-R test.

Further support for this diagnosis was seen in the 24-point discrepancy between the Verbal and Performance IQs on the WISC-III in favor of the latter. This relationship suggested a general verbal deficiency. Using Bannatyne's WISC subtest recategorization, his lowest score was on conceptual abilities, his highest on spatial abilities.

Additional testing indicated that Richard's trouble appeared to be in the auditory area. He scored very low on auditory reception, memory, and verbal expression on the auditory discrimination test. Both auditory and visual associations were very low, while visual-motor was high.

From a visual point of view, his problem appeared to be at the associative rather than the input level. Letters or word forms were perceived correctly, without reversal, but their symbolic significance was not grasped. Hence, he was unable to associate words with one another in such a manner as to furnish meaning or give him an understanding of a given sentence. It was anticipated that Richard would fail to profit under normal classroom practices and remedial classes if the emphasis was upon visual input (reception), figure-ground, and spatial orientation.

His ability to write from dictation (auditory) was impaired. When asked to write

Case Example 10–2. *(Continued)*

"The boy came home," he was able to reproduce only the initial consonant of each word except for the word *The,* which he knew by rote. However, Richard's capacity to copy from printed material to script or vise versa was intact. This is often referred to as a type of dysgraphia, which has been a constant finding in children with a primary reading (developmental deficit) problem.

Each of the cases presented provides valuable information for practitioners in helping to determine a differential diagnosis. The data provided from the MPDT-R lends support to its being selected as one of the instruments used in a psychoeducational-clinical battery of tests.

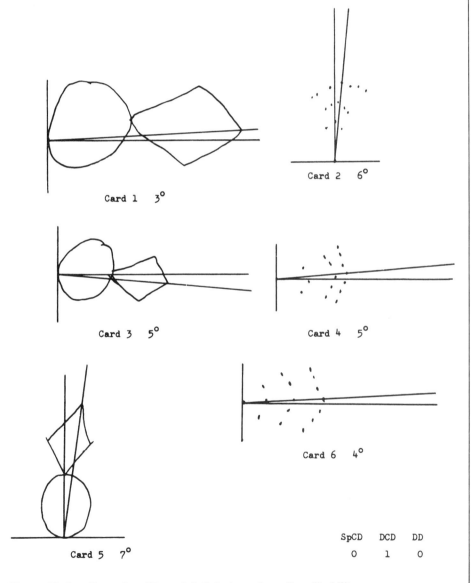

Figure 10–2. Case of auditory deficit (primary) reading disability

CONCLUSION

The MPDT-R has been demonstrated to be a very useful instrument in the applied as well as clinical areas of assessment. We need to reiterate that *no single test* has been shown to be completely adequate for individual diagnosis. A battery of tests whose findings are integrated with supporting data from observational and interviewing data should always be utilized by the clinician. However, no matter how valuable any instrument may be, diagnosis cannot rest on the single finding of that test score alone. The MPDT-R does offer a unique opportunity to psychologists to assess visual-motor-perceptual skills based on research and clinical investigation and should be included as part of a psychological or educational battery. The MPDT-R has been shown to be useful in helping to differentiate children who have difficulties in receptive disturbances (problems in visual perception) from those with expressive problems (difficulty with execution of the designs). The MPDT-R offers the clinician much promise as an important instrument in the administration of a comprehensive psychoeducational battery, whether in a school or agency setting.

REFERENCES

Bauman, E., & St. John, J. (1971). The usefulness of some tests of visual perception. *Psychology in the Schools, 8,* 347–349.

Bender, L. (1938). A visual motor test and its clinical use. Research Monograph, 3. New York: American Orthopsychiatric Association.

Bender, W.D. (1992). *Learning disabilities: Characteristics, identification, and teaching strategies.* Boston: Allyn & Bacon.

Buckley, P.D. (1978). The Bender-Gestalt Test: A review of reported research with school age subjects. *Psychology in the Schools, 3,* 327–338.

Buros, O. (1966). *The sixth mental measurement yearbook.* New Brunswick, NJ: Gryphon Press.

Carroll, J.L., Fuller, G.B., & Lindley, K.E. (1989). Visual motor ability of children with articulation disorders. *Perceptual and Motor Skills, 69,* 32–34.

Clawson, A. (1959). The Bender-Gestalt as an index of emotional disturbance. *Journal of Projective Techniques, 23,* 198–206.

Engin, A., Walkenshaw, D., Carlton, G., & Calabria, K. (1976). Comparative prediction of second grade reading and mathematical achievement using the BG and MPDT. Paper presented at the National Association of School Psychologists, Kansas City.

Fredrick, D., & Fuller, G.B. (1973). Visual motor performance: Delineation of the perceptual deficit hypothesis. *Journal of Clinical Psychology, 29,* 207–209.

Fredrick, D., Fuller, G.B., & Hawkins, W. (1969). Relationship between perception (input) and execution (output). *Perceptual and Motor Skills, 29,* 923–934.

Fuller, G.B. (1962). Introduction of a new orientation for Wertheimer's Gestalt figures to be called the Minnesota-Percepto Diagnostic Test. Phase I: Children. Paper presented at the Minnesota Psychological Association meeting, Minneapolis.

Fuller, G.B. (1963). A further study on rotation: Crossvalidation. *Journal of Clinical Psychology, 19,* 127–128.

Fuller, G.B. (1969). *The Minnesota Percepto-Diagnostic Test, 28,* 1–81 (Monograph Supplement).

Fuller, G.B. (1982). *Minnesota Percepto-Diagnostic Test-Revised.* Brandon, UT: Clinical Psychology Publishing.

Fuller, G.B. (1992). Differential diagnosis of disturbed adolescents with the MPDT-R. *Perceptual and Motor Skills, 74,* 1139–1142.

Fuller, G.B., & Carroll, J. (1989). Diagnostic efficacy and stability of the Minnesota Percepto-Diagnostic Test with psychotic and nonpsychotic psychiatric patients. *Perceptual Motor Skills, 69,* 1202–1203.

Fuller, G.B., & Chugnon, G. (1962). Factors influencing rotation in the Bender-Gestalt performance of children. *Journal of Projective Techniques, 13,* 168–172.

Fuller, G.B., & Doan, G.H. (1992). Differentiation of Alzheimer and cerebrovascular patients with the MPDT-R. *Perceptual and Motor Skills, 75,* 715–721.

Fuller, G.B., & Friedrick, D. (1979). Visual motor test performance: Race and achievement. *Journal of Clinical Psychology, 35,* 621–623.

Fuller, G.B., & Goh, D.S. (1981). Intelligence, achievement, and visual-motor performance among learning disabled and emotionally impaired children. *Psychology in the Schools, 18,* 261–268.

Fuller, G.B., & Laird, J.C. (1963a). Comments and findings about rotations. *Perceptual and Motor Skills, 16,* 673–680.

Fuller, G.B., & Laird, J.C. (1963b). The Minnesota Percepto-Diagnostic Test. *Journal of Clinical Psychology 16,* 1–33. (Monograph Supplement).

Fuller, G.B., & Levine, M.N. (1987). Comparison of the efficacy of the MPDT-R and Bender Gestalt in assessing brain damaged adolescents. *Journal of Psychoeducational Assessment, 3,* 194–199.

Fuller, G.B., Thomas, A.R., & Vance, B. (1987). Ethnic differences on the MPDT-R. *Diagnostique, 13,* 21–27.

Fuller, G.B., & Vance, B. (1993). Comparison of the MPDT-R and Bender-Gestalt in predicting achievement. *Psychology in the Schools, 30,* 220–226.

Fuller, G.B., & Vance, B. (1995). A comparison of three native American groups and a Caucasian group on the MPDT-R. *Psychology in the Schools, 32,* 12–17.

Fuller, G.B., & Wallbrown, F.H. (1983). Comparison of the MPDT and Bender-Gestalt: Relationship with achievement criteria. *Journal of Clinical Psychology, 39,* 985–988.

Goldstein, K. (1939). *The organism.* New York: American Book.

Goldstein, K., & Scheerer, M. (1941). Abstract and concrete behavior: An experimental study with special tests. *Psychological Monographs, 53,* 32–57.

Hallahan, D., & Cruickshank, W. (1973). *Psychoeducational foundations of learning disabilities.* Englewood Cliffs, NJ: Prentice-Hall.

Halpan, V. (1955). Rotation errors on Bender-Gestalt. *American Journal of Mental Deficiency, 59,* 484–489.

Hutt, M.L., & Breskin, G.J. (1960). *The clinical use of the Bender-Gestalt Test.* New York: Greene & Stratton.

Kitay, A.D. (1972). Review of the Bender-Gestalt. In O.K. Buros (Ed.), *Seventh Mental Measurement Yearbook* (pp. 161–162). Highland Park, NJ: Gryphon Press.

Koffka, K. (1935). *Principles of gestalt psychology.* London: Kegan Paul.

Koppitz, E.M. (1958). The Bender-Gestalt Test and learning disturbances in young children. *Journal of Clinical Psychology, 14,* 292–295.

Koppitz, E.M. (1963). *The Bender-Gestalt Test for young children.* New York: Greene & Stratton.

Koppitz, E.M. (1973). Bender-Gestalt test performance and school achievement: A 9-year study. *Psychology in the Schools, 10,* 280–284.

Mann, L. (1971). Psychometric phrenology and the new faculty psychology. The case against ability testing and training. *Journal of Special Education, 5,* 3–14.

Mayes, L., & Vance, B. (1992). Using three different types of assessment data for diagnostic purposes. *Psychological Reports, 70,* 83–88.

Palmer, J.O. (1983). *The psychological assessment of children.* (2nd ed.). New York: Wiley.

Salvia, J., & Ysseldyke, J. (1995). *Assessment* (6th ed.). Boston, MA: Houghton Mifflin.

Sattler, J. (1988). *Assessment of children* (3rd ed.). San Diego: Jerome M. Sattler.

Snow, J.H., Hartlage, L.C., Hynd, G.W., & Grant, D.H. (1983). The relationship between the Lauria-Nebraska Neuropsychological Battery-Children's Revision and the MPDT-R with learning disabled students. *Psychology in the Schools, 20,* 415–419.

Taylor, D.L., Kauffman, D., & Partenio, I. (1984). The Koppitz Development Scoring System for the Bender-Gestalt: Is it developmental? *Psychology in the Schools, 21,* 186–192.

Vance, H.B. (1981). Intellectual factors of reading disabled children. *Journal of Research and Development in Education, 14,* 11–23.

Vance, H.B., Fuller, G.B., & Ellis, R. (1983). Discriminant function analysis of LD-BD children's scores on the WISC-R. *Journal of Clinical Psychology, 3,* 749–753.

Vance, H.B., Fuller, G.B., & Lester, M.L. (1986). A comparison of the MPDT-R and the Bender-Gestalt. *Journal of Learning Disabilities, 19,* 211–214.

Vance, H.B., Lester, M., Thatcher, R. (1983). Interrater reliability of expert versus novice scoring of the Minnesota Percepto-Diagnostic Test. *Psychology in the Schools, 4,* 420–424.

Wallbrown, F.H., & Fuller, G.B. (1984). A five-step procedure for the clinical use of the MPDT-R in neuropsychological assessment of children. *Journal of Clinical Psychology, 40,* 220–229.

Wallbrown, J.D., Wallbrown, F.H., & Engin, A. (1977). The validity of two clinical tests of visual motor perception. *Journal of Clinical Psychology, 33,* 491–495.

Walters, R. (1976). *The relationship of reflection-impulsivity, visual-motor perception, and reading ability in third-grade children.* Unpublished master's thesis, Central Michigan University, Mt. Pleasant, MI.

Witt, J.C., Elliott, S.N., Gresham, F.M., & Kramer, J.J. (1988). *Assessment of special children: Test and problem-solving process.* Boston: Scott, Foresman/Little.

Wyne, M.D., & O'Connors, P.D. (1979). *Exceptional children: A developmental view.* Lexington.

Chapter 11

ASSESSING ADAPTIVE BEHAVIOR

MARYANN DEMCHAK AND SARAH DRINKWATER

Adaptive behavior refers to the ability of an individual to meet the demands of the everyday environment and encompasses self-sufficiency as well as social competence. The importance of adaptive behavior in assessment and program planning has increased due to the stringent assessment mandates of Public Law 101–476 (previously P.L. 94–142) and a stronger emphasis on the adaptive behavior component in the definition of mental retardation. Because adaptive behavior is distinct from intelligence and academic ability (McGrew & Bruininks, 1989), assessment of adaptive behavior provides unique information for the multidisciplinary assessment process (Reschly, 1990). This unique information contributes to both classification of and instructional programming for individuals with disabilities.

HISTORY AND DEVELOPMENT

Adaptive behavior is grounded in the history of the treatment and identification of individuals with mental retardation. Horn and Fuchs (1987) discuss this history with an emphasis on the role of adaptive behavior. Prior to 1820 adaptive behavior was used primarily to identify those individuals unable to function in society. This assessment was informal and focused on those who were physically deformed or behaviorally deviant. The nineteenth century (1820–1890) saw an emphasis on training programs that targeted skills needed for meeting the social demands of the larger community. Adaptive behavior took a minor role in identification of and intervention planning for individuals with mental retardation in the early twentieth century (i.e., 1890–1940). During this time the primary emphasis was on intelligence scores. In recent years (i.e., 1940 to the present), a greater emphasis has been placed on adaptive behavior for identification and program planning, and the systematic assessment of adaptive behavior has been stressed. Edgar Doll (1935), one of the primary advocates of emphasizing adaptive behavior, developed a measure of social maturity (i.e., adaptive behavior) to be used in conjunction with intelligence tests in identifying individuals as mentally retarded.

Contributions of Edgar Doll

Edgar Doll is the major pioneer in the assessment of adaptive behavior. His view that the primary criterion of *mental deficiency* must address social incompetence led to the development of the Vineland Social Maturity Scale (Doll, 1935). He stressed that it was important to look at the whole person and not simply at intelligence; it was insufficient to define mental retardation according to intelligence test scores alone (Doll, 1940). The scale was developed as a means of assessing social adequacy in terms of self-sufficiency, which becomes more complex with increasing age. Thus, the scale provided a means of investigating problems in the area of mental retardation that were previously not researched due to the lack of instrumentation. In addition to viewing adaptive behavior as developmental in nature, another of Doll's contributions was the recognition of the importance of environmental demands and opportunities. These expectations and opportunities influence the development of skills in adaptive behavior. For example, if an individual is never expected to perform a particular skill or provided with opportunities to perform the behavior, it is unlikely that the individual will develop that particular skill in that setting. Even though his specific categories are no longer used, Doll also established the perception of adaptive behavior as encompassing a variety of areas (e.g., self-help dressing, locomotion, occupation, self-direction; Doll, 1935, 1953, 1965). Another continuing contribution relates to methodology used to assess adaptive behavior; Doll's scale required the use of significant others as respondents in providing information regarding a person's performance in the area of social competence. Adaptive behavior instruments continue to use this format today.

The Increasing Emphasis of Adaptive Behavior in Mental Retardation Definitions

Although Doll advocated for a number of years that it was insufficient to assess only intelligence in the identification of individuals with mental retardation, it was not until 1959 that the American Association on Mental Retardation (AAMR), previously the American Association on Mental Deficiency, included adaptive behavior in its definition of mental retardation. Heber (1961) defined mental retardation as "subaverage general intellectual functioning which originates during the developmental period and is associated with impairment in adaptive behavior" (p. 3). Thus, a person with a low IQ score who did not display significant limitations in the area of adaptive behavior could not be identified as mentally retarded. The 1973 AAMR definition of mental retardation included a stronger emphasis on adaptive behavior by stating that deficits in adaptive behavior must exist concurrently with significantly subaverage general intellectual functioning and must be evident during the developmental period (Grossman, 1977 in Patton & Jones, 1994). Grossman (1983) further expanded the definition of mental retardation to recognize that significantly subaverage general intellectual functioning can result in or be associated with concurrent impairments in adaptive behavior. Once again, these impairments must be displayed during the developmental period.

In 1992 the AAMR published a new definition of mental retardation that was intended to represent a major paradigm shift in how mental retardation is viewed (Luckasson et al., 1992). The new definition and classification system highlights a specification of supports needed by the individual. Greater importance is placed on the interaction of the person who is mentally retarded with his or her environment than on viewing any deficits as the problem of the individual. The current definition retains the emphasis on significantly subaverage intellectual functioning existing concurrently with limitations in the area of adaptive skills, manifested prior to the age of 18 years.

In addition to defining mental retardation, the AAMR also clarified each of the key components of their mental retardation definition. Initially, definitions of adaptive behavior did not include a recognition that adaptive behavior is relative to one's age and culture. However, Grossman (1983) incorporated these important emphases in his definitions, stating that impairments in this area are reflected in marked limitations in meeting the requirements for personal independence and social responsibility expected for the age and cultural group of the individual. Luckasson and others (1992) further clarified the significance of adaptive behavior by delineating, for the first time, specific areas of adaptive skills. These authors also differentiated *adaptive behavior* from *adaptive skills*. Adaptive behavior refers to the broader construct of the individual's performance in meeting environmental demands. Adaptive skills is intended to suggest an assortment of skills in which an individual can have strengths at the same time that limitations may be present. In designating 10 adaptive skill areas, the authors specify that to be classified as mentally retarded an individual must have limitations in as few as two of the areas (as well as have significantly subaverage intellectual functioning).

Unfortunately, adaptive behavior assessment did not become a standard part of school assessment until the mid-1970s (Reschly, 1982). Even then, little guidance was offered to school psychologists regarding adaptive behavior definition, criteria, and assessment instruments (Patrick & Reschly, 1982). These authors also noted the absence of guidelines for combining the results of intelligence and adaptive behavior tests in classification decisions. However, in more recent years, there has been an increased emphasis on using adaptive behavior scales as part of the comprehensive assessment process (Hutton, Dubes, & Muir, 1992).

OVERVIEW OF ADAPTIVE BEHAVIOR

Although there are various definitions of adaptive behavior, the most commonly cited is that of the AAMR. "Adaptive behavior is defined as the effectiveness or degree with which individuals meet the standards of personal independence and social responsibility expected for age and cultural group" (Grossman, 1983, p. 1). Key components of adaptive behavior emphasize typical performance and not ability, increasing complexity as a function of age, cultural expectations, personal independence and social skills, and environmental demands.

Typical Performance

Whereas assessment of intelligence focuses on a person's abilities, assessment of adaptive behavior stresses an individual's typical performance. What is important is actual behavior and not abilities or constructs that are believed to underlie behavior. The emphasis of adaptive behavior lies within meeting the everyday demands of the individual's environment (Grossman, 1983). Thus, an individual would be scored deficient in a particular area if he or she possesses a skill but does not routinely perform it without assistance or prompting. For example, a young man possesses the skill to complete purchases at a store independently but, instead, allows care providers to make his purchases for him. Although this man has the necessary skills, he would be identified as being deficient in this particular area because he does not typically perform this task. For the person to be considered competent, the skill must be completed by the individual, not for the individual (Schmidt & Salvia, 1984). It is also important to examine typical performance in the context of community settings that are characteristic of the person's same-age peers (Luckasson et al., 1992).

Increasing Complexity with Age

What is viewed as appropriate adaptive behavior varies as a function of age. Expectations for a preschool child are much different from what is expected of a school-aged child, adolescent, or an adult. Grossman (1983) identified changing areas of emphasis for various age groups during infancy and early childhood (1–4), childhood and early adolescence (1–4 and/or 5–8), and late adolescence and early adulthood (1–7 and/or 8):

1. Sensorimotor skills development
2. Communication skills (including speech and language)
3. Self-help skills
4. Socialization (development of ability to interact with others)
5. Application of basic academic skills in daily life activities
6. Application of appropriate reasoning and judgment in Mastery of the environment
7. Social skills (participation in group activities and interpersonal relationships)
8. Vocational and social responsibilities and performance (p. 25)

As can be seen, the criteria for judging adaptive behavior change with the age of the individual, becoming increasingly more complex. There is an increasing emphasis on meeting the demands of the environment. By the time an individual reaches adulthood, adaptive behavior examines the degree to which the individual is independent in the community and in a vocation. Increasing social participation and conforming to community standards is also examined. Luckasson and colleagues (1992) continue this emphasis on the developmental relevance of specific adaptive skills; they state that it is important to consider the relevance of specific skills based on the relevance to the person's age.

Cultural Expectations

In addition to meeting age expectations, a person must also satisfy cultural expectations. Behaviors considered to be adaptive, or appropriate, will vary from culture to culture as well as within subcultures in the same country. For example, in many areas of the United States an important personal hygiene skill involves shaving. However, in some subcultures in the United States and Europe, shaving facial hair for men and body hair for women is not expected. It is particularly important to examine cultural expectations when evaluating social functioning (i.e., items focusing on interpersonal relationships; Reschly, 1989). It should be noted that cultural demands are not static; social expectations change with time (Schmidt & Salvia, 1984).

Personal Independence and Social Skills

The AAMR definition stresses meeting the standards of practical intelligence (i.e., maintaining and sustaining one's independence in the activities of daily living) and social intelligence (i.e., comprehending social expectations and how to behave within social situations; Luckasson et al., 1992). Even though the AAMR definition is viewed as the authoritative source, it neglected to identify specific domains of adaptive behavior until the 1992 definition and classification system. Hence, a variety of adaptive behavior domains and subdomains have been used in adaptive behavior scales and research. Currently, the AAMR definition specifies and defines the following 10 adaptive skill areas: communication, self-care, home living, social, community, self-direction, health and safety, functional academics, leisure, and work (Luckasson et al., 1992). Although this new specificity is welcomed by some (e.g., Reiss, 1994; Smith, 1994), others criticize the domains on the basis that no single, current adaptive behavior scale assesses all these areas and that no factor analytic research confirms that the 10 adaptive skill areas exist and are independent of one another (MacMillan, Gresham, & Siperstein, 1993). However, it should be noted that these criticisms are viewed by some as invalid (Reiss, 1994).

Although a salient concept does not exist, adaptive behavior is a unique construct that does not overlap with intellectual and academic abilities (McGrew & Bruininks, 1989). There is a wide range in the literature in the number of adaptive behavior domains and subdomains identified. As was previously mentioned, the AAMR identifies 10 adaptive skill areas. Holman and Bruininks (1985) analyzed existing adaptive behavior instruments and research and identified a different set of 10 broad clusters and 45 more subdomains of adaptive behavior. Although there are a large number of adaptive behavior domains and the names can vary, Reschly (1989) summarizes this information in four general domains: independent functioning (e.g., toileting, self-feeding, self-dressing, use of leisure time, environmental mobility), social functioning (e.g., avoiding inappropriate behaviors, appropriate sharing, appropriate communication), functional academics (e.g., money handling, following a schedule), and vocational responsibilities and performance (e.g., searching for a job, specific job skills). Although broad domains are sufficient for classification purposes, greater detail is necessary when assessing adaptive behavior for instructional planning. There does seem to be consistent agreement that adaptive behavior refers to meeting the demands of daily life to achieve personal and social self-sufficiency. This general agreement is reflected in the fact that adaptive behavior scales are fairly similar and typically include the same basic domains of behavior (Reschly & Gresham, 1988).

Environmental Demands

This last key component addresses situational specificity of adaptive behavior. The varying environmental demands are unique to the individual and incorporate interactions with others at school, at home, and in the community. Any assessment of adaptive behavior must take into consideration performance in these various settings. It is inappropriate to assess behavior in one setting while excluding others; level of independence can vary markedly from one environment to another. This variability occurs as a result of unique expectations and demands of significant others in assorted settings. In addition, these variable expectations and demands can influence the overall development of adaptive behavior (Reschly, 1990). Finally, knowledge of environmental demands provides crucial information for programming purposes. What is adaptive, or appropriate, in one setting may not be in another setting or at another time; that is, adaptive behavior is dynamic rather than static and dependent on time and place.

RELATIONSHIP OF MALADAPTIVE BEHAVIOR TO ADAPTIVE BEHAVIOR

Maladaptive behavior (e.g., self-injurious behaviors, stereotypic behaviors, physical and verbal aggression, disruptive and destructive behaviors), a two-dimensional construct, is typically labeled *social* (i.e., externally directed) or *personal* (i.e., internally directed; McGrew & Bruininks, 1989). Although maladaptive and adaptive behavior are distinct constructs (McGrew & Bruininks, 1989), it is beneficial to assess the presence of maladaptive behaviors because they may interfere with achieving adaptive behaviors (Sparrow & Cicchetti, 1987). In their review of research on adaptive behavior and mental retardation, Bruininks, Thurlow, and Gilman (1987) showed that not only does maladaptive behavior interfere with attaining adaptive behavior, it also limits integration into schools, interferes with family acceptance, limits employment, and interferes with integration into social settings. According to Bruininks et al. (1987), successful identification and intervention with these behaviors is vital if the individual is to develop more adaptive behaviors and is to be integrated fully within society. In some adaptive behavior scales (e.g., Vineland Adaptive Behavior Scales, Scales of Independent Behavior), the relationship between adaptive and maladaptive behaviors is addressed in ascertaining the individual's proficiency in meeting the demands of his or her environment.

Recent approaches to intervening with maladaptive behaviors place more emphasis on the relationship between adaptive and maladaptive behaviors than did past approaches. Currently, an emphasis is placed on conducting a functional assessment prior to designing intervention procedures (Demchak, 1993). One aspect of functional assessment is identifying appropriate and functionally equivalent behaviors that can be targeted as alternatives to the maladaptive behaviors. These alternative behaviors frequently fall in the adaptive behavior domains of communication, recreation, and social skills; the maladaptive behavior occurs because the individual may not have an appropriate adaptive behavior for the situation (Demchak & Bossert, 1996). Discussing the methodology for completing functional assessments of maladaptive behaviors is beyond the scope of this chapter. (See Demchak & Bossert, 1996; O'Neill, Horner, Albin, Storey, & Sprague, 1990).

ADAPTIVE BEHAVIOR INSTRUMENTS

Vineland Adaptive Behavior Scales

One of the most well known adaptive behavior instruments, the Vineland Adaptive Behavior Scales (Harrison, 1985; Sparrow, Balla, & Cicchetti, 1984a,b), a revision of the Vineland Social Maturity Scale (Doll, 1935, 1965), is composed of three versions: the Survey Form, the Expanded Form, and the Classroom Edition. Each of these versions contains items in the following domains: communication, daily living skills, socialization, and motor skills. Additionally, the Expanded and Survey Forms also assess maladaptive behavior. Scoring options include usually performed (2 points), sometimes/partially performed (1 point), never exhibited (0 points), no opportunity for performance, and don't know. This scoring system allows credit for emerging skills and behaviors that are partially performed. According to the authors, the major purposes of the Vineland are diagnostic evaluation, program planning, and research. Each form of the Vineland may be more appropriate for one or more of these functions based on its organization, content, and comprehensiveness.

The Survey Form (Sparrow et al., 1984b), which utilizes a semistructured interview format, consists of 297 items and targets individuals from birth through 18 years or low functioning adults. It is designed to be used for general assessment purposes highlighting strengths and areas of need. This form can be completed in 20 to 60 minutes.

The Expanded Form (Sparrow et al., 1984a), containing all items in the Survey Form plus additional items for a total of 577, is a more comprehensive assessment instrument designed to ultimately develop educational or habilitative plans. It also uses a semistructured interview format (requiring 60 to 90 minutes), with a caregiver or parent, and is appropriate for use with the same individuals as the Survey Form. In addition, the Expanded Form includes a Program Planning Profile that provides an in-depth illustration of an individual's capabilities. This profile assists the practitioner in pinpointing particular skills for intervention. Those areas with the highest scores provide a base for expanding behaviors, whereas weaker domains identify potential behaviors for acquisition training.

The Classroom Edition (Harrison, 1985) is comprised of 244 items assessing adaptive behavior in the classroom. This edition contains some items from the Survey and Expanded Forms plus additional items related to academic functioning. Unlike the other versions of the Vineland, this edition employs a questionnaire completed independently by the teacher in approximately 20 minutes. Even though the teacher completes the questionnaire, a trained examiner will likely need to score it and interpret the results. The Classroom Edition is appropriate for students 3 years through 12 years of age.

To the authors' credit, the Vineland is one of the most psychometrically sound adaptive behavior instruments available. Each of the three versions summarizes research on standardization, reliability, and validity in its own technical manual. The standardization sample involved over 3,000 participants representing a cross-section of the United States population and including individuals with disabilities. A review of the reliability and validity research illustrates technical adequacy (see Salvia & Ysseldyke, 1995).

Scales of Independent Behavior

Another well-known adaptive behavior instrument is the Scales of Independent Behavior (SIB; Bruininks, Woodcock, Weatherman, & Hill, 1984). The SIB, a comprehensive measure (226 items) of adaptive behavior and functional independence, is comprised of four broad domains: motor skills, social and communication skills, personal living skills, and community living skills. These four areas are further divided into 14 subscales, which further delineate specific skills and behaviors (40 to 50 minutes' administration time). Overall performance of an individual is summarized with a broad independence score, indicating a combined total score. Additional components of the SIB are a short-form version consisting of 32 items for screening (10 to 15 minutes administration time), an early development scale of 32 items for use with young children (10 to 15 minutes), and a scale of problem behaviors (8 to 10 minutes) that targets maladaptive behavior. The scoring options include a score of 0, which indicates the individual never performs the behavior; 1, which indicates the individual does the task but not well; 2, indicating the individual performs the task fairly well; and 3, illustrating the task is performed very well. The SIB is intended for a variety of assessment, program planning, and evaluation purposes with individuals from infancy through adulthood.

Assessors can generate five profiles from the results of the SIB. Two percentile rank profiles, based on age, illustrate an individual's performance compared with that of others the same age. One of these percentile rank profiles also includes a comparison of level of intelligence. The subscale profile enables an interviewer to plot an individual's raw scores and to compare the individual's subscale scores. The fourth profile, the training implications profile, contains information on the individual's relative performance index based on age, level of functioning, and suggested training range. Last, the problem-behaviors profile outlines the frequency and severity of the individual's problem behaviors.

Salvia and Ysseldyke (1995) provide a summary of the technical adequacy of the scale, detailing reliability and validity information as well as norming information. The SIB appears to be quite valid, with variable reliability statistics.

Inventory for Client and Agency Planning (ICAP)

The ICAP (Bruininks, Hill, Weatherman, & Woodcock, 1986) is an adaptive behavior measure composed of 77 items and designed to assess comprehensively the status (e.g., diagnosis, marital status, medical characteristics), adaptive behavior, and needs of clients (20-minute administration time). Its primary purpose is to aid interventionists in screening, monitoring, managing, and evaluating services provided to clients. The ICAP should be completed by a respondent who has known the client for at least 3 months and also sees the client on a daily basis. Domains included in the ICAP are motor skills, social and communication skills, personal living skills, and community living skills.

Examiners score each item individually using a quality descriptor score. A score of 0 indicates that the client never performs the task and a score of 1 reflects a poor performance of the task. If an individual performs a behavior fairly well a score of 2 is recorded, and a score of 3 indicates that the individual does the task very well. Similar to the SIB, overall adaptive behavior performance is summarized within the broad independence score. The ICAP also includes a problem-behavior scale (8 to 10 minutes) for assessing difficult behaviors that may affect personal and community adjustment.

Technical information on the psychometric adequacy of the ICAP is contained in the examiner's manual. Norming standards as well as the sampling procedures used with the 1,764 subjects are discussed. Several reliability and validity studies were conducted with the subjects and indicate adequate psychometric properties.

AAMR Adaptive Behavior Scales

The AAMR Adaptive Behavior Scales (ABS) are composed of two versions: the School scale (Lambert, Nihira, & Leland, 1993) and the Residential and Community scale (Nihira, Leland, & Lambert, 1993). Part 1 of each of these versions addresses personal independence and daily living and contains items in the following nine domains: independent functioning, physical development, economic activity, language development, numbers and time, prevocational/vocational activity, self-direction, responsibility, and socialization. The ABS-School scale further divides these domains into 18 subdomains. The ABS-Residential and Community contains an additional domain in the area of domestic activity for a total of 10 domains that are broken into 21 subdomains. Part 2 of both the ABS-School and the ABS-Residential and Community is concerned with social behavior and is intended to assess behaviors that pertain to personality and behavior disorders. The School scale contains seven domains: social behavior, conformity, trustworthiness, stereotyped and hyperactive behavior, self-abusive behavior, social engagement, and disturbing interpersonal behavior. The Residential and Community scale includes these seven domains as well as the additional domain of sexual behavior in Part 2.

Scoring differs for each part of the instrument. In Part 1, the evaluator is asked to complete two different types of items. The first item requires the evaluator to select the highest level of behaviors displayed by circling the number of the statement that best represents the behavior the person being rated typically exhibits in the targeted area. Other items in Part 1 require the evaluator to determine whether the person being rated can perform specified tasks and to circle either the number in the "Yes" column or that in the "No" column. Part 2 scoring options include: the behavior never occurs (0 points), the behavior occurs occasionally (1 point), and the behavior occurs frequently or habitually (2 points). According to the authors, the purposes of the ABS-School and the ABS-Residential and Community are the same and include identification of strengths and weaknesses, diagnosis, documentation of progress, and research.

The ABS-School can be completed either as an interview with an individual well acquainted with the person being rated or as a questionnaire to be completed by the rater. Administration time is not specified. The authors state that the instrument is intended for use with individuals "up through 21 years of age" (Lambert et al., 1993, p. 7). However, users should note that the sample includes individuals who are not mentally retarded, ages 3 through 18 years; individuals with mental retardation in the sample are ages 3 through 21 years.

As with the ABS-School the ABS-Residential and Community can be completed either as an interview or by the rater completing it directly. Again, administration time is not specified. The authors state that the instrument is appropriate "for use with individuals up through 79 years of age" (Nihira et al., 1993, p. 5). However, users should be cautioned that the instrument was validated only with individuals who were mentally retarded, ages 18 through 60+.

Technical information on both versions of the ABS is included in each examiner's manual. Sampling procedures and norming standards are discussed.

APPLICATION OF ABS TO IDENTIFICATION AND CLASSIFICATION

The major functions of adaptive behavior assessment encompass screening, classification, and developing as well as evaluating teaching or intervention programs (Taylor, 1993). Regardless of the purpose of assessment, it is essential that the adaptive behavior instrument selected is psychometrically sound. Many adaptive behavior scales that do not have adequate reliability and validity information continue to be used (Hutton et al., 1992). Scales that are norm referenced are more appropriate for use in supporting classification decisions whereas criterion-referenced inventories are better suited to program planning (Browder, 1991; Reschly, 1989).

Assessment of adaptive behavior is an essential component when identifying individuals who are mentally retarded. If deficits in adaptive behavior do not exist concurrently with significantly subaverage general intellectual functioning, the person cannot be classified as mentally retarded (Luckasson et al., 1992). The 1992 AAMR definition and classification system specifies that limitations in adaptive skills must occur in two of the 10 identified adaptive skill areas (Luckasson et al., 1992). Although Luckasson and her colleagues do provide some guidelines regarding limitations (e.g., they occur within the context of age-appropriate community settings) in adaptive skills, they do not provide any specific cut-off scores. They further caution that the adaptive skill instrument used must be appropriately normed and standardized.

Although assessment of adaptive behavior is not essential for identification of other disabilities, it has implications for other areas (e.g., emotional disorders, learning disabilities, physical disabilities). Harrison and Robinson (1995) recommend assessing adaptive behavior for all students with disabilities or suspected disabilities. The form of this assessment could include use of a standardized adaptive behavior scale and observations in different settings and with different respondents in order to develop a comprehensive picture of the individual. More appropriate classification decisions will be made and more appropriate program selection will result when adaptive behavior is assessed and considered in these decisions (Reschly, 1989). In the following paragraphs we discuss the application of adaptive behavior assessment to identification and classification of individuals with behavior disorders, learning disabilities, physical disabilities, and sensory impairments.

Sparrow and Cicchetti (1987) found that impairments in adaptive behavior positively correlate with severity of psychological disturbance. These authors also found that specific deficits occurred in interpersonal skills, coping strategies, and leisure skills. Major difficulties were found to exist in socialization and maladaptive behavior. Assessment of adaptive behavior will help to differentiate children with behavior problems from their nondisabled peers and thus should be an integral component of the whole assessment process (Sparrow & Cicchetti, 1987). The National Association of School Psychologists (1995) stresses that students with emotional or behavioral disorders must receive a collaborative and interdisciplinary assessment that includes assessing adaptive skills in both school and out of school settings to determine the extent of adaptive behavior limitations. Although students with emotional or behavioral disorders may display deficits in adaptive skill areas such as self-care or work skills and adjustment, it is more likely that limitations will be displayed in the areas of social skills and peer relationships (Merrell, 1994).

Adaptive behavior scales are not often used in classification decisions in the area of learning disabilities because the emphasis tends to be on academics. Additionally, students with learning disabilities tend to be treated as a homogeneous group. However, results from adaptive behavior instruments reveal that subgroups may exist and this information may influence classification decisions. Weller and Strawser (1987) reviewed the performance of students classified as learning disabled and found that they could be further divided into five subgroups that focused on specific adaptive behavior deficits (e.g., poor independent work habits, socialization). Knowing that these subgroups exist can impact how these students are identified and classified and can subsequently influence programming.

Assessment of those with physical disabilities, similar to assessment of students with learning disabilities, has also neglected adaptive behavior. With these students the emphasis tends to be on medical issues (e.g., occupational therapy, physical therapy), intelligence, and academic progress (Pollingue, 1987). Pollingue (1987) suggests that adaptive behavior scales can provide valuable knowledge that may influence classification and placement issues by contributing information on amount and type of assistance needed in meeting demands of daily living.

Last, the use of adaptive behavior measures with low incidence populations (e.g., hearing and visual impairments) is in its infancy due to complex issues. These issues include impaired sensory input, appropriate assessment techniques, and adapted scoring procedures (Meacham, Kline, Stovall, & Sands, 1987). Even though these issues have not been resolved, adaptive behavior scales can provide useful information on the adaptive efforts of individuals with sensory impairments. Individuals with visual impairments may exhibit limitations in self-help and other adaptive skill areas partly due to their visual impairment and partly because of overdependence on others (Davidson & Dolins, 1993). Other adaptive skill areas in which these individuals may display deficits include social and play skills (Bradley-Johnson, 1995). Similarly, children who are deaf or hard-of-hearing may also display limitations in the social/emotional area (Vess & Douglas, 1995). Thus, the assessment of adaptive behavior can be important for classification and placement as well as program planning.

The above categorical descriptors are typically applied to school-age children and older individuals; however, it is not always appropriate to apply these labels to preschoolers. The label typically used with this population is *developmentally delayed*. Developmental delays may be displayed in self-help, motor, cognition, social, and/or communication domains. Assessment of adaptive behavior has particular relevance with preschoolers because it may help practitioners identify delays in these domains. Identification of these delays may help to qualify a child to receive special services; that is, adaptive behavior assessment may be one component of the multisource assessment. Some of the most common areas screened for preschool children include communication, gross- and fine-motor skills, social/emotional development, and self-help skills (Gridley, Mucha, & Hatfield, 1995), all common areas on adaptive behavior instruments.

There are several reasons for the increased emphasis on adaptive behavior in all disability areas and across all ages of individuals. First, the expansion of the AAMR definition of mental retardation to include adaptive behavior has had a major influence on the assessment of adaptive behavior. Second, litigative and legislative decisions have influenced the use of adaptive behavior scales. For example, various court cases (e.g., *Larry P. v. Riles, Diana v. the Board of Education*) contributed to the nondiscriminatory evaluation components of Public Law 101–476 and Public Law 99–457. As a result there are more stringent assessment guidelines to be followed: (1) Tests cannot be racially or culturally discriminatory; (2) tests must be administered in the native language or mode of communication; (3) no single evaluation can be used as a sole criterion; (4) trained personnel must administer tests; (5) tests must be validated for the purpose used; and (6) accommodations must be made for physical and sensory disabilities. Additionally, assessment must be conducted in all areas related to the suspected disability and must utilize multisource measures. This variety of sources can include teacher observations, parent report, and aptitude and achievement tests as well as adaptive behavior scales. Not only is multifactored assessment required by current law, it also provides a more holistic approach to classification decisions (Reschly, 1981). Thus, more emphasis must be placed on adaptive behavior to describe typical patterns of behavior. Third, Public Law 101–476 and Public Law 99–457 recognize the importance of including parents in the educational decision-making process. A key way to involve parents in assessment is in the area of adaptive behavior. Parents and significant others are often the respondents on adaptive behavior measures and have vital information pertaining to their child's performance. Last, Public Law 101–476 mandates transition services for all students with disabilities, beginning no later than 16 years of age. Effective transition planning is unlikely to occur in the absence of a comprehensive assessment. Assessment for transition planning should include evaluation of skills related to community living and maintaining employment (e.g., daily living skills, personal management, social skills, vocational skills; Levinson, 1995).

APPLICATION OF ABS TO INSTRUCTIONAL PROGRAM PLANNING

Educational program planning involves delineating individual goals and objectives to address students' strengths and areas of need. Adaptive behavior measures can provide useful information for programming for individuals who are physically disabled (Pollingue, 1987), learning disabled (Weller & Strawser, 1987), sensory impaired (Meacham et al., 1987), or mentally retarded (Langone & Burton, 1987). Additionally, there are programming implications for individuals with mild to severe disabilities and for preschool children as well as school-aged children, adolescents, and adults.

General Program Planning

Program planning requires the use of instruments that thoroughly cover relevant areas. Unfortunately, most current adaptive behavior scales provide only an overview of the individual's adaptive performance without providing information regarding specific skills (Harrison & Robinson, 1995). The results are best used as a guide to identify general strengths, areas mastered, and needs for future independence. This global picture of an individual can be especially beneficial for the practitioner who is unfamiliar with the person assessed. Although more in-depth assessment will be needed when planning for an unfamiliar person, the adaptive behavior results can narrow the amount of additional assessment by helping the practitioner identify priority areas. It is essential that this additional, specific assessment occur as part of the comprehensive process. Without the specific assessment, the global results of the adaptive behavior instrument would not be particularly useful in developing instructional programs (Berg, Wacker, & Steege, 1995).

To conduct a comprehensive evaluation, appropriate assessment practices require the use of multiple sources (e.g., parents, teachers), multiple settings (e.g., home, school, community), and multiple methods (e.g., interview, observation). Especially important, for comparative purposes, is the use of at least one standardized adaptive behavior inventory for identifying deficits in this area (Reschly, 1989). When adaptive behavior deficits are used as part of the justification for special-education classification, it is imperative that adaptive behavior goals are included in the individual education plan (Reschly, 1990).

Planning for Specific Instructional Programs

Although broad goals can be identified from the results of standardized adaptive behavior inventories, specific instructional objectives require more in-depth assessment in the form of ecological, or environmental, inventories. These inventories are completed in the individual's current and future environments in order to identify specific skills needed in those settings. Conducting ecological inventories paired with providing instruction in the natural settings enhances the probability of skill generalization and maintenance. Although the methodology for completing ecological inventories has been emphasized in the area of severe disabilities (Brown et al., 1979), these procedures have been used less frequently in the area of mild disabilities. However, this methodology has valuable implications for individuals with either severe or mild disabilities.

Severe Disabilities

One of the best practices in severe disabilities is a functional curriculum that is developed using ecological inventories (Browder, 1991). The process for completing these inventories is delineated by Brown et al. (1979) as follows: (1) identify functional curricular domains (i.e., domestic, community, leisure, vocational), (2) identify current and future environments, (3) identify subenvironments within each environment, (4) specify activities that occur within each subenvironment, and (5) delineate the skills required to complete each activity.

Table 11–1. Sample ecological inventory for the community domain

Domain: Community	*Environment:* Fast Food Restaurant
Subenvironment:	Counter area
Activity:	Ordering
Skills:	Go to the counter
	Stand in line
	Move forward with line
	Place order when asked
	Pay for order when asked
	Pick up tray or bag and leave counter
Subenvironment:	Eating area
Activity:	Eating meal
Skills:	Go to eating area
	Scan for empty table
	Go to empty table and sit down
	Eat meal
	Collect trash on tray or in bag
Subenvironment:	Trash area
Activity:	Throwing away trash
Skills:	Go to trash area
	Throw trash in receptacle
	Place tray on top of receptacle

Table 11–2.   Factors to consider in prioritizing goals

1. Is the targeted activity appropriate for the chronological age of the individual?
2. Can the targeted activity be taught using materials appropriate for the chronological age of the individual?
3. Is the targeted activity needed on a daily basis?
4. Can the targeted activity be taught regularly across settings and using different materials?
5. Will performance of the targeted activity increase interactions with nonhandicapped peers?
6. Is the targeted activity needed in current and future environments?
7. Is the targeted activity a critical activity (i.e., if the individual is not taught to perform the activity will someone else need to do it for him or her)?
8. Can the targeted activity be taught in the natural context in which it will be needed?
9. Is it a preference of the family or caregivers that the individual be taught the targeted activity?
10. Is it a preference of the individual to learn the targeted activity?
11. Can the individual partially (or independently) participate in the targeted activity?

One useful strategy for obtaining this information involves interviews, conducted by the primary service provider, with significant others, teachers, and other service providers. Berg and colleagues (1995) recommend that these semistructured interviews focus on (1) skills in which the student is independent or requires little assistance, (2) skills that must still be mastered, (3) any behavior problems displayed, (4) identification of activities, foods, and social attention that might serve as potential reinforcers, (5) methods used to communicate (verbal and nonverbal), and (6) priority skills for instruction as well as priority problem behaviors for elimination. The IMPACT Curriculum (Neel & Billingsley, 1989) contains two excellent examples of interview formats: one for parents or care providers in the home setting and the other for teachers in the school setting.

Additionally, the practitioner may visit the home, future school placement, and various community sites (e.g., restaurants, stores, parks, and possible places of employment). Table 11–1 provides an example of a completed ecological inventory for one environment within the community domain. Ecological inventories provide numerous potential goals for instruction, which need to be prioritized. The questions in Table 11–2 can be used to assist the practitioner in selecting goals as priorities for instruction. For each potential goal the practitioner would ask each of the questions listed in the table. Those goals receiving the largest number of "Yes" answers would be higher priorities than other potential goals. However, further assessment is needed in the areas targeted as priorities to identify specific skills needed as well as to identify potential adaptations.

Discrepancy analyses (i.e., student repertoire inventories), which compare the performance of individuals with disabilities to those without, are used to target specific behaviors needed for successful performance of the activity. The steps for conducting discrepancy analyses are as follows: (1) identify the skills performed by peers without disabilities to complete a specific activity, (2) observe the individual with disabilities and record whether the person is able to complete the steps, (3) complete a discrepancy analysis of the person's behavior to identify why the person is unable to perform the step (e.g., unable to state what is desired because the person is nonverbal and lacks a communication system), and (4) specify what should be done (i.e., teach the skill directly, develop an adaptation, teach a related skill). For these who are nonverbal, the targeted option may be to provide them with communication cards and then teach them to use those cards to place their order. Table 11–3 provides an example of completed discrepancy analysis. Completing discrepancy analyses addresses an area that Langone and Burton (1987) believe to be the cornerstone for assessing learner progress: comparison to persons without disabilities.

Mild Disabilities

With individuals with mild disabilities (e.g., mild mental retardation, learning disabilities, behavior problems) adaptive behavior, if assessed, is done so with an emphasis on identification as opposed to an emphasis on programming. However, adaptive behavior has valuable implications for planning for inclusion of students with disabilities in general-education classrooms as well as for transition to postsecondary activities. Inclusion of students with mild disabilities may be more successful if practitioners employ environmental analyses to identify appropriate goals and objectives. By surveying the future environment (i.e., general-education classroom) to delineate specific activities and skills, the teacher can target the behaviors relevant for success in that environment. If teachers neglect to conduct ecological inventories, it is likely that skills targeted in the special-education envi-

Table 11–3.   Sample discrepancy analysis for the community domain

Student: Karen   *Domain:* Community   *Subenvironment:* Counter Area
Date: 2/2/96   *Environment:* Fast Food   *Teacher:* Carl Morgan
          Restaurant

Nondisabled Person Inventory		Student Inventory	Discrepancy Analysis	What-to-do Options
Activity:	Ordering			
Skills:	Go to the counter	+		
	Stand in line	+		
	Move forward with line	−	Stands in same place	Teach to step forward when person in front moves forward
	Place order when asked	−	Is nonverbal	Teach to use a communication card that gives her order
	Pay for order when asked	−	Gives wrong amount of money	Teach to use next dollar strategy to pay for order
	Pick up tray or bag and leave counter	+		

Code: + = correct response; − = incorrect response.

ronment will not be those that are most important for success in the inclusive setting (Horn & Fuchs, 1987). Targeting relevant goals and objectives may result in smoother transition to the inclusive setting and may also lead to more positive attitudes from general educators (Horn & Fuchs, 1987).

Anderson-Inman, Walker, and Purcell (1984) suggest using methodology similar to ecological inventories for program planning with students with mild disabilities. Their process, referred to as transenvironmental programming, emphasizes preparing students placed in resource-room programs for reentry into mainstreamed classrooms. Step 1 focuses on assessing the target environment (i.e., the regular classroom) to identify critical behavioral expectations of the setting to ensure that students entering the class can meet those expectations. These authors provide examples of two instruments that can be used to identify the behavioral and academic demands of the inclusive classroom. Step 2 stresses intervening in the special-education environment to prepare the student for the general-education class. Thus, it is necessary to teach, systematically, the social and academic skills as well as the skills related to academic success (e.g., asking for help, following directions) necessary for success in the inclusive environment (i.e., those behaviors identified in Step 1). Generalization of skills across settings is the emphasis of Step 3. Specific strategies for enhancing generalization of behavior (e.g., using natural contingencies, programming common stimuli, self-management procedures, general case instruction) are discussed elsewhere (Albin & Horner, 1988; Stokes & Baer, 1978; Stokes & Osnes, 1988). The final step of the transenvironmental programming model emphasizes the importance of evaluating student performance in the target environment. This evaluation provides critical information as to the success of the intervention and also provides ongoing data for altering the intervention program if it has not been successful.

Environmental analyses are also beneficial in planning for community-based instruction and transition to postsecondary activities. Conducting ecological inventories can result in functional goals and objectives that may lead to greater skill generalization following completion of school. In the past, the importance of transition was primarily emphasized for those individuals with more severe disabilities. However, Public Law 101–476 requires that transition services be part of the IEP process for all students with disabilities by the age of 16 years and annually thereafter. For successful transition planning, practitioners cannot rely on what is thought to be needed but must address the interests and preferences of the student and move beyond traditional teaching approaches in the classroom. Langone (1990) and Cronin and Patton (1993) outline methodology that can be used to develop appropriate curriculum for students with mild to moderate disabilities. Langone stresses that it is important to apply the principle of *community validity* in determining whether particular goals and objectives are meaningful for a specific student. To determine if curriculum content is community valid, Langone recommends completing a community needs assessment by (1) interviewing parents, guardians, students, and employers (Table 11–4 provides examples of interview questions pertaining to individuals with mild disabilities), (2) having these same individuals complete questionnaires, and (3) conducting direct observations. Langone (1990) and Cronin and Patton (1993) suggest structuring observations, conducted in community environ-

Table 11–4.   Sample interview questions for program planning for students with mild disabilities

Student Questions
1. What are your goals related to obtaining a job?
2. How would you find a job in this area?
3. What besides academics does school offer you? What are you interested in?
4. Do you need a college degree or further education to attain your job goals?
5. How do you spend your free time?
6. With whom do you spend your free time?

Questions for Former Students
1. Do you have problems in social situations?
2. Do you have transportation difficulties in getting to your job (e.g., public transportation schedules, fares)?
3. What do you think was the best/most important thing you learned in school?
4. What was the least helpful?
5. What skills did you have to learn in order to live on your own?
6. Are there any jobs you would rather do?
7. Why have you not tried to get these jobs?

Questions for Employers
1. What does an individual need to know for this job?
2. What could stop you from hiring an individual with a disability?
3. Is the site accessible?
4. How do you feel about a job coach being on site?
5. What are the specific job skills needed?
6. Is there a dress code?
7. Are there benefits with the job?
8. Would you hire this individual for long-term or short-term employment?

Parent/Caregiver Questions
1. Does your son/daughter use time concepts for daily activities?
2. What do you anticipate for your son/daughter in the future after schooling is completed?
3. What basic or functional academic skills do you think your son/daughter needs for the future?
4. Are there any academic skills that would be directly usable at home or in the community if your son/daughter could do them?
5. Does your son/daughter interact with same age peers in the neighborhood?
6. What kind of family recreational activities do you do?
7. What responsibilities does your son/daughter have at home?
8. What jobs or personal hygiene/grooming skills would you like your son/daughter to perform independently at home?
9. Can your son/daughter go to a store, buy something, and get change?
10. Can your son/daughter recognize signs within the community?

ments, in a format similar to the ecological inventories previously described. The environments are broken down into subenvironments; the observer indicates the specific activities, or major life demands, that occur there and the skills needed to complete the activities. By subsequently completing discrepancy analyses, the practitioner can identify specific objectives for a particular student. By employing this methodology with students with mild disabilities prior to developing the IEP, it is likely that teachers will develop more appropriate goals and objectives that emphasize teaching individuals meaningful skills needed for successful independent living upon completion of school. If skills are not community valid, they would not be given a high priority in the IEP (Langone, 1990). This approach to assessment and subsequent teaching also emphasizes moving beyond the instruction in the classroom and teaching in the community where the particular skills are, and will be, needed. It also requires integrating life skills content into the ongoing curriculum (Cronin & Patton, 1993).

By following this approach, it is also likely that teachers will move beyond traditional approaches for teaching academics to students with mild disabilities. Instead, more emphasis will probably be placed upon *functional academics*. Functional academics refers to those skills necessary for basic literacy and basic knowledge of concepts of time and number (Reschly, 1989). With this approach to teaching academics there is an emphasis on teaching reading, writing, and mathematics as they relate to everyday demands. Academic skills would be taught in the context of functional activities (e.g., managing a bank account, grocery shopping for one's self or family, planning menus, reading and following recipes/directions), using natural materials, and in the context of a variety of natural environments. The previously discussed strategies of ecological inventories (i.e., community or environmental inventories) and discrepancy analyses are once again the means for determining the specific academic content meaningful for a particular student.

Grenot-Scheyer, Eshilian, and Falvey (1989) provide an adaptation to the ecological inventory process to aid practitioners in developing reading content. After specifying the curriculum domain, the environment, the subenvironment, and the activity, the practitioner identifies key vocabulary for that activity. An abbreviated example of this approach is provided:

Domain: Vocational

Environment: High School

Subenvironment: Home Living Skills Class

Activity: Baking

Key Vocabulary: Nouns used in activity

    1. Appliances: Oven, mixer

    2. Kitchen "Tools": Measuring cup, teaspoon, tablespoon, etc.

In addition to identifying nouns used in the activity, the teacher would also specify verbs, modifiers, and descriptors, as well as prepositions.

Table 11–5. Sample ecological inventory incorporating functional academics

Domain: Community	*Environment:* Fast Food Restaurant
Subenvironment: Counter Area	*Activity:* Ordering

Skills: Go to counter
Stand in line
    Check time to determine appropriate menu board (e.g., breakfast or lunch)
    Read menu board to select desired item(s)
    Determine if enough money for desired item(s)
Move forward with line
Place order when asked
Pay for order when asked
    Determine appropriate amount of money to give counterperson
    Wait for change
    Count change
Pick up tray or bag and leave counter

The ecological inventory approach can also be used to identify functional mathematics content. Following implementation of the basic steps of the strategy (i.e., identifying the curriculum domains, environments, subenvironments, and activities), the practitioner reviews the activity to identify the money concepts needed to perform the activity, time concepts needed for independent performance, essential measurement concepts, and necessary problem-solving skills (Ford et al. in Grenot-Scheyer, Eshilian, & Falvey, 1989). Table 11–5 provides an example of an ecological inventory that incorporates functional academics (i.e., reading and mathematics) in ordering a meal in a restaurant. Once again, a discrepancy analysis would be completed to identify the specific skills needed by the student.

Preschoolers with Disabilities

The use of adaptive behavior scales with preschoolers with disabilities is not a widespread practice. However, appropriate and functional programming for preschoolers with disabilities is an issue for many early interventionists. Ecological inventories and discrepancy analyses, previously discussed, provide a framework for identifying appropriate goals and objectives, including participation in ongoing activities in the integrated preschool setting. Similar to the Anderson-Inman et al. (1984) transenvironmental programming approach is the Vincent et al. (1980) and Salisbury and Vincent (1990) criterion of the next environment model for planning for preschoolers with disabilities. This model enables practitioners to evaluate early childhood programs to determine relevant skills for programming to enhance success in current and future environments. To ascertain relevant survival skills for smoother transitions, four strategies are recommended: kindergarten tryouts, follow-up of children who already transitioned, kindergarten teacher-generated skills, and direct observation of potential classrooms for integration. Assessing adaptive behavior is an ongoing process that only begins in the preschool years.

Summary of Best Practices

It is most important that assessment of adaptive behavior be relevant for all individuals with disabilities, regardless of type or severity, and for preschoolers and adults. Successful use of adaptive behavior assessment in general and specific program planning for students with mild to severe disabilities requires implementation of a variety of best practices. Third-party respondents must be people who know the individual well in a variety of settings so that they do not resort to guessing about an individual's typical performance. It is insufficient to base assessment of adaptive behavior on only performance in classroom or program situations. Rather, performance in home and community environments must also be considered for a comprehensive profile of the individual. Also necessary for this complete profile is consideration of information from various sources: standardized adaptive behavior instruments, interviews with significant others, and direct observation of the individual in the natural environment. Results from this multisource assessment has implications both for classification and instructional programming. If assessment of adaptive behavior is used as part of the multisource assessment process for identification and classification, it is imperative that psychometrically sound instruments are used. While the global score obtained from adaptive behavior scales may contribute to classification decisions and general goals, more information is needed for developing specific objectives for instructional programming. If results from an adaptive behavior scale contribute to classification and placement decisions, adaptive behavior, generally or in specific domain(s), should be addressed within the individualized program plans for the individual. Using standardized instruments that are comprehensive in addressing various domains and include items that range from low to high in complexity and skill development (Cone, 1987) can narrow the amount of subsequent detailed assessment needed. However, designing instructional objectives and programs requires more specific assessment (e.g., ecological inventories, transenvironmental programming) in the natural environment.

Placing an emphasis on adaptive behavior in specific program planning for students with mild to severe disabilities leads to a variety of best educational practices. Subsequent instruction pertaining to the goals and objectives developed through assessment emphasizing adaptive behavior requires use of natural environments and materials to be most successful. Additionally, the targeted skills should be taught in the context of meaningful activities and not in isolation to ensure maximum success. As is evident from the above discussion, it becomes necessary to target different goals and objectives for students with mild disabilities than what has been typically targeted in the past (Cronin & Patton, 1993). By following these guidelines, it enhances the probability that individuals with mild to severe disabilities will be more likely to generalize and maintain skills; that is, they will be more successful in meeting the demands of their everyday environments.

ISSUES AND FUTURE DIRECTIONS

Although the above strategies and procedures are documented as best practices, there continues to be a need to encourage practitioners to implement them in many situations. For example, assessment of adaptive behavior, relevant for individuals with all types of disabilities, continues to be emphasized only for those who are mentally retarded. It is recommended that practitioners utilize assessment of adaptive behavior for classification and programming decisions for other types of disabilities (e.g., learning disabilities, behavior disorders, sensory impairments, physical disabilities). In addition, adaptive behavior assessment is appropriate for individuals of all ages, including preschoolers.

One important role of adaptive behavior measurement is use in planning for future educational placements, employment, and living arrangements. More emphasis needs to be placed on strategies such as Anderson-Inman and others' (1984) approach to planning for reintegration of students with mild disabilities, use of the criterion of the next environment model with preschoolers with disabilities (Salisbury & Vincent, 1990), planning for transition from school to postschool activities, and targeting functional academics with students with mild disabilities. Finally, more work needs to be done to bring the methodology of ecological inventories and discrepancy analyses to all practitioners who work with individuals with severe disabilities to help these individuals participate more fully in their communities.

In addition to the issues that involve practitioner implications, there are standardization and adaptive behavior construct concerns that continue to need attention. Although many of the recent, well-known adaptive behavior instruments include preschool children in their norming sample, the numbers may not be adequate. Also, as early childhood special education is a relatively new field, the content of adaptive behavior items should be reviewed to be sure it is ecologically valid and appropriate for young children.

Another major area of concern relates to the issue that there is no clear concept of adaptive behavior (McGrew & Bruininks, 1989; Salvia & Ysseldyke, 1995). Numerous definitions of adaptive behavior contribute to wide variability in the number of domains and subdomains on individual adaptive behavior instruments affecting validity. If domains are inadequately covered on a particular instrument, this inadequacy could unfairly influence classification or programming decisions.

CONCLUSION

Adaptive behavior is a dynamic construct influenced by the individual's age, environment, and culture. Assessing adaptive behavior provides a useful, overall profile of the individual with implications for classification and instructional programming. Including adaptive behavior as part of the multisource assessment process will contribute to sounder classification and placement decisions. According to Reschly (1981), assessment of adaptive behavior is essential in order to guarantee that educational programs for students with disabilities are functional and effective rather than dead-end and inferior. Since we can effectively modify and teach adaptive behavior, it is imperative that we do so to enhance the likelihood that individuals with disabilities will be successful in present and future environments.

REFERENCES

Albin, R.W., & Horner, R.H. (1988). Generalization with precision. In R.H. Horner, G. Dunlap, & R.L. Koegel (Eds.), *Generalization and maintenance: Life-style changes in applied settings* (pp. 99–120). Baltimore: Paul H. Brookes.

Anderson-Inman, L., Walker, H., & Purcell, J. (1984). Promoting the transfer of skills across settings: Transenvironmental programming for handicapped students in the mainstream. In W.L. Heward, T.E. Heron, D.S. Hill, & J. Trap-Porter (Eds.), *Focus on behavior analysis in education* (pp. 17–37). Columbus OH: Merrill.

Berg, W.K., Wacker, D.P., & Steege, M.W. (1995). Best practices in assessment with persons who have severe or profound handicaps. In A. Thomas & J. Grimes (Eds.), *Best practices in school psychology III* (pp. 805–816). Washington, DC: National Association of School Psychologists.

Bradley-Johnson, S. (1995). Best practices in planning effective instruction for students who are visually impaired or blind. In A. Thomas & J. Grimes (Eds.), *Best practices in school psychology III* (pp. 1133–1140). Washington, DC: National Association of School Psychologists.

Browder, D.M. (1991). *Assessment of individuals with severe disabilities: An applied behavior approach to life skills assessment* (2nd ed.). Baltimore: Paul H. Brookes.

Brown, L., Branston-McClean, M.B., Baumgart, D., Vincent, L., Falvey, M., & Schroeder, J. (1979). Using the characteristics of current and subsequent least restrictive environments in the development of curricular content for severely handicapped students. *AAESPH Review, 4,* 407–424.

Bruininks, R.H., Hill, B.K., Weatherman, R.F., & Woodcock, R.W. (1986). *Examiner's Manual: Inventory for Client and Agency Planning.* Allen, TX: DLM Teaching Resources.

Bruininks, R.H., Thurlow, M., & Gilman, C.J. (1987). Adaptive behavior and mental retardation. *The Journal of Special Education, 21,* 69–88.

Bruininks, R.H., Woodcock, R.W., Weatherman, R.F., & Hill, B.K. (1984). *Interviewer's Manual: Scales on Independent Behavior.* Allen, TX: DLM Teaching Resources.

Cone, J.D. (1987). Intervention planning using adaptive behavior instruments. *Journal of Special Education, 21,* 127–148.

Cronin, M.E., & Patton, J.R. (1993). *Life skills instruction for all students with special needs.* Austin, TX: PRO-ED.

Davidson, P.W., & Dolins, M. (1993). Assessment of the young child with visual impairment and multiple disabilities. In J.L. Culbertson & D.J. Willis (Eds.), *Testing young children: A reference guide for developmental, psychoeducational, and psychosocial assessments* (pp. 237–261). Austin, TX: PRO-ED.

Demchak, M. (1993). Functional assessment of problem behaviors in applied settings. *Intervention in School and Clinic, 29,* 89–95.

Demchak, M., & Bossert, K.W. (1996). *Assessing problem behaviors.* Washington, DC: American Association on Mental Retardation.

Doll, E.A. (1935). A genetic scale of social maturity. *The American Journal of Orthopsychiatry, 5,* 180–188.

Doll, E.A. (1940). The social basis of mental diagnosis. *Journal of Applied Psychology, 24,* 160–169.

Doll, E.A. (1953). *The measurement of social competence: A manual for the Vineland Social Maturity Scale.*

Doll, E.A. (1965). *Vineland Social Maturity Scale: Condensed Manual of Directions.* Circle Pines, MN: American Guidance Service.

Grenot-Scheyer, M., Eshilian, L., & Falvey, M.A. (1989). Functional academics. In M.A. Falvey (Ed.), *Community-based curriculum* (2nd ed., pp. 285–320). Baltimore: Paul H. Brookes.

Gridley, B.E., Mucha, L., & Hatfield, B.B. (1995). Best practices in preschool screening. In A. Thomas & J. Grimes (Eds.), *Best practices in school psychology III* (pp. 213–225). Washington, DC: National Association of School Psychologists.

Grossman, H.J. (1977). *Manual on terminology and classification in mental retardation* (2nd ed.). Washington, DC: American Association on Mental Deficiency.

Grossman, H.J. (1983). *Classification in mental retardation.* Washington, DC: American Association on Mental Deficiency.

Harrison, P.L. (1985). *Vineland Adaptive Behavior Scales: Classroom Edition Manual.* Circle Pines, MN: American Guidance Service.

Harrison, P.L., & Robinson, B. (1995). Best practices in the assessment of adaptive behavior. In A. Thomas & J. Grimes (Eds.), *Best practices in school psychology III* (pp. 753–762). Washington, DC: National Association of School Psychologists.

Heber, R. (1961). A manual on terminology and classification in mental retardation (2nd ed.). [Monograph supplement]. *American Journal of Mental Deficiency, 64.*

Holman, J.G., & Bruininks, R.H. (1985). Assessing and training adaptive behaviors. In K.C. Lakin & R.H. Bruininks (Eds.), *Strategies for achieving community integration of developmentally disabled citizens* (pp. 73–104). Baltimore: Paul H. Brookes.

Horn, E., & Fuchs, D. (1987). Using adaptive behavior in assessment and intervention: An overview. *The Journal of Special Education, 21,* 11–26.

Hutton, J.B., Dubes, R., & Muir, S. (1992). Assessment practices of school psychologists: Ten years later. *School Psychology Review, 21,* 271–284.

Lambert, N., Nihira, K., & Leland, H. (1993). *Adaptive Behavior Scale-School* (2nd ed.). Austin, TX: PRO-ED.

Langone, J. (1990). *Teaching students with mild and moderate learning problems.* Boston: Allyn & Bacon.

Langone, J., & Burton, T.A. (1987). Teaching adaptive behavior skills to moderately and severely handicapped individuals: Best practices for facilitating independent living. *The Journal of Special Education, 21,* 149–165.

Levinson, E.M. (1995). Best practices in transition services. In A. Thomas & J. Grimes (Eds.), *Best practices in school psychology III* (pp. 909–915). Washington, DC: National Association of School Psychologists.

Luckasson, R., Coulter, D.L., Polloway, E.A., Reiss, S., Schalock, R.L., Snell, M.E., Spitalnik, D.M., & Stark, J.A. (1992). Mental retardation: Definition, classification, and systems of supports (9th ed.). Washington, DC: American Association on Mental Retardation.

MacMillan, D.L., Gresham, F.M., & Siperstein, G.N. (1993). Conceptual and psychometric concerns about the 1992 AAMR definition of mental retardation. *American Journal of Mental Retardation, 98,* 325–335.

McGrew, K.S., & Bruininks, R. (1989). The factor structure of adaptive behavior. *School Psychology Review, 18,* 64–81.

Meacham, F., Kline, M.M., Stovall, J.A., & Sands, D.I. (1987). Adaptive behavior and low incidence handicaps: Hearing and visual impairments. *The Journal of Special Education, 21,* 183–196.

Merrell, K.W. (1994). *Assessment of behavioral, social, and emotional problems.* New York: Longman.

National Association of School Psychologists. (1995). Students with emotional/behavioral disorders. In A. Thomas & J. Grimes (Eds.), *Best practices in school psychology III* (pp. 1219–1221). Washington, DC: Author.

Neel, R.S., & Billingsley, F.F. (1989). *IMPACT: A functional curriculum handbook for students with moderate to severe disabilities.* Baltimore: Paul H. Brookes.

Nihira, K., Leland, H., & Lambert, N. (1993). *Adaptive Behavior Scales-Residential and Community* (2nd ed.). Austin, TX: PRO-ED.

O'Neill, R.E., Horner, R.H., Albin, R.W., Storey, K., & Sprague, J.R. (1990). *Functional analysis of problem behavior: A practical assessment guide.* Sycamore, IL: Sycamore Publishing.

Patrick, J.L., & Reschly, D.J. (1982). Relationship of state educational criteria and demographic variables to school-system prevalence of mental retardation. *American Journal on Mental Deficiency, 86,* 351–360.

Patton, J.R., & Jones, E.D. (1994). Definitional perspective. In M. Beirne-Smith, J.R. Patton, & R. Ittenbach (Eds.), *Mental retardation* (4th ed., pp. 56–98). Columbus, OH: Merrill.

Pollingue, A. (1987). Adaptive behavior and low incidence handicaps: Use of adaptive behavior instruments for persons with physical handicaps. *The Journal of Special Education, 21,* 117–125.

Reiss, S. (1994). Issues in defining mental retardation. *American Journal of Mental Retardation, 99,* 1–7.

Reschly, D.J. (1981). Psychological testing in educational classification and placement. *American Psychologist, 36,* 1094–1102.

Reschly, D.J. (1982). Assessing mild mental retardation: The influence of adaptive behavior, sociocultural status, and prospects for nonbiased assessment. In C.R. Reynolds & T.B. Gutkin (Eds.), *The handbook of school psychology* (pp. 209–242). New York: Wiley.

Reschly, D.J. (1989). Incorporating adaptive behavior deficits into instructional programs. In G.A. Robinson, J.R. Patton, E.A. Polloway, & L.R. Sargent (Eds.), *Best practices in mild mental disabilities* (pp. 39–63). Reston, VA: Council for Exceptional Children.

Reschly, D.J. (1990). Best practices in adaptive behavior. In A. Thomas & J. Grimes (Eds.), *Best practices in school psychology II* (pp. 29–42). Washington, DC: National Association of School Psychologists.

Reschly, D.J., & Gresham, F.M. (1988). Adaptive behavior and the mildly handicapped. In T.R. Kratochwill (Ed.), *Advances in school psychology* (Vol. 6, pp. 249–282). Hillsdale, NJ: Erlbaum.

Salisbury, C.L., & Vincent, L.J. (1990). Criterion of the next environment and best practices: Mainstreaming and integration 10 years later. *Topics in Early Childhood Special Education, 10*(2), 78–89.

Salvia, J., & Ysseldyke, J.E. (1995). *Assessment* (6th ed.). Boston: Houghton Mifflin.

Schmidt, M.W., & Salvia, J. (1984). Adaptive behavior: A conceptual analysis. *Diagnostique, 9,* 117–125.

Smith, J.D. (1994). The revised AAMR definition of mental retardation: The MRDD position. *Education and Training in Mental Retardation and Developmental Disabilities, 29,* 179–183.

Sparrow, S.S., Balla, D.A., & Cicchetti, D. (1984a). *Vineland Adaptive Behavior Scales: Interview Edition Expanded Form Manual.* Circle Pines, MN: American Guidance Service.

Sparrow, S.S., Balla, D.A., & Cicchetti, D. (1984b). *Vineland Adaptive Behavior Scales: Interview Edition Survey Form Manual.* Circle Pines, MN: American Guidance Service.

Sparrow, S.S., & Cicchetti, D.V. (1987). Adaptive behavior and the psychologically disturbed child. *The Journal of Special Education, 21,* 89–100.

Stokes, T.F., & Baer, D.M. (1978). An implicit technology of generalization. *Journal of Applied Behavior Analysis, 10,* 349–367.

Stokes, T.F., & Osnes, P.G. (1988). The developing applied technology of generalization and maintenance. In R.H. Horner, G. Dunlap, & R.L. Koegel (Eds.), *Generalization and maintenance: Life-style changes in applied settings* (pp. 5–19). Baltimore: Paul H. Brookes.

Taylor, R.L. (1993). *Assessment of exceptional students: Educational and psychological procedures* (3rd ed.). Boston: Allyn & Bacon.

Vess, S., & Douglas, L. (1995). Best practices in program planning for children who are deaf or severely hard of hearing. In A. Thomas & J. Grimes (Eds.), *Best practices in school psychology III* (pp. 1123–1132). Washington, DC: National Association of School Psychologists.

Vincent, L.J., Salisbury, C., Walter, G., Brown, P., Gruenewald, L.J., & Powers, M. (1980). Program evaluation and curriculum development in early childhood/special education: Criteria of the next environment. In W. Sailor, B. Wilcox, & L. Brown (Eds.), *Methods of instruction for severely handicapped students* (pp. 303–328). Baltimore: Paul H. Brookes.

Weller, C., & Strawser, S. (1987). Adaptive behavior of subtypes of learning disabled individuals. *The Journal of Special Education, 21,* 101–115.

Part III

Assessing Special Populations

Chapter 12

DEVELOPMENTAL ASSESSMENT: EVALUATION OF INFANTS AND PRESCHOOLERS

KORESSA KUTSICK MALCOLM

A request to assess a child who has not reached school age is often distressing for many psychoeducational diagnosticians. Few clinicians receive specialized training in infant and preschool assessment and because of this the instruments available for this purpose are not familiar tools. Many of the tests look cumbersome and complicated with all their objects. Examiners may recall vague information that these instruments were flawed in terms of validity, reliability, and other statistical components. In many cases, examiners just do not know which tests they should administer. To complicate matters, there are the preschool children themselves. These children typically do not have prior experience in sitting still for any type of structured activity. They squirm and grab at all the assessment toys. They want to work on the floor and not at a table. They refuse to give back a particular test object. Their articulation skills may be so poor that their speech is unintelligible. You ask them to do something and they look at you as if you are not speaking in their native language. Many will not leave their parents in order to go to the evaluation room.

These factors have led some psychologists, diagnosticians, speech pathologists, and other educationally based professionals to exclaim, "I don't know what to do with these little guys." Reports have been filed stating that a young child was untestable. The first premise of this chapter is that there is no such thing as an untestable child. Some children, especially the very young child who might possess a variety of disabilities, pose greater challenges to the assessment process than do others. Nevertheless, they can be evaluated. The purpose of this chapter is to discuss guidelines, issues, techniques, and instruments relevant to the evaluation of young children. The history of preschool assessment will also be reviewed. It is hoped this information will provide the evaluator of preschoolers with an appropriate framework for completing developmental assessments.

HISTORY AND DEVELOPMENT

Interest in the assessment of the developmental status of infant and preschool children can be traced to the turn of the twentieth century. The creation of instruments for preschool assessment follows the general history of psychological testing. Early attempts to examine intellectual functioning of young children were undertaken in order to gather data for theories of cognitive development that were emerging during the late 1800s and early 1900s. Educational, governmental, and military needs to classify individuals for training purposes fostered the development of techniques to assess ability. Binet and Simon, in the first decades of the 1900s, pioneered intellectual testing with the development of the early Binet scales. Hall and Gesell, with their clinics for the study of child development, sparked continued interest in the assessment of young children. Terman and Merrill (1937) revised the Binet scales and included items developed for preschool children. The number of published assessment instruments has increased dramatically and continually since the 1930s.

During the 1940s instruments specifically designed for the assessment of infants and preschoolers emerged. Two of the most used tests of that era were the Cattell Infant Intelligence Scale (Cattell, 1940), which was designed for children ages newborn through 2 years, and the Leiter International Performance Scale (Leiter, 1948) for children ages 2 to 18 years. For the next several years researchers examined the predictive nature of such instruments. Little correlation was found between scores on infant and preschool tests and later school success.

Serious attention to the special assessment needs of the preschool child was not achieved until the 1960s. With the advent of Head Start and other early intervention programs came the need to mark and follow the developmental status of large numbers of children. By 1971, over 120 preschooler and kindergarten tests had been developed (Hoepfner, Stern, & Nummedal, 1971). Unfortunately, statistical properties, standardization procedures, and measurement practices plagued many of these instruments.

The Head Start program of the 1960s marked the beginning of an era of governmental and legislative actions that have had major impacts on the education of children in the United States. Federal mandates especially influenced the development of special education for handicapped children and created an incredible demand for intellectual and academic assessment instruments. Public Law 94–142, the Education for All Handicapped Children Act, passed in 1975, set the stage for widespread efforts to educate all handicapped children. Public Law 94–142 held that public school systems must provide free and appropriate educational services for handicapped children ages 2 to 21 in the least restrictive environment. Initial and reevaluations of these children were mandated by this law. In 1986, the federal government enacted Public Law 99–457, the Education of the Handicapped Act Amendments, which extended the intent of 94–142 to children from birth. The diagnosis of handicapping conditions in school-age and preschool children has led to a multimillion-dollar test publishing industry. Advances in test construction are leading to larger and more comprehensive test batteries with statistical properties that far surpass the early psychometric tests. The development of good preschool tests has lagged behind those for older children. The 1980s, however, marked the beginning of new-found interest in the improvement and development of preschool assessment instruments.

MAJOR INSTRUMENTS

For the past two decades, four instruments have dominated the field of developmental assessment: the Bayley Scales of Infant Development (Bayley, 1969); the McCarthy Scales of Children's Abilities (McCarthy, 1972); the Stanford-Binet Intelligence Scales (Terman & Merrill, 1937); and the Wechsler Preschool and Primary Scale of Intelligence (Wechsler, 1967). Three of these tests have undergone revisions in recent years. The fourth edition of the Stanford-Binet was published in 1986; the revised edition of the Wechsler Preschool and Primary Scale of Intelligence became available in 1989; and the second edition of the Bayley Scales was released in 1993. All three of these instruments currently hold dominant positions in the assessment of preschool children. A revision of the McCarthy Scales is currently being considered.

Extensive and comprehensive reviews of the Bayley, McCarthy, Binet, and Wechsler scales are available in a number of sources (e.g., Sattler, 1982; Anastasi, 1988; and in the Buros Mental Measurement Yearbooks). In order to allow space for discussion of other useful but less well publicized preschool tests, only brief descriptions of these instruments will be presented in this chapter.

The Bayley Scales of Infant Development

The Bayley Scales of Infant Development were constructed to assess the mental, motoric, and behavioral functioning of children ages newborn through 2 years, 6 months (Bayley, 1969). The second edition of this test (BSID-II), published in 1993, continues to provide procedures for assessing the mental, motor, and behavioral functioning of young children. Several changes were made in the revision of this test, however. The second edition of the Bayley updated the normative information for the test, which reflects a better representation of the U.S. population. A second feature of the revised test is that it expanded the age range from 1 to 42 months. The original Bayley was developed to assess children ages 2 through 30 months. With the exception of additional items, reorganization of the test materials, and changes in scoring, the Mental and Motor scales of the BSID-II are quite similar to those of the original test. A very positive feature of the BSID-II is the expansion and formalization of the infant behavior rating scale. The Behavior Rating Scale (BRS), formerly called the Infant Behavior Record on the original Bayley, is completed by the examiner after the evaluation session. The sets of questions presented in the BRS provide ratings in the areas of Attention/Arousal, Orientation/Engagement, Emotional/Regulation, and Motor Quality. A combined rating is also computed. The BRS may prove to be a useful index in monitoring signs of early behavioral problems in young children. This scale should hold good research promise for those wishing to conduct longitudinal studies regarding factors such as early temperament, activity levels, and awareness, and their relationships to later developmental issues (Matheny, Dolan, & Wilson, 1976).

Since the BSID-II is relatively new, extensive literature regarding its reliability and validity are not yet available. Information presented by Bayley (1993) in the BSID-II manual indicated that strong positive reliability coefficients were obtained when scores on the BSID and BSID-II were compared. Given the large numbers of test items on the BSID-II that were the same or quite similar to the BSID, this is not surprising. Test-retest and interscorer reliability information presented in the manual was also respectable. Validity information presented in the BSID-II manual is less impressive. The information on the validity of the BSID-II rests on the assumption that since the BSID-II and BSID are so similar, and since the BSID had good research behind it to establish its validity, then the BSID-II must also be as valid an infant test as the BSID. Studies are needed to substantiate this assumption. As with most infant tests, the predictive validity of the BSID-II for functioning in later stages of childhood and adulthood will probably be limited. All infant tests are best used as measures of a child's current developmental status.

Administration of the BSID-II requires thorough familiarity with the large number of assessment items comprising the Mental and Motor scales. The number of toys and various manipulatives utilized in a BSID-II administration continues to pose challenges in organization and maintenance for those who give this test. The materials are attractive to children and are necessary to tap into the wide range of abilities young children between the ages of 1 month and 40 months can demonstrate. Examiners who use the BSID-II should have knowledge of general measurement principles and techniques as well as knowledge of child development.

One disadvantage of the BSID-II, as was true of the BSID, is that the scale does not yield separate domain scores for abilities tapped by the Mental and Motor scales. Bayley continues to assert that an infant's abilities are so intermeshed that they cannot be separated into discrete factors or domains. In an age where a child's eligibility for preschool special-education services depends on documentation of delays in separate areas of functioning, examiners often have wished that the Bayley provided separate domain scores for areas such as cognition, language, and fine- and gross-motor functioning. Some researchers (Haskett & Bell, 1978; Reuter & Craig, 1976) developed alternative recategorization systems for the BSID. None have yet been proposed for the BSID-II. Bayley herself does not advise that such systems be developed or utilized with the new test.

The McCarthy Scales of Children's Abilities

The McCarthy Scales of Children's Abilities (MSCA; McCarthy, 1972) is a comprehensive developmental battery that assesses the intellectual and motor development of children ages 2 years, 6 months to 8 years, 6 months. The test is comprised of 18 subtests, which are organized into 5 scales. These scales include the Verbal scale, which taps a child's verbal expression and conceptual thinking; the Quantitative scale, which measures a child's understanding of numbers; the Perceptual Performance scale, nonverbal response activities, which assess a child's ability to reason without words; a Memory scale, which assesses short-term auditory and visual memory; and the Motor scale, which addresses the child's fine- and gross-motor functioning. Scores on the first three of these scales combine to form the General Cognitive Index (GCI), an overall measure of a child's current developmental status. The GCI has a mean of 100 and a standard deviation of 16. Each of the five domain scores carry means of 50 and standard deviations of 10.

Psychometric properties of the McCarthy are good. The test was standardized on 1,032 children stratified by race, geographic region, father's occupation, and urban-rural dimensions as reflective of the 1970 census. Reliability data for the MSCA is strong. Test-retest coefficients for the GCI and separate subscales run in the .90s. Internal consistency ranges from the high .70s to low .90s for the five scales and GCI (McCarthy, 1972, p. 34). The validity of the MSCA has been established in numerous publications (e.g., Nagle, 1979; Davis & Walker, 1976). Correlations with other instruments such as the WPPSI and Stanford-Binet Scale, Form L-M generally range from the low .70s to low .80s.

The administration of the MSCA usually takes 60 to 90 minutes. This is a long time to maintain a small child in structured activities. What helps keep a child on task is that the motor subtests are placed in the middle of the battery and allow the child to walk, jump, skip, toss and catch beanbags, and stretch a bit. The majority of tasks that comprise the McCarthy are very child oriented. The puzzles, blocks, pictures, and xylophone typically can hold a child's interest. The activities also move along quickly, which helps to keep a preschooler on task (Berk, 1979).

Kaufman (1977) outlined the major limitations of the MSCA. He thought the administration of the test required a great deal of clerical work and was difficult to learn. In addition, he cited the following weaknesses in the test relevant to practitioners:

1. The MSCA could be administered only by a psychologist.
2. The test lacked items that require social comparisons or judgments.
3. The Motor scale is not a stable measure after age 6 years, 6 months.
4. There was not sufficient ceiling for children over age 7.
5. The score range of the McCarthy is 50 to 150, so it is not a good measure to use with children who are functioning at or below trainable levels of mental retardation or who are highly gifted.
6. There is not enough of a base for the youngest children. The test seems too difficult for children under 3 years of age.

Kaufman also had found that a 15-point discrepancy exists between the GCI and Full Scale WPPSI IQs and Stanford-Binet Scale, Form L-M IQs for LD children, with the GCI being lower. If the McCarthy is used as a measure of ability in the diagnostic process of determining whether a child is learning disabled, an evaluator would not be as likely to uncover a significant ability achievement split as with the WPPSI. In turn, a number of children who would have been found eligible to receive special-education services if the Wechsler test had been used, would go without services. Kaufman does not recommend the use of the MSCA in the evaluation of LD children for these reasons.

The WPPSI and the WPPSI-R

One of the four major preschool assessment batteries to undergo a recent revision is the Wechsler Preschool and Primary Scale of Intelligence. A downward extension of the Wechsler Intelligence Scale for Children-Revised (1989), perhaps the most commonly used test of intellectual ability in school-aged children, the WPPSI was published in 1967 for use with children ages 4 years to 6 years, 6 months. In 1985, the Psychological Corporation began a review of the strengths and weaknesses of this test, which led to the revision of the WPPSI.

The WPPSI-R, published in 1989, maintains a striking similarity to the old WPPSI. Those who worked on the development of this revision wanted a final product that was a close relation to the original version so that users would find it easy to pick up and master yet that reflected improvements in test procedures and measurement theory. The WPPSI-R maintained 48% of the WPPSI items. There were five major changes in the test. These included an expansion on the age range from 3 years to 7 years, 3 months; larger, more colorful artwork; addition of an object assembly task; the development of a crack back manual; and a redesign of the record form, which now highlights examiner information and provides a tear-away score sheet that examiners can easily remove from the rest of the test to save file space.

The WPPSI-R consists of 12 subtests that comprise performance and verbal scales. The Performance scale consists of six subtests, including Object Assembly, Geometric Design, Mazes, Picture Completion, and Animal Pegs. The Verbal scale contains the Information, Comprehension, Arithmetic, Vocabulary, Similarities, and Sentences subtests. Each of the WPPSI-R subtests has a mean of 10 and a standard deviation of 3. The Performance, Verbal, and Full Scale IQ scores, like all of the Wechsler tests, carry a mean of 100 and a standard deviation of 15.

The WPPSI-R was standardized on 1,700 children randomly selected and reflective of the 1986 U.S. census in terms of region, age, gender, ethnicity, and parental education and occupation levels. Norm sets were broken into 17 groupings for ages 3 years to 7 years, 3 months. Reliability data sited in the manual is good. Internal consistency correlations were generally above .80 for all age groups. Test-retest reliabilities for the scaled scores ranged from .88 to .91. Test-retest coefficients for the individual subtests were not as strong, however. These ranged from .52 for Mazes and .59 for Object Assembly to .82 for Picture Completion. Three types of validity are reported in the WPPSI-R manual. These include construct, concurrent, and discriminant. Clean two-factor performance and verbal solutions have been obtained in factor analytic studies of the WPPSI-R. (For those familiar with factor structures of the WISC-R, it is interesting to note that the WPPSI-R has not been found to carry the freedom from distractibility factor.) This factor structure was thought to lend good support to the construct validity of the test. In terms of concurrent validity, correlations between the WPPSI and WPPSI-R have been in the mid-.80 range; between the fourth Stanford-Binet (Thorndike, Hagan, & Sattler, 1986) and WPPSI-R, in the .80 to .90 range. Low-moderate correlations have been found between the WPPSI-R and Kaufman Assessment Battery for Children. In terms of discriminant validity, it was generally found that children who scored low on the WPPSI-R also scored low on other tests of ability. There is little information available regarding the predictive validity of the WPPSI-R, due to its recent publication date.

The administration of the WPPSI-R generally takes 75 minutes. At times, the administration process becomes quite painful. This is especially true for the Block Design subtest, which with its demonstrations, second trials, and ceiling rules seems to go on forever. It is very difficult to keep a young child interested in the WPPSI-R, even with the improvements in graphics and materials.

Two changes noted in the WPPSI-R will have ramifications for its use in the identification of special-needs children. One of these changes is that the IQ score range has been expanded. The WPPSI-R yields IQs from 41 to 160; the WPPSI from 55 to 155. This change will allow the WPPSI-R to be useful in the identification of children who possess abilities in the trainable range of mental retardation. It also seems that the WPPSI-R yields less inflated IQ scores than did the WPPSI. A recent study by Kaplan (in press) found that for a group of thirty 4 1/2- to 5-1/2-year old children the WPPSI yielded a mean Verbal score of 123, mean Performance score of 124, and mean Full Scale score of 126, whereas for the same group of children the mean WPPSI-R Verbal score was 117, the mean Performance score was 114, and the mean Full Scale score was 118. The greatest ramification of this factor will be felt in the diagnosis of young learning disabled children. With lower WPPSI-R IQ scores, it may be more difficult to document ability achievement splits. As such, fewer young children may be diagnosed as learning disabled.

Even though the changes in the WPPSI-R reflect advances in test and measurement practices, the instrument still has some weaknesses. The most relevant of these for the practitioner are presented below.

1. There are no specified directions for adapting testing procedures to fit a child's handicapping condition and still maintain the integrity of the standardization of the test.

2. Even though some subtests allow examiners to demonstrate items to a child, the test does not provide sample teaching items that are often necessary and useful when working with children who have little experience in formal educational or testing activities.

3. The WPPSI-R has a limited item floor. Some children can obtain a raw score of zero (which means they could not do any of the items in the subtest) and still obtain a scaled score as high as 6. Because of this, the WPPSI-R may not yield an accurate measure of abilities in lower functioning children.

Despite its faults, the WPPSI-R does mark advances in test construction. Early reviews of the test hold it may become the best measure of abilities of preschool children available. Time will tell if this will be the case.

The Stanford-Binet

Since 1937, the Stanford-Binet has been the instrument of choice for the assessment of a young child's abilities. The major reason for this was that it was perhaps the most extensive battery available for preschool children in its day. The 1937 Binet Scales extended its age range down to a 2-year-old level (Terman & Merrill, 1937). Items were added to this version that were appropriate for children ages 2 to 5.

Twenty-three years later, in 1960, a revision of the scales was undertaken. Items and normative data were updated and the test incorporated the deviation IQ as the index of intellectual ability.

During the 1960s, 1970s, and early 1980s, the 1960 Stanford-Binet (known as Stanford-Binet, Form L-M) was a primary measure of abilities in preschool children. Test items were organized in 6-month intervals based on developmental age appropriateness for the youngest of children and then by year intervals after age 5 (Terman & Merrill, 1973).

Items at the preschool level were very much based on activities young children typically encounter, such as block stacking, bead stringing, and so forth. The Stanford-Binet Form L-M (SB-LM) yielded a single IQ score for a child. This became a source of criticism of the L-M form because the test tapped more than one area of functioning. It was difficult to determine a child's strengths or weaknesses in specific ability areas from his or her performance on the SB-LM. It was also difficult to determine the impact of a child's particular handicapping condition on his or her test performance because only one overall score was obtained and items were not separated by domains. Examiners would have to estimate the ability level of a child who could not perform particular kinds of items due to a physical handicap. Despite these weaknesses, the test items for young children contained materials they enjoyed (small cars, blocks, beads, tiny household objects). Administration of the test was quick at this age level, and relatively reliable and valid test scores were obtained. In 1986, the Stanford-Binet was again revised and the fourth edition was published (SB-IV; Thorndike, Hagan, & Sattler, 1986). A wide variety of content was retained from the L-M form but the test authors updated, reorganized, and added items. The SB-IV yields four area scores as well as an overall measure of intelligence. The area scores include Verbal Reasoning, Abstract/Visual Reasoning, Quantitative Reasoning, and Short-Term Memory. Fifteen separate tests now comprise the SB-IV. Not all children are administered all 15 tests. Authors of the SB-IV developed an adapted-levels approach for examiners to follow in selecting appropriate subtest starting points for administration. Examiners begin the administration of the SB-IV with the vocabulary subtest. A child's score on this test indicates which other subtests are administered and what level is an appropriate starting point for that child so that beginning items are neither too easy nor too difficult.

The SB-IV composite score has a mean of 100 and standard deviation of 16. Each of the area scores also have this mean and standard deviation. Raw scores on the 15 individual tests are converted to a "standard age score" with a mean of 50 and standard deviation of 8.

Reliability data for the composite and area scores are good for a test of this magnitude. Kudar-Richardson and test-retest reliabilities are at and above the .90 range. The reliability of the individual subtests, however, is not as strong, ranging from .73 to .97 for KR-20 reliabilities and .28 to .83 for test-retest coefficients. Similar patterns were noted for the validity of the SB-IV when compared to other tests. The SB-IV area and composite scores correlated moderately highly to highly with other measures of abilities (i.e., WISC-R, WPPSI). The individual subtests did not fare as well. It is also important to note that the factor analytic properties of the SB-IV do not support the breakdown of the subtests into the five area scores

(Sattler, 1990). The ramifications of the reliability and validity data available on the SB-IV for examiners is that the composite score is the most acceptable description of a preschool child's abilities. Interpretation of strengths and weaknesses at the subtest level and, perhaps, even at the area level may not yield accurate descriptors of a child's functioning status.

In terms of its appeal to young children, the SB-IV seems to have lost some of the attractiveness older versions possessed. Fewer objects are available for the child to manipulate. Children do not seem as interested in the tasks presented. Many examiners have lamented how few items lower functioning preschoolers might be given for their test scores, and how raw scores of 0 can yield even low-average test results. Because of these factors, the SB-IV may be of less value as a measure of abilities in preschoolers than was its predecessors.

NEWER DEVELOPMENTAL ASSESSMENT BATTERIES

Changes in federal and state laws, which created or expanded special-education services for handicapped infants and preschoolers, brought greater need for assessment tools appropriate for this population. Within the past few years, a number of new tests have been developed for the young child. Many of these instruments may rival the traditional developmental tests in terms of their utility and value in the diagnostic assessment of children newborn through age 5. The most promising of these tests are presented below.

The Miller Assessment for Preschoolers

Published by the Psychological Corporation in 1982, the Miller Assessment for Preschoolers (MAP; Miller, 1982) is one of the most comprehensive of the newer developmental batteries. This test is appropriate for children ages 2 years, 9 months through 5 years, 8 months. Sensory motor and cognitive abilities are tapped by the test. Five developmental indexes are yielded for a child's performance. The Foundations Index provides information about the child's motor and sensory functioning. The Coordination Index examines gross-, fine- and oral-motor functioning. The Verbal Index, the index probably most similar to traditional measures of ability, consists of items that measure auditory and visual memory, sequencing, comprehension, association, and verbal expression. The Nonverbal Index, one of the most valuable of the test, provides information about a child's memory, sequencing, visualization, and mental manipulations that do not require verbal response. This index would be particularly useful with a child whose severe articulation or language delays interferes with his or her performance on tasks requiring verbal responses to demonstrate cognitive functioning. The final index of the MAP is the Complex Tasks Index. Test items in this grouping require a child to interpret visual-spatial information, which is presented in a variety of ways. Test items that comprise the MAP have a strong neurological basis and are similar to activities found on neuropsychological batteries.

The MAP was standardized on 1,200 preschoolers stratified by age, race, sex, geographic location, socioeconomic level, and urban/rural residence. Adequate reliability and validity data is provided in the manual; however, additional research is needed to strengthen this data. Percentile scores are available for a child's overall test performance and for the five performance indexes.

The test activities of the MAP are very appealing to children. Tasks are presented in a game format. Test administration is generally completed in less than 30 minutes. The clinician will need to spend some time becoming familiar with the testing procedures and materials, as all the objects that are appealing to a young child take some management on the examiner's part to correctly present to the child. Individuals who would be eligible to administer the MAP include psychologists, masters-level educators, educational diagnosticians, program coordinators, preschool specialists, preschool speech pathologists, and others trained in test/measurement theory and practice and in early childhood development.

The MAP is a unique preschool assessment battery. It offers some different information and taps different functioning areas than do other batteries of its kind. The MAP would be a good addition to a battery of tests given to young children. It also has good research potential.

The Battelle Developmental Inventory

The Battelle Developmental Inventory (BDI; Newborg, Stock, Wnek, Guidubaldi, & Svinicki, 1984) is a standardized assessment battery for children from birth to 8 years. It is becoming a popular test among teachers of handicapped infants and preschoolers, as it is one of few comprehensive batteries administered by teachers that yields standard scores. The BDI consists of 341 items grouped into five domains: Personal-Social, Adaptive, Motor, Communication, and Cognitive. The domains are separate entities. An evaluator may choose to administer all five or any one of the separate domains, depending on need. A screening test composed of 96 of the total test items is also available.

Administration of the BDI incorporates a number of data-gathering techniques. Sources of data collected about the child's ability to perform any of the test items can include direct assessment; parent, caregiver, or teacher interviews; and observations of the child in a home or center setting. A 3-point scoring system (0 for no response or no opportunity to perform the action, 1 for partial or sometime performance, and 2 for a full response) allows examiners to identify emerging skills and develop educational strategies to foster these. Administration time is estimated at less than 1 hour for children under the age of 3 years and 1.5 to 2 hours for children over age 3. Testing may be completed during several sessions to save fatigue on the child and examiner. Some evaluation teams even assign various BDI domains to different team members to administer.

The BDI was standardized on 800 children (a relatively small sample) who were representative of 1981 U.S. census data for race and sex and who resided in 24 states and 4 geographic regions. Children with high and low incidence handicapping conditions were included in the standardization group. Reliability and validity information reported in the manual is modestly adequate, although additional data is needed regarding these dimensions of the test. A number of derived scores can be obtained for each of the test domains, including percentiles, z scores, T scores, deviation quotients, and normal curve equivalents. One weakness of the BDI, however, is that the norm tables report scores only to a deviation quotient of 65. The manual describes procedures for computing lower scores; however, this opens the possibility of calculation errors.

The BDI contains one feature that is very useful for those who must assess children with particular physical handicapping conditions. Test instructions carry specific information as to how an item can be adapted for a child who is physically, visually, or hearing impaired. These adaptations can theoretically be made without interfering with the normative character of the test.

One aspect of the BDI that needs to be addressed is that the test can be purchased with or without test materials. Buying the test without the stimuli certainly cuts down on cost. Those using the test gather their own materials per specifications for each item. Gathering one's own test materials, however, would seem to lead to problems regarding standard administration and raise questions regarding validity of test scores. Subtle changes in materials might alter the difficulty of an item. In such cases, examiners would have to be cautious when comparing their subjects' test performance to those of other children in the normative sample. Even when a complete test kit is bought, examiners may still need to purchase materials such as a beeper ball, as a few items necessary to adapt a test activity for a handicapped child are not included.

The BDI is a useful instrument for the identification of strengths and weaknesses in young handicapped children and, thus, in aiding program development. It can also be used to chart a student's progress and to help determine the effectiveness of educational interventions. The format of the test lends itself well to the development of individual educational plans. Because of these applications, the BDI is finding a place among the tests educators of preschool handicapped children routinely use.

The Cognitive Abilities Scale

One of the most difficult children to test is the child 2 to 3 years old. Because the child is too old and developmentally advanced for infant tests such as the Bayley and too young for the tasks required of the preschool batteries such as the McCarthy, it is very difficult to obtain precise measures of the 2-year-old's functioning status.

Noting this problem in her own work with children, Bradley-Johnston (1987) developed an assessment instrument specifically designed for children ages 2 to 3. The Cognitive Abilities Scale (CAS; Bradley-Johnston, 1987) provides for a norm-referenced assessment tool to be used in the diagnosis of developmental delays and to ascertain a child's skill acquisition in five basic areas. These areas are Language, Reading, Mathematics, Handwriting, and Enabling Behaviors. The Language subtest assesses a child's ability to use and understand spoken words. The Reading subtest measures readiness skills such as handling a book, picture identification, and listening comprehension. The Mathematics subtest assesses various quantitative concepts and early rote and rational counting. The Handwriting subtest assesses pre-writing skills such as early drawing of shapes and lines and pencil grasp. The Enabling Behaviors subtest is less achievement oriented than the first four tests. This subtest taps a child's auditory and visual memory.

Administration of the CAS can be accomplished within 30 to 45 minutes. Materials required for administration include a manual, a record booklet and manipulables such as toys, a picture book, and a storybook. Although the materials are a bit cumbersome to access, as they are stored in a cloth bag, they help keep the child interested in the testing procedure.

The CAS provides percentiles and standard scores. The overall test score has a mean of 100 and a standard deviation of 15. The subtests have means of 10 and a standard deviation of 3. Five hundred thirty-six children comprised the norming sample and were representative of residence, parent occupation, ethnicity, and gender and age characteristics of the U.S. population. The reliability and validity data available for the CAS is adequate although, like so many of the tests for young children, additional information is needed in these areas.

Although not a thorough battery, the CAS may find a use as a bridge between the infant and preschool tests. The CAS would be a good test to include when evaluating a child 2 to 3 years old.

ASSESSMENT OF ACHIEVEMENT IN THE PRESCHOOL CHILD

Until recently, the assessment of achievement in children who were not yet in kindergarten was an unheard of concept. With needs to document delays for special-education preschool placements and for program evaluation, this area of assessment has come to light.

The assessment of achievement in preschool children generally involves tapping their acquired knowledge of pre-academics or readiness skills. This knowledge includes color and shape recognition, quantity, and quality dimensions. As the child approaches kindergarten age, this knowledge may also include pre-reading and pre-writing skills such as letter identification, name printing, and various drawing tasks. Only a few individually administered tests of achievement are available specifically for the preschool child. A number of these are presented below.

Bracken Basic Concept Scale

The Bracken Basic Concept Scale (BBCS; Bracken, 1984) is probably the most comprehensive individually administered achievement test for young children. A total of 258 concepts (not all of which are administered to a single child) are assessed by this scale. Items are grouped into seven subscales. These include a School Readiness Composite, which will be discussed below as it plays a role in the testing procedure of this scale. Other BBCS subtests are Direction/Position, Social/ Emotional, Size, Texture/Material, Quantity, and Time/Sequence, which all measure concepts as their titles imply. A screening test is also available in the BBCS. The administration of the Bracken is very simple and straightforward. Materials needed include the manual, stimulus booklets, a record booklet, and a pen or pencil. The stimulus materials are pictorial and are presented in an easel format, which aids administration. There is no need to fumble through boxes and test kits for manipulables. Not having concrete objects to manipulate can make this test somewhat boring to very young children. The test moves along quickly, however, which helps keep children on task. Responding is limited to requiring the child to point to one of four quadrants that pictorially represents a particular concept named by the examiner. For example, if the examiner asks, "Show me which is big," the child would point to one of four choices that demonstrates the concept "big." The manual discusses phrasing and prompts that examiners may use to help children understand the required task. For example, it is permissible to encourage a child to "look at all the pictures and choose the best answer" and to "look at this picture, this picture, this one, and this one" in order to elicit the correct response from a child.

The diagnostic scale of the Bracken begins with six separate subtests that comprise the School Readiness Composite Scale. These subtests tap the child's knowledge of colors, letters, numbers, shapes, directions, and positions. The child's combined raw score on these subtests determines a recommended starting level for administration of the subsequent scales. Basals on the subsequent tests are established by working from the starting point and moving backwards or forwards as necessary until three consecutive passes are achieved. Ceilings are established once three consecutive failures are obtained. Raw scores on these subtests can be used to obtain standard scores (with a mean of 100 and standard deviation of 15), percentiles, and age equivalency. Responses are recorded by marking each item as being passed or failed. The child's response choice is also coded on presented circles. The author of the test recommends drawing slash marks through the circles, but coloring them in works well.

The BBCS was normed on 1,109 children who were representative of U.S. population demographics. Reliability and validity information for the test provided in the manual is adequate, but based on small sample sizes. Additional information is needed to support the validity and reliability of the BBCS.

The BBCS may be utilized by those professionals and paraprofessionals within school and clinical settings who are trained in basic psychoeducational test administration and interpretation. This would include educational diagnosticians, teachers of special-education students, school and clinical psychologists, and speech and language pathologists.

One of the most useful features of the BBCS is that it lends itself well to the development of individualized education plans (IEPs). A checklist is provided that allows examiners to mark which concepts a child has mastered. Recommendations for concepts that need to be developed stem nicely from this list and are readily understandable for parents as well as professionals. This list can also be used to chart progress a child has made from pre- to postinterventions; therefore, it could also serve as a program evaluation and child progress documentation tool.

The BBCS represents a positive step in the developmental history of preschool assessment instruments. It should prove to be a useful addition to diagnostic batteries used with young children. Its greatest value will probably come in its role of documenting a young child's level of preschool knowledge acquisition for use in identifying ability achievement discrepancies. A revision of this test is currently being considered by the test's author and publisher.

The Boehm Test of Basic Concepts-Preschool Version

Another norm-referenced test of general achievement for the preschool child is the Boehm Test of Basic Concepts-Preschool Version (Boehm, 1986). The Boehm-Preschool taps 26 basic receptive vocabulary and grammar concepts that a child 3 to 5 years old typically encounters in his or her world. This test is a downward extension of the Boehm Test of Basic Concepts. Administration of the Boehm-Preschool takes approximately 15 minutes and is easily accomplished. Children are asked to point to a picture that best represents a concept presented by an examiner. Scoring is a simple pass/no pass system. Raw scores yield percentiles and *T* scores.

The Boehm-Preschool was standardized on 433 children, a small sample but one that did represent race, region, and socioeconomic dimensions proportionate to those of the U.S. population. Reliability and validity information presented in the manual is good, although somewhat limited in terms of sample size and number of studies conducted.

The Boehm-Preschool is a good instrument to use to screen children who might need additional testing to determine if they need special-education services. It would also be a useful tool to use to supplement the educational portions of evaluations conducted with children ages 3 to 5 years.

Learning Accomplishment Profile

The Chapel Hill Project in North Carolina generated a series of assessment tools useful in documenting the educational needs of young children. These instruments include the Early Learning Accomplishment Profile (E-LAP; Glover, Perminger, & Sanford, 1978) for newborn through 3 years; the Learning Accomplishment Profile-Revised (LAP; Sanford & Zelman, 1981) for children ages 3 to 6; the Learning Accomplishment Profile-Diagnostic Edition (LAP-D; LeMay, Griffin, & Sanford, 1977) for children 3 to 5; and the Learning Accomplishment Profile-Standardized Assessment (Nehring, Nehring, Bruni, & Randolph, 1992) for children ages 30 to 72 months. The E-LAP, LAP, and LAP-D are criterion- rather than norm-referenced tests. A standardization of the LAP-D was undertaken to allow for the use of the test for comparative purposes.

The non-normative versions of the LAP are best used by those who work with a child in an educational program. The developers of these tests advocated their use as pre- and postmeasures of a child's developmental status. They are good measures to use for program effectiveness evaluations. The tests were not designed as tools to diagnose handicapping conditions or to determine eligibility for special services, although they are frequently inappropriately used for such purposes. The developers of the standardized version of the LAP-D maintain that test scores obtained can be used to identify children in need of special services. Standard scores can be computed and used to identify and document delays in development.

The technical data available for the early LAP tests are questionable. The tests were constructed based on "expert review" of the type and age appropriateness of items. The LAP-D manual does offer some reliability data, which is promising but limited. The technical report for the standardized version of the LAP-D indicates better examination of reliability and validity for this test. Additional research into the utility of the LAP-D Standardized Assessment will be needed to solidify this test's place in the realm of preschool assessment.

Administration of the LAP tests require rather extensive examiner familiarity. The test materials are numerous and it takes practice to become familiar with their manipulation and presentation. The administration time for the LAP tests varies by child, but typically involves 1 hour for a complete administration. The LAP subtests tap similar areas of a child's functioning. These areas include fine- and gross-motor skills, cognition, language, self-help, and social/emotional status. The self-help subscales were deleted from the LAP-D Standardized Assessment test.

The Brigance Diagnostic Inventory of Early Development

Another criterion-referenced instrument available to those who work with preschool children is the Brigance Inventory (Brigance, 1978). The Brigance can be administered to children from birth through age seven. This test covers a number of developmental tasks, including gross- and fine-motor functioning, self-help skills, speech/language skills, and general knowledge. For older preschoolers and young primary-grade students, the Brigance also taps basic readiness skills such as reading common signs, printing upper- and lowercase letters, and early numerical knowledge.

Some of the materials necessary to administer the Brigance must be gathered by examiners, although the printed matter is provided. Technical data available regarding the Brigance is limited. Criterion-referenced tests typically do not present the elaborate details of the test's development as do the norm-referenced tests.

Perhaps the most useful feature of the Brigance is that its response booklet allows for the continuous assessment of a child. An examiner can use one response booklet to record a child's performance during numerous administrations of the test. Different-colored pens or pencils can be utilized to chart the child's progress over administrative sessions. In a glance, examiners can note what skills a child has acquired over time.

ASSESSMENT OF EMOTIONAL STATUS IN PRESCHOOLERS

The evaluation of a preschooler's emotional status should focus on her social skills, temperament, attachment to others, frustration tolerance, and general behavior patterns. Unfortunately, measures of these attributes are almost nonexistent for the very young child.

A few experimental tests exist for the assessment of an infant's emotional status. Some limited tests are available for older preschoolers, highlighted below. For the most part, however, examiners will need to rely on observational data, analysis of related test data, parental responses to questionnaires, and parts of various available tests in order to assess personality factors in children under the age of 5.

Social Competency

The reader may recall that most of the preschool tests reviewed in this chapter contained subtests or domains that addressed social functioning (for example, the Social Emotional scales on the BDI and BBCS.) Examiners can combine these subtests and administer them in order to directly assess a child's knowledge of various social skills. Most of the tasks utilized in these tests involve a child's identification of facial expressions, moods depicted in various settings, and interactions between individuals. Socio-grams, simple assessment tools that ask questions such as "Who would you eat lunch with?" can be developed to fit an examiner's need. Such tools can be used with preschoolers if administered in an interview format. The sociogram is helpful in determining which child may be least popular among peers. These questions can also help document that a child's behavior or emotional difficulties are interfering with peer relationships.

More formalized measures of social competency in the preschool child include the Kohn Social Competence Scale-Revised (Kohn, Parnes, & Rosman, 1979) for children ages 3 to 6 years, the California Preschool Social Competency Scale (Levine, Freeman, & Lewis, 1969) for children ages 4 years to 6 years, 6 months, and the Children's Behavior Scale (Stott, 1962) for 4 years to 6 years, 6 months. The reliability and validity data on all three of these tests need development; however, the scales can provide some information as to the level of social skill development a young child has acquired.

Behavior

A few general behavior rating scales are available that were specifically designed for the child under five. One of the most widely used is the Preschool and Kindergarten Edition of the Burks' Behavior Rating Scale (Burks, 1977). This scale is comprised of 105 items grouped into 18 behavior domains that address such aspects of the child as self-concept, anger control, intellectual functioning, aggressiveness, and dependency. The Burks' Preschool can be completed by a parent, caregiver, and/or teacher. Responses from one individual or a number of individuals can be easily plotted to provide an overview of impressions of a child.

Another rating scale designed specifically for the young preschool child is the Preschool Behavior Questionnaire (PBQ; Behar & Stringfield, 1974). The PBQ is a teacher-completed scale consisting of 36 items. Three behavioral characteristics (Hostile-Aggressive, Anxious-Fearful, and Hyperactive-Distractible) are derived from this scale. The Preschool Burks' and the PBQ have adequate reliability and validity data. Each can be used to determine general behavioral difficulties in young children.

One important factor to remember regarding the behavioral and emotional assessment of preschool children is that such assessments should not be geared only toward the identification of characteristics of the child. The young child's social and emotional functioning is perhaps as dependent upon family and cultural variables as it is on more genetically predisposed characteristics such as temperament. Parental styles, socio-economic conditions, discipline techniques, and parental expectations, to name a few, can have great impact on a child's emotions and behaviors.

Temperament

Temperament is the genetically determined components of a child's emotional nature. Included in this construct are the child's ability to adapt to change, speed of response, general mood, pattern of sleep and wakefulness, and interaction style with others (Thomas, Chess, & Karn, 1977). Infant temperament scales have been used primarily for research purposes. These tools can provide examiners with general data regarding a child's basic personality structures. Data obtained from these scales can be used to assist parents in learning how to interact with their children, what discipline strategies may be most effective, and which ideas may enhance the child's social and emotional functioning.

SCREENING INSTRUMENTS

In clinical and school settings, examiners often have need of reliable and valid methods of obtaining basic information about a child's developmental status. Many physicians now utilize short developmental screening inventories to ascertain whether additional, more comprehensive (and more costly) evaluations are needed. School systems often conduct mass screenings of preschool children—also to determine whether these children are exhibiting signs of developmental delays that might warrant full special-education eligibility evaluations. Several screening tests are available that can be utilized in these cases. The most popular of these are presented below. Most of these tests have not undergone the extensive development of reliability and validity as have the major developmental tests. As the term "screening" implies, these instruments should be used to obtain only a rough measure of a child's current developmental status. By nature of their content and their brevity, screening tests do not contain enough items to provide a comprehensive view of the child.

The Developmental Indicators of the Assessment of Learning-Revised (DIAL-R)

The DIAL-R (Mardell-Czvdnowski & Goldenberg, 1983) is typically administered in a team format, with professionals and trained paraprofessionals administering the sets of items that comprise the motor, concepts, and language domains of the test. Total test time is about 20 to 30 minutes, depending on the child's age and level of cooperation, and the examiner's familiarity with the materials. The DIAL-R is appropriate to use with children ages 2 through 6 years. Scores for each of the three domains are categorized into three possible areas: potential problem, average, or potentially advanced. Users of this screener will find that at the lower age levels, children need to pass few if any items to obtain scores considered to be within the average range. Also, for older preschoolers, there is not enough of a range of items that would give accurate findings for placement into the potentially advanced category. The DIAL-R is best used with the 3- to 5-year-old population. It has less value when screening very young children or those who might be considered for additional evaluations to determine placement into educational programs for gifted children.

The Screening Test of the Battelle Developmental Inventory (BDI)

The BDI Screening Inventory (Newborg et al., 1984) utilized direct assessment, naturalistic observations, and/or parent interview to obtain information on a child's functioning in the areas of personal social skills, adaptive behavior, motor skills, communication, and cognition. The BDI Screening test can be used with children ages 2 through 8 years. With a total of 96 items, the BDI Screening test offers one of the more comprehensive assessments for instruments of its kind. The flexibility in using observational or interview data is helpful when children are not cooperative for formal administration of test items. Administration time can vary a good bit with this test, depending on the form of data collection used (interview or direct assessment) and the child's cooperation. This screening test may take up to 1 hour to complete, which does not lend itself well to mass screenings.

The Denver Developmental Screening Test (DDST)

The DDST (Frankenburg, Dodds, Fandal, Dazuk, & Cohrs, 1975) can also be a rather lengthy test to administer. It consists of 186 items divided into five scales: physical, self-help, social, academic, and communication. The test can be used with children from birth to age 9 years. Direct assessment and caregiver interview can be used to obtain an estimate of a child's developmental status.

THE EVALUATION OF PLAY

Through play, a child learns about the world. The experiences and knowledge a child gains in play provide major contributions to the development of all aspects of functioning. Evaluators who have worked with preschool children, however, have tended to overlook assessing this aspect of the child's functioning. There are a few inventories available to document the developmental appropriateness of a child's play. Few reports contain sections that summarize the nature and form of a child's play behavior. For the professional who would like to include an evaluation and discussion of play in a comprehensive evaluation of a young child, the following information is provided.

There are no formal tests of play being marketed at this time. A few tests, such as Assessing Linguistic Behaviors (Olswang, Stoel-Gammon, Coggins, & Carpenter, 1987) and the Wisconsin Behavior Rating Scale (Song, Jones, Lippert, Metzgen, Miller, & Borreca, 1983) contain nice subtests that provide some structured procedures for observing and evaluating play skills. Paget (1990) has noted that various experimental/research methods for the evaluation of play have been discussed in the literature (e.g., the Symbolic Play Scale Checklist) and the Peer Play Scale. These measures, however, are not normed, nor do they offer enough information about their statistical or functional properties to allow for their use much beyond research settings.

Application of basic developmental theories to understand and analyze the appropriateness of observed behavior is an alternative to direct assessment of play. Piagetian principles (of object permanence, for example, conservation, and symbolic thought) are used by developmental psychologists to determine the level of cognitive maturation represented in play activities. Paget (1990), for example, examined the development of symbolic thought through observations of preoperational-aged children.

When observational approaches to analyzing play are used, the examiner is faced with choices as to environments in which the play should occur. Some examiners gain access to preschool classrooms that can offer a child a selection of activities and materials. At times, it may be appropriate to allow the child to engage in free play alone or with other children. If not enough information can be gathered from free play, examiners might set out specific toys (such as those that involve different levels of container play, block manipulations, imagination). A child will sometimes perform specific actions with such toys in free play that they would not in more formalized assessment situations. Some examiners choose to observe a child's play in the home environment. This offers opportunities to see the child as he or she tends to function on a daily basis with familiar materials. When brought into clinical settings, children often are so overwhelmed that they have little interaction with materials presented in that setting. Observations of home play also allow examiners the opportunity to observe play that may occur between the child and parent, other siblings, and neighbors. It is also often helpful to make note of toys available in the home. This allows the examiner to determine whether there are appropriate materials available for the child to use in play. If the child has few or no toys, attempts can be made to provide these (via donations or toy lending libraries) so that the child has the opportunity to act on emerging cognitions.

ISSUES IN PRESCHOOL ASSESSMENT PRACTICES

Instrument Selection

One of the most important rules of thumb to keep in mind about choosing the instruments to evaluate a young child is that no one instrument will address all aspects of a child's functioning. Some of the larger batteries will tap a number of domains, but never all. For example, the WPPSI-R is reported to tap verbal and performance abilities; however, it does not have items that assess gross-motor functioning. For the most part, examiners will find they need to combine subtests and tasks from a number of instruments in order to obtain comprehensive information about a child. This becomes especially true for the child who possesses a handicapping condition that prevents his or her performance on certain parts of batteries, which in turn would cause Full Scale scores to be less than accurate representations of a child's functioning. A common example of this would involve a child between the ages of 2 and 5 who possesses a severe speech and language handicap. When choosing assessment tools for such a child, the examiner may not wish to select instruments that completely involve expressive language skills as a response format. Obviously a child who could not talk would not do very well on such instruments. Errors in diagnosis can be made when the handicapping condition is not taken into account when assessment instruments are selected, administered, and interpreted. Children who could not express themselves verbally might end up with test scores and diagnoses indicative of mental retardation rather than of a speech and language impairment. Faulty recommendations and treatments could result that would limit effectiveness of interventions and cause the child more harm than good. Case Example 12–1 addresses the selection of tests and parts of tests needed to assess a young child.

Case Example 12–1. Assessing children with physical disabilities

---

Ted is a 39-month-old child who has a medical diagnosis of cerebral palsy with involvement of the lower and upper extremities. He is not ambulatory and he has no motor control in his right arm and hand. Ted does have some mobility in his left arm and hand, which permits him to use a pointing response. Ted's vision, hearing, and expressive language skills appear to be intact.

In this case, since Ted is not ambulatory, gross-motor assessment tasks requiring running, kicking, or ball bouncing would not be in order. His performance on tasks involving complex fine-motor movements would not provide a true image of his overall abilities since activities requiring these skills would measure the degree to which his physical handicap prevented him from completing these tasks rather than other aspects of his functional capabilities. Examiners may want to have this information, but should not rely on object manipulation activities to obtain a complete view of this child.

For Ted, the most appropriate kinds of task that could be used to assess his potential for learning as well as his acquired knowledge would be those requiring verbal expression or limited physical dexterity, such as pointing to objects or pictures. In terms of specific instruments and subtests, the following would be appropriate tools to administer to Ted.

Cognitive functioning:	WPPSI-R: Verbal subtests
	Stanford-Binet-IV: Verbal, Quantitative and Memory subtests
	McCarthy Scales of Children's Abilities: Verbal, Quantitative, and Memory subtests (with the possible exception of tapping sequence, which involves a motoric response)
Pre-Academic Skills:	Bracken Basic Concept Scale
	Boehm Preschool
	Brigance Inventory of Early Development

Case Example 12–2.   Selecting developmentally appropriate tests

---

Mary was 4 years, 8 months old when referred to a local preschool handicapped program after her mother discovered educational services for young children were available. Although the child had been followed by public health agencies since birth, delays in functioning had not been noted. Mary's mother thought her daughter might "be a little slow" since her other child, a boy in kindergarten, had recently been found eligible for special services.

Very little background data was available for Mary. Her medical records indicated no significant physical or health factors. By the mother's report, Mary obtained developmental milestones at age-appropriate levels. Her chronological age was used to select the first instruments administered to her, the WPPSI-R and the BBCS.

It soon became evident that Mary's abilities and skills were at levels well below her chronological age. With the exception of Object Assembly and Comprehension on the WPPSI-R, Mary obtained raw scores of 0 on all other WPPSI-R & BBCS subtests. Given that the lower age limits on these instruments is 3 years and 2 years, 6 months, respectively, examiners knew they needed to drop back and find tests that tapped functional abilities below these levels. With the administration of the WPPSI-R and BBCS the examiners knew what Mary could not do, but had no idea what she could do.

For subsequent assessment sessions, examiners pulled subtests from the McCarthy (lower age limit 2 years, 6 months) and the Bayley scales and Brigance inventories to obtain accurate measures of Mary's functioning. Her developmental delays were pervasive, as she was found to be functioning at an 18- to 24-month level in all areas.

An evaluator could attempt to administer some tasks that require minor object manipulations just to see what Ted would do with them (for example, perceptual performance items on the McCarthy such as block building and puzzle solving). As long as these tasks reflect the extent of the child's physical handicapping condition and this is communicated appropriately in a report, it would be appropriate to attempt to administer such items.

Another consideration in the selection of appropriate assessment tools for young children is the possible need to move to lower levels of tests. This need may be encountered when it is not possible to acquire enough background information on a child before testing to estimate approximate functioning levels (see Case Example 12–2).

Rapport

Building and maintaining rapport with the preschool child involves different techniques than those used with older children. A young child is often fearful of strangers and unwilling to work with an examiner. Time must be spent gaining the child's trust. A good way to acquire trust is to spend time with the child in the presence of the mother and/or father. Typically, an examiner can engage the parent in a structured interview and gather data about the family and child while giving the child a chance to become accustomed to him or her.

In cases where a child is extremely reluctant to be alone with an examiner there is no need to make the evaluation a traumatic experience. It is also rather pointless to try and test a child who is screaming for the parent. In these situations, a parent may be asked to sit with the child during the evaluation, which is often enough to calm the child and allow him or her to work at the testing tasks. Before this arrangement is attempted, however, it is wise to discuss with the parents the fact that they may not help their child to perform any of the requested tasks. It is very difficult for the parent to watch the testing, especially as the child reaches tasks he or she cannot do. By discussing the parent's role prior to the evaluation, an examiner can help ensure that the test performance reflects the child's, not the parent's, functioning.

Home versus Center Testing

When a child is not yet attending school, a question of where to test arises. Many professionals prefer to have a child brought to their clinical setting. The advantage of clinics and other center-based evaluation rooms is that greater controls can be put on the environment. Generally when a center-based evaluation room is utilized, examiners can ensure that the room is quiet and relatively free of distractions, that furnishings are clean and child size, and that necessary testing materials are close at hand. Testing a child in a clinical setting can create problems, however. Young children often are frightened of new surroundings. They may be so fearful or guarded in the clinical setting that their test performances are adversely affected. Children unaccustomed to new surroundings can also be so stimulated by the testing environment that they spend all their energies in exploratory behaviors. In either situation, the clinical setting creates barriers to ascertaining true measures of the child's functioning.

An alternative to a clinical evaluation site is testing in the child's home. On their home turf, children tend to be more spontaneous and outgoing. Time needed to build rapport and gain cooperation can be reduced when the examiner meets a child at home, and test results may be less susceptible to a child's shyness, stranger anxiety, and other *in vivo* factors. Testing in the home, however, also carries limitations. Examiner safety is one. Unfortunately, many homes and neighborhoods are plagued by violence and crime. Examiners should never travel to homes where there are strong possibilities of harm. In one situation, a mother who was contacted to schedule the evaluation of her 3-year-old cursed the examiner profusely before she angrily agreed to set a date. Information about the mother indicated she had spent time in prison for attempted murder and drug-related convictions. Her older children had been removed from her custody, and she was fearful the 3-year-old was being evaluated for possible removal. In fact, the evaluation was requested by the local school system to determine the child's eligibility for preschool special-education services. Given the mother's phone manners and history of incarceration, the examiner requested that a large male supervisor accompany her to the child's home. Fortunately, the mother was very pleasant and the evaluation occurred without incident. Risk to one's own safety should always weigh heavily in decisions regarding where to test. Other adverse factors related to home testings are:

1. It is difficult to ensure adequate work spaces or furniture at which to work.
2. Other children in the home may want to participate in the test activities.
3. Some children have few restraints placed on them at home and behave much less appropriately than they would at a school or clinical setting.

The choice of where to test depends on personal preferences and pragmatic concerns such as transportation for families and work space available in schools and clinics. For those who opt to do home testings it is helpful to consider taking along some extra materials in addition to the tests themselves. A list of these materials include:

1. *A vinyl tablecloth* that can be spread on a floor to provide a clean work area for babies or children and examiners.
2. *A small folding table* such as a TV tray, in case the family does not have a table at which to work. A TV table with short legs can be put atop a tablecloth so the child and examiner can sit on the floor and have adequate tabletop working space.
3. *A box of toys,* perhaps good used items, which can be left with the child who wants to keep them and cries.

Criterion versus Norm-Referenced Testing

A debate has arisen as to whether criterion-referenced testing is more appropriate for preschool children than is norm-referenced testing. Some evaluators feel the use of norm-referenced tests leads to diagnostic labels that in turn set up certain expectations for a child. The decision as to what type of test is used depends on the assessment needs of the child and evaluator. When a child is tested to determine eligibility for a special program, norm-referenced tests should be the instruments of choice. These tests, by nature of their design, provide for a comparison of the child being tested to some predetermined norm. The comparison allows examiners to document specific delays and their magnitude. Norm-referenced tests also tend to have better well-defined statistical properties (such as reliability and validity) than do criterion-referenced tests. This data can be used to provide justification for a test's use in the diagnosis or classification of a child.

Criterion-referenced tests, such as the Brigance and LAP-D, are useful tests for examiners who simply want to mark the progress a child makes over time. These tests usually break skills into very specific actions. They also tend to be more direct in the assessment of particular skills. These features of criterion-referenced tests make them somewhat more appealing to educators who must develop specific education plans for a child and communicate with parents regarding details of a child's functioning.

ADDITIONAL ASSESSMENT PROCEDURES

This chapter has focused on the use of specific tests to measure a young child's developmental status. Even the best of these tests, in and of themselves, cannot provide a complete picture of a child. Children do not live in isolated vacuums. The score an infant or preschool child obtains on any measures of functioning can be as much a reflection of environment and caretakers as it is of biologic development. For this reason, a truly comprehensive evaluation of a young child must include information about her pre- and postnatal experiences, socioeconomic history, and health care. Information regarding the parents' attitude toward the child, their care of their son or daughter, discipline techniques, and resources available to their family should also be obtained. In many clinical settings, evaluations of children tend to focus just on presenting problems or behaviors of a given child. It is not uncommon for preschool personnel to receive reports on a child in their center from some clinical setting describing some terrible behaviors or delays that lead to some significant psychological diagnosis, which is not reflective of the child in the educational setting he or she attends on a daily basis. A common example of this seems to involve children who are referred to clinical settings for evaluations of possible attention-deficit/hyperactivity disorder. If the child is noncompliant and overly active during the attempts to evaluate him at the clinic, and if the parents present with complaints of difficulties in managing the child in the home setting, the less experienced examiner might jump to the diagnosis of ADHD. Review of the child's functioning in other settings might yield information that would change this diagnosis and subsequent treatment recommendations.

Let us suppose that a more experienced examiner was working with this case. The presenting data, direct assessment, observational data, and parent reports all point toward the ADHD diagnosis. The examiner, however, knows that the child was attending a preschool program. She sends out questionnaires and behavioral rating scales to the personnel at this center. Compilation of this data indicates no significant discrepancy problem in the data she has regarding the child's behavior in various settings. On follow-up interviews with the preschool staff and the child's parents, it is found that the parents do not set consistent limits or schedules with their children. Structured learning activities are not set up in the home. Several family stressors, including marital discord and the recent death of a favorite grandparent, are noted. It is also found that with subsequent sessions, the child becomes more friendly and compliant with the examiner and with formal evaluation procedures. This examiner would hold off on the diagnosis of ADHD and recommend interventions for the family. The child would not be the focus of treatment. Treatment options in this case might include parenting classes, marriage counseling, family therapy, and coordination of home and preschool communication so that all of those working with this child can explore and learn the techniques that seem to work best.

Case Example 12–3.   Preschool evaluation report

REASON FOR REFERRAL

Harry was referred for this psychoeducational evaluation after a preschool screening conducted by his school system indicated he might be experiencing significant developmental delays.

BACKGROUND INFORMATION

Harry is 4 years, 10 months old and currently lives with his biological parents. He has been attending a private preschool program in his community. Harry's teacher reported the boy experiences attending and off-task behavioral difficulties that were not typical of the other children in his program. Harry's medical history is significant for a number of at-risk factors. At the age of 18 months he began to experience severe seizures, which were found to be related to the presence of a right temporal-parietal arachnoid cyst. A shunt was placed to drain fluid from the cyst and his seizures were treated with phenobarbital. Reports from Harry's physician indicated normal medical functioning at the time of this evaluation. Recent physical examinations indicated no significant neurologic findings; however, abnormal EEG spiking had been noted in previous hospital reports.

BEHAVIORAL OBSERVATIONS

Harry was asked to spend 3 days attending the preschool program for children with developmental disabilities in his local school district. Observations of Harry in this setting found him to be an energetic little boy. He initiated interactions with the other children and with adults. He played with a variety of toys and materials. Harry could use words and short sentences to express himself. It was noted, however, that he had some difficulty answering questions with appropriate responses. He could give related information but not the specific content requested. Harry followed the routine of the classroom nicely and adjusted to group activities well. He appeared to be a happy, curious child.

Harry's evaluation was conducted over the course of 2 separate days in order to prevent him from becoming unduly fatigued by the assessment process. During the evaluation, Harry had some difficulty attending to structured activities. He was very distractible and he demonstrated an impulsive response style, even for his age. Harry displayed a bit of stubbornness as he would put his head down on his arms when he could not have his way. He responded quickly, however, to requests to comply with directions. Throughout the verbal segments of this evaluation, Harry demonstrated difficulty processing questions and retrieving appropriate information. Many times he tended to give related but inappropriate content for questions.

Harry responded well to firm requests to comply with directions and to the use of positive reinforcement (stickers) for appropriate behavior and effort. His performance on the various tasks comprising this evaluation was thought to be a valid indicator of his abilities and skills.

METHODS OF EVALUATION

Wechsler Preschool and Primary Scale of Intelligence-Revised (WPPSI-R)

McCarthy Scales of Children's Abilities (MSCA): Memory & Motor scales

(continued)

Case Example 12–3.   *(Continued)*

Bracken Basic Concept Scale (BBCS)

Battelle Developmental Inventory (BDI): Personal, Social, Adaptive, & Communication scales

Burks' Behavior Rating Scale-Preschool and Kindergarten Edition

RESULTS

Harry's WPPSI-R performance indicated he is experiencing significant delays in the development of his intellectual abilities. His general functioning was found to be from 12 to 24 months behind levels expected for his chronological age. Harry's nonverbal abilities were found to be within a range of 2 to 3 standard deviations below means established for children his age, indicating significant deficits in this area of functioning. His verbal abilities were somewhat better developed, in a range of 1 to 2 deviations below means for Harry's age. Specific intellectual weaknesses identified were in the areas of perceptual motor functioning, general information, and arithmetic reasoning.

The MCSA Motor and Memory subtests were administered to Harry in order to gain information about his abilities in these areas. His gross-motor skills were found to be age appropriate. He demonstrated right-hand dominance. His balance and general coordination was good. Harry's fine-motor functioning was found to be significantly delayed. He obtained age equivalency of 3 years on all of his drawings. His work indicated perceptual motor weaknesses consistent with his WPPSI-R performance. In terms of his memory, Harry demonstrated significant weakness in his ability to recall verbal information of any kind, be it word or numerical data. His performance on all of the tasks requiring short-term auditory recall of sentences, words, or numbers was at a 2-year developmental equivalency. When the memory tasks did not require a verbal response, Harry was able to give a stronger performance. His visual memory was assessed to be at a 3 1/2-year level.

Academic skill testing conducted with Harry indicated delays in a number of concept areas. His basic skills of color recognition, number concepts, and letter and shape identification, as measured by the BBCS, were at the first percentile for children his age. Harry did not consistently identify colors, letters of the alphabet, or shapes. He could not count rotely or rationally. Harry has not yet developed an understanding of concepts such as different and same. His knowledge of social and emotional concepts, size dimensions, quantity concepts, textures, and materials were all at levels below the tenth percentile for his age. Strengths Harry demonstrated involved his knowledge of direction (i.e., up, down) and of time (night, day). These strengths were within the low-average range.

Harry's mother was asked to complete a Burks' Behavior Rating Scale in order to summarize her impressions of her son's behavior. From the information gathered on this scale, Harry's attention span, impulse control, and intellectual status were seen as his greatest areas of weakness. Harry's mother also indicated her son could be resistive to directions and authority. All other areas of his behavior and emotional and mental status were seen as being appropriate for his age.

SUMMARY AND RECOMMENDATIONS

The results of this evaluation indicated Harry is experiencing significant developmental delays in the areas of cognition, language, perceptual motor functioning, and

Case Example 12–3.   *(Continued)*

preacademic skills. These delays represented magnitudes of 25 to 50 percent. Harry's behavior is characterized by impulsivity, a short attention span, and a tendency to resist authority. He responds well to behavior management techniques. It is recommended that Harry participate in a center-based preschool program available to children who have developmental disabilities. Other recommendations for Harry include:

1. Share the results of this evaluation with Harry's physician and the medical staff who monitor his physical and neurologic status, pending permission to do so. Harry's receiving preschool teacher and these professionals should communicate regularly in order to monitor the boy's developmental status as well as the possible effects of his medication and past medical problems on his learning experiences.

2. Harry's preschool program should emphasize language building experiences to help him improve his functional communication competency.

3. Behavior management techniques designed to reinforce appropriate behaviors would be useful in building Harry's on-task behavior and his compliance with directions from those who work with him. A firm and consistent management style will also help reduce his resistance to authority.

4. Harry's parents should be provided each week with a short list of activities that they can do at home to help build Harry's basic skills in color recognition, counting, and so forth.

5. Harry's parents should be encouraged to continue to allow their son to care for as many of his own needs as possible (such as grooming and dressing) to keep these skills strong.

CONCLUSION

The assessment of a preschool child poses difficult challenges to examiners who may be more accustomed to working with older children. A number of new tests and revised versions of traditional instruments are helping evaluators face these challenges. Test developers are becoming more sensitive to the assessment needs of the young child and are designing tests—creative yet relatively fun for the child to take—that tap a number of abilities and skills. Selection and proper administration of various batteries and parts of tests allow examiners to obtain complete reviews of a child's developmental status. Although some tests for preschoolers still need work to develop reliability and validity data, they hold great promise in the task of evaluating the young child.

REFERENCES

Anastasi, A. (1988). *Psychological Testing* (6th ed.). New York: Macmillan.

Bayley, N. (1969). *Bayley Scales of Infant Development: Manual.* San Antonio, TX: The Psychological Corporation.

Bayley, N. (1993). *Bayley Scales of Infant Development-Second Edition: Manual*. San Antonio, TX: The Psychological Corporation.

Behar, L.B., & Stringfield, S.A. (1974). A behavior rating scale for the preschool child. *Developmental Psychology, 10,* 601–610.

Berk, R.A. (1979). The discrimination efficiency of the Bayley Scales of Infant Development. *Journal of Abnormal Child Psychology, 7,* 113–119.

Boehm, A.E. (1986). *Boehm Test of Basic Concepts-Preschool Version*. San Antonio, TX: The Psychological Corporation.

Bracken, B.A. (1984). *Bracken Basic Concept Scale: Manual*. San Antonio, TX: The Psychological Corporation.

Bradley-Johnson, S. (1987). *Cognitive Abilities Scale: An educationally relevant measure for two- and three-year old children*. Austin, TX: PRO-ED.

Brigance, A.H. (1978). *Brigance (R) Diagnostic Inventory of Early Development*. N. Billerica, MA: Curriculum Associates.

Burks, H.F. (1977). *Burks' Behavior Rating Scales: Preschool and Kindergarten Edition*. Los Angeles: Western Psychological Services.

Cattell, P. (1940). *The measurement of intelligence of infants and young children*. New York: Psychological Corporation.

Davis, E.E., & Walker, C. (1976). Validity of the McCarthy Scales for southwestern rural children. *Perceptual and Motor Skills, 42,* 563–567.

Frankenburg, W., Dodds, J., Fandal, A., Dazuk, E., & Cohrs, M.(1975). *Denver Developmental Screening Test Manual*. Denver, CO: Ladoca Project & Publishing Foundation.

Gerkin, K.C., Hancock, K.A., & Wade, T.H. (1978). Comparison of the Stanford-Binet Intelligence Scale and the McCarthy Scales of Children's Abilities with Preschool Children. *Psychology in the Schools, 15,* 468–472.

Glover, M.E., Perminger, J.L., & Sanford, A.R. (1978). *Early accomplishment profile*. Winston-Salem, NC: Kaplan.

Gottfried, A.W., & Brody, D. (1975). Interrelationships between and correlates of psychometric and Piagetian scales of sensorimotor intelligence. *Developmental Psychology, 11,* 379–387.

Haskett, J., & Bell, J. (1978). Profound mental retardation: Descriptive and theoretical utility of the Bayley Mental Scale. In C.E. Meyers (Ed.), *Quality of life in severely and profoundly mentally retarded people* (pp. 327–352). Washington, DC: American Association on Mental Deficiency.

Hoepfner, R., Stern, C., & Nummedal, S.C. (1971). *CSE-ERIC preschool/kindergarten test evaluations*. Los Angeles: UCLA Graduate School of Education.

Kaplan, C.H. (in press). Bright children and the revised WPPSI: Concurrent validity. *Journal of Psychoeducational Assessment*.

Kaufman, A. (1977). *Clinical evaluation of young children with the McCarthy Scales*. New York: Grune & Stratton.

Kaufman, A.S., & Kaufman, N.C. (1972). *Clinical evaluation of young children with the McCarthy Scales*. New York: Grune & Stratton.

Kohn, M., Parnes, B., & Rosman, B. (1979). *Kohn Social Competence Scale-Revised*. New York: William A. White Institute of Psychiatry, Psychoanalysis, & Psychology.

Leiter, R.G. (1948). *International Performance Scale*. Chicago: Stoelting.

LeMay, D.W., Griffin, P.M., & Sandford, A.R. (1977). *Learning Accomplishment Profile-Diagnostic Edition*. Winston-Salem, NC: Kaplan.

Levine, S., Freeman, F.F., & Lewis, M. (1969). *California Preschool Social Competency Scale*. Palo Alto, CA: Consulting Psychologists Press, 1969.

Lichtenstein, R., & Ireton, H. (1984). *Preschool screening: Identifying young children with developmental and educational problems.* San Antonio, TX: Psychological Corporation.

Mardell-Czvdnowski, C., & Goldenberg, D. (1983). *Developmental Indicators for the Assessment of Learning-Revised.* Circle Pines, MN: American Guidance Service.

Matheny, A.P., Dolan, A.B., & Wilson, R.S. (1976). Within pair similarity on Bayley's Infant Behavior Record. *Journal of Genetic Psychology, 128,* 263–270.

McCarthy, D. (1972). *Manual for the McCarthy Scales of Children's Abilities.* New York: The Psychological Corporation.

Miller, L.J. (1982). *Miller Assessment for Preschoolers.* San Antonio, TX: Psychological Corporation.

Nagle, R.J. (1979). The McCarthy Scales of Children's Abilities: Research implications for the assessment of young children. *School Psychology Digest, 8*(3) pp. 319–325.

Nehring, A.D., Nehring, E.F., Bruni, J.R., & Randolph, P.L. (1992 pre-press release). Learning Accomplishment Profile Standardized Assessment-Examiner's Manual. Winston-Salem, NC: Kaplan.

Newborg, J., Stock, J.R., Wnek, L., Guidubaldi, J., & Svinicki, J. (1984). *The Battelle Developmental Inventory.* Allen, TX: DLM Teaching Resources.

Nicolich, L. (1977). Beyond sensorimotor intelligence: Assessment of symbolic maturity through analysis of pretend play. *Merril-Palmer Quarterly, 23,* 89–101.

Olswang, L.B., Stoel-Gammon, C., Coggins, T.E., & Carpenter, R.L. (1987). *Assessing linguistic behaviors: Assessing prelinguistic and early linguistic behaviors in developmentally young children.* Seattle: University of Washington Press.

Paget, K.D. (1990). Best practices in the assessment of competence in preschool-age children. In A. Thomas & J. Grimes, *Best Practices in School Psychology-II* (pp. 107–119). Washington, DC: National Association of School Psychologists.

Paget, K.D., & Bracken, B.A. (1983). *The Psychoeducational assessment of preschool children.* Orlando, Fla.: Grune & Stratton, Inc., Harcourt Brace, Jovanovich, Publishers.

Ramey, C.T., Campbell, F.A., & Nicholson, J.E. (1973). The predictive power of the Bayley Scales of Infant Development and the Stanford-Binet Intelligence Test in a relatively constant environment. *Child Development, 44,* 790–795.

Reuter, J., & Craig, S. (1976). *Bayley Scales of Infant Development Kent Scales Profile* [First Chance Project Grant #0E6 0074 02678]. Kent, OH: Kent Developmental Metrics.

Roszkowski, M.J. (1989). Review of the Bayley Scales of Infant Development. In J.C. Conoley & J.K. Kramer (Eds.), *Tenth Mental Measurements Yearbook.* Lincoln: The University of Nebraska Press.

Sanford, A.R., & Zelman, J. (1981). *Learning Accomplishment Profile-Revised.* Winston-Salem, NC: Kaplan.

Sattler, J.M. (1982). *Assessment of children's intelligence and special abilities.* Boston: Allyn & Bacon.

Song, A., Jones, S., Lippert, J., Metzgen, K., Miller, J., & Borreca, C. (1983). *Wisconsin Behavior Rating Scale.* Madison: Central Wisconsin Center for the Developmentally Delayed.

Stott, D.H. (1962). Personality at age four. *Child Development, 33,* 287–311.

Terman, L.M., & Merrill, M.A. (1937). *Measuring intelligence.* Boston: Houghton Mifflin.

Thomas, A., & Chess, S. (1977). *Temperament and development.* New York: Brunner/Mazel.

Thomas, A., Chess, S., & Karn, S. (1977). Parent and teacher temperament questionnaire for children 3–7 years of age. In A. Thomas & C. Chess (Eds.), *Temperament and development.* New York: Brunner/Mazel.

Thorndike, R.L., & Merrill, M.A. (1973). *Technical Manual for the Standford-Binet Intelligence Scale: 1972 Norms edition.* Boston: Houghton Mifflin.

Thorndike, R.L., Hagen, E.P., & Sattler, J.M. (1986). *Technical Manual: Stanford-Binet Intelligence Scale: Fourth Edition.* Chicago, IL: Riverside.

Vietz, P.M., & Vaughn, H.G. (1988). *Early identification of infants with developmental disabilities.* San Antonio, TX: The Psychological Corporation.

Wechsler, D. (1967). *Wechsler Preschool and Primary Scale of Intelligence.* San Antonio, TX: The Psychological Corporation.

Wechsler, D. (1974). *Wechsler Intelligence Scale for Children-Revised.* San Antonio, TX: The Psychological Corporation.

Wechsler, D. (1989). *Wechsler Preschool and Primary Scale of Intelligence-Revised.* San Antonio, TX: The Psychological Corporation.

Chapter 13

PSYCHOEDUCATIONAL ASSESSMENT OF CULTURALLY AND LINGUISTICALLY DIVERSE CHILDREN AND YOUTH

MARGARET R. ROGERS

At this time in the history of American psychology, it is difficult to say what constitutes best practices when conducting psychoeducational assessments with culturally and linguistically diverse (CLD) youngsters. This is especially true when working with cases involving linguistic minority children, who present a special challenge to evaluators for several reasons. First, most evaluators are not, by and large, specifically trained in the dynamics of assessments with bilingual or limited-English-proficient children (Ochoa, Delgado-Rivera, & Ford, 1994). Second, the assessment technology as a whole has not kept pace with the need for ecologically valid and methodologically sound procedures in this area. Although significant advancements have been made in the last 15 years in the technical adequacy of some of the most popular and widely used assessment measures, overall there is a serious shortage of appropriate instrumentation. Third, the traditional child-centered assessment paradigm, which frequently relies heavily on the use of norm-referenced instruments, is of limited utility with many CLD youngsters. Fourth, empirical evidence supporting the use of specific assessment practices is underdeveloped (e.g., use of interpreters). As the knowledge base in this area expands and changes, so will our understanding and confidence about what constitutes best practices in providing assessment services to CLD children.

In light of these considerations, this chapter is designed to synthesize the extant literature relevant to conducting psychoeducational assessments with CLD children and youth. The main focus is to assist psychologists and educational diagnosticians in considering the ethical, psychometric, and ecological/cultural influences that contribute to effective practices in assessing minority children and to describe the strengths and limitations of current assessment technology in applications with these populations. The chapter is written as a professional resource and guide for practicing school psychologists, regular and special educators, and graduate students who are training to become psychologists or educational diagnosticians.

DEFINITIONS

The focus of the chapter is on working with racially, ethnically, culturally, and linguistically diverse youngsters. *Racial/ethnic minority* children and youth will refer to individuals belonging to African American, Hispanic (Mexican American, Latino, Puerto Rican, etc.), Pacific Islander (Samoan, Hawaiian, etc.), Native American (Sioux, Cherokee, etc.), Asian American (Chinese, Japanese, Vietnamese, Cambodian, Korean), or biracial groups. The children and adolescents who represent these groups have been born and raised in the United States, have immigrated to this country, or may be refugees. It is clear that whereas minority group members may share a number of similarities, heterogeneity and diversity exist among these groups as well. The characteristics that distinguish members of one group from those of another can range from physical attributes (e.g., skin pigmentation, facial features) to social and cultural experiences (e.g., similar family origins, social and political histories and captivities, religious beliefs). Members of these groups may also be considered culturally diverse to the extent that they share cultural and social backgrounds and experiences different from those of the dominant culture.

Culturally diverse children may also be linguistically diverse in that their native language may not be English. Limited English proficient (LEP) children are those who speak a language other than English in addition to demonstrating some English language skills. LEP children's proficiency and competency in speaking their native language and English ranges from a mastery over both languages, to mastery over one and limited fluency in the other, to mastery over neither language. LEP children frequently come from home environments in which a primary language other than English is spoken and use of English within the home varies considerably.

The focus here will be on the psychoeducational assessment of racially, ethnically, culturally, and linguistically diverse children. First, the ethical considerations that shape assessment practices will be discussed. Second, psychometric issues relevant to working with CLD youngsters will be identified. The assessment process will extend from prereferral activities to follow-up. The process will emphasize a systematic approach to data gathering using the most psychometrically sound and ecologically valid procedures available. Special attention will be given to promoting an ecological approach to assessment that considers the social, cultural, and linguistic context of each child. Because all human experience occurs within a context, it is crucial that we consider how children's behavior, attitudes, and values are defined and shaped by the cultural context in which they occur.

LEGAL CONSIDERATIONS

To a large extent, considerations regarding how best to assess and educate minority children are guided by federal, state, and local legislation, and by litigation outcomes. Over the last few decades, the courts and Congress have become increasingly more active in influencing the direction of educational and psychological services within the schools. The impact of these legal proceedings on the education of children, in general, and minority children, in particular, is tremendous. Because of the profound influence these cases and legislative acts have had in shaping current educational policies and assessment practices that pertain to CLD children, it is important that those who work with CLD children understand the legal precedents that are involved. By becoming aware of these legal influences and changes, professionals will be better equipped to provide assessment services within the prescribed legal parameters. For a description of some of the most important court cases and legislative acts pertinent to CLD youth, readers are referred to Fischer and Sorenson (1996) and Rogers (1993). What follows is a succinct summary of the court decisions and legislative acts that have had enormous consequences for the way minority children are evaluated and educated in U.S. schools. Specifically, the evaluation of minority children now must be based on (1) multidisciplinary assessments involving information gathered from a variety of sources and methods, (2) assessments conducted in the child's native language as well as English, (3) assessments that protect children from selection and administration practices that are racially and culturally discriminatory, (4) clearly specified procedures for assessing linguistically diverse children, and (5) informed parental consent and notification of rights to due process.

ETHICAL CONSIDERATIONS

Psychologists performing psychoeducational evaluations are guided by legal mandate, by the ethical standards and principles developed by the National Association of School Psychologists (NASP, 1992) and the American Psychological Association (APA, 1992), and by the testing standards delineated in the *Standards for Educational and Psychological Testing* (American Educational Research Association, American Psychological Association, & National Council on Measurement in Education, 1985). The new *APA Ethical Principles of Psychologists and Code of Conduct* (1992) provides some of the most explicit statements to guide professional service delivery. Specifically, *Human Differences* (Part 1.08) states that psychologists have an ethical responsibility to consider the impact of age, race, ethnicity, gender, socioeconomic status (SES), language, disability, religion, national origin, and sexual orientation on individual functioning and psychological well-being. The principle also calls for psychologists to be ethically responsive by becoming cross-culturally competent through training, supervision, or consultation with diverse groups (APA, 1992). This principle makes central psychologist's obligation to consider each client's unique constellation of cultural and linguistic characteristics when providing psychological services.

The ethical guidelines of both the APA and NASP provide psychologists with general standards that help to define and regulate many aspects of professional practice and conduct. In addition, APA recently developed and published more specific principles to help guide service delivery to CLD clients in the *Guidelines for Providers of Psychological Services to Ethnic, Linguistic, and Culturally Diverse Populations* (APA, 1993). It should be noted that although the *Guidelines* help to guide the services of doctoral-level psychologists, it makes sense for nondoctoral psychologists and education diagnosticians to adhere to them as well.

In addition to ethical principles and associated relevant guidelines, professional assessment practices should also be informed by the *Standards for Educational and Psychological Testing* (American Educational Research Association et al., 1985). The *Standards,* currently under revision, serve as the authoritative document on the development, use, interpretation, and evaluation of tests and are a useful resource for professionals who assess minority children because they clearly specify characteristics of tests that evaluators should consider when selecting and using assessment instruments. The 1985 edition of the *Standards* includes one entire chapter (Chapter 13) exclusively devoted to testing linguistically diverse youngsters that is crucial reading for those who work with these populations.

PROFESSIONAL PREPARATION AND QUALIFICATIONS

Given the specialized nature of assessment practices with minority children, it is suggested that those learning how to perform and those already conducting psychoeducational evaluations with CLD youngsters receive extensive instruction in areas that relate to quality service delivery with CLD clients. Recently, it has been argued that psychologists have been far too focused on developing the psychometric properties of assessment instruments for use with groups or individuals with particular characteristics and far too unfocused on the cross-cultural competencies of the psychologists who are using the particular instrument (Ponterotto & Alexander, 1996). Although improving the technical qualities of methods is important, what should be most important is the cross-cultural understanding, skill, and expertise of the psychologist. As Ponterotto and Alexander (1996) point out, "a 'culture-bound' (or biased) assessment device in the hands of a well-trained multicultural practitioner is preferred over a 'culture-fair' instrument in the hands of a poorly trained (multicultural) practitioner" (p. 652).

To develop cross-cultural competencies, evaluators need to be well informed about a range of topics, including language development, second-language acquisition, nonbiased assessment techniques, culturally sensitive environmental and individual evaluation procedures, and culturally appropriate intervention strategies. Each of these topics is considered to be vitally important in preparation for work with minority children and their families. In addition to content knowledge in these areas, prepared evaluators need competencies in three important areas.

First, evaluators should have extensive coursework and training in the construction, selection, use, and interpretation of tests. Any good psychological tests and measurement text (e.g., Anastasi's *Psychological Testing,* 1988) should be required reading along with the *Standards.* It is strongly believed that better training in testing and measurement, with a special emphasis on the limitations of norm-referenced tests, will prevent the inappropriate use of standardized tests with all children.

In addition to specialized training in tests and measurement, evaluators need to develop a knowledge base in cross-cultural psychology to be able to provide culturally sensitive and meaningful assessment services. The schools, just like any other major American institution, are places where biased institutional policies and practices are created and maintained. Bias may be found in the school curriculum (through texts containing distortions, unrealistic depictions, invisibility, stereotyping, etc.), in the school climate (e.g., an environment that implicitly seems to accept sexual harassment between students, school personnel, faculty-students), in referral and/or assessment practices, or in school policies (e.g., segregation, tracking, etc.). Therefore, it is essential that psychologists working with CLD school-age youngsters become skilled in assessing the degree to which bias is present and negatively impacting the school environment and community. Not only must psychologists be well versed in identifying bias, they must also be skilled in developing, implementing, and evaluating techniques designed to eliminate bias, prejudice, and oppression that exists on an individual and/or institutional level.

According to Nuttall, De Leon, and Valle (1990), one way that psychologists can become more sensitive to cultural issues is by evaluating their own value systems, cultural backgrounds, and personal identities to understand better how these processes influence their professional practices. Learning more about the environmental characteristics and the psychosocial climate of the child's school, home, and community can provide the evaluator with a broader and more complete understanding of the child's experiential base and how those experiences affect academic achievement and interpersonal adjustment. Evaluators interested in learning more about the unique social, political, and familial experiences of different cultural, racial, and ethnic groups are encouraged to consult one of a number of excellent resources (e.g., Helms, 1992a; Nuttall et al., 1990; Takaki, 1989; Taylor Gibbs & Huang, 1989).

Third, as part of the training process it is vitally important that students have firsthand exposure to and supervised casework experience with racial, ethnic, and linguistic minority children during practica and internship. Students need to learn how to adopt a cultural lens that considers the impact of language and culture at each step in the problem-solving process. Through structured practical experiences students will be able to synthesize information drawn from coursework with hands-on experiences to systematically develop their cross-cultural competencies. Special attention during the applied component of training should be paid to learning how to locate, secure, and tap into community, home, and/or school-based resources. Information from these sources will help to place each child's evaluation within its appropriate cultural context.

PSYCHOMETRIC CONSIDERATIONS

A critical skill in assessing CLD children is being sensitive to and knowledgeable about the psychometric characteristics of assessment procedures. Best practices dictate that evaluators use the most well-developed, objective, reliable, valid, and systematic data-gathering methods available. Special attention must be focused on carefully selecting and using appropriate techniques and instruments given the nature of the presenting problem along with considerations regarding the child's racial/ethnic, cultural, linguistic, and socioeconomic background.

Part of the reason evaluators need to be particularly careful in the selection and administration of assessment procedures with CLD children is the long and contro-versial history psychological tests have had in applications with these populations. Few subjects in the testing movement have captured heightened emotional debate as has the use of traditional testing devices with CLD youngsters (Reynolds & Brown, 1984). At the heart of much of the debate has been the issue of whether standardized tests are discriminatory and biased when used with racial/ethnic minor-ity children. In part, these arguments have been propelled by the fact that children from different racial/ethnic groups have historically been overrepresented or, in some cases, underrepresented among special-education populations, allegedly as the result of bias inherent in tests.

As a consequence, the technical adequacy of tests has come under intense scru-tiny. Experts in testing (e.g., Anastasi, 1988; Salvia & Ysseldyke, 1991) have pointed out a number of problems in measuring the abilities and skills of minority children. Problems with inadequate representation among standardization groups, inappropriate test content, and questionable item relevancy have all been cited as significant difficulties with traditional standardized tests (Fradd, Barona, & Santos de Barona, 1989). The technical characteristics that have proved to be most prob-lematic will be highlighted so that evaluators will be cognizant of features of assess-ment devices that need to be critically analyzed when selecting a norm-referenced instrument for use with a CLD youngster.

Adequate Representation within the Standardization Sample

One concern arises when tests and test data are used as if the test norms adequately reflect the individual or group being assessed. Some instruments have excluded African Americans, Hispanics, and other minority groups in the norming process and sampled only Whites when standardizing the instruments. This practice limits the applicability of the test norms to the White group only. Other tests have in-cluded minorities during the norming process but underrepresented their overall numbers. Further, some test developers have included minority groups in adequate numbers but have not evenly sampled these groups in terms of other major popula-tion characteristics such as SES. Over- or underrepresenting lower-, middle-, or upper-SES minorities in the standardization group sacrifices the accuracy and utility of the test norms. A norm-referenced test designed to represent the current demo-graphics of children in the United States needs to include samples of minority and majority group members in proportion to the latest data from the U.S. Bureau of the Census in terms of age, sex, race, SES, size of community, and geographic location. A good rule of thumb is that a test selected for use should have norms that were developed within the last 15 years. Salvia and Ysseldyke (1991) recommend that test publishers develop new norms for tests every 15 years. Given the rapidly changing demographics in the United States, this suggestion seems warranted.

Test Content

The content of a test can be problematic when different groups perform differently on test items. When groups can be distinguished on the basis of their performance on test items such that some items are more difficult for members of different groups, those items are considered to be biased (Reynolds & Kaiser, 1990). Two methods have been employed to eliminate item bias. First, test developers and publishers have appointed expert review teams to scrutinize test content for objectionable and potentially biased items. Then identified items have been removed from the item pool. This approach has received more support from a public relations perspective than it has from an empirical point of view (Reynolds & Kaiser, 1990).

The second, more methodologically sound approach, has been to subject test items to statistical analysis during test development and modify or discard items from the final item pool that evidence race or gender bias. Careful evaluators will need to review test manuals to ensure that item bias procedures have been undertaken and that selected instruments have empirically demonstrated a lack of bias across minority groups. Choosing tests that have eliminated biased items will effectively minimize this source of error from the evaluation process.

A second way that test content can be problematic concerns the testing materials. Anastasi (1988) points out that a test may contain pictures, words, or illustrations that exert an undesirable influence on the testing situation for the minority child. For example, a test may contain stereotypical pictures, offensive words, or pictures that depict only one racial group. Exposure to these stimuli during a standardized test administration could affect a minority child's motivation to perform at optimal levels.

A third though indirect way the test content can be problematic is that its results might be misused to predict the future potential of a child who has not been exposed to and has not had an opportunity to learn the test material. This is particularly problematic with achievement testing. Generally speaking, it is not appropriate to use test results gathered under these conditions for predictive purposes. By thoroughly reviewing test materials and stimuli for potentially objectionable characterizations and questionable or irrelevant content before conducting an assessment, an evaluator can more carefully screen and select instruments accordingly.

Construct Validity

The construct validity of a test may also be a concern when the test evidences factorial invariance across racial/ethnic minority groups. Test developers and publishers need to report empirical evidence in the test manual that attests to the stability of the factor structure of a test for various majority and minority groups. When such information is not reported either in the manual or in the extant literature, the instrument is considered to be of limited practical utility because it is impossible to independently judge the factorial stability of the measure.

Other Test-Related Concerns

In addition to the technical qualities of tests, Anastasi (1988) recommends that evaluators consider other test-related factors that influence the validity of an assessment and have an impact on the meaningfulness of test results of minority children.

Such factors as previous exposure to standardized testing situations, motivation to perform well, and the rapport established between test taker and evaluator are all variables that may have an impact on test validity. To deal with these effects, Anastasi proposes several suggestions. First, evaluators should retest children with alternate versions of the test in cases where the validity of the test administrations is questioned. Second, evaluators should provide test takers with an adequate period of time to become oriented to the test procedures and environment before beginning formal testing. Third, evaluators should provide children with opportunities to practice test-taking skills. It should be noted that some of the more recently developed individually administered intelligence tests and academic achievement measures have responded to these suggestions by including sample (practice) items and by developing and publishing alternate test forms. Many of these instruments will be highlighted in the section of this chapter dealing with critical components of the assessment process.

To summarize, it is important for practitioners to carefully evaluate the technical merits and qualities of an instrument before selecting it for use with a particular minority child. Tests must have representative and appropriate norms, must contain test materials that sensitively reflect multicultural experiences, and should not exhibit item bias or factorial invariance. Also, evaluators should consider the recommendations of Anastasi (1988) when planning assessments with CLD children.

CRITICAL COMPONENTS OF THE ASSESSMENT PROCESS

This section serves as a practical guide for evaluators to follow in performing culturally sensitive, appropriate, and accurate assessments with racially, ethnically, culturally, and linguistically diverse clients. Special attention is devoted to minimizing and/or eliminating possible sources of bias at each step in the assessment process. Alternatives to traditional assessment practices are described. The most important components of the assessment process are prereferral activities, pre- and postassessment multidisciplinary team meetings, record review, environmental assessment, language proficiency assessment, cognitive assessment, academic achievement assessment, report writing, and follow-up activities.

Prereferral Activities

Evaluators can assist their school systems in preparing to meet the educational and psychological needs of minority children in two important ways: by educating and upgrading the skills of those who provide services to minority youngsters and by participating in school-based prereferral teams.

Educational Efforts

A primary objective of practitioners working in multicultural and multilingual settings is to engage in ongoing educational efforts (e.g., in-service workshops) with the school faculty and staff. One important way that evaluators can foster the professional development of school personnel is to draw attention to environmental variables and circumstances that influence children's academic and social performance and progress. The ongoing educational efforts should be designed to help school personnel learn about (1) how to identify and confront expressions of racism, sexism, classism, ableism, and heterosexism embedded in their schools, (2) issues that commonly confront minority members of the school community and neighborhood, and (3) cultural and social characteristics of the diverse groups of minority students that attend the school. It is vitally important that school faculty and staff work individually and collectively to identify, challenge, and confront oppressive educational and social practices that they encounter in their schools. The specific foci of these educational efforts may be wide ranging and may include workshops about how to examine instructional materials for racial and gender bias (Banks, 1994; Sadker, Sadker, & Long, 1993), how to transform curricula to represent a multicultural pluralistic approach to education (Banks, 1993), and how to use anti-bias instruction in the classroom (Derman-Sparks, 1993).

The in-service workshops may also explore and describe the cultural matches/mismatches that may exist between a minority child's home environment and the culture of the school. Finally, the information disseminated should also inform educators and administrators about the legal, ethical, and psychometric issues associated with assessing minority children.

Educational outreach efforts should include developing liaison relationships with members of the local community to further ensure that the assessment is culturally anchored and grounded (Barnett, Collins, Coulter, Curtis, Ehrhardt, Glaser, Reyes, Stollar, & Winston, 1995). The community representative should be selected because experiences and/or training make him or her familiar with the cultural characteristics and context of various local minority groups and because he or she is willing to serve as a cultural consultant to the schools. Enlisting the assistance and support of CLD community members in the problem-solving process helps to expand the range of expertise that is brought to bear on educational decisions. It may also lead to enhanced intervention acceptability and utility (Barnett et al., 1995) because it increases the likelihood that solutions will be culturally relevant and responsive. School personnel involved in arranging for a cultural consultant should be sensitive to the need to form a relationship between the school and the consultant that is an equitable one.

Prereferral Teams

Another objective of the evaluator is to participate in and contribute to the school-based prereferral team. The prereferral team is usually the first group to speak with the person who referred the child. If teacher referred, it is a good idea to contact the child's caretaker(s)/parent(s) during the prereferral phase to enlist support in helping to define and solve the problem. Through contacts with the family, the evaluator has an opportunity to become better acquainted with the caretakers' perception of the problem, the sociocultural context of the home, and other home-related factors that influence the child's social and academic development and experiences.

When a CLD child is initially referred to the team, close attention needs to be paid to the reasons for the referral. In a meta-analysis of the teacher expectation research, Dusek and Joseph (1983) report that teacher expectations about student academic and social skills are frequently based on initial impressions about the student's race, social class, and physical attractiveness. Reasons for referral based on these variables alone in the absence of objective data are never sufficiently justified. When these types of referrals arise, consultation with the referral source is recommended to help clear up misperceptions and revise stereotypical or biased thinking. In addition, reasons for referrals based on other sources of bias (institutional, systemic) should also be ruled out before proceeding with an individual evaluation. In the case of referrals involving limited-English-proficient Hispanic children who have just immigrated to the United States, Wilen and van Maanen Sweeting (1986) suggest that many presenting problems may be temporary problems associated with adjusting to new surroundings. They advise practitioners to carefully consider the context of the child's current life experiences and assess problem severity and chronicity before proceeding with a formal assessment.

Presenting problems that survive this process will proceed through the problem-solving activities employed by the prereferral team. When working with CLD youngsters, the ethnic validity of the problem-solving process becomes particularly important (Barnett et al., 1995). Ethnic validity refers to "the degree to which problem identification and problem solving are acceptable to the client in respect to the client's belief and value systems, as these are associated with the client's ethnic/cultural group" (p. 221). Within this context, the problem-solving process incorporates information about the cultural variables impacting the problem at each step. Using a cultural framework, the goals of the prereferral team are to clearly define and prioritize presenting problems, gather and review baseline data, identify solutions that have been tried but have failed, pinpoint alternative solutions, monitor the implementation of interventions, and help the teacher to evaluate intervention effectiveness. Proceeding through the problem-solving process will assist in supplying valuable information about instructional strategies that have and have not worked. Test-teach-test techniques are strongly recommended as part of the data-collection process. If the interventions attempted at this level are not successful and the team has eliminated teacher and/or systemic bias as the basis for the referral, the child will be referred to the multidisciplinary team for a more in-depth evaluation.

Preassessment Multidisciplinary Team Meeting

Once a CLD youngster has been referred to the multidisciplinary team, team members need to objectively review the referral information and supplementary data collected by the prereferral team and decide if a more thorough and comprehensive individual assessment appears warranted. If the team decides to proceed with further assessments, the child's parent(s) need to be notified formally. Keep in mind that these early meetings with the parents will set the tone for future interactions, and every effort should be made to treat parents in a culturally sensitive and respectful manner. Poorer families may not have a telephone, and some parents may be illiterate or may not speak English. In these cases, a home visit with evaluator, parents, and cultural consultant and/or interpreter is recommended. Prior to the meeting, the evaluator will need to make sure that the cultural consultant and interpreter understand that all interactions with the family are confidential.

The early meetings with the parents are an excellent opportunity to obtain information about the family's customs and language preferences. For CLD children, Miller (1984) recommends that evaluators use this opportunity to find out the name the child prefers to be called during the evaluation. He notes that cross-cultural differences exist in terms of how a person prefers to be addressed and points out the importance of ascertaining the family's customs about names to prevent misunderstandings. For LEP or bilingual children, Sattler (1988) advises evaluators to use a home language survey with the parents to gather information about the languages used between the child and his or her siblings and parents at home. He suggests that evaluators inquire about the languages depicted in the television programs the child watches and the language the parents use when reading to the child. Gathering this type of information at this stage will help guide interactions with the child and his or her family during remaining portions of the assessment.

Parents who have recently arrived in the United States or are new to the school district or to special-education procedures, will have a high need for information regarding the evaluation process and the implications of the process. Therefore, during the meeting the evaluator will also need to ensure that the parents are completely informed of their legal rights and options as well as what an assessment entails. The notification of plans to evaluate should be written in language the parents understand and should specify the type of evaluation(s) that will be carried out, the parents' legal options and rights to due process, and a request for their written consent to the evaluations.

Once parental consent has been secured, the multidisciplinary team needs to decide how the assessments will be organized. Experienced evaluators have pointed out the advantages of extending the different assessments over a multiday period. For example, Chamberlain and Medinos-Landurand (1991) suggest that when LEP or bilingual children require multiple evaluations, the assessments should be carried out in a sequential rather than simultaneous manner. This allows children time to become accustomed to the demands of one-to-one assessments and reduces the likelihood that they will feel overwhelmed. Employing a less intensive assessment schedule also affords the various specialists time to analyze the child's performance after each assessment and to make decisions about the need for continued data collection (Chamberlain & Medinos-Landurand, 1991).

Review of Records

If the records have not already been examined during prereferral, the next step in the assessment process is to review the child's cumulative folder. Children who immigrate to the United States may have school records from their native country and these should be requested. In reviewing the file, pay close attention to the child's school history. For example, note interruptions in schooling, location and number of schools attended, grades enrolled in and completed, language(s) used in former classrooms, report-card grades and achievement test scores, history of retentions, and special services previously received. Any information about the educational system and curricula the child has been exposed to along with specific academic skills the child has mastered are helpful to ascertain. Additional information regarding the child's developmental and medical history as well as current health status should be noted, and appropriate referrals for vision and hearing screening should be made.

Environmental Assessment

When performing psychoeducational assessments of CLD children, an environmental assessment is an essential component of the process in helping the evaluator understand the social context of the child. The environmental assessment includes a systematic analysis of the characteristics of the classroom, school, home, and community environments in which the child functions. Psychologists who work in schools need to use their organizational assessment skills to critically examine the norms, culture, climate, power centers, and power relationships that exist within their schools. For example, psychologists need to be cognizant of organizational variables that promote achievement for CLD youngsters as well as systemic barriers and discriminatory practices that hinder achievement and adjustment (e.g., tracking). Part of the organizational assessment should also focus on the overt and hidden agendas and value systems of those in power in the school system because those values communicate powerful messages about what is important in the educational experience (Banks, 1994; Sarason, 1982).

In focusing on the immediate context and experiences of the referred child, behavior that may be considered appropriate within the context of the home or community may not be construed similarly within the classroom. Therefore, it is important to identify and document the cultural similarities and differences within the settings so that the child's performance can be interpreted within an appropriate cultural framework. Minority children may be exposed to cultural practices at school that are embedded in the majority culture orientation of the school they attend and curriculum they are exposed to but that are not consistent with their home and community experiences (Huang & Taylor Gibbs, 1992). These cultural mismatches in norms and expectations between the home and school may create confusion for the child and can affect assessment performance as well as day-to-day functioning in the classroom.

For example, research has suggested that cultural mismatches between the participation structures of children's home and school environments can affect academic success. Participation structures refer to rules that define acceptable behavior in different situations. Au and Mason (1981) studied the reading achievement of Hawaiian children and found that the children experienced significant gains in reading skills after the participation structures of the classroom were changed to be more compatible with those operating at home. They found that the children's home environments were characterized by overlapping interactions where family members freely interrupted each other when conversing. When reading instructions at school were modified to accommodate this overlapping conversational style, reading achievement improved. This research underscores the value and importance of collecting information from the home and school environments of CLD children.

Many of the techniques employed in environmental assessments are similar to the methods used by ethnographers in the study of diverse cultures. The techniques include but are not limited to interviews, observations, work samples, checklists, and peer nomination techniques. Interviews, observations, and work samples will each be examined more closely in turn.

Interviews

The evaluator will want to conduct interviews with all relevant individuals who are linked to the referred child, including the child. Interviews may be informal and relatively unstructured or structured depending on the referral question and preferences of the evaluator and interviewees. If teacher referred, preobservation interviews with the teacher provide an opportunity to gather further information about the reasons for the referral and help to clearly define the presenting problem(s). In clarifying the nature of the concerns, it is valuable to gather frequency, severity, duration, antecedent, and consequent information. The interviews should also be used to ascertain the extent of the teacher's previous experiences with CLD children.

There are a number of structured approaches to conducting interviews and observations that are readily available. A valuable option is The Instructional Environment Scale II (TIES II; Ysseldyke & Christenson, 1996), which combines an observational system with teacher, caretaker, and student interviews. The TIES has several attractive features. Chief among them is that the TIES incorporates the perspectives of those key people who are typically most invested in the youngster's educational experience. Second, the TIES II provides a systematic format for analyzing important features of the instructional environment that likely have an impact on instructional success and skill acquisition.

In addition to obtaining information about the instructional environment, interviews with the child and caretaker(s)/parent(s) and sometimes extended family members are also important in contributing to an understanding of the child's cultural and linguistic background and current family context. Henning-Stout (1994) reinforces the importance of including the youngster in the interviews and suggests directly questioning the child about his or her academic skills, social adjustment, motivation to learn, and instructional needs. Catarino (1991) recommends conducting part of the parent interview with the child present so the evaluator will be able to observe parent-child conversations and make note of any differences that exist in the child's linguistic skills or communicative style within the home and school environments.

Depending on the background of the child, the evaluator may want to gather information from the caretaker(s)/parent(s) about the family's origins as well as cultural background. For example, if a family has recently immigrated to the United States the evaluator will want to determine the length of time the family has lived at their present residence, the locations of previous residences, and the extent of their involvement with their new community. This will give an indication of the degree of their acculturation to the new area and prevailing culture. Has the family left their native country because of war or are they seeking political asylum? Are there any social or political stresses that are having an impact on their child's situation? Has the child lost relatives or witnessed acts of war? Is the family living in the United States legally? Did the parents experience a change in job status when they moved? What do the parents do for a living? Have there been family separations? Do extended family members live with them? All of these considerations will have an impact on the child's psychological functioning and will need to be considered as factors that may be influencing school behavior and academic performance.

The evaluator will also want to assess the parents' attitude toward education. Do they value an education? What are their own educational backgrounds and experiences? What are their expectations for their child's education? Do the parents help the child with homework assignments? What are the child's study habits? Is there evidence that the family spends time together? Do the parents read to themselves or to their children? What are the consequences for school success or failure? Answers to these questions give an indication of the child's psychosocial environment and the parents' attitudes toward achievement and schooling.

Information about the child's medical and developmental history also needs to be gathered. Were developmental milestones met? Has the child had any significant medical problems? Questions concerning previous diagnoses will be important when dealing with children from some racial/ethnic groups because of their high-risk status (e.g., Native Americans and fetal alcohol syndrome). How does the family treat medical problems? What are the parents' attitudes toward children with handicaps or illnesses? What is the child's place in the birth order? How many siblings does the child have? Are there opportunities to play with same-age and same-language peers? What is the child's age? Miller (1984) advises that there are variations among cultures regarding how a child's age is calculated and suggests that reports about a child's age may need to be verified through appropriate channels.

Does the child have any chores or household responsibilities? What is the division of labor in the home? Does the family value cooperation or competition more? Is the child encouraged to become independent? Are there noticeable differences in the way sons and daughters are treated? What are the roles of the mother and father in the family? How is the child disciplined? Finally, the evaluator will want to informally assess the communication mode and style between the parents and their children. Is it mostly nonverbal or verbal? Is eye contact and gesturing important? What language is used? Accurate documentation of this information will help the evaluator to have a better understanding of the sociocultural and linguistic context of the child's home environment.

Observations

Careful collection of observational data throughout the problem-solving and assessment process will provide information about how the youngster functions across settings. Some combination of one-to-one assessment and classroom, school, home, and community observations will typically be desired. The evaluator will want to pay special attention to any indications of cultural mismatches between home/community and school environments and the ways that school personnel and the youngster cope with the inconsistencies. Evidence of the child's motivational and problem-solving styles should also be noted.

To increase the precision and accuracy of the collected data, structured observations of operationalized target behaviors are recommended. The evaluator should make sure that data are collected within a variety of instructional contexts. Does the child work well independently and in small and large groups? Also, how does he or she relate to peers and teachers? It is advisable that these observations include comparisons with same-age culturally/linguistically similar and culturally/linguistically different peers. The observations will provide a wealth of information about the match between the child's behaviors, the task at hand, and the behaviors of others within his or her environment. To gather information about how the child fits in with his or her community, Correa (1989) recommends that the evaluator attend social events and community-based meetings in the child's home environment.

Work Samples

Obtaining work samples of day-to-day assignments and tests is an invaluable way to better understand and assess the relationship between task requirements and the child's skill. Evaluators can use the work samples to perform a task analysis of academic assignments across the subjects that challenge the youngster and gain a more complete picture of skill strengths and weaknesses. Collecting work samples over a multiweek period is optimal because it allows the evaluator to monitor skill acquisition and difficulties over time. For LEP or bilingual children, the work samples should be collected for academic tasks completed in both English and the child's native language.

ONE-TO-ONE ASSESSMENTS

There is considerable variation in the reasons for carrying out psychoeducational evaluations. There are however features of psychometrically sound and valid assessments that should be remembered regardless of the purpose of the evaluation. First, the most reliable, valid, and appropriate techniques should be selected for use during the evaluation. Depending on the purpose of the assessment, appropriate techniques may be curriculum based or screening or diagnostic norm-referenced tools based on locally or nationally derived norms. Second, bilingual children will need to have each assessment performed separately in both languages with instruments that are technically sound in each language. When technically adequate procedures are not available, the evaluator will need to use single-subject design methodology to collect baseline, intervention, and postintervention data to help determine the child's strengths and weaknesses.

Third, to ensure that assessments are an accurate reflection of the child's competencies and skills, it is desirable to have the parents observe the evaluations through a one-way mirror, if the setting permits. The parents should be asked to render their judgment about the validity of the child's performance. Did the child demonstrate what he or she is capable of doing? Is this the way the child usually behaves? These questions are important in establishing the validity of the assessment and must be asked. For assessments that necessitate norm-referenced techniques, a fourth practice that will enhance validity is the use of testing-of-limits

(TOL) procedures (Sattler, 1988). Once the standardized test administration is completed, the evaluator can employ TOL to determine the strategies the child used to solve incorrectly answered questions. TOL procedures are especially useful with children who have little experience with the demands of one-to-one assessments and with those who have not been taught a specific skill being assessed.

Language Proficiency Assessment

The assessment of language proficiency needs to be the very first one-to-one evaluation conducted with LEP or bilingual youngsters because the language(s) used for all subsequent assessments and the interpretations made of assessment results are based on the competencies shown during this initial evaluation. Generally speaking, children who are clearly monolingual should be evaluated in their dominant language, whereas bilingual children need to be evaluated in both languages. Current legal and ethical guidelines dictate that bilingual children should have all assessments performed in their native language and in English by a specialist fluent in both languages.

Whoever conducts the language proficiency evaluation (usually the speech and language specialist) needs to be aware of current research and theory regarding the acquisition of first and second languages. The evaluator should perform a thorough assessment of the child's speaking, writing, and reading skills and receptive and expressive abilities using both informal and formal data collection techniques. Fradd et al. (1989) suggest collecting three 15-minute oral-language samples as part of the informal assessment. They point out that the child's teacher may be in the best position to obtain these samples because he or she has the most sustained contact with the child. Both the teacher and the specialist who performs the assessment will want to pay close attention to and document any idiosyncrasies in the child's speech that reflect differences in dialect or regional variations in speech patterns. Close collaboration between the specialist, parents, teacher, and psychoeducational evaluator will help to define the child's linguistic abilities.

The purpose of the language proficiency evaluation is to determine the extent of the child's fluency in English and in the native language. The evaluation will distinguish children whose native language skills are intact and well developed but whose English skills are just emerging from children who show delays in native language skills and in learning skills. Children who are bilingual will show a range of linguistic competencies and their expertise in either language will be dependent on their age, ability level, language(s) of instruction, and amount of exposure to their native language and English. Clinical observations suggest that younger children generally take less time than older children to acquire a second language (Cummins, 1984). Also because of differences in ability level and rate of learning, mentally retarded children usually take longer than children who are not mentally retarded to learn a second language. Gifted children may learn to speak a second language at an accelerated pace.

Cummins (1984) notes that most bilingual children acquire the ability to converse in a second language before they can use the second language on more academic or cognitively demanding tasks. He suggests that children's ability to converse in a second language appears within the first 2 years of exposure to the language, whereas the ability to use a second language to function effectively in an academic setting takes from 5 to 7 years. Cummins' studies suggest that speech and language specialists will need to assess both conversational and more academically focused language skills during the language proficiency evaluation in order to gather information that will be most predictive of the child's language abilities in academic settings. The specialist will need to be thoroughly familiar with the specific skills various instruments are designed to assess in order to accomplish this objective.

Other researchers have suggested that as children acquire a second language, they experience a period of regression in their first language skills (Fradd et al., 1989). These findings suggest that as bilingual children acquire increasing fluency with a second language, frequent assessments of their language skills are warranted. In fact, Ortiz and Garcia (1985) recommend against using the results from language proficiency assessments that are more than 6 months old because of the variability seen in children's language skills when they are acquiring a second language.

Use of Interpreters

Evaluators who are monolingual will need to refer bilingual children to a well-trained and qualified bilingual specialist for this phase and, if needed, for the remaining portions of the evaluation. Ethically and legally this is the most prudent action to take. In the past, monolingual evaluators who have been confronted with referrals of bilingual children have questioned the feasibility of using test interpreters rather than bilingual specialists. In these cases, Figueroa (1990) recommends against the use of poorly trained interpreters and views the use of well-trained interpreters as problematic.

Interpreters may not be trained in test administration procedures, may substitute words, may speak a different dialect, or may engage in subtle prompting behaviors that exert an influence on the child's responses (Nuttall, Medinos-Landurand, & Goldman, 1984). In addition, translating a test that has been developed and normed in English may not yield a technically equivalent form of the test. Translators may substitute words that are more difficult than the original words and this will influence the psychometric properties of the test. Overall, Figueroa (1990) calls into question the validity of evaluations conducted by interpreters because of the lack of empirical evidence supporting the use of interpreters. Therefore, it is advisable that monolingual evaluators locate bilingual specialists in their community or region and employ their services when a bilingual child has been referred for an evaluation.

Cognitive Assessments

The information provided by the environmental and language-proficiency assessments will help to guide the selection of cognitive and educational assessment devices to fit the unique characteristics and assessment needs of the referred CLD child. In most states in the United States, an evaluation for special-education eligibility will need to be based on a carefully selected combination of cognitive, academic achievement, and behavioral techniques and measures because no one technique provides an adequate sample of the child's skills and competencies. For many referrals, the current realities of the federal definitions for special education eligibility dictate that some form of cognitive assessment be conducted. At the same time, the ultimate responsibility for using norm-referenced cognitive assessment instruments as part of a comprehensive psychoeducational evaluation rests with the practicing psychologist. Many scholars (e.g., Armour-Thomas, 1992; Helms, 1992b) are critical of the use of standardized cognitive assessment devices with minority youngsters and suggest that psychologists discontinue their use altogether.

It is clear that no currently published cognitive assessment instrument is appropriate for all children. Therefore, psychologists will need to use their own best judgment about the characteristics and needs of the referred youngster and critically examine the psychometric properties of the range of instruments that are available before determining whether a test is available that provides the best fit with the child's characteristics in relation to the assessment questions. In some situations, this may mean forgoing a cognitive assessment as part of the overall evaluation. In other situations, a cognitive assessment will be warranted. For those situations, the next two portions of the chapter draw attention to the advantages and disadvantages of some of the most widely used norm-referenced assessment devices in applications with minority children and youth. First, a sample of the major intellectual assessment devices (e.g., Kaufman Assessment Battery for Children, Stanford-Binet Intelligence Scale-Fourth Edition, Wechsler Intelligence Scale for Children-Third Edition, Wechsler Preschool and Primary Scale of Intelligence-Revised) used with preschool and school-age youngsters will be reviewed and will be followed by a discussion of alternatives to these more conventional measures. Then, some of the more popular norm-referenced academic achievement instruments will be reviewed. All reviews emphasize the technical dimensions of the instruments that are relevant to assessing CLD youngsters and that have the potential to affect the validity of the evaluation.

Specifically, each test was analyzed with respect to the following characteristics:

1. Does the test contain an adequate and representative standardization sample?
2. Have the test authors employed a minority review panel and/or statistical item-analysis procedures to detect biased items?
3. Is the reliability and validity of the scale established and documented?
4. Are diverse racial/ethnic groups represented in the test materials through pictures and other illustrations?
5. Does the test contain sample or practice items?
6. Is a parallel or alternate form available?
7. Is there empirical evidence supporting the use of the instrument with English-as-a-Second-Language (ESL) students?
8. Has a Spanish version of the test been developed and properly normed?

Kaufman Assessment Battery for Children

The Kaufman Assessment Battery for Children (K-ABC; Kaufman & Kaufman, 1983) is a test of intelligence and achievement designed for use with children between the ages of 2 years, 5 months to 12 years, 5 months. The scale contains 10 mental processing subtests and 6 supplementary achievement subtests. It yields a total Mental Processing Composite (MPC) score that has a mean of 100 and a standard deviation of 15. It has been lauded for including normal, exceptional, and gifted children in the standardization sample and is considered to be one of the most user friendly of the major intelligence scales. The K-ABC was also the first in the most recent generation of intelligence tests that attempted to respond to many of the criticisms of traditional intellectual measures vis-a-vis uses of the scales with minority children. In applications with minority populations, the K-ABC has many attractive and distinctive features.

First, in comparison to other major intelligence tests, the K-ABC contains many tasks that do not require expressive language skills. This is a positive feature for evaluators concerned with the impact of regional or dialectical speech differences on test performance. A second important feature is that a Spanish version of the scale is available for use with Spanish-speaking Mexican children that was normed on a Mexican sample. A third desirable feature is that test items were analyzed during test development by both a panel of minority experts and by statistical procedures to identify biased items. As a result, objectionable items were revised or eliminated from the final version of the scale, and test stimuli reflect pictures of diverse multicultural groups.

Fourth, each of the mental processing subtests is preceded by an unscored sample item, and the first two scored items are designated as teaching items to help familiarize children with task demands and provide experience in test taking. Fifth, the mean MPC yielded by the scale for minority groups comes closer to the mean MPC for Whites than do the full scale quotients of other similarly developed intelligence instruments. The 15-point discrepancy between minority groups and Whites on the Wechsler Intelligence Scale for Children-Revised is narrowed to 0 to 7 points on the K-ABC. The largest discrepancy on the K-ABC occurs between African American school-aged children and Whites (African American mean MPC = 93.7, White mean MPC = 100), followed by Navajo Indians (mean MPC = 94.2), and Hispanics (MPC = 97.5). A mean MPC reported for a small sample of Sioux Indians (100.6) most closely approximates the White sample MPC. A sixth attractive feature of the K-ABC is that the manual provides sociocultural norms by SES and race (African American and White) for those interested in comparing the test taker's performance with other children from similar racial and SES groups.

The K-ABC also has a number of shortcomings in its applications with minorities. Although the norm group approximated the 1980 U.S. census data in terms of White, African American, Hispanic, and Other groups (Native American, Pacific Islander, Asian), the sample underrepresented Hispanics and African Americans at the lower-SES level and overrepresented both groups at the upper-SES level. This upward bias may contribute to the closer approximations seen between the MPCs of Whites and minority groups. The SES imbalance also suggests that the scale is most representative of African Americans and Hispanics at the middle-SES levels.

Two other limitations of the K-ABC are concerned with the test authors' recommendations for adapting the scale for use with non-English-speaking children. First, the authors suggest that the English version of the scale can be used for non-English-speaking children with the aid of an interpreter. Toward that end, the manual provides Spanish as well as English directions. However, there is no evidence that the Spanish instructions or interpreters were part of the test development or standardization process, and LEP and/or bilingual children were not included in the norm groups. Therefore, this recommendation is not based on sound assessment principles. In addition, the authors promote the Nonverbal scale (composed of a selection of Mental Processing subtests) as an alternative for use with non-English-speaking children age 4 years to 12 years, 5 months; but, again, since the norms did not include LEP children, comparisons with this population would be of limited usefulness. Therefore, caution should be used in employing the English version of the K-ABC with non-English-speaking children.

Stanford-Binet Intelligence Scale-Fourth Edition

The Stanford-Binet Intelligence Scale-Fourth Edition (SB-IV; Thorndike, Hagen, & Sattler, 1986) represents the latest revision in the long and distinguished history of Binet intelligence scales. It is used with children, adolescents, and young adults between the ages of 2 and 23. This revision contains 15 subtests, 6 new and 9 retained from the previous version. Several steps were taken during the development and standardization of the scale to respond to the special characteristics of racial/ethnic minority children.

For instance, items from the Stanford-Binet Intelligence Scale Form L-M criticized for ethnic bias were removed from the latest version, and the test now contains a sampling of pictures that represent ethnically diverse people. In addition, two independent panels of minority experts analyzed test items for possible bias while the scale was being revised. Moreover, statistical procedures identified biased items that were eliminated from the final version of the scale. Many of the subtests begin with sample items. Finally, concurrent validation studies reported in the manual that support this type of validity were based on samples that adequately represented minority group members.

Despite these efforts, three major concerns have been expressed about the psychometric qualities of the scale. First, the accuracy of the norms has been questioned (Cronbach, 1989). Although the standardization sample approximated the 1980 U.S. census data on the basis of ethnicity and the norm group includes Whites, African Americans, Hispanics, Asians, Pacific Islanders, and Native Americans, the upper-SES level was oversampled for these groups and weighting procedures were needed to adjust for the effects. Thus, the norms are not considered to be an accurate reflection of the populations they are supposed to mirror.

Second, the reliability of the scale has yet to be determined using large and representative samples of minority youngsters. The test-retest reliability studies reported in the manual did not include adequate numbers of minority children. Third, the construct validity of the scale and, specifically, the stability of the factor structure across minority groups has not yet been demonstrated. In order to conclude that the scale is measuring the same constructs for different groups of people, empirical evidence supporting the factorial stability of the scale is needed.

There are a number of other less technical concerns about the SB-IV that may limit its usefulness with minority individuals. Like the Wechsler scales, the SB-IV requires verbal skills on at least half of its subtests. Evaluators concerned about testing children who speak a different dialect than standard English will need to pay attention to the youngster's verbal responses to reduce the likelihood of scoring errors. Also, to date, a Spanish version of the scale has not been developed and marketed.

Wechsler Intelligence Scale for Children-Third Edition

The Wechsler Intelligence Scale for Children-Third Edition (WISC-III; Wechsler, 1991) is the latest version of the WISC scale to be revised and renormed and is designed for use with youngsters age 6 years to 16 years, 11 months. It contains a total of 13 subtests; 12 of the subtests were retained from the WISC-R and include modifications, and the 13th subtest is the new Symbol Search scale. The WISC-III has a number of laudable features. First, the test developers not only employed a panel of minority experts to review the items for bias but also used item analysis procedures on the test results of an oversample of more than 400 ethnic minority children to identify biased items. Items that showed bias were either eliminated or reworded. Second, the manual specifically states that evaluators who use the test with CLD youngsters should receive formal training with similar populations. Third, to reduce the verbal demands placed on the test taker at the beginning of testing, the subtests have been resequenced so that the introductory subtest is now a Performance one rather than a Verbal subtest. In addition, three subtests (Similarities, Picture Arrangement, and Object Assembly) begin with sample items.

The standardization sample approximates the 1988 U.S. census data in terms of proportional representation of Whites, African Americans, Native Americans, Aleuts, Asian Americans, Pacific Islanders, Hispanics, and Other minority groups. Seven percent of the sample was classified as handicapped, 5% as gifted, and only English-speaking children were represented in the standardization group. The test does not contain a parallel form or alternate Spanish version nor does it provide administration instructions and normative data for use with ESL students.

Wechsler Preschool and Primary Scale of Intelligence-Revised

The Wechsler Preschool and Primary Scale of Intelligence-Revised (WPPSI-R; Wechsler, 1989) is a completely renormed, downward and upward extension of the original WPPSI scale and is designed for use with children between the ages of 3 years and 7 years, 3 months. The WPPSI-R contains 12 subtests, 6 representing the Verbal subtests and the remaining 6 comprising the Performance subtests. The scale contains several noteworthy advancements over its predecessor. For example, a panel of minority experts reviewed each item for bias and made recommendations for item revision or exclusion. Also, items were statistically analyzed for bias using data compiled from 400 minority children, and biased items were eliminated. Two of the subtests contain pictures of racial/ethnic children and all but one include a sample item.

The standardization sample is excellent and approximates 1986 U.S. Bureau of the Census data regarding sex, age, geographic region, ethnicity, and parental occupation and education characteristics. Altogether, the sample is composed of Whites (70.1%), African Americans (15.3%), Hispanics (11.2%), and Other (3.4%) minority groups. However, there is no evidence that LEP children were included in the sample, and a Spanish version of the scale is not available. Evidence for internal, interrater, and test-retest reliability of the scale suggests that the highest reliabilities are for the full scale. Construct, concurrent, and predictive validity studies are also reported in the manual.

Alternative Cognitive Measures

Alternative cognitive instruments have been employed to supplement and in some cases replace conventional norm-referenced assessment techniques. Depending on the instrument, these alternative tools can be useful in providing further information about the child's present functioning and potential for future learning. A handful of intelligence instruments have been translated into Spanish (e.g., the K-ABC and the WISC-R) and are available for use with Spanish-speaking children. Other scales that have been used with minority children to supplement more conventional techniques include a group of nonverbal scales that primarily measure reasoning skills. They are the Test of Nonverbal Intelligence (Brown, Sherbenou, & Johnson, 1982), the Columbia Mental Maturity Scale (Burgemeister, Blum, & Lorge, 1972), the Raven's Progressive Matrices (Court & Raven, 1986), and the Leiter International Performance Scale (Leiter, 1948).

These nonverbal scales have been targeted for use with CLD children for a number of reasons. One reason is that evaluators have assumed that nonverbal scales are more culture fair than conventional intelligence scales because they eliminate the culture loading dimension of tests that rely on verbal abilities. The culture loading of more traditional tests has often been cited as the reason minorities perform less well than majority children on the scales. However, Anastasi (1988) cites a number of studies showing that minority children achieve higher overall scores on the more traditional scales than on the nonverbal devices. Another reason nonverbal scales have been used with LEP or bilingual children is that they do not require verbal responses. However, none of the nonverbal scales has been normed on LEP youngsters, which makes using the scales for normative comparisons inappropriate.

Two major disadvantages of nonverbal scales limit their usefulness with minority children. First, the scales exhibit a number of psychometric weaknesses. For example, the norms for the Leiter are not only quite dated but are based on a very small and homogeneous sample of 289 children. Second, little evidence exists that suggests a relationship between performance on nonverbal tests of intelligence and academic success in the classroom. Therefore, evaluators are urged to exercise caution in the use of nonverbal devices with minority children, and when these devices are employed they should not be used in isolation.

Two other alternative intelligence measures discussed in the literature as supplementary devices are the Cartoon Conservation Scales (DeAvila & Havassy, 1975) and Learning Potential Assessment Device (LPAD; Feuerstein, 1979). The Cartoon Conservation Scales are based on Piaget's theory of cognitive development and require the child to demonstrate an understanding of conservation concepts on a series of paper-and-pencil tasks. The LPAD is based on a test-teach-test assessment paradigm in which the evaluator engages in a teach-assess-teach-assess loop. Unfortunately, although both approaches appear promising, neither has been systematically employed or researched. They thus cannot be recommended for use until more empirical evidence is documented.

Academic Achievement Assessment

Depending on the reason for referral and the characteristics/needs of the referred youngster, the evaluator will need to make a decision about the scope and type of academic achievement assessments that should be conducted. Recent findings about the overlap between standardized reading achievement tests and the actual content of reading curriculum (e.g., Bell, Lentz, & Graden, 1992; Good & Salvia, 1988) suggest that the meaningfulness of testing outcomes can be seriously compromised because many standardized tests do not cover material that students are taught. As the primary purposes of most academic assessments are to gain meaningful information about the student's skill strengths and weaknesses and determine the best approaches to instruction, a norm-referenced academic assessment device may not be the best choice for a given child. Curriculum-based and criterion-referenced measures and assessments are alternatives receiving growing endorsement in the literature, most recently with bilingual Hispanic students (e.g., Baker & Good, 1995). In her book *Responsive Assessment,* Henning-Stout (1994) also discusses a range of promising non-norm-referenced assessment strategies. Interested readers and evaluators are encouraged to check into these valuable resources to assess their meaningfulness in use with their particular clientele.

For those situations in which a norm-referenced academic assessment seems warranted, the following section discusses some of the major individually administered, standardized academic achievement tests. Special attention will be devoted to the qualities of the tests that are relevant when assessing minority children.

Kaufman Test of Educational Achievement

The Kaufman Test of Educational Achievement (K-TEA; Kaufman & Kaufman, 1985) is a test of academic achievement composed of five subtests: Mathematics Applications, Mathematics Computation, Reading Decoding, Reading Comprehension, and Spelling. The K-TEA is used with children and adolescents age 6 years to 18 years, 11 months. The standardization group approximated the 1983–1984 U.S. Bureau of the Census data in terms of proportionately representing Whites, African Americans, Hispanics, Native Americans, Alaskans, Asians, and Pacific Islanders. During test development, test items were statistically analyzed for bias, and many that showed bias were eliminated. However, 12 items that showed race or gender bias were incorporated into the final version of the scale in a counterbalanced manner. Internal and test-retest reliability estimates of the scale are satisfactory. Content and construct validity also appear to be adequately established.

Drawbacks of this scale in its use with minority groups include the lack of a parallel form, the lack of a Spanish version of the test, and the lack of sample items. In addition, unlike the colorful and attractive stimuli comprising the K-ABC, all of the K-TEA pictures are achromatic and do not seem inviting. A handful of the pictures depict the physical characteristics of multicultural children.

Woodcock-Johnson Psycho-Educational Battery-Revised

The Woodcock-Johnson Psycho-Educational Battery-Revised (WJ-R; Woodcock & Johnson, 1989) is an updated, expanded, and renormed version of the original 1977 scale. It consists of nine standard subtests and five supplementary subtests that assess reading, mathematics, written language, and knowledge skills of people aged 2 to 90. The WJ-R has a number of advantages over the K-TEA in applications with minority youngsters. First of all, it contains parallel forms A and B, and both forms have pictures of minority children, use multicultural names in the test stimuli, and contain colorful and appealing illustrations. Second, item bias procedures were employed to detect items that proved to be more difficult for members of minority groups. Six of the subtests begin with sample practice items. The standardization sample did not include anyone with less than 1 year of experience with English, and test authors caution against using the scale with ESL children. They also clearly state that the scale should not be used with an interpreter and recommend using the Bateria Woodcock Psycho-Educative en Español (Woodcock, 1982) for Spanish-speaking youngsters.

The methods employed to standardize the scale were impressive. Although the standardization sample approximated 1980 U.S. census data, minority groups were slightly overrepresented among the 6,359 subjects. The norm group was composed of White (78.6%), African American (16.9%), Hispanic (9.3%), Asian/Pacific Islander (3.2%), and Native American (1.3%) individuals. Stringent SES selection procedures were also employed to ensure adequate representation in terms of parental and community characteristics.

KeyMath-Revised

The KeyMath-Revised (Connolly, 1988) is an expanded version of the original KeyMath test and assesses mathematics skills within the three broad areas of Basic Concepts, Operations, and Applications. Alternate forms A and B are designed to be used with youngsters in grades K through 9. Test pictures and wordings reflect a multicultural influence, and the manual reports that test items were reviewed for possible bias during a national calibration study. Those items identified as biased were then revised or excluded from the final scale. However, the manual is unclear whether this review process was based on subjective or statistical procedures. The scale contains no sample items. Stratified sampling procedures were employed to match 1985 U.S. census data and although Whites, African Americans, Hispanics, Native Americans, Pacific Islanders, and Asians were represented in appropriate numbers, there was a slight underrepresentation of individuals from the Southwestern and Northeastern portions of the United States. The content validity and construct validity of the scale have been demonstrated, as have internal and alternate form reliability.

Test of Written Language-2

The Test of Written Language-2 (Hamill & Larsen, 1988) is designed to assess mechanical and more substantive aspects of written language skill in youngsters age 7 to 17. The scale contains parallel forms A and B, each of which is composed of 10 subtests. Sample items begin a handful of these subtests. The manual does not report the use of any item analysis procedures to reduce or eliminate racial or gender bias. The norm sample approximates the Statistical Abstract of the United States in terms of ethnicity (e.g., White, 84%; African American, 12%; Hispanic, 9%; American Indian, 3%; Asian, 1%; and Other, 4%). The test authors recommend against the use of the scale with non-English-speaking youngsters and instead suggest the Pruebo de Lectura y Lenguaje Escrito (Hamill, Larsen, Wiederholt, & Fountain-Chambers, 1982), which assesses written Spanish skills and was normed on 2,300 children age 8 to 16 residing in Mexico and Puerto Rico.

Woodcock Reading Mastery Test-Revised

The Woodcock Reading Mastery Test-Revised (WRMT-R) (Woodcock, 1987) contains the Word Identification, Word Attack, Word Comprehension, Passage Comprehension, Visual Auditory Learning, and Letter Identification subtests designed to assess the reading skills of kindergartners to individuals age 75 and older. The WRMT-R is a revision and renorming of the 1973 Woodcock Reading Mastery Test. Several subtests begin with sample items, and alternate forms G and H are available for retesting purposes. During test development, statistical procedures were used to detect biased items. The norm group for youngsters in grades K to 12 matches the 1980 U.S. census data and Whites, African Americans, Native Americans, Asians/Pacific Islanders, and Hispanics are adequately represented. A minor disadvantage of the WRMT-R is that all of the illustrations are achromatic and do not seem to depict minorities. In fact, the physical characteristics of those shown in the pictures are quite dated and remind the reviewer of hairstyles from the 1950s and 1960s.

Postevaluation Multidisciplinary Team Meeting

After the various assessments have been conducted, the multidisciplinary team will reconvene with some combination of the following people participating: school administrator, regular and special-education teachers, bilingual teacher, speech and language specialist, psychoeducational evaluators, caretakers/parents and extended family members, cultural consultant, and any other personnel involved with the case. If the child's parents speak a language other than English, a well-trained interpreter who is sensitive to the dynamics and requirements of multidisciplinary team meetings should attend.

The purposes of the postevaluation meeting are to discuss the results of the assessments, provide feedback to the parents about their child's performance, and determine the child's educational and social needs. Care needs to be taken to interpret the assessment results within an appropriate and relevant linguistic and cultural context. If the child received lower scores on the norm-referenced assessments than were expected, Anastasi (1988) and Chamberlain and Medinos-Landurand (1991) advise evaluators to consider carefully reasons why the low scores occurred. For example, was the child tested on material that was unfamiliar or that had not been taught? Was the content of the test inconsistent with the child's cultural experiences? Were techniques used to familiarize the child with the testing environment? Were technically adequate tests chosen and used? Did the child seem motivated during the assessments? If the parents had an opportunity to observe the assessments, did they feel that the child's performance accurately reflected the child's true abilities?

The results of all assessments and the implications of them should be simply and clearly communicated to the parents and the other members of the multidisciplinary team in understandable language. During the meeting, the parents will need to be given enough time to formulate and ask questions and process the feedback they receive. If the child is eligible for special education services, the parents' input regarding the decision should be sought and incorporated into the team decision-making process. The practical and legal ramifications of any decisions made during the meeting should be clearly described.

Report Writing and Follow-up Activities

After the child's strengths and weaknesses have been identified, recommendations for intervention need to be developed and implemented. The evaluator should periodically monitor the child's progress by consulting with teachers and family members on an ongoing basis. Both successful and unsuccessful interventions should be documented in the child's records. Careful documentation will assist the multidisciplinary team in building a database on each child so that intra- and interindividual comparisons of academic progress can be made.

A written report should be generated for each evaluation. The psychoeducational assessment report should indicate the race/ethnicity of the child and his or her parents, the languages spoken at home and during the assessments, and any deviations in standardization that occurred during the administration of norm-referenced instruments. The specific instruments and techniques used should be clearly indicated, and the dates of administration along with the time each test required should be documented. In addition, any steps taken by the evaluator to improve the validity of the assessments should be noted. In general, the report should contain sufficient detail so that readers will understand the exact protocol followed during the assessment.

CONCLUSION

The major aim of this chapter has been to assist psychologists and educational diagnosticians in performing culturally meaningful and technically sound assessments with diverse children and youth. Based on legal, ethical, and psychometric considerations, several recommendations for conducting assessments with CLD children appear warranted. First, evaluators working in multicultural and multilingual schools need to critically evaluate each referral they receive and screen out those that reflect individual or systemic bias. Only referrals that survive rigorous scrutiny should proceed to an individually focused evaluation. Second, evaluators should tailor each assessment to meet the unique cultural and linguistic needs of the youngsters they work with. This is accomplished by carefully selecting data collection techniques, interpreting evaluation results within their appropriate cultural context, and basing educational decisions on data derived from multiple sources, methods, and settings. Third, when selecting norm-referenced measures, test manuals need to be reviewed carefully to ensure that psychometric indicators are suitable for the individual test taker. The norms must contain a representative sample that matches the characteristics of the referred child, and the reliability and validity of the scale should be well documented. In select cases, locally normed instruments may be the measures of choice.

Fourth, assessment procedures used with minority children need to be supported by current research. Ethically, it is the evaluator's responsibility to be aware of available research in the field and translate the empirical evidence into professional practice. Finally, the evaluator needs to develop a network of professional and community contacts and resources that will assist in providing culturally relevant and meaningful psychological services with minority children. The chapter closes with a case study that involves a scenario not altogether rare for those who work in urban schools in the United States. The case has been left unresolved so that readers will have an opportunity to consider how they would apply the ideas and findings presented in the chapter to address the issues that the case raises. The intention is to provide evaluators with a chance to challenge their problem-solving and decision-making skills in relation to an actual case involving a CLD youngster.

Case Example 13–1. Evaluation of a culturally and linguistically diverse youngster

REASON FOR REFERRAL AND PRESENTING INFORMATION

Alfredo M., an 11-year-old immigrant from Mexico, has attended Papillion Elementary School for the last 18 months. Currently a fifth-grader in an English-speaking class, he is demonstrating significant problems in reading and written language skills. Alfredo's primary language is Spanish but his conversational English is good. His teacher reports that he has low-average math skills and that his progress in other subject areas is satisfactory. No educational records are available from the school he attended in Mexico, nor are any medical records or early developmental history information available. Alfredo is the oldest of four boys brought to live in the United States by their maternal grandparents after the boys' parents were killed in an accident. At the present time, they are all living on a temporary basis with their maternal aunt and her family (husband and two children) and their grandparents.

On the basis of this presenting information, how would you proceed with the data collection process? What questions do you have and how would you want to go about answering them? What specific actions would you take to better understand and address Alfredo's educational needs?

REFERENCES

American Educational Research Association, American Psychological Association, & National Council on Measurement in Education. (1985). *The standards for educational and psychological testing*. Washington, DC: American Psychological Association.

American Psychological Association. (1992). Ethical principles of psychologists and code of conduct. *American Psychologist, 47,* 1597–1611.

American Psychological Association. (1993). Guidelines for providers of psychological services to ethnic, linguistic, and culturally diverse populations. *American Psychologist, 48,* 45–48.

Anastasi, A. (1988). *Psychological testing*. New York: Macmillan.

Armour-Thomas, E. (1992). Intellectual assessment of children from culturally diverse backgrounds. *School Psychology Review, 21,* 552–565.

Au, K.H., & Mason, J.M. (1981). Social organization factors in learning to read: The balance of rights hypothesis. *Reading Research Quarterly, 17,* 115–152.

Baker, S.K., & Good, R. (1995). Curriculum-based measurement of English reading with bilingual Hispanic students: A validation study with second-grade students. *School Psychology Review, 24,* 561–578.

Banks, J.A. (1993). Approaches to multicultural curriculum reform. In J.A. Banks & C.A.M. Banks (Eds.), *Multicultural education: Issues and perspectives* (2nd ed.) (pp. 195–214). Boston: Allyn & Bacon.

Banks, J.A. (1994). *Multiethnic education: Theory and practice* (3rd ed.). Boston: Allyn & Bacon.

Barnett, D.W., Collins, R., Coulter, C., Curtis, M.J., Ehrhardt, K., Glaser, A., Reyes, C., Stollar, S., & Winston, M. (1995). Ethnic validity and school psychology: Concepts and practices associated with cross-cultural professional competence. *Journal of School Psychology, 33,* 219–234.

Bell, P.F., Lentz, F.E., & Graden, J.L. (1992). Effects of curriculum test overlap on standardized achievement test scores: Identifying systematic confounds in educational decision making. *School Psychology Review, 21,* 644–655.

Brown, L., Sherbenou, R.J., & Johnson, S.K. (1982). *Test of Nonverbal Intelligence*. Austin, TX: PRO-ED.

Burgemeister, B., Blum, L.H., & Lorge, I. (1972). *Columbia Mental Maturity Scale*. New York: The Psychological Corporation.

Catarino, L.C. (1991). Step-by-step procedures for the assessment of language minority children. In A. Barona & E.E. Garcia (Eds.), *Children at risk: Poverty, minority status, and other issues in educational equity* (pp. 269–282). Washington, DC: National Association of School Psychologists.

Chamberlain, P., & Medinos-Landurand, P. (1991). Practical considerations for the assessment of LEP students with special needs. In E.V. Hamayan & J.S. Damico (Eds.), *Limiting bias in the assessment of bilingual students* (pp. 111–156). Austin, TX: PRO-ED.

Connolly, A.J. (1988). *KeyMath-Revised*. Circle Pines, MN: American Guidance Service.

Correa, V.I. (1989). Involving culturally diverse families in the educational process. In S.H. Fradd & M.J. Weismantel (Eds.), *Meeting the needs of culturally and linguistically different students: A handbook for educators* (pp. 130–144). Boston: College-Hill.

Court, J.H., & Raven, J.C. (1986). *Manual for Raven's Progressive Matrices and Vocabulary Scales: Coloured Progressive Matrices*. London: Lewis.

Cronbach, L.J. (1989). Review of the Stanford-Binet Intelligence Scale: Fourth Edition. In J.V. Mitchell, Jr. (Ed.), *Tenth mental measurements yearbook* (pp. 773–775). Lincoln, NE: Buros Institute of Mental Measurement.

Cummins, J. (1984). *Bilingualism and special education: Issues in assessment and pedagogy.* San Diego: College-Hill.

DeAvila, E.A., & Havassy, B. (1975). *Cartoon Conservation Scales.* Corte Madera, CA: Linguametrics Group.

Derman-Sparks, L. (1993). Empowering children to create a caring culture in a world of differences. *Childhood Education, 66*–71.

Dusek, J.B., & Joseph, G. (1983). The bases of teacher expectancies: A meta-analysis. *Journal of Educational Psychology, 75,* 327–346.

Feuerstein, R. (1979). *The dynamic assessment of retarded performers: The learning potential assessment device, theory, instruments, and techniques.* Baltimore: University Park Press.

Figueroa, R.A. (1990). Best practices in the assessment of bilingual children. In A. Thomas & J. Grimes (Eds.), *Best practices in school psychology II* (pp. 93–106). Washington, DC: National Association of School Psychologists.

Fischer, L., & Sorenson, G.P. (1996). *School law for counselors, psychologists, and social workers.* New York: Longman.

Fradd, S.H., Barona, A., & Santos de Barona, M. (1989). Implementing change and monitoring progress. In S.H. Fradd & M.J. Weismantel (Eds.), *Meeting the needs of culturally and linguistically different students: A handbook for educators* (pp. 63–105). Boston: College-Hill.

Good, R., & Salvia, J. (1988). Curriculum bias in published norm-referenced reading tests: Demonstrable effects. *School Psychology Review, 17,* 51–60.

Hamill, D.D., & Larsen, S.C. (1988). *Test of Written Language-2: Manual.* Austin, TX: PRO-ED.

Hamill, D.D., Larsen, S.C., Wiederholt, J.L., & Fountain-Chambers, J. (1982). *The Pruebo de Lectura y Lenguaje Escrito.* Austin, TX: PRO-ED.

Helms, J.E. (1992a). *A race is a nice thing to have: A guide to being a white person.* Topeka, KS: Content Communications.

Helms, J.E. (1992b). Why is there no study of cultural equivalence in standardized cognitive ability testing? *American Psychologist, 47,* 1083–1101.

Henning-Stout, M. (1994). *Responsive assessment: A new way of thinking about learning.* San Francisco: Jossey-Bass.

Huang, L.N., & Taylor Gibbs, J. (1992). Partners or adversaries? Home-school collaboration across culture, race, and ethnicity. In S.L. Christenson & J.C. Conoley (Eds.), *Home-school collaboration: Enhancing children's academic and social competence* (pp. 81–109). Silver Spring, MD: National Association of School Psychologists.

Kaufman, A.S., & Kaufman, N.L. (1983). *Kaufman Assessment Battery for Children Manual.* Circle Pines, MN: American Guidance Service.

Kaufman, A.S., & Kaufman, N.L. (1985). *Kaufman Test of Educational Achievement Comprehensive Form Manual.* Circle Pines, MN: American Guidance Service.

Leiter, R.G. (1984) *Leiter International Performance Scale.* Chicago: Stoelting.

Miller, N. (1984). The case history in a cross-cultural milieu. In N. Miller (Ed.), *Bilingualism and language disability: Assessment and remediation* (pp. 169–176). San Diego: College-Hill.

National Association of School Psychologists. (1992). *Professional conduct manual: Principles for professional ethics and standards for the provision of school psychological services.* Washington, DC: National Association of School Psychologists.

Nuttall, E.V., DeLeon, B., & Valle, M. (1990). Best practices in considering cultural factors. In A. Thomas & J. Grimes (Eds.), *Best practices in school psychology-II* (pp. 219–233). Washington, DC: National Association of School Psychologists.

Nuttall, E.V., Medinos-Landurand, P., & Goldman, P. (1984). A critical look at testing and evaluation from a cross-cultural perspective. In P.C. Chinn (Ed.), *Education of culturally and linguistically different exceptional children* (pp. 42–62). Reston, VA: The Council for Exceptional Children.

Ochoa, S.H., Delgado-Rivera, B., & Ford, L. (1994, August). *School psychology training pertaining to bilingual psychoeducational assessment.* Paper presented at the American Psychological Association annual convention, Los Angeles, California.

Ortiz, A.A., & Garcia, S.B. (1985). *Characteristics of limited English proficient Hispanic students in programs for the learning disabled: Implications for policy, practice, and research.* Austin, TX: The University of Texas, Handicapped Minority Research Institute on Language Proficiency.

Ponterotto, J.G., & Alexander, C.M. (1996). Assessing the multicultural competence of counselors and clinicians. In L.A. Suzuki, P. Melle, & J.G. Ponterotto (Eds.), *Handbook of multicultural assessment: Clinical, psychological, and educational applications* (pp. 651–672). San Francisco: Jossey-Bass.

Reynolds, C.R., & Brown, R.T. (1984). Bias in mental testing: An introduction to the issues. In C.R. Reynolds & R.T. Brown (Eds.), *Perspectives on bias in mental testing* (pp. 1–39). New York: Plenum Press.

Reynolds, C.R., & Kaiser, S.M. (1990). Test bias in psychological assessment. In T.B. Gutkin & C.R. Reynolds (Eds.), *The handbook of school psychology* (pp. 487–525). New York: Wiley.

Rogers, M.R. (1993). Best practices in assessing minority or ethnically different children. In B. Vance (Ed.), *Best practices in assessment for school and clinical settings.* (pp. 399–440). Brandon, VT: Clinical Psychology; New York: Wiley.

Sadker, M., Sadker, D., & Long, L. (1993). Gender and educational equity. In J.A. Banks & C.A.M. Banks (Eds.), *Multicultural education: Issues and perspectives* (2nd ed.) (pp. 111–128). Boston: Allyn & Bacon.

Salvia, J., & Ysseldyke, J.E. (1991). *Assessment* (5th ed.). Boston: Houghton Mifflin.

Sarason, S.B. (1982). *The culture of the school and the problem of change* (2nd ed.). Boston: Allyn & Bacon.

Sattler, J.M. (1988). *Assessment of children: Third edition.* San Diego: Jerome M. Sattler.

Takaki, R. (1989). *Strangers from a different shore: A history of Asian Americans.* New York: Penguin.

Taylor Gibbs, J., & Huang, L.N. (Eds.). (1989). *Children of color: Psychological interventions with minority youth.* San Francisco: Jossey-Bass.

Thorndike, R.L., Hagen, E.P., & Sattler, J.M. (1986). *The Stanford-Binet Intelligence Scale: Fourth Edition.* Chicago, IL: Riverside.

Wechsler, D. (1989). *Wechsler Preschool and Primary Scale of Intelligence-Revised: Manual.* San Antonio, TX: The Psychological Corporation.

Wechsler, D. (1991). *Wechsler Intelligence Scale for Children-Third Edition: Manual.* San Antonio, TX: The Psychological Corporation.

Wilen, D.K., & van Maanen Sweeting, C. (1986). Assessment of limited English proficient Hispanic students. *School Psychology Review, 15,* 59–75.

Woodcock, R.W. (1982). *Bateria Woodcock Psycho-Educative en Español.* Allen, TX: DLM Teaching Resources.

Woodcock, R.W. (1987). *Woodcock Reading Mastery Test-Revised: Manual.* Allen, TX: DLM Teaching Resources.

Woodcock, R.W., & Johnson, M.D. (1989). *Woodcock Johnson Psycho-Educational Battery-Revised: Manual.* Allen, TX: DLM Teaching Resources.

Ysseldyke, J.E., & Christenson, S.L. (1987). *The Instructional Environment Scale.* Austin, TX: PRO-ED.

Chapter 14

THE DIAGNOSIS AND ASSESSMENT OF AUTISTIC DISORDERS

RONALD C. EAVES AND ABEER M. AWADH

The diagnosis and assessment of autistic disorders has long been a source of confusion for practitioners for three reasons. First, the early assumption that autism has a psychogenic rather than biogenic etiology burdened the field for three decades. Today, the overriding majority of practicing professionals accept that the cause of autistic disorder is biological. The second source of confusion hinges on the better way to characterize autistic disorder. That is, should it be viewed as an effective or a cognitive dysfunction? Third, does autistic disorder represent a spectrum of severe early childhood disorders or a unique disorder with a single symptomatology, course, and prognosis?

HISTORY AND DEVELOPMENT

Leo Kanner

Originally, Kanner (1943) presented early infantile autism as a unique affective disorder, representing approximately 10% of individuals with childhood psychoses. He considered the inability of such children "to relate themselves in the ordinary way to people and situations from the beginning of life" (Kanner, 1943, p. 26) as the primary disorder of autism. Later, Kanner presented two principle diagnostic criteria of early infantile autism, which "are always present and indispensable for the inclusion of any child in the category of early infantile autism" (Kanner, 1954, p. 380): the obsessive insistence on the preservation of sameness and extreme autistic aloneness or self-isolation. He believed that all other symptoms of autism could be explained on the basis of these two criteria.

Although Kanner suggested that autism has biogenic underpinnings, the field focused on his depiction of the parents as "cold, detached, humorless perfectionists . . . [who] treat their children about as meticulously and impersonally as they treat their automobiles" (1954, p. 384). Thus, for at least 30 years, parents bore the brunt of most assignations as to the cause of early infantile autism.

Bernard Rimland

It was not until Rimland (1964) published his classic work, *Infantile Autism,* that a strong case was made for a biogenic etiology of autism. The points he made to support his contention were:

1. Some clearly autistic children are born of parents who do not fit the autistic parent personality pattern.
2. Parents who do fit the description of the supposedly pathogenic parent almost invariably have normal, non-autistic children.
3. With very few exceptions, the siblings of autistic children are normal.
4. Autistic children are behaviorally unusual "from the moment of birth."
5. There is a consistent ratio of three or four boys to one girl.
6. Virtually all cases of twins reported in the literature have been identical, with both twins afflicted.
7. Autism can occur or be closely simulated in children with known organic brain damage.
8. The symptomatology is highly unique and specific.
9. There is an absence of gradations of infantile autism which would create "blends" from normal to severely afflicted (pp. 51–52).

Rimland also presented evidence that autism should be considered a cognitive rather than an affective disorder. Specifically, he argued that "the child with early infantile autism is grossly impaired in a function basic to all cognition: the ability to relate new stimuli to remembered experience" (1964, p. 79). He further averred that this cognitive impairment has two "interdependent consequences: 1. The child cannot understand relationships nor think in terms of concepts, symbols, analogies or abstractions; and 2. He cannot integrate his sensations into a comprehensible whole—his perception of the world is vague and obscure" (p. 79). Rimland introduced a neural theory to explain autistic disorder. Among several possible sources of the disorder, he favored a dysfunctional reticular formation as a likely culprit, citing the work of Hebb (1955), Lindsley (1958), Magoun (1958), and many others to undergird his position.

More Recent Developments

Both Kanner and Rimland considered autism to be a unique disorder, not to be confused with disorders in the much larger set of children diagnosed with childhood schizophrenia, symbiotic psychosis, childhood psychosis, and atypical development. Nevertheless, practitioners and researchers seized upon the term, and by the mid-1970s the vast majority of children with very severe behavioral disorders were being diagnosed as autistic. Although there was no classification for autism at all in the first or second editions of the *Diagnostic and Statistical Manual of Mental Disorders* of the American Psychiatric Association (*DSM;* 1952, 1968), by 1987 when the revised third edition of the *DSM* was published (*DSM-III-R*), autistic disorder was the only distinct classification available. Other previously used labels (e.g., childhood onset pervasive developmental disorder, Heller's syndrome, atypical pervasive developmental disorder, disintegrative psychosis) were relegated to the ambiguous category known as *pervasive developmental disorder not otherwise specified*. The schizophrenia classification could be used only if the child met the criteria for adult forms of schizophrenia. As Rimland (1994) recently put it, " 'Childhood schizophrenia' was not an attractive term—'autism' sounded much better" (p. 5). There were also political purposes behind the shifting definitions and diagnoses. For instance, Rutter and Schopler (1988) noted that the definition promoted by the National Society for Autistic Children was primarily intended to obtain propitious social policy for children with autistic disorder and their families.

The confusion caused by the events of the last 50 years has had three important implications. First, much of the research that has been conducted has had little impact because of the different definitions used to identify subjects. Today, there are no less than seven definitions in use by various organizations in the United States and other parts of the world: Autism Society of America (ASA; Ritvo & Freeman, 1978); Creak (1961, 1964); *DSM-III-R* (APA, 1987), and now, *DSM-IV* (APA, 1994); the ninth edition of the *International Classification of Diseases* (*ICD-9;* World Health Organization, 1977), and now the 10th edition (*ICD-10;* World Health Organization, 1992); and Rutter (1978). When differing criteria are used to identify subjects with autistic disorder, it is difficult if not impossible to reconcile the conflicting results that are frequently reported in the literature.

Because of the many definitions in use and the broader diagnostic standards that have evolved, prevalence estimates have generally been on the increase. Older estimates of autistic disorder usually fell in the range from 4 to 6 per 10,000 children. More recently, estimates commonly range from 7 to 14 cases per 10,000 (Locke, Banken, & Mahone; 1994). Even more striking is the total range among prevalence estimates: from 2 to 21 children with autistic disorder for every 10,000 youngsters (Ritvo et al., 1989). Such large fluctuations do not bode well for planning services, for determining etiology, or more fundamentally for the validation of autism as an identifiable syndrome.

Unfortunately, until the confusion over definition and diagnosis is overcome, there will be little progress in the discovery of effective treatment approaches for children with autism. To date, the most effective interventions have not been unique to children with autistic disorder. Rather, the same treatments are found to be similarly effective with a wide array of youngsters with moderate and severe disabilities. In lieu of research on instructional programs designed for autistic children, most practitioners assume "that the principles that apply to the assessment and treatment of . . . one population are also relevant to [autism]" (Oswald, Ellis, Singh, & Singh, 1994, p. 147).

Given the current heterogeneity of behavior symptoms across individuals, a prominent recent trend in the literature has been the search for meaningful subgroups of individuals with autism (e.g., Borden & Ollendick, 1994; Eaves, Ho, & Eaves, 1994; Sevin et al., 1991; Siegel, Anders, Ciaranello, Bienenstock, &

Kramer, 1986; Volkmar, 1987; Wing & Attwood, 1987). There are important reasons for attempting to subclassify individuals in a heterogeneous group. First, different subgroups may have different etiologies. Second, like the various forms of cancer and fever, different subgroups may demand different treatments. Finally, course and prognosis may vary, depending upon the etiology and treatment of the subgroup.

It should be noted that the trend toward identifying subtypes of autism in some ways brings the field back to where it was in the late 1940s and 1950s. To summarize, Kanner introduced a unique subtype of childhood psychosis. By the 1970s the field had embraced the term, labeling nearly all severe behavioral disorders among children as autism. Finally, it is ironic that the search is on once again for meaningful subtypes. Nevertheless, the current state of affairs is not a linear return to the Kanner and Rimland eras. Today, a much more diverse group of scholars and practitioners are using far more sophisticated techniques in the investigation of autistic disorder. Given this growing interest and improved methodology, there is hope that the future of individuals with autism will be brighter.

CURRENT DEFINITIONS

Five definitions have seen the most use over the past 20 years. The *DSM* and *ICD* have undergone recent changes, but given the influence of the parent organizations (American Psychiatric Association and World Health Organization) there seems little doubt that they will continue to have a powerful influence on the field.

Creak (1961) and the British Working Party

Creak's (1961, 1964) definition represented the combined thought of the British Working Party, a group of 13 clinicians and researchers who questioned whether autism represented a distinct diagnostic category as Kanner maintained. Their definition was intended to identify early forms of childhood psychosis and not early infantile autism *per se*. Creak's paper included nine criteria developed following observations of 100 children labeled psychotic: (1) gross and sustained impairment of emotional relationships with people; (2) apparent unawareness of personal identity to a degree inappropriate for age; (3) pathological preoccupation with particular objects or certain characteristics of them, without regard to function; (4) sustained resistance to change in the environment and persistent efforts to maintain or restore sameness; (5) abnormal perceptual experience; (6) frequent acute, excessive, and seemingly illogical anxiety; (7) speech either lost, never acquired, or failing to develop; (8) distortion in motility pattern; and (9) background of serious retardation in which islets of normal or exceptional intellectual function or skill may appear. Although the definition is now dated, the authors of two currently popular assessment instruments (i.e., Autism Behavior Checklist and Childhood Autism Behavior Rating Scale) used it in the development of their scales. Consequently, the impact of the Creak definition continues to be felt.

Autism Society of America

The current definition adopted by the ASA is an outgrowth of the definition written by Ritvo and Freeman (1978). The latest version is published in each issue of *Advocate,* the newsletter of the ASA. According to the May–June 1996 issue, autism "typically appears during the first 3 years of life" (p. 3). Further, the ASA considers autism to be a neurological disorder with the following behavioral symptoms: (1) disturbances in the rate of appearance of physical, social, and language skills; (2) abnormal responses to sensations (i.e., sight, hearing, touch, balance, smell, taste, reaction to pain, and the way the body is held); (3) speech and language delayed or missing, though specific thinking capacities may be present; and (4) abnormal relating to people, objects, and events. Severely disabled individuals may exhibit extreme self-injury, repetitive behavior, and aggression (*Advocate,* 1996, May–June).

Rutter (1978)

Following a discussion of the issues surrounding the diagnosis and definition of autism, Rutter (1978) defined autism in terms of four essential criteria: (1) onset before 30 months of age; (2) impaired social development with a number of special characteristics that are not consistent with the child's intellectual level; (3) delayed and deviant language development, also with a number of special characteristics that are not consistent with the child's intellectual level; and (4) insistence on sameness (e.g., stereotyped play patterns, aberrant preoccupations, or resistance to change). Rutter "strongly recommend[ed] that, in order to ensure comparability, all investigators define their samples in this way" (1978, p. 156).

Diagnostic and Statistical Manual of Mental Disorders (DSM)

There are many reasons why the *DSM* has undergone three fairly rapid revisions over the past 16 years. Originally used more or less exclusively by psychiatrists as a loose guide for their practice, it is now commonly employed by widely diverging disciplines and lay people to resolve educational hearings and legal disputes, to plan needed services, to appropriate funds, and to summarize current thinking about mental disorders within the United States and the rest of the world. In recent years, technology has served to shrink the globe, research has grossly expanded the amount of information available about mental disorders, and the need to coordinate more closely with international bodies like the World Health Organization has become more apparent. Thus, the *DSM* has taken on much greater importance since the 1980 revision.

DSM-III

The authors of the *DSM-III* chose not to use such terms as *atypical children, symbiotic psychosis,* and *childhood schizophrenia.* They also chose not to represent such childhood disorders as psychoses because they "bear little relationship to the psychotic disorders of adult life" (APA, 1980, p. 86). Instead, the term *pervasive developmental disorder* was adopted because it described "most accurately the core clinical disturbance: many basic areas of psychological development are affected at the same time and to a severe degree" (p. 86). Included among the pervasive developmental disorders were infantile autism, childhood onset pervasive developmental disorder, and atypical pervasive developmental disorder. Childhood onset pervasive developmental disorder, as implied by the name, was said to occur after 30 months of age but before age 12. Unlike infantile autism, the criteria focused heavily on affective disturbances: excessive anxiety, unexplained rage, and self-mutilation. The label *atypical pervasive developmental disorder* was to be used when criteria were not met for infantile autism or childhood onset pervasive developmental disorder.

The following are the diagnostic criteria for infantile autism as delineated by the *DSM-III* (APA, 1980):

A. Onset before 30 months of age

B. Pervasive lack of responsiveness to other people (autism)

C. Gross deficits in language development

D. If speech is present, peculiar speech patterns such as immediate and delayed echolalia, metaphorical language, pronominal reversal

E. Bizarre responses to various aspects of the environment (e.g., resistance to change, peculiar interest in or attachment to animate or inanimate objects)

F. Absence of delusions, hallucinations, loosening of associations, and incoherence as in schizophrenia (pp. 89–90)

A comparison shows that the Rutter (1978) and *DSM-III* (1980) definitions have much in common, though there are differences in the criteria that are highlighted as primary, features offered as examples of primary criteria, and associated features. For instance, Rutter's primary criterion of "insistence on sameness" becomes one example of the autistic child's "bizarre responses to various aspects of the environment" in the *DSM-III*. Further, Rutter agreed that delusions and hallucinations were unlikely to develop in children with autism, but he did not include this exclusionary statement in his definition as did the authors of the *DSM-III*.

DSM-III-R

Below is a summary of the diagnostic criteria for autistic disorder according to the *DSM-III-R* (APA, 1987):

At least 8 of the following 16 items must be present. At least two items from A, one item from B, and one item from C must be included.

A. Qualitative impairment in reciprocal social interaction as manifested by:
   1. marked lack of awareness of the existence of feelings of others
   2. no or abnormal seeking of comfort at times of distress
   3. no or impaired imitation

    4. no or abnormal social play

    5. gross impairment in ability to make peer friendships

B. Qualitative impairment in verbal and nonverbal communication and in imaginative activity as manifested by:

    1. no mode of communication

    2. markedly abnormal nonverbal communication

    3. absence of imaginative activity

    4. marked abnormalities in the production of speech, including volume, pitch, stress, rate, rhythm, and intonation

    5. marked abnormalities in the form or content of speech, including stereotyped and repetitive use of speech

    6. marked impairment in the ability to initiate or sustain a conversation with others, despite adequate speech

C. Markedly restricted repertoire of activities and interests as manifested by:

    1. stereotyped body movements

    2. persistent preoccupation with parts of objects

    3. marked distress over changes in trivial aspects of environment

    4. unreasonable insistence on following routines in precise detail

    5. markedly restricted range of interests and preoccupation with one narrow interest

D. Onset during infancy or childhood.

The 1987 revision of the *DSM-III* made three important changes. First, the labels within pervasive developmental disorders changed. Infantile autism was changed to autistic disorder, childhood onset pervasive developmental disorder was dropped, and atypical pervasive developmental disorder became pervasive developmental disorder not otherwise specified. The diagnostic disposition of affective disturbances emphasized in childhood onset pervasive developmental disorder (e.g., excessive fearfulness, giggling for no apparent reason, and wrist-biting) appeared as associated features in autistic disorder.

Second, the number of primary criteria was reduced from six to four. That is, the criterion excluding features associated with schizophrenia (e.g., delusions, hallucinations) was dropped, and the two criteria involving language development and speech were collapsed into one criterion.

Third, the diagnostic criteria of the *DSM-III-R* increased significantly in specificity and explicitness. The 16 items describing the criteria were accompanied by behaviorally worded examples, making the determination of their presence or absence easier. Beyond that, the definition explicated for the first time a specific number of items that must be present in order to make the diagnosis of autistic disorder. Finally, the age of onset was expanded from age 30 months to include all the childhood years.

The changes in the definition of autism increased the prevalence of autism substantially (Hertzig, Snow, New, & Shapiro, 1990; Spitzer & Siegel, 1990). For instance, Hertzig et al. (1990) showed that among 75 children with pervasive developmental disorders, 41% met the *DSM-III* criteria for infantile autism, while 71% of the same children met the *DSM-III-R* criteria for autistic disorder.

DSM-IV

More changes took place with the publication of the *DSM-IV* (APA, 1994). First, three subtypes of pervasive developmental disorders were added: Rett's disorder, childhood disintegrative disorder, and Asperger's disorder. With regard to autistic disorder, the three primary criteria were retained but the number of items describing the criteria was reduced from 16 to 12 and there was some movement of items across criteria. Below is a summary of the *DSM-IV* definition of autistic disorder.

At least 6 of the following 12 items must be present. At least two items from A, one item from B, and one from C must be included.

A. Qualitative impairment in social interaction as manifested by
   1. marked impairment in the use of multiple nonverbal behaviors
   2. failure to develop peer relationships appropriate to developmental level
   3. lack of spontaneous seeking to share enjoyment, interests, or achievements with others
   4. lack of social or emotional reciprocity
B. Qualitative impairment in communication
   1. delay in, or total lack of, the development of spoken language
   2. in individuals with adequate speech, marked impairment in the ability to initiate or sustain a conversation
   3. stereotyped or repetitive use of language or idiosyncratic language
   4. lack of various, spontaneous, make-believe play or social imitative play appropriate to developmental level
C. Restricted repetitive and stereotyped patterns of behavior, interests, and activities
   1. encompassing preoccupation with one or more stereotyped and restricted patterns of interest that is abnormal in intensity or focus
   2. apparently inflexible adherence to specific, nonfunctional routines or rituals
   3. stereotyped or repetitive motor mannerisms
   4. persistent preoccupation with parts of objects
D. Delays or abnormal functioning in social interaction, language as used in social communication, or symbolic and imaginative play prior to 3 years of age
E. The disturbance is not better accounted for by Rett's disorder or childhood disintegrative disorder

Although it is too soon to complete a summary evaluation of the *DSM-IV* changes in the pervasive developmental disorders classification, there are preliminary points of likely concern. First, the addition of three new subtypes of pervasive developmental disorders will probably draw criticism, if only because their construct validity has yet to be demonstrated. Second, the reduction in the number of items used to describe the three primary criteria for autistic disorder is likely to cause consternation among clinicians and researchers alike. The reduction in items, taken together with the fewer behavioral examples offered in the new definition, could cause another round of changes in prevalence estimates. Further, the change in definition does little to assuage, and probably exacerbates, preexisting problems in comparing research results across studies that employed different definitions of autistic disorder. Finally, age of onset has changed once again, and the requirement that delays or abnormal functioning in social interaction, language, or symbolic play must be present before 3 years is new. Given these and other issues that are likely to arise, it seems doubtful that a gold standard for the diagnosis of autistic disorder has yet arrived.

THEORY

Over the past five decades research has revealed a great deal about human functioning. The contributions have come from diverse disciplines: anthropology, child development, education, neurology, psychology, and sociology, just to name a few. The knowledge base is now so robust that writers have begun to integrate research findings into broad-based theories of human behavior (Calvin, 1989, 1996; Damascio, 1994; Eaves, 1993a; Kagan, 1994; Ornstein, 1991, 1995). These theories are relevant to the etiology, diagnosis, and treatment of autistic disorder (cf., Kinsbourne, 1980, 1987).

Figure 14–1 illustrates the major elements and functions of the human brain. The brain contains five interactive physical units: sensory system brain stem, limbic system, cerebrum, and cerebellum. The brain stem is the most archaic component of the human brain. Aside for its role in modulating the autonomic nervous system, the brain stem, via the reticular activating system (RAS), has been tied to the degree of arousal experienced by the organism. The RAS receives environmental stimulation from the major sensory pathways and classifies that stimulation according to its adaptive importance.

As shown in Figure 14–2, adaptively unimportant environmental stimuli are habituated; that is, stimuli that do not affect our lives (e.g., a speck on a wall, a falling leaf) are ignored. Two kinds of stimuli lead to arousal and capture our attention: adaptively important stimuli and novel stimuli. The reason adaptively important stimuli (e.g., food, shelter, hated enemies) cause arousal is straightforward. Because such stimuli either enhance or threaten our lives, they demand that we attend to them. Enhancing (or reinforcing) stimuli cause an orienting response; this can be indicated by a number of salient behaviors (e.g., reduced heart rate, looking at the stimuli, ears pricked up, stalking, etc.). Threatening (or punishing) stimuli cause a defensive response evidenced by an array of behaviors indicating the organism's rejection of the stimuli (e.g., aggressive attack, increased heart rate, fearful flight, ears laid back, etc.). Novel stimuli cause arousal because we don't yet know whether they are adaptively important or unimportant. To the extent that a novel stimulus might cause us pain or pleasure, it is critical that we familiarize ourselves with it and eventually classify it as adaptively important or unimportant.

Following the classification of the environmental stimuli, the RAS projects that information to the limbic system and cerebrum for further processing (see Figure 14–1). Although the processing of the limbic system and cerebrum is much more

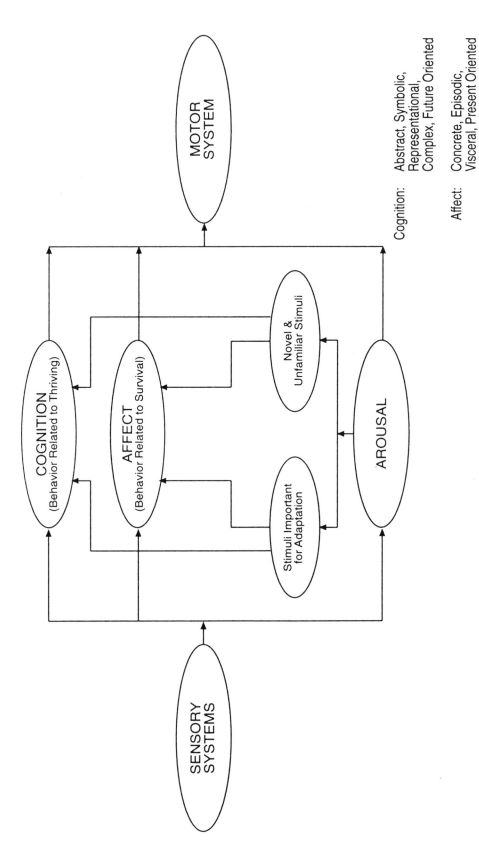

Figure 14–1. A model for human behavior

© 1993 Ronald C. Eaves

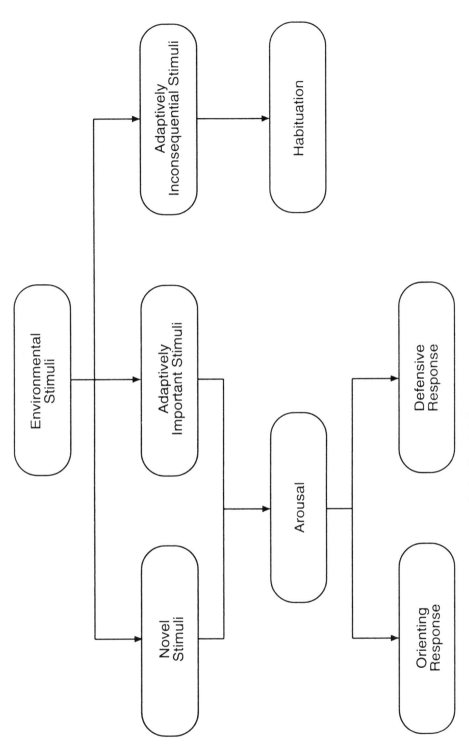

Figure 14–2.   Relationship between arousal stimuli and their responses

© 1993 Ronald C. Eaves

sophisticated than that of the RAS, without the active participation of the RAS a state of arousal cannot be achieved (Lindsley, 1958). It is as if the RAS must inform the higher levels of the brain whether it likes the stimuli or not before higher-order decisions can be made.

The limbic system, sometimes referred to as the transitional cortex, is a neurological component shared by humans, the primates, and all mammals. It provided our ancestors with a revolutionary adaptive advantage: species possessing a limbic system can learn from their own experience. Thus, mammals go through a relatively lengthy developmental period during which they learn a vast number of adaptive routines that enhance their survival. Other species are largely at the mercy of the neurological networks with which they are born.

That the adaptive routines learned by mammals via the limbic system are affective in nature was first proposed by Papez (1937). Affective adaptive routines deal with concrete, episodic events that are closely linked to short-term survival, particularly during emergencies. Such episodic events can be perceived directly through the senses and are commonly accompanied by visceral sensations. Examples of adaptive routines associated with the limbic system include the finding of food, water, and shelter (exploratory behavior); avoiding and escaping dangerous circumstances (flight); stalking and killing prey (aggression); mating (reproduction); ensuring safety; and resting. Because of their ability to learn from their own direct experience, mammals are not devoted to a single food source, climate, or terrain. Instead, they are able to adapt to a wide variety of environmental niches.

The cognitive system is most closely associated with the cerebral cortex. In the animal kingdom, primates possess the most complex cerebrums; their greatest elaboration is found in humans. The cerebrum is the most recent component of the brain to evolve, and it is the last to mature. It is generally considered to be the source of abstract thinking, symbolic conceptualization, and future planning, as well as deductive and inductive reasoning. Unlike other components of the brain, the cerebrum considers objects, events, and ideas representationally; that is, without directly perceiving them through the senses.

It is the ability to deal with problems abstractly that explains the impressive adaptive advantage proffered by the cerebrum: humans can learn complex relationships and adaptive routines for dealing with those relationships without direct experience. Lower-order mammals must risk injury and death as they learn adaptive routines through direct experience. Humans, through their ability to abstract, forewarn their offspring about environmental dangers and teach routines for avoiding them. In modern societies, children spend some 25% of their days in school learning how to live successfully in a civilized world that demands relatively high levels of abstract reasoning and the ability to plan ahead.

John Huhlings Jackson (1958) was the first prominent writer to advance the concept that functions have a vertical organization in the human brain. Thus, each neurological function has a low-level representation, a middle-level representation, and a high-level representation. Although he considered the spinal cord and brain stem to embody low-level representation and the cerebrum to be involved in high-level representation, Jackson did not implicate the elements of the limbic system in middle-level representation, presumably because the affective functions of that portion of the brain were not known until Papez wrote his ground-breaking article in 1937. Papez' theory was appealing because it suggested that "emotion, which had no known anatomic substrate, was a product of the limbic lobe, which had no recognized function" (Kolb & Whishaw, 1980, p. 24).

One might ask why the brain is organized into three levels. The answer concerns the fact that each level represents a major evolutionary development. The brain stem provided more sophisticated autonomic functions than did the spinal cord alone. The affective (limbic) system allowed mammals to learn adaptive routines directly through their own life experiences. The cognitive system (cerebrum) made it possible for humans to learn adaptive routines symbolically, without the need for direct experience. These components were accretionary; that is, each component was added onto earlier, more archaic components. Although each structure conferred fundamentally new behavioral adaptations upon the species, the more archaic structures did not cease to function. Consequently, it was necessary for each new system to integrate its activity with the extant systems. Thus, newer structures may exert superordinate control over older structures, given the right circumstances. For instance, during periods of perceived danger, the limbic system of mammals can supersede the normal functioning of the brain stem and temporarily increase heart rate, breathing, and perspiration, while the function of the digestive system is shut down. When environmental events allow the luxury of careful deliberation before choosing a response, the cognitive system (cerebrum) may well supersede the more ancient systems. On the other hand, "insofar as environmental events call for functions directly related to a particular brain structure, newer structures may be unable to supersede"; therefore, "in times of imminent danger [e.g., attack by a wild bear], the normal function of the limbic system cannot easily be overridden by the [cerebral] cortex of the brain" (Eaves, 1993a, p. 11).

The assessment procedures to follow are based on the theory just outlined and more fully elaborated by Eaves (1993a). As it relates to autism, the approach is similar to Ornitz' (1989) model, which suggested that autism is caused by "a dysfunction of the neuronal networks in the brain stem and diencephalon that are involved in the initial processing of sensory input" (p. 174). He further averred that "distorted sensory input, when transmitted to higher centers, becomes distorted information, and . . . this in turn becomes the basis of the deviant language and social communication [found in autistic children]" (p. 174). Dawson and Lewy (1989) presented a similar model, which also involves the cortical-limbic-reticular loop. Their formulation includes oversensitive novelty detectors in the cortex, overactive excitatory neurons in the hippocampus, and unresponsive RAS and thalamic synchronizers to explain such phenomena as the reduced P3 response and reduced habituation to novel stimuli that are commonly found in autism.

In simple terms, the thrust of these models is that information is disrupted along various of the neural pathways connecting the reticular, limbic, and cortical systems. In the most severe cases of autism, the individual is unable to make *affective or cognitive sense* of his or her environment. This leads to the development of behavioral repertoires that appear peculiarly maladaptive to an observer. Such repertoires are governed by the arousal system acting alone, as it were, since neither a concrete (i.e., limbic) nor abstract (i.e., cerebral) understanding of environmental stimuli has been attained. Examples of behavior governed by the arousal system include self-stimulation (hand flapping, spinning, finger flicking, fascination with textures); affective and cognitive indifference (lack of eye contact, rejection of affection, lack of emotion, mutism); fascination for objects; and resistance to change. Those individuals with autism who gain some concrete understanding of their world engage in behavior marked by its affective, or limbic, content. Examples of such behavior include peculiar eating habits, aggression and conduct disorders (bites, pulls hair, self-injury, crying, whining, screaming), distorted affect, and chronic fear. Finally, autistic individuals who attain a degree of abstract appreciation of their world develop behavior marked by its cognitive content. Such individuals exhibit an array of speech and language symptoms (misuse of pronouns, repetitive speech, unusual prosody), uneven development of learned skills, and savant behavior.

ASSESSMENT

Historically, the classification of autism depended heavily on the judgment and expertise of the clinician. Unfortunately, not many public school personnel had much experience with the condition, and far too often children with autistic disorder were misdiagnosed and placed in classrooms for the retarded or multihandicapped. Although the problem remains in the schools today, four trends are reducing the number of gross mistakes being made.

A new generation of instruments is available that is a clear improvement over instruments of the past. Although they are not of high enough quality to rely on for important classification decisions, a good deal is known about their psychometric properties (e.g., norms, reliability, validity). This has not been as true in the past. In addition, the new instruments have made the assessment process more accessible to parents and teachers. Although these individuals may lack knowledge about measurement, they are often intimately familiar with the child to be assessed. Instruments like the Autism Behavior Checklist and Pervasive Developmental Disorder Rating Scale formalize the contributions that teachers and parents can make in the assessment process.

A growing trend over the last two decades has been the interdisciplinary team approach. This means that public schools depend on the unique expertise of a wide array of individuals in order to reach important diagnostic and placement decisions. Thus, an assessment team might include parents, a school psychologist, a special educator with a background in autism, a speech and language therapist, regular classroom teachers, and other professionals from the school and community. By employing individuals with diverse knowledge and skill, fewer misclassifications of children with autism occur.

Because of the interdisciplinary approach, better training programs, and the increased number of children with autism attending public schools, staffs have more knowledge and experience with autism than has been true in the past. As schools become more inclusive, accommodating children with autism in regular classes when it is reasonable, this trend will lead to even more improvement in this area.

Parents are now more knowledgeable about their rights than they were 20 years ago. Public Law 94–142 (now the Individuals with Disabilities Education Act) explicitly provided parents the right to participate in decision making about their children and the right to due process when parent and school recommendations are in conflict. The ASA has no doubt been influential in promoting such legislation. It has also provided parents with extensive information about services, relevant agencies, books, and videotapes through its newsletter, *Advocate*. Finally, many well-publicized legal suits have made parents aware that they can have a powerful influence in gaining services for their children.

In the diagnosis of autism, it is important that the assessment team have a clear concept of the salient features that comprise the condition. While any of the definitions reviewed earlier in this paper could be used to glean those characteristics commonly associated with autism, they lack theoretical underpinnings that can be used to estimate the severity of the problem, the strengths and weaknesses within the construct of autistic disorders, or to suggest relevant treatment approaches. A recommended starting point is to adopt an organization that identifies the arrangement and interrelation of the components of autistic disorder. One such organization is A Taxonomy of Goals and Objectives: Autistic Disorder (TOGOAD; Eaves, 1966a). Figure 14–3 displays a layout of this taxonomy. Ideally, such an organization not only shows the theoretical structure of autistic disorder, but, like TOGOAD, also contains written goals and objectives for each element in the taxonomy. Such a document provides three important advantages: (1) it guides the assessment process, ensuring that selected instruments estimate the desired elements of autistic disorder; (2) it reduces the labor of writing goals and objectives for individualized education programs; and (3) it ensures that there is a direct link between assessment outcomes and instructional design.

Even with the improvements mentioned above, clinical judgment and experience remain the most critical aspects of the assessment process. Although the remainder of this chapter emphasizes the psychometric elements of assessing autistic disorder, the extant technology is not so sophisticated that it can overcome a poorly trained, inexperienced, or unintelligent practitioner.

The assessment of individuals incorporates three related phases: screening, clinic assessment, and follow-up assessment (Eaves & McLaughlin, 1977). In this section, each of these components will be discussed and followed by a case study to illustrate each process.

Screening

Screening is a quick, inexpensive means for making tentative judgments about a child's's status in a variety of domains. No child would formally be classified as autistic during this phase of assessment. Instead, one of two decisions would be made: The child is not a candidate for autistic disorder or the child might have autistic disorder; additional assessment is required before a formal judgment is made. Four assessment methods are appropriate to use during screening.

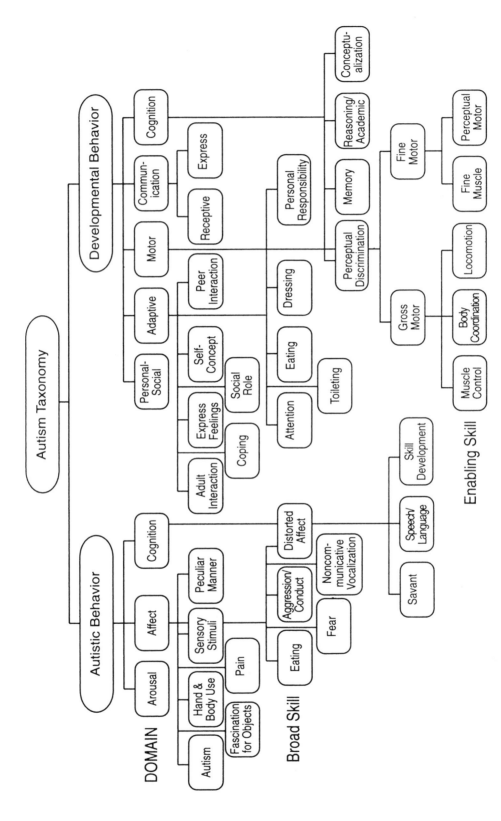

Figure 14–3. Autism taxonomy

© 1993 Ronald C. Eaves

Informal consultation. The first assessment method, informal consultation, is a process during which the assessor discusses the client with individuals who have extensive contact and knowledge about him or her (e.g., parents, teachers, siblings). Although there is no structured plan for the consultation, the assessor may ask for information about onset, family history, specific features of the client's symptoms, and so on.

Inspection of previously collected data. When this method is used, the assessor studies files, reports, and other permanent products that may provide insight into the client's developmental history, medical history, prior experiences, and idiosyncratic behavior. In this method it is important for the assessor to remain aware that a particular file may contain data that are either objective or subjective, that may be valid or suspect. It is important to weigh the evidence carefully, looking for both consistencies and inconsistencies that heighten the clinician's insights about the child and his or her environment. Thus, the assessor may be able to judge that the client has received competent (or incompetent) help from the professional community in the past. Likewise, the assessor may interpret the parents' attitudes and expectations as reasonable (or unrealistic).

Structured interviews. These range from norm-referenced instruments to intake interviews that obtain information about the history and current status of the client. As a rule, only norm-referenced interviews provide psychometric data that allow potential users to evaluate the quality of the instrument. Unlike informal consultation, structured interviews have guidelines for data collection, prescribed questions to ask, systematic means for recording responses, directions for summarizing the responses, and suggestions for interpreting the summaries. Among the most frequently used structured interviews in the assessment of autistic disorder are adaptive behavior scales. For example, the Vineland Adaptive Behavior Scales-Interview Edition (VABS-IE; Sparrow, Balla, & Cicchetti, 1984) assesses three domains of adaptive behavior (i.e., Communication, Daily Living Skills, and Socialization), which form the Adaptive Behavior Composite when combined.

Screening devices. These instruments use a wide variety of terms in their titles: checklist, rating scale, inventory, questionnaire, opinionnaire, and so on. Screening devices usually require that a caregiver (e.g., teacher, clinician, or parent) identify which behaviors in an array of such behaviors are exhibited by a client. In checklists, the presence of a problem behavior is indicated by placing a check next to the item. Rating scales require the respondent to indicate the degree to which the behavior is present by marking a value on a multipoint scale. Thus, a zero may indicate *no problem,* one may indicate a *mild problem,* and two may indicate that the behavior is a *severe problem* for the client. Many screening devices exist that claim to estimate the extent to which an individual exhibits autistic behavior. The Childhood Autism Rating Scale (Schopler, Reichler, & Renner, 1988), the Autism Behavior Checklist (Krug, Arick, & Almond, 1995), and the Pervasive Developmental Disorder Rating Scale (Eaves, 1993b) are three examples of such screening devices.

Case Example 14–1.   Screening the autistic child—John

John first came to the autism clinic at 7 years of age. He appeared to be a healthy and attractive boy of average height and weight. John's mother, Donna Arnold, reported that he displayed unusual behavioral patterns early in his development; even as a baby he seemed remote and uninvolved with the world around him. Inasmuch as John had an older brother and sister, Donna was an experienced mother. Thus, she became concerned when the usual mother-child bonding patterns failed to develop. For instance, John did not exhibit the typical shrugging of his shoulders and infant smile in anticipation of being picked up by his mother. In addition, he was an indifferent eater. During the first 3 months of his life, John rarely nursed at his mother's breast for more than a few moments. Attempts to bottle-feed him were not very successful either. According to Donna, John seemed most content when left alone in his cradle. When removed, he became immediately fretful for several minutes, after which he was content to remain in his mother's arms. When she returned him to his cradle, he once again became fretful. It appeared to his mother as if John became upset whenever any change occurred.

As John grew older, other signs of his affective and cognitive indifference became apparent. Both Donna and her husband, Bob, agreed that their son rarely made sustained eye contact with either of them. When tentative eye contact *was* made, John seldom followed their movements as children frequently do. Even when they sat directly in front of him, both parents had the feeling that John was looking through them rather than at them. John's lack of interest in social contact was manifested in a number of other ways. For instance, his brother, Sam, characterized John's normal facial expression as "just a blank; it's like he's in a world of his own." Although he learned not to become upset when others hugged him, there was no mistaking that John was relieved when such expressions of affection were finished. Although he spent a lot of time with his cousins and neighborhood peers, he showed no interest in them; he always preferred solitary activities. On occasions when others interrupted these solitary activities, John responded defensively by crying or throwing tantrums.

During his second and third year, self-stimulatory behavior appeared with progressive embellishments. For instance, John spent periods of 20 to 30 minutes simply staring at his hands. Later, he began to spread his fingers apart and move his hand back and forth between his eyes and any source of bright light. After a time engaged in this behavior, John sometimes became agitated and, with a wide-eyed, hysterical look on his face, began shaking his hands up and down rapidly. This action was accompanied by a loud screeching noise ("Eeee! Eeee! Eeee!"). At other times, John held his fingers in a stiff, distorted manner, followed by an odd flicking motion of his index finger. Other behaviors that John engaged in included back-and-forth or side-to-side rocking, the dangling of long, flexible materials (belts, cords, pony tails), and lining up wooden blocks (he rarely stacked them as most children do).

Throughout his life, John consistently preferred to interact with inanimate objects rather than living things. Objects that moved, whether alive or mechanical, caused him to react with fear and to withdraw. Thus, the family dog and pet bird, along with mechanical toys and kitchen appliances (e.g., the electric mixer) were avoided. Objects that he liked were those that did not move of their own accord (e.g., blocks, photo albums, dolls). Yet, he did not play with the objects he liked in expected ways. For instance, dolls were held by the foot as often as by the hand. He commonly pushed

Case Example 14–1.   *(Continued)*

his wooden car, not on its wheels, but upside down. John was also attracted to unusual objects; he rarely passed up the opportunity to listen to the crinkly sound made by cellophane being crumpled. He also seemed to be fascinated by the texture of materials. When he found a texture that attracted him, John rubbed the material with his fingers or against his cheek. He particularly liked rubbery materials like pencil erasers, but he also seemed to enjoy the touch of soft, smooth cloth. His preference for certain textures and objects was compulsive; it was a rare occasion when John did not have an eraser or piece of cloth in his pocket or within easy reach.

In spite of John's physically attractive, intelligent appearance, it was obvious that his cognitive development lagged well behind that of other children his age. For instance, Donna believed that John "understands quite a lot," but admitted that his receptive language was difficult to assess because he usually ignored the speech of others. On the other hand, John's communicative speech was limited to only a few dozen words. When confronted with circumstances involving abstract, symbolic material (e.g., listening to stories, watching movies, looking at magazines), John's attention was rarely engaged for more than a few moments.

Unquestionably, John's most disturbing characteristic was his increasingly severe self-injurious behavior. To the best of Donna and Bob's recollection, John began hitting his chin with a closed fist when he was 4 to 5 years of age. Initially, the blows carried no injurious force and did not alarm his parents. But the force of his blows increased and so did the variety of his self-destructive acts as he grew older. During his visit to the autism clinic, John was observed striking his chin with considerable force. According to his parents, this hitting had become more frequent during the past year. A thick callous on his right hand was stark evidence of his hand-biting behavior, which occurred when John became agitated. Finally, John had recently begun to pick at his hands and arms, causing them to bleed. Allowing the resulting sores to heal had also been a problem because John picked away scabs as soon as they formed over the wound.

During their visit to the center, Donna and Bob were interviewed to obtain an estimate of John's adaptive behavior. The results of the Vineland Adaptive Behavior Scales-Interview Edition are displayed below. According to his parents' report, John's overall performance in adaptive behavior revealed a significant handicapping weakness. Paired comparisons between the domains resulted in no significant differences (95% confidence level). Thus, these data were consistent with other evidence obtained during the screening phase. They also implied that John was equally weak in the Communication, Daily Living Skills, and Socialization domains.

Domain	*Standard Score*	*95% Confidence Interval*	*Percentile*	*Age Equivalent*
Communication	40	33–47	< 0.1	< 1–00
Daily Living Skills	47	40–54	< 0.1	1–07
Socialization	49	41–57	< 0.1	< 1–00
Adaptive Behavior Composite	45	40–50	< 0.1	< 1–00

Note: Standard scores have a mean of 100 and a standard deviation of 15.

Two screening devices were completed during John's visit: the Pervasive Developmental Disorder Rating Scale (PDDRS) and the Autism Behavior Checklist (ABC).

(continued)

Case Example 14–1.   *(Continued)*

The *PDDRS* is a screening device designed to correspond to the theory outlined in the theory section of this chapter. Indeed, a factor analysis of the ratings of 325 children with pervasive developmental disorders resulted in three second-order factors: Arousal, Affect, and Cognition. The results of the PDDRS are presented below. Donna and Bob's ratings suggested that John's behavior was consistent with that of children with autistic disorder. John's composite score was equal to or greater than 99% of the 325 children who comprised the PDDRS norm group. Consistent with other screening evidence obtained, the results indicated that John's most extreme behavior occurred in Arousal (e.g., autistic aloneness, self-stimulation) and Affect (e.g., eating problems, fear, self-injury). The data suggested that while aberrant Cognitive Behavior (e.g., speech and language anomalies, savant behavior, uneven skill development) was not so extreme as Arousal and Affect, John's score placed him above the 50th percentile when compared to the norm group. The scores obtained for the ABC corresponded closely with the PDDRS results. Each of his ABC scores (i.e., Sensory, Relating, Body and Object, Language, Social and Self-Help, and Total) were above the means of the norm group consisting of children with autism.

In summary, the screening evidence obtained through informal consultation, structured interviews, and screening devices all consistently support the inference that John exhibits severe delays and disabilities associated with pervasive developmental disorders/autism and adaptive behavior. Based on these results, the clinic team decided to conduct a more time-consuming and costly clinic assessment.

Domain	Standard Score	Percentile
Arousal	132	98
Affect	144	>99
Cognition	103	58
Pervasive Developmental Disorder Composite	138	99

Note: Standard scores have a mean of 100 and a standard deviation of 15.

Clinic Assessment

The purpose of the clinic assessment phase is to obtain more valid estimates of the child's status in relevant domains. These estimates allow the assessment team to confirm or deny the weaknesses tentatively identified during screening. The process demands more time, expense, and clinical expertise than the screening phase, but such demands are warranted when important, often long-term, diagnostic decisions are to be made.

As before, it is critical to select instruments that correspond closely with the theoretical model and taxonomic structure of autism adopted by the school or agency. The Pervasive Developmental Disorder Observation Schedule (PDDOS; Eaves, 1996b), like the PDDRS, was constructed to estimate performance in the three domains incorporated in Eaves' (1993a) theory and the TOGOAD: Arousal, Affect, and Cognition. Other relatively elaborate assessment systems are the Psycho-

Case Example 14–2.   Clinic assessment of the autistic child—John

An important aspect of clinic assessment is to investigate the possibility that a client exhibits characteristics consistent with diagnoses other than autism. Such assessment should include a neurological examination, which may reveal a syndrome with a known biological etiology distinct from, or associated with, autism (e.g., Lesch-Neyen syndrome, fragile X syndrome). In John's case, no contradictory evidence was found. On the other hand, magnetic resonance imaging showed hypoplasia of cerebellar vermal lobules VI and VII, a characteristic found by Courchesne (1989) to be more frequent among people with autism than normal controls.

A speech and language assessment provides detailed information about the quantity and quality of the client's development, along with the clinician's impressions regarding the most accurate diagnosis (e.g., autism versus severe developmental language disorder). An audiological examination may uncover a significant hearing loss, a condition that may be confused with autism. According to the speech and language specialist, although John exhibited severe communication disabilities, she considered the overall results to support the diagnosis of autistic disorder. The audiological examination led to the conclusion that John's hearing was in the normal range.

Finally, a test of intelligence should be administered in order to estimate the client's cognitive functioning. Although it may not be used as a diagnostic criterion for an individual client, one of the more consistent findings reported in the literature of people with autism is the higher performance IQs that they attain relative to verbal IQ. Overall intelligence test performance is also an important index of prognosis (as is speech and language development); individuals with higher IQs and better communication skills exhibit more improvement across time. For clients with significant speech and language disabilities, it is important to select an intelligence test that does not demand comprehension and use of language beyond their ability (e.g., Coloured Progressive Matrices [Raven, 1993], Columbia Mental Maturity Scale [Burgemeister, Blum, & Lorge, 1972], Kaufman Brief Intelligence Test-Matrices subtest [K-BIT; Kaufman & Kaufman, 1990], and the Matrix Analogies Test [Naglieri, 1985]). Given John's lack of communication skills and low tolerance for interpersonal interaction, the school psychologist administered the K-BIT. Inasmuch as the K-BIT requires only about 20 minutes to administer, it was completed in its entirety. Although John showed little interest in the Vocabulary items, he was able to respond appropriately to a number of the items in the Matrices subtest. The results of the examination were as follows (standard scores have a mean of 100 and a standard deviation of 15): (1) Composite standard score = 40, 95% confidence interval = 31–49, percentile rank < 0.1; (2) Vocabulary standard score = 40, 95% confidence interval = 31–49, percentile rank < 0.1; (3) Matrices standard score = 48, 95% confidence interval = 36–60, percentile rank < 0.1. Such results are primarily between 3 and 4 standard deviations below the population mean and are consistent with the finding that approximately 60% of children with autism have IQs below 50 (Ritvo & Freeman, 1978).

The assessment team used the PDDOS to evaluate the degree to which John displayed autistic behavior. Like the PDDRS, the PDDOS was designed to correspond to the theory outlined earlier. Thus, measures of Arousal, Affect, and Cognition are obtained, which can be compared to the PDDRS ratings to determine the extent to which

(continued)

Case Example 14–2. *(Continued)*

the two sets of estimates correspond. The rationale is that if two independently derived estimates of autistic behavior obtained by different methods both support the diagnosis of autistic disorder then the confidence of the final diagnosis is increased significantly.

The PDDOS uses a continuous time-sampling format; that is, the assessor observes the client for a 10-second interval, followed by a 5-second interval for recording the behavior just observed. This observe-record-observe sequence is repeated until 14 minutes have elapsed. Ideally, 14-minute samples of behavior are obtained in a variety of environmental settings (e.g., home, school, work, recreation), with the client engaged in different tasks or activities, in the presence of different people, and at different times of day. Such variety not only provides a more representative sample of

Pervasive Developmental Disorder Observation Schedule

Record Sheet

Child: _John Arnold_   Teacher: _Betty Brown_

School: _Achievement Center_   Date: _12/12/96_

Setting: ☐ Home   ☒ School   ☐ Vocation   ☐ Recreation   ☐ Other

Describe: _self-contained_

Task/Activity: _Cutting shapes_

☒ Group of _3_   ☐ Individual   Adult/Pupil Ratio: _6/1_

Observer: _Alice Best_   Reliability Checker: _none_

~~Arousal~~ Affect ~~Cognition~~	~~Arousal~~ ~~Affect~~ Cognition	Arousal Affect Cognition	~~Arousal~~ ~~Affect~~ Cognition	~~Arousal~~ ~~Affect~~ Cognition	Arousal ~~Affect~~ Cognition	Arousal ~~Affect~~ Cognition	Arousal Affect Cognition
Arousal Affect Cognition	Arousal Affect Cognition	~~Arousal~~ Affect Cognition	~~Arousal~~ Affect Cognition	Arousal Affect Cognition	Arousal Affect Cognition	~~Arousal~~ Affect Cognition	~~Arousal~~ Affect Cognition
~~Arousal~~ ~~Affect~~ Cognition	~~Arousal~~ ~~Affect~~ Cognition	~~Arousal~~ ~~Affect~~ Cognition	Arousal ~~Affect~~ Cognition	Arousal ~~Affect~~ Cognition	~~Arousal~~ ~~Affect~~ Cognition	~~Arousal~~ ~~Affect~~ Cognition	Arousal ~~Affect~~ Cognition
Arousal Affect Cognition	Arousal Affect Cognition	Arousal Affect Cognition	Arousal Affect Cognition	Arousal Affect Cognition	~~Arousal~~ Affect Cognition	~~Arousal~~ Affect Cognition	~~Arousal~~ Affect Cognition
~~Arousal~~ ~~Affect~~ Cognition	Arousal ~~Affect~~ Cognition	Arousal ~~Affect~~ Cognition	~~Arousal~~ Affect Cognition	~~Arousal~~ Affect Cognition	~~Arousal~~ ~~Affect~~ Cognition	Arousal ~~Affect~~ Cognition	~~Arousal~~ Affect Cognition
~~Arousal~~ Affect Cognition	~~Arousal~~ ~~Affect~~ Cognition	~~Arousal~~ ~~Affect~~ Cognition	Arousal ~~Affect~~ Cognition	Arousal Affect Cognition	Arousal Affect Cognition	~~Arousal~~ Affect Cognition	~~Arousal~~ Affect Cognition
~~Arousal~~ ~~Affect~~ Cognition	Arousal ~~Affect~~ Cognition	Arousal Affect Cognition	~~Arousal~~ Affect Cognition	~~Arousal~~ Affect Cognition	~~Arousal~~ ~~Affect~~ Cognition	~~Arousal~~ ~~Affect~~ Cognition	~~Arousal~~ ~~Affect~~ Cognition

Scores: Arousal = _32_ /56 = _57_ %

Affect = _26_ /56 = _46_ %

Cognition = _0_ /56 = _0_ %

Composite = _42_ /56 = _75_ %

Figure 14–4.   An example of a completed pervasive developmental disorder observation schedule record sheet

Case Example 14–2.   *(Continued)*

behavior, it also helps to identify those environmental circumstances most problematic for the client. Thus, systematic observation serves a dual purpose: it facilitates judgments about the classification of the client and it provides baseline data that can be used for instructional planning.

Figure 14–4 illustrates a completed PDDOS record sheet, and Figure 14–5 summarizes eight 14-minute observations of John's behavior while engaged in a variety of

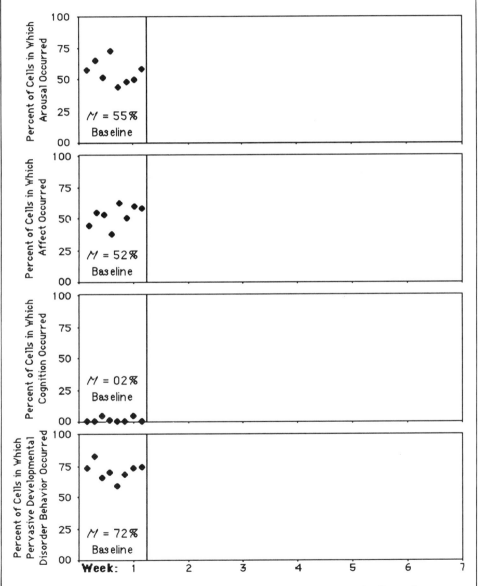

Figure 14–5.   Summary estimates of John's autistic behavior on the Pervasive Developmental Disorder Observation Schedule

(continued)

Case Example 14–2.   *(Continued)*

activities in the autism clinic, at home, and in school. Because the data were stable across days, activities, and settings, they were plotted together in Figure 14–5. The results support the screening findings. First, John exhibited some form of pervasive developmental disorder during 72% of the 448 observation intervals. Such a high score is indicative of autistic disorder and provides independent support of the PDDRS Composite score (SS = 138). John's two highest scores on the PDDOS were Arousal (M = 55%) and Affect (M = 52%), which contrasted with his Cognitive score (M = 02%). The same pattern occurred on the PDDRS, where Arousal and Affect were the two highest scores (SS = 132 and 144, respectively) and Cognition was lower (SS = 103).

This pattern (i.e., high levels of Arousal and Affective behavior, together with a low Cognition score) is characteristic of school-aged children with relatively severe autism. Greater evidence of cognitive behavior, even though it reflects peculiar or distorted language and abstract skill development, indicates a better prognosis for the individual. That is because modern society places great demands on a person's ability to deal effectively with complexity and abstraction. Those who are not linguistically facile, who cannot grasp symbolic concepts, and who fail to generalize those concepts find it very difficult to adapt in today's technological environment.

In addition to the provision of evidence useful in the classification of individuals, the PDDOS provides three other benefits. First, it reveals the broad forms of pervasive developmental disorder (i.e., arousal, affect, and cognition) that are most severe and require more intensive remediation. Second, the data plotted in Figure 14–5 represent a baseline that can be used as a benchmark in judging the overall success of interventions across long periods of time. By obtaining PDDOS data every 2 to 4 weeks, one can judge whether the attainment of specific objectives leads to a more general improvement in behavior. Third, by writing copious notes immediately following each PDDOS session, the assessor identifies a number of enabling and specific behaviors that will guide follow-up assessment. In John's case, the observer noted 11 specific behaviors that contributed most to his inflated PDDOS scores: chin hitting, hand biting, skin picking, hand flapping, finger flicking, looking at hands, noncompliance, uncommunicative vocalizations, lack of eye contact, rejecting affection, and rejecting changes.

The curriculum for an individual with autism should include traditional domains appropriate to his developmental levels. All of the evidence indicated that John's developmental attainment was far below his chronological age of 7 years. Consequently, the team member responsible for assessing overall development administered the Battelle Development Inventory (BDI; Newborg, Stock, Wnek, Guidubaldi, & Svinicki, 1984) to John. The results are displayed below.

Domain	Developmental Quotient	Percentile	Age Equivalent (mos.)
Personal-Social	04	< 01	04
Adaptive	29	< 01	28
Motor	48	< 01	46
Communication	16	< 01	35
Cognitive	48	< 01	15
BDI Total	23	< 01	22

Note: Standard scores have a mean of 100 and a standard deviation of 15.

Case Example 14–2. *(Continued)*

The BDI was intended for use with children from birth through 8 years of age but, unfortunately, the tabled standard scores are truncated at 65 (i.e., 2.33 SDs below the mean). John performed well below that level. Consequently, the examiner resorted to a practice that is ordinarily viewed with reproach by measurement experts: she calculated developmental quotients (DQ = [age equivalent ÷ chronological age] × 100) for each of the BDI scores. Developmental quotients can easily lead to misinterpretations when treated as if they were standard scores, but in this instance they provided a more accurate picture of John's performance than did the standard score of 65 assigned in the BDI norm tables. Although one must be careful about interpreting the apparent differences between pairs of BDI scores, it was clear that John's performance could be characterized as reflecting moderate to severe disabilities in all domains. The BDI Total score indicated a severe developmental disability. While the quantitative results of the BDI were somewhat unsatisfactory, the examination did reveal a number of potential enabling and specific skills that the team was able to assess in follow-up assessment. For instance, John intermittently used his own name, and he was heard to utter 13 other recognizable words that were used to communicate: mama, daddy, Sam, Alabama, beroom (bedroom), blanket, Daw (Darwin, the family dog), house, juice, poop (toilet), go, g'bye, 911, and Petey (pet bird). Although the number of words used spontaneously was small, the variety of phonemes provided a rich base on which to build.

---

educational Profile-Revised: Volume I (Schopler, Reichler, Bashford, Lansing, & Marcus, 1990), the Adolescent and Adult Psychoeducational Profile: Volume IV (Mesibov, Schopler, Schaffer, & Landrus, 1988), and the Autism Screening Instrument for Educational Planning-2 (Krug et al., 1995). Each of these systems obtains assessment data for the purpose of developing educational programs for children and/or adults with autistic disorder.

Follow-Up Assessment

The purpose of the follow-up assessment phase is to obtain valid estimates of the child's achievement of enabling and specific skills. The primary assessment methods used are systematic observation and criterion-referenced (or curriculum-based) tests. In Bloom, Hastings, and Madaus' (1971) terms, the process involves formative evaluation using absolute criteria for mastery. Formative evaluation implies that data will be collected frequently so that inadequate instructional procedures can be modified with little wasted time. Absolute mastery criteria are standards for minimally acceptable performance that require complete or nearly complete attainment of the skill (e.g., 95% accuracy).

The enabling and specific skills assessed in follow-up assessment are those that once attained combine with other mastered skills and ultimately lead to mastery of important, large domains. For example, consider the child who frequently bites other children who interfere with his or her play. In the Taxonomy of Goals and Objectives: Autistic Disorder (see Figure 14–3) such behavior is classified as a form of aggressive conduct. Aggressive conduct is classified as one enabling form of affective behavior. Affect is a broad form of behavior that characterizes children with autistic disorder. The idea is to master the multiplicity of specific behaviors such that, gradually, enabling skills, broad skills, and—ultimately—domains are mastered by the student.

The instructional procedures used for individuals with autism are brief but labor intensive. For instance, instruction and practice for a single skill may last only 10 minutes, but an efficient instructor will usually complete procedures for 10 to 12 skills in a 2-hour session. It is not unusual for instructors to work on 20 to 30 different skills each day, often repeating the instructional procedures 2 to 3 times for each skill. It is necessary to work on specific skills (e.g., eye contact) because skills at higher taxonomic levels (e.g., autism) are too complex and contain too many elements to expect measurable improvement over the short term. Instead, skills are taught using discrete trials (i.e., rapidly implemented trials that result in easily observable correct or incorrect responses). For example, a common beginning skill for many children with autism is the discriminative stimulus (S^D) "Look at me." A discrete trial might consist of noting whether the child engages in at least 2 seconds of face-to-face eye contact with the instructor, with a response latency of less than 5 seconds.

Because of the need to identify a large number of specific skills suitable for intervention, the follow-up assessment of individuals with autism is extensive. Ordinarily the assessment team can expect to assess a range of specific forms of autistic behavior (e.g., arousal, affect) as well as specific developmental skills from five domains: personal-social, adaptive, motor, communication, and cognition. The formal results of clinic assessment as well as the observations of the assessment team should be used to identify enabling and specific skills that require follow-up assessment.

Case Example 14–3.   Follow-up assessment of the autistic child—John

---

This assessment phase incorporated the use of 16 instruments that provided pretest or baseline data on 46 specific objectives. The process required 8 days during which a special educator and an aide collected data. The following table contains a list of some of the skills that were identified for instruction. Three of the instruments used in follow-up assessment are described below.

Arousal	*Affect*	*Cognition*
Eye Contact	Self-Injury	Critical Information
1 second	hitting chin	full name
2 seconds	biting hand	address
5 seconds	picking skin	city/state
Hand Use	Eating	phone number
flapping hands	finishing plate	emergency number
flicking fingers	picky eating	parents' names
looking at hands	Aggressive Conduct	birth date/age
Fascination for Objects	noncompliance	Expressive Pointing
soft cloths	whining, crying	Matching
erasers (rubber)	biting/scratching others	object to object

Case Example 14–3.   *(Continued)*

Sensory-Stimulation	Resisting Changes	picture to object
rectal digging (smell)	Fear/Anxiety	color to color
dangling	fears moving objects	letters/numbers
crinkling cellophane	anxious in crowds	Receptive Language
mouthing objects	fears loud noises	one-step commands
Reclusiveness	Toileting	body parts
withdraws to bedroom	bladder	Verbal Imitation
withdraws to closet	bowel	vowels/consonants

The most troubling behavior for John's parents and his teacher was the high frequency with which he engaged in self-injury. Three specific self-injurious behaviors
were noted during screening and clinic assessment: chin hitting, hand biting, and skin
picking. The Self-Injury Observation Schedule (SIOS; Eaves, 1993c) was constructed
and used to obtain a reliable and valid estimate of the rate of self-injurious behavior.
Unlike the PDDOS, which uses a time-sampling format, the SIOS employs event
sampling. That is, each self-injurious behavior is defined as a separate event, and each
such event is recorded every time it occurs. For instance, chin hitting was defined as
follows: "The child hits his own chin or jaw with his open hand or fist. Ordinarily, this
action results in an audible noise, but the observer need not hear the hit in order to
record an instance of the behavior. Each hit should be recorded as a separate event.
Do not record instances in which the child holds both hands under his chin and claps
them together" (Eaves, 1993c, p. 3). John's self-injury was observed over 8 days in a
variety of settings (i.e., home, school) and circumstances (i.e., work, free time, and
lunch). Figure 14–6 illustrates the results.

Most importantly, the SIOS results indicated that John engaged in high levels of
self-injury. Overall, he emitted an average of 5.47 self-injurious acts per minute. Chin
hitting was most frequent ($M = 2.70$ hits per minute), followed by hand biting ($M =
1.92$ bites per minute) and skin picking ($M = 1.68$ picks per minute). Clearly, it was
important to design an intervention strategy that would effectively reduce these behaviors. Fortunately, the conditions maintaining the self-injury became apparent during
data collection. As indicated in Figure 6, John's acts of self-injury dropped significantly
during lunch and free play, activities that placed few demands on him. The special
educator and aide presented the team with a convincing case that John used self-injury
to encourage others to stop making demands on him and to leave him alone. Indeed,
Bob and Donna admitted that when John abused himself they often stopped trying to
get him to complete his task and either focused on the self-injurious behavior or
withdrew altogether. The assessment team was fairly certain that the behavior could be
extinguished by simply ignoring it and working through the task at hand. In any case,
the specific objective selected from the TOGOAD that identified self-injury as an
important weakness for John read as follows:

Using standard procedures for the Self-Injury Observation Schedule, John's emission of
chin hitting, hand biting, and skin picking will each equal .07 acts per minute or less; his
overall emission of self-injury will equal .20 acts per minute or less; behavior rates will be
averaged over at least three observation sessions of 15 minutes each.

(continued)

Case Example 14–3.   *(Continued)*

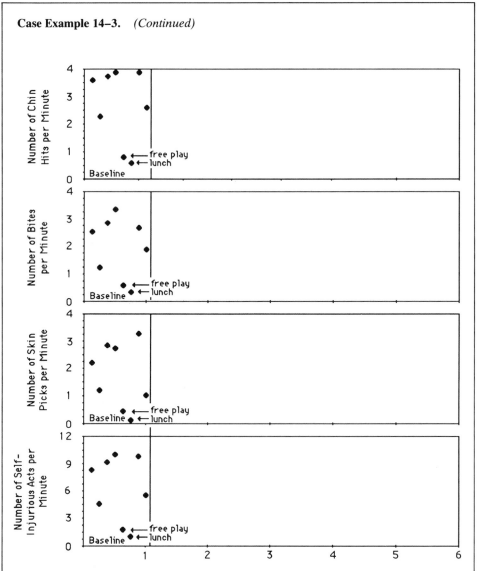

Figure 14–6.   Summary estimates of John's behavior on the Self-Injury Observation Schedule

Lack of eye contact was another behavior that seriously hindered attempts to teach John adaptive skills. Follow-up assessment of eye contact consisted of presenting him with the S^D "John, look at me," an average of 50 times each assessment day. The results showed that John made eye contact (within 5 seconds) with the person making the request on 3.25% of such occasions. He was much more likely to engage in self-injurious behavior following the S^D ($M = 14.25\%$) than to comply by making eye contact. When eye contact *was* made, it was fleeting, rarely lasting more than a second or two. Using an improvised lesson, the special educator determined that John's eye contact improved quickly when he was reinforced for eye contact with enthusiastic praise and edibles such as corn chips and sugar-coated corn flakes. This result sug-

Case Example 14–3.   *(Continued)*

gested that improved eye contact could be readily achieved using discrete trials and reinforcement. Given its status as a central prerequisite for the attainment of most adaptive skills, the assessment team strongly recommended that improved eye contact be given priority at the beginning of his treatment. Therefore, the assessment team selected the following specific objective for John from the TOGOAD:

> Given the request, "John, look at me," at least 50 times throughout the day, he will make face-to-face eye contact with the person making the request within 5 seconds and maintain it for at least 5 seconds; mastery is inferred when John meets the criteria for eye contact 95% of the 50 or more times requested over the course of one day.

Another set of specific skills that should be given priority in the assessment of children with autism is mastery of critical personal information. Although John's parents indicated that it was not a problem for him, some children wander away from caregivers if left alone even momentarily. It is crucial that such children be able to provide others with information that will help them locate the child's parents. Figure 14–7 illustrates John's responses to Set One of the Critical Personal Information Test (CPIT; Eaves, 1996c).

Critical   Personal   Information   Test

Child: *John Arnold*   Mediator: *Betty Brown*
Agency: *Achievement Center*   Date: *12/12/96*
Setting: *self-contained classroom*
Examiner: *Alice Bist*   Reliability Checker: *none*

Directions: Ask each question precisely as it is displayed below. Score 1 if the child's response matches the expected response. Otherwise, score 0. For errors, record the child's precise response beside the Expected Response.

Set One
Time Start: *9:35*   Time Stop: *9:36.42* Total Time: *1.42*   minutes

Question	Expected Response	Error Response	Score
What is your name?	John Arnold	*John · Q - NR*	0
What is your address?	401 3rd Avenue	*NR*	0
What city do you live in?	Opelika	*Alabama*	0
What state do you live in?	Alabama	*Alabama*	1
What is your phone number?	(334) 844-5943	*911*	0
What is your mother's name?	Donna Arnold	*Mama*	0
What is your father's name?	Bob Arnold	*Daddy*	0
When was your birthday?	January 16, 1989	*NR*	0
How old are you?	7 years old	*Held up 5 fingers*	0
Tell the emergency phone number.	911	*911*	1
		Total:	2

Figure 14–7.   An example of a completed Critical Personal Information Test

(continued)

Case Example 14–3.   *(Continued)*

Random Set		Time in Minutes				Score
One	_/_ minutes	_25_ seconds =	_1.42_ minutes	_2_		
Two	_/_ minutes	_36_ seconds =	_1.60_ minutes	_2_		
Three	_/_ minutes	_44_ seconds =	_1.73_ minutes	_1_		
		Totals:	_4.75_ minutes	_5_		
Percent Correct = _17_		Correct Responses per Minute = _1.05_				

Figure 14–7.   *(Continued)*

Brief tests like the CPIT tend to be quite unreliable. For instance, the 95% confidence interval for a raw score of 6 on the CPIT is 2 to 10 (20 to 100%); in other words, 10-item tests, used alone, provide little information about a child's mastery. However, by repeating the test items, one effectively increases the number of scorable responses and thus increases test reliability (Eaves, 1979). The standard CPIT repeats the 10 items three times in random order, which provides 30 scorable responses. The 95% confidence interval for John's total raw score of 5 was 1 to 9 (3 to 30%). Consequently, the assessment team could be quite confident of John's need to master the critical personal information skills, and they selected the following specific objective from the TOGOAD: "given a standard administration of the Critical Personal Information Test, John will respond orally with at least 93% accuracy; The duration of the 30-item test will not exceed 3 minutes."

CONCLUSION

The diagnosis and assessment of autistic disorder is an arduous process that demands considerable expertise in its conduct. While screening and clinic assessment can be completed in as little as a day or two, 1 or 2 weeks should be set aside for follow-up assessment. At its completion, an instructor should have identified enough specific objectives to keep busy for 4 to 6 months. The reader is encouraged to inspect Catherine Maurice's (1993) curriculum for Michel in order to gain an idea of the scope and sequence of an autistic child's instructional program.

Most people who are working with these youngsters for the first time are amazed at the number of skills taught each day. Actually, research shows that, when the instruction of individuals with autism is fast-paced and intensive, specific objectives are attained much more rapidly. It is critical that assessment procedures provide a base that can be used to document successful and unsuccessful instructional strategies. Without such precise follow-up assessment data, it is difficult if not impossible to identify weak instructional strategies and to modify them without wasting significant amounts of time. In addition, without preinstructional documentation of baseline and pretest levels of performance, it is commonplace for parents and professional personnel alike to see progress that simply isn't there.

REFERENCES

American Psychiatric Association. (1952). *Diagnostic and statistical manual of mental disorders* (1st ed.). Washington, DC: Author.

American Psychiatric Association. (1968). *Diagnostic and statistical manual of mental disorders* (2nd ed.). Washington, DC: Author.

American Psychiatric Association. (1980). *Diagnostic and statistical manual of mental disorders* (3rd ed.). Washington, DC: Author.

American Psychiatric Association. (1987). *Diagnostic and statistical manual of mental disorders* (3rd ed., revised). Washington, DC: Author.

American Psychiatric Association. (1994). *Diagnostic and statistical manual of mental disorders* (4th ed.). Washington, DC: Author.

Bloom, B., Hastings, J., & Madaus, G. (1971). *Handbook of formative and summative evaluation of student learning.* New York: McGraw-Hill.

Borden, M.C., & Ollendick, T.H. (1994). An examination of the validity of social subtypes in autism. *Journal of Autism and Developmental Disorders, 24,* 23–37.

Burgemeister, B.B., Blum, L.H., & Lorge, I. (1972). *Columbia Mental Maturity Scale.* San Antonio, TX: The Psychological Corporation.

Calvin, W.H. (1989). *The cerebral symphony: Seashore reflections on the structure of human consciousness.* New York: Bantam Books.

Calvin, W.H. (1996). *How brains think.* New York: Basic Books.

Courchesne, E. (1989). Neuroanatomical systems involved in infantile autism: The implications of cerebellar abnormalities. In G. Dawson (Ed.), *Autism: Nature, diagnosis, and treatment* (pp. 119–143). New York: Guilford Press.

Creak, M. (1961). Schizophrenia syndrome in childhood: Progress report of a working party. *Cerebral Palsy Bulletin, 3,* 501–504.

Creak, M. (1964). Schizophrenia syndrome in childhood: Further progress report of a working party. *Developmental Medicine and Child Neurology, 6,* 530–535.

Damascio, A.R. (1994). *Descartes' error: Emotion, reason, and the human brain.* New York: Avon Books.

Dawson, G., & Lewy, A. (1989). Reciprocal subcortical-cortical influences in autism: The role of attention mechanisms. In G. Dawson (Ed.), *Autism: Nature, diagnosis, and treatment* (pp. 144–173). New York: Guilford Press.

Definition of autism. (1996, May–June). *Advocate, 28*(3), 3.

Eaves, R.C. (1993a). A theory of human behavior. In R.C. Eaves & P.J. McLaughlin (Eds.), *Recent advances in special education and rehabilitation* (pp. 3–29). Austin, TX: PRO-ED.

Eaves, R.C. (1993b). *Pervasive Developmental Disorder Rating Scale.* Opelika, AL: Small World.

Eaves, R.C. (1993c). *Self-Injury Observation Schedule.* Opelika, AL: Small World.

Eaves, R.C. (1996a). *Taxonomy of goals and objectives: Autistic disorder.* Opelika, AL: Small World.

Eaves, R.C. (1996b). *Pervasive Developmental Disorder Observation Schedule.* Opelika, AL: Small World.

Eaves, R.C. (1996c). *Critical Personal Information Test.* Opelika, AL: Small World.

Eaves, R.C., Ho, H.H., & Eaves, D.M. (1994). Subtypes of autism by cluster analysis. *Journal of Autism and Developmental Disorders, 24,* 3–22.

Eaves, R.C., & McLaughlin, P.J. (1977). A systems approach to the assessment of the child and his environment: Getting back to basics. *Journal of Special Education, 11,* 99–111.

Eaves, R.C., McLaughlin, P.J., & Foster, G.G. (1979). Some simple statistics for classroom use. *Diagnostique, 4,* 3–12.

Hebb, D.O. (1955). Drives and the CNS (conceptual nervous system). *Psychological Review, 62,* 243–254.

Hertzig, M.E., Snow, M.E., New, E., & Shapiro, T. (1990). *DSM-III* and *DSM-III-R* diagnosis of autism and pervasive developmental disorder in nursery school children. *Journal of the American Academy of Child and Adolescent Psychiatry, 29,* 123–126.

Jackson, J.H. (1958). *Selected writings of John Huhlings Jackson.* In J. Taylor (Ed.), New York: Basic Books.

Kagan, J. (1994). *Galen's prophesy.* New York: Basic Books.

Kanner, L. (1943). Autistic disturbances of affective contact. *Nervous Child, 2,* 217–250.

Kanner, L. (1954). To what extent is early infantile autism determined by constitutional inadequacies? *Proceedings of the Association of Research on Nervous and Mental Disorders, 33,* 378–385.

Kaufman, A.S., & Kaufman, N.L. (1990). *Kaufman Brief Intelligence Test.* Circle Pines, MN: American Guidance Service.

Kinsbourne, M. (1980). Do repetitive patterns in children and animals serve a dearousing function? *Journal of Developmental and Behavioral Pediatrics, 1,* 39–42.

Kinsbourne, M. (1987). Cerebral-brainstem relations in infantile autism. In E. Schopler & G.B. Mesibov (Eds.), *Neurobiological issues in autism* (pp. 107–125). New York: Plenum.

Kolb, B., & Whishaw, I.Q. (1980). *Fundamentals of human neuropsychology.* New York: W.H. Freeman.

Krug, D.A., Arick, J.R., & Almond, P.J. (1995). *Autism Screening Instrument for Educational Planning.* Austin, TX: PRO-ED.

Lindsley, D.B. (1958). Psychophysiology and perception. In *Current trends in the description and analysis of behavior* (pp. 48–91). Pittsburgh, PA: University of Pittsburgh Press.

Locke, B.J., Banken, J.A., & Mahone, C.H. (1994). The graying of autism: Etiology and prevalence at fifty. In J.L. Matson (Ed.), *Autism in children and adults: Etiology, assessment, and intervention* (pp. 37–57). Pacific Grove, CA: Brooks/Cole.

Magoun, H.W. (1958). *The waking brain.* Springfield, IL: Charles C. Thomas.

Maurice, C. (1993). *Let me hear your voice: A family's triumph over autism.* New York: Fawcett Columbine.

Mesibov, G., Schopler, E., Schaffer, B., & Landrus, R. (1988). *Adolescent and Adult Psychoeducational Profile: Volume IV.* Austin, TX: PRO-ED.

Naglieri, J.A. (1985). *Matrix Analogies Test-Expanded Form.* San Antonio, TX: The Psychological Corporation.

Newborg, J., Stock, J.R., Wnek, L., Guidubaldi, J., & Svinicki, J. (1984). *The Battelle Developmental Inventory.* Allen, TX: DLM/Teaching Resources.

Ornitz, E.M. (1989). Autism at the interface between sensory and information processing. In G. Dawson (Ed.), *Autism: Nature, diagnosis, and treatment* (pp. 174–207). New York: Guilford Press.

Ornstein, R. (1991). *The evolution of consciousness.* New York: Prentice Hall.

Ornstein, R. (1995). *The roots of the self.* New York: HarperCollins Publishers.

Oswald, D.P., Ellis, C.R., Singh, N.N., & Singh, Y.N. (1994). Self-injury. In J.L. Matson (Ed.), *Autism in children and adults: Etiology, assessment, and intervention* (pp. 147–164). Pacific Grove, CA: Brooks/Cole.

Papez, J.W. (1937). A proposed mechanism of emotion. *Archives of Neurology and Psychiatry, 38,* 724–744.

Raven, J.C. (1993). *Coloured Progressive Matrices.* San Antonio, TX: The Psychological Corporation.

Rimland, B. (1964). *Infantile autism.* Englewood Cliffs, NJ: Prentice-Hall.

Rimland, B. (1994). The modern history of autism: A personal perspective. In J.L. Matson (Ed.), *Autism in children and adults: Etiology, assessment, and intervention* (pp. 1–11). Pacific Grove, CA: Brooks/Cole.

Ritvo, R., Freeman, B., Pingree, C., Mason-Brothers, A., Jorde, O.L., Jenson, W., McMahon, W., Petersen, P., Mo, A., & Ritvo, A. (1989). The UCLA-University of Utah epidemiologic survey of autism: Prevalence. *American Journal of Psychiatry, 146,* 194–199.

Ritvo, R., & Freeman, B.J. (1978). National Society for Autistic Children definition of the syndrome of autism. *Journal of Autism and Developmental Disorders, 8,* 162–170.

Rutter, M. (1978). Diagnosis and definition of childhood autism. *Journal of Autism and Developmental Disorders, 8,* 139–161.

Rutter, M., & Schopler, E. (1988). Autism and pervasive developmental disorders: Concepts and diagnostic issues. In E. Schopler & G. Mesibov (Eds.), *Diagnosis and treatment of autism* (pp. 15–37). New York: Plenum.

Schopler, E., Reichler, R.J., Bashford, A., Lansing, M.D., & Marcus, L.M. (1990). *Psychoeducational Profile-Revised: Volume I.* Austin, TX: PRO-ED.

Schopler, E., Reichler, R.J., & Renner, B.R. (1988). *The Childhood Autism Rating Scale.* Los Angeles: Western Psychological Services.

Sevin, J.A., Matson, J.L., Coe, D., Love, S.R., Matese, M.J., & Benevidez, D.A. (1991). *Empirically derived subtypes of pervasive developmental disorders: A cluster analysis.* Unpublished manuscript.

Siegel, B., Anders, T.F., Ciaranello, R.D., Bienenstock, B., & Kramer, H.C. (1986). Empirically derived subclassification of the autistic syndrome. *Journal of Autism and Developmental Disorders, 16,* 275–293.

Sparrow, S., Balla, D., & Cicchetti, D.A. (1984). *Interview edition, expanded form manual, Vineland Adaptive Behavior Scales.* Circle Pines, MN: American Guidance Service.

Spitzer, R.L., & Siegel, B. (1990). The *DSM-III-R* field trial of pervasive developmental disorders. *Journal of the American Academy of Child and Adolescent Psychiatry, 29,* 855–862.

Volkmar, F. (1987). Diagnostic issues in the pervasive developmental disorders. *Journal of Child Psychology and Psychiatry, 28,* 365–369.

Wing, L., & Attwood, A. (1987). Syndromes of autism and atypical development. In D.J. Cohen & A. Donnelan (Eds.), *Handbook of autism and pervasive developmental disorders* (pp. 3–19). New York: Wiley.

World Health Organization. (1977). *International statistical classification of diseases, injuries, and causes of death* (9th ed.). Geneva: Author.

World Health Organization. (1992). *International statistical classification of diseases, injuries, and causes of death* (10th ed.). Geneva: Author.

Chapter 15

VOCATIONAL ASSESSMENT OF SPECIAL NEEDS LEARNERS

G. FRANKLIN ELROD, DENNIS G. TESOLOWSKI, AND
SANDY D. DEVLIN

OVERVIEW

Defining Vocational Assessment

Many terms have been used in labeling the assessment of vocationally related skills. Terms such as *career assessment, vocational evaluation,* and *vocational assessment* are often used synonymously. In practice, however, these three terms refer to processes that have distinct origins, definitions, and purposes. The following section provides a brief overview of each of these processes.

Career Assessment

Career assessment involves an examination of an individual's progress along a career development continuum. Just as there are stages, for example, in cognitive development, language acquisition, and reading proficiency, so too are there stages to career development. Career development is viewed as a lifelong process wherein individuals assume various roles from birth through the preschool and elementary-school years to secondary and postsecondary education, continuing into one or more vocations, and ending with the retirement years.

Career development models (see, e.g., Brolin, 1978, 1983, 1989; Clark & Kolstoe, 1990; Halpern, 1985; Kokaska, Gruenhagen, Razeghi, & Fair, 1985) take a holistic view of an individual's career, focusing not only on vocational roles (e.g., employee) but also on the other roles that a person assumes during a lifespan. These other roles could include, for example, student, parent, citizen, volunteer, and homemaker. It follows, therefore, that career assessment encompasses the totality of this holistic career experience, examining functional, personal, and social skills as well as occupational readiness.

The authors would like to express their appreciation for the assistance of Mr. Ray Minge, Consultant for Vocational Special Needs Education, Union County (OR) Educational Service District, and to the New Concepts Corporation of Tucson, Arizona, in the development this chapter.

Vocational Evaluation

Emanating primarily from the field of rehabilitation, vocational evaluation focuses on a narrow set of outcomes. Rather than the holistic, paid and nonpaid roles that comprise a career assessment model, vocational evaluation is conducted "to determine individual competencies, needs, and adjustments for placement in a work environment" (Veir, 1987, p. 214). Vocational evaluation as a separate entity has drawn from the fields of psychology, vocational and industrial education, occupational therapy, military training, medicine, and workshop settings. Stated another way, the function of vocational evaluation is to identify an individual's physical, mental, and emotional abilities, limitations, and tolerances in order to predict his or her current and future employment potential and adjustment. The goals of vocational evaluation seek to answer the following four questions:

- Is the individual ready to decide on a vocational training curriculum?
- If so, which course or program of study is best suited to the individual?
- If not, which of the individual's weaknesses need strengthening?
- What plan would promote changes in the individual or the environment to enhance the individual's decision on a vocational training program? (Roberts, 1970).

Thus, vocational evaluation addresses various domains, all directed at facilitating the progress of an individual toward job training and eventual job placement. Vocational evaluation, therefore, often involves the use of simulated or actual work settings to better gain a perspective of specific tasks (e.g., sorting, alphabetizing) that may be relevant to success on a particular job.

Vocational Assessment

Expanding on the domains of vocational evaluation while retaining an occupational orientation, vocational assessment affords equal weight to traditional educational variables. In other words, the examination of academic and sociobehavioral variables is viewed as an integral part of the process of determining vocational program placement by identifying needed support services and curricular adjustments with the ultimate goal of facilitating job training and placement. Thus, vocational assessment has been defined as "a comprehensive process conducted over a period of time, involving a multidisciplinary team . . . with the purpose of identifying individual characteristics, education, training, and placement needs, which provide educators the basis for planning an individual's program" (Dahl, Appleby, & Lipe, 1978, p. 103).

Vocational assessment (differs from the two other diagnostic approaches discussed above in that:

- Vocational assessment is not as holistic as career assessment (i.e., nonpaid roles are rarely the focus).

- Vocational assessment is a more ongoing process than vocational evaluation, often extending from the beginning of secondary schooling through actual job placement.
- Vocational assessment gives equal weight to educational variables (which is also true of career assessment).

Because vocational assessment is multidisciplinary the process may be completed by a variety of professionals including regular and special educators, guidance counselors, school administrators, and vocational educators. Parents can also lend valuable information to this assessment process. It should be emphasized that data gleaned from vocational assessment should not be used merely to screen students from a vocational program but should also provide insight as to how some vocational courses may be adapted, or support services provided, to enhance students' potential for success (Elrod, 1987a).

Historical Perspective

A form of vocational assessment was introduced more than 2,300 years ago when Plato proposed a series of tests for the guardians of his ideal republic (Odiorne & Miller, 1971). Situational work evaluation techniques were also mentioned by Gideon in the Biblical book of *Judges* (Chap. 7) when he selected 300 warriors to fight the Midianites (Jaffee, 1965; Tesolowski & Morgan, 1980).

However, based on more recent history, the systematic study of work potential seems to have spanned a period of approximately 65 to 75 years, beginning with World War I. Neff (1968) identified the following four approaches to vocational assessment:

- Mental testing
- Job analysis
- Work samples
- Situational assessment

Any history of vocational assessment must necessarily focus on legislative enactments, which in turn drive programs and specific themes. Key legislation with provisions focusing on vocational assessment and training can be subdivided into categories representing fields from which they have emanated. Three fields that have had a major impact on vocational assessment are vocational education, rehabilitation, and special education (Phelps & Frasier, 1988). These three categories are discussed from a historical perspective below, along with the umbrella civil rights provisions mandated by the Americans with Disabilities Act (U.S. Congress, 1990a).

Vocational Education

The early years of the twentieth century in the United States were ones of growing industrialization, expanding agricultural production, and increasing numbers of immigrants from other lands. The continuing and urgent need for a well-trained work force was the major impetus for the enactment of the Smith-Hughes Act (U.S. Congress, 1917). This act was the outcome of the work of the Commission on National Aid to Vocational Education, which viewed vocational training as a necessary ingredient to "democratize the education of the country" (Commission on National Aid to Vocational Education, 1914, p. 12).

Another major event that prompted a renewed interest in vocational education was the Soviet Union's successful launching of Sputnik in 1957. Concerns surfaced that students in the United States lacked technical knowledge. These concerns were translated into action with the passage of the National Education Act (U.S. Congress, 1958). This act emphasized the need for occupational training by earmarking funds for the preparation of skilled technicians, supporting students interested in higher education, and providing $15 million for the construction of area vocational education programs (Nystrom & Bayne, 1979).

During the early to mid-1960s, the Civil Rights Movement absorbed much of the energy of the United States. It suddenly became clear that equal occupational opportunities were only valid when they were accompanied by comprehensive vocational training. Thus, the Vocational Education Act (U.S. Congress, 1963) was passed to open vocational programs to disadvantaged populations by providing more vocational guidance and career planning services. This act also provided funds for developing programs for students with academic, social, or other disabilities of such severity that they impaired the students' chances of completing regular vocational education programs.

In 1968, through the Vocational Education Amendments (U.S. Congress, 1968), monies were set aside to be used expressly for disadvantaged and disabled populations. As a result, a state was required to spend at least 10% of its total federal vocational education allotment on programs for disadvantaged students and one-half of that on programs for students with disabilities. These earmarked funds were enacted to bolster the Vocational Education Act of 1963, which by itself did not achieve the desired gains for these target student populations.

The Carl D. Perkins Vocational and Technical Education Act (U.S. Congress, 1984) is the only legislative enactment that mentions vocational assessment (Veir, 1987). Continuing the theme of providing for vocational programs for disabled and disadvantaged populations, the Perkins Act mandated "an assessment of the interests, abilities, and special needs of a [disabled or disadvantaged] student with respect to completing successfully the vocational education program" (U.S. Congress, 1984).

The most recent vocational education legislative initiative has underscored the relationship between traditional academics and vocational training. The Carl D. Perkins Vocational and Applied Technology Education Act Amendments (U.S. Congress, 1990b) promote a shift in vocational education from a job-skills orientation toward a vehicle for learning academics and thinking skills, and for linking thought to action (Wirt, 1991). Increasingly, therefore, vocational assessment must be viewed as a key bridge.

Thus, since the turn of the century, vocational education has sought to offer contemporary training to all students, including those with disadvantages or disabilities. Legislation emanating from that field has enunciated this theme. With the passage of the Perkins Act of 1984 and the subsequent amendments of 1990, the assessment of vocational skills has now become an integral component of the over-all assessment menu available for use with students.

Rehabilitation

With the passage of the Rehabilitation Act of 1973 (U.S. Congress, 1973), the federal government broadened the concept of rehabilitation from one focusing primarily on the outcome of competitive employment to one also including interme-diate outcomes such as sheltered or homebound employment (Phelps & Frasier, 1988). Of course, the most noteworthy sections of the Rehabilitation Act, Sections 503 and 504, promote affirmative action and anti-discriminatory policies, respec-tively, on behalf of persons with disabilities. The act, however, also authorized the use of an individualized written rehabilitation program (IWRP), which required:

- A statement of long-range rehabilitation goals and related objectives
- A statement of specific rehabilitation services to be provided
- Projected dates for initiation and duration of services
- Objective evaluation criteria
- Where appropriate, a detailed explanation of the availability of a client assis-tance project (Phelps & Frasier, 1988, p. 14)

Thus, the guidelines for development of the IWRP, which closely parallel those for development of the individualized education plan (IEP), either directly or indirectly implied that some form of assessment be conducted. If individualized goals and objectives were to be provided, these provisions would have to be based on the needs of an individual client. Thus, an assessment of a client's vocational abilities and limitations would have to be conducted. In addition, the IWRP guidelines specifi-cally mention that "objective evaluation criteria" be developed to assess a client's progress toward rehabilitation. Such an evaluation would necessarily involve an ongoing vocational assessment of a client's skills relative to the skills the client possessed prior to commencement of the individualized rehabilitation program.

New directions in rehabilitation and training were initiated with the passage of the Rehabilitation Act Amendments (U.S. Congress, 1974) and the Rehabilitation, Comprehensive Services, and Developmental Disabilities Amendments (U.S. Con-gress, 1978). The 1974 amendments provided for community service employment and projects for training persons with severe disabilities in "real work settings" (Phelps & Frasier, 1988, p. 16). The amendments of 1978 strengthened affirmative action provisions for persons with disabilities. This strengthening was so pro-nounced that the amendments have been interpreted as entitlements that permit persons with disabilities to receive services as a right rather than as a privilege (Kiernan & Payne, 1982).

The contributions of the field of rehabilitation have augmented and, in some cases, preceded efforts from education in the vocational preparation of persons with disabilities. In general, while providing a foundation of antidiscrimination and affirmative action, rehabilitation legislation established the basis for IWRP develop-ment. These guidelines directly and indirectly promoted the use of assessment and evaluation in working with individual clients.

Special Education

The Education for All Handicapped Children Act (EAHCA; U.S. Congress, 1975) established a foundation for providing a free, appropriate, public education for all students with disabilities. This act includes vocational education under the rubric of the education that must be free, appropriate, and public (Hursh & Kerns, 1988). Under guarantees of the EAHCA, the provision of least restrictive environment (LRE) is most pertinent to vocational assessment. By linking the concept of LRE with the concept of vocational education, the thrust of vocational assessment should therefore identify a student's strengths and limitations relative to vocational training and to the greatest extent possible promote the education of students with disabilities in the least restrictive vocational setting.

The Education of the Handicapped Act Amendments (U.S. Congress, 1983) initiated the allocation of grants for developing programs for secondary special-education and transition services. This initiative was directed at reducing high levels of unemployment among individuals with disabilities while enhancing better service coordination among the various agencies (including schools) that provide job preparation and occupational orientation services (Phelps & Frasier, 1988).

A policy thrust from the U.S. Office of Special Education and Rehabilitation Services in the mid-1980s (see Will, 1984) prompted the development of educational programs that would foster the occupational outlook of students with disabilities. At approximately the same time, several statewide follow-up studies underscored the need to better prepare students with disabilities for the world of work (Edgar, Levine, & Maddox, 1986; Hasazi, Gordon, Roe, Hull, Finck, & Salembier, 1985; Mithaug, Horiuchi, & Fanning, 1985). As a result of that policy initiative and these follow-up studies, special educators became more cognizant of incorporating career, prevocational, and vocational goals and objectives into students' individualized education plans. Thus, the assessment of variables relative to these three domains emerged as a programmatic influence, which currently continues to be evidenced.

The most recent special-education legislation is the Individuals with Disabilities Education Act (IDEA; U.S. Congress, 1990c). With regard to assessment practices, IDEA establishes that "transition services" must be based on an individual student's needs, which encompass that student's vocational interests. Furthermore, IDEA stipulates that a student's individualized education plan (IEP) must provide a statement of needed transition services, beginning no later than age 16 and continuing annually thereafter. For students who might possess more serious disabilities, the transition statement can begin on the IEP at age 14 or younger.

Civil Rights

The theme of serving Americans with disabilities has been revitalized with the passage of the Americans with Disabilities Act (ADA; U.S. Congress, 1990a). This act is intended to extend and protect the civil rights of Americans with disabilities, thereby ending the unjustified segregation and exclusion of such persons from the mainstream of American life. Congress, in enacting this piece of legislation, focused on the fact that 43 million Americans have one or more physical or mental disabilities, and that this number is increasing as the population as a whole ages.

Congress furthermore had to come to terms with the fact that Americans with disabilities often encounter discrimination in such critical areas as employment, housing, public accommodations, education, transportation, communication, recreation, health services, voting, and access to public services. This is to provide legal recourse for discrimination against persons with disabilities, just as is currently available for discrimination based on race, color, sex, national origin, religion, and age. Justin Dart of the President's Committee on Employment of People with Disabilities indicated that the ADA establishes "a clear and comprehensive prohibition of discrimination on the basis of disability" (Dart, 1990, p. 1).

With regard to assessment, Section 102, Title 1 of the ADA specifically directs employers to use tests that measure the job skills of an applicant rather than reflect the applicant's disability. It follows, therefore, that vocational assessment conducted in the educational setting should focus on the student's skill level while addressing adaptations that can facilitate successful completion of vocational training.

FORMAL ASSESSMENT OF VOCATIONAL SKILLS

Work Sample Evaluation

Historical Background

The relatively short history of work sample evaluation is described in Pruitt's (1977) text. He stated that the first work sample, developed by Munsterberg, was a model of a street car designed to try out prospective operators for the Boston Railroad Company. The second oldest reference by Pruitt indicated that a standardized work sample was developed in the late 1920s to select garment machine operators (Treat, 1929).

During the past 50 years, literally thousands of noncommercial work samples have been developed in rehabilitation facilities throughout the United States. However, the first commercial work evaluation system, commonly referred to as The TOWER System, was developed by the Institute for the Crippled and Disabled (1959) in New York. This system was formally titled TOWER: Testing, Orientation, and Work Evaluation in Rehabilitation. Since the early 1970s, numerous commercial work sample systems have been developed by private entrepreneurs and through government-sponsored funding.

Definition of a Work Sample

Nadolsky (1977) stated that numerous definitions of the term *work sample* are available and that the essential components of these definitions are consistent with one another. In a discussion of standardized work samples, Anastasi (1961) stated:

> the [work sample] task set for the subject is similar to the work he is to perform on the job. The representativeness of the behavior sample and the closeness with which the task duplicates actual job conditions are essential considerations. For practical expediency, work samples are sometimes presented in the form of "miniature," "analogy," or "simulated" tests. (p. 468)

When discussing the work sample approach to vocational evaluation, Neff (1968) defined a work sample as "a 'mock-up'—a close simulation—of an actual industrial operation, not different in its essentials from the kind of work a potential worker would be required to perform on an ordinary job" (p. 178).

Finally, a working definition was created by Task Force Number 7 of the Vocational Evaluation Project (1975) as a part of the "Glossary of Terms Used in Vocational Evaluation." This task force defined a work sample as

> a well defined work activity involving tasks, materials, and tools which are identical or similar to those in an actual job or cluster of jobs. It is used to assess an individual's vocational aptitude, worker characteristics, and vocational interests. (p. 92)

Commercial Work Samples

The definition of the term *work sample* has established the parameters for using simulated tasks that are closely associated with occupations in the labor market. Numerous commercial work samples have been developed since the early 1970s. Generally, activities included in work sample systems are designed to be as realistic as possible, as compared to the actual work to be performed.

Benefits Associated with Work Samples

Students with special instructional needs (e.g., disadvantaged students and students with disabilities) can benefit from participating in work sample activities because these activities provide practical, hands-on experiences that cannot readily be assessed by written industrial tests or through on-the-job observation in actual work environments (Neff, 1968). Work samples often incorporate tools, technology, and standards associated with actual employment. In addition, work sample technologies are usually designed to emphasize psychomotor (performance) skills rather than cognitive (verbal or written) skills. Professional educators working as evaluators in this process are able to observe the actual work-related performance of students with special needs. It is possible to gather useful information about students' work capacity, manipulative skills, interpersonal skills, physical abilities, and work habits. It is extremely important for this information to be utilized when identifying students' strengths and limitations, determining appropriate vocational program placement, establishing realistic career goals, identifying the need for program or equipment modifications, and for placing students in jobs in the labor market (Sarkees & Scott, 1986).

Advantages of Using Commercial Work Samples

One of the primary advantages of using commercial work samples in the assessment process is that they tend to motivate students with special needs. This high level of motivation is attributed to the similarity of work sample procedures to actual job tasks. The students appear to enjoy participating in psychomotor-oriented tasks much more than pencil-and-paper tasks. Neff (1968) indicated that the virtue of the work sample approach is its strong reality orientation, its close simulation of actual work demands, and the unparalleled opportunity it affords to observe actual work behaviors in a reasonably controlled setting.

By observing the performance of students with special needs on work sample technologies, skilled evaluators can acquire useful data that assists them in predicting functional levels associated with occupational abilities, aptitudes, attitudes, tolerances, and limitations. Students are required to participate in hands-on experiences and often must exhibit the ability to follow verbal directions. The ultimate advantage for students with special needs is the potential for selecting an appropriate vocational education program, and eventually acquiring an appropriate job in the local community (Sarkees & Scott, 1986).

Availability of Commercial Work Samples

Numerous commercial work sample technologies are available. Researchers and authors such as Botterbusch (1987), Pruitt (1977), Sarkees and Scott (1986), and Scarpati (1989) have reported the specific advantages and disadvantages of many individual work sample systems. The most comprehensive comparison of vocational assessment and evaluation systems was conducted by Brown, McDaniel, and Couch (1994). Their publication, entitled *Vocational Evaluation Systems and Software: A Consumer's Guide,* systematically compares commercially produced work sample systems and accompanying software packages. This source, which is must reading for anyone who wants to learn more about the advantages and disadvantages of work sample systems.†

Table 15–1 displays corporate names and addresses for selected commercial work samples, dexterity tests, and work simulators. It is suggested that these companies be contacted for specifics on validity, reliability, and use of the samples listed.

A Vision of Work Sampling Technologies of the Future

Several corporations that produce and market *work simulators* are listed in Table 15–1. These high technology work simulators, which appear to have evolved from work sampling technology, seem to be on the cutting-edge of vocational evaluation and assessment procedures. Futuristic work simulators are expanding the boundaries of traditional work sampling technologies and curriculum-based assessment procedures. They are making it possible to gather more valid data related to many of the following critical vocational assessment areas: vocational interests and values, career awareness, physical skills, functional academic skills, aptitudes and worker traits, specific vocational skills, work behaviors and attitudes, learning style, related functional living skills, career decision-making skills, job-seeking skills, and personal understanding of oneself and the world of work (Peterson & Peterson, 1986).

The Critical Aspect of Collecting and Using Valid Data

Data collected through the vocational assessment process is generally used to determine the direction of each special needs student's adult life. More specifically, this

†Available through: Ronald Fry, Manager, The Rehabilitation Resource, Stout Vocational Rehabilitation Institute, School of Education and Human Resources, University of Wisconsin-Stout, Menomonie, WI 54751.

Table 15–1. Corporate names and addresses for selected commercial work sample technologies

Corporation/Address	Work Sample Names
Attainment Company P.O. Box 103 Oregon, WI 53575	Work Skill Development Package
Baltimore Therapeutic Equipment 7455-L New Ridge Road Hanover, MD 21076–3105	Bolt Box Assembly Tree
Baltimore Therapeutic Equipment 1202 Bernard Drive Baltimore, MD 21223	BTE Work Simulator, Model WS10 BTE Work Simulator, Model WS20
Career Evaluation Systems, Inc. 7788 Milwaukee Ave. Niles, IL 60648	Career Evaluation System
Easy Street Environments Health Services Marketing, Ltd. 6908 East Thomas Road, Suite 201 Scottsdale, AZ 85251	Work Hardening, Office & Factory Modules
Dr. Edward Hester University of Kansas Lawrence, KS 66045	Hester Evaluation System
ICD Rehabilitation and Research Center 340 East 24th St. New York, NY 10010	TOWER Worksamples Micro-TOWER
Jastak Associates 1526 Gilpin Ave. Wilmington, DE 19806	Wide Range Employment Sample Test (WREST)
Loredan Biomedical, Inc. 1632 DaVinci Ct. P.O. Box 1154 Davis, CA 95617	LIDO WorkSET
McCarron-Dial P.O. Box 45628 Dallas, TX 75245	McCarron-Dial Work Evaluation System
New Concepts Corporation 2341 S. Friebus Ave., Suite 14 Tucson, AZ 85713	Singer Worksamples
Physio-Tek, Inc. P.O. Box 190 Martinez, CA 94553	Human Engineering Center

Table 15–1.   *(Continued)*

Corporation/Address	Work Sample Names
Piney Mountain Press, Inc. P.O. Box 333 Cleveland, GA 30528	Skills Assessment Module Prevocational Assessment Screen
Prep, Inc. 1007 Whitehead Road Ext. Trenton, NJ 08638	Coats Worksamples
Psychological Corporation 1001 Polk Street San Francisco, CA 94109	Crawford Small Parts Bennett Hand Tool
S.A.V.E. Enterprises P.O. Box 5871 Rome, GA 30161	Systematic Approach to Vocational Education
Talent Assessment, Inc. P.O. Box 5087 Jacksonville, FL 32247	Talent Assessment Program
Valpar International Corporation P.O. Box 5767 Tucson, AZ 85703–5767	Valpar Component Worksamples MESA Computerized Screening Tool Valpar 17
Vocational Assessment Consultants P.O. Box 64401 Virginia Beach, VA 23464	Vocational Assessment System
Vocational Research Institute Jewish Employment and Vocational 1528 Walnut Street, Suite 1502 Philadelphia, PA 19102	JEVS Worksamples
Work Evaluation Systems Technology 1950 Freeman Long Beach, CA 90804	WEST 1 & 2 Lifting WEST 3 Comprehensive Weight WEST 4 Upper Extremity WEST Bus Bench WEST Tool Sort
Work Recovery, Inc. 2341 S. Friebus Ave., Suite 14 Tucson, AZ 85713	ERGOS Work Simulator
The Work System Lake Forest Health Services 31740 Franklin Fairway Farmington Hills, MI 48018	The Work System: Work Simulations for Sustained Productivity

information is used to identify in which vocational education program a student will be allowed to participate and, possibly, to ascertain that student's eventual job placement when he or she exits the school system. Certainly, the importance of this information is magnified when the lifelong ramifications of these decisions are reflected upon. The concern about using valid data on which to base decisions has led to the evolution of work simulators. This new breed of work sampling technology focuses on the concept of *physical/functional capacities assessment.*

While educational agencies (i.e., the public schools) may not be assessing students to determine whether they should be hired, they *are* making decisions that will very likely affect the entirety of these students' adult working lives. After all, decisions are being made that relegate individual students to specific vocational education programs and, possibly, eventual job placement. Consequently, the importance of using objective, valid data based upon actual occupational standards is critical to the assessment process.

Physical/Functional Capacities Assessment

Work sampling technologies and curriculum-based vocational assessment rating instruments have often focused on collecting useful data related to physical and functional abilities. However, the data generated through these processes is often subjective. In work simulator approaches, physical and functional capacities assessment is a highly structured, interdisciplinary, individualized evaluation program designed to provide a benchmark of the individual's physical and vocational functioning. It includes a baseline assessment of physical performance that is related to the physical and functional demand factors defined by the U.S. Department of Labor (Work Recovery Incorporated, 1988, p. 4). Drawing from the fields of ergonomics (the science of maximizing comfort on the job) and engineering, work simulator technology has resulted in a system that focuses on the examinee by considering the education, emotions, aptitudes, interests, attitudes, and other relevant data needed to become a successful worker.

The ERGOS™ Work Simulator (Work Recovery Incorporated, 1989), for example, has five component units that are used to collect functional capacities assessment data. These components are:

1. Strength measurement simulation
2. Whole body range of motion simulation
3. Work endurance simulation
4. Standing work tolerance simulation
5. Seated work range and upper extremity simulation (Brandon & Snyder, 1989, p. 215)

The work simulator approach provides a step toward more valid and reliable assessment data. The more valid and reliable vocational assessment can become, the more confidence we can have in predicting vocational potential. In fact, the ERGOS™ Work Simulator is currently being used in a demonstration project to test Social Security claimants with a potential cost savings of $54.5 million to $129.6

million (Work Recovery Incorporated, 1995). As a whole, formal vocational assessment is evolving toward this more valid and reliable assessment process.

INFORMAL ASSESSMENT OF VOCATIONAL SKILLS

An alternative to the norm-referenced instrumentation of formal assessment, criterion-referenced informal assessment has gained in popularity in recent years. A rationale for using informal assessment procedures often focuses on its economic advantages, its ease of administration, and its direct application to instruction (Elrod, Isbell, & Braziel, 1989). Specific objectives of informal vocational assessment include the following:

- The identification of students with learning problems
- The identification of students who may be potential failures
- The diagnosis of students' academic strengths and limitations
- The gleaning of information to assist in curricular and instructional modification
- The assistance in the identification of appropriate classroom materials based on needed classroom skills
- The use of classroom teachers or other personnel familiar with the curriculum in the design of the assessment instrument (Wisconsin Vocational Studies Center, 1980)

Classroom-Based Techniques

Informal assessment techniques can address prevocational skills that influence success in vocational training and vocationally related skills that have direct bearing on vocational achievement. Such skills as work habits, occupational interests and knowledge, academic skill level, and personal-social skills can be assessed informally. Classroom-based assessment techniques that evaluate a student's *typical performance* rather than *optimal performance* as might be gleaned in a more formal testing situation (Tindal & Marston, 1990). Classroom-based assessment can be conducted by regular and special educators, with ongoing evaluation being conducted by vocational educators. Parents may also be a part of the informal vocational assessment intake process.

As displayed in Table 15–2, academic and occupational skills can be self-assessed in an informal fashion. By using a simple Y (yes) or N (no) response mode, elementary-age children can self-report their own perceptions regarding their academic skills and their work habits. The behaviors identified in Table 15–2 are applicable to both school and work situations (Elrod et al., 1989). Such a scale can be paired with self-monitoring behavioral techniques. While not being vocational assessment, per se, such an evaluation, if conducted with preadolescents, can assist in building critical work habits that will later have a direct bearing on a student's potential for vocational success. If necessary, the teacher conducting the assessment may read the scale items to account for lower reading skill levels of all or some of the children in the class.

Table 15–2.   Sample student academic/occupational self-evaluation scale

Academic/Occupational Skills

I enjoy keeping my desk neat.	Y	N
I enjoy writing letters to my friends.	Y	N
I enjoy answering questions in class.	Y	N
I like to do crossword puzzles.	Y	N
I like to play sports.	Y	N
I can count money easily.	Y	N
I like to think about what I will be when I grow up.	Y	N
I plan my own schedule.	Y	N
I enjoy taking care of others.	Y	N
I like to watch adults at work.	Y	N
I enjoy talking on the telephone.	Y	N
I like to run.	Y	N
I enjoy going to new places.	Y	N
I like people to count on me.	Y	N
I like to learn about inventors.	Y	N
I can draw maps well.	Y	N
I enjoy earning money.	Y	N
I like to save money.	Y	N
I complete all of my homework.	Y	N

Source: "Assessing Transition-Related Variables From Kindergarten Through Grade 12: Practical Applications" by G.F. Elrod, C.H. Isbell, and P.M. Braziel, 1989, *Diagnostique, 14,* p. 253. Copyright 1989 by the Council for Educational Diagnostic Services. Adapted by permission.

An important but nonetheless neglected aspect of classroom-based vocational assessment is teacher self-evaluation. Assessment of vocationally related skills should not be simply an annual activity for reporting purposes. The information gleaned from such assessment practices must be incorporated into instruction at all grade levels. Table 15–3 provides a teacher self-evaluation scale that can be used weekly or monthly as a reminder to infuse career/vocational concepts into the existing curriculum (Elrod et al., 1989). A modified version of this scale can be used to facilitate a carryover of instruction in vocationally related skills with parents.

Determining a student's vocational interests has been identified as a key dimension of vocational assessment (Veir, 1987). While outstanding commercially produced vocational interest scales exist, such as the AAMD-Becker Reading-Free Vocational Interest Inventory (Becker, 1975), the Self-Directed Search, Form E (Holland, 1985), and the Wide Range Interest and Opinion Test (Jastak & Jastak, 1974), the classroom teacher, through a structured interview process, can assess a student's career interests. As presented in Table 15–4, a series of questions addressing vocational preference and student knowledge about those preferences can indicate a degree of career maturity (Elrod et al., 1989).

While the evaluation instrument shown in Table 15–5 may not appear to be vocational in nature, it is actually a component of the Alternative Learning Program (ALPs) Assessment Battery (Looslie, 1991) of the Union County (Oregon) Educational Service District. As an informal diagnostic tool, the ALPs Battery is

Table 15–3.   Example of teacher self-evaluation scale

Self-Evaluation Scale Items			*Rating*		
I integrate transition-related skills within basic skills objectives.	1	2	3	4	5
I encourage parental involvement in curricular decisions.	1	2	3	4	5
I select classroom activities which are applicable to real-life settings.	1	2	3	4	5
I use a concrete approach in demonstrating problem solving.	1	2	3	4	5
I use a "hands-on" approach to teaching.	1	2	3	4	5
I maintain a classroom environment which stimulates independence.	1	2	3	4	5
I am consistent with my behavior management.	1	2	3	4	5
I implement student self-management techniques.	1	2	3	4	5
I create opportunities for group interaction.	1	2	3	4	5
I seek support of other professionals with regard to program planning.	1	2	3	4	5
I assign classroom duties to promote proper work attitudes.	1	2	3	4	5

Rating Scale: 1 = Almost never; 2 = Occasionally; 3 = About half of the time; 4 = Usually; 5 = Almost always.
Source: "Assessing Transition-Related Variables From Kindergarten Through Grade 12: Practical Applications" by G.F. Elrod, C.H. Isbell, and P.M. Braziel, 1989, *Diagnostique, 14,* p. 254. Copyright © 1989 by the Council for Educational Diagnostic Services. Reprinted with permission.

composed of three domains: reading, mathematics, and language arts. Each of these three skill areas are requisite competencies to success in the ALPs course for students with behavior disorders. The content of the program is a school-based production enterprise that includes manufacturing, advertising, sales, and reinvestment of profits. Therefore, reading, mathematics, and language arts are essential skills for success in the ALPs curriculum. As a pretest, the ALPs Battery can determine the support that each student will need to complete the program successfully. The ALPs Battery is also correlated with skills the students will need if they elect to take the General Education Diploma (GED) examination. Thus, in the case of the ALPs course, traditional academics are viewed as essential for competent performance in the school-based enterprise.

In a pure sense, a program such as the ALPs is not considered a vocational

Table 15–4.   Sample vocational interest interview questions

1.   What job would you like to have when you finish your education?
2.   Do you like to work (play) inside or outside?
3.   Do you like to work (play) alone or with others?
4.   Do you like to have it quiet when you work (play)?
5.   Would you be willing to move in order to get a job?
6.   Would you mind working in the evenings or on weekends?
7.   Would you mind receiving further training to become a better employee or receive a promotion?
8.   What kind of yearly salary do you feel is reasonable?
9.   Would you prefer a desk job or a job where you can use your physical skills?
10.   Would you prefer working for a large company or a small business?

Source: "Assessing Transition-Related Variables From Kindergarten Through Grade 12: Practical Applications" by G.F. Elrod, C.H. Isbell, and P.M. Braziel, 1989, *Diagnostique, 14,* p. 255. Copyright © 1989 by the Council for Educational Diagnostic Services. Reprinted with permission.

Table 15–5.   Selected items from ALPs Assessment Battery

Mathematics
6) 4038 + 2379 + 401 =
7) $2.69 + $3.74 =
34) 8 5/12 − 3 2/3 =
39) Sam has 4 coins in his pocket: a 50-cent piece, a quarter, a dime, and a penny. How much money does Sam have in change?
44) Terry applied for a typing job that required a typing speed of at least 65 words per minute. She was given a 6-minute timed typing test. Terry typed 348 words. How many words per minute did Terry average on this test?

Language Arts
Choose the option that makes the sentence correct.
_____ 2.   _____ both excellent softball players.
      a. Their
      b. Theirs
      c. They're
_____ 3.   The President talked, laughed, and _____.
      a. he was joking.
      b. joked.
      c. he joked.
Choose the correct sentence.
_____ 2.   a. Sandy, will you please give me a call?
      b. Sandy will you please give me a call?
      c. Sandy, will you please give me a call.

Reading
[The following items are based on reading passages.]
Select the correct response.
_____ 2.   If you follow the advice in the passage, what does the author predict will happen?
      a. The car will break down within a week.
      b. You will save money by buying a new car.
      c. You will have found a good mechanic.
      d. The car will never break down.
      e. You will have found a car worth buying.
_____ 4.   The main purpose of this passage is to:
      a. give factual information on buying a car.
      b. tell you which model of car to buy.
      c. get you to look under the hood carefully.
      d. get you to hire a mechanic.
      e. warn you about used car salesmen.

program. It is not a course designed to prepare students for a specific occupation (e.g., plumbing, drafting, or welding). However, some students, such as those with behavior disorders, are usually underrepresented in traditional vocational programs. Thus, it can be argued that since a program such as ALPs does, in fact, prepare students for the world of work in a generic sense, it *does* constitute some degree of vocational training. And, if ALPs can be perceived as a generic vocational program promoting generalizable vocational skills (Greenan, 1983), then the ALPs Battery can be perceived as an informal vocational assessment.

Curriculum-Based Vocational Assessment

Curriculum-based vocational assessment (CBVA) has been defined as "a continuous process used to answer questions about the instruction and special service needs of individual students as they enter into and progress through specific vocational education programs" (Albright, Cobb, Sarkees, & Kingsbury, 1989, p. 144). Thus, rather than a program screening device, or a pre- and posttest procedure, CBVA is an ongoing process evaluating not only student progress but also the effect of specific instructional interventions. Distinguishing features of CBVA are as follows:

1. A response to the information needs of personnel at three stages: during the selection and planning of a student's vocational program; as the student progresses through the program; and during the transition of the student from school to competitive employment or postsecondary education.
2. An assessment activity tied directly to the student's vocational education curriculum.
3. A collaboration of personnel responsible for providing vocational instruction and special services to the student.
4. The use of criterion-referenced, performance-based, and direct procedures for determining student achievement.
5. An adaptation to community-based training environments at both the secondary and postsecondary levels (Albright et al., 1989, p. 144).

While CBVA has been defined and various approaches offered (see, e.g., Albright & Cobb, 1988; Ianacone & Leconte, 1986; Stodden, Meehan, Bisconer, & Hodell, 1989), the operationalizing of CBVA is still open to interpretation. Two factors influence this openness. First, by definition, CBVA is a *process,* not a single, standardized assessment instrument or test battery. This process may vary based on the type of vocational program, setting, and personnel. Second, by nature CBVA is *flexible* and can be adapted, not only across vocational courses but to community work sites as well. Variables influencing this flexibility include instructional pedagogy, availability and type of equipment used in instruction, adopted course text (if any), and desired outcomes (i.e., course adaptation, identification of student strengths and limitations, and community placement).

The development of a foundation of an established process on which to base CBVA, therefore, can enhance its application and exportability. As an alternative assessment approach, curriculum-based assessment has been applied to academic skills (Fuchs, Deno, & Marston, 1983), individualized education plan goals and objectives (Fuchs & Fuchs, 1986), regular-classroom instruction (Bursuck & Lessen, 1985), and the screening and referral process (Marston, Mirkin, & Deno, 1984). Such alternatives provide established processes and procedures from which CBVA can be developed and applied across vocational programs and community work sites.

A curriculum-based assessment approach proposed by Bursuck and Lessen (1987) is particularly pertinent to CBVA applications. The reasons for the relevance of this approach are:

- The use of task types (e.g., see/write, hear/write behaviors) with which to categorize competency behaviors
- The development of probes based on the categorized competency behaviors
- The use of a "work habits" assessment domain
- The application of ecological assessment through an environmental inventory

The following section, therefore, applies the Bursuck and Lessen model to CBVA. Using a vocational course in general metals, specific competency behaviors are identified and categorized into task types. This categorization is followed by work habit variables that can be assessed and by dimensions of the classroom environment that can be examined for adaptation purposes. General metals is a competency-based course providing the student with the knowledge and skills

Table 15–6.   See/write behaviors for general metals course

Copy a drawing with dimensions.
Copy safety rules.
Identify in writing various metals (e.g., brass, bronze).
Draw a ruler depicting increments to 1/64″
Identify in writing:
  Measuring tools
  Layout tools
  Cutting tools
  Filing tools
Identify in writing metal working machinery
Compute in writing:
  Multiple digit addition with regrouping
  Multiple digit subtraction with regrouping
  Multiple digit multiplication with regrouping
  Multiple digit division with regrouping
  Addition of fractions with unlike denominators
  Subtraction of fractions with unlike denominators
  Conversion of fractions to decimals
  Addition of decimals
  Subtraction of decimals
Copy notes from class demonstrations

Table 15–7. See/say behaviors for general metals course

Orally identify safety rules.
Orally recall procedures for starting and stopping metal working machinery.
Orally recite procedures for proper operation of metal working machinery.
Orally identify techniques for bending, cutting, and filing machine work.
Orally convert fractions to decimals using charts.
Orally identify drill and tap sizes from charts.

necessary in metal manufacturing (e.g., casting, sheet metal, gas welding, soldering, and ornamental iron work).

Task Types

The curriculum-based assessment model proposed by Bursuck and Lessen (1987) includes four task types: see/write behaviors, see/say behaviors, hear/write behaviors, and think/write behaviors. These four task types are applied, as described below, to the general metals course. A fifth task type, learn/perform behaviors, is added to the model to reflect the performance nature of vocational education courses.

A course in general metals includes several see/write competency behaviors (see Table 15–6). Some of these behaviors (e.g., those involving arithmetic computations) can be taught in the special class and reinforced in the vocational class. Thus, CBVA can assist in detecting generalizable skills applicable across various vocational course offerings (Greenan, 1983, 1987). The results of CBVA with the general metals course indicate substantial amounts of written work, more so than may be imagined by most special educators or diagnosticians. Additionally, a behavior such as "copy notes from a class demonstration" is a skill uniquely different from taking lecture notes in a traditional class setting. Although this note-taking skill is often taught in the special class, gleaning important information from in-class demonstrations is less emphasized. In such an instance, the vocational instructor can underscore important points during the demonstration using verbal and visual cues while this skill is being taught.

Table 15–7 displays see/say competency behaviors for general metals. Some of these behaviors (e.g., "orally convert fractions to decimals") can be converted into in-class probes whereby the instructor can quickly assess a student's knowledge or application of a procedure.

Some of the hear/write competency behaviors (e.g., "list safety rules," "spell related terms") may also be taught in a special class (see Table 15–8). It is noteworthy that CBVA clearly defines the importance of safety in a vocational course such as general metals. A mention of safety is found in four of the five domains used as task type categories.

Table 15–8. Hear/write behaviors for general metals course

List safety rules from memory.
Spell related terms from dictation.
Write class lecture notes.
List machinery operating procedures from lecture.

Table 15–9.   Think/write behaviors for general metals course

Make a drawing of a metal assembly.

Draft parts of a product to be manufactured.

Think/write behaviors, indicating that a novel outcome is expected from the synthesis of prior knowledge, are displayed in Table 15–9. An interesting factor related to the think/write behaviors (both of which involve drafting) is that other identified skills (e.g., "proper line weight" and "correct labeling and dimensions") are prerequisites to success. Thus, an initial examination of curricular requirements in a given vocational class may spawn the need to assess (and teach) such behaviors.

Because of the application and performance nature of vocational education, a fifth competency domain—learn/perform behaviors—was added to the four domains proposed by Bursuck and Lessen (1987). These learn/perform behaviors (shown in Table 15–10) focus on a demonstrated synthesis of knowledge, much of which combines behaviors from the other four competency domains. Thus, "demonstrate proper techniques for casting" can be viewed as a synthesis of the following behaviors:

1. See/write behaviors: copying safety rules; identifying various metals; and copying notes from class demonstrations
2. See/say behaviors: orally identifying safety rules; and orally converting fractions to decimals
3. Hear/write behavior: listing safety rules

Using information gained from the task-type analysis, assessment probes are designed to evaluate specific competencies. Table 15–11 provides a listing of 20 terms from the general metals course that are incorporated into a spelling probe. These same terms can be used to assess knowledge of key concepts. Some probes that are performance-based in nature may have a timed element derived from industrial standards.

Work Habits

Beyond the assessment of tasks related to specific vocational courses, CBVA should evaluate a student's work habits across several settings.

Table 15–10.   Learn/perform behaviors for general metals course

Demonstrate safety rules in shop setting.

Demonstrate proper welding procedures.

Perform proper procedures in using metal working machinery.

Demonstrate proper techniques for:

    Casting

    Forming

    Bending

Exhibit proper procedures when finishing a product.

Table 15–11. Spelling probe from general metals course

abrasive
adhesion
alloy
aluminum
anvil
beryllium
brazing
chisel
cohesion
copper
corrosion
ductility
embossing
ferrous
forge
galvanized
malleability
metallurgy
oxidation
pewter

Work habits and behaviors can be assessed using a Likert-type scale wherein specific behaviors are targeted (see Table 15–12). To glean the generalizability of these behaviors, it is suggested that such an evaluation be conducted simultaneously in different settings. For example, on a given day a regular teacher, a special-education teacher, a vocational instructor, and an employer (if work experience is an option) can complete the same rating scale on a specific student. Evaluated behaviors can thus be assessed across various environments in which the student is expected to perform. While the rating scale shown in Table 15–12 is teacher designed, there are some prepackaged, researched work-habits assessment tools available (see Rosenberg & Tesolowski, 1979; Rusch, Schutz, Mithaug, Stewart, & Mar, 1982).

Ecological Assessment

Evaluating the vocational environment in which a student performs can facilitate that student's success in that environment. Uses of ecological assessment are:

- The identification of instructionally relevant variables that can be influenced by the teacher or supervisor.
- The determination of whether a particular vocational course or work experience site is suitable for a given student.
- The distinguishing of achievement problems that are student centered or teacher centered (Bursuck & Lessen, 1987).

Thus, appropriate vocational ecological assessment should evaluate both teacher (supervisor) and student behaviors in an antecedent/behavior/consequence manner

Table 15–12.   Work habit rating scale

Student: _____

Date: _____   Evaluation Site: _____

Rater: _____

Work Behavior		Rating			
1. Dresses appropriately.	1	2	3	4	5
2. Is well-groomed.	1	2	3	4	5
3. Attends class (work) regularly.	1	2	3	4	5
4. Is punctual.	1	2	3	4	5
5. Demonstrates initiative.	1	2	3	4	5
6. Works well independently.	1	2	3	4	5
7. Works well with peers.	1	2	3	4	5
8. Works well with authority figures.	1	2	3	4	5
9. Is receptive to constructive criticism.	1	2	3	4	5
10. Shows pride in work.	1	2	3	4	5
11. Keeps neat work area.	1	2	3	4	5
12. Completes tasks on time.	1	2	3	4	5
13. Asks questions, if needed.	1	2	3	4	5
14. Accepts new responsibilities.	1	2	3	4	5
15. Solicits additional tasks (duties) when finished with a task (duty).	1	2	3	4	5

Rating Scale: 1 = Never observed; 2 = Observed sometimes; 3 = Observed about half of the time; 4 = Observed often; 5 = Always observed.

Source: "Assessing Transition-Related Variables From Kindergarten Through Grade 12: Practical Applications" by G.F. Elrod, C.H. Isbell, and P.M. Braziel, 1989, *Diagnostique, 14,* p. 257. Copyright by the Council for Educational Diagnostic Services.

(Bursuck & Lessen, 1987). Some of the variables included in the assessment device shown in Table 15–13 have been determined to correlate positively with academic achievement (Anderson, Evertson, & Brophy, 1979), success in vocational training (Elrod, 1987b), and job performance (Salzberg, McConaughy, Lignugaris/Kraft, Agran, & Stowitschek, 1987).

Specific alterations in the Bursuck and Lessen (1987) ecological assessment device were incorporated into the instrument displayed in Table 15–13. To make the instrument more applicable to vocational programs, the terms *teacher* and *supervisor* are used interchangeably to address work experiences in which an employer/supervisor rather than a teacher would be the focus of the evaluation. In addition, instead of focusing solely on academic responses (i.e., correct/incorrect answers), the vocational environment would necessarily include *performance* of skills. Thus, both successful and unsuccessful performance scenarios are used. It should be noted that the device displayed in Table 15–13 reflects only a partial ecological screening, since it focuses primarily on student-teacher (or supervisor)-peer behaviors in successful and unsuccessful situations. Other variables that can be assessed via an ecological survey would include the following: the physical setting of the vocational course/work site, the worker/student-supervisor/teacher ratio, the type of equipment needed, and the specific type of clothing necessary on the job (e.g., steel-toed work boots).

Table 15–13.   Ecological assessment instrument for vocational programs

1. Teacher (supervisor) response to successful performance:
   _____   a. immediate reinforcement
   _____   b. delayed reinforcement
   _____   c. no reinforcement
2. Student response to successful performance:
   _____   a. positive
   _____   b. negative
   _____   c. no response
3. Peer response to student's successful performance:
   _____   a. positive
   _____   b. negative
   _____   c. no response
4. Teacher (supervisor) response to unsuccessful performance:
   _____   a. immediate corrective feedback
   _____   b. delayed corrective feedback
   _____   c. modeling of correct performance
   _____   d. requiring of student to imitate correct performance
   _____   e. no corrective feedback
   _____   f. punishment/sarcasm
5. Student response to unsuccessful performance:
   _____   a. guessed
   _____   b. self-corrected
   _____   c. gave up
   _____   d. attempted alternative response: _____
   _____   e. sought assistance from: _____
   _____   f. became negative/hostile
6. Peer response to student's unsuccessful performance:
   _____   a. positive/encouraging
   _____   b. negative/discouraging
   _____   c. no response

By using a CBVA model that incorporates curricular task evaluation, work habits assessment, and an ecological screening, the evaluator can come to know the variables that directly affect a student's potential for success in a specific vocational program. At various points in the ongoing assessment process the evaluator must use the data to address these decision points:

1. Is the vocational course suitable for the student?
2. If so, what skills does the student need for successful course completion?
3. Can skill deficits be strengthened?
4. Can these skills be taught cooperatively by vocational and special education?
5. Can the vocational course be adapted to assist the student in overcoming these skill deficits?

Recent trends in CBVA promote a seamless approach between assessment and site-based training that reinforces the notion "that assessment is an integral part of teaching and learning" (Cartwright, Cartwright, & Ward, 1995, p. 486). Such a model does not separate vocational evaluation from site-based job training. Kohler (1994) describes an on-the-job evaluation and training process for students with mild disabilities in which student performance was assessed in three skill categories: (1) work-related behaviors (e.g., displays initiative, seeks assistance), (2) generalized skill outcomes (e.g., follows oral directions, displays appropriate attitude to the public), and (3) specific skill outcomes (e.g., makes change accurately, accurately records customer order). A seamless, employment-focused curriculum provides relevant, real-world, hands-on vocational evaluation and training for students with disabilities. Many of the assessed skills in such a model are generalizable to other occupations and thus promote flexibility in employment outcomes.

Vocationally Related Social Skill Assessment

Gathering information about a student's social skill development is an often neglected aspect of vocational assessment. While it is readily accepted that a potential employee must be able to meet the technical qualifications of a job before being hired, it is sometimes assumed that that employee already has the skills needed to enhance interpersonal relationships within the work environment (Sargent, 1991). In truth, the rehabilitation literature indicates that the opposite is true; most individuals with mild and moderate disabilities who lose jobs do so not because of their inability to perform the tasks associated with the job or because they are not productive workers but because they exhibit socially inappropriate behavior while at work.

The typical student develops social skills through incidental learning and maturation. Since students with cognitive deficits experience very little incidental learning, the special-education teacher must structure lessons to teach specific social skills as they relate to employability. The structured lesson should include demonstration of the specific skill being taught, prompting through environmental cues, and practice of the skill in several environments to ensure generalization (Berkell & Brown, 1989).

Specific social skills related to vocational success may include but are not limited to:

- Responding to criticism
- Asking for feedback
- Responding to authority
- Initiating a conversation
- Respecting the personal space of others
- Making a complaint

Each social skill targeted as a goal for transition to employment should be assessed informally through a checklist used by the teacher (see Table 15–14). Later, through a checklist that initiates self-evaluation, the student can track his or her own job-related social skill development (see Table 15–15).

Informal vocational assessment strategies can facilitate school-to-work transition by being relatively inexpensive, flexible, seamless in integrating evaluation and

Table 15–14.   Sample checklist for teacher use evaluating responding to authority

Student Name: _____

Date: _____

Person in Authority/Title: _____

Circle Y (Yes) or N (No) for the following behaviors

1.   Did student respond to authority by returning his/her greeting in a   Y   N
     friendly way.
2.   Did student make eye contact with authority figure?   Y   N
3.   Did student follow directives immediately?   Y   N
4.   Was student respectful?   Y   N

Observer: _____

Site: _____

Working Conditions: _____

Task(s) Assigned: _____

_____

---

training, instructionally relevant, and reflective of the local job market. These advantages can foster assessment results that in turn can promote successful integration into the world of work.

Assessment of vocational skills must be translated into valid annual goals and short-term objectives on an individual basis. A thorough vocational assessment report should address interests and aptitudes with prescriptions as to prospective vocational education approaches. A student's strengths and limitations related to training in a specific vocational program must be clearly defined.

A vocational evaluation report should be readable and reflect specific test results. If formal assessment batteries are used, the tests and subtests should be briefly described as to their content and the specific skills assessed. Results should relate to specific occupations and job listings in the *Dictionary of Occupational Titles* (*DOT;* U.S. Department of Labor, 1977).

Table 15–15.   Sample checklist for self-evaluation of responding to authority

Name: _____

Date: _____

Person in Authority/Title: _____

Circle Y (Yes) or N (No) for each of the following:

1.   Did you return the person's greeting?   Y   N
2.   Did you face the person and make eye contact?   Y   N
3.   Did you do what the person asked you to do immediately?   Y   N
4.   Did you act glad to do what the person asked you to do?   Y   N

Job Site: _____

Your Duties: _____

_____

Case Example 15–1.   Vocational assessment

ANYTOWN HIGH SCHOOL
1234 PINEWOOD AVENUE
ANYTOWN, USA

DATE: January 22, 1991
STUDENT: John Doe
AGE: 15
GRADE: 10
EXAMINER: P. Smith
EVALUATION DATES: January 10, 11, 14, 1991
ASSESSMENT DEVICES USED: Vocational Interest Assessment System (VIAS)
New Concepts Engine Service Work Sample
New Concepts House & Industrial Wiring Work Sample
Apticom: Aptitudes E,F,K,M, & P

BACKGROUND INFORMATION
John Doe is a student with learning disabilities who is mainstreamed for all but one period of the school day. He is a likable young man who is cooperative and presents himself well in public. John's parents divorced when he was 10 years of age, and he is currently living with his mother. He has one younger sister, 11 years old, who is also living at home with the mother. John is an athletic young man, who possesses an interest and skill in working with his hands. John's work history includes a summer job as a stock boy with Miller Hardware and a job as a part-time kitchen helper at the high school.

Strengths. With regard to John's relative strengths, the following characteristics are pertinent:

- Excellent attendance
- Punctual
- Neat appearance
- Cooperative with peers, authority figures
- Seeks assistance as needed
- Good mechanical ability

Limitations. John's relative limitations are as follows:

- Poor conceptualization skills
- Poor attention span
- Low frustration tolerance
- Does not work well under pressure
- Lacks self-confidence
- Slow work pace

(continued)

Case Example 15–1.   *(Continued)*

Primary Learning Mode. John acquires material most effectively when it is presented through an audio/visual means (e.g., a film), or through actual hands-on instruction.

ASSESSMENT RESULTS

Vocational Interests. Results of the VIAS showed that John demonstrated a high degree of interest in the following areas:

- Electrical/electronics
- Trade and industrial-mechanical
- Engineering technology

Test Performance. New Concepts Engine Service Work Sample: This work sample measures the ability to learn and perform several of the basic tasks commonly performed in mechanical repair jobs. The tasks explored in this work station most closely resemble those performed by Automobile Mechanics, *DOT #*602.261–010. Both time and accuracy scores should be taken into consideration as they relate to recommended jobs.

Accuracy	5 errors
Time	107 minutes

New Concepts House & Industrial Wiring Work Sample: This work sample measures the ability to learn and perform several of the basic tasks commonly performed in entry-level jobs in the wiring trades. The tasks explored in this work station most closely resemble those performed by an Electrician's Helper, *DOT #*829.684–022. Both time and accuracy scores should be considered as they relate to recommended jobs.

Accuracy	6 errors
Time	205 minutes

Apticom: Aptitude E
Measures the ability to move the hand and foot in coordination with each other in accordance with presented visual stimuli.

Results   54th percentile

Apticom: Aptitude F
Measures the ability to move the fingers and manipulate small objects with the fingers rapidly and accurately.

Results   91st percentile

Apticom: Aptitude K
Measures the ability to coordinate eyes and hands or fingers rapidly and accurately in making precise movements with speed. Ability to make a movement response accurately and quickly.

Results   60th percentile

Case Example 15–1. *(Continued)*

Apticom: Aptitude M
Measures the ability to move the hands easily and skillfully. To work with the hands in placing and turning motions.

Results   54th percentile

Apticom: Aptitude P
Measures the ability to perceive pertinent detail in objects or in pictorial or graphic material. To make visual comparisons and discriminations and see slight differences in shapes and shadings of figures and widths and lengths of lines.

Results   56th percentile

Physical Demands Reported:
The physical demand level of John's profile indicates a level of lifting 50 pounds maximum with frequent lifting and/or carrying of objects weighing up to 25 pounds. This level may be re-verified on specific job sites.

Analysis of Test Performance.
Engine Service Work Sample:
   Accuracy: John's near average accuracy score suggests that he should not require more supervision than most trainees or workers. His score also indicates an ability to learn and perform fairly accurately a multistep process through a combination of verbal instructions, hands-on learning, and learning strategy applications. John may also benefit from training if a higher level of accuracy is required for satisfactory job performance. His accuracy suggests that he should be comfortable working with hand tools, such as those used in mechanical repair jobs.
   Time: John's slightly below average time score suggests that he would benefit from practice in learning to perform tasks of this nature quickly. He might also benefit from training to achieve the level of speed required for satisfactory job performance. John's score also suggests that he may not be comfortable working with hand tools, such as those used in mechanical repair jobs, at least at present.

House and Industrial Wiring Work Sample:
   Accuracy: John's low score suggests that he will likely require more supervision than most trainees or workers. His score also indicates that he would benefit from practice in learning to perform a multistep process accurately. John would also benefit from training to achieve the higher level of accuracy required for satisfactory job performance. His accuracy also suggests that he is not comfortable working with small hand tools used in entry-level wiring trades.
   Time: John's near average score suggests that he felt fairly comfortable with the task. His score also reflects a tendency to try to work quickly in performing work-related tasks. John's score also suggests that he should—with development of accuracy— eventually be comfortable with small hand tools used in entry-level wiring occupations.

Apticom: Aptitude E
John's score suggests that he has the aptitude to work fairly comfortably at tasks that require skilled or easy coordination of the eyes, hands, and feet, such as is required of workers operating sewing machines, forklifts, and motor vehicles.

(continued)

Case Example 15–1.   *(Continued)*

Apticom: Aptitude F

John's excellent score suggests that he has the aptitude to work very comfortably at tasks that require fast or accurate finger movement as is required of bank tellers, electronics workers, and data-entry operators.

Apticom: Aptitude K

John's score suggests that he has the aptitude to work fairly comfortably at tasks that require rapid and accurate coordination of the eyes, hands, and fingers in making precise movements with speed. This level of aptitude is required for a person to work comfortably as a telephone-answering service operator, clerk typist, stenographer, veterinarian, librarian, audit clerk, mail clerk, clothes designer, illustrator, general duty nurse, calculating-machine operator, bindery worker, coding clerk, restaurant manager, forester, diesel mechanic, automobile painter, and forester aide.

Apticom: Aptitude M

John's near average score suggests that he has the aptitude to work fairly comfortably at tasks that require skillful or easy hand movement as is required of electronics mechanics, sheet metal workers, electronics assembly workers, printer compositors, surgical technicians, or machine packagers.

Apticom: Aptitude P

John's near average score suggests that he has the aptitude to perceive pertinent detail in objects or in pictorial or graphic material. However, this score also indicates that he may encounter some difficulties in making visual comparisons and discriminations in very fine shapes and shadings of figures and widths and lengths of lines. This higher level of aptitude is needed in interpreting dental X rays, photographic materials or flight charts.

SUMMARY AND RECOMMENDATIONS

For vocational training and work, John's strengths consist of:

1. An ability to learn and perform a multistep process fairly accurately, using hand tools for mechanical repair jobs.
2. An ability to learn and perform fairly quickly work tasks using hand tools for entry level jobs in the wiring trades.
3. Good form perception.
4. Good motor coordination.
5. Excellent finger dexterity.
6. Good manual dexterity.

For vocational training and work, John's limitations consist of:

1. A need for practice in learning to perform quickly when working with hand tools for mechanical repair jobs.
2. A need for extended practice in learning to perform a multistep process accurately, using small hand tools for entry level jobs in the wiring trades.
3. Fair eye-hand coordination.

The subject (John Doe) described in Case Example 15–1 is a student with a mild disability. He possesses enough skills so that with minimal support services he can be educated in the least restrictive vocational setting. In addition to the summary and recommendations noted in the case study, a multidisciplinary examination of the assessment results can delineate roles and responsibilities of vocational, regular, and special education.

In John Doe's case, for example, some of his limitations can be addressed in the special class and reinforced in both vocational and regular education. John's first limitation is his work pace. While the results specifically target a mechanical orientation, work pace can be taught and reinforced in other settings as well. An annual goal on John's individualized education plan might be written as follows: "John Doe will decrease the length of time it takes him to complete an assigned task."

This effort to influence John's work pace can also be reinforced in the regular classroom. Cooperating regular teachers can monitor the time it takes John to complete assignments given in class. These regular teachers can also reinforce on-time task completion by providing verbal or visual cues as reminders of expired time or off-task behaviors. Parents can even monitor John's on-time task completion performance at home.

John's second limitation, performing a multistep process when using hand tools for entry-level wiring jobs, provides another opportunity for multidisciplinary cooperation. The special educator and vocational educator can cooperatively design a learning strategy wherein each step of using the hand tool can be identified and applied to a mnemonic device to facilitate recall of the steps. Such a strategy development process has been used to promote acquisition and application of steps in improving academic performance (Deshler, Schumaker, & Lenz, 1984; Deshler, Schumaker, Lenz, & Ellis, 1984) and classroom participation (Ellis, 1989) among students with learning disabilities. Strategy instruction has also been applied in teaching steps to successful job interviewing (Julian, 1987).

As stated earlier in this chapter, the primary purpose of the vocational assessment of students with disabilities is to support their education in the least restrictive vocational setting. Thus, cooperation among special, regular, and vocational education can enhance a student's progress toward successful completion of a vocational training program.

CONCLUSION

As the field of vocational education evolves to reflect a more technically oriented job market, so too will the nature of vocational assessment change to meet this evolution. The skills needed for success in technological fields will be increasingly less distinguishable from more traditional academic subjects. As a part of the tech-prep initiative being implemented in some states, traditional subject content such as that found, for example, in biology is being integrated into vocational courses such as vocational-agriculture. A major factor that will continue to differentiate vocational education will be its application of those academic skills in a work environment. The notion that students who cannot perform successfully in traditional subject areas will be able to find a haven in vocational education will simply not be valid. Success in vocational education will increasingly depend on the possession of the requisite academic and social skills and work behaviors that reflect the needs of a society more oriented toward information processing. Recent educational reform efforts have made the erroneous assumption that students already possess the necessary work habits (as identified in Table 15–12) and need only more intensive academic or vocational preparation. To the extent that the instruction of work habits is ignored in new curricular policy thrusts, these well-intentioned reform initiatives will produce less than hoped for outcomes. For this reason, this chapter has offered suggestions regarding the assessment of vocationally relevant social skills.

As vocational education integrates more traditional academic content into its course offerings, the abdication of responsibility for vocational assessment (which has been viewed as the primary domain of vocational education) will be less justifiable. It will be more incumbent upon regular educators, special educators, counselors, and school psychologists to participate actively in the vocational assessment process. Tesolowski and Wichowski (1984) found that instructors and counselors were making vocational placement decisions on available work sample results even though neither group had sufficient training in vocational assessment to accurately interpret the test outcomes. Only through a truly multidisciplinary assessment approach will the abstract nature of certain traditional school subjects be minimized through relevant vocational applications and proper vocational program placement decisions be implemented. This multidisciplinary approach will require a collaborative theme to vocational assessment, which means that more than just vocational education must be involved in this assessment process.

As this nation engages in a serious examination of the unintended consequences of welfare dependency, students must exit the kindergarten through 12th-grade system with the skills to further their education, enter the competitive work force, or transition into a combination of both. For those citizens who have become dependent on a public assistance program that is destined to change in the next 10 years, "the American dream of success through hard work, sturdy self-reliance, and personal responsibility seems increasingly stale" (Armey et al., 1994, p. 17). It has been noted, for example, that within the broader context of transition training, preparing students with disabilities for the world of work can enhance individual empowerment (Szymanski, 1994). Overreliance on government support by an ever-increasing subset of the nation's population not only destroys individual initiative and empowerment but impacts the economy as a whole. A glance into the not-too-distant future reveals that unless the "bottom fifty percent" of the population can be trained to operate and maintain the technology developed by the "smartest twenty-five percent," new high-tech processes cannot be employed (Thurow, 1993) or, if they are employed, will be employed in foreign labor markets.

The twenty-first century will evidence a change in the way vocational education, and education in general, is evaluated, especially by the general public and elected officials at the local, state, and national levels. No longer will inputs and outcomes be confused as signs of educational excellence. Inputs—for example, class size, the number and type of computers in a school district, the number of programs focusing on special groups (i.e., at-risk, violent, or gifted students), and the average annual dollars spent educating each child—will become less important to taxpayers and the officials they elect. Specific outcomes as found in standardized test scores, the number of students exiting the school system who successfully enter higher education, and the number of students who enter the competitive work force with the prerequisite skills to perform entry-level job duties will be the bottom line in determining educational effectiveness (Elrod, in press). To the extent that proper, multidisciplinary vocational assessment can foster instructional interventions that can ultimately result in empowerment, self-worth, and, above all, competitive employment at an independent living wage for the special needs student, vocational education can be the vanguard of accountability of American education in the twenty-first century.

REFERENCES

Albright, L., & Cobb, R.B. (1988). Curriculum-based vocational assessment: A concept whose time has come. *The Journal for Vocational Special Needs Education, 10,* 13–16.

Albright, L., Cobb, R.B., Sarkees, M.D., & Kingsbury, D. (1989). Formative field test evaluation of a curriculum-based vocational assessment training program. In G.F. Elrod (Ed.), *Career education for special needs individuals: Learning, earning, contributing.* Reston, VA: Division on Career Development of the Council for Exceptional Children.

Anastasi, A. (1961). *Psychological testing* (2nd ed.). New York: Macmillan.

Anderson, L.M., Evertson, C.M., & Brophy, J.F. (1979). An experimental study of effective teaching in first-grade reading groups. *The Elementary School Journal, 79,* 193–223.

Armey, D., Forbes, M.S., Jr., Friedman, M., Gramm, P., Postrel, V., Roback, J., Shelton, J., & Smith, F.L., Jr. (1994, Summer). Serfdom USA: How far have we traveled down Hayek's 'road'? *Policy Review, 69,* 14–21.

Becker, R.L. (1975). *AAMD-Becker reading-free vocational Interest Inventory.* Washington, DC: American Association of Mental Deficiency.

Berkell, D.E., & Brown, J.M. (1989). *Transition from school to work for persons with disabilities.* White Plains, NY: Longman.

Botterbusch, K. (1982). *Vocational assessment and evaluation system.* Menomonie, WI: University of Wisconsin-Stout, Materials Development Center.

Brandon, T.L., & Snyder, L. (1989). Work Recovery Center, Piedmont Hospital, Atlanta, Georgia. In L. Ogden-Niemeyer & K. Jacobs (Eds.), *Work hardening—State of the art* (pp. 209–221). Thorofare, NJ: Slack.

Brolin, D.E. (1978). *Life centered career education: A competency based approach.* Reston, VA: The Council for Exceptional Children.

Brolin, D.E. (1983). *Life centered career education: A competency based approach* (rev. ed.). Reston, VA: The Council for Exceptional Children.

Brolin, D.E. (1989). *Life centered career education: A competency based approach* (3rd ed.). Reston, VA: The Council for Exceptional Children.

Brown, C.D., McDaniel, R.S., & Couch, R.H. (1994). *Vocational evaluation systems and software: A consumer's guide.* The University of Wisconsin—Stout, The Rehabilitation Resource.

Bursuck, W.D., & Lessen, E.I. (1985). Curriculum-based assessment: Increasing the participation of regular educators in mainstreaming. *ICEC Quarterly, 34,* 25–26.

Bursuck, W.D., & Lessen, E.I. (1987). A classroom-based model for assessing students with learning disabilities. *Learning Disabilities Focus, 3,* 17–29.

Carl D. Perkins Vocational Education Act of 1984 (PL 98–524).

Cartwright, G.P., Cartwright, C.A., & Ward, M.E. (1995). *Educating special learners* (4th ed.). Belmont, CA: Wadsworth.

Clark, G.M., & Kolstoe, O.P. (1990). *Career development and transition education for adolescents with disabilities.* Boston: Allyn & Bacon.

Commission on National Aid to Vocational Education (1914). *Report of the Commission on National Aid to Vocational Education* (together with hearings held on the subject). U.S. House of Representatives, 63rd Congress, second session, Doc. No. 1004 (Vol. 1, p. 12). Washington, DC: U.S. Government Printing Office.

Dahl, T., Appleby, J., & Lipe, D. (1978). *Mainstreaming guidebook for vocational educators teaching the handicapped.* Salt Lake City: Olympus.

Dart, J. (1990, Fall). ADA: Landmark declaration of equality. *Worklife: A Publication on Employment and People with Disabilities, 3,* 1.

Deshler, D.D., Schumaker, J., & Lenz, B.K. (1984). Academic and cognitive interventions for LD adolescents: Part I. *Journal of Learning Disabilities, 17,* 108–117.

Deshler, D.D., Schumaker, J., Lenz, B.K., & Ellis, E.S. (1984). Academic and cognitive interventions for LD adolescents: Part II. *Journal of Learning Disabilities, 17,* 170–179.

Edgar, E., Levine, P., & Maddox, M. (1986). *Statewide follow-up studies of secondary special education students in transition.* Working paper of the Networking and Evaluation Team, Child Development and Mental Retardation Center, University of Washington, Seattle.

Ellis, E.S. (1989). A metacognitive intervention for increasing class participation. *Learning Disabilities Focus, 5,* 36–46.

Elrod, G.F. (1987a). Transition-related assessment: The foundation of preparation for postsecondary success. In G.F. Elrod (Ed.), *Transition-related assessment* [Monograph]. *Diagnostique, 12,* 127–130.

Elrod, G.F. (1987b). Academic and social skills pre-requisite to success in vocational training: Perceptions of vocational educators. *The Journal for Vocational Special Needs Education, 10,* 17–21.

Elrod, G.F. (in press). Using proper restraint techniques as a means of last resort. In J. Blendinger (Ed.), *Positive response to school violence: Creating safe schools.* Mississippi State, MS: Social Science Research Center, Mississippi State University.

Elrod, G.F., Isbell, C.H., & Braziel, P.M. (1989). Assessing transition-related variables from kindergarten through grade 12: Practical applications. *Diagnostique, 14,* 247–261.

Fuchs, L.S., Deno, S., & Marston, D. (1983). Improving the reliability of curriculum-based measures of academic skills for psychoeducational decision making. *Diagnostique, 8,* 135–149.

Fuchs, L.S., & Fuchs, D. (1986). Curriculum-based assessment of progress toward long-term and short-term goals. *Journal of Special Education, 20,* 69–82.

Greenan, J.P. (1983). Identification and validation of generalizable skills in vocational programs. *Journal of Vocational Education Research, 8,* 46–71.

Greenan, J.P. (1987). Generalizable skills instruction. In G.D. Meers (Ed.), *Handbook of vocational special needs education* (2nd ed.). Rockville, MD: Aspen.

Halpern, A.S. (1985). Transition: A look at the foundations. *Exceptional Children, 51,* 479–486.

Hasazi, S.B., Gordon, L.R., Roe, C.A., Hull, M., Finck, K., & Salembier, G. (1985). A statewide follow-up on post-high school employment and residential status of students labeled "mentally retarded." *Education and Training of the Mentally Retarded, 20,* 222–234.

Holland, J.L. (1985). *The Self-directed Search-Form E.* Odessa, FL: Psychological Assessment Resources.

Hursh, N.C., & Kerns, A.F. (1988). *Vocational evaluation in special education*. Boston: College-Hill Press.

Ianacone, R.N., & Leconte, P.J. (1986). Curriculum-based vocational assessment: A viable response to a school-based service delivery issue. *Career Development for Exceptional Individuals, 9,* 113–120.

Institute for the Crippled and Disabled (1959). *TOWER: Testing, orientation, and work evaluation in rehabilitation*. New York: Author.

Jaffee, C.L. (1965). Assessment centers find management potential. *Bell Telephone Magazine, 44,* 18–24.

Jastak, J., & Jastak, S. (1974). *Wide Range Interest and Opinion Test*. Wilmington, DE: Guidance Associates of Delaware.

Julian, M. (1987, March). *Strategy applications to enhance job interviewing skills*. Paper presented at the annual conference of the South Carolina Division on Career Development, Columbia, SC.

Kiernan, W.E., & Payne, M.E. (1982). Hard to train: A history of vocational training for special needs youth. In K.P. Lynch, W.E. Kiernan, & J.A. Stark (Eds.), *Prevocational and vocational education for special needs youth*. Baltimore: Paul H. Brookes.

Kohler, P.D. (1994). On-the-job training: A curricular approach to employment. *Career Development for Exceptional Individuals, 17,* 29–40.

Kokaska, C.J., Gruenhagen, K., Razeghi, J., & Fair, G.W. (1985, October). Division on Career Development's position statement on transition. In D.E. Brolin (Ed.), *Proceedings of the International Conference on the Decade of the Disabled: Transition to work and adult life* (p. 28).

Looslie, K.M. (1991). *ALPs assessment battery*. Island City, OR: Union County Educational Service District.

Marston, D., Mirkin, P., & Deno, S. (1984). Curriculum-based measurement: An alternative to traditional screening, referral and identification. *Journal of Special Education, 18,* 109–117.

Mithaug, D., Horiuchi, C., & Fanning, P. (1985). A report on the Colorado statewide follow-up survey of special education students. *Exceptional Children, 51,* 397–404.

Nadolsky, J.N. (1977, July). *The use of work samples in the vocational evaluation process*. Paper presented at the Rehabilitation Forum on Systems of Vocational Evaluation, Rehabilitation Services Education, Auburn University, Auburn, AL.

Neff, W.S. (1968). *Work and human behavior*. Chicago: Aldine Press.

Nystrom, D.C., & Bayne, G.K. (1979). *Occupation and career education legislation* (2nd ed.). Indianapolis: Bobbs-Merrill.

Odiorne, G.S., & Miller, E.L. (1971). Selection by objectives: A new approach to managerial selection. In W.L. French & D. Hellriegel (Eds.), *Personnel management and organization development: Fields in transition* (pp. 218–236). New York: Houghton Mifflin.

Peterson, M., & Peterson, D. (1986). Assessment: A resource in vocational instruction of special needs students. *The Journal for Vocational Special Needs Education, 8,* 13–16.

Phelps, L.A., & Frasier, J.R. (1988). Legislative and policy aspects of vocational special education. In R. Gaylord-Ross (Ed.), *Vocational education for persons with handicaps*. Mountain View, CA: Mayfield.

Pruitt, W.A. (1977). *Vocational (work) evaluation*. Menomonie, WI: Walt Pruitt Associates.

Roberts, C.L. (1970). Definitions, objectives, and goals in work evaluation. *Journal of Rehabilitation, 36,* 13–15.

Rosenberg, H., & Tesolowski, D.G. (1979). *Florida International Diagnostic-prescriptive Vocational Competency Profile*. Chicago: Stoelting.

Rusch, F.R., Schutz, R.P., Mithaug, D.E., Stewart, J.E., & Mar, D.K. (1982). *The vocational assessment and curriculum guide*. Seattle: Exceptional Education.

Salzberg, C.L., McConaughy, E.K., Lignugaris/Kraft, B., Agran, M., & Stowitschek, J.J. (1987). Behaviors of distinction: The transition from acceptable to highly valued worker. *The Journal for Vocational Special Needs Education, 10*, 23–28.

Sargent, L.R. (1991). *Social skills for school and community: Systematic instruction for children and youth with cognitive delays*. Des Moines, IA: The Council for Exceptional Children.

Sarkees, M.D., & Scott, J.L. (1986). *Vocational special needs* (2nd ed.). Alsip, IL: American Technical Publishers.

Scarpati, S. (1989). Assessing vocational abilities. In H.L. Swanson & B.L. Watson (Eds.), *Educational and psychological assessment of exceptional children*, 2nd ed. (pp. 309–337). Columbus, OH: Merrill.

Stodden, R.A., Meehan, K.A., Bisconer, S.W., & Hodell, S.L. (1989). The impact of vocational assessment information on the individualized education planning process: Supporting curriculum-based assessment. *The Journal for Vocational Special Needs Education, 12*, 31–36.

Szymanski, E.M. (1994). Transition: Life-span and life-space considerations for empowerment. *Exceptional Children, 60*, 402–410.

Task Force Number 7, Vocational Evaluation Project (1975). Glossary of terms used in vocational evaluation. *Vocational Evaluation and Work Adjustment Bulletin, 8*, 85–93.

Tesolowski, D.G., & Morgan, T.E. (1980). Selecting educational administrators: The assessment center technique. *NASSP Bulletin, 64*, 107–115.

Tesolowski, D.G., & Wichowski, C.P. (1984). Perceived equity of admission standards and practices utilized in public occupational education programs. *Journal of Industrial Teacher Education, 21*, 25–42.

Thurow, L. (1993). *Head to head: The coming economic battle among Japan, Europe, and America*. New York: Warner Books.

Tindal, G.A., & Marston, D.B. (1990). *Classroom-based assessment: Evaluating instructional outcomes*. Columbus, OH: Merrill.

Treat, K. (1929). Tests for garment machine operators. *Personnel Journal, 8*, 19–28.

U.S. Congress (1917). *Smith-Hughes Act*.

U.S. Congress (1958). *National Education Act*.

U.S. Congress (1963). *Vocational Education Act*, Public Law 88–210.

U.S. Congress (1968). *Vocational Education Act Amendments of 1968*, Public Law 90–576.

U.S. Congress (1973). *Rehabilitation Act of 1973*, Public Law 93–112.

U.S. Congress (1974). *Rehabilitation Act Amendments of 1974*, Public Law 93–516.

U.S. Congress (1975). *Education for All Handicapped Children Act*, Public Law 94–142.

U.S. Congress (1978). *Rehabilitation, Comprehensive Services, and Developmental Disabilities Amendments*, Public Law 95–602.

U.S. Congress (1983). *Education of the Handicapped Act Amendments*, Public Law 98–199.

U.S. Congress (1984). *Carl D. Perkins Act*, Public Law 98–524.

U.S. Congress (1990a). *Americans with Disabilities Act*, Public Law 101–336.

U.S. Congress (1990b). *Carl D. Perkins Vocational and Applied Technology Education Act Amendments*, Public Law 101–392.

U.S. Congress (1990c). *Individuals with Disabilities Education Act*, Public Law 101–476.

U.S. Department of Labor (1977). *Dictionary of occupational titles*. Washington, DC: Author.

Veir, C.A. (1987). Vocational assessment: The evolving role. In G.D. Meers (Ed.), *Handbook of vocational special needs education* (2nd ed.). Rockville, MD: Aspen.

Will, M. (1984). *OSERS programming for the transition of youth with disabilities: Bridges from school to working life.* Washington, DC: Office of Special Education and Rehabilitative Services.

Wirt, J.G. (1991). A new federal law on vocational education: Will reform follow? *Phi Delta Kappan, 72,* 425–433.

Wisconsin Vocational Studies Center (1980). *Puzzled about educating special needs students?* University of Wisconsin, Madison: Author.

Work Recovery, Incorporated (1988). *ERGOS training manual.* Tucson, AZ: Author.

Work Recovery, Incorporated (1989). *ERGOS Work Simulator.* Tucson, AZ: Author.

Work Recovery, Incorporated (1995). *Work Recovery, Inc. confirms Allsup, Inc.'s selection of ERGOS technology for proposed Social Security project.* Tuscon, AZ: Author.

Chapter 16

ASSESSING CHILDREN WITH MENTAL RETARDATION

BRUCE GORDON, DONALD H. SAKLOFSKE, AND
DENISE K. HILDEBRAND

Issues surrounding the assessment of children with mental retardation have been interwoven with many of the key developments and debates in the field of psychology. In 1992, the American Association on Mental Retardation (AAMR) issued a revised definition of mental retardation, billing it as a major paradigm shift in the conception of the disorder (Luckasson et al., 1992). This chapter explores the challenges and opportunities presented by the new definition to the endeavor of assessing children with mental retardation according to the four dimensions specified by the AAMR. Finally, a case study will demonstrate the application of the new definition in the assessment and planning of interventions for children with mental retardation.

The 1992 Definition

The AAMR definition describes mental retardation as

> substantial limitations in present functioning. It is characterized by significantly subaverage intellectual functioning, existing concurrently with related limitations in two or more of the following applicable adaptive skill areas: communication, self-care, home living, social skills, community use, self-direction, health and safety, functional academics, leisure, and work. Mental retardation manifests before age 18. (Luckasson et al., 1992, p. 5)

At first glance, the new definition does not appear to be radically different from the previous revision (Grossman, 1983). The three core elements remain: (1) subaverage intellectual functioning, (2) adaptive skills deficits, and (3) occurrence before age 18. One major change from 1983 is that adaptive behavior is now broken down into 10 specific subdomains. Four assumptions have been added to underpin the definition. The first assumption is that assessment will consider cultural and language differences. The second assumption is that adaptive skills deficits must occur within relevant environments for the child. The third states that weaknesses in some adaptive skills often coexist with strengths in others. The final assumption declares that with proper support over time, people with mental retardation do improve in their ability to function.

A very significant change from the previous definition involves subclassification. The previous system partitioned mental retardation by IQ level (mild, moderate, severe, and profound). The current scheme describes what levels of support the child requires across different life situations. Mental retardation is no longer synonymous with the person but is rather a disability that varies according to the interaction between the person, his or her capabilities, the environment, and the levels of support provided to the client. For example, earlier descriptions such as "Bill is moderately mentally retarded" have been replaced by "Bill is a person with mental retardation, who evidences weaknesses in his communication and academic skills but also manifests relative strengths in his social and leisure skills." The impact of the disability will vary depending on the situation. Bill's mental retardation will be a much more significant impairment in a classroom with minimal special-education support than it will be when he goes to a baseball game in his community with neighborhood children.

The new definition outlines a three-step process for diagnosis and assessment, and involves consideration of four dimensions:

Dimension I: Intellectual Functioning and Adaptive Skills
Dimension II: Psychological/Emotional Considerations
Dimension III: Physical/Health/Etiology Considerations
Dimension IV: Environmental Considerations

The first step involves making the actual diagnosis. The second includes the identification of the client's strengths and weaknesses across the four dimensions. Key environments such as home and school are assessed to see how they assist or hinder the child's development, and consideration is given to what would be the ideal environment to foster maximum growth. The third step involves creating a profile of the supports the child requires across each of the four dimensions.

The 1992 definition changes the emphasis in assessment from classification to designing effective treatment plans for children with mental retardation.

DIMENSION I: INTELLECTUAL FUNCTIONING AND ADAPTIVE SKILLS

Intellectual Functioning

The first step in the three-step process outlined by the 1992 definition involves consideration of whether a diagnosis of mental retardation is appropriate. The initial stage of that process involves assessment of the child's intellectual functioning. The child must demonstrate significantly subaverage intellectual functioning, which is defined by AAMR as a score approximately 2 standard deviations or more below the mean (i.e., a standard IQ score of approximately 70 to 75; Luckasson et al., 1992). Critics (MacMillan, Gresham, & Siperstein, 1995) have expressed concern regarding the lack of precision in the IQ cutoff score. For example, it is not clearly stated whether 75 is the absolute cutoff point for consideration of a diagnosis of mental retardation—or 75 plus the standard error of measurement. This has implications for the identification of mental retardation in children. Luckasson et al. (1992) counter that the cutoff point for IQ is not more precisely defined because of the role that clinical judgment plays in the interpretation of test results leading to a diagnosis of mental retardation. The imprecision of tests and measurement error should alert clinicians to the fact that IQ scores can only be an estimate of a likely range of functioning. Diagnosis of individuals with IQ scores close to the upper cutoff point should rely on sound clinical judgment with primary consideration given to whether deficits are seen in adaptive behavior skills.

A very large number of intelligence tests are available and this can pose a selection problem for practitioners. These tests vary in psychometric quality (e.g., standardization and norms, reliability, validity), their appropriateness for particular individuals and groups (e.g., younger children, children with sensory impairments, etc.), and the way that they define and consequently assess intelligence (see the special 1990 issue of the *Journal of Psychoeducational Assessment* entitled *Intelligence: Theories and Practice*). The test selection procedure will also be guided by the kinds of questions to be addressed, which range from assessment for diagnosis of mental retardation to the need for prescriptive information.

Traditionally, the role of intelligence tests in the assessment of mental retardation has been to determine a child's general level of intellectual and cognitive ability relative to a preset score cutoff (IQ = 70). For this reason, tests that sample a broad range of abilities, following the Binet tradition, are most often employed. While these tests may not be appropriate for some children with severe intellectual impairment, it is still necessary to estimate general intellectual functioning (g) by employing more specific tests or test combinations (e.g., Raven's Matrices, Peabody Picture Vocabulary Test-Revised). Some of the most often used g measures include the Wechsler Preschool and Primary Scale of Intelligence-Revised (Wechsler, 1989); Wechsler Intelligence Scale for Children-Third Edition (WISC-III; Wechsler, 1991), and Wechsler Adult Intelligence Scale-Revised (Wechsler, 1981), soon to be replaced by the WAIS-III. The Stanford-Binet Intelligence Scales-Fourth Edition (SB-IV; Thorndike, Hagan, & Sattler, 1986) continues to be frequently used by clinicians because it covers the early childhood to adult age ranges. A limitation of both the WISC-III and the SB-IV is that neither test was intended for the assessment of more cognitively impaired (Sattler, 1992).

Still within the g tradition, the Differential Ability Scales (Elliott, 1990) is gaining increasing acceptance in the assessment of children with mental retardation. The Woodcock-Johnson Psycho-Educational Battery-Revised (Woodcock & Johnson, 1987), grounded in the Horn-Cattell *Gf-Gc* theory of intelligence, may also be used in the identification of children with mental retardation (Evans, Carlsen, & McGrew, 1993). More recent models have emphasized such aspects of cognition as attention, processing, and planning (e.g., Das, Naglieri, & Kirby, 1994; Naglieri & Das, 1990) and would appear to have greater potential for differential diagnosis and program development. Finally, the suspicion or even recognition of mental retardation often occurs during infancy. Children with recognizable syndromes such as

Down Syndrome or who have suffered severe neurological damage pre- or postnatally may be referred for assessment at a very early age. In such cases, the Bayley Scales of Infant Development-Second Edition (Bayley, 1993) are often employed to obtain a mental development index.

The Wechsler Intelligence Scale for Children-Third Edition

The WISC-III was published in 1991 and like earlier versions measures general intelligence (Full Scale IQ—FSIQ) as well as Verbal (VIQ) and Performance (PIQ) intelligence. The six subtests in the Verbal scale and seven tests included in the Performance scale also yield four factors: Verbal Comprehension, Perceptual Organization, Freedom from Distractibility, and Processing Speed. Of interest is that a sample of children with mental retardation reported in the WISC-III manual earned their highest scores on the Processing Speed Index. The WISC-III retains great popularity among psychologists and educators because it is part of the Wechsler family of tests dating back to 1939. There is a wealth of valuable information available to guide examiners in the clinical use of the WISC-III (Kaufman, 1994). The WISC-III was carefully standardized and has excellent psychometric properties (Sattler, 1992). Kamphaus (1993) states,

> The WISC-III possess an extraordinary research base that can be used to guide assessment practice. The WISC-III possesses many admirable psychometric properties. It is a good measure of "g"; it has ample criterion-related validity, a modern norming sample, and excellent reliability estimates for the composite scores. (p. 157)

When employing the WISC-III with children with mental retardation, there are several considerations to keep in mind. The limited floors of the FSIQ, VIQ, and PIQ restrict the use of the WISC-III to children who manifest less severe intellectual disability. The WISC-III FSIQ only extends downward to a score of 40. However, this is 4 standard deviations below the mean and together with expert clinical observation should at least indicate that the child is either mildly, moderately, or quite severely cognitively impaired. Still, the examiner should consider the use of the WPPSI-R or SB-IV for 6-year-old children who are below average in intellectual ability. This raises another consideration for the examiner. While the WISC-III FSIQ shows quite a high correlation with IQ and total ability scores obtained from other general ability tests (e.g., Differential Ability Scales), it should be remembered that these IQ scores are not interchangeable and, in fact, may be quite different.

There is some evidence from earlier studies of the WISC-R that children with mental retardation earn lowest scores on the Information, Similarities, and Vocabulary subtests, while highest scores are found on the Picture Completion and Object Assembly subtests (Kaufman, 1979; Mueller, Dash, Matheson, & Short, 1984). However there does not appear to be a characteristic and reliable PIQ > VIQ discrepancy that would assist in differential diagnosis or serve as a diagnostic indicator. Kamphaus (1993) offers some excellent examples to guide examiners when there is a VIQ/PIQ score difference (e.g., PIQ = 88, VIQ = 60, FSIQ = 72). If there is evidence suggesting more severe impairment in verbal comprehension or extremely poor fine- and gross-motor skills, it may be necessary to ensure that consideration is then given to either VIQ or PIQ scores as well as the FSIQ. Such score variations also reinforce the need to ensure that a diagnosis of mental retardation does not rest solely on an IQ score.

The new norms for the WISC-III will certainly yield lower scores than would be obtained on the older WISC-R or from tests normed some years before the WISC-III standardization. For example, the WISC-III manual reported that a 2-year interval between testing on the WISC-R and WISC-III resulted in a 9-point lower score for children with mental retardation. This finding must be considered at the time of first assessment as well as at retesting. While these children tend to manifest greater stability of IQ, artifacts due to normative factors and test floor and ceiling effects may produce spurious interpretations of IQ test data. Another statistical artifact that must be considered is regression to the mean. Thus, a retest IQ score that is slightly higher than earlier results from the same test may simply reflect regression effects. Of course, intelligence test scores may be less stable in instances involving neurological damage or deteriorating conditions (e.g., Tay-Sachs Disease), or in response to either medical (e.g, Phenylketonuria or PKU) or environmental interventions such as language enrichment or the Pass Remedial Program (Das, 1993; Das et al., 1994).

The greatest utility of the WISC-III still lies in its strength as a measure of general intellectual ability. Various guidelines have been suggested to promote accurate and responsible test interpretation. For example, Kamphaus (1993) outlines an integrative method of test interpretation and illustrates its application with the Wechsler scales. Further, Kaufman (1994) advocates five basic tenets as a guide to individualized WISC-III interpretation:

The WISC-III subtests measure what an individual has learned.

The WISC-III subtests are samples of behavior and are not exhaustive.

The WISC-III assesses mental functioning under fixed experimental conditions.

The WISC-III is optimally useful when it is interpreted from an information-processing model.

Hypotheses generated from WISC-III profiles should be supported with data from multiple sources (pp. 6–14).

The Differential Ability Scales

A newer measure of cognitive ability that has strong utility for working with children with mental retardation is the Differential Ability Scales (DAS) designed by Colin Elliott (1990). The DAS consists of two test batteries, one for preschoolers (2 years, 6 months to 5 years, 11 months) and another for school-age children (6 years to 17 years, 11 months). Our clinical experience has been that preschoolers find the majority of the tasks very appealing to try even when the items are difficult for them to fully succeed on. The school-age battery for the DAS involves a set of six core subtests to assess overall cognitive ability and three diagnostic subtests to explore memory and information-processing skills. The main advantage to the school-age battery as compared to measures such as the WISC-III and SB-IV is its ability to produce a reliable and valid estimate of overall cognitive ability in a significantly shorter assessment time. The school-age DAS typically takes about half an hour less to administer than the WISC-III. This saving of time can be a very important consideration for children with shorter attention spans and allows the clinician to use the time saved to explore other assessment issues. The DAS also uses an adaptive testing model in which the child spends the majority of the assessment time working on items of moderate difficulty, thereby minimizing the time spent on too hard or too easy items. The effect is that children typically experience less failure before moving on to another test activity.

The DAS also provides more opportunity for the clinician to distinguish between moderate and severe intellectual disabilities. An extrapolation formula allows calculation of an estimate of overall cognitive ability down to the fifth standard deviation below the mean—as compared to the WISC-III and SB-IV in which minimum possible scores are at the fourth standard deviation. The extrapolation formula allows use of the preschool battery with school-age children with severe and profound intellectual deficits. This results in an assessment where children experience a greater degree of success, thereby providing insight into what they are able to do and their problem-solving approaches.

A significant weakness of the DAS for assessing preschoolers with developmental delays is the lack of tasks involving expressive language skills. Preschoolers are only required to provide one-word answers, such as found on the picture-naming task. While less reliance on verbal skills can be an asset in looking at the developmental skills of children from different cultural or linguistic backgrounds, it also limits the ability of the clinician to assess the child's verbal reasoning skills when short phrases or sentences are required. Partial compensation is provided by a Verbal Comprehension subtest that requires the child to carry out increasingly complex verbal directions using a set of toys. This subtest seems to be quite sensitive to detecting language-processing weaknesses in preschoolers above and beyond their general developmental delay.

The Cognitive Assessment System

One of the newest measures of cognitive ability is the Cognitive Assessment System (CAS; Das & Naglieri, 1996). The CAS represents an effort to anchor the assessment of cognitive abilities in current theories of cognition and information processing. The CAS uses the PASS model (Das et al., 1994) to explore children's intellectual strengths and weaknesses—PASS is an acronym for the four major cognitive processes outlined by the model: planning, attention, successive (processing), and simultaneous (processing). Planning involves creating a goal, selecting a strategy to achieve it, and then evaluating the effectiveness of the plan. Attention involves regulating arousal and alertness. Successive processing utilizes sequential or serial-order coding of information for problem solving, while simultaneous processing codes information by integrating distinct bits of information into a unified whole.

The PASS model and the CAS have great potential for assessing the cognitive abilities of children with mental retardation. In keeping with the spirit of the 1992 AAMR definition of mental retardation, the CAS could provide a profile of the child's strengths and weaknesses across the four major cognitive processes surveyed by the PASS model rather than just a global estimate of overall intellectual impairment.

Das, Kirby, and Jarman (1979) argue that children with mental retardation show their greatest weaknesses in the planning component. Naglieri, Das, and Jarman (1990) found empirical support for planning as the most significant weakness in a study comparing children with mental retardation to nondisabled children across the four components of the PASS model. Gordon and Saklofske (1994) used the developmental-difference paradigm (Hodapp, Burack, & Zigler, 1990) along with the PASS model to describe the cognitive development of children with mental retardation. Their findings suggest that planning and simultaneous processing abilities are quite similar for both children with mild mental retardation and nondisabled children; the exception was a slower rate and lower asymptote in ultimate level of performance for the mental retardation group. However, the development of successive processing abilities showed significant differences between the two groups that went beyond simply a slower rate. These studies suggest that the PASS model and the CAS may provide a particularly fruitful framework for better understanding and description of the intellectual strengths and limitations of children with mental retardation.

Adaptive Behavior

The notion of adaptive behavior has been included in descriptions of mental retardation beginning with Goddard's (1907) recognition that individuals may still function adequately within their environments given appropriate training and supports despite limitations in intellectual functioning. One of the earliest scales of adaptive behavior was the Vineland Social Maturity Scale, which was intended to assist in the description of social competencies of individuals with mental retardation.

Currently, "adaptive behavior refers to the quality of everyday performance in coping with environmental demands" (Grossman, 1983, p. 42). In contrast to the more abstract construct and measurement of intelligence, adaptive behavior focuses upon those skills required to engage in self-care and to interact appropriately with others within an individual's environment. While various descriptions of adaptive behavior have been posited in recent years (e.g., Bruininks, Thurlow, & Gilman, 1987), the AAMR (1992) describes adaptive behavior as a composite of the following adaptive skills: communication, self-care, social skills, community use, self-direction, health and safety, functional academics, leisure, and work skills. Further, the AAMR indicates that limitations in adaptive skills must occur in at least two areas.

Concern has been raised regarding the identification of the 10 adaptive skill areas, as they have not been theoretically or empirically derived (Macmillan, Gresham, & Siperstein, 1993). The assessment of adaptive behavior is then complicated by the fact that no instruments have been developed that comprehensively assess these ten adaptive skill areas (Macmillan et al., 1995). Additional concerns pertain to cultural differences in behavior and its outcomes that may confound test scores and resulting interpretations. Because child-rearing practices vary across cultures, parental expectations of a child's behavior may differ from those of main-stream society. Cultural sensitivity must go hand in hand with expert clinical judgment when assessing children from different cultures on all four dimensions proposed by the AAMR.

Further criticisms of the assessment of adaptive behavior relate to the continuing ambiguity regarding the components of adaptive behavior, the overlap or independence of adaptive skills and intelligence, and the potential misuse of adaptive behavior data in the diagnosis of mental retardation (Beirne-Smith, Patton, & Ittenbach, 1994). Despite these criticisms, there is consensus that both personal independence and social responsibility are critical components in both the diagnosis of and prescriptive planning for individuals with mental retardation.

Adaptive Behavior Scales

Numerous adaptive behavior scales have been developed for use in assessing this component of mental retardation. Commonly used scales are the Adaptive Behavior Inventory for Children (Mercer & Lewis, 1977), the AAMD Adaptive Behavior Scale (Nihiri, Foster, Shellhaas, & Leland, 1975), the AAMD Adaptive Behavior Scale, School Edition (Lambert, Windmiller, Tharinger, & Cole, 1981), and the Vineland Adaptive Behavior Scales (VABS; Sparrow, Balla, & Cicchetti, 1984).

As a revision of the Vineland Social Maturity Scale, the Vineland Adaptive Behavior Scales are composed of three separate editions: one classroom edition and two interview editions for use with parents or primary caregivers. The classroom edition of the VABS is presented in a checklist format to be completed by the classroom teacher. Designed for children ages 3 to 13, it permits the assessment of adaptive skills within the classroom environment.

The two interview editions yield data on five different adaptive skill areas/subdomains, including communication, daily living skills, socialization, motor skills, and maladaptive behavior. A composite score can also be generated based on the first four subdomains. The two editions are appropriate for assessing children from birth to 18 years of age. While the VABS is one of the most widely used and psychometrically sound of the adaptive behavior scales, "the test will have its greatest use with mildly and moderately handicapped students, although the expanded form contains many items that are appropriate for individuals with severe handicaps" (Taylor, 1989, pp. 237–238). Taylor further suggests that the VABS can assist in classification, placement, and educational programming decisions.

DIMENSION II: PSYCHOLOGICAL/EMOTIONAL CONSIDERATIONS

The 1992 AAMR definition places a great deal of importance on mental health concerns for people with mental retardation, assigning a separate dimension of the classification system for consideration of these issues. Historically, these concerns have often been ignored with some debate as to whether people with mental retardation were capable of experiencing mental health problems because of their diminished intellectual capacity (Levine, 1989; Scheerenberger, 1983).

Current research suggests that children with mental retardation do experience the same types of psychological disorders as other children (Lovell & Reiss, 1993) and at a much higher rate than their peers who are not mentally retarded (Reber, 1992). Rutter's Isle of Wight epidemiological study (Rutter, Graham, & Yule, 1970) estimated that children with mental retardation were four to five times more likely to experience psychological disorders than typical children. Research studies have produced greatly varying estimates of the rate of psychopathology in children with mental retardation ranging from 11% to 70% (Einfeld & Tonge, 1996a; Lovell & Reiss, 1993; Reiss, 1990).

A number of theories have been offered to explain why children with mental retardation are at higher risk for psychological problems. Reber (1992) argued that increased rates of psychopathology may be another manifestation of the organic pathology that caused the intellectual disability in the first place. Others have pointed to the increased stress children with mental retardation experience from repeated learning failure, family stress and dysfunction, and peer rejection (Kobe & Mulick, 1995). Levine (1989) suggested that another reason for the higher rate of psychological problems in children with mental retardation is that their problems tend to either be ignored or not identified at an early stage. Furthermore, once the difficulty is identified, mental health services may not be as readily available as it is for typical children. Fewer than 10% of children with mental retardation and a major psychiatric disability had seen a mental health specialist according to Einfeld and Tonge's (1996b) epidemiological study of Australian children. Research suggests that much psychopathology in children with mental retardation goes undiagnosed (Reiss, Levitan, & Szyszko, 1982). Reiss et al. argue that clinicians tend to interpret symptoms of psychopathology in children with mental retardation as being part of the intellectual disability and not as symptomatic of a distinct psychological problem. This tendency to use mental retardation to overexplain a child's behavior is known as diagnostic overshadowing.

Studies examining rates of psychopathology across levels of intellectual disability have found conflicting results. Some suggest higher rates for children with severe mental retardation (Myers, 1987), while others find higher rates for children with mild to moderate disabilities (Borthwick-Duffy & Eyman, 1990). Einfeld and Tonge (1996b) found significantly lower rates of psychopathology in children with profound mental retardation compared to those with mild, moderate, and severe levels. Types of psychopathology tend to differ depending on level of intellectual disability. Children with mild to moderate mental retardation tend to show more problems with anxiety and disruptive behaviors while those with severe and profound disabilities show more stereotyped, autistic, and self-injurious behavior (Einfeld & Tonge, 1996b; Lovell & Reiss, 1993).

Assessment Issues

The assessment, diagnosis, and treatment of psychopathology in children with mental retardation is a difficult endeavor even for clinicians experienced in working with this population. Communication difficulties often limit the child's ability to verbally explain his or her feelings and experiences, and until recently there has been a lack of psychometric tools for addressing these clinical issues. Instead, the clinician must often rely on careful observation of the child and thorough interviewing of parents and teachers (Lovell & Reiss, 1993).

Kobe and Mulick (1995) argue that psychopathology in children with mental retardation is usually the result of a combination of biological and environmental factors. They see the goal of assessment as determining the extent to which each of these factors plays in the child's presenting problem. Their experience has been that both biological and environmental factors need to be addressed for a successful treatment plan.

Kobe and Mulick propose four major components for good assessment. First, a medical consultation should be arranged to assess what physical or health factors might influence the presenting problem. Consideration must be given to how chronic illnesses, medication side effects, or health changes might contribute to the child's problem. Second, psychological assessment is recommended to understand the child's strengths and weaknesses both in terms of cognitive abilities and adaptive skills. Third, Kobe and Mulick strongly recommend applied behavior analysis to determine what events trigger the problem and what function it serves for the child. Finally, an assessment should be made of the child's environments and how they influence the problem behavior. This assessment should include the determination of the expectations and demands on the child in each setting as well as the exploration of what a typical day is like for the child.

Behavioral Checklists

Questionnaires such as the Child Behavior Checklist (CBC; Achenbach, 1991) and the Personality Inventory for Children (PIC; Lachar, 1982) have proven to be reliable, valid, and efficient means of assessing psychopathology in children. Clinical experience is that these instruments can be helpful in better understanding psychological problems for children with mental retardation but that the results must be interpreted with caution. Nanson (1990) has shown that the CBC is useful in assessing behavior problems in children with fetal alcohol syndrome. However, Aman, Tasse, Rojahn, and Hammer (1996) caution that scales designed for typical children may not be effective for children with mental retardation since the expression of psychopathology can be significantly different in this population. For example, children with mental retardation typically show elevations on the Psychosis scale of the PIC (Levine, 1989). This appears to occur because of the large number of items on the scale inquiring about adaptive skills such as toilet training and social skills. Careful analysis of the responses on this scale for children with mental retardation often reveals the concerns are more about developmental difficulties than actual psychotic symptomatology.

Recently, a number of new scales have been specifically designed to assess psychopathology in children with mental retardation. The Aberrant Behavior Checklist (ABC; Aman, Singh, Stewart, & Field, 1985) was designed to measure drug treatment effects in adolescents and adults with mental retardation. The ABC requires a caregiver to rate 58 items describing symptoms of psychopathology on a 4-point scale. The original factor analyses by Aman et al. indicated a five-factor solution with scales measuring irritability, withdrawal, hyperactivity, stereotypies, and inappropriate speech. More recent research (Freund & Reiss, 1991; Marshburn & Aman, 1992; Rojahn & Helsel, 1991) found the ABC has clinical utility in assessing psychopathology in children with mental retardation and has a similar factor structure for children and adults and adolescents. Rojahn and Helsel (1991) found support for criterion validity but noted some concerns with test reliability.

The Developmental Behavior Checklist (DBC; Einfeld & Tonge, 1995) is a modification of the CBC and, like its predecessor, features both a parent and a teacher version. The DBC consists of six scales measuring anxiety, autism, communication disturbances, and disputive, self-absorbed, and antisocial behaviors. Einfeld and Tonge (1995) argue that the DBC has good internal consistency and interrater and test-retest reliability. In addition, the scales are both specific and sensitive in identifying clinically significant behavior problems.

The Nisonger Child Behavior Rating Form (CBRF; Aman et al., 1996) is normed for children with mental retardation from 3 to 16 years old. The Nisonger CBRF consists of two sections, one examining problem behaviors and the other focusing on adaptive or prosocial behaviors. Factor analysis of the parent version identifies six factors: conduct problems, insecurity/anxiety, hyperactivity, self-injury/stereotypies, self-isolation, and oversensitivity. The teacher version shares the first five factors but its sixth factor is labeled *irritability*. Items encompass behaviors such as tantrums, mood swings, and frustration. According to Aman et al., the Nisonger CBRF shows high internal consistency and interrater reliability and demonstrates good concurrent validity with the ABC.

The Reiss Scales for Children's Dual Diagnoses (Reiss & Valenti-Hein, 1994) is designed for children ages 4 to 21 years and requires that two caregivers rate behaviors on a 3-point scale. The Reiss covers 10 scales, measuring anger/self-control, anxiety, attention, autism, conduct disorder, depression, self-esteem, psychosis, somatoform behavior, and withdrawal. There is some indication that this scale is best used with children with mild and moderate intellectual disabilities since some degree of self-report is required (Hurley & Sovner, 1992).

Other scales have been aimed at more specific assessment goals. The Diagnostic Assessment for the Severely Handicapped (Matson, Gardner, Coe, & Sovner, 1991) focuses on the symptoms of psychopathology seen specifically with children and adults with severe and profound intellectual disabilities. The Adolescent Behavior Checklist (Demb, Brier, Huron, & Tomor, 1994) is a self-report measure designed to detect psychological problems in adolescents with mild or borderline intellectual disabilities. Items are read to the client who then responds verbally; a minimum of a fourth-grade reading level is required to comprehend the material.

Hurley and Sovner (1992) provide a number of recommendations for the use of psychopathology checklists with children who have mental retardation. First, the clinician must recognize that checklists cannot be used as the sole method of assessment but rather as part of a comprehensive diagnostic process that involves clinical interviews and a medical evaluation. They also suggest that it can be facilitative to use two different checklists in an attempt to establish concurrent validity for any diagnostic hypotheses. Similarly, the use of two or more caregivers as raters can provide a better picture of the extent of the presenting problem.

Hurley and Sovner argue for the importance of using clinical judgment in interpreting test scores. They reiterate Kobe and Mulick's (1995) concern that the standard cutoff of +2 standard deviations for considering behavior as clinically significant may not be appropriate with current scales designed for children with mental retardation. Most scales are not based on a random sample of children with mental retardation but rather on groups referred to clinics for behavioral or developmental difficulties. Even with a random sample, prevalence data show that this population has a much higher rate of psychopathology so the traditional standard-deviation cutoff of 2 is probably not sensitive enough. Rather, they propose considering scores at the 85th percentile or above as clinically significant.

Exercising sound clinical judgment also means doing a careful item-by-item analysis of the responses on each scale. A positive endorsement of an item inquiring about suicidal behavior or hallucinations requires follow up regardless of what the overall scale score is.

Finally, to interpret a checklist it is important to know just exactly what types of children the norms were based on and who the raters are. For example, parent ratings on the Nisonger CBRF are based mostly on the mother's ratings (Aman et al., 1996). It may be difficult to generalize the ratings to fathers. Our clinical experience has been that fathers tend to rate symptoms as less severe than mothers do. Thus, it would be important to consider seriously a father's rating of a scale score at the 80th percentile on a scale primarily normed on a mother's responses.

Clinical Interviews

A vital part of the assessment process of psychological strengths and weaknesses is the clinical interviews with the child, family, and teachers. Kobe and Mulick (1995) indicate interviews are likely to be more successful with children with mental retardation if they are conducted over a series of short sessions rather than in one long interview. Obviously, language must be matched to the child's developmental level. They also encourage an awareness of the possibility of leading children to an answer or encouraging compliance. One child had made vague complaints of feeling dizzy and seeing spots at times. The consulting neurologist suspected migraine headaches and queried the child about whether the spots he saw were like the aura often associated with migraines. He did this by drawing an elaborate diagram of an aura and asking the child whether this was what he saw. The boy readily agreed— and now when asked about the spots will reproduce a very good reproduction of the neurologist's original diagram. To this day, it is unclear whether the boy is actually experiencing auras or had this phenomenon suggested by the neurologist's line of questioning.

For children who find a lengthy verbal exchange difficult, play interviews offer an excellent method for gathering information. As the name suggests, this method combines play and verbal questioning with the clinician titrating the level of each according to the client's needs. The interview takes place in a playroom stocked with a variety of toys appropriate to the child's developmental level. The verbal questions are selected from Achenbach's Semi-structured Clinical Interview for Children and Adolescents (McConaughy & Achenbach, 1994), which covers topics such as feelings about family, friends, and school. Questions are interspersed throughout the play. For children who find talking about themselves difficult, the process may be framed in a game format. The child is told that he and the clinician are playing a game called *scavenger hunt* and that while they play with the toys it is the clinician's job to find out a number of things about the child (e.g., favorite subject in school). It is not just the answers to the questions that are important but also the process of the play interview that provides valuable information. How the child relates to the clinician and utilizes the play materials can have diagnostic utility.

For children with more severe disabilities and limited communication skills, the verbal questions can be curtailed and the focus put instead on the play and interaction. Since many children with mental retardation can have difficulty verbalizing their feelings or giving a good history of the presenting problem, careful clinical interviews of parents and other significant caregivers is important. Lovell and Reiss (1993) argue that interviews should include inquiries about neurovegative signs such as changes in sleep, appetite, or energy, since these may be particularly sensitive markers for psychopathology in children with mental retardation. Kobe and Mulick (1995) suggest that drawing a timeline of occurrence of symptoms and other significant events in the child's life based on information gained from family and teachers can be quite helpful in sorting out potential influences and antecedents on the presenting problem.

DIMENSION III: PHYSICAL/HEALTH/ETIOLOGY CONSIDERATIONS

Dimension III of the AAMR's (1992) multidimensional definition of mental retardation focuses on etiology as well as health and physical considerations. The AAMR (1992) advocates that health and physical factors can have a significant impact on functioning as well as "assessment, environmental factors, and the need for supports and services" (p. 61). Thus, the psychologist should be alert to the influence and effects of health and physical factors when conducting both intellectual and adaptive skills assessments.

Turning to etiological considerations, there is a growing list of causes of mental retardation as well as diagnostic labels. An examination of the AAMR (1992) description of disorders in which mental retardation may occur is very lengthy and is viewed under the following headings:

Prenatal onset: including chromosomal disorder, syndrome disorder, inborn error of metabolism, developmental disorder of brain formation, environmental influence.

Perinatal onset: including intrauterine disorders, neonatal disorders.

Postnatal onset: including head injury, infection, demyelinating disorder, degenerative disorder, seizure, disorder, toxic-metabolic disorder, malnutrition, environmental deprivation, hypoconnection syndrome (pp. 81–91).

The etiology of mental retardation can be most parsimoniously viewed as either biological or psychosocial. However, the *Diagnostic and Statistical Manual of Mental Disorders-Fourth Edition* (*DSM-IV;* 1994) states that no clear etiology can be determined in 30 to 40% of individuals who have undergone extensive diagnostic evaluations for mental retardation. The *DSM-IV* lists four predisposing factors that reflect a biological basis, including:

Heredity (about 5%) such as inborn errors of metabolism and chromosomal aberrations.

Early alterations of embryonic development (about 30%) such as chromosomal changes and toxin-induced prenatal damage.

Pregnancy and perinatal problems (about 10%) including oxygen deprivation, prenatal or birth trauma, and viral infections.

General medical conditions acquired in infancy and childhood (about 5%) including infections and poisoning.

A fifth predisposing factor includes a mixture of environmental (e.g., social and linguistic deprivation; caretaker neglect or abuse) and other severe developmental and mental disorders (e.g., Asperger's Disorder, Autistic Disorder). The prevalence of these influences is estimated at 15 to 20%. Mental retardation that is suspected to have an environmental cause as well as those cases where no clear biological cause can be found is frequently referred to as *familial retardation.* Sattler (1992) states that most milder forms of mental retardation (IQ range 50 to 70) fall into the familial grouping in contrast to the severe levels of retardation that more often have an organic or biological basis. Further, mild retardation characterizes about 85% of children with mental retardation.

Following a diagnosis of mental retardation, consideration of etiological factors may further contribute to both a description of the client and to program development and implementation. However, evaluation of the description of etiological factors serves more than one agency or party—such as the school or medical profession. The multifactorial approach to etiology recommended by the AAMR first identifies four groups of causal factors: biomedical, family, behavioral, and educational. A second component of causality relates to who is affected by a diagnosis of mental retardation (i.e., the parents, the diagnosed person, or both). Finally, the AAMR (1992) suggests that "these concepts concerning the multifactorial and intergenerational origins of mental retardation have important implications for prevention" (p. 71). Thus, clinical evaluation for etiology is much more than a disconnected exercise; it is one that has considerable implications for program development and prognosis.

DIMENSION IV: ENVIRONMENTAL CONSIDERATIONS

Positive environments contribute significantly to growth in cognitive development and social skills in children with mental retardation (Luckasson et al., 1992). Dimension IV of the 1992 AAMR definition requires assessment of which environments are important to the child, how each helps or hinders the child's development, and what would be the optimum environment to facilitate the child's growth.

Luckasson et al. outline three key characteristics of positive environments. First, they provide opportunities for the child to learn and grow. Second, they foster well-being by providing for such needs as physical safety, material comforts, and community participation. Finally, positive environments promote stability by providing a sense of predictability and control for the child.

One way of assessing environments is to analyze how they facilitate or inhibit five optimum environmental characteristics (Luckasson et al., 1992). The first of these characteristics is community presence, or being able to share in the typical places of community life that are important for all children. A second related characteristic of optimum environments is community participation, or having the experience of being part of a community of people and friends. A third characteristic is choice, or having a sense of power and control over one's life. The fourth characteristic is competence, or having the opportunity to learn and do meaningful activities. The final characteristic of positive environments is respect, or truly being valued. Analysis of how well an environment facilitates these characteristics involves watching the child in the setting, coming to an understanding of what happens there or who is involved, and determining what else the child or family wants to do there or do more of.

Two key environments for children with mental retardation are home/family and school. This section will explore important assessment issues and tools for each.

Home/Family: Assessment Issues

For families, the experience of mental retardation has changed significantly over the years. Previously, many children with mental retardation lived away from home in institutions. Today, the vast majority of children with mental retardation grow up with their parents and siblings. They may remain in their parental homes well into adulthood. Mental retardation can be a very significant and long-term stressor on family function.

Wikler (1981) suggests three ways mental retardation can impact negatively on the family. The first is by increasing parental stress levels as care-giving demands are intensified, financial pressures mount, and parents experience difficulty finding information about how to help their child. The second possible negative impact on the family is social isolation as the family finds less time for friends and community contacts because of increased caregiving demands. Finally, there can be an increase in behavior and psychological problems with other siblings in the family. Some studies have found higher divorce rates and a greater incidence of marital problems for families living with mental retardation (Gath, 1985), but others find no significant difference when factors such as socioeconomic status are controlled for (Wikler, 1981). Other research reports that siblings experience more anxiety, greater conflicts with parents, and poorer interpersonal relationships than do children from families without mental retardation (Crnic, Friedrich, & Greenberg, 1983). However, Wilson, Blacher, and Baker (1989) found that siblings of children with severe intellectual disabilities coped very well and were able to see a number of positive aspects from having a disabled sibling as part of the family.

Obviously, mental retardation is not a uniform stressor across all families, marriages, and siblings. Crnic et al. (1983) proposed a model to explain why some families experience great stress and others adapt well. They argue that the family's response to mental retardation depends on the interaction of three factors: stress, coping resources, and ecological contexts. Stress can be increased or reduced by the availability of coping resources such as extended family networks and problem-solving skills. Similarly, stress is mediated by the ecological contexts or key environments in which the family is involved and by how well these help or hinder their overall adjustment.

Our clinical experience has been that two key aspects of the home/family environment requiring assessment are the psychological health of each parent and the health of the marriage. Families draw their strength from parents, and a vicious circle can develop where the impact of the disability compromises the health of the parents or the marriage, which results in their having fewer resources and less energy to devote to the children. This can result in deterioration in the behavior of the children, which in turn further compromises the parents' personal psychological health. Good assessment should consider strengths and weaknesses in the parents' psychological health and the marriage relationship. Good treatment plans require consideration of what can be done to maximize both. Similarly, siblings may receive less attention to their needs as the focus of the family is drawn to the child with mental retardation (Dyson, Edgar, & Crnic, 1989). Their needs should be considered to provide a total picture of family health.

Home/Family: Assessment Tools

One useful instrument in assessing the psychological health of parents and the marriage relationship is the Parenting Stress Index-Third Edition (PSI-3; Abidin, 1995). This scale evaluates three distinct aspects of stress a parent may be experiencing. The Child Domain looks at characteristics of the child that may be producing stress. These include attention problems, adaptability, how demanding the child is, mood, how much the child reinforces the parent, and how acceptable the child is to the parent. The Parent Domain addresses characteristics of the parent that influence stress. These include competence as a parent, sense of isolation, attachment to the child, physical health, role-restriction, depression, and support from spouse. A Life Stress scale measures other stressors for the parent occurring outside of the parental relationship. Abidin (1995) presents evidence that the PSI-3 has good internal consistency and test-retest reliability as well as showing concurrent validity with a number of other measures of family functioning and parent stress. The PSI-3 has been found to be an efficient means of identifying whether a parent is experiencing clinically significant levels of stress and of generating hypotheses for what the specific sources of that stress are.

The Parenting Satisfaction Scale (PSS; Guidubaldi & Cleminshaw, 1994) evaluates a parent's degree of satisfaction regarding three aspects of parenting: their own parenting performance, their relationship with their child, and their happiness with their spouse's parenting performance. The PSS may be a useful conversation starter with families regarding their level of satisfaction or happiness with their own parenting and how this may impact upon the development of their children.

Just as play interviews can be useful in evaluating the child's psychological status, family play sessions can be valuable in assessing family functioning. This process can be quite structured, as with the Marschak Interaction Method (Jernberg, 1991) where parent and child are required to complete a series of tasks such as feeding the child or playing a competitive game together. It can also be quite nondirective. Having the family go to a playroom stocked with toys appropriate for their child's developmental level and instructing them to have fun with the toys is a useful approach. As the play progresses, different combinations of family members can be asked to play together in order to assess how specific groupings relate. Finally, the family is requested to clean up the playroom, which allows observation of how they approach and execute completion of a task together. We have found this method provides a great deal of information about parenting skills, attachment to the child, energy level of the parents, and allegiances/alignments within the family.

School: Assessment Issues

With the passage of Public Law 94–142, school-based special-education services for children with mental retardation were legislated in the United States. Although other countries (e.g., Canada, Australia) do not have federal legislation mandating the provision of special-education services, many school districts within these countries have adopted practices that reflect the intent of Public Law 94–142. For example, they have mandated the development and implementation of assessment protocols and individual education plans (IEPs) for children with special needs (e.g., mental retardation). Moreover, numerous states and provinces have legislated that individuals with mental retardation must receive public school education until the age of 21 (AAMR, 1992).

The identification of children with mental retardation may be made during infancy and early childhood if there is known etiology (e.g., Down Syndrome). However, children who are delayed in acquiring cognitive and behavioral skills and who do not have an identified etiology may be labeled as "developmentally delayed, disadvantaged, or most simply *at risk*" (Polloway, 1987, p. 12). These children may be placed in early intervention programs (according to P.L. 99–457) with the intent of follow-up evaluations prior to or at the time of entry into the school system.

According to Public Laws 94–142 and 99–457, assessment practices must be multidisciplinary; that is, a variety of team members must contribute to the assessment process. Depending on the nature and extent of the disabling condition, assessment teams may comprise both school-based and community-based personnel such as school psychologists, classroom and special-education teachers, parents, occupational and/or physical therapists, speech/language pathologists, and social workers (Orelove & Sobsey, 1991; Rainforth, York, & Macdonald, 1992; Taylor, 1989).

As a function of their traditional assessment role within the multidisciplinary team, school psychologists typically conduct formal and informal assessments in order to facilitate both placement and programming decision making. For educational placement decisions, school psychologists are required to identify those children who perform below the cutoff score on tests of intellectual functioning (e.g., SB-IV) and demonstrate deficits in adaptive skills (e.g., Vineland Adaptive Behavior Scales). Within the context of the school environment, these limitations pertain to a variety of adaptive skill areas, such as communication, self-care, social skills, self-direction, use of community resources, and functional academics. For educational programming decisions (e.g., development of the IEP), school psychologists may assess the student's academic performance (using norm-referenced and curriculum-based tests), conduct interviews with parents and teachers to prioritize skill acquisition needs, and observe the student in the classroom and school setting to evaluate behavior and ascertain whether program goals and objectives are being met (AAMR, 1992; Fiscus & Mandell, 1983; Gajar, Goodman, & McAfee, 1993).

The development of the IEP reflects the processes of assessment: diagnosis, placement, program planning, program implementation, and evaluation (Fiscus & Mandell, 1983). The IEP specifies "the student's present level of educational performance, state[s] annual goals and instructional objectives, identif[ies] the educational and related services to be provided, and specif[ies] objective criteria for evaluating attainment of objectives" (Rodger, 1995, p. 235). The AAMR recommends that the nature and extent of required supports also be identified within the school environment and incorporated into the IEP (AAMR, 1992). As conceptualized by the AAMR, these supports may range in intensity (intermittent, limited, extensive, and pervasive), may be applicable to all or particular adaptive skills, and may be required in some or all of an individual's environments. Of course, the duration of the required supports may vary from ongoing/long term to short term. A complementary document to the IEP is the individualized transitional plan (ITP). In addition to the annual goals and objectives stated in the IEP, the ITP should include transition services required by the students to ensure that they achieve "appropriate vocational, academic, and social goals for their lives in postsecondary school settings" (Gajar et al., 1993, p. 179).

Since the inception of the IEP process, however, concerns have been raised regarding its efficaciousness. A review of the literature (e.g., Rainforth et al., 1992; Skinner, 1991; Smith, 1990) suggests that the IEP process can be facilitated through the inservicing of parents, teachers, and support service personnel. For example, inservicing regarding collaborative decision making, conflict resolution, and caseload management should be done periodically as team members (particularly school-based) may be replaced annually (Rodger, 1995). The IEP must also be of such quality and content that it will have credibility with those members (e.g., classroom and special-education teachers) directly responsible for implementing the goals and objectives pertaining to instructional programming (Rodger, 1995).

Assessment Tools

Within the school venue, assessment tools may vary from formal measures (e.g., standardized norm-referenced tests of intelligence) to informal measures (e.g., direct observation of the student in the classroom). Although intelligence tests and adaptive behavior scales are routinely used by school psychologists to ascertain whether an individual has mental retardation, a variety of other assessment tools and/ or approaches may be used depending on the nature and extent of the disability.

Recently, alternative methods for assessing student performance have been advocated; these approaches will be described here briefly.

Transdisciplinary Approach to Assessment

The transdisciplinary approach to assessment and educational programming was developed in order to address concerns regarding the isolated and potentially redundant practices of multidisciplinary teams. The model is particularly useful for children with multiple disabilities and "is characterized by a sharing, or transferring, of information and skills across traditional disciplinary boundaries" (Orelove & Sobsey, 1991, p. 11). Team members are encouraged to assess children within their natural environments through behavioral observations conducted jointly. Traditional assessment techniques may be employed if further information is required; however, the focus of the assessment is on the natural context within which the child functions. Indirect service is the primary means through which intervention is conducted; team members (e.g., psychologists) serve as consultants to the teacher or service designate.

Collaborative Assessment Approach

The collaborative assessment approach is similar to the transdisciplinary approach in that assessments are conducted within the students' natural environments while they are performing typical activities. Although formal assessments may be conducted by specific team members, collaboration on the part of the team members at the initial stages of the assessment will help to ensure that appropriate and relevant programs and intervention plans are developed (Rainforth et al., 1992).

The assessment process consists of four steps (which may overlap):

Planning the assessment—establishing the assessment team, identifying priorities regarding assessment of particular environments.

Assessing the student—development of an ecological inventory that is based on performance expectations of age-appropriate peers without disabilities; target student's performance (with and without assistance) is then assessed against performance indicators in the inventory.

Analysis of the target student's and peers' performance discrepancies.

Diagnostic assessments by individual team members consisting of both formal and informal assessment strategies (Rainforth et al., 1992).

The goal of the collaborative assessment approach is to produce an integrated IEP that will have the most utility for the student's instructional environment. Intervention practices extend beyond the transdisciplinary approach in that both indirect and direct services are provided.

CONCLUSION

The assessment of children with mental retardation has advanced significantly in recent years. The administration of an intelligence test for classification purposes has only given way to an ongoing multimethod and multisource assessment process. The AAMR has proposed a four-dimensional description of mental retardation, which recognizes intellectual functioning and adaptive skills, psychological needs, physical and health considerations, and environmental factors.

Best practices in assessment may not only result in a diagnosis of mental retardation but also have utility for the development and implementation of comprehensive educational and vocational programs. Further, the promotion of personal and social well-being is a critical factor in the assessment of children with mental retardation. Clearly, assessment must be cast within a collaborative multidisciplinary framework.

Case Example 16–1 illustrates the best practices in assessment of mental retardation.

Case Example 16–1.   Assessing mental retardation

Bobby is a 9-year-old boy who had previously been diagnosed with mild to moderate mental retardation under the 1983 classification system. He was referred again for psychological assessment because of parental concerns regarding delayed cognitive and social development. Bobby complained to his parents that he did not have any friends, was not invited to play sports with the other boys, and was called "stupid" by other children in his neighborhood. In addition, Bobby's parents found him to be quite stubborn at times; he exhibited temper tantrums when frustrated.

STEP 1: DIAGNOSIS OF MENTAL RETARDATION

Although a diagnosis of mental retardation had been made when Bobby was 6 years old, assessment of his cognitive abilities and adaptive behavior skills was repeated to help identify current strengths and weaknesses in these areas.

The results of the current intellectual assessment along with those obtained from previous assessments are shown below. Bobby continues to present with a mild to moderate intellectual impairment with no significant difference between his verbal and performance abilities.

9 years old	WISC-III	
	Full Scale IQ	55
	Verbal Scale IQ	58
	Performance Scale IQ	60
7 years old	WPPSI-R	
	Full Scale IQ	53
	Verbal Scale IQ	54
	Performance Scale IQ	60

(continued)

Case Example 16–1.   *(Continued)*

6 years old	WPPSI-R	
	Full Scale IQ	58
	Verbal Scale IQ	65
	Performance Scale IQ	58
5 years old	Stanford-Binet L-M	
	Composite IQ Score	68

Bobby's adaptive behavior skills were assessed using the Vineland Adaptive Behavior Scales-Interview Edition. These results along with those from his last assessment are shown below. Bobby displays moderate deficits in all three subdomains which is consistent with the previous assessment. There has been a decline in his daily living-skill standard score since his previous assessment. An inspection of the items indicates that this is primarily due to lower scores on toileting items. Bobby had been completely independent in his toileting skills on the last assessment but is now having many fecal-soiling incidents.

Vineland Adaptive Behavior Scales	*9 Years Old*	*7 Years Old*
Communication	52	58
Daily living skills	42	64
Socialization	53	53
Adaptive composite	46	54

The most recent assessment data show that Bobby continues to present with significant subaverage intellectual functioning and adaptive skill limitations in communication, self-care, and social skills. The diagnosis of mental retardation remains appropriate.

STEP 2: CLASSIFICATION AND DESCRIPTION: PROFILE OF
STRENGTHS AND WEAKNESSES

Dimension I: Intellectual Functioning and Adaptive Skills.
 Intellectual Functioning: Previously described
Adaptive Skills:

A. Communication Skills

Strengths: able to express himself clearly in full sentences.

Weaknesses: often has trouble understanding verbal directions.

B. Social Skills

Strengths: very friendly, sociable, and polite; teachers enjoy working with him; has one close friend with whom he plays regularly.

Weaknesses: has a hard time understanding rules of organized games; tends to become excluded as a result; has a difficult time controlling his anger when denied his own way at home; responds with temper tantrums.

Dimension II: Psychological/Emotional Considerations. In order to assess Bobby's psychological and emotional strengths and weaknesses, his parents were asked to complete the Child Behavior Checklist. Their responses were similar and showed clinically significant elevations on the Uncommunicative, Social Withdrawal, Hyperac-

Case Example 16–1.   *(Continued)*

tive, Aggressive, and Delinquent subscales. Their descriptions of Bobby present a profile of a boy who is self-conscious and who has a hard time talking about his feelings. They see him as a boy who is not liked by other children his age (he tends to play with younger children in the neighborhood). He has a high activity level and difficulties with concentration and impulse control. Bobby tends to be quite disobedient at home, often breaks things, and demands a lot of attention. He is described as quite stubborn and moody.

Bobby's teachers have been asked to complete the school version of the Child Behavior Checklist; these data are forthcoming. However, in an interview, his teachers indicated that they thought he was not experiencing behavioral difficulties in the classroom or on the playground.

Bobby participated in a play interview using a semi-structured clinical interview as previously described in the chapter. Bobby related well to the interviewer and engaged easily in a variety of play activities. He did not identify concerns when asked about possible difficulties at home or school. Interestingly, he forgot to include himself in a family drawing; when reminded, he drew himself outside of the house in which the rest of his family was situated.

Dimension III: Physical/Health/Etiology Considerations. No etiology has ever been determined for Bobby's mental retardation. When he was 6 years old he was seen by a child psychiatrist who made an additional diagnosis of attention-deficit hyperactivity disorder. Bobby was prescribed Ritalin, which greatly improved his attentional skills but also had the side effects of increased irritability and loss of appetite. His medication was changed to Dexedrine, which reduced the side effects but was also less effective in controlling attentional problems.

Dimension IV: Environmental Considerations. Bobby's parents completed the Parent Stress Index to better describe their strengths and weaknesses as a family. Again, their responses were quite similar. All of the stress subscales from the Child Domain were above the 95th percentile. Bobby was described as a child who was extremely demanding, very hyperactive, and very different from the child they had expected prior to his birth. This suggested that Bobby's parents were still in the process of accepting Bobby's disability. There were no clinical elevations on the stress subscales from the Parent Domain. Bobby's parents did not indicate any significant problems with their sense of competence as parents, feelings of isolation, their own physical health, or the level of support they received from each other. In fact, their responses suggested that they may have been unwilling to admit to some stresses frequently experienced by parents. Interestingly, on the scale measuring stressful life events in the previous year, the father indicated a marital reconciliation while the mother did not.

Bobby's family, including his parents and younger brother, participated in a family play session. In general, the family had a great deal of fun playing together. They presented as quite loving with primarily positive relationships with each other. However, it was noted that when the whole family played together, the father tended to be less involved, often retreating to a corner while the play went on around him. When

(continued)

Case Example 16–1. *(Continued)*

the mother left the room, the father was much more involved and showed a great deal of patience and energy in explaining to Bobby how a table hockey set worked.

STEP 3: PROFILES AND INTENSITIES OF NEEDED SUPPORTS

The assessment identified a number of supports that would benefit Bobby.

1. *Communication:* Bobby was described as having difficulty following verbal directions. A speech/language pathologist also assessed Bobby and indicated he presents with a severe receptive language processing disorder. This is compounded by his attentional difficulties. Speech/language therapy was initiated to help build receptive language skills. Parents and teachers were instructed to be aware of the difficulty, to make sure that they had Bobby's attention when giving directions, to keep directions short, using simple language, and to ensure that Bobby understood the content and meaning of the verbal communication.

2. *Self-care:* A number of behavioral interventions were considered to help with the fecal soiling difficulty. However, the psychologist requested a consultation with the family pediatrician to look at possible medical factors before proceeding.

3. *Social Skills:* A social skills program was begun at the school to help Bobby with some of the interaction problems he was experiencing with other children. The program focused on assisting Bobby to understand the rules of games he wanted to play. Direct intervention on the playground further facilitated his interactions with the other children.

4. *Psychological/Emotional Considerations:* Bobby was taught several anger management and relaxation strategies to build his repertoire of strategies to use when he felt frustrated. A course of individual play therapy was initiated to address his self-esteem issues and his sense of being different from the other children in his class.

5. *Physical/Health Considerations:* The family pediatrician concluded that Bobby's fecal soiling was the result of a severe constipation problem. Medical therapy was initiated to correct the problem. Once the constipation difficulty was addressed, Bobby's toileting skills returned to their former level of complete independence. In addition, the pediatrician continued to consult with the family regarding the medication used to assist Bobby with his attentional difficulties.

6. *Environmental Considerations:* Bobby's parents were experiencing a great deal of stress from a number of behaviors stemming from his short attention span and intellectual disability. Behavioral strategies were recommended. After several sessions, the parents reported that Bobby's behavior was better controlled and much less frustrating to them.

Given the apparent lack of ongoing communication between the school and Bobby's parents, it was recommended that the school-based team members and the parents review the IEP to determine the appropriateness of current educational programming and grade placement.

Several other supports were also suggested to the parents. Previously, the parents indicated that they had not been out together as a couple for over 5 years. The parents agreed to a respite evening together every week. Following several of these outings, they agreed that marital therapy might be helpful in addressing a number of issues relating to parental roles.

Luckasson et al. (1992) provide a model to profile needed supports that includes

Case Example 16–1.   *(Continued)*

support functions and intensity levels of required supports. The table below demonstrates how the model might be used to describe the supports from which Bobby could benefit. As an alternative to this approach, we have found that a list of the required supports may suffice for our purposes in clinical practice.

Dimension/Area	Support Function	Activities	Intensity
Intellectual Functioning and Adaptive Skills			
Communication	Teaching	SLP assessment and treatment	Intermittent and extensive
Self-Care	Teaching	Assistance with rebuilding toileting skills after medical therapy	Intermittent
Social Skills	Teaching	Teaching functional play skills for playground use	Limited
Psychological/ Emotional Considerations	Teaching and behavioral support	Anger management	Limited
		Teaching skills for relaxation	Limited
		Play therapy	Limited
Physical/Health Etiology	Health assistance	Medical assessment & therapy for fecal soiling	Intermittent
	Health assistance/ behavioral support	Medication to assist with attentional problems	Extensive
Environmental Considerations Home/Family	Behavioral support	Consultation with family re: behavior strategies	Extensive
	In-home living assistance	Respite for parents	Extensive
School	Health assistance support	Marital therapy	Limited
		Coordination of services	Extensive
	Support	Increase familial involvement in IEP process	Extensive
		Review optimal environment (e.g., placement and program)	Limited

REFERENCES

Abidin, R.R. (1995). *Parent Stress Index: Third Edition*. Odessa, FL: Psychological Assessment Resources.

Achenbach, T.M. (1991). *Manual for the Child Behavior Checklist/4–18 and 1991 Profile*. Burlington, VT: University of Vermont, Department of Psychiatry.

Aman, M.G., Singh, N.N., Stewart, A.W., & Field, C.J. (1985). The Aberrant Behavior Checklist: A behavior rating scale for the assessment of treatment effects. *American Journal of Mental Deficiency, 89,* 485–491.

Aman, M.G., Tasse, M.J., Rojahn, J., & Hammer, D. (1996). The Nisonger CBRF: A child behavior rating form for children with developmental disabilities. *Research in Developmental Disabilities, 17,* 41–57.

American Psychiatric Association (1994). *Diagnostic and statistical manual of mental disorders* (4th ed.). Washington, DC: Author.

Bayley, N. (1993). *Manual for Bayley Scales of Infant Development* (2nd ed.). San Antonio, TX: The Psychological Corporation.

Beirne-Smith, M., Patton, J.R., & Ittenbach, R. (1994). *Mental Retardation: Fourth Edition.* New York: MacMillian College Publishing Company.

Borthwick-Duffy, S.A., & Eyman, R.K. (1990). Who are the dually diagnosed? *American Journal on Mental Retardation, 94,* 586–595.

Bruininks, R.H., Thurlow, M., & Gilman, C.J. (1987). Adaptive behavior and mental Retardation. *Journal of Special Education, 21,* 69–88.

Crnic, K.A., Friedrich, W.N., & Greenberg, M.T. (1983). Adaptation of families with mentally retarded children: A model of stress, coping, and family ecology. *American Journal of Mental Deficiency, 88*(2), 125–138.

Das, J.P. (1993). Neurocognitive approach to remediation: The PREP model. *Canadian Journal of School Psychology, 9,* 157-173.

Das, J.P., Kirby, J.R., & Jarman, R.F. (1979). *Simultaneous and successive cognitive processes.* New York: Academic Press.

Das, J.P., & Naglieri, J.A. (1996). *The cognitive assessment system.* Chicago: Riverside.

Das, J.P., Naglieri, J.A., & Kirby, J.R. (1994). *Assessment of cognitive processes.* Needham Heights, MA: Allyn & Bacon.

Demb, H.B., Brier, N., Huron, R., & Tomor, E. (1994). The Adolescent Behavior Checklist: Normative data and sensitivity and specificity of screening tools for diagnosable psychiatric disorders in adolescents with mental retardation and other developmental disabilities. *Research in Developmental Disabilities, 15,* 151–165.

Dyson, L., Edgar, E., & Crnic, K. (1989). Psychological predictors of adjustment by siblings of developmental disabled children. *American Journal on Mental Retardation, 94*(3), 292–302.

Einfeld, S.L., & Tonge, B.J. (1996a). Population prevalence of psychopathology in children and adolescents with intellectual disability, I: rationale and methods. *Journal of Intellectual Disability Research, 40,* 91–98.

Einfeld, S.L., & Tonge, B.J. (1996b). Population prevalence of psychopathology in children and adolescents with intellectual disability, II: epidemiological findings. *Journal of Intellectual Disability Research, 40,* 99–109.

Einfeld, S.L., & Tonge, B.J. (1995). The Developmental Behavior Checklist: The development and validation of an instrument to assess behavioral and emotional disturbance in children and adolescents with mental retardation. *Journal of Autism and Developmental Disorders, 25,* 81–104.

Elliott, C.D. (1990). *The Differential Ability Scales.* Toronto: The Psychological Corporation.

Evans, J.H., Carlsen, R.N., & McGrew, K.S. (1993). Classification of exceptional students with the Woodcock-Johnson Psycho-Educational Battery-Revised [Monograph series]. *Journal of Psychoeducational Assessment,* 6–19.

Fiscus, E.D., & Mandell, C.J. (1983). *Developing individualized education programs.* St. Paul, MN: West Publishing Company.

Freund, L.S., & Reiss, A.L. (1991). Rating problem behaviours in outpatients with mental retardation: Use of the Aberrant Behavior Checklist. *Research in Developmental Disabilities, 12,* 435–451.

Gajar, A., Goodman, L., & McAfee, J. (1993). *Secondary schools and beyond: Transition of individuals with mild disabilities.* New York: Macmillan.

Gath, A. (1985). Parental reactions to loss and disappointment: The diagnosis of Down's syndrome. *Developmental Medicine & Child Neurology, 27,* 392–400.

Gordon, B., & Saklofske, D.H. (1994). New approaches to the developmental-difference debate. *Developmental Disabilities Bulletin, 22,* 54–72.

Grossman, H.J. (1983). *Classification in mental retardation.* Washington, DC: American Association on Mental Deficiency.

Guidubaldi, J., & Cleminshaw, H.K. (1994). *Parenting Satisfaction Scale.* San Antonio, TX: The Psychological Corporation.

Hodapp, R., Burack, J.A., & Zigler, E. (1990). *Issues in the developmental approach to mental retardation.* New York: Cambridge University Press.

Hurley, A.B., & Sovner, R. (1992). Inventories for evaluating psycho-pathology in developmentally disabled individuals. *The Habilitative Mental Healthcare Newsletter, 11,* 45–49.

Jernberg, A.M. (1991). Assessing parent-child interactions with the Marschak Interaction Method (MIM). In C.E. Schaeffer, K. Gitlin, & A. Sandgrund (Eds.), *Play Diagnosis and Assessment* (pp. 493–516). New York: Wiley.

Kamphaus, R.W. (1993). *Clinical assessment of children's intelligence.* Boston: Allyn & Bacon.

Kaufman, A.S. (1979). *Intelligent testing with the WISC-R.* New York: Wiley.

Kaufman, A.S. (1994). *Intelligent testing with the WISC-III.* New York: Wiley.

Kobe, F.H., & Mulick, J.A. (1995). Mental retardation. In R.T. Ammerman & M. Hersen (Eds.), *Handbook of Child Behavior Therapy in the Psychiatric Setting* (pp. 153–180). Toronto: Wiley.

Lachar, D. (1982). *Personality Inventory for Children. Revised formal manual supplement.* Los Angeles: Western Psychological Services.

Lambert, N., Windmiller, M., Tharinger, D., & Cole, L. (1981). *AAMD Adaptive Behavior Scale, School Edition.* Washington, DC: American Association on Mental Deficiency.

Levine, M.N. (1989). *Mental retardation handbook.* Los Angeles: Western Psychological Services.

Lovell, R.W., & Reiss, A.L. (1993). Dual diagnoses: Psychiatric disorders in developmental disabilities. *Pediatric Clinics of North America, 40,* 579–592.

Luckasson, R., Coulter, D.L., Polloway, E.A., Reiss, S., Schalock, R.L., Snell, M.E., Spitlanik, D.M., & Stark, J.A. (1992). *Mental Retardation: Definition, classification, and systems of supports.* Washington, DC: American Association on Mental Retardation.

MacMillan, D.L., Gresham, F.M., & Siperstein, G.N. (1993). Conceptual and psychometric concerns about the 1992 AAMR definition of mental retardation. *American Journal on Mental Retardation, 98,* 325–335.

MacMillan, D.L., Gresham, F.M., & Siperstein, G.N. (1995). Heightened concerns over the 1992 AAMR definition: Advocacy versus precision. *American Journal on Mental Retardation, 100,* 87–97.

Marshburn, E.C., & Aman, M.G. (1992). Factor validity and norms for the Aberrant Behavior Checklist in a community sample of children with mental retardation. *Journal of Autism and Developmental Disorders, 22,* 357–373.

Matson, J.L., Gardner, W.I., Coe, D.A., & Sovner, R. (1991). A scale for evaluating emotional disorders in severely and profoundly mentally retarded persons: Development of the Diagnostic Assessment for the Severely Handicapped (DASH) Scale. *British Journal of Psychiatry, 159*, 404–409.

McConaughy, S.H., & Achenbach, T.M. (1994). *Manual for the semi-structured clinical interview for children and adolescents.* Burlington: University of Vermont, Department of Psychiatry.

Mercer, J., & Lewis, J. (1977). *System of multicultural pluralistic assessment.* New York: The Psychological Corporation.

Mueller, H.H., Dash, U.N., Matheson, D.W., & Short, R.H. (1984). WISC-R subtest patterning of below average, average, and above average IQ children: A meta-analysis. *Alberta Journal of Educational Research, 30*, 68–85.

Myers, B.A. (1987). Psychiatric problems in adolescents with developmental disabilities. *Journal of the American Academy of Child and Adolescent Psychiatry*, 74–79.

Naglieri, J.A., & Das, J.P. (1990). Planning, attention, simultaneous, and successive (PASS) cognitive processes as a model for intelligence. *Journal of Psychoeducational Assessment, 8*, 303–337.

Naglieri, J.A., Das, J.P., & Jarman, R.F. (1990). Planning, attention, simultaneous and successive cognitive processes as a model for assessment. *School Psychology Review, 19*, 423–442.

Nanson, J. (1990). Behavior in children with fetal alcohol syndrome. In W.I. Fraser (Ed.), *Key issues in mental retardation research.* London: Blackwell.

Nihiri, K., Foster, R., Shellhaas, M., & Leland, H. (1975). *AAMD Adaptive Behavior Scale.* Washington, DC: American Association on Mental Deficiency.

Orelove, F.P., & Sobsey, D. (1991). *Educating children with multiple disabilities: A transdisciplinary approach* (2nd ed.). Baltimore: Paul H. Brookes.

Polloway, E.A. (1987). Transition services for early age individuals with mild mental retardation. In R.N. Ianacone & R.A. Stodden (Eds.), *Transition issues and directions* (pp. 11–24). Reston, VA: The Council for Exceptional Children.

Rainforth, B., York, J., & Macdonald, C. (1992). *Collaborative teams for students with severe disabilities: Integrating therapy and educational services.* Baltimore: Paul H. Brookes.

Reber, M. (1992). Mental retardation. *Psychiatric Clinics of North America, 15*, 511–522.

Reiss, S. (1990). Prevalence of dual diagnoses in community-based day programs in the Chicago metropolitan area. *American Journal on Mental Retardation, 94*, 578–585.

Reiss, S., Levitan, G.W., & Szyszko, J. (1982). Emotional disturbance and mental retardation: Diagnostic overshadowing. *American Journal of Mental Deficiency, 86*, 567–574.

Reiss, S., & Valenti-Hein, D. (1994). Development of a psychopathology rating scale for children with mental retardation. *Journal of Consulting and Clinical Psychology, 62*, 28–33.

Rodger, S. (1995). Individual education plans revisited: A review of the literature. *International Journal of Disability, Development, and Education, 42*(3), 221–139.

Rojahn, J., & Helsel, W.J. (1991). The Aberrant Behavior Checklist with children and adolescents with dual diagnosis. *Journal of Autism and Developmental Disorders, 21*, 17–28.

Rutter, M., Graham, P., & Yule, W. (1970). *A neuropsychiatric study in childhood.* London: Heinemann.

Sattler, J.M. (1992). *Assessment of children: Revised and updated third edition.* San Diego: Jerome M. Sattler.

Schalock, R.L., Stark, J.A., Snell, M.E., Coulter, D.L., Polloway, E.A., Luckasson, R., Reiss, S., & Spitalnik, D.M. (1994). The changing conception of mental retardation: Implications for the field. *Mental Retardation, 32*, 181–193.

Scheerenberger, R.C. (1983). *A history of mental retardation.* Baltimore: Paul H. Brookes.

Skinner, M.E. (1990). Facilitating parental participation during individualized education program conferences. *Journal of Educational and Psychological Consultation, 2,* 285–289.

Smith, S.W. (1990). Individualized education programs (IEPs) in special education—from intent to acquiescence. *Exceptional Children, 56,* 6–14.

Sparrow, S.S., Balla, D.A., & Cicchetti, D.A. (1984). *Vineland Adaptive Behavior Scales.* Circle Pines, MN: American Guidance Service.

Tasse, M.J., Aman, M.G., Hammer, D., & Rojahn, J. (1996). The Nisonger Child Behavior Rating Form: Age and gender effects and norms. *Research in Developmental Disabilities, 17,* 59–75.

Taylor, R.L. (1989). *Assessment of exceptional students: Educational and psychological procedures* (2nd ed.). Englewood Cliffs, NJ: Prentice Hall.

Thorndike, R.L., Hagan, E.P., & Sattler, J.M. (1986). *Technical Manual, Stanford-Binet Intelligence Scale: Fourth Edition.* Chicago: Riverside.

Wechsler, D. (1981). *Manual for the Wechsler Adult Intelligence Scale-Revised.* San Antonio, TX: The Psychological Corporation.

Wechsler, D. (1989). *Manual for the Wechsler Preschool and Primary Scale of Intelligence-Revised.* San Antonio, TX: The Psychological Corporation.

Wechsler, D. (1991). *Manual for the Wechsler Intelligence Scale for Children-Third Edition.* San Antonio, TX: The Psychological Corporation.

Wikler, L. (1981). Chronic stresses of families with mentally retarded children. *Family Relations, 30,* 281–288.

Wilson, J., Blacher, J., & Baker, B.L. (1989). Siblings of children with severe handicaps. *Mental Retardation, 27*(3), 167–173.

Woodcock, R.W., & Johnson, M. (1989). *Woodcock-Johnson Psycho-Educational Battery-Revised.* Chicago: Riverside.

Author Index

Subject Index

AAMD-Becker Reading-Free Vocational Interest Inventory, 431
Aberrant Behavior Checklist (ABC), 463–464
The Abilities of Man, 163
Absolute mastery criteria, 409
Academic achievement, 278–279, 281, 377–379
Activity units (AUs), 24
Actuarial assessment strategy, 68–69, 134
Adaptive behavior, 246–247
 age-appropriate behavior, 300–301
 best practices in assessment of, 317
 cultural expectations and, 301–302
 definition of, 299, 318
 domains of, 301–302
 environmental demands on, 302
 future of assessment of, 317–318
 history of assessment of, 297–299
 identification of other disabilities using assessments of, 306–309
 instruments for assessment of, 303–306, 461
 maladaptive behavior and, 302–303
 measured for instructional program planning:
 general planning, 309
 in mild disabilities, 312–316
 for preschoolers with disabilities, 316
 in severe disabilities, 310–312
 mental retardation and, 298–299, 306, 460–461
 typical performance, 300

Adaptive Behavior Inventory for Children, 461
Adaptive skills, 299
ADHDEXPERT, 41
Adjustment Scales for Children and Adolescents (ASCA), 143–144
Adolescent and Adult Psychoeducational Profile: Volume IV, 409
Adolescent Behavior Checklist, 464
Adolescent psychological status, 136–137
Adult neuropsychological battery, 71–72
Advocate (ASA newsletter), 389, 399
AEPS Family Report Instrument, 2
Aesthetics of test appearance, 200
Affective indifference, 398
Affirmative action, 422
Age, 357
Aggregation principle, 271
Aggression, 135
Alternative assessment, 16, 34–40
Alternative Learning Program (ALP) Assessment Battery, 431–434
Alzheimers Disease, 284
American Association on Mental Deficiency (AAMD), 201, 298
 AAMD-Becker Reading-Free Vocational Interest Inventory, 431
 Adaptive Behavior Scale, 461
American Association on Mental Retardation (AAMR):
 Adaptive Behavior Scales (ABS), 305–306

definition of adaptive behavior, 460
definition of retardation, 247, 298–299, 301, 454–455, 466
etiology of retardation, 467
individualized education plan (IEP), 471
American Educational Research Association, 218, 226, 357
American Psychiatric Association, 388
American Psychological Association, 134, 218, 226
 Ethical Principles of Psychologists and Code of Conduct, 226, 357
Americans with Disabilities Act, *1990* (P.L. 101–336), 420, 423–424
Anomia, 76
Anterior cortex, 67
Antidiscrimination, 422
Antisocial behavior, 256
Anxiety:
 depression and, 145, 257
 as effecting test performance, 205, 206, 207
 Hamilton Anxiety Scale, 95
 MMPI and, 137, 139
Appearance of patients, 149
Aptitude/achievement discrepancies, 181
Aptitude-treatment interactions (ATIs), 183, 241
Arena assessment, 7–8, 40
Army Individual Performance Scales, 199
Arteries, brain, 65–66
Articulation disorders, 285–286
Artificial intelligence, 98
Asperger's disorder, 392, 467
Assembly Tree, 427